SOLDIERS, SAINTS, AND SHAMANS

NATHANIEL MORRIS

SOLDIERS, SAINTS, and SHAMANS

Indigenous Communities and the Revolutionary State in Mexico's Gran Nayar, 1910–1940

THE UNIVERSITY OF ARIZONA PRESS
TUCSON

The University of Arizona Press
www.uapress.arizona.edu

We respectfully acknowledge the University of Arizona is on the land and territories of Indigenous peoples. Today, Arizona is home to twenty-two federally recognized tribes, with Tucson being home to the O'odham and the Yaqui. Committed to diversity and inclusion, the University strives to build sustainable relationships with sovereign Native Nations and Indigenous communities through education offerings, partnerships, and community service.

First paperback edition 2022

ISBN-13: 978-0-8165-4102-7 (hardcover)
ISBN-13: 978-0-8165-4693-0 (paper)

Cover design by Leigh McDonald
Cover photo: *Mist on the Mountains near Huaynamota* by Nathaniel Morris
Typeset by Leigh McDonald in Garamond Premier Pro 10/13.5 and Eldon WF (display)

Publication of this book is made possible in part by the proceeds of a permanent endowment created with the assistance of a Challenge Grant from the National Endowment for the Humanities, a federal agency.

Library of Congress Cataloging-in-Publication Data
Names: Morris, Nathaniel, 1986– author.
Title: Soldiers, saints, and shamans : indigenous communities and the revolutionary state in Mexico's Gran Nayar, 1910–1940 / Nathaniel Morris.
Description: Tucson : The University of Arizona Press, 2020. | Includes bibliographical references and index.
Identifiers: LCCN 2020011735 | ISBN 9780816541027 (hardcover)
Subjects: LCSH: Indians of Mexico—History—20th century. | Cora Indians—History—20th century. | Huichol Indians—History—20th century. | Tepehuan Indians—History—20th century. | Nahuas—History—20th century. | Mexico—History—Revolution, 1910–1920—Participation, Indian. | Mexico—History—1910–1946.
Classification: LCC F1234 .M867 2020 | DDC 972/.3408997454—dc23
LC record available at https://lccn.loc.gov/2020011735

Printed in the United States of America
♾ This paper meets the requirements of ANSI/NISO Z39.48-1992 (Permanence of Paper).

To the elders of the Gran Nayar. This book would never have existed without you—far less the story it tells.

Gracias, ch'dió tímuaranáchite'e, taxchaab, pamparios, xi mo se.

CONTENTS

ILLUSTRATIONS

FIGURES

MAPS

TABLE

NOTE ON ETHNIC NOMENCLATURE

THIS BOOK CONCERNS, above all, the four Indigenous peoples of the Gran Nayar, often known, both in Spanish and English, as the Coras, Huichols, Southern Tepehuanos (sometimes spelled Tepehuanes), and Mexicaneros. Each people has their own language, all belonging to the Uto-Aztecan family. Cora (Náayari) and Huichol (Wixárika) constitute the family's Corachol branch (to which various other now-extinct local languages also belonged). Southern Tepehuano (divided between the O'dam and Audam dialects) and its closely related but now-extinct variant Tepecano belong to the Tepiman branch (along with the Northern Tepehuano, Pima, and Tohono O'odham languages). Finally, the language of the Mexicaneros is a peripheral dialect of Nahuatl.

Increasingly, members of the first three groups would prefer that outsiders call them by their own names for themselves rather than use the terms Spanish missionaries and administrators first imposed on them as part of an ongoing process of physical, political, and cultural subjugation that was accompanied by brutal violence and the despoliation of their lands. Over the following chapters, then, I use the terms *Náayari* (singular) or *Náayarite* (plural) in place of "Cora" and "Coras," *Wixárika* (singular) and *Wixáritari* (plural) in place of "Huichol" and "Huichols," and *O'dam* (singular and plural) in place of "Tepehuano" or "Tepehuanos" (as to try and use both *O'dam* and *Audam* would, I fear, become rather confusing). The Mexicanero endonym actually comes from their own language (in common with many other Nahuatl-speaking groups throughout Mexico), and I will therefore continue to refer to them as *Mexicaneros*.

ACKNOWLEDGMENTS

THIS BOOK BEGAN with a letter I sent to my "long-lost" uncle, Chris French, in Santa María del Oro, Nayarit, when I was nineteen years old. Thank you, Chris, for replying and for welcoming me into your Mexican home, which was where, looking east toward the mountains, I first set eyes on the Gran Nayar. Thanks also to the rest of my Mexican family—Amelia, Cristian, Karen, Carlos "El Oso," Casey, Danny, Analía, Haley, Aide, Lilia, Fernando, and Lya (QEPD)—for ensuring that a bed, food, and plenty of coffee (and, when necessary, beer) were never far away during breaks from fieldwork, whether on the shores of La Laguna, at Rancho La Querencia, or in Tepic.

Although I stumbled on the Gran Nayar before arriving at Oxford University as an undergraduate, I would never have been able to study the history of the region and its peoples without the help of Professor Alan Knight, to whom I owe an enormous debt of gratitude. His patience, guidance, good humor, and keen insights into Mexican history, society, politics, and culture(s) inspired me to stick with research into Latin American themes over the course of a decade and eventually to research and write the doctoral thesis on which this book is based. Any factual errors, boring passages, theoretical misunderstandings, or ridiculously long sentences herein are almost certainly the result of my ignoring his good advice. I am also very grateful to Professor David Parrott and Mr. Robin Lane Fox at New College, Oxford, for their help, guidance, and general encouragement throughout my studies—and for letting me in as an undergraduate in the first place! I would also like to thank the Arts and Humanities Research Council, the New College Reynolds Fund, and Oxford University's Faculty of History for their financial and logistical support during my time as a student.

My greatest thanks, however, must go to the people of the Gran Nayar, without whose kindness and generosity I could not even have begun to research and write this book. Despite the poverty and violence that blights the region, my local friends made sure I always had a roof over my head and some blankets to warm me during cold nights. Even when food was in short supply, there was always a pile of steaming tortillas waiting for me at the end of each day's work. And although many people were bemused by my interest in the history of their communities, they were always happy to help me find local elders they thought might be willing to share their memories and stories of *la revolución*, and in many cases accompanied me to translate these stories from Náayari, Wixárika, O'dam, or Mexicanero into Spanish. In Santa Catarina, I am especially grateful to Don Samuel Robles and his family, in particular his sons, Hugo and Braulio; in San Miguel Huastita, to Juan and Ofelia Salvador and Don Rosalio "Chalillo" Salvador Carillo (QEPD); in Tuxpan de Bolaños, to Josefina Salvador, Catarino "Chuwa" Bañuelos, and Don Salvador Sánchez; in Santa María Ocotán, to Santiago Cumplido, Carmela and Elizabeth Soto Gurrola, and, between there and Durango, to her son, Honorio Mendía Soto; in Cerro de las Papas, to Don Saturnino Solís Mendoza (QEPD); in Llano Grande, to Secundino; in San Francisco de Paula, to Don Fernando Muñiz and his son, Pedro; and in Presidio de los Reyes, to Silvino and Silvia and their family. I owe extra thanks, in Santa Teresa, to Doña Rita (QEPD) for delicious food and *té de laurel*, to Ambrosio Castañeda, for the *craic*, and to Oscar and Nacho Álvarez and their father, Don Pedro, for giving me the chance to serve for five years as a "devil" in the community's Semana Santa festival and for protecting me from the occasional rowdy *borrado* looking to *chingar el gabacho*. And, above all, I am grateful to all of the elders who agreed to share their stories with me. This book is dedicated to them and to the communal authorities who gave me permission to stay in their communities and carry out this research, despite sometimes unfortunate precedents set by irresponsible anthropologists and new-age idiots searching for peyote and cultural "purity." I hope that I have here been able to do justice to their trust and their generosity and that I have fulfilled my vague promises that, in some small way, my work might help them hold on to their history and *costumbre* in the face of multiple outside pressures.

Of course, my research also involved countless months in archives outside the Gran Nayar. Staff members at numerous different archives were instrumental to the success of my documentary research. I owe special thanks to Gustavo Villanueva, without whom my work at the Aurelio Acevedo Robles archive at the National Autonomous University of Mexico (UNAM) would have been almost impossible, and to Armando Casas, who not only helped me penetrate Durango's state archives but also offered me warm friendship and a better understanding (if not necessarily a deep appreciation) of heavy metal music. I am also grateful for the friendships of innumerable Mexican colleagues, who offered me stimulating conversation, vital insights into the cultures and histories of the Gran Nayar and its inhabitants, and tacos, *tlayudas*, and many fine mescals besides. In particular, in Zacatecas, many thanks to Mark and Susana Lawrence; in Durango, to Antonio Reyes, Bridget Zavala, and Selene Galindo; in Zamora, to Paul Liffman; and in Mexico City, to Regina Lira, Johannes Neurath, Anahí Luna, and Margarita Valdovinos. Thanks also to Efraín Rangel, Philip Coyle, Jay Fikes, Jesús Jáuregui, and Víctor Téllez Lozano for sharing their research with me, and to Jean Meyer and Ben Fallaw, who were both generous enough to read early drafts of this book and give me valuable feedback on it. On a less academic note, thanks also to the staff and guests at Guadalajara's Hostel Tequila (QEPD)—above all José Juan, Gaby, Fernando, Oscar, Max, Pedro, Maja, and Laura—who did little for my productivity but made sure my stays in the city were some of the best times of my life.

I am also very grateful to the support of my colleagues, friends, and family in London, Oxford, and elsewhere. Bryce and Claudia shared their home with me in San Francisco, while Mark, Ben, Luis, and Ally all traveled thousands of miles to visit me in Mexico. The rest of the boys—Adam, Alex, Pete, Christian, Rob, Marc, Dom, Mike, Matt, James, and John—all patiently endured my endless stories of *la sierra* in London pubs and helped me to keep it together in the face of academic pressures. Thanks also to Philip Knox, who graciously took on more than his fair share of work in terms of Balkan side projects because of my long absences in Mexico. Benjamin Smith and Wil Pansters provided me with a much-needed postdoctoral job on their epic Narco-Mex research project and were kind enough to build in breaks in my workload so I could continue writing this book at the same time. Working with them was fun and instructive, and I've become a better historian for it. Thanks also to Paulo Drinot, Thom Rath, William Booth, and all the other organizers of, and presenters and attendees at, the IHR History of Latin America Seminars for providing such a collegiate space for academic exchange and for welcoming my participation even as an unemployed and precariously unaffiliated "independent scholar." On that note, a big shout out is due to Sonja at the Streatham Jobcentre for helping me negotiate the horrors of Universal Credit during my time on the dole, which allowed me to put the finishing touches to this book. I am also inordinately grateful to the Leverhulme Foundation and UCL for rescuing me from post-postdoctoral unemployment. And many, many thanks to Kristen Buckles at the University of Arizona Press for her support in making this book a physical reality, as well as to the anonymous peer reviewers for their incisive feedback and constructive critiques of previous drafts of this book, and to Stacey Wujcik and the rest of the Arizona team, and my copyeditor, Kat Thomas, for all the help with the rest of the publication process.

Finally, my most heartfelt love and thanks go to my family. Without my parents, Ben and Philippa, this book would still be nothing but a "twinkle in the eye"—as would I. So, thank you, Mum and Dad—I'd never have been inspired to write this book had you not instilled in me a deep curiosity about the world, a somewhat anarchist political streak, and the desire to constantly question the decisions of the powerful. My apologies if those same qualities made me a deeply annoying child! Thanks also to my brother and sister, Jake and Henrietta, who never ceased to encourage me over the course of my studies, despite my neglect of brotherly duties in the name of this research; and to Rachel, Stephen, Immy, and Issy—"the neighbors"—who were always similarly supportive. Extra thanks are also due to Dad for his invaluable editorial insights, and to Tallulah for the same—without you both this damn thing would be at least a thousand pages long and no one would ever have wanted to publish it, let alone read it! All of my love to Tallulah for less dryly academic reasons, too: I'll be forever grateful to you for so graciously putting up with the way my research has so often taken me far away from you and from our home in London; for supporting me through my doubts about the feasibility of finishing this book and of becoming a "real" historian; and for reminding me that sometimes it's normal to be stressed (even if it barely, ahem, ever happens to me). Thank you for your laughter, your risottos, and your love. *Te amo, nena.*

ABBREVIATIONS

Auts. Trads.	Autoridades Tradicionales
CAN	Comisión Nacional Agraria
CLA	Comité Local Agraria
CSOC	Confederación Socialista de Obreros y Campesinos
DAI	Departamento de Asuntos Indígenas
DECI	Departamento de Educación y Cultura Indígena
DEFD	Director de Educación Federal de Durango
DEFJ	Director de Educación Federal de Jalisco
DEFN	Director de Educación Federal de Nayarit
DEI	Departamento de Educación Indígena
Dept. Agrario	Departamento Agrario
DERICI	Departamento de Escuelas Rurales y Incorporación Cultural Indígena
DOF	Diario Oficial de la Federación
Fed.	Federal
GN	Guardia Nacional (Cristera)
Gob. Dgo.	State Governor of Durango
Gob. Jal.	State Governor of Jalisco
Gob. Nay.	State Governor of Nayarit
Jefe Pol.	Jefe Político
JOM	Jefe de Operaciones Militares
LNDLR	Liga Nacional Defensora de la Libertad Religiosa
n.d.	No Date

PM	Presidente Municipal
PNR	Partido Nacional Revolucionario
POED	Periódico Oficial del Estado de Durango
POEJ	Periódico Oficial del Estado de Jalisco
POEN	Periódico Oficial del Estado de Nayarit
Proc. de Pueblos	Procurador de Pueblos
Rep.	Representative
Res. Pres.	Resolución Presidencial
Sec. Gob	Secretaría de Gobernación
Sec. Guerra	Secretaría de Guerra
SEP	Secretaría de Educación Pública

THE CACIQUES OF THE GRAN NAYAR

SIERRA NÁAYARI, NAYARIT

Evaristo Castañeda, Náayari cacique and defensa commander in Santa Teresa
León Contreras, Náayari cacique and defensa commander in Jesús María
Eutimio Domínguez, Náayari cacique of the Náayari Baja region, from San Juan Corapan
Eusebio González, Náayari cacique and defensa commander in San Pedro Ixcatán
Mariano Mejía, mestizo cacique of Náayari Alta region, later a local cristero commander
J. Jesús Meza, mestizo army officer, official head of defensas of the Sierra Náayari
Mariano Solís, Náayari leader of La Mesa, former bandit and later municipal president

SIERRA WIXÁRIKA, JALISCO

Juan Bautista, Wixárika cacique and commander of San Sebastián's cristero forces
Agustín Carrillo, Wixárika cacique and defensa commander in Santa Catarina
Agustín Mijares Cosío, Wixárika teacher and pro-government leader in Santa Catarina
Patricio "Mezquite," Wixárika cacique, leader of San Sebastián's Carrancista forces
Nieves and Petronilo Muñoz, father and son, heads of Huajimic's ruling mestizo clan
Pedro Quintanar, mestizo Carrancista cacique of Huejuquilla, later cristero general
Griseldo Salazar, Mezquitic's pro-government mestizo cacique and defensa commander

José "Pepe" Sánchez, mestizo cristero leader from near Mezquitic
Cenobio Sánchez de la Cruz, Wixárika cacique and defensa commander in Tuxpan
Clemente Villa, Wixárika Carrancista commander and cacique of San Andrés

SIERRA O'DAM, DURANGO

Valente Acevedo, mestizo cristero commander from near San Bernardino
Ascensión "Chon" Aguilar, O'dam defensa commander from Xoconoxtle
Gregorio Aguilar, father of Ascensión, Carrancista fighter and defensa commander
Dámaso Barraza, O'dam defensa commander in Yonora, later cristero general
Florencio and Frumencio Estrada, mestizo cristero commanders from Huazamota
José María Gutiérrez, O'dam cacique of San Francisco Ocotán
Porfirio Mayorquín, mestizo from Acaponeta, cristero commander in Durango
Sixto Mendía, O'dam cacique and defensa commander in Santa María Ocotán
Trinidad Mora, mestizo from Santiago Bayacora, commander of Durango's cristeros
Nabor, Vicente, and Tiburcio Muñoz, heads of Huazamota's ruling mestizo clan
Primo Ortiz, former cacique of Huazamota, overthrown there by los Muñoz
Cosme Solís, O'dam cacique and defensa commander in Santa María Ocotán
Macario and Ireneo Valdés, O'dam cristero leaders from Temoaya
Federico Vázquez, mestizo cristero commander, last of Mexico's cristero rebels

SOLDIERS, SAINTS, AND SHAMANS

INTRODUCTION

ON A HOT June morning in 1928, a column of eighty federal soldiers set out across the mountains of southern Durango in search of a group of rebels who, in the name of "Christ the King," had declared a holy war on Mexico's revolutionary government. Around midday, the nervous conscripts and their Indigenous O'dam guides began to climb the ridge known locally as Cerro de las Papas (Potato Hill). As they passed along a narrow path bounded on both sides by sheer rock walls, the O'dam rolled up their white cotton trousers and pulled red bandanas from their shoulder bags. When the soldiers asked them why, their leader, Luciano Carrillo, replied simply that they were hot.

Satisfied with this answer, the federal commander, Colonel José Ruiz, mounted on a magnificent white horse, motioned his men onward. A handful of earth and pebbles slid down onto the path a few meters ahead of him, but he paid no attention and continued forward. Then a boulder crashed toward him from the forested slopes above, and wheeling around on his startled horse, Ruiz shouted for his men to halt. The crack of gunfire began to echo about the mountains, and Ruiz saw first one and then another of his men fall to the ground. Carrillo's O'dam, marked out from the soldiers by their rolled-up trousers and bandanas, seemed oblivious to the bullets. The federals scrabbled frantically for shelter, but they found little cover on the barren mountainside. Luciano Carrillo and the other O'dam had led the soldiers straight into a trap in which most of them would succumb to the bullets and boulders of *cristero* guerrillas led by Carrillo's ally, the O'dam warlord Juan Andrés Soto.[1]

The massacre at Cerro de las Papas remains the most notorious of the battles that took place in the mountains of southern Durango during the Mexican Revolution, a thirty-year period of violent upheaval that began with a popular uprising against the dictatorship of Porfirio Díaz in 1910 and ended with the consolidation of the modern Mexican state in the late 1930s, during the radical presidency of Lázaro Cárdenas. The pines that stand in the forests near Cerro de las Papas are today still scarred by cristero bullets, reminding local people of the ambush there, which has passed into O'dam lore and continues to be celebrated in their stories and songs. A nearby government-run school is even named, somewhat ironically, after the school-burning rebel Juan Andrés Soto, while the name of another local landmark—Nabat bo', or "the reclining mestizo"—commemorates the spot where the O'dam rebels killed Colonel Ruiz himself.

The O'dam homeland in southern Durango is part of a wider cultural-geographical region known as the *Gran Nayar*: a 20,000 km² expanse of mountains and canyons that stretches into the neighboring states of Nayarit, Jalisco, and Zacatecas. The Gran Nayar comprises one of northwestern Mexico's most ethnically diverse areas. In addition to the O'dam, it is the homeland of the Indigenous Wixárika, Náayari, and Mexicanero peoples, all closely linked by culture, history, geography, trade, and religious practice. A Spanish-speaking mestizo minority also lives in the region.[2] All of these groups played active roles in the civil wars that followed the overthrow of Díaz; in the coups, countercoups, and military rebellions that accompanied the revolutionary power struggles of the 1920s; in the Cristero Rebellion, or *cristiada*, that consumed much of Mexico between 1926 and 1929; and in the land reforms, "socialist" education programs, and renewed cristero violence of the 1930s. Like that of Juan Andrés Soto, the names of the Gran Nayar's other revolutionary-era leaders have also passed into local legend: men like Wixárika cristero chief Juan Bautista, pro-government Náayari militia leader Eutimio Domínguez, and the mestizo Mariano Mejía, who fought for the Carrancistas before raising the communities of Nayarit's mountains against the revolutionary regime—an act immortalized in the nationally famous ballad "Valentín de la Sierra."

Despite the vibrancy of local oral traditions concerning the revolution, only a handful of scholars have explored how the upheavals of this period affected the Gran Nayar. This is all the more surprising given the existence of a substantial body of research into other aspects of Náayari, Wixárika, O'dam, and Mexicanero history,[3] not to mention a profusion of ethnographic studies into their cultures, religious practices, and use of the hallucinogenic peyote cactus.[4] This lack of academic interest in the role the Gran Nayar's inhabitants have played in modern Mexican history is directly related to their status as amongst the least assimilated Indians in the Americas, which has given rise to popular images of them as living in a timeless vacuum. It is also a consequence of the idea—prevalent in Mexico since the colonial era—that Indian "history" is that of

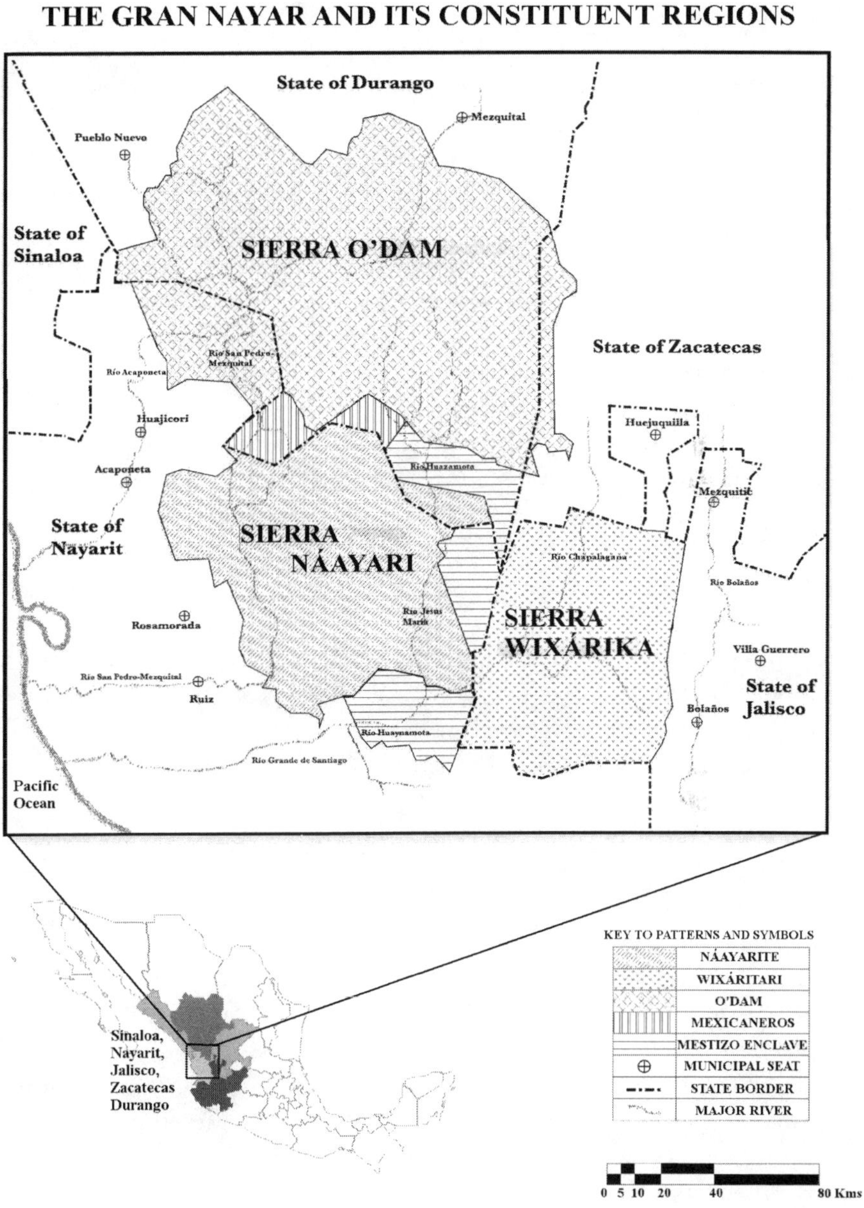

MAP 1 Overview of Gran Nayar. Map by the author, based on Plan Lerma, *Operación HUICOT*.

the glorious pre-Hispanic past, leaving their descendants worthy of interest only to anthropologists and a few romantics interested in folklore.[5]

However, Náayari, Wixárika, O'dam, and Mexicanero memories of the Mexican Revolution have a significance that goes beyond the folkloric. On closer examination, stories like that of the ambush at Cerro de las Papas—at first glance a simple tale of canny Catholic guerrillas defeating foolhardy federal interlopers—raise important questions about the nature of many of the developments of the revolutionary period. In the 1920s, revolutionary statesmen and rebel ideologues alike claimed that the Cristero Rebellion was motivated by Catholic zealotry, while more recently, historians have argued that support for the rebels was predicated less on belief and more on the cultural, social, and political consequences of Catholic practice.[6] But both of these interpretations are challenged by the fact that only a few of the O'dam guerrillas who mounted the attack at Cerro de las Papas were even baptized Catholics and most arrived at the ambush fresh from celebrating a shamanic ritual, or mitote, that dated back to pre-Hispanic times and was viewed by the church as incompatible with orthodox Catholic practice.[7]

Indeed, Náayari, Wixárika, O'dam, and Mexicanero religious traditions are so heterodox that Pope John XXIII declared their homeland terra nullius (no-man's-land) in 1962 and sent Franciscan missionaries to convert them to the "true faith." Even the pope could make little headway in the Gran Nayar, whose peoples today continue to practice their distinctive ethnic religions, complete with complex cosmologies, rituals, mythological epics, and, in the case of the Wixáritari, purpose-built pagan temples, all of which fascinate anthropologists and cause their mestizo neighbors to disparage them as heathens. What, then, led so many of the region's Indigenous inhabitants to join the Catholic insurgents of the 1920s and 1930s to the extent that the last cristeros in the country to lay down their arms were Wixáritari and O'dam?

Furthermore, the rebels' ruse was only successful because many other local people had declared their support for the government and had played a key role in regional anti-cristero campaigns, working with federal forces as guides and auxiliary fighters. Only by feigning such sympathies were Carrillo and his O'dam cristeros able to lure Colonel Ruiz into their trap. Why then did so many of the Gran Nayar's Indigenous inhabitants choose to turn against their rebellious ethnic compatriots and align themselves with a government that actively sought to curb their cherished cultural and political autonomy in the name of revolutionary nation-building?

The participation of the Náayarite, Wixáritari, O'dam, and Mexicaneros in the popular mobilizations and revolutionary infighting that preceded the first Cristero Rebellion, and in the agrarian reform and second Cristero Rebellion that followed it, raises additional questions about the dynamics of the Mexican Revolution while also challenging widespread ideas about the Gran Nayar itself. Although geographers, anthropologists, and historians have often represented the region's peoples as "closed off in their own ethnocentric worlds,"[8] they threw themselves into the events of the revolutionary period with such gusto that bloody interethnic conflicts and intracommunal "civil wars" broke out throughout the Gran Nayar. While some of the region's culturally distinct and politically self-governing communities may have been carried along by the violence that swept Mexico between 1910 and 1940, others were genuinely attracted to the rival ideologies of Villistas or Carrancistas, cristeros, and radical agrarian reformers. At the same time, their unique and markedly magical ways of understanding the world also helped to shape these sympathies, with important effects on their societies and cultures and on the local, regional, and national outcomes of the Mexican Revolution and, therefore, on the emergence of the Mexican nation-state as we know it today.

To make sense of this complex history, this book—the first systematic study of the participation of the Gran Nayar's inhabitants in the Mexican Revolution—initially explores how and why the Náayarite, Wixáritari, O'dam, and Mexicaneros took part in the "armed phase" of the revolution, between 1910 and 1920. Alan Knight has convincingly argued that although it resulted in the dramatic reconfiguration of both state and nation,[9] the armed revolution consisted of a multitude of popular rural movements "motivated by local concerns."[10] Above all, these concerns related to threats to local political and/or cultural autonomy, which inspired to action those independent-minded and often mountain-dwelling revolutionary actors Knight classes as *serranos*, or, alternatively, to the usurpation of peasant lands, which drove *agraristas* to take up arms in their defense.[11] However, as Knight himself has pointed out, the distinction between the two groups is not always rigid.[12] This is certainly true in the case of the Gran Nayar, where local revolutionaries viewed the political and cultural autonomy of their communities as inseparable from their continued control of communal lands—all of which were under severe pressure on the eve of the revolution.

Náayari, Wixárika, O'dam, and Mexicanero leaders sought to use, with some success, the tumult of the revolution's armed phase to reassert their political autonomy and reclaim control of lost territory. However, the regime that rose from the ashes of Porfirian Mexico soon threatened their gains. In common with contemporary nationalists throughout the world,[13] Mexico's revolutionary ideologues saw the consolidation of the modern nation-state as dependent on the reformation of previous "activities and cultural forms that have provided modes of organization, social practice and identity."[14] The destruction of "primitive" Indigenous political structures, languages, and "superstitions" throughout rural Mexico was envisaged as an essential part of this process.

This project, which involved corporatist, state-managed agrarian reform, violent anticlerical crackdowns, and education programs designed to replace native languages with Spanish and to challenge traditional gender and age roles within Indigenous communities,[15] inherently threatened not only the political autonomy but also the ways of life, the worldviews, and even the basic ethnic identities of many of Mexico's Indigenous inhabitants. In the Gran Nayar, it paved the way for a violent confrontation between highly autonomous Indigenous peasant communities and an expansionist revolutionary state: a clash between practitioners of subsistence agriculture and promoters of capitalist development, rival Indian generations and political factions, and distinct visions of the world, religion, and daily life.

These clashes produced some of the most severe defeats that the Mexican government's state- and nation-building programs suffered during this period, with sometimes counterintuitive consequences. Thus members of "traditionalist" Indigenous factions, who upheld a resolutely pagan religious tradition and defined themselves in opposition to local mestizos, became an important force within the Catholic-inspired, mestizo-dominated cristero rebel movements of the 1920s and 1930s. Similarly, the federal educational programs so often lauded for bringing literacy and "progress" to rural Mexico instead precipitated both passive resistance and violent opposition throughout the Gran Nayar, which extended to the burning of schools and even the murder of several teachers. And the radical land reforms of left-leaning President Lázaro Cárdenas (1934–40), ostensibly designed to liberate the Mexican peasantry from social and economic oppression, instead facilitated the usurpation of Indigenous lands by mestizo ranchers and gave rise to many of the violent conflicts between local communities that still define life in the region today.

At the same time, the story of Náayari, Wixárika, O'dam, and Mexicanero interactions with the revolutionary state is not exclusively one of coercion, oppression, and resistance. Despite widespread local opposition to schools, influential minority factions supported their establishment in the hope of winning the government's support for their agrarian or territorial claims, believing that teachers would provide their communities with links to a government that promoted the idea of agrarian reform to shore up its legitimacy. Some, particularly the warlords and caciques (political bosses) who had risen to influence during the armed phase of the revolution, also had vested interests in promoting revolutionary political and economic change, which offered them avenues to power and wealth previously inaccessible in their traditionally gerontocratic and subsistence-based societies.[16] Some of these leaders, whom I will refer to as *cosmopolitans*,[17] also saw the arrival of schools and mestizo immigrants in their communities as undermining the "conservative" factions with whom they increasingly competed for power.[18]

Throughout the region, however, the Indigenous identities of members of both factions continued to be defined by *el costumbre*: an interlocking complex made up of descent group and communal-level ritual practices, church-based festivals, and faith in the power of saints, ancestors, and pre-Hispanic gods. These were themselves bound up with cyclical conceptions of history and a belief that shifting subsistence agriculture, hunting, and gathering were sacred activities in which all "real people"—that is, the Indigenous inhabitants of the Gran Nayar—were obliged to participate. Thus unless they were willing to cease to be "Indians" by giving up costumbre entirely, even the region's more aggressively "cosmopolitan" leaders remained to some extent bound to the "old ways," even as political, social, and economic convulsions encouraged the integration of new gods, saints, and ceremonies into older politico-religious systems.

Contradictions and ambiguities therefore characterize the history of the revolution in the Gran Nayar. Unpicking these can also shed light on the inner contradictions of the Mexican Revolution itself. Thus the divergent responses of the region's inhabitants to the developments of this period were tied not just to their own cultural, historical, and religious idiosyncrasies but also to the disparate ways in which outsiders claiming to represent either the Revolution or the Catholic Church—including soldiers, teachers, agronomists, priests, and rebels—enacted supposedly uniform national-level policies in the Gran Nayar between 1910 and 1940. The reality of such discrepancies challenges widely held interpretations of developments across Mexico as a whole in this period, casting doubt, for example, on the idea that the revolutionary state gradually evolved into an actor that genuinely negotiated with Indigenous Mexicans over the direction of social, political, and economic reforms.[19] The nature of the interactions between local people and government officials, military commanders, and rebel leaders also complicates views of the revolution's rural teachers as noble martyrs in the service of popular liberation from oppression, poverty, and "backwardness"[20] and narratives of the cristero rebellions as either heroic "crusades" mounted by pious Catholic peasants against a Jacobinic state or as the self-interested efforts of regressive fundamentalists and wealthy landowners to overthrow a popular regime and roll back agrarian reform.[21] Delving into Náayari, Wixárika, O'dam, and Mexicanero participation in the revolution additionally highlights the hitherto neglected importance of communal militias—the so-called defensas sociales—in shaping state formation at both local and regional levels and in putting down the little-studied second Cristero Rebellion, which in the Gran Nayar was at least as devastating as the first cristiada.

The significance of the story presented in this book extends even beyond Mexico's borders, as the processes of resistance and accommodation to caciquismo (boss politics), Catholic evangelization, factional violence, assimilatory pressures, and counterinsurgency operations that shook the Gran Nayar all have their counterparts elsewhere in the Global South. The case studies presented here can therefore provide insights into the dynamics of rural violence and the cultural, religious, and sociopolitical effects of state-building across much of rural Latin America[22] and above all into the causes and nature of clashes between Indigenous groups and national political movements in countries such as Peru, Nicaragua, and Colombia, and beyond as far as India and Vietnam.[23] These insights are all the more relevant today given the critical importance of minority peoples—including Kurds, Druze, and Tuareg—in so many of the conflicts that still wrack the "decolonized world" and the vital role that religious faith and belief in the supernatural—so essential to shaping the revolution in the Gran Nayar—still plays in politics around the globe.

TIME, SPACE, AND HISTORY IN THE GRAN NAYAR

Given the extent to which the beliefs, rituals, and other dictates of costumbre still permeate every aspect of Náayari, Wixárika, O'dam, and Mexicanero life, from farming and hunting to politics and warfare, the revolution was locally experienced—and is today remembered—as both a political and a supernatural event: an era of widespread intercommunal and factional conflict, when the still-unfinished agrarian reform that today divides the region first began; but also a time when local warlords channeled occult forces to defend their communities from raiders and when miraculous statues of Catholic saints resisted the attacks of bandits or soldiers, or even took on human form to lead the charge against their enemies.

It is natural, then, to find historical narratives of the Mexican Revolution embedded in the modern ceremonial practices of the Gran Nayar's inhabitants, whether in the form of bandolier-draped dancers demanding gold from village elders in Tuxpan de Bolaños; painted "devils" shouting their allegiance to the Carrancistas, Villistas, or cristeros in Santa Teresa; or glazed-eyed peyote pilgrims in Santa Catarina irreverently yelling "Long live the supreme government!" as they romp around their ritual dance grounds. Many of the political outcomes of the revolution are also conceived in terms of their effects on local ethno-religious identities, for they resulted in the written word becoming more politically important than traditional oral narratives. Within the local imaginary, the revolution therefore marks a watershed between a time of "savagery" during which forebears practiced costumbre "properly" and retained control of their ancestral lands and a postrevolutionary era of territorial and cultural loss accompanied by the arrival of "modern" forms of social organization and national-level political and cultural influence on local life.

This conception of history has a profound effect on the way the inhabitants of the Gran Nayar today understand their relationships with the Mexican government, the country's mestizo majority, and, indeed, one another. However, it also poses a challenge for outsiders seeking to construct a "rationalist" narrative based on local sources,[24] as these often ignore questions of ideology or wider political context when explaining historical actors' behavior, instead stressing their "lack of civilization" or possession of supernatural abilities harnessed through costumbre. The fact that there are few people left in the Gran Nayar today who are old enough to remember the revolution poses another set of problems, as the testimonies of second-hand informants frequently compress events and mix up the identity of key characters, so that Pancho Villa becomes a cristero leader or Manuel Lozada ends up fighting the Carrancistas.[25]

Scholars wishing to use written records to piece together the regional story of the revolution face a rival set of difficulties. Only a handful of secondary accounts relating to the revolution in the Gran Nayar have ever been published, in large part because of outsiders' stereotypes of the region and its peoples. The Wixáritari, for example, have long been one of Mexico's most prominent Indigenous peoples, popularly regarded as a "tribe of artists," whose colorful designs adorn everything from T-shirts and tequila bottles to the buses of Nayarit's capital city, Tepic. But because their culture is held up as an archetypal example of a tradition "untarnished" by outside influences, few Mexicans, whether revolutionary government officials or scholars, politicians, or journalists writing more recently, believe they could have contributed much to such a grand and inherently national event as the revolution. Their Náayari, O'dam, and Mexicanero neighbors, meanwhile, are usually portrayed either as "closed," inward-facing primitives or, more recently, as dangerous cartel gunmen. In both cases, they are viewed as living in a Wild West backwoods that is too isolated from mainstream Mexican society for their forebears to have been involved in matters of national import. Local leaders do not feature in the Mexican state's official revolutionary hagiographies, and unlike the similarly rugged, Indigenous-majority regions of Sonora, Puebla, or Oaxaca, the Gran Nayar remains entirely absent from most Mexicans' mental maps of the period.

Archival documents are therefore the main written sources for local participation in the revolution. However, the few archives that still exist in the Gran Nayar itself have all suffered much from rebel attacks, insects, rainy-season storms, and the local custom of burying important papers "to keep them safe." State and federal archives contain rather more information, but much of this is still hard to use, as documents authored by local people usually provide only fragmentary snapshots of happenings in their communities or the wider region. The records produced by outsiders are similarly fragmentary and are additionally colored by ethnic and political bias and condescension toward the Indigenous people with whom they are concerned.

Given these problems, I have used what Paul Friedrich calls an *anthrohistorical* approach in order to construct the narrative framework of this book. I supplemented "personal letters, personal documents, local chronicles, published history, numbers, legal files, and laws" taken from a wide range of Mexican archives with "participant observation, gossip, [and] common sense" obtained through fieldwork.[26] In my search for documents, I spent several years working in the state archives of Jalisco and Durango,[27] the archives of both the Archdiocese of Guadalajara and the Franciscan

Mission at Zapopan, cristero archives in Mexico's National Autonomous University, and a range of federal archives in Mexico City. With regard to the latter, the reports of local teachers and zone inspectors stored in the Mexican national archives (AGN) proved particularly rich in information on politics, society, and culture in the Gran Nayar during the revolution. Meanwhile, two semiautobiographical novels—Antonio Estrada's *Rescoldo* and Ángel Menendez's *Nayar*—provided invaluable additional information in relation to the second Cristero Rebellion in the region.

Over the course of the more than five years it took to research this book, I also spent months at a time living in the communities of the Gran Nayar. I walked, rode horses, and hitched rides in the backs of pickup trucks in search of the region's surviving eyewitnesses to the revolution, managing to interview forty-six different informants, most of them extremely elderly. Their reminiscences were vital to filling gaps in the historical record left by the nonexistence, loss, or destruction of documents, gave me access to counterhegemonic narratives missing from existing documents, and, above all, provided me with the details of how the inhabitants of the Gran Nayar—both human and otherworldly—both experienced and participated in the revolution. While gathering this oral testimony—including songs as well as interviews—I lived with Náayari, Wixárika, O'dam, and Mexicanero families. I ate their food, slept on their floors, learned a little (far too little) of their languages, and listened to their own stories—often sad, sometimes hilarious—of life in the region. Fieldwork also helped me to grasp the scale of the Gran Nayar's rugged geography and its varied, often severe climates and gave me a chance not only to observe but also to take part in local ceremonies and festivals. Helping to prepare ritual feasts, dancing, praying, drinking, and, in Santa Teresa, running laps and fighting other stick-wielding "devils" helped me to understand how local rituals express both collective memories and more far-reaching mythical-historical narratives, all of which have been inflected to some degree by local experiences of the revolution.[28]

Fieldwork in the Gran Nayar was not always easy, however, and I found myself facing many of the same problems the emissaries of the revolutionary state had encountered long before I arrived in the mountains. Mexico's drug war today hinders outsiders' penetration of the Gran Nayar just as rebel activity did during the revolution, and it ultimately prevented me from reaching one of the region's two Mexicanero communities. I was also sometimes accused of being a "gringo spy" working for the DEA—not a comfortable situation when your accusers are carrying guns.[29] Dispersed local settlement patterns, widespread monolingualism, and a simple aversion to contact with outsiders—the latter often a consequence of bitter struggles to maintain cultural and political autonomy in the face of outside threats—also complicated my research.

In particular, older women were reluctant to talk to me, which compounded the notable lack of local female perspectives present in the documentary record. The latter is a product both of patriarchal systems of Indigenous governance—hence local women didn't sign, far less write, petitions and other letters—and the fact that Indigenous women were frequently unwilling to even be seen by the outsiders who produced the other half of the documentary record.[30] I did eventually manage to carry out interviews with some women, which helped me to learn more about female experiences during the revolution. Thanks to the importance of the Gran Nayar's women in transmitting their cultures to subsequent generations, male elders also told me stories passed down to them by their mainly monolingual mothers and grandmothers (although in their telling, such tales are likely inflected by male perspectives).

To compensate for these problems and to shore up the ethnographical side of my investigation, I turned to the pioneering research of early anthropologists and explorers such as Carl Lumholtz and Konrad Theodor Preuss, both of whom traveled widely in the Gran Nayar in the two decades before the outbreak of the revolution. Their work provided the foundations of my analysis of the region's transformation during the first half of the twentieth century. And my analytical methodology was also influenced by the way in which Preuss, in particular, used the similarities and differences between the Gran Nayar's four peoples as the basis for deeper and more comprehensive analyses of each.[31] I also drew freely from the more recent research of Mexican scholars—many of them associated with Mexico's Escuela Nacional de Antropología e Historia (ENAH) and/or the Universidad Nacional Autónoma de Mexico (UNAM)—who have led an important shift away from the idea of the Wixáritari, above all, as representatives of "uncorrupted" pre-Hispanic traditions, and of the Gran Nayar as a whole as a mystical backwater separated from modern Mexico by a distance of hundreds of miles and thousands of years.[32] Instead, they have helped to locate the region's cultures and costumbre within wider Mesoamerican, colonial, Porfirian, or modern Mexican contexts.[33]

The end result of this research is a fine-grained, microhistorical analysis of change and continuity in the Gran Nayar over the course of a period of great national ferment, as seen through the eyes of mestizo teachers, state governors, municipal authorities, cristero rebels and federal generals, and, most important, the local people themselves. The book begins with an outline of the cultural, social, and economic history of the Gran Nayar and its peoples from pre-Hispanic times to the outbreak of the revolution, which includes a discussion of the origins and development of the idea of the region as a remote, hermetically sealed world—a misconception key to the revolutionary state's local policies and one that continues to sustain popular perceptions of the area today (chapter 1). It then explores local participation in the armed phase of the revolution between 1910 and 1920 (chapter 2) and suggests why some of the Gran Nayar's communities were more deeply involved than others and how this involvement led to the rise of caciques in many communities formerly governed only by elders and cargo-system hierarchies. Continuing on in chronological order to the early Sonoran period (1920–26), chapter 3 shows how the emergence of caciquismo combined with the effects of revolutionary state-building to foster increased intracommunal factional conflicts in some parts of the Gran Nayar and growing intercommunal conflicts in others.

This leads to a discussion (chapter 4) of the way in which these burgeoning conflicts, together with the historical and cultural particularities of each of the region's Indigenous communities, influenced local participation on either side of the first cristiada, as well as what this participation entailed. Chapter 5 returns to the issue of revolutionary state-building by examining the state's renewed attempts to "integrate" the Gran Nayar following the de facto defeat of the cristero rebels in 1929 and the ways in which continued factional conflict exacerbated preexisting tensions and led to the outbreak of another round of cristero violence in the region in 1934. The final part of the book explores local participation in this rebellion and its results at local, regional, and national levels, as well as the outcomes of the "socialist education" policies and agrarian reform enacted in the Gran Nayar between 1934 and 1940, during the presidency of Lázaro Cárdenas (chapter 6).

Many Náayarite, Wixáritari, O'dam, and Mexicaneros might struggle to understand this analysis as constituting a history, given that their histories are traditionally enshrined in ritual actions, in cyclical conceptions of time, and in complex mythical narratives. But even if my work is essentially an artifact of the same European-mestizo world whose intrusion into their time and space it itself seeks to analyze, it does at least try to respect and to reflect the ways in which the inhabitants of the Gran Nayar understand the world and their own place within it. At the same time, I hope to contribute to mainstream understandings of the revolution by showing that despite their long-standing absence in the historiography, the Náayarite, Wixáritari, O'dam, and Mexicaneros played a range of active roles in the Mexican Revolution. The nature of this participation varied from community to community (or even between factions from the same community) and changed over time, conditioned by local and regional historical and cultural idiosyncrasies; by the alliances or conflicts that existed both between and within different communities; and by the reactions of local people to the violence unleashed by the overthrow of Díaz and to the revolutionary government's subsequent attempts to "integrate" them into the Mexican nation. Thus, not all O'dam supported the cristeros, nor were all Náayarite Carrancistas; in fact, it is clear that between 1910 and 1940 there was as much—if not more—fighting between different communities of the same ethnic group, and between rival factions within the same communities, as there was between Wixáritari, say, and Náayarite, or "Indians" and "mestizos."

In conclusion, however, I argue that all of the different strategies that Náayari, Wixárika, O'dam, and Mexicanero communities, factions, and individuals employed during this tempestuous period to counter threats to their political autonomy and cultural identities, and to simultaneously obtain outside support in the context of agrarian, factional, or personal struggles, allowed them to shape the postrevolutionary settlement within the Gran Nayar and influence the course of the revolution across western Mexico as a whole. In some ways, the end result of this dual process of resistance and accommodation to the pressures and opportunities offered by the revolution was a Gran Nayar much changed by mestizo immigration, the rise of bicultural caciques, the development of new communal power structures and religious practices, the emergence of new conflicts or alliances between communities, and, in a few communities in particular, a shift toward an increasingly monetized and extractive local economy.

However, as Claude Lévi-Strauss noted more than half a century ago, Indigenous societies are far more flexible than is still often popularly imagined and are "not only capable of conserving what exists, or of retaining briefly a crumbling past, but also of elaborating audacious innovations, even though traditional structures are thus profoundly transformed."[34] And so, especially given the centrality of ideas of creation and re-creation to the cultures of the region's Indigenous peoples,[35] their participation in the Mexican Revolution did not, except in a few specific cases, fundamentally alter their identities as Náayari, Wixárika, O'dam, or Mexicanero. Furthermore, the regional postrevolutionary settlement was in fact far from settled: it remained a "work in progress" into the era of unchallenged PRI (Partido Revolucionario Institucional, or Institutional Revolutionary Party) hegemony in Mexico,[36] as the communities of the Gran Nayar continued to resist mestizo immigration and caciquismo, defend their rights to political and cultural autonomy, and petition for agrarian reform. As, indeed, they continue to do today.

1

THE GRAN NAYAR

From Conquest to Revolution

THE GRAN NAYAR is approximately the size of the U.S. state of New Jersey (or the Mexican state of Hidalgo) and forms part of Mexico's Sierra Madre Occidental mountain range. Politically, it includes some or all of the municipalities of El Nayar, La Yesca, Acaponeta, Huajicori, Ruiz, and Rosamorada in Nayarit; Mezquitic, Bolaños, and Huejuquilla in Jalisco; Mezquital and Pueblo Nuevo in Durango; and (to a much smaller degree) Valparaíso in Zacatecas. The region's volcanic plateaus are overlooked by tall peaks (the highest of which, Cerro Gordo, reaches 3,340 m) and are cut through by the Bolaños, Acaponeta, Santiago, Huaynamota, Chapalagana, San Pedro-Mezquital, Huazamota, and Jesús María Rivers (whose canyons drop to a minimum of 400 m above sea level).

Areas above 1,000 m are generally temperate, but at lower altitudes the prevailing climate is subtropical and often extremely hot. Across the region as a whole, the climate also fluctuates between a wet season between June and September and a harsh dry season that lasts from October until May. Geographically, the Acaponeta and San Pedro-Mezquital Rivers divide the mountains of the Gran Nayar from the coastal plains and mangrove swamps of Nayarit and Sinaloa to their west, while to the east, the canyon of the river Bolaños separates the region from the arid highlands of central Mexico. The Huaynamota and Santiago Rivers and the peaks of the Transvolcanic Belt mark the Gran Nayar's southern boundary.

However, the region is better defined in cultural terms, as those lands inhabited by the Náayarite, Wixáritari, O'dam, and Mexicaneros. State boundaries and the territories of each ethnic group roughly coincide, as the 5,000 km^2 Náayari homeland (or Sierra Náayari, divided between the Náayari Baja to the west and the Náayari Alta to the east) is located almost completely within Nayarit, making up nearly 18 percent of the state's total area;[1] the traditional homeland of the Wixáritari (the Sierra Wixárika) comprises some 4,000 km^2, or 5 percent, of the area of the much larger state of Jalisco (although some of this territory has been annexed to Nayarit, which has also hosted a significant Wixárika diaspora since the revolution); while the O'dam and Mexicanero territories of the Sierra O'dam occupy more than 9,000 km^2, or 7.5 percent, of Durango's total area (although one historically mixed O'dam-Mexicanero community and several exclusively Mexicanero hamlets lie across Durango's border with Nayarit). A few small villages have also long been inhabited by mestizos, known locally as *vecinos* (neighbors).

The Gran Nayar is today one of Mexico's poorest and most marginalized regions and is seen by the people of surrounding regions as wild and remote.[2] However, since the early 1980s scholars have challenged the idea that such peripheral areas have ever been truly isolated,[3] and the ancestors of the Gran Nayar's modern inhabitants are today recognized as having raided and traded both with neighboring Indigenous peoples and later with the Spaniards who sought to conquer them; served as *indios flecheros* (Indian archers) in the armies of the viceroy, while resisting Jesuit and Franciscan efforts to evangelize them; fought both as insurgents and royalists during the Mexican struggle for independence; and then, during the mid-nineteenth century, formed the core of the rebel army of Manuel Lozada, who for twenty years ruled much of western Mexico as an autonomous peasant republic. The Gran Nayar's current links—both voluntary and involuntary—to the national and international narcotics trade meanwhile place the region and its inhabitants firmly in the Mexican mainstream.[4]

It is not surprising, then, to find that the Náayarite, Wixáritari, O'dam, and Mexicaneros were active participants in the revolution, which spawned conflicts they are still struggling to resolve. But if the revolution was so important locally, why does the idea of the Gran Nayar's isolation from all national events and processes remain so prevalent? The answer lies in the fact that although hundreds of years of exchange with the wider world has helped to shape their languages, beliefs, practices, and sociopolitical structures, the Náayarite, Wixáritari, O'dam, and Mexicaneros have simultaneously managed to hold on to a high level of cultural and political autonomy. This led representatives of the colonial regime, and their nineteenth-century successors, to develop and disseminate the idea of the Gran Nayar as a space cut off from the rest of Mexico by geography and the "savagery" of its inhabitants. To understand how and why these same inhabitants participated in the events of the revolutionary period, it is not enough to explore the nature of their cultures and societies at the end of the Porfiriato and their development over the course of many centuries of exchange with external forces. We must also understand the way in which these same external forces

COMMUNITIES OF THE SIERRA NÁAYARI (AND THEIR NEIGHBORS)

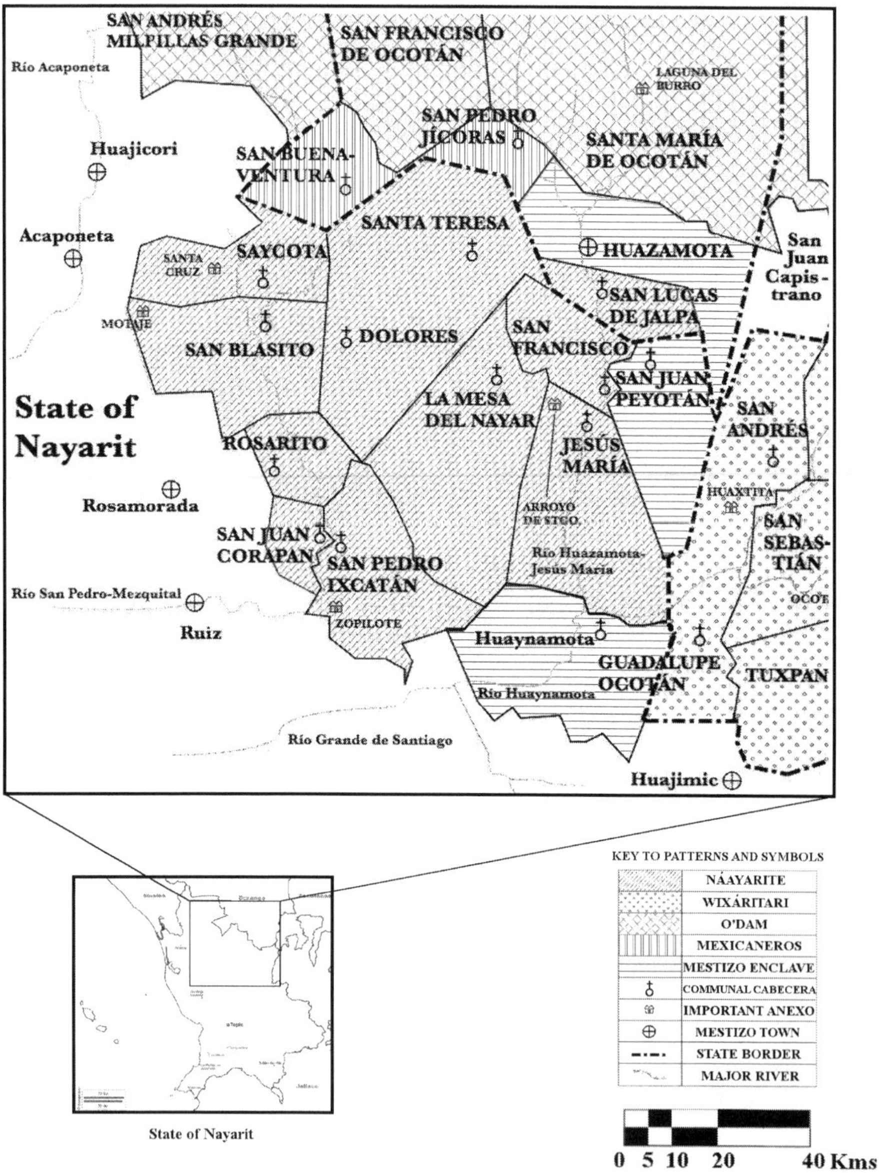

MAP 2 Nayarit, close-up with scale. Map by author, based on Plan Lerma, *Operación HUICOT*.

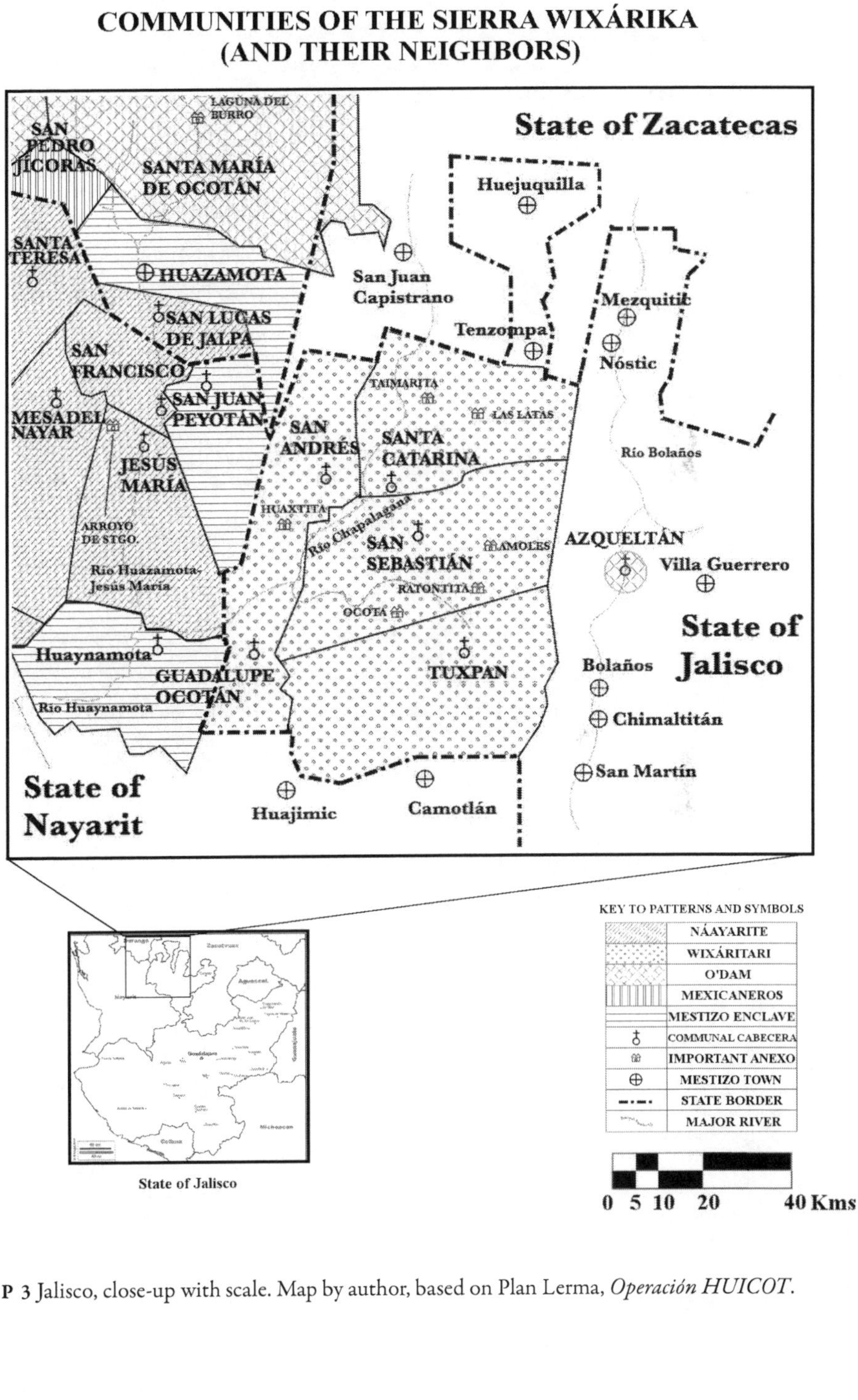

MAP 3 Jalisco, close-up with scale. Map by author, based on Plan Lerma, *Operación HUICOT*.

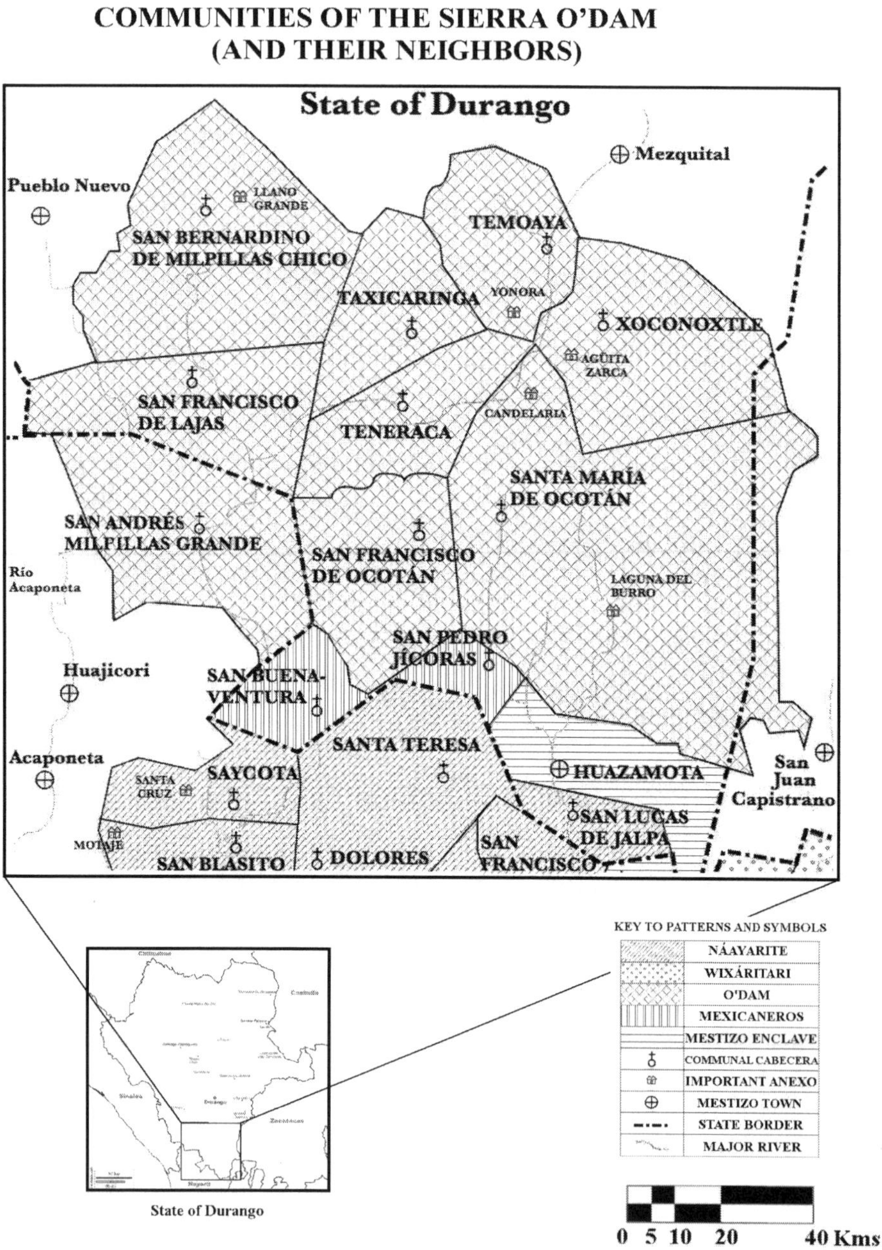

MAP 4 Durango, close-up with scale. Map by author, based on Plan Lerma, *Operación HUICOT*.

consistently refuted this reality, which led Porfirian and revolutionary officials alike to enact insensitive—and often outright antagonistic—policies in the Gran Nayar, garnering the sometimes violent opposition of many of the region's inhabitants and cementing the myth of their isolation.

THE GEOGRAPHY AND CULTURAL ECOLOGY OF THE GRAN NAYAR

The Gran Nayar's inhabitants have always depended for survival on subsistence agriculture, the success of which relies on their dispersion across the region's varied ecological niches. The rivers and seasonal streams that run through the low-lying subtropical zones are rich in fish, turtles, and crustaceans, and crops and fruit trees can be planted directly on their banks (although the soil is often poor and vulnerable to flooding). The scrublands that spread up the sides of the canyons, densely grown over with small trees, bushes, and cacti, are more versatile still, providing fertile soil for planting, a wide range of edible vegetation for gathering, and pasture for livestock. Above these scrublands, between 1,000 m and 1,400 m altitude, are forests of scrub oak that lack much useful flora and fauna, but the pine forests that dominate areas above 1,400 m provide firewood and material for building houses, a habitat rich in game (especially deer, boar, and squirrels), a huge range of edible and medicinal plants and mushrooms,[5] and grassy forest clearings on which to graze livestock.

To make the most of these varied resources, the Náayarite, Wixáritari, O'dam, and Mexicaneros traditionally live not in compact villages but in rancherías—small settlements consisting of a few wood or adobe-brick huts—scattered throughout the mountains. Each ranchería is inhabited by two or more nuclear families belonging to the same clan, or *descent group*, who have usage rights over nearby lands and are also free to raise crops and livestock on any other vacant part of their community's territory. Although both wild and domesticated animals and gathered and cultivated fruits, vegetables, mushrooms, cacti, and agaves form an important part of local diets, the inhabitants of the Gran Nayar have historically depended above all on stores of squash, beans, and maize to get them through the lean months of the dry season. These crops are grown in small plots—known in much of Mexico as *milpas* and locally as *coamiles*—cleared using slash-and-burn techniques and shifted every few years. Given the region's rugged terrain, even today many coamiles are still tended with only machetes and *coas* (digging sticks).[6]

Although all of a ranchería's inhabitants work together to gather wild foods and raise livestock, men perform most of the work in the fields, hunt, and collect firewood, while women prepare food, look after young children, and make clothes using homespun wool from locally reared sheep, and since the late nineteenth century, an unbleached cotton cloth known as *manta*, sold by itinerant traders or bought in mestizo market towns. Children take part in all these activities as soon as they are able. During the rains, some members of the family stay in the ranchería to look after the crops while others head to temporary ranches in the highlands where they pasture cattle and make cheese.[7] The inhabitants of different rancherías also come together to participate in ritualized, reciprocal collective labor, vital to intensive agricultural tasks such as clearing land and bringing in the harvest.[8]

Despite the controversy that surrounds the practice today, polygyny seems to have helped ease the burden of this life on individuals of both genders and remains prevalent throughout the Gran Nayar.[9] In general terms, the region's women and children were also more highly respected and better treated by men than in many other rural areas of the country. Although until the mid-twentieth century, Mexican law stipulated that married women were "under the control of their husband and required his permission to exercise most legal acts,"[10] in the Gran Nayar women were free to divorce their common-law husbands and did not give up their economic independence on marrying but could inherit property and goods from their families and pass these on to their own daughters.[11] Meanwhile, regardless of the status of their parents, no child was regarded as illegitimate, and adoption was an easy and widespread way of making sure children were provided for.

In addition to these subsistence strategies and attitudes toward gender roles and family structure, the Náayarite, Wixáritari, O'dam, and Mexicaneros share the same basic religious beliefs and cosmology, which are themselves rooted in wider Mesoamerican traditions. They conceive of the world as a concave gourd bowl (also a female deity) surrounded by water on all sides. Above this gourd goddess are the heavens, ruled over by another female deity, the golden eagle. Below the earth is a "dark, cavernous underworld" linked by a tunnel to the sky. The male god of the sun is associated with the deified ancestors and with hunting, as are other similarly "arid" and "austere" deities such as fire, wind, the Morning Star, and the deer, who is also the peyote cactus. Creation and fertility, and thus water and agriculture, are the preserve of female deities, including those of maize, squash, the rains, and local lakes and rivers.[12] However, "there exist at least as many deities as there are human beings . . . and just as amongst humans, there are many distinct gods who share the same name."[13] Religion and ritual permeate all aspects of life, as "even in the most insignificant activities, they invoke the multitude of their gods and ancestors, trying to win their support through offerings and prayers."[14] Belief in gods' multiple identities also extends into religious practice, as shamans not only mediate between gods, ancestors, and the population at large but also, in the context of some rituals, temporarily become gods themselves.[15]

The gourd world that humans, animals, gods, spirits, and ancestors together inhabit is seen as divided into four parts, at the center of which is the Gran Nayar itself. The boundaries of the latter are marked at each of its four cardinal points and again at its center by geographical features—mountain peaks, caves, lakes, and springs—that are also deities and/or ancestors themselves. Similar sets of sacred landmarks, or *mojoneras*, traditionally mark the boundaries of the communal territories into which the Gran Nayar is divided and the descent group territories into which the latter are split. The idea of the universe as a structure of endless worlds-within-worlds, with each one a concentric circle defined by its four cardinal points and center, has given rise to a sacred numerology centered on the number five.

The peoples of the Gran Nayar, like many Mesoamerican groups, hold maize to be the sacred origin of all life and tell that the gods created man from maize dough. Alongside maize grown for consumption in the form of tortillas, tamales, or atole, each Náayari, Wixárika, O'dam, and Mexicanero descent group sows its own special "ancestral" variety, handed down from generation to generation, for exclusive ritual use. But activities such as trade and war have also shaped local worldviews and ritual practices. Before the conquest, the region lay at the intersection of important trade routes that connected Aridoamerica to the central Mexican plateau, the Pacific littoral, and the great civilizations of Mesoamerica. The ancestors of the Náayarite, Wixáritari, O'dam, and Mexicaneros were warriors and traders as well as farmers and hunters, controlling the flow of commercially and/or ritually important goods such as turquoise, feathers, animal skins, seashells, peyote, and salt through the mountains,[16] and trade remains important to local livelihoods.[17] Memories of ancient economic and cultural connections have survived in local costumbre, for example in pilgrimages to the Pacific Coast, where they once obtained salt and which is regarded as both a "chaotic" region of fetid fertility and the land of the dead,[18] whose souls take the form of the tiny flies that swarm in the mangrove swamps.[19] Likewise, Wixáritari still travel hundreds of miles east to "hunt" peyote in the deserts of San Luis Potosí, where the sun was born and the deified ancestors reside.[20]

The costumbre of the Náayarite, Wixáritari, O'dam, and Mexicaneros is inseparable from the landscape in which they live, which the gods brought into being to replace previous worlds destroyed as part of an ongoing "cosmic battle" between light and darkness, order and chaos, aridity and fertility. The story of this creation is inscribed in the geography of the Gran Nayar and the surrounding regions, which is strewn with thousands of sites identified with the gods and ancestors and their stories. Journeys along the region's caminos reales—trails hacked out of the mountains during the colonial era or earlier, which link the region's rancherías with one another and with the rest of Mexico—double as pilgrimages along sacred routes that, like the songlines of Australia's Aboriginal peoples, retrace and connect together the hundreds of different narratives that make up the epic history of the creation.[21] In the Gran Nayar, land is simultaneously culture, identity, and history.

This history is not a linear progression of events but rather a web of similar or contrasting categories of event, which, like the sacred sites with which they are identified, are "not temporally removed but spatially removed."[22] Such an understanding of the past is characterized, above all, by "its lack of remoteness." The gods created all of the world's races at the same time as the world itself: first bringing into being the peoples of the Gran Nayar, and then the Spaniards/Mexicans, and then the "gringos" (white foreigners). A sense of the more recent arrival of the Spaniards, and their introduction of iron tools, money, and cattle, is embedded within local historical memory through their conceptual association with the cult of the (Spanish) Catholic saints, but the appearance of all these in the Gran Nayar is nonetheless projected back to the mythical past.[23] The conquest is thus part of the creation, while the nineteenth-century rebel leader Manuel Lozada becomes Jesus Christ himself, betrayed and killed by "Jews" not in Jerusalem but in Mexico City.[24]

The ritualized recitation of parts of this cyclical, categorizing, and somewhat freewheeling history constitutes an essential element of ceremonies known as *mitotes*, which are central to the religious practices of the Gran Nayar's inhabitants. These ceremonies ensure, amongst other things, that the ancestors will grant the participants health, protection, plentiful rains, and a successful harvest and are therefore timed to coincide with the different stages of maize cultivation. Mitotes usually involve long sessions of fasting and feature sacrifices to the gods, the hunting of deer, the use of "holy water" gathered at sacred springs to bless adults and baptize children, and often the consumption of specially brewed alcoholic drinks and/or peyote. Most culminate in several nights of dancing around a sacred fire at the center of a dedicated ritual space called a *patio* (or in the case of the Wixáritari, in a temple called a *tuki*).[25] Depending on whether they are being celebrated at descent group or communal level, mitotes are held either at the ranchería of a clan elder or at a sacred space close to the center of a community. Descent group mitotes emphasize shared kinship bonds and the parallels between the life cycles of humans and maize through the ritual use of sacred "family" maize and the initiation of children while celebrating the harvest.[26] Communal mitotes meanwhile stress the unity of the community and, at a higher level, the eternal struggle between light and darkness.

Mitotes also involve pilgrimages to, and along, the boundaries of either communal or descent group territories to ritually maintain the stability and integrity of these borders, as well as the bonds amongst the individuals living within them.[27] Mitotes additionally serve to showcase the purity and abnegation of the elders in charge, legitimizing their ritual-political authority over the rest of the participants. These rituals therefore embody and reinforce comprehensive local ways of understanding both their local environments and the universe as a whole.[28] Given the tendency of the peoples of the Gran Nayar to view identity not as a fixed oneness but rather as an aggregation of multiple, transmutable equivalences, sacred sites such as mitote patios and boundary markers represent, through synecdoche, the universe itself.[29] By a similar logic, the rituals performed at these places are not reenactments of the original creation of the universe but a continuation of this same act itself.[30] Such actions propitiate the non-human forces—spirits, animals, gods, and ancestors—who control nature and ensure the physical and spiritual health of individuals, descent groups and communities, and peace, not just in the Gran Nayar but throughout the world. They also guarantee that world's very existence: for the Náayarite, Wixáritari, O'dam, and Mexicaneros believe that if they give up their costumbre, the cycle of world destruction will begin again, and the universe, no longer re-created through ritual, will not only cease to exist but will never have existed in the first place.[31]

CONQUISTADORS, CATHOLICS, AND PRIEST-KINGDOMS: THE GRAN NAYAR, 1530-1810

Even from a "rationalist" historical perspective, the Náayari, Wixárika, O'dam, and Mexicanero belief that their world came into being at the same time as the conquest is actually fairly accurate. It was only from the 1530s, when Spanish conquistador Nuño Beltrán de Guzmán arrived in western Mexico, that the Gran Nayar began to evolve into a cultural-geographical space distinct from the surrounding regions. After wantonly slaughtering much of the local population, Guzmán incorporated the areas today inhabited by the Náayarite and Wixáritari into the province of Nueva Galicia. Thirty years later, Basque adventurers in search of new silver mines finally conquered the lands of the O'dam to the north, which became part of the rival imperial province of Nueva Vizcaya.[32]

Disagreements between the two provinces over their borders and the devastation wrought by the Mixtón War (1532–42) between the Spaniards and an alliance of rebellious western Mexican tribes obstructed the foundation of Spanish military garrisons—or *presidios*—in the Gran Nayar. After the end of the Mixtón War, the region became a classic "shatter zone,"[33] a safe haven for Indigenous refugees fleeing Spanish domination, including "defeated but still well-organized Caxcans and trans-Tarascan groups."[34] These groups continued to violently resist Franciscan attempts to missionize them, most famously during the Tepehuan Revolt of 1616–20, which destroyed much of Nueva Vizcaya's colonial infrastructure.[35]

After the defeat of the O'dam rebels in 1620, Spanish soldiers and Franciscan missionaries based in Zacatecas renewed their evangelizing efforts.[36] However, the

O'dam, who had "neither lords nor kings" and were instead led by ritual specialists,[37] refused to move permanently to the new concentrated settlements established by the missionaries. Instead, they regularly headed back to their ranches in the mountains to hunt, gather, and participate in mitote rituals,[38] or fled permanently to remote parts of the sierra to avoid forced labor in the Spanish mines or on haciendas.[39] As the seventeenth century progressed, however, the Franciscans gradually managed to settle some O'dam. They founded a mission at San Bernardino de Milpillas Chico, with a dependent settlement—or *visita*—at San Francisco de Lajas;[40] refounded an old mission at Huazamota, with visitas at San Pedro Jícoras, San Antonio de Padua, and San Lucas de Jalpa; and established a third mission at Mezquital, with visitas at Temoaya, Xoconoxtle, Taxicaringa, Teneraca, Santa María Ocotán, and San Francisco Ocotán.[41]

Each of these settlements was centered around a church whose resident *santitos* (images or statues of saints) were integrated by local people into their costumbre as "Spanish gods," regarded as the originators of innovations, such as cattle and currency, that had arrived with the Spaniards. Although the Franciscans entrusted the cults of these gods to newly formed communal *cofradías* (sodalities), the shamans who led the local mitote ceremonies managed to cement their preexisting authority by monopolizing communication with the santitos,[42] who sent them messages through "dreams or accidents."[43]

To the south of the O'dam, the upheaval of the conquest prompted several Indigenous polities in what is today the Sierra Náayari and the western part of the Sierra Wixárika to unite into a single kingdom.[44] It remained independent until 1722, when it became the last Indian realm in Mexico to fall to the Spanish.[45] Dominated by the ancestors of today's Náayarite, it was governed by a politico-religious leader known as the Tonatí, or Rey Nayar.[46] Spanish colonial sources referred to the inhabitants of this polity as *nayaritas* (hence the names Gran Nayar or Nayarit for their homeland, and their own name for themselves, Náayarite). Their number included "gentile" and apostate Indigenous people from across western Mexico, escaped African slaves, renegade *castas* (mixed-race people), and even a few Spaniards.[47] Although neither Catholic missionaries nor Spanish soldiers were permitted to enter the Rey Nayar's kingdom, his subjects traded in salt and livestock with the inhabitants of nearby coastal regions, and some worked seasonally in the mines of Durango and Zacatecas.[48]

As a result of such contacts, the nayaritas began to adopt elements of the Catholic faith into their costumbre.[49] However, their priest-kingdom was ultimately held together by resolutely non-Christian practices, such as mass mitote ceremonies—which at this point featured human sacrifice—overseen by the Tonatí. His capital at La Mesa became the focal point of a "centralized political and religious tradition"[50] that united the region's disparate descent groups, themselves defined by participation in family-level mitotes.[51] Although the military capacity of this unified population was key to their resistance to Spanish expansion, colonial-era missionaries and soldiers—just like the teachers and military commanders of the 1920s and 1930s—preferred to use geography to explain the continued independence of the Tonatí's kingdom, describing the region as "furious and horrible. . . . It is not even possible to ride horseback in this country."[52]

Many of the Wixáritari living to the east of the proto-Náayari homeland also owed allegiance to the Tonatí. However, at a lower level they were governed by their own politico-religious councils, each one based at a particular tuki temple (plural: *tukite*) and headed by a ceremonial specialist called a *kawiteru* (plural: *kawiterusixi*). These specialists and their councils were drawn from the descent groups living in the area around each tuki and headed the rituals that held each group together as a political unit. However, as the Spaniards established mines, missions, and military colonies staffed by Nahuatl-speaking settlers on the eastern borders of the Sierra Wixárika,[53] the Wixáritari came into increasing contact with the colonial world. In general, the Wixáritari adopted a policy of "alternately accommodating, appropriating and resisting colonial Spanish institutions through a shifting strategy of commercial exchanges, mercenary services, apostasy, and raiding, sometimes against their Indigenous neighbours."[54] By 1649, some of the Wixáritari of the Huejuquilla valley to the north of the modern Sierra Wixárika had been settled at Tenzompa,[55] while missions were also founded at Ostoc and Huajimic in the south.[56] By 1727, the Franciscans had penetrated what is today the Sierra Wixárika proper, establishing a mission at San Sebastián with visitas at San Andrés and Santa Catarina.[57]

The inhabitants of these new Wixárika settlements, along with many O'dam from farther north,[58] took part in the final conquest of the Náayari priest-kingdom in 1722. But despite this apparent accommodation to Spanish rule, a few years later the colonial authorities accused the Wixáritari of San Andrés and Santa Catarina of conspiring with rebellious Náayarite.[59] Meanwhile, just as in the Sierra O'dam, the Catholic ceremonialism and civil-religious hierarchies that the missionaries imposed on the Wixáritari were integrated into the existing politico-religious framework of their costumbre. The different tukite became the centers of districts—still governed by councils of kawiterutsixi—into which each community's territory was subdivided. Catholic churches meanwhile evolved into something like communal tuki temples, consecrated not just to particular saints but also to the Wixárika deities with whom they became closely associated. Just as the influence of the kawiterutsixi was validated by their leadership of tuki-centered ceremonial cycles,[60] the power of the new communal authorities was legitimized by new communal rituals held in the new churches. The evolution of an additional role for the kawiterutsixi as advisers to these authorities linked ritual-political innovations back to older power structures and ensured the cohesion of each community's multiple tuki districts.[61]

A similar phenomenon occurred in the area of the Náayari priest-kingdom after it was brought under Spanish control. The Jesuits, rather than the Franciscans, were made responsible for evangelizing most of the defeated Náayarite and eventually congregated them into missions at Jesús María, La Mesa, Santa Teresa, San Juan Peyotán, San Juan Corapan, Rosarito, and Huaynamota.[62] They also settled a group of Indigenous Tecualmes at San Pedro Ixcatán, where they soon abandoned their original language for Nahuatl.[63] The Franciscans also settled a mixture of Náayarite and Nahuatl-speakers at Saycota, San Blasito, and San Buenaventura.[64] Within each of these new settlements—some of which doubled as military presidios—elements of Catholic ceremonialism, such as the cult of the santitos, were absorbed into Náayari costumbre,[65] and even after the Náayarite returned to their dispersed ranches following the expulsion of the Jesuits from Mexico in 1767, they continued to use the missions and their churches "as ceremonial and assembly centres."[66] By the late eighteenth century, the Náayarite thus possessed "a half-digested Christianity but a well organized and functioning civil-religious hierarchy,"[67] which held together their disparate descent groups in the absence of the Tonatí and allowed them to continue to mobilize effectively against external threats.

MEXICAN INDEPENDENCE, MANUEL LOZADA, AND THE CONSOLIDATION OF COSTUMBRE, 1810-1873

The outbreak of the Mexican War of Independence in 1810 ushered in a renewed period of political and cultural autonomy for the inhabitants of the Gran Nayar. Many embraced the pro-independence cause and forced the Franciscans to flee their missions in 1811.[68] The violence also caused population movements that may have resulted in local Nahuatl speakers—the people we now know as Mexicaneros—arriving in southern Durango.[69] After Mexico won its independence in 1821, Liberal and Conservative factions of the national elite embarked on a thirty-year struggle for control of the young nation. As central and state governments were constantly overthrown and reordered, few officials took it on themselves to visit the "wild" Indians of the Gran Nayar. Meanwhile, although the Catholic Church engaged in intensive evangelical activity across much of the country—to the extent that some scholars see the nineteenth century as the era of Mexico's "second spiritual conquest"[70]—none of the Gran Nayar's communities had a resident priest until the 1890s[71] because of regional volatility and the local population's poverty and because "the secular clergy were not accustomed to the lifestyle imposed on them by the remoteness of the mountains."[72] Franciscan missionaries from Zacatecas worked amongst the Wixáritari between 1843 and 1859,[73] but their presence was sporadic, and they mainly occupied themselves with the destruction of "idolatrous" native shrines (which were nonetheless quickly rebuilt).[74] And even those few Náayarite, Wixáritari, O'dam, and Mexicaneros who were baptized remained distrustful of official representatives of the Catholic faith, whom the Náayarite, for example, believed "carried disease in their cassocks."[75]

Support for the revolutionary movement of mestizo peon-turned-bandit chief and agrarian reformer Manuel Lozada allowed the Gran Nayar's inhabitants to maintain their political and religious autonomy into the 1870s and thus avoid the deleterious effects of the mid-century Liberal Reform Laws.[76] Between 1853 and 1873, Lozada ruled almost all of what is today the state of Nayarit (then the Seventh Canton of Jalisco), and much of the surrounding area, as an independent peasant republic.[77] First rising to prominence through an alliance with Tepic's commercial elite, who resented the political and economic interference of their rivals in the state capital of Guadalajara, Lozada soon began to help the region's peasants take back territory lost because of the Reform, which had mandated the division and distribution of communal and church-owned lands and opened them up for purchase by speculators and large landowners.[78] Federal troops intervened in the early 1850s on behalf of Lozada's enemies and pursued him and his followers into the mountains of the Sierra Náayari.

However, the Náayarite regarded the appearance of government soldiers in their homeland as a threat to their autonomy and many joined Lozada. They soon made up the backbone of his proto-*agrarista* army, despite their communities having been little affected by the Reform.[79] Some Wixáritari supported Lozada for the same reasons their Náayari neighbors did,[80] or as a reaction to the Franciscans' destruction of their sacred sites and the invasion of their lands by mestizos.[81] Lozada also won some support in southern Durango, particularly in Huazamota and San Lucas.[82] Indigenous support for Lozada's movement provided journalists and politicians with the opportunity to condemn it as a "caste war" aimed at the "destruction of the white race," compounding colonial ideas of the Gran Nayar as a remote and impenetrable bastion of savagery.[83]

Over the course of the sixty or so years from the War of Independence to the death of Manuel Lozada, the religious beliefs, cultural forms, and sociopolitical structures that still define life in the Gran Nayar took definitive shape. As often occurs in the absence of priests or government officials, local people subverted and transformed external ideas as they incorporated them into their own discourses.[84] The sign of the cross became a symbol of the four cardinal points, while the Virgin of Guadalupe and the Aztec Eagle—symbols of the Mexican Catholic Church and state respectively—became twin avatars of the eagle goddess of the heavens.[85] In the same way, given their propensity to stack numerous different ideas inside one another like so many Russian dolls, the inhabitants of the Gran Nayar imbued Catholic festivals with pagan meanings, converting them into surreal burlesques of the practices originally introduced by the Franciscans or Jesuits.[86]

These church-based fiestas, which included Lenten carnivals, rowdy Easter passion plays, and the name days of locally venerated saints, now celebrated not only the story of Christ and the lives of his followers but also the eternal conflict between light and darkness; thus for the Náayarite and some Wixáritari and Mexicaneros, Easter festivals that reenacted Christ's death and resurrection became wild celebrations of fertility and disorder.[87] Catholic saints were meanwhile "completely assimilated into the framework of pagan concepts and Indigenous spirituality,"[88] as God the Father, the resurrected Christ, the Virgin, and saints such as James, Michael, and Sebastian were identified with arid, "austere" deities like the sun and the ancestors, while the "dead" Christ was conflated with the deities of fertility and the underworld.[89]

The santitos of the region's churches were regarded as gods that had "existed since the beginning of the world" and offered prayer arrows, gourds, flowers, raw cotton (representing rain clouds), alcohol, and animal sacrifices.[90] They were often dressed in the costumes used by a community's ritual dancers or carried other markers of local ethnic identity.[91] Each community's eponymous santito was regarded as its literal founder: a god who in ancient times had appeared suddenly—and miraculously—in a nearby sacred space, such as a cave. Shamans then persuaded them to move to their current positions through prayer, fasting, and sacrifices and by constructing churches for them to live in. Each community then coalesced around these new ritual centers.[92] As in Indigenous communities throughout Latin America, such foundation stories conspicuously neglect all mention of missionaries or Spanish soldiers and instead symbolically affirm local power over "foreign" santitos and the privileged nature of the relationship between these and the community as a whole, which in the Gran Nayar was not mediated by the institutional church or its representatives.[93]

Just as the cults of santitos became part of costumbre and local mythical histories, the santitos became sacred sites in themselves, integrated into the physical networks of the holy that crisscrossed the Gran Nayar. Their name days became important celebrations in their home communities, and some particularly powerful santitos might receive Indigenous (and sometimes mestizo) pilgrims from across the region or even be loaned out to neighboring communities on special occasions. For the population of the Gran Nayar, as for many of Mexico's other Indian peoples,[94] the celebration of such festivals helped to counterbalance the division and atomization of Indigenous society promoted by colonial "parcelization" policies by fostering both ritual and social exchange between groups that might otherwise have little opportunity to mingle.[95]

Church-based ceremonialism also underpinned the autonomous political systems being constructed in the Gran Nayar. Each former Jesuit or Franciscan mission became the ceremonial capital, or cabecera, of a self-governing republic that encompassed the lands to which the Spanish Crown had given its inhabitants collective title during the colonial period. These territorial claims were based on documents known as *títulos virreinales*, venerated by local people as objects of great power that, in the far distant "origin times," had been brought to their communities from Mexico City by the deified ancestors, or even Jesus Christ himself.[96] These stories transformed textual "monarchic relics" into genuinely religious (although hardly orthodox Catholic) relics,[97] which, as in other Indigenous regions, were considered proof of each community's "god-given right" to its lands.[98]

Aside from a sacred título virreinal, the Gran Nayar's communal cabeceras contained little more than a church to house its santitos, a space for the celebration of communal mitotes, a jail, the "courthouse" (*casa real*) that served as the headquarters of the communal authorities, and houses and a special maize field for the exclusive use of these officials.[99] Although the rest of each community's inhabitants came to its cabecera only a few times a year, membership of a community remained more important in the Gran Nayar than wider "tribal" or ethnolinguistic identities. However, such membership was not only contingent on birthright, as although their communities were certainly "corporate," they were not necessarily "closed," and Indigenous people who settled in a different community because of marriage or commercial interests could become *comuneros* through participation in communal mitotes, church-based fiestas, and assemblies.[100]

Each community was ruled by a group of male officeholders who together constituted a cargo hierarchy known as the *gobierno tradicional*, or traditional government. A defining feature of cargo systems—not just locally but throughout Latin America—is that their members are not paid for their services, which are instead seen as a personal "sacrifice" on the community's behalf. After serving their term, officeholders "return to their everyday occupations as ordinary citizens. Respect in the community, experience in lesser posts, and the financial resources to take time away from farming are the main prerequisites for election."[101] In the Gran Nayar, each official was nominated for and confirmed in their post via a series of rituals that legitimized their exercise of power. Once in office, they were also responsible for ensuring that communal costumbre was performed correctly, further blurring the lines between ritual and political life.

At the head of each gobierno was a small council of elderly ritual specialists (the *consejo de ancianos*) who led communal costumbre, nominated those who would fill the civil-religious *cargos* (rotating offices) that made up the second tier of communal government, and advised the latter during their time in office. An elder became eligible for membership of the consejo only if he had himself worked his way through the complete cargo system hierarchy. *Consejeros* were often the ritual leaders of their community's most influential descent groups, which helped to knit together communal- and kinship-level political organizations. Although consejeros were appointed for life, they were usually elderly by the time they became eligible for such roles, and the makeup of the consejo was subject to frequent change as its members died and were replaced.

The second layer of a community's traditional government was loosely divided between church and courthouse cargo hierarchies, both rooted in systems of governance that missionaries had established throughout colonial Mexico. However, in the Gran Nayar their origin was attributed to Christ himself and associated with the worship of the sun and the morning and evening stars.[102] Courthouse officials served one-year terms and carried ceremonial staffs—or *varas de mando*—that were regarded not as mere symbols of authority but as gods who constituted the essence of authority in themselves.[103] These offices (or rather the varas with which they were associated) formed a pyramid at whose apex was the *gobernador* (communal governor). He and his seconds were responsible for resolving conflicts between different members of the community, helping the elders to oversee and themselves funding communal costumbre, and maintaining the integrity of the community's territory. Below such senior offices came "military" cargos with roots in the Spanish colonial militia system,[104] including *capitán* (captain), *alférez* (second lieutenant), and *sargento* (sergeant), who often played an important role in rowdy communal Easter festivals. At the bottom of the courthouse hierarchy were the *alguaciles*, or *topiles* (sheriffs), young men who formed a kind of communal police force and acted as messengers and enforcers of the governor's rulings.

Church offices, such as that of the *fiscal* (treasurer) and *mayordomo* (steward), were also common in Indigenous communities across Mexico, having originally been created by missionaries to oversee local cofradias that were absorbed into communal cargo systems during the mid-nineteenth century.[105] In the Gran Nayar, the fiscal acted as sacristan of the community's church and was also in some cases responsible for the upkeep of its mitote patio. *Mayordomías* (stewardships) were jointly assigned to married couples, who were given responsibility for organizing the cult of one of the community's santitos for one-, three-, or even five-year terms. Such roles were the most important public political openings for women in the Gran Nayar, although women were also assigned more strictly religious roles related to communal mitotes[106] and frequently played key "behind the scenes" roles in community politics, either as advisers to male relatives with courthouse cargos or as healers or even shamans.

In some Mexican Indigenous communities, it was believed that only elderly men "who had worked all the way up the cargo system, possessed sufficient wisdom to speak on community affairs."[107] But in the Gran Nayar, while consejeros wielded significant political influence, decisions about important issues that affected the whole community were reached by consensus at assemblies in which all adult members of the community (including women and youths over the age of fifteen) were expected to take part. An assembly could last several days, and an individual's ability to influence the debate depended not just on age or standing in the community but on their talent as a public speaker.[108] This was linked to the vital role that elegant oratory—including the ritualized recitation of prayers and mythical-historical narratives, often over the course of several consecutive days and nights—played in local ceremonial life, making the Indigenous peoples of the Gran Nayar, like their Yaqui or Mazatec contemporaries, highly "sensitive to 'fine words'" in political as well as religious settings (as far as the two could be separated in the first place).[109]

However, despite the evolution of these complex structures of communal governance, membership of a descent group remained just as important to the identities of the Gran Nayar's inhabitants as membership of a community. Ritual activity, overseen by male elders who inherited their offices for life from fathers or uncles,[110] defined the makeup and structure of each descent group and united the inhabitants of dispersed rancherías into subcommunal political and territorial blocs, which often developed into communal political factions. The rancherías of particularly sizeable or politically powerful descent groups might be grouped around a larger settlement, known as an *anexo*, featuring a small chapel or mitote patio at which rituals halfway between those of the descent group proper and the community were carried out. Among the Náayarite and Wixáritari, descent was traced bilaterally. An individual was therefore eligible to participate in the descent group mitotes of both their mother and father, and of both of their parents' parents, and so on.[111] Among the O'dam and Mexicaneros, descent was reckoned more restrictively; individuals took part only in the mitotes of their father's family, limiting them to membership of a single descent group synonymous with their paternal surname.[112] It is impossible to know for sure how many members different descent groups had in this period but as is the case today, their sizes likely varied a great deal, fluctuating across time as some expanded and others died out.[113]

Descent groups were always exogamous (or out-marrying), and alliances between them were often shored up through marriage. Because of the lack of Catholic priests in the sierra, such unions were officiated over by elders and were therefore unrecognized by the church. Some Náayari parents apparently arranged the marriages of their children without consulting them, often for political reasons.[114] And while most Wixárika, O'dam, and Mexicanero couples came together of their own volition, the parental consent necessary to cement a union might be withheld if a match was deemed impolitic.[115] As in much of rural Mexico, alliances between different descent groups could also be cemented via the church-based institution of compadrazgo (godparenthood), which ritually tied together a child's father and godfather (*compadres*) or mother and godmother (*comadres*).[116] Although less important than kinship or simple friendship in deciding political allegiances, compadrazgo still helped to reinforce personal ties to particular communal factions[117] and to ritualize economic and/or political alliances between Indians and mestizos, given that the latter inherently lacked descent group affiliations.[118]

Although the Náayarite, Wixáritari, O'dam, and Mexicaneros each recognized that, culturally and linguistically, they constituted separate peoples, they also believed that they all shared a common ancestry, acknowledged that their worldviews and costumbres were similar, and saw themselves as collectively inhabiting a territory much larger than any one ethnicity's homeland. These ideas were reinforced by the cults of regional saints, and even more important, by regular pilgrimages to ancestral holy places whose importance extended beyond the boundaries of any one community or ethnic group. These included Teekata, within the Wixárika community of Santa Catarina; Tuakamuta, near the Náayari community of La Mesa; and Cerro Gordo, on the boundary between the O'dam communities of Lajas and San Bernardino. The prominence of such sites conveyed special influence on the communities that controlled access to them. But the existence of such conceptual and ritual links failed to create much ethnopolitical solidarity amongst the four peoples of the Gran Nayar as a whole or the communities amongst which the Wixárika, O'dam, and Mexicanero populations were split.

Loose political bonds *did* exist between the different Náayari communities. These were founded on pilgrimages and ritual exchanges carried out by communal authorities at sacred sites across the Náayari homeland—practices that first emerged during the era of the Náayari priest-kingdom[119] and developed further between 1853 and 1873, during the rule of Manuel Lozada.[120] While each Náayari community constituted a self-governing entity—as guaranteed by Lozada's defense of each community's "right to absolute independence and sovereignty"[121]—the practice of intercommunity costumbre, with the Náayari "capital" of Jesús María at its center, facilitated the political and military coordination of the region's authorities in defense of pan-communal interests. To this end, Lozada and his Náayari lieutenant, Dionisimo Gerónimo, presumably in coordination with the local traditional authorities, annually appointed a "governor of the indigenous territories" to rule the Sierra Náayari as a whole,[122] as well as subordinate politico-military officials to serve as Lozada's representatives in each of the region's communities.[123] In contrast to the chronically divided communities of their Indigenous neighbors, the Náayarite therefore enjoyed into the early twentieth century a politico-military cohesion that, while less solid than that of the Yaqui communities of Sonora,[124] is perhaps comparable to the solidarity that existed between the Eleven Pueblos of Michoacán.[125]

TERRITORIAL CONFLICTS AND ETHNIC TENSIONS: THE GRAN NAYAR UNDER PORFIRIO DÍAZ

In 1869, the government in Mexico City elevated Jalisco's seventh canton to the status of a federal military district, formally asserting central authority over Manuel Lozada's strongholds in place of Jalisco's weak state government. The creation of the new entity—named after its capital, Tepic—gave rise to long-running territorial disputes with the neighboring states of Jalisco, Zacatecas, and Durango. In the short term, these conflicts weakened the jurisdiction of all four entities over the Gran Nayar. However, Lozada's defeat and death in 1873 deprived the Náayarite, Wixáritari, O'dam, and Mexicaneros of an important protector and left them vulnerable to the political, cultural, and territorial pressures unleashed on Mexico during the rule of Porfirio Díaz (a period known as the Porfiriato).

Díaz acceded to the presidency in 1876 and quickly sought to expand central government control over peripheral regions. In central and southern states, Porfirian reforms converted communities into municipalities and their cargo systems into municipal governments, binding them—in theory—to regional and central authorities.[126] However, de jure authority over the Gran Nayar was instead handed to the prefects of distant market towns. In each of the region's communities, these prefects created new civil and paramilitary offices—such as *juez auxiliar* (assistant judge) and *jefe del cuartel* (chief of staff)—to locally represent Porfirian authority.[127] But in practice these offices were usually assigned to Indigenous people who already held cargos within their traditional communal governments, or they became cargos in themselves, integrated into preexisting communal power structures "through curious ceremonies."[128] Instead of establishing state authority over the Gran Nayar, the new officials continued to answer to local elders and communal assemblies and to "obey in everything the traditional governor."[129]

In this period, a few government employees were also sent into the Gran Nayar to work as teachers and otherwise represent the government. However, few Indigenous parents allowed their children to attend the new schools,[130] and if teachers tried to make local people pay taxes or otherwise meddled in communal politics, they were forced out by their hosts. Many therefore abandoned their roles as servants of the state and instead served the gobiernos tradicionales as scribes.[131] Unlike their equivalents in comparable Indigenous regions of Mexico, mestizo officials therefore amassed little real power in the Gran Nayar during the Porfiriato.[132] It was only when the Indians left their mountains that regional authorities were able to exert any real power over them, for example by fining them for wearing their traditional costumes in urban areas (which spurred the development of a lively trade in rented trousers in cities such as Tepic and Colotlán).[133]

Economic pressures, rather than political reforms or the forced wearing of trousers, posed by far the greatest threat to the communities of the Gran Nayar. The region constituted "an unknown country" for the people of nearby cities like Tepic,[134] and in general the Gran Nayar's inhabitants were far less integrated into regional markets than the Indigenous peoples of central Mexico,[135] or even those of the country's northern and southern peripheries.[136] However, trade along western Mexico's caminos reales still linked lowland merchants and cattle ranchers to the inhabitants of the Gran Nayar, some of whom also took advantage of religious obligations to do business in the towns they passed en route to distant sacred sites.[137]

The most important regional signifier of wealth and prestige in this period—and thus the single most important trade commodity—was cattle (which were also revered in religious terms by the regional Indigenous groups, in particular the Wixáritari).[138] Mestizo muleteers journeyed into the mountains to exchange manta, machetes, salt, and raw cane sugar for Indigenous-raised livestock.[139] The growing wealth of the Indigenous people involved in such commerce led to the emergence of economic divisions in the Gran Nayar's traditionally egalitarian communities. Norwegian explorer Carl Lumholtz, who visited the region at the turn of the century, observed that in the Sierra Wixárika, where "formerly nothing was owned individually except the house, some dogs, and the corn gathered at the harvest," some now owned "cattle, mules and horses, sheep and hens, and a number of iron implements," as well as money. The latter was spent on "cotton cloth and red flannel," glass beads ("considered good investments, as diamonds are among Americans"), and brandy.[140] Shamans benefited disproportionately from the new influx of cash and luxury goods into the Gran Nayar, for in return for curing their patients they might charge "from ten to fifteen dollars, or its equivalent in naturalia" and "return from a professional tour . . . with eight or ten cows as net profit, beside sheep, goats, and donkeys."[141]

Much of this new wealth was either "buried in great secrecy" or ritually redistributed, mainly through the sacrifice of animals, as "even where only a few hens are owned profits must be shared with the gods." Livestock numbers were also kept down by disease, accidents, and the depredations of wolves, bears, and other predators (including bandits). Around half of the Wixárika population owned no livestock at all, while "the well-to-do have a few cows, two or three mules, half a dozen sheep, and several hens. Only three or four [Wixáritari] . . . own [large] herds of cattle."[142]

During his time in Nayarit, Lumholtz also met Náayarite who had become rich through submitting to "fasting and restrictions for a month, or even a year" in order to win the favor of the "master of the mountain," for the "belief that the mountains are the masters of all riches—of money, cattle, mules, sheep, and shepherds—is common among the tribes of the Sierra Madre."[143] Although Lumholtz neglects to mention the exact quantity of wealth these Náayarite had amassed, we can assume that the general economic situation in the Náayari, O'dam, and Mexicanero communities was little different from that prevailing in the Sierra Wixárika, where, Lumholtz concluded that

> the few who are well off and could afford better things live no better than the others; they eat their tortillas and beans and sleep on the floor, as they always did, and know no

> better. On the other hand, the disadvantages are very manifest. Since the acquisition of domestic animals, the people have begun to realise that there are rich and poor in this world, and those who own little are filled with envy of their more opulent relations. In order to attend to a number of animals, it is necessary to employ helpers, and thus the foundations are laid for social distinctions which not so long ago were entirely unknown among them.[144]

By the end of the nineteenth century, the regional cattle trade had obviously begun to threaten the socioeconomic equilibrium of the Gran Nayar's communities. It also jeopardized their territorial integrity, as mestizo ranchers increasingly penetrated the Gran Nayar in search of pasture for their own cattle. As in other marginal parts of the country, both the Porfirian state and the Catholic Church encouraged mestizos to squat and, eventually, permanently settle "unused" Indigenous lands.[145] Both institutions saw these mestizo "pioneers" as potential military auxiliaries and ambassadors of civilized values who would spearhead the parcelization of communal lands in accordance with Liberal legislation and open up the region's natural resources to "productive" use. Given that Náayari, Wixárika, O'dam, and Mexicanero costumbres, agricultural practices, and political autonomy were all closely intertwined with and dependent on access to large tracts of land, the influx of mestizo settlers endangered not just the integrity of their communities, but their very existence as distinct peoples. Thus they "strenuously resisted all attempts of the Mexican Government in this direction. To have everybody plant corn and graze his cattle where he pleases is happiness to them and in accord with their condition of life, which asks for nothing more than sufficient food and shelter for all."[146]

Much of what we know about the struggles of Náayarite, Wixáritari, O'dam, and Mexicaneros to resist these threats is based on the reports of the foreign explorers, ethnologists, and collectors of plants, animals, and human skulls, who arrived in the region in the late nineteenth century. In addition to Lumholtz, they included Aleš Hrdlička, a Czech doctor; Konrad Theodor Preuss, a German ethnologist; and Léon Diguet, a French photographer and collector. These men came in search of either "primitives" who resembled "early man"[147] or the last heirs of the Aztecs, whose modern beliefs and practices might shed light on those of the civilizations destroyed by the conquest.[148] They were reluctant to undermine their reputations as adventurers by pointing out the long history of contact between the peoples of the Gran Nayar and the surrounding regions,[149] and they instead described the local Indians as geographically isolated and forgotten by time, which pleased their sponsors and captured the imaginations of domestic and foreign publics. However, while reinforcing popular ideas of the Gran Nayar as cut off from the rest of the world, their accounts of day-to-day life in the region also evince the complexities of each people's cultures and the ways in which both individuals and communities were now fighting to preserve their identities, worldviews, and ways of life.

Preuss noted that because of their dispersed settlement patterns and seasonal migrations "it is difficult to calculate the approximate size of the Indian population" but suggested their numbers were declining through the absorption of outlying populations into regional mestizo society.[150] However, the rough estimates of Preuss and other foreign visitors, taken together with Porfirian census data (shown in table 1), provide a conservative but still fairly accurate picture of the demographics of the Gran Nayar, at least compared with later counts, which were handicapped by revolutionary violence and the laziness of local census takers.

TABLE 1 Population estimates for Indigenous peoples of the Gran Nayar, 1890–1910

	NÁAYARITE	WIXÁRITARI	O'DAM	MEXICANEROS[a]
1896 Census[b]	2,868	2,181	—	—
Lumholtz (1890s)[c]	2,500	4,000	3,000	—
1900 Census[d]	4,205	4,427	3,011	271
Preuss (1906)[e]	5,000	5,000	—	<1,000
Hrdlička (1908)[f]	3,187	3,818	3,221	—
1910 Census[g]	7,468	4,427	8,441[h]	—
Diguet (1911)[i]	3,000	5,000	—	—
Average	4,032	4,121	4,418	<635

[a] Early census takers ignored the Mexicaneros and subsequently failed to distinguish their language from other Nahuatl dialects, making it hard to separate Durango and Nayarit's native Mexicaneros from Nahuatl-speaking migrants from elsewhere.

[b] INEGI, *Estadísticas Históricas*, i, 119.

[c] Lumholtz, *Unknown Mexico*, i, 469, 492; ii, 100.

[d] INEGI, *Estadísticas Históricas*, i, 119.

[e] Preuss, *Fiesta, Literatura y Magia*, 169–70.

[f] Hrdlička, *Medical Observations*, 6–7, based on data from November 1904.

[g] INEGI, *Estadísticas Históricas*, i, 119.

[h] This high figure is likely due to the amalgamation of Durango and Nayarit's O'dam with the "Tepehuanes del Norte" of Chihuahua.

[i] Diguet, *Por tierras occidentales*, 91, 130.

The dramatic disparities between many of these estimates mean that they should all be treated with caution, but the average totals over this fifteen-year period do suggest that the Náayari, Wixárika, and O'dam populations were tiny compared with Mexico's major Indigenous peoples, such as the Zapotecs, Tzotzils, or Tarahumara, but roughly comparable to groups such as the Amusgo, Cuicateco, or Huave (although the Mexicanero population was much smaller still).[151] These averages also suggest that the Gran Nayar in this period had a population density of only 0.66 inhabitants per km^2: less than a tenth of the Mexican national average, in 1900, of 6.89 inhabitants per km^2. The Gran Nayar therefore remained more marginal in relation to regional—and indeed national—economic and political systems than many of Mexico's other Indigenous regions, which helps to explain why its inhabitants were able to maintain a much greater relative level of autonomy during the Porfiriato.

We lack demographic figures for the Gran Nayar's mestizos, but they clearly constituted only a fraction of the region's total population. The majority of these mestizos were settlers from the market towns given official jurisdiction over the Gran Nayar,[152] while others came from smaller, formerly Indian settlements on the very edges of the Gran Nayar itself.[153] They arrived via the regional network of caminos reales, which increasingly acted as conduits for the flow of migrants into the mountains as well as for commerce between the highlands and neighboring areas. While the renegades and refugees who had taken refuge in the Gran Nayar in previous centuries had been quickly assimilated into Indigenous populations, the colonists of the Porfirian era had no intention of integrating into the region's communities.[154] Instead, seeking pasture for their cattle, they claimed Indigenous lands for themselves, using Porfirian agrarian reform laws and church counterclaims to their advantage. Often, as in the Yaqui Valley and other areas of Mexico then undergoing similar colonization campaigns, the settlers enjoyed the direct backing of both institutions.[155] Many settlers also used armed force—as had been applied to their own Indian forebears only recently—to overcome local resistance to their encroachments.[156]

In the Sierra Wixárika of Jalisco, now divided between the municipalities of Mezquitic and Bolaños, Preuss noted that the Wixáritari feared "that their lands would be taken from them, and thus they distrust outsiders."[157] The formerly Wixárika pueblo of Tenzompa invaded Santa Catarina's lands,[158] while the hacienda of San Juan Capistrano expanded into the territory of both Santa Catarina and San Andrés. San Andrés' anexo of Guadalupe Ocotán, founded by Wixáritari fleeing the mestizo takeover of Huajimic, was threatened by the descendants of those same mestizo invaders, backed by the authorities in Tepic, which wanted to expand their jurisdiction eastward into what had until then been Jalisco.[159] Meanwhile mestizos from Bolaños and El Salitre (renamed Villa Guerrero in 1921) invaded Azqueltán, the last bastion of Jalisco's much-diminished Tepecano population, forcing many of the latter to abandon their language and heterodox religious practices. Soon after, the victorious colonists began to use Azqueltán as a staging area for their invasion of San Sebastián.[160]

Josefino missionaries from Zacatecas also arrived in the Sierra Wixárika in this period. The secular clergy had rarely visited the Wixáritari in previous years, "as the latter are unsociable and the former do not speak their language."[161] However, the Josefinos now attempted to fully evangelize the Wixáritari, establishing a first mission in San Sebastián in 1902 and a second in San Andrés a year later. While they had little success in converting local people to Catholicism,[162] their "recruitment" of Wixárika children for schooling in Zacatecas (often without the permission of their parents),[163] and their encouragement of mestizo colonization, had an important impact on both communities. By 1908, one hundred settlers were living in San Andrés,[164] while another fifty mestizo families had settled in and around San Sebastián and its anexo, Tuxpan.[165] In contrast, although the people of Santa Catarina were "great travelers" who came "much in contact with the whites," their community lacked a permanent mission and was therefore home to only one mestizo: a government teacher "whose work fails to achieve any result."[166]

Of course, trade, friendship, and ritual exchange had never exclusively defined the relations amongst the Gran Nayar's different communities, or amongst its different ethnic groups as a whole.[167] As in the rest of Mesoamerica, intercommunal disputes over territory were "a regular, highly patterned feature of the cultural landscape . . . [that] sometimes continue[d] for decades, even centuries" and involved making ritual claims to land through boundary-marking ceremonies and pilgrimages, writing petitions to the government, and engaging in brawls that might involve "considerable bloodshed."[168] However, the growing pressure the mestizo settlement exerted on the landholdings of the Gran Nayar's communities exacerbated existing conflicts and gave rise to new ones.

In 1887, the authorities of both San Sebastián and San Andrés accused Santa Catarina of invading their communal territories, while Santa Catarina's leaders subsequently traveled to Guadalajara to counter-accuse San Andrés of stealing their lands, and in 1890 took their complaints all the way to President Díaz. Tensions also emerged between the inhabitants of San Sebastián and Wixárika refugees from the extinct community of Ostoc, who had founded a new settlement—Tuxpan—within lands controlled by San Sebastián.[169] The inhabitants of Tuxpan had pretensions to autonomy, but those of San Sebastián regarded Tuxpan and the lands around it as an indivisible part of their community. The budding political-territorial conflict between these two groups would later help to determine the course of the cristero rebellions in the region.

Mestizo immigration and Porfirian land reform similarly threatened the O'dam communities of Durango, now divided amongst the municipalities of Mezquital,

Pueblo Nuevo, and Huazamota. The latter had once been home to Mexicaneros, who were pushed out by mestizo settlers to "the two miserable hamlets of San Antonio [de Padua] and San Pedro [Jícoras], located on the upper banks of the [Huazamota] river."[170] Mestizos also began to settle lands that belonged to Taxicaringa, Xoconoxtle, and Temoaya, situated on the northern edge of the Sierra O'dam,[171] as well as San Bernardino Milpillas Chico, whose inhabitants were by now "much mixed with Mexicans."[172] Meanwhile, Santa María and the neighboring community of Xoconoxtle together won government certification of their joint ownership of around 421,000 hectares of communal territory,[173] but immediately lost 120,000 hectares—the so-called Predio de la Montaña—to a mestizo lawyer as payment for his help in the case. The owners of San Juan Capistrano—the same hacienda then invading the Wixárika lands to its south—also took advantage of the poorly defined state boundary between Zacatecas and Durango to begin claiming large parts of Santa María Ocotán's lands to its north.[174]

Just as in the Sierra Wixárika, inter-Indian conflict in the Sierra O'dam soon began to spike. Some clashes involved factions that were defined and structured according to their origins in different parts of the same communal territory,[175] as in the case of Santa María Ocotán, where descent groups living in the important anexo of Candelaria el Alto accused those living near the communal cabecera of "abusing" them.[176] Meanwhile, Taxicaringa, Temoaya, San Bernardino, San Francisco de Lajas, and San Andrés Milpillas Grande fought amongst themselves over the location of the borders between them.[177] Durango's state government was forced to intervene in the conflict between Lajas and San Andrés, as the border between them doubled as the state border between Durango and the Territory of Tepic.[178]

The encroachments of San Andrés Milpillas's inhabitants into Durango was in turn related to the pressures unleashed by the division and privatization of communal lands in the Territory of Tepic, which was one of the ten Mexican entities most affected by this process during the Porfiriato.[179] The O'dam and Mexicaneros then living in Tepic's municipalities of Huajicori and Acaponeta, whose lands lay close to roads and railways now being built along the Pacific coast, were hit particularly hard. Many O'dam fled communities in these areas to escape "the advancing 'neighbours'" and settled in San Andrés Milpillas Grande. Their arrival tipped the ethnic balance in this traditionally mixed Mexicanero-O'dam community toward the latter[180] and perhaps prompted some local Mexicaneros to move north toward Lajas, contributing to the tensions between the two communities. Meanwhile, Indigenous people who refused to leave their homes nearer the coast—including the O'dam of Quiviquinta and the Mexicaneros of Picachos—shed their distinct ethnic identities altogether. Emigration and acculturation thus brought about a drastic decline in Tepic's O'dam and Mexicanero populations.[181]

By the end of the Porfiriato, the formerly Náayari community of San Juan Peyotán had also been transformed into "an almost completely mestizo settlement,"[182] as had Huaynamota, once home to Mexicaneros and a few Náayarite.[183] The Náayarite of San Pedro Ixcatán were threatened by expansion of nearby haciendas,[184] and similar pressures prompted the Náayarite of San Lucas, on the disputed border between Tepic and Durango, to travel to Guadalajara in an unsuccessful search for their colonial titles.[185] The Sierra Náayari's single resident priest, based in Jesús María, encouraged around one hundred mestizos to settle in and around that community,[186] while a number of other "impecunious Mexicans" also lived in nearby San Francisco (although they were not permitted to take over local lands but were instead employed as peons by the local Náayarite).[187]

In general, the Náayarite were better insulated from the threat of mestizo colonization than their Wixárika, O'dam, and Mexicanero neighbors. Their communities lay in the most inaccessible parts of Acaponeta, Rosamorada, Santiago Ixcuintla, and the so-called Subprefectura de la Sierra (officially part of the municipality of Tepic), and thanks to the difficulties of local transport and communication, the wealth of more productive land available to ranchers, speculators, and landowners elsewhere, and Náayari support for a series of small-scale regional uprisings in the years following Manuel Lozada's death,[188] most Náayarite retained control of their traditional territories into the twentieth century. This fact, combined with the ritual-political links that existed between their communities, also curbed the development of internecine conflicts between them.

Ultimately, although a few Náayarite, like their neighbors, responded to the pressures of mestizo settlement and prevalent national discourses of Indian "primitivism" by abandoning their costumbre,[189] most continued to tenaciously oppose the colonization of their homeland by outsiders. Lumholtz noted that, in general, the Náayarite had "very strong objections to unions with [mestizos],"[190] and Preuss reported that "they don't want to know anything of the outside world," describing them as "a haughty people, skilled in the use of weapons, and whom one might not want to bump into up a mountain."[191] In fact, the vast majority of the Náayarite, Wixáritari, O'dam, and Mexicaneros encountered by Lumholtz, Preuss, et al. in this period were "still thoroughly Indian, and proud of it."[192]

All four groups continued to regard their distinct beliefs, practices, and languages as superior to those of mestizo Mexicans,[193] and they fought hard to hold on to their cultural, political, and territorial autonomy, whether this entailed using the presence of literate mestizo officials—or even foreign explorers—to their own advantage or, conversely, becoming "defiant and disagreeable" toward outsiders.[194] The Náayarite of Santa Teresa, for example, implored Lumholtz "to ask the Mexican Government to let them keep their old customs, which [the communal authorities] had heard they were going to prohibit" and to "use [his] influence toward preventing the whites from settling in the vicinity, since they were eager to get at the big forests."[195] Meanwhile, the O'dam of Teneraca and San Francisco Ocotán violently opposed mestizo settlement in their communities,[196] and in Santa María Ocotán, the largest of the O'dam communities, "if a mestizo appeared . . . the alférez and his drum called together the inhabitants, and with pushes and shoves, without saying a word, they would expel him from Santa María."[197]

Ultimately, both strategies were fairly effective. Although Porfirian reforms ended each community's de jure political autonomy, and many also lost de facto control of portions of their traditional landholdings, most Náayarite, Wixáritari, O'dam, and Mexicaneros still prayed to the same gods as their ancestors (even if some of these deities had taken on additional identities since the conquest); led lives that were still regulated by the dictates of traditional authorities, elders, and ritual specialists (although one or two of these might now have an additional "official," government-approved title); paid no taxes (even when these were demanded by the local municipal authorities);[198] grew their own food and raised their own cattle on lands to which they still held legal title; spoke little Spanish;[199] ignored the local representatives of the church (who rarely visited their communities anyway);[200] and only tolerated the presence of government functionaries if they proved themselves useful. They continued to maintain "a very close relationship with their gods, to whom they dedicate a huge amount of their lives, a fact of which they are extremely proud,"[201] and Preuss noted that "there are few primitive peoples that have a 'living literature' as rich as that of the tribes [of the Gran Nayar]."[202]

On the eve of the revolution, then, the Náayarite, Wixáritari, O'dam, and Mexicaneros still held on to their Indigenous identities, communal lands, and a much higher level of autonomy vis-à-vis both church and state than that enjoyed by many of Mexico's other Indigenous groups,[203] to the extent that Hrdlička described them as still "practically self-governing tribes."[204] And although the Porfirian state by now regarded the Gran Nayar as "pacified territory,"[205] and Lumholtz and other foreign explorers, in line with the positivism and social Darwinism that dominated contemporary views of native societies,[206] predicted that "these primitive people will soon disappear by fusion with the great nation to whom they belong,"[207] Hrdlička was ultimately correct when he noted that the Náayarite, Wixáritari, O'dam, and Mexicaneros had "not given up the thought of armed resistance" to the threats that outsiders posed to their lands, cultures, and ways of life.[208]

2

THE "ARMED PHASE" OF THE REVOLUTION IN THE GRAN NAYAR, 1910–1920

IN OCTOBER 1910, after fraudulent elections in which Porfirio Díaz won a landslide victory, dissident political leader Francisco I. Madero issued his Plan de San Luis Potosí, urging the nation to rise up against the dictatorship on November 20. Across the country, peasants, workers, and members of the provincial middle classes answered Madero's call, setting in motion the decade-long "armed phase" of the revolution and an additional twenty years of rebellions, coups, and state-building efforts before a consolidated one-party state finally emerged from the tumult.

Náayari, Wixárika, O'dam, and Mexicanero participation in the events of 1910–20 has been ignored by all but a handful of scholars, and there are few (if any) eyewitnesses to them left in the Gran Nayar today. But oral accounts compiled by anthropologists since the 1930s, and second- and third-hand stories gathered during my own fieldwork in the region, attest to the far-reaching local effects of the revolution. Such testimony centers above all on the rise of local warlords, who grew powerful with the help of supernatural forces, defended their communities from bandits, and took back lands stolen by mestizo invaders, but who soon began to challenge the legitimate authority of elders, cargo holders, and costumbre.

Although chronologically vague, these local accounts, used in careful combination with the reports of revolutionary leaders, military telegrams, locally written petitions, and memoirs published after the event, provide enough information to reconstruct the story of the armed revolution in the Gran Nayar: from the arrival of the first supporters of Madero in the region in 1911, to the rise of communal militias headed by warlords from 1916 onward, to the final "pacification" of the Gran Nayar around the end of the decade. These sources show that many Náayarite, Wixáritari, O'dam, and Mexicaneros took an active interest in the activities of armed groups operating in and around their homelands and tried to confront or cooperate with these external forces to their own advantage, while others sought to flee the fighting and the growing threat of conscription.

Unlike the Yaqui or Mayo, many of whom sided on a "tribal" basis with either the Villistas or Carrancistas, the inhabitants of the Gran Nayar, whose primary loyalties lay with community rather than ethnicity, behaved rather more like the highlanders of Chiapas,[1] forming alliances with different revolutionary actors at the communal (or even subcommunal) level to fulfill specific local objectives. Bridging the gap between Knight's *serrano* and *agrarista* categories, these goals extended from simple self-defense to the pursuit of personal advantage, increased communal autonomy, and the restoration of communal lands lost during the Porfiriato. The specific methods used to this end could differ greatly from one community to another, depending on the historical, geographical, and sociocultural conditions of each, as well as on the specific local "facts on the ground," which often shifted dramatically from one day to the next.[2] However, by the end of the period, most of the region's warlords had pledged allegiance to Carranza's Constitutionalist faction, often in exchange for weapons and recognition as legitimate revolutionary actors. In the short term, emergent national- and state-level Constitutionalist administrations had little choice but to tolerate the de facto autonomy of these caciques and their militias.[3] But the behavior of these leaders (and in many cases their very existence) led to the growth of the internal discord and factional feuds that would increasingly define politics—and indeed everyday life—within the communities of the Gran Nayar in the 1920s.

THE MADERISTA REVOLUTION IN THE GRAN NAYAR, 1910–1913

Soon after Madero launched his Plan de San Luis Potosí, the Mexican Revolution reached the mountains of Durango, Zacatecas, Jalisco, and the then-federal Territory of Tepic (which in 1917 became the state of Nayarit). Rugged and sparsely inhabited, the mountains constituted perfect terrain for rebel guerrilla operations. With events at the national level moving rapidly, Madero's old friend Luis Moya declared against Díaz, assembled an armed force in Chihuahua, and marched south toward his hometown of Chalchihuites, Zacatecas, on the state border with Durango and Jalisco. Antonio Amaro, Justo Ávila, Pánfilo Natera, and Félix and Santos Bañuelos all rallied to Moya's cause,[4] and by February 1911 the rebels had taken most of the major towns to the north and east of the Sierra Wixárika (including the regional municipal seat of

Mezquitic),[5] as well as the town of Mezquital, Durango, whose authorities governed, at least on paper, much of the Sierra O'dam.[6] Although an expeditionary force set out from Tepic for the Sierra Náayari, "with the object of protecting those pueblos and preventing an invasion by the rebels of Zacatecas and Durango,"[7] it failed to achieve its objectives. Luis Moya took the city of Zacatecas in April, and Tepic itself fell to Maderista forces under Martín Espinosa and his nephew, Juventino, in May, without a shot being fired.[8] A few days later, Madero and Pascual Orozco defeated the federal army at Ciudad Juárez and forced President Díaz from power.

The collapse of regional Porfirian authorities[9] and the rise to power of new Maderista state and municipal governments had important consequences for some of the Gran Nayar's communities. After Madero was elected president in November 1911, Alberto Robles Gil became governor of Jalisco and launched a series of administrative reforms, adjusting political boundaries and posting new authorities to previously autonomous communities. Within the municipality of Mezquitic, San Andrés Cohamiata was named the center of a new "political and judicial precinct" encompassing the entire Sierra Wixárika.[10] However, the precinct's headquarters was soon moved to the more accessible San Sebastián.[11] According to the local jefe político, this was because San Andrés, at 180 km from Mezquitic, was so far from the municipal seat that documents took fifteen days to arrive there,[12] if they arrived at all—for the Chapalagana River became impassable during the rains, cutting off all communications.[13] However, an alternative government report indicates that

> the Wixáritari of San Andrés opposed the presence of political commissioners, and also expelled the teacher of the government-run school, who dedicated himself to extorting them, and instead sent their children to a Catholic school.[14]

Although the people of San Andrés ejected all representatives of the state from their community, they and their neighbors continued to tolerate—for the moment—the presence of both Josefino missionaries and mestizo settlers. The bishop of Zacatecas was even able to spend several weeks in Santa Catarina in January 1912, where he oversaw the destruction of a Wixárika shrine without provoking much opposition.[15] It seems that the Wixáritari felt that the state posed a more obvious threat to their autonomy than did a few ineffective missionaries and mestizo immigrants.

The people of Santa Catarina—described by Lumholtz as "the men of the world among the tribe"[16]—also came into close contact with anti-Madero rebels during this early stage of the revolution. In March 1912, shortly after the bishop's visit, the community's traditional government informed Governor Robles Gil that many local people wanted to join bands of "Zapatistas" active nearby. These rebels probably belonged to the forces of Camilo Rentería, a rancher, sometime bandit chief, and grandson of one of Manuel Lozada's regional commanders during the 1860s, who was based in Huaynamota, just on the other side of the frontier with Tepic.[17] Similar friendly contacts with Cheche Campos,[18] who took refuge in Santa Catarina after razing the rival mestizo pueblo of Huejuquilla to the ground in December, were probably the basis for a local federal commander reporting in the same month that "the Wixáritari have now armed themselves."[19] Such contacts do not, however, contradict Rojas's assertion that around this time another group of Wixáritari—perhaps from neighboring San Sebastián, which had a long history of conflict with Santa Catarina—aided a Maderista general, Cándido Aguilar, by capturing and sending him "some of the rebels who had interned themselves in the Sierra."[20]

Meanwhile, in the Territory of Tepic continuous fighting obstructed any attempts to extend central or local government authority over the Sierra Náayari. Pascual Orozco's revolt against Madero had been seconded locally by an ex-federal lieutenant, Miguel Guerrero,[21] who raised a force that raided along the western edge of the sierra.[22] Guerrero then joined forces with Camilo Rentería in Huaynamota,[23] and together the rebels attacked Tepic on April 29. Although they were repelled with losses—to the extent that the federal commander claimed that Rentería himself had died in the battle[24]—the city's elite were alarmed by the sudden appearance of a rebel army at their gates, and Tepic's Chamber of Commerce warned President Madero that

> this city lacks a sufficient garrison of federal soldiers under a commendable military leader . . . it remains threatened by numerous, malicious armed individuals and the Indians of the Sierra. . . . It is well-known that former lieutenant Guerrero intends to take Tepic and here gather his forces for a subsequent attack on Guadalajara, and we invoke the disagreeable memory of the chieftain Lozada, to demonstrate the damage that a determined man can cause the nation once in possession of Tepic.[25]

Although references to Indian rebellion had long been used by the elites of both Tepic and Guadalajara to tarnish political opponents like Manuel Lozada and to elicit federal intervention in local disputes by invoking the specter of a Yucatan-style "caste war,"[26] the chamber's appeal probably also reflected the real presence of Náayari and Wixárika individuals amongst Rentería's troops.[27] And just as the memory of Lozada remained a byword for the dangers of Indigenous rebellion amongst Tepic's elite, so too it seems likely that those Náayarite and Wixáritari who decided to join Rentería—himself a descendent of one of Lozada's lieutenants—were encouraged to do so by memories of their former successes under Lozada.[28]

The fears of Tepic's elite were soon confirmed, for news of Renteria's death proved premature, and it transpired that the rebel leader was in fact alive and in Huaynamota with two hundred fighters.[29] Rentería and Guerrero's forces skirmished with federal troops throughout the summer, and by July the number of "bandits" active in the territory had reached more than eight hundred men.[30] The authorities' use of the term *bandit* to vilify revolutionaries was common throughout Mexico in this period, but it is important to note that many early revolutionary leaders—including such major figures as Emiliano Zapata—had much in common with Hobsbawm's figure of the "social bandit" and often struggled to form cohesive social movements from the even more "bandit-like" local rebels who formed the backbone of their forces.[31] In the Sierra Náayari, the depredations of the latter turned local people against Rentería. Anticipating the important role they would play in defeating local Villistas-turned-bandits a few years later, the Náayarite of the Jesús María region, angered by Rentería's attempts to levy "forced loans" on them, attacked his men and forced them to flee the region in disarray.[32] However, Rentería's rebels seem to have regrouped farther to the south by the end of the year, when "groups of bandits" were once again reported as roaming the mountains around Huajimic, "robbing horses and saddles from anyone they find in possession of them."[33]

The experiences of the O'dam and Mexicaneros during the early stages of the revolution were rather similar. With much of Durango also dominated by Pascual Orozco's "Colorado" rebels,[34] there was little if anything the state's Maderista authorities could do to impose their control over peripheral areas, including the southern municipalities of Mezquital and Pueblo Nuevo. Thus the O'dam and Mexicanero inhabitants of these areas, like their Náayari neighbors, had more contact with the rebels than with representatives of the government. This led the prefect of Mezquital to worry, in late 1912, that the "natives of Yonora may join the bandits"[35]—an indication of the threat that an O'dam rebellion would pose to government control of the municipal seat and a portent of the vital part that Dámaso Barraza, cacique of Yonora and Temoaya, would play in subsequent stages of the revolution (and, indeed, in the cristiada).

In the Territory of Tepic, the collusion of the smaller local O'dam and Mexicanero population with rebel forces led government troops to round up the inhabitants of San Andrés Milpillas Grande and forcibly congregate them in Acaponeta.[36] Some of their neighbors in Durango were similarly exiled as a result of federal counterinsurgency tactics.[37] Both government-enforced exile and incorporation into rebel bands led to increased O'dam and Mexicanero interaction with mestizo Mexicans and with the culture and politics of the nation-state that existed beyond the borders of their homeland. Those who stayed behind became nomads, forced to roam the sierra in search of food and safety. Many ended up in previously uninhabited areas far from their original homes, which put pressure on the old borders between their communities, giving rise to new territorial disputes that would shape their subsequent participation in the revolution.

FROM HUERTA'S COUP TO REVOLUTIONARY CIVIL WAR, 1913–1915

In February 1913, over the course of the ten days known as the *Decena Trágica*, President Madero was deposed and then assassinated by his foremost military chief, General Victoriano Huerta (a native of far-northern Jalisco and apparently of Wixárika descent on his mother's side).[38] Venustiano Carranza, the Maderista governor of Coahuila, refused to recognize Huerta and was joined in his opposition by Francisco "Pancho" Villa in Chihuahua, Emiliano Zapata in Morelos, and Álvaro Obregón in Sonora, all of whom turned their arms on Huerta, the federal army, and Pascual Orozco (whom Huerta had promoted to the rank of general, in the process transforming Orozco's "Colorado" rebels into federal auxiliaries). An all-out civil war ensued, and as it progressed, disparate groups of revolutionaries and bandits—often indistinguishable in our sources, given the vague and politically prejudiced language of official reports[39]—passed back and forth through the Gran Nayar. In the context of this upheaval, any tenuous steps either Huerta or his rivals took toward establishing their authority over the region (and other similar areas) ground to a halt.[40]

In the Sierra Wixárika, plans to establish a postal service linking Mezquitic with Santa Catarina and San Sebastián, aimed at fomenting the region's economic development,[41] were abandoned, and the "precinct headquarters" earlier established in San Sebastián was forgotten. Rebel bands raided across northern Jalisco as a whole,[42] and although the threat they posed was cavalierly dismissed by Huerta's commander in Mezquitic,[43] local federal troops soon found themselves in a hopeless position, with the regional capital of Colotlán "destroyed by revolutionary fires" and its garrison left "without arms or ammunition."[44] The renewed conflict crept ever closer to the Wixárika communities as the Tepecanos of nearby Azqueltán declared against Huerta (and thus against their old enemies, the "counterrevolutionary" mestizo caciques of El Salitre).[45] Meanwhile, farther to the north, rebels under Domingo and Mariano Arrieta and Calixto Contreras took the city of Durango from pro-Huerta forces in June 1913.[46] Pancho Villa played a key role in the ensuing revolutionary campaign, and his División del Norte soon dominated the center-north of Mexico, while Álvaro Obregón took control of Sonora and Sinaloa. By early 1914, as forces under Obregón's ally Lucio Blanco moved from Sinaloa into Tepic en route to Guadalajara, revolutionary forces surrounded the Gran Nayar on all but its southwestern flank.[47]

Ivor Thord-Gray, a Swedish adventurer and mercenary who had joined Villa's forces on a bet with a friend and ended up serving as a colonel in Obregón's cavalry division under General Blanco, wrote an account of the 1913–14 Tepic campaign in which he directly discusses the participation of the Indigenous peoples of the Gran Nayar. Although Thord-Gray has a tendency to exaggerate the daring of his own exploits and the importance of his role in the revolution, he was also an amateur ethnologist who took a keen interest in the Indigenous cultures he encountered in Mexico (he later wrote an English-Tarahumara dictionary), and his descriptions of the Gran Nayar, its inhabitants, and their attitudes in this period are often perceptive.

Blanco sent Thord-Gray into the Sierra Náayari in May 1914 in search of a federal cavalry force reported as active in the region. Near the Náayari community of Saycota he was joined at his campfire by "an old Indian with a family of four" who had been hiding from federal troops and "had not eaten anything for some time except roots and maggots." Although by May—the end of the dry season—supplies often grew scarce in the Gran Nayar, the explicit link made between hiding and hunger suggests the presence of armed outsiders who had obstructed the access of local civilians—particularly women and children—to stored food supplies and probably disrupted the normal agricultural cycle. Such disruption likely explains why the five O'dam whom Thord-Gray met soon afterward had left their homes in southern Durango and were armed with "short bow, arrows and machetes." They agreed to join Thord-Gray outside Acaponeta a few days later, together with six other O'dam whom they had recruited to the revolutionary cause and who proved invaluable, killing eight of Huerta's federals in a skirmish soon after, each "with an arrow [to] the back." The O'dam took the federals' rifles and ammunition, but much to their disgust the soldiers' horses "automatically became the property of the army."[48] That they instantly agreed to join Thord-Gray's troops when promised rifles and money indicates that, as in many rural regions of Mexico, the revolutionary unrest had seriously disturbed life in the Sierra O'dam, driving local people from their homes in search of supplies and security, the latter in the form of arms.

Thord-Gray returned to the Gran Nayar after taking part in the victorious battle for Tepic on May 16, 1914. Just as Obregón had his battalions of Yaquis and Mayos, so was Blanco interested in the fighting potential of the Náayarite and O'dam, whom he had heard "would make good material for soldiers under their own chiefs, especially 'If you promise them absolute control over their own land, affairs and religion.'" He therefore sent Thord-Gray off toward "[Wixárika] Country" in search of a federal cavalry force that some Tepecano scouts had reported moving south across the sierra from Zacatecas. Thord-Gray and his fifty-three men (mainly Yaquis) were guided by two O'dam, one Náayari, and one Wixárika and took with them twenty Winchester carbines, with fifty rounds per gun, in the hope of arming local Indigenous men to fight for Blanco's cause.

Thord-Gray wrote of the expedition that "the whole territory seemed deserted, and we met only two half-starved Indians in four days," probably reflecting the flight of most inhabitants in the wake of local fighting. Passing through Huajimic, where his Indigenous guides did not trust the local mestizos, they arrived in Guadalupe Ocotán, which he described as "very run-down looking, especially the temple and the god-houses" and where he recruited two more Wixárika scouts. Thord-Gray's party then crossed into Jalisco, heading through the territory of San Sebastián to Ocota, one of the community's most important anexos and the home of Thord-Gray's Wixárika guide, José. Although Thord-Gray describes the Wixáritari as "not anywhere near as warlike as their neighbours, the Náayari," the men of Ocota, just like the O'dam he had earlier recruited, were eager to get their hands on the Winchesters. José and his father, "a famous singing-shaman" (probably the kawiteru of Ocota's tuki temple)

> spent the early part of the morning trying to persuade me to issue the fifteen guns to his men in the community of Octota. About twenty men were presented as responsible enough. When I informed José and his father that the remainder would be selected from other settlements, it started a strong remonstrance against the idea. They advised me forcefully to confine the recruiting to their community only; outside men could not be mixed with theirs as it would invite trouble. The old man said, "If you pick men from two or more settlements, they will soon quarrel and break up into several parties, each group being members of their own community under their own recognized leader."[49]

After moving on to San Sebastián itself, Thord-Gray found only reluctant and unreliable allies. One of the Yaquis guarding their party's weapons was killed in the night with a Wixárika arrow, and Thord-Gray struggled to prevent the other Yaquis from massacring San Sebastián's inhabitants in revenge. The next day, after an unsuccessful search for the perpetrators, who the locals claimed must have been from elsewhere—presumably the rival community of Santa Catarina, to the borders of which their manhunt took them—Thord-Gray was eager to leave the area, especially as he only narrowly escaped an attempt on his own life in his camp that evening.

At the last minute, he decided to leave one gun with his guide's father in Ocota and then made a deal with San Sebastián's traditional government, arming the governor, the community's chief "shaman," and a group of local men in exchange for their help in spreading rumors of a "huge" rebel army marching through the sierra toward Bolaños and Chimaltitán. This ruse successfully panicked the local federal garrisons, allowing Thord-Gray's men to take both towns with barely a shot fired. They then rejoined Obregón's forces near Tepic. On their return, Blanco and the other generals were eager to know about the potential of the Gran Nayar's Indians as revolutionary fighters. "I advised them not to waste any more time on the [Wixáritari]," Thord-Gray replied, "but did recommend them as excellent trackers and scouts, [although] suspicious by nature."[50]

Three key points emerge from Thord-Gray's account of his time in the Gran Nayar. First, although the intertribal solidarity prevalent amongst Sonora's Yaquis and Mayos allowed them to be "formed into individual regiments" within Obregón's army,[51] there existed little solidarity between the Wixárika communities, or even the tuki districts into which they were subdivided. Instead, each Wixárika community was "a complete little state, with its own government and headman," which was not conducive toward turning the Wixáritari into an effective revolutionary fighting force, least of all for service outside their communal territories. Second, although Thord-Gray asserts that each of these "mini-states" had "little truck with outsiders"[52] and hardly "knew or cared of the world outside their tribe,"[53] his actual narrative of the expedition shows that while they probably cared little about the ideologies or programs professed by the different revolutionary factions, the Wixáritari were in fact well informed about regional military developments. Wixárika informants gave him valuable information regarding the movements, activities, and even the morale of federal troops active in the Sierra Wixárika and beyond, as far as Mezquitic, Colotlán, Bolaños, and even Tlatenango, Zacatecas—where, for example, they reported that "the Federal regiment . . . was shanghaiing peons and Indians to work for them and sometimes into the army."[54] Thord-Gray's testimony is also early evidence of the way in which the Wixáritari, Náayarite, O'dam, and Mexicaneros sought to use the revolution to their advantage. In the following years, as fighting in the Gran Nayar grew fiercer and the number of armed groups roaming the region increased, local people would increasingly form alliances with these outsiders, not only to obtain the arms, ammunition, and horses emphasized by Thord-Gray but also to pursue bolder, more obviously political objectives, such as the defense of their communal landholdings and political autonomy.

PARAMILITARIES AND POWER STRUGGLES: THE RISE OF THE GRAN NAYAR'S DEFENSAS

After rebel victories forced Huerta from power in July 1914, tensions grew between Carranza and Obregón on one side and Villa and Zapata on the other. A new civil war soon broke out between the rival revolutionary factions. In spring 1915, Villa was defeated in the Bajío. Much of his army dispersed and some elements headed into the Gran Nayar, pursued by Carrancista forces. This development served to increase contacts—both friendly and hostile—between the region's Indigenous communities and armed outsiders and paved the way for the local establishment of Carrancista-armed self-defense militias, which, according to one rather disapproving observer, transformed "savages with bows and arrows" into "savages with carbines and mausers."[55] In turn, this led to the rise of a new generation of Náayari, Wixárika, O'dam, and Mexicanero leaders who can be defined, according to Knight's cacical grading system, as bottom-level local (or even sublocal) *caciquillos*, some of whom survived the revolution to emerge in the 1920s as higher-level "municipal" or even "regional" caciques.[56]

Although hacendados and other wealthy citizens had in many areas already armed "white guard" militias to protect their persons and property,[57] the rural defensas that emerged across Mexico from late 1915 were an expression of "a shift in the popular mood," as villagers, exhausted by the constant depredations of armed groups of all stripes, banded together to defend themselves.[58] Villistas-turned-bandits, often supported by local mestizos, posed the greatest threat to the Gran Nayar's Indigenous communities, who looked to the Carrancistas for support. Some formed defensas after the Carrancistas occupied a community, asked the traditional authorities to select a suitable leader or picked one from amongst them, and charged them with organizing a militia. In other cases, Carrancista commanders lent official recognition to preexisting militias on condition they pledge allegiance to Carranza. The Carrancistas gave these groups whatever arms they could spare (generally bolt-action rifles known as *cerrojos*), although because of shortages, many defensas initially armed themselves with bows and arrows, slings, machetes, or the ever-versatile *coa* digging stick.[59] As in other peripheral regions of Mexico, the size of the Gran Nayar's defensas varied from five to more than forty members,[60] fluctuating according to the availability of weapons, the severity of external threats, and the value of the prizes to be won through armed action.[61]

Regardless of how they were selected, most defensa commanders were young men capable of mediating between their communities and the outside world. Given the long histories of contact between the Gran Nayar and nearby mestizo towns, and the way in which local shamanic practices encouraged individuals to assume multiple contradictory identities, there were always a few individuals in each community who could act simultaneously as Indian *and* mestizo.[62] In some cases, these men were actually mestizos themselves, albeit with close ties to local Indigenous majorities. If they had some military training, their command of a defensa was all the more authoritative—so much the better if they were wealthy (in this period synonymous with cattle ownership) and therefore had the means to supply some of a defensa's material needs and more to lose from Villista raids.

Across much of Mexico, the communal defensas set up after 1915 played a vital role in Carrancista operations against Villista guerrillas, but when not on official campaign, they were usually subject to little Carrancista oversight. In addition to functioning as politically vital mediating institutions between community and outside forces,[63] many defensas soon became vehicles for personal and factional interests,[64] and their commanders, thanks to the combination of armed force and the new financial and political opportunities available to them, established themselves as local strongmen, somewhere between "petty caudillos" and "municipal caciques."[65] In spite of strongly worded reminders that they were not to act as policemen, levy fines, or otherwise usurp the powers of weakly constituted (or nonexistent) civil authorities,[66] the "external protection" that these leaders provided their communities was often "complemented, [or] even outstripped, by internal extortion."[67]

The Carrancistas knew that without local support, harnessed through the defensas and their commanders-turned-caciques, they would struggle to wipe out Villismo and banditry in the more remote parts of the country.[68] The Carrancista government therefore further rewarded the loyalty of these men—like Gabriel Barrios in the Sierra Norte de Puebla and Francisco Antillón in Namiquipa, Chihuahua—with arms, political support, and pledges of noninterference in local matters, which in turn boosted both the de facto power and the perceived legitimacy of the *cacicazgos* that they established.[69] However, the Náayarite, Wixáritari, O'dam, and Mexicaneros had preserved a much higher level of autonomy vis-à-vis the Mexican state than that enjoyed by Barrios's Nahuas or the mestizos of Namiquipa. They were accustomed to being governed not by caciques, merchants, or Catholic priests, but by politico-religious cargo holders selected by communal consensus and the dreams of a gerontocracy of ritual specialists. The emergence of military-orientated communal leaderships in this period thus caused more controversy in the Gran Nayar than elsewhere in Mexico.[70]

It is important to note that the emergence of the Gran Nayar's defensas and the rise of their commanders to political importance had some conceptual and historical antecedents. The power of the region's traditional governments had always been similarly rooted in the ability of elders and officeholders to mediate between their communities and external agents—although the latter were not mestizo military commanders but gods, ancestors, and other nonhumans.[71] Nor was military caciquismo an entirely new phenomenon in the region, especially amongst the Náayarite, in whose communities some level of politico-military caciquismo had been institutionalized during the rule of Manuel Lozada. Indeed, as Philip Weigand and Paul Liffman have pointed out, the "power shift to younger, bicultural war chiefs during a crisis is a broad historical pattern among central Uto-Aztecan peoples."[72] To that end, the traditional power structures in many of the Gran Nayar's communities included "military cargos" (such as capitán or alférez), which sometimes came with three-year terms in place of the usual one-year limit, squaring the need for temporary military control of a community during wartime with costumbre-based forms of authority overseen by communal elders.

Previously, however, once the immediate military threat passed, local war leaders receded into the political background. But many of the Gran Nayar's defensa commanders-turned-caciques were reluctant to give up their newfound power and growing wealth. As the threat of Villista raids began to ebb, and with it their original raison d'être, they sought to bolster their positions by pursuing the same kind of policies that had long resonated well with Indigenous populations throughout Mexico: above all the expulsion of outsiders from their communities and the restitution of lost landholdings.[73] Some scholars have argued that such actions represent no more than the attempts of caciques to seize control of the essential peasant means of production—land—for themselves.[74] But Paul Friedrich argues that in Michoacán, cacique-promoted *agrarismo* helped peasants to take back more territory in a shorter space of time than would have been possible otherwise. Gilbert Joseph, meanwhile, points out that dichotomies of cacical "good and evil" are often artificial.[75] The latter view is borne out in the case of the Gran Nayar, where, in the short term, defensa commanders successfully combined strong local support, firepower, and contacts with state- and federal-level political and military leaders to win back lost lands for their communities, which in turn helped them to maintain their own status.

The concentration of power in the hands of these leaders also disrupted the traditional political equilibrium in the Gran Nayar's egalitarian societies, where political influence was traditionally diffused amongst individuals, descent groups, and communal hierarchies via the annual rotation of cargos and other ritual mechanisms (such as accusations of witchcraft, which could even destroy the influence of powerful shamans).[76] As leaders without ritually defined term limits, whose power rested on their guns and status as intermediaries, the defensa commanders' very existence challenged the authority and legitimacy of patriarchal hierarchies defined by gender, age, ritual, and communal support. In the long term, then, the rule of the defensa commanders polarized the communities of the Gran Nayar and gave rise to violent factional disputes,[77] locally validating Knight's general judgment that "the only good cacique is—if not a dead cacique—at least a short-lived cacique."[78]

THE DEFENSAS OF THE SIERRA WIXÁRIKA AND THE RISE AND FALL OF COLONEL MEZQUITE

Colonel Patricio Mezquite—known to many Wixáritari today as *el Meki*—is the first of the caciques of the Gran Nayar for whom we possess reliable information. The story of his bloody career and his demise at the hands of his own followers is an early example of a young, ambitious, and wealthy Indigenous leader using the availability of powerful "foreign" allies to secure for himself an unprecedented level of influence, only for this to generate enough local opposition to precipitate his own downfall.

Mezquite rose to power in the Sierra Wixárika at a time of widespread violence in the north of Jalisco. The municipal seat of Mezquitic had been governed by a pro-government administration for several years, as had the nearby town of Huejuquilla, where Carrancista forces put local rancher (and future cristero general) Pedro

Quintanar in charge of a detachment of seventy-five men.[79] But Villista remnants still controlled much of the countryside, raiding ranches and skirmishing with the local defensas. Anthropologist Robert Zingg retrospectively described Mezquite as a "Villista general,"[80] and Beatriz Rojas, who also claims that the majority of Wixáritari were Villista sympathizers, reiterates this idea.[81] Philip Weigand, however, argues that because local mestizos backed the Villistas, the Wixáritari of San Sebastián, seeking "renewed comunidad autonomy . . . declared against Villa (and, therefore, against the local vecinos). Revolutionary ideology had little or nothing to do with the choice."[82]

The latter version is corroborated by the reports of contemporary Josefino missionary Calixto Guerrero, according to whom el Meki was a San Sebastián notable named Juan Patricio de la Torre, nicknamed *Mezquite* for his thorny and unbending nature (like the mesquite tree).[83] Guerrero claimed to have officiated at Mezquite's Catholic marriage ceremony—a rare thing for a Wixárika to undergo in this period, suggesting that Mezquite, like many of Mexico's Indigenous caciques,[84] was already adept at moving between his own communal, Indigenous world and that of the mestizo Mexico that surrounded it. Father Guerrero subsequently helped to persuade San Sebastián's elders to appoint Mezquite communal governor for two years running from 1913, "during which time he became rich." As was usual in the Gran Nayar, his wealth likely consisted of cattle. In return for Guerrero's political support, Mezquite used his influence as governor, his wealth, and the patron-client ties that came with the latter (through the generous provision of cattle for communal rituals and festivals, for example) to secure the Josefinos the labor they needed to construct a new headquarters in San Sebastián. His missionary allies rewarded him for this assistance by giving him three hundred pieces of clothing donated by Catholic groups in Mexico City, which Mezquite himself handed out to San Sebastián's inhabitants, further cementing his local influence.

However, the alliance of convenience between Mezquite and the Josefinos fell apart as Villista forces took refuge in the Sierra Wixárika from 1915, transforming it into a "theatre for the horrors of war and the crimes that accompany it." In May 1916, Villista commander Félix Díaz arrived in San Sebastián with one hundred and twenty men,[85] terrorizing the inhabitants and roughing up the Josefinos and their assistants. They stayed sixteen days, devouring all the grain and animals they could find, until Carrancista general Carlos Martínez arrived with four hundred men and drove them out. The rival groups alternately occupied San Sebastián some eight times, until the local Carrancistas, "realizing that only those who knew the region's terrain could prevent the rebels occupying the Sierra, armed forty Wixáritari and granted one of them the rank of colonel."

It is not surprising that the military rank went to Mezquite, or that the men of his community were willing to support his leadership—for he was a locally influential

Spanish speaker who knew how to deal with mestizos and owned enough cattle to feed his followers. As commander of a militia, Mezquite became more influential still, as

> this new squadron, who knew the land and were armed not just with guns, but with the ferocity of their natural instincts, began to operate against the rebels and obtained great victories. Carried away by their triumphs and believing they had the government's full support to commit whatever outrages they pleased, they took for their headquarters the same mission building they had previously viewed with great respect, doing whatever they wanted with that which they found inside. And as the mestizo colonization of their lands had never pleased them, now that they were armed and in complete control of their territory, they cast out the mestizo settlers without mercy, taking from them whatever they wished, murdering some of them and proclaiming their dislike for the missionary priest because he had brought the mestizos.[86]

The Josefinos and the surviving mestizo colonists fled to San Andrés, but Mezquite's defensa and a detachment of Carrancistas arrived there soon after, in search of the Zacatecan Villista (and amateur bullfighter) general Tomás Domínguez,[87] rumored to have taken refuge in the community. Domínguez escaped, much to the fury of the Carrancistas, who promptly murdered the four unfortunate men they found in the community's jail, looted the church and stabled their horses inside, and took the mission buildings as their headquarters. They were on the cusp of also murdering Calixto Guerrero's brother, Father Moisés, and his assistant, when the men were saved by the intervention of "a Wixárika, Clemente Villa, who served as the squadron's guide and had the rank of lieutenant colonel."[88]

Villa, a native of San Andrés, then established a defensa there as well, which served as the foundation of a cacicazgo that would last into the 1920s. Together with Mezquite, he forced out San Andrés's remaining twenty mestizo families (some of whom were refugees from elsewhere, including San Sebastián). Guerrero claims that

> all the Wixáritari, carried away for a moment by their savage instincts, vomited thunder and lightning from their eyes and mouths against the priest and the mestizos, accusing them of stealing their lands by having lived there.

However, Guerrero used his previous friendship with Mezquite to save the lives of the terrified mestizos, who, with ropes already around their necks, stood beneath the trees at the edge of San Andrés, waiting to be hanged en masse. They then fled the sierra for Huejuquilla and Mezquitic, or accompanied Guerrero himself to San Juan Capistrano, where the hacienda's chaplain received in solemn ceremony the sacred image of San José they had "rescued" from San Sebastián. "Such are God's trials!" concluded

Guerrero. "With cruelty the Wixáritari dismissed His Chasteness, the missionaries and mestizos, blighting themselves forever with the ignominy of ingratitude. Father forgive them for they know not what they do!"[89]

Having cleared their lands of missionaries and mestizos, the Wixárika defensas helped Carrancista troops defeat northern Jalisco's remaining Villistas, many of them Tepecanos from Azqueltán.[90] Then, in October 1918, the Wixáritari crossed into Nayarit with Carrancista soldiers under Colonel Lacarra, Huazamota's defensa under Primo Ortiz, and the defensas of San Juan Capistrano and Huejuquilla under Pedro Quintanar. Together they attacked Huaynamota, the last stronghold of Villista commander Félix Díaz, "sowing panic and death and after a hard-fought shootout taking the pueblo, which the rebels had turned into a warehouse for the products of their looting and pillaging."[91]

Guadalajara's *El Informador* reported that "those who acted with most valor were the aforementioned guerrilleros Ortiz and the Wixárika who has made himself feared throughout the Sierra for his bravery and audacity." Oral accounts are more explicit in their descriptions of Mezquite's "bravery," however.

> All those whom Lacarra's soldiers took captive were delivered to the Wixáritari as prisoners, while they headed back from the campaign. They never should've done it. On their return they found all of the Villistas hanged from the highest pine trees. Those Wixáritari were heartless, although the Villistas were also unforgivable.[92]

Although local mestizos have always looked down on their "savage" Wixárika neighbors, reports of the Wixárika defensas' brutality are sufficiently widespread that there must be some truth to them.[93] But such violence failed to trouble the Carrancistas with whom Mezquite collaborated in this period, and after Carranza himself became president in May 1917, Mezquite's behavior only became more extreme, as he took advantage of his alliance with the revolution's victors to raid the mestizos living around the Sierra Wixárika's frontier with Nayarit.

In early 1919, Father Francisco del Real reported that Mezquite and his men had murdered "thirty-eight Christians young and old at a ranch near Amatlán [de Jora, Nayarit],"[94] forcing him to flee the region with four hundred other parishioners.[95] Mezquite also drove into exile many of the inhabitants of Camotlán and Huajimic, who had territorial conflicts with both San Andrés and San Sebastián.[96] In Camotlán, del Real was able to save the local church's ornaments, but the priest lamented that from Huajimic,

> I couldn't bring anything, because I feared meeting el Mezquite, who doesn't pardon the life of anyone. A few days after he chased out the local believers, I heard the Wixárika

> robbed the church of anything they could use, and smashed the rest. Their barbarity reached the level of mockingly putting Lord San José in the jail, and then imitated a firing squad and shot him to pieces.[97]

The mestizo priest naturally regarded the theft and "execution" of Huajimic's santito as a sacrilegious outrage: an example of the iconoclasm for which many Carrancistas became famous[98] and of the heathen disrespect of the Wixáritari for the True Faith. However, similar acts have been typical of periods of political upheaval across the world,[99] as holy images are "looted and confiscated as the spoils of war . . . or cunningly stolen from their owners to enhance the prestige of the burglars."[100] Such acts also had direct regional antecedents. The Tepecanos of Azqueltán once fought a ruinous war with their neighbors "over a miraculous image of San Lorenzo,"[101] while Manuel Lozada had "confiscated" sacred images from towns that opposed his rule in order to symbolically punish his enemies and as "part of a broader scheme to construct a new religious centre in Lozada's headquarters."[102]

Furthermore, the San José that Mezquite and his men destroyed was not just any saint, but rather Huajimic's patron. Jailing and executing the "Spanish god" whom the Wixáritari regarded as Huajimic's eponymous founder and primary source of spiritual strength was therefore less an example of either Wixárika or Carrancista anticlericalism and more a symbolic punishment meted out to their long-standing mestizo rivals. In fact, if San José had survived his ordeal—thereby miraculously proving his "innocence"—he would probably have been adopted by the Wixáritari and taken off to replace the San José recently taken from San Sebastián by the Josefinos.[103]

Thanks to their victories over settlers, missionaries, Villistas, and even the "gods" of rival communities, the Wixáritari of San Sebastián, in contrast with many of Mexico's other Indigenous groups, saw the decade of armed revolution as

> a golden age—a time without mestizos, without priests, during which the maize grew fat and the harvests were good (and went untaxed), and their native ceremonies flourished and could be practiced without Catholic censure.[104]

Ironically, however, Mezquite himself began to challenge traditional norms. "He got bigheaded!" as one elder in Tuxpan expressed it; "if he had curbed his excesses nothing would have happened to him, but no, he kept on with them, because he liked it."[105] According to an elderly female informant, Mezquite started to "rob" Wixárika girls from other communities,[106] and his regime descended from being one that respected communal consensus and the advice of the elders to "a despicable dictatorship, based on terror."[107] He raided Santa Catarina and San Sebastián's semi-independent anexo of Tuxpan, killing many of their inhabitants and driving others into exile.[108] And his attacks on Wixárika rivals within San Sebastián itself culminated in a massacre that left "several dozen dead, whose bones can still be seen" near the community's cabecera.[109]

Mezquite also overplayed his hand with the region's mestizos: Wixárika informants today describe his raiding major towns, including Chimaltitán, San Martin de Bolaños, Villa Guerrero, and perhaps even Colotlán,[110] while in the 1930s, Zingg's sources reported Mezquite once sold "four cows from some mestizo traders, and then sent his men to kill them in the high Sierra and bring back the animals."[111] The region's new Carrancista commander, the notoriously hard-line General Francisco de Santiago, was worried by the threat that out-of-control Wixárika militarism posed to regional political stability,[112] and in 1919, Carrancista troops, aided by some of Mezquite's own disaffected followers,[113] arrested Mezquite at his ranch.[114] Weigand claims the soldiers then murdered the infamous Wixárika cacique "under pretext of the *ley fuga*" (i.e., shot while trying to escape),[115] but some Wixárika informants claim that it was in fact the Wixáritari themselves who "bumped him off" so as to put a permanent end to his abuses.[116]

MARIANO MEJÍA, EUTIMIO DOMÍNGUEZ, AND CACIQUISMO IN THE SIERRA NÁAYARI

In the Territory of Tepic, the formation of defensas sociales played a similarly important part in Carrancista efforts to combat remnant Villistas and generalized banditry, while also upsetting local political systems and setting the stage for intracommunal factional conflicts. In the Náayari communities, defensas made up of local notables and their allies, armed by the Carrancistas, began to coalesce at around the same time as their equivalents in the Sierra Wixárika, and in response to the same pressures, given the ease with which Villistas raiders moved between the two regions.[117] In stark contrast with earlier Carrancista policy in central Mexico, where in 1914–15 they had ruthlessly purged local political elites,[118] in late 1916, the Carrancista jefe político in the Territory of Tepic, General Torres Sur, decided to work with the preexisting authorities in the Sierra Náayari rather than reform or replace them.[119] This boosted the authority of local militia commanders, who further consolidated their local cacicazgos during the fighting that followed Carranza's elevation, in January 1917, of the Territory of Tepic to the category of a "Free and Sovereign State," called *Nayarit* after the Náayari priest-king who had once ruled the region.[120] General Jesús M. Ferreira, whom Carranza appointed the new state's governor, alleged that local rural unrest was the fault of "agitators who, hiding behind constitutional guarantees, intensify the insane ambitions of the illiterate classes" and began "a fierce and energetic action" to stop

Nayarit falling "in the same conditions as those of the time of Lozada."[121] However, Ferreira's campaign in the countryside only aggravated the violence in the countryside, which "increased in such an alarming manner that, during the last days of Ferreira's administration, it was nearly impossible to travel across the state."[122] Across Nayarit, the growing rural disorder increased the dependence of the Carrancista authorities on defensas sociales, while the defensas' roles as protectors of their communities from bandits bolstered their local legitimacy.

By early 1919, when General Francisco de Santiago, fresh from his successful anti-Villista campaign in neighboring parts of Jalisco,[123] seized power in Nayarit,[124] de facto control over the entire Sierra Náayari lay in the hands of two Carrancista-aligned defensa commanders: Mariano Mejía in the Náayari Alta and Eutimio Domínguez in the Náayari Baja. Domínguez, remembered with pride in his home community of San Juan Corapan "for having been one of our indigenous brothers who fought on the side of the revolutionary government headed by don Francisco I. Madero,"[125] was a full-blooded Náayari born in 1882.[126] His father was also a native of Corapan and a relatively wealthy rancher, while his mother, according to some accounts, was originally from San Francisco—reflecting the strong links of trade, kinship, and ritual that still linked together the different Náayari communities. Domínguez seems to have been an early participant in the revolution in Nayarit—perhaps joining the forces of ex-federal lieutenant Miguel Guerrero, then active on the outskirts of the Náayari Baja in early 1912, or those of Thord-Gray in 1914. He eventually returned home to San Juan with a wounded knee (which never fully healed, forcing him to spend most of the rest of his life on horseback)[127] and the rank of colonel in Carranza's Constitutionalist army.[128] There he established a defensa to defend his father's cattle and his community from the raids of the "bandits" then active in the area.[129]

After his father's death in one of these raids, Domínguez inherited what was left of his herds.[130] This enabled him to sponsor ceremonies that increased his status within the descent groups he belonged to, while his status as a ranking military officer and his command of a well-armed defensa limited the opposition of rival families or factions to his increasing influence in San Juan and neighboring communities. He not only appeared to his Náayari compatriots as "one of us" but also as a natural leader possessed of supernatural powers. He was known to spend much of his time fasting and praying to his community's santitos, "so that nothing would happen to his men." Thanks to Domínguez's asceticism, the five devoted bodyguards who always surrounded him in battle were reputed to have been practically bulletproof, their white cotton shirts and trousers "shot full of holes, but not a scratch on their bodies."[131]

However, Domínguez also spoke good Spanish and had learned to read and write while in the army. His intellect would later impress SEP officials, who rather patronizingly described him as a "Náayari Indian of relative culture."[132] Like other Indigenous caciques in this period, from Oaxaca to Michoacán, he used his literacy, charisma, and military prowess to successfully negotiate the violent and alien world of revolutionary mestizo politics while also playing up his ethnicity in order to present himself as a "noble Indian."[133] Domínguez acted as a bridge between Náayarite and outsiders, allowing him to consolidate his influence over the rest of the Náayari Baja—whose communal defensas sociales were all under his control by 1920—while simultaneously developing his clout with the state government, which would come to depend on him to harness the collective military potential of the Náayarite during the first Cristero Rebellion.

Domínguez's friend and then-ally Mariano Mejía was an even more powerful figure. Unlike the Náayari Domínguez, Mejía was born in 1879 in the increasingly "mestizoized" community of Huaynamota[134] and was later described by the famous Mexican author Juan Rulfo as a "mestizo of Náayari blood."[135] Oral sources agree that his mother was a local "Indian"[136] and his father a mestizo rancher from Arandas, Jalisco. However, although unable to speak the Náayari language[137] and despite traditional Náayari distrust toward mestizos, Mejía become one of the many "white and mestizo ethnic brokers" to raise a powerful and predominantly Indigenous force during the revolution.[138] By 1920 he represented Carranza's government throughout the entirety of the Náayari Alta and beyond into neighboring parts of Durango and Jalisco.[139]

Mejía was orphaned as a boy when ex-Lozadista rebels killed his father and his mother fled Huaynamota.[140] Mejía's uncle, a priest, adopted him and took care of his education,[141] allowing him to become, like Domínguez, one of the few literate individuals in the Sierra Náayari. Mejía arrived in Jesús María some years before the revolution with "a chest full of gold coins" left to him by his father. He invested in cattle and soon become a wealthy rancher,[142] able to hire mestizos from across the region to work on his farmstead in Jesús María's anexo of Arroyo de Santiago.[143] Mejía was also careful to win the favor of his Indigenous neighbors. As a mestizo, he naturally lacked Náayari descent group relations, but he married a Náayari woman and also established alternative Catholic-style ritual kinship ties with other Náayarite—such as the local Contreras family—via compadrazgo.[144] He hired Náayarite as well as mestizos to help him with his herds and crops, establishing patron-client ties with his neighbors.[145] Such economically grounded patron-client relationships were rare then in the Gran Nayar, as its inhabitants were subsistence agriculturists who only occasionally worked as wage laborers. But Mejía's establishment of such ties with local Náayarite allowed him to expand his regional influence, which would further increase during the revolution.

In the absence of any official documentation relating to Mejía's military career, and given the vagueness of oral sources, it is impossible to be certain of his early revolutionary activities. Rojas claims he was originally a Villista,[146] but oral accounts agree that Mejía was not an active revolutionary of any kind and never left the sierra to fight for a particular faction. Instead, he was simply a rich and literate local mestizo who also commanded the respect of many Náayarite—a man with huge potential, then, to become a "revolutionary" cacique in the *serrano* tradition.[147] Given the high level of autonomy already enjoyed by the Náayarite in this period, the Villista faction's pro-autonomy, *serrano* tendencies would not have compensated, at least in the eyes of wealthy individuals like Mejía, for their tendency to rob and pillage; for as Rojas points out, "At this point, Villismo and banditry were practically the same thing."[148] Just as in the cases of Eutimio Domínguez and Patricio Mezquite, Mejía's wealth—in particular his extensive herds—would have been natural targets for the Villista bands roaming the sierra. It is not surprising, then, that at some point during the revolutionary civil war,[149] Mejía obtained arms from the Carrancistas for himself and eleven men—probably selected, as usual, from amongst his peons, in-laws, and compadres[150]—to set up a militia in Arroyo de Santiago "to preserve order there."[151] It was a natural alliance of convenience: the Carrancistas increased their influence in the sierra by allying with an important local figure, while the alliance gave Mejía the opportunity to protect both his own private property and his adopted community, enabling him to further increase his local power and prestige.[152]

Only after he actively demonstrated his loyalty to the Carrancistas, however, could Mejía extend his authority beyond Jesús María. According to local interviewees, a rebel leader called José Gallegos, most likely a Villista from Zacatecas, at some point took refuge in the Sierra Náayari.[153] When the Constitutionalist authorities in Tepic heard of his presence, they ordered Mejía to assassinate him. Mejía accordingly invited Gallegos to join his defensa in a raid on local "bandits" and then murdered him as they ate lunch in the mountains.

The versions of this story told by Mejía's grandsons attribute supernatural powers to Gallegos: "He had a huge devil painted on his back, which stopped bullets or anything else hitting him." He was so fearsome that when Mejía invited him to come on the expedition, Gallegos refused to even bring a gun, preferring a huge knife instead.[154] Later, as Gallegos drank water from a brook, one of Mejía's men grabbed the knife, while another tried to pin him from behind, but such was Gallegos's strength that even without his weapon "he knocked them down, dead!" Eventually one member of the defensa lassoed the unfortunate rebel chieftain

> and caught up his head, so he was hanging from a tree. . . . Then they started shooting him, and then they stabbed him in the neck, but the man was still talking, saying, "*Caray*! You traitors! Let me go!"

Mejía and his men, unable to kill Gallegos, finally thought of taking off his shirt, revealing the devil tattooed across his back.

> Then they stripped his skin off with a knife, took off all of the devil, and then he began to die, so they cut his throat—and even then he was trying to talk—so they took him to where a deep pothole was, and threw him down inside, and there, now headless, completely fucked up, there he died.[155]

It is natural that Mejía's descendants should exaggerate Gallegos's powers, and thus the strength of their own famous forebear. But the mythical elements of the story also fit within a well-documented Latin American tradition of attributing supernatural qualities to influential leaders,[156] thereby bolstering their charismatic power and legitimizing their authority.[157] Emiliano Zapata is the most famous Mexican leader to have been subjected to such mythification,[158] but much the same was also done to Eutimio Domínguez and, more importantly, to Manuel Lozada, to whom many Náayarite and Wixáritari still attribute occult powers.[159]

Even discounting the similarities between the supernatural tales told about Mejía and Lozada, it is clear that the general precedent set by the latter must have helped boost local acceptance of Mejía's influence fifty years later. Just as Lozada, aided by his Náayari lieutenant Dionisio Gerónimo, overcame traditional Náayari antipathy toward mestizos to dominate the entire Sierra Náayari, so too Mejía was helped by his Náayari compadre León Contreras to rise from commanding eleven men in Arroyo de Santiago to controlling the defensas of every Náayari and mestizo community in the Náayari Alta.[160] His influence even extended beyond state lines as far as Huazamota and San Lucas in Durango[161] and San Andrés in Jalisco,[162] which, significantly, were the only communities outside the Territory of Tepic to sign Lozada's 1870 political manifesto,[163] further reflecting the parallels between the two men's careers and spheres of influence. Nugent and Alonso have signaled the "importance of popular forms of historical memory and their strategic deployment in political struggle" during the revolution,[164] and it would seem that, as in the cases of contemporary Indigenous mobilizations in Puebla and the Yucatán,[165] Mejía successfully tapped into Náayari memories of their forebears' participation in the conflicts of the nineteenth century to unite them against the threat that bandits and Villistas now posed to them.

Like Manuel Lozada, both Mejía and Domínguez also exercised their power at the local level through subordinate military commanders. Mejía won the allegiance of the rest of the Náayari Alta's defensas—or even managed to select new Spanish-speaking commanders for them himself—by supplying them with cerrojo rifles obtained from his Carrancista allies, which replaced the muskets, slings, and bows and arrows they had previously depended on.[166] Each community's defensa remained responsible for the defense of its local interests, pursuing local bandits and more minor delinquents. However, "when they needed to take care of something big [Mejía and/or Domínguez] called them all together, and off they went to wherever the real danger was."[167]

The ability of Mejía and Domínguez to establish themselves as paramount authorities in the Sierra Náayari no doubt owed much to the prior existence of a centralized politico-military command amongst the Náayarite, both during the rule of Lozada and in the era of the Rey Nayar. In turn, by calling together all of the defensas of the Sierra Náayari to undertake larger-scale military operations, Mejía and Domínguez boosted their effectiveness as military commanders, and thus the strength of their claims to legitimate military and political authority over the region and its inhabitants. They played an important role in Francisco de Santiago's pacification campaign in Nayarit in 1919 (to the extent that Mejía was on first name terms with the general), which won their cacicazgos the state government's full recognition.[168] And their unifying influence not only helped to strengthen the collective ability of the Náayarite to defend themselves but also impeded the outbreak of internecine conflicts that might otherwise have fractured the bonds between their communities. This brought to the region a level of political stability that local people initially welcomed after the chaos of the early years of the revolution. Into the 1920s, however, as the threat posed to Náayari communities by bandit gangs receded and the pursuit of their own personal commercial and political interests increasingly tied Mejía, Domínguez, and their subordinates to the revolutionary state, resistance to their authority grew, engendering factional conflicts throughout the region.

CACIQUES, CARRANCISTAS, AND CROSS-STATE CONFLICT IN THE SIERRA O'DAM

In the mountains of southern Durango, O'dam and Mexicanero defensas also played an important role in the fighting between Carrancistas and remnant Villista forces. Their growing power spurred the development of new regional cacicazgos and the outbreak of complex intercommunal and interethnic conflicts, some of which spilled over into Nayarit, Jalisco, and Zacatecas. The most important early O'dam cacique, Dámaso Barraza, first appears in our sources in August 1917, in relation to a Durango-wide "pacification" campaign recently launched by new state governor Domingo Arrieta. Barraza took part in this campaign as a federal captain charged with coordinating operations against the Villistas in the municipality of Mezquital, but he soon became a powerful regional leader in his own right and would later be one of Mexico's first cristero generals. He was born in 1879 in Yonora,[169] an anexo of San Miguel Temoaya. Although Jean Meyer describes Barraza as both a "mestizo"[170] and an "acculturated O'dam,"[171] local oral accounts agree that, like most of Temoaya's inhabitants until after the revolution, he was a fluent O'dam speaker who still took part in both communal and family mitotes,[172] hence his nickname—"El Indio."[173]

With practice of costumbre came membership of the Barraza descent group, which in the usual O'dam style consisted of all those who took part in the same family-level mitotes as he did and which would form the basis of the communal faction that grew up around his leadership. Through his marriage to Nieves Valdés,[174] Barraza also gained the support of many of her kinsmen, including Macario and Ireneo Valdés, who were founding members of Yonora's defensa (and would also later become cristero commanders).[175]

A physically powerful man and a charismatic leader, Barraza was described some years later as

> a huge man, stocky, so mean-looking that just seeing him scared me; he wore a fringed suede jacket, and matching fringed trousers, a big sombrero turned up at both sides, big spurs that sung out as he walked, a .45 in his belt and a rifle in his hand.[176]

Meyer asserts that Barraza began his career as a Villista—an idea he uses to highlight the supposedly strong links between Villismo and the cristeros[177]—but Barraza was more closely associated with Durango's regional caudillos, the Arrieta clan, than with any national-level faction. This does not rule out his having fought at one time as part of Villa's División del Norte,[178] but it is more probable that Barraza, who like Eutimio Domínguez and Mariano Mejía was a (relatively) wealthy rancher,[179] rose to a position of regional military and political power through alliances with whichever revolutionary forces would provide him with arms to defend himself, and his community, against bandit gangs and rebel raids.[180] Barraza eventually threw in his lot with the Carrancistas, in this case represented by the Arrietas, who probably saw in Barraza a commander cut from the same *serrano* cloth as themselves and a useful ally against the Villistas who threatened their own wider control of the state.[181]

In 1917, "First Captain" Barraza commanded a well-equipped militia based near his ranch in Yonora and took advantage of his position to take back communal territory lost to ranchers from Mezquital's municipal seat,[182] ordering them to attend "a meeting in Yonora, where he told them the land wasn't theirs, and if they didn't leave he'd kill them all."[183] However, Barraza also worked with the defensa of Mezquital in local anti-Villista campaigns,[184] especially after Villa himself reentered northern Durango in August 1917 and began a new recruitment drive across the state.[185] Despite the activities of both defensas, however, the depredations of Villista bandits and renegade federal troops in southern Durango increased over the following months.[186] Widespread violence, banditry, and the Spanish influenza epidemic severely disrupted local agricultural production,[187] meaning that 1918 was remembered locally as the worst year of the revolutionary period: "the year of hunger."[188]

Because of the threat of rebel raids and the flight of local officials, it was impossible to hold municipal elections in southern Durango in March 1918, while an "absolute lack of funds"[189] caused by the ongoing regional economic crisis forced Mezquital's defensa to disband. Many of the town's inhabitants therefore left their homes for the safety of the nearby mountains.[190] Although by May there were up to four hundred Villistas active in the region,[191] Barraza's Carrancista militia remained intact and scored a number of victories against the rebels, including at the hacienda of El Capulín (where Barraza would also rout a superior federal force during the cristiada).[192] Barraza was lauded by the citizens of Mezquital as "he who has hit the enemy hardest, so that they have not returned to attack this town."[193] However, because of the failure of the state government to pay for the upkeep of his force, Barraza left Mezquital for the hacienda of El Refugio, whose owners had hired him and his O'dam fighters to protect their property—a somewhat ironic turn of events given that in much of the rest of Mexico, it was the enmity between hacendados and Indigenous villagers that had in the first place triggered the uprisings that became the revolution.[194]

By the end of the year, as Carrancista operations forced the Villistas of northern and western Mexico to disperse into ever more remote areas, the O'dam and Mexicaneros, like their Náayari and Wixárika neighbors, found themselves on the frontlines of a new round of violence.[195] The threat of rebel raids and a dramatic rise in generalized banditry fostered the growth of Carrancista-armed—but essentially politically and economically autonomous—defensa forces in communities elsewhere in the Sierra O'dam,[196] including Santiago Teneraca, Santa María Ocotán, San Bernardino de Milpillas Chico, and Xoconoxtle.[197]

Although some of these militias may already have been active for several years, from 1918 their leaders began to seek formal recognition by the region's mestizo civil authorities. In Pueblo Nuevo, the municipal government acknowledged that, as it was unable to provide security for the region's inhabitants, "the locals take care of the persecution of bandits as a collective task."[198] Durango's state government therefore recognized the right of Pueblo Nuevo's communities to form defensas under their own leaders and to confiscate any property found in rebel hands to pay for their own upkeep.[199] A similar system likely prevailed in Mezquital. But although southern Durango's Indigenous inhabitants were legally entitled to defend themselves against bandits, some of their militias turned to banditry themselves, raiding and plundering their neighbors.

In December 1918, for example, José María Gutiérrez, the assistant governor of San Francisco Ocotán, wrote to Domingo Arrieta, asking him to

> give us the right to our defence so we are not threatened by an invasion of armed men like those carried out by the leaders of various of the pueblos that surround us . . . we want to live freely as we have always lived peacefully for many years and we don't want to involve ourselves in any kind of revolution but rather be under the orders of your superior authority.[200]

Arrieta authorized the community to organize its own defensa force, adding that the state government would then "certify as leader of said force the person whom you designate"—which perhaps unsurprisingly turned out to be Gutiérrez himself.[201] Unlike Dámaso Barraza, Mariano Mejía, or Eutimio Domínguez—all of whom had formed armed groups independently of preexisting communal power structures—Gutiérrez was a high-ranking member of his community's traditional government, and the defensa that he founded in San Francisco Ocotán was therefore—at least initially—still accountable to the communal assembly and local ritual-political officeholders. In affirming Gutiérrez as head of San Francisco's defensa, Durango's revolutionary officials meanwhile followed exactly the same procedures in relation to the O'dam authorities as their Porfirian predecessors had done; that is, they claimed de jure power over Indigenous communal power structures that in reality remained completely autonomous.

However, although the formation of a defensa in San Francisco Ocotán did not initially lead to conflicts within the community, the defensa owed its very existence to the conflicts that already existed between San Francisco and its neighbors—conflicts that meshed with broader disputes over the location of Durango's borders with Nayarit. José María Gutiérrez alleged that those who had been attacking San Francisco de Ocotán were not "bandits" or "Villistas" but rather the Mexicaneros of San Buenaventura and San Pedro Jícoras, in Durango, and the O'dam, Mexicaneros, and mestizos of San Andrés Milpillas and Picachos, across the state line in Nayarit.[202] He claimed that these interlopers from another state had not only invaded San Francisco but had also tried to force the authorities of San Buenaventura to "declare independence from the authorities of this state and annex themselves to the neighboring state of Nayarit."[203]

By playing up the affront to Durango's pride that the actions of Nayarit's defensas represented and by invoking the threat they also posed to the integrity of the state itself, Gutiérrez secured the support of Durango's government. Arrieta ordered the defensas of San Andrés and Picachos, and the inhabitants of San Buenaventura, to halt their attacks on San Francisco[204] and commanded San Buenaventura's traditional government, whose loyalty Gutiérrez had so effectively called into question, to "bring to the attention of this government any kind of attempt made by the authorities of Nayarit to exercise jurisdiction there."[205]

Grateful for this support, in December Gutiérrez informed the state government that

> this pueblo desires to learn of the new laws and reforms, and of the official government bulletin, the Federal Constitution and other books of law that will serve as their base, for their administration from this courthouse, and also the other regulations that will be useful for the same, and in virtue of our all being illiterate natives . . . we only hope

> that you will send us these tools because they are very important, or at least tell us where we need to ask for them.[206]

Both the defensa and the traditional authorities of San Francisco thus made their loyalty to the new revolutionary order in Durango explicit, even as their plea for information about what this revolutionary order actually consisted of demonstrated just how far removed from the control of any outside forces they, and the community as a whole, still remained.[207]

In the far southeast of the Sierra O'dam, in the municipality of Huazamota, which bordered not only Nayarit but also Jalisco and Zacatecas, the growth of local defensa forces also inflamed internal conflicts. In the mestizo-inhabited municipal seat, a faction headed by Vicente, Tiburcio, and Nabor Muñoz challenged the power of the local cacique, Primo Ortiz, who for the past twenty years had governed with an iron fist the mestizos of Huazamota, the Mexicaneros of San Pedro Jícoras, and the Náayarite of San Lucas de Jalpa.[208] After Ortiz declared for the Carrancistas, the Muñoz clan allied with the Villistas of northern Jalisco in an attempt to unseat their rival.[209] However, in the face of local Villista losses—including the massacre of Félix Díaz's men at Huaynamota in October 1918, in which Ortiz played an important role—los Muñoz returned to Huazamota and swore to retire to private life in exchange for Ortiz's pardon. But in July 1919, Ortiz complained to the governor of Durango that the young upstarts were once again conspiring against him "with the aim of getting their hands on the leadership of the militia which is at my command." He accused them of allying to this end with Felipe Ángeles—a one-time Carrancista general who, after deserting to the Villistas and then fleeing into exile, had recently returned to Mexico to lead an abortive rebellion against Carranza.[210] Ortiz thus charged his local rivals with treachery against not only himself but against Carranza, and at the same time, he symbolically equated the legitimacy of his own control of Huazamota with that of Carranza's rule over the nation.[211]

In response to these accusations, Domingo Arrieta confirmed Ortiz in his post and authorized him to apprehend "these troublemakers" and send them to the state capital. In the meantime he ordered Ortiz to prepare for upcoming statewide "extraordinary municipal elections"[212]—a sign that the Carrancista pacification campaign in Durango was bringing a measure of political stability to much of the state. However, while Ortiz was lobbying Arrieta in the state capital—some 250 km north from Huazamota across the mountains—Tiburcio Muñoz traveled to Jesús María, Nayarit, only around 50 km south along the Jesús María River. There he obtained from Mariano Mejía a letter of recommendation safeguarding "their persons, lives, interests and arms, as they are honorable people."[213] Mejía also wrote separately to Domingo Arrieta, advising him that the people of Huazamota

> are not in agreement with the militia commander of their pueblo for certain motives that would be lengthy to enumerate and knowing my obligation is to watch over the sons of this pueblo I find myself obliged to proclaim to you in agreement with General Francisco de Santiago, since this neighboring pueblo borders the state of Nayarit, for which I beg you to do this pueblo a favor, and help in all the ways you can Mr. Tiburcio Muñoz, as well the others who represent the pueblo, for he is a person who has never stained the cloth of his honor.[214]

The support of Mejía—and by association of Mejía's powerful ally General de Santiago—for Ortiz's rivals caused an about-turn in the attitude of Governor Arrieta, who two weeks later ordered Ortiz to step down as commander of Huazamota's defensa in favor of Vicente Muñoz (who, in self-consciously revolutionary style, slammed Ortiz as being a corrupt old "capitalist").[215] Arrieta thanked Mariano Mejía for "the goodwill that you have demonstrated in providing guarantees to the people of the Municipality of Huazamota," asked him to pass on "extensive thanks to General Francisco de Santiago, on the part of the governor of this entity," and requested both men help Vicente Muñoz "bring his task to a successful end."[216]

However, Ortiz refused to give up control of Huazamota or to hand over to Vicente Muñoz and his newly reconstituted defensa "not one rifle nor a single bullet."[217] Instead, he rallied his own regional allies, including the defensas of Mezquitic and Huejuquilla (in Jalisco), and San Juan Capistrano (in Zacatecas).[218] The inhabitants of the latter wrote to Durango that they had previously fought alongside Ortiz and the defensas of Mezquitic and Huejuquilla—as well as the "honorable men of San Juan Peyotán" (Nayarit)—in defense of the entire cross-border region, which they accused the Muñoz clan of terrorizing during their time as Villistas. They claimed that they would be the first to suffer if the Muñoz clan again rose against the government—which, given their treacherous characters, they were liable to do.[219]

Against Ortiz's alliance with the defensas of San Juan Capistrano, Mezquitic, and Huejuquilla, the Muñoz brothers and their supporters—who Vicente claimed numbered fifty-five men[220]—formed an alliance of convenience with O'dam leader Gregorio Aguilar, who headed the defensa of Santa María Ocotán (which bordered Huazamota to the north).[221] Aguilar was in fact a native of Xoconoxtle, where he remained an important communal leader, but since 1915 had commanded an "armed band" in Candelaria, an anexo of Santa María.[222] By 1918, he commanded the same captain's rank as fellow O'dam cacique Dámaso Barraza, with whom he worked closely to defeat bandits active on the northern side of the Sierra O'dam, allowing him to cultivate friendly contacts with municipal and state government officials.[223] Further south, however, he had already clashed with Primo Ortiz, complaining to the state government in May 1919 that Ortiz and his forces "continually molested" the people of

Santa María Ocotán.[224] Given the long-standing territorial disputes between Huazamota and Santa María, it is hardly surprising that a feud would develop between their leaders. The alliance between Aguilar and los Muñoz—the enemies of his enemy—was a natural consequence of this conflict.[225]

The Durango state government was alarmed by the prospect of cross-border warfare breaking out between rival Carrancista-aligned defensas in its southernmost municipality and so decided to nominate Antonio Gutiérrez, a supposedly neutral local notable, to the position of the defensa's new commander in Huazamota. The Muñoz clan refused to acquiesce, calling Gutiérrez a "blind instrument of Mr. Ortiz, which we believe to be prejudicial to the entire pueblo."[226] The intransigence of both sides inevitably led to violence, which ended in a battle between Gutiérrez, Ortiz, and fifty armed mestizos on one side and one hundred mestizos, O'dam, and Mexicaneros under los Muñoz and Gregorio Aguilar on the other. In the end, Gutiérrez was defeated and captured, Ortiz escaped, and the surviving members of the losing faction sent desperate petitions to the Durango state government, asking that

> you would order that Gregorio Aguilar retire from here and ask from the government of Tepic that Mr. Mariano Mejía provide guarantees to Mr. Antonio Gutiérrez, in case they have not killed him already, and the other people of order in that place.[227]

However, Aguilar also wrote to the state government, declaring triumphantly that he had fought only to defend "order" in the region and that

> I left Huazamota in the possession of Mr. Muñoz and it appears that the authorities are now working together well and the militia commander continues to tenaciously pursue Ortiz so that soon there will be tranquillity in the pueblo which is what the inhabitants desire.[228]

Aguilar's victory allowed him to increase his influence across ethnic and communal lines: in addition to controlling the O'dam of Santa María Octotán and Xoconoxtle, he was now a kingmaker in mestizo Huazamota, while the Mexicaneros of nearby San Pedro Jícoras were grateful to him for deposing the "abusive" Ortiz.[229] Aguilar used his growing political influence—and his legal right as a defensa commander to dispose of property "confiscated" from his enemies—to become a wealthy rancher.[230] However, Durango's military commander-in-chief accused Aguilar of interference in local political matters beyond his remit as a defensa commander and promised to support Gutiérrez against him.[231] Meanwhile, the state government itself was sufficiently confused by the factional violence and the conflicting reports and complaints of both sides that it commissioned an official named Adolfo Bermúdez to broker a peaceful settlement between them.[232]

Bermúdez arrived in Huazamota at the end of October 1919. He reported that the inhabitants, fearing for their lives amid the violence, had completely abandoned the municipal seat, but after assuring them that the state government would guarantee their safety, most returned to their homes. The defensa, now firmly in the hands of the Muñoz faction, temporarily handed over its weapons to a neutral figure until elections could decide its new leader.[233]

On October 30, Vicente Estrada, acting head of the provisional local government and a close ally of los Muñoz, was elected the new defensa commander, and Tiburcio Muñoz replaced him as chief civil authority. Bermúdez approved these appointments, which were promptly seconded by the state government. The Muñoz faction had gained total politico-military control of Huazamota.[234] However, the support of Bermúdez (and by extension of Durango's state government) for the mestizo Muñoz clan did not extend to their O'dam ally Gregorio Aguilar. Instead, Bermúdez, like Durango's military authorities, saw the power of Aguilar and the region's other chief Indigenous cacique, Dámaso Barraza, as a problem and warned that

> justice here has been for various years in the gift of only the chiefs of the Security Forces or Defensa commanders, true caciques who are absolute in its administration, employing the most barbarous procedures. I gathered reports that these chiefs, especially those of Santa María Ocotán and of Yonora, still proceed as I have indicated. Furthermore, during my stay in this pueblo [of Huazamota], I received innumerable complaints about the aforementioned chiefs; complaints of which, apparently, the Supreme Government is already aware.[235]

CONCLUSIONS

Despite popular perceptions of the Náayarite, Wixáritari, O'dam, and Mexicaneros as passive subjects who have always been isolated from national events, it is clear that members of all four groups (as well as the local mestizo minority) played an active part in the armed phase of the revolution. By 1914, many had joined, on an individual basis, the revolutionary bands then operating in the Gran Nayar before, from 1915, whole communities entered into the fighting between Villista guerrillas and the Carrancista forces pursuing them.

It was in this context that, under the leadership of small-scale warlords, many of the Indigenous inhabitants of the Gran Nayar—no strangers to warfare in the first place—secured arms and allies and began to turn the presence of external forces in and around their homelands to their own advantage. By the end of the decade of armed revolution, this process left control of the entire Sierra Náayari in the hands of two men—the Náayari Eutimio Domínguez and the mestizo Mariano Mejía—who from being "local caciques" had risen to become "municipal" or, in the latter's case, "regional" caudillos.[236] By contrast, the death of Patricio Mezquite left the Sierra Wixárika split between local cacicazgos—such as that of Clemente Villa—which encompassed no more than one community and in which defensa commanders shared power with gobiernos tradicionales. The situation amongst the O'dam and Mexicaneros meanwhile lay somewhere between these two extremes, in that the influence of a few caciques, such as Gregorio Aguilar and Dámaso Barraza, spanned several communities, while a multitude of lower-level caciques continued to rule smaller, communal fiefdoms in alliance (as in the case of San Francisco de Ocotán) with traditional local authorities.

In the Sierra Náayari, the power of the region's two caciques—tied to local memories of mass mobilization under Lozada (and even the Tonatí) and to the existence of long-standing ritual and political ties between communities—served to limit the outbreak of internecine violence caused by the emergence of defensas. However, in both the Sierra O'dam and the Sierra Wixárika, many defensas engaged in intercommunal warfare and factional feuding, linked to struggles for regional influence, intercommunal territorial and political disputes, and broader territorial conflicts between the states of Durango, Nayarit, and Zacatecas.

Although the Sierra Náayari was as yet free from either intercommunal or factional violence, the death of Mezquite in the Sierra Wixárika and the ego-driven conflicts amongst Primo Ortiz, the Muñoz family, and Gregorio Aguilar in the Sierra O'dam proved a sign of things to come for the inhabitants of all three regions. In large part, the growth of such internecine conflicts across the Gran Nayar was part and parcel of the dynamics of revolutionary caciquismo across Mexico and beyond. Scott has observed that in times of social, political, and economic volatility, local leaders often amass new power and wealth at the expense of previous forms of social cohesion "founded on tenancy, employment and charity." As the rich have less need to "cultivate" the poor, they become increasingly dependent on the support of outside forces—such as allies in government—for their continued control of village life.[237] Knight shows that this was certainly the case in Mexico, where, as the revolution wore on, it became increasingly difficult to distinguish between those caciques "who enjoyed substantial local support" and "those whose power derived from above," given their propensity "to shed their popular support in favour of the endorsement of the centre and/or of local elites."[238]

Although the Gran Nayar's defensas helped the region's communities to better defend themselves from raiders and other menaces, including the mestizo settlement that threatened their communities from within, there would always be local people who looked askance at their ties to outsiders, especially when they took advantage of such ties to pursue personal political interests and to increase their wealth (usually in the form of cattle). Into the 1920s, as those defensa commanders who survived the armed phase of the revolution associated themselves ever more closely with outside forces to fortify their positions and expand their herds, such resentment would only increase.

3

SCHOOLS, STATE-BUILDING, AND COMMUNAL AUTONOMY UNDER THE SONORANS, 1920–1925

IN LATE 1919, Mexico began to prepare for elections to choose Carranza's successor as president. General Álvaro Obregón saw himself as rightfully next in line, but Carranza backed a more malleable, non-military figure. Obregón ran for the presidency anyway, but Carranza so obstructed his candidacy that in April 1920, Obregón launched an uprising with fellow Sonoran generals Adolfo de la Huerta and Plutarco Elías Calles. The Sonoran forces quickly drove their former commander-in-chief out of Mexico City, and a few weeks later he was ambushed and killed as he tried to reach loyalist forces. De la Huerta assumed power as interim president and was succeeded in December 1920 by Obregón, whose accession heralded the beginning of a six-year period of revolutionary consolidation under the so-called Sonoran dynasty.

In this period, neither de la Huerta, Obregón, or Calles (who became the third Sonoran president in 1924) deviated from long-standing Liberal aims of building a stable Mexican nation-state defined by "capitalist development, national integration, and anticlericalism." But given the chaotic situation from which the country was only just beginning to emerge, they were forced to "employ a new range of institutional and political techniques" in their state-building drive. Despite their nationalism, their policies were also influenced by an "admiration for what they saw as the material progress and dynamism" of contemporary U.S. society.[1] This chapter looks at the methods the Sonoran regime used in its attempts to "incorporate" the Gran Nayar and its independent-minded inhabitants into the Mexican nation-state between 1920 and 1926; the ways in which local individuals, factions, and communities reacted to these efforts; and the consequences of such interactions for the Gran Nayar, the wider region, and even Mexico as a whole.

INSTRUMENTS OF SONORAN STATE-BUILDING IN THE GRAN NAYAR

In much of Mexico, a variety of federal institutions, state and municipal administrations, and the country's armed forces—at this point still under the control of numerous semiautonomous revolutionary generals—took part in the Sonoran state-building project.[2] However, the generals responsible for the military zones that corresponded to Nayarit, Jalisco, Durango, and Zacatecas, keen to profit during the limited time that Obregón and Calles permitted them to stay in their commissions,[3] tended to ignore the Gran Nayar in favor of wealthier regions.[4] Adolfo de la Huerta's failed 1923 rebellion also divided the army and further weakened its presence in the Gran Nayar. Similarly, while state and municipal governments appointed police and defensa commanders in other similarly peripheral areas,[5] these civilian authorities were no more able than their Porfirian predecessors to extend their power into the Gran Nayar. Independent-minded local defensa commanders were instead left to jostle for control of their communities with local cargo hierarchies.

Some historians argue that the military caciques who challenged Indian power structures across Mexico from the mid-nineteenth century remained loyal to traditional ideals of reciprocity and communalism while opening up new economic and political opportunities for young people and women.[6] But these interpretations often underplay the violence of cacical authority and the depth of local resistance to growing cacical power,[7] both of which typified the factional power struggles that rocked the Gran Nayar in this period. It was in the midst of such tensions—which in the Sierra Wixárika had already led to the murder of Patricio Mezquite—that officials working for the federal government's chief state-building dependencies arrived in the region.

The weakness of most federal agencies in the Gran Nayar is evident in their failure to collect much local statistical and demographic data, usually an essential tool for "defining reality in accordance with particular interests and for establishing routines to benefit the structure of domination."[8] Census takers barely penetrated the Gran Nayar in 1921: out of nearly two million speakers of Indigenous languages above the age of five registered across Mexico, they managed to record details of only 341 Náayarite and 364 Wixáritari (less than 10 percent of these groups' estimated populations in 1910). The census registered a more impressive 1,834 speakers of "Tepehuano," but most were Northern Tepehuanos (Odami) from Chihuahua, unrelated to the O'dam—or Southern Tepehuanos—of Durango.[9]

Sonoran efforts to assimilate the Gran Nayar into the Mexican nation therefore centered on the activities of the Secretariat of Education (Secretaría de Educación Pública, or SEP) and the National Agrarian Commission (Comisión Nacional Agraria, or CNA). The Carrancistas had created the latter in 1916 to judge the validity of peasant collectives' requests for grants of state land (*dotación de ejidos*) or of communal petitions for the restitution of territory (*restitución de tierras*) lost since the reform. The CNA passed on its recommendations to the president, who had the final say on each case in the form of a "presidential resolution." However, the Carrancistas and their Sonoran successors alike viewed wide-ranging agrarian reform as a threat to the stability of the economy and of society itself.[10] Early agrarian legislation was thus designed to limit the scale and scope of peasant claims to land. Even launching a claim itself was difficult and required peasants to nominate an agrarian council—the Comité Particular Ejecutivo—to oversee their claims. The transfer of a communal claim to the control of a small group often caused confusion and factional discord, turning some peasants against the very idea of agrarian reform.[11] Moreover, widows and other female heads of household were ruled ineligible to participate in such processes, and thus to claim plots of land, removing from them a right they had enjoyed since the colonial era. This engendered further grassroots opposition to agrarian reform.[12]

Meanwhile, "political considerations frequently outweighed pragmatic, technical or economic considerations regarding the ultimate disposition of the land or the (legally defined) 'legitimacy' of the claim."[13] Regional elites often took control of the Local Agrarian Commissions (Comisiones Locales Agrarias, or CLAs) responsible for deciding which claims were worthy of further examination by the CNA, obstructing claims that threatened their interests and in many parts of the country enlisting the help of the military to crush agrarista political organizations.[14] Meanwhile, many of those claims for either restitución (restitution) or dotación (grant) that did reach the CNA were ignored, delayed, or rejected, as the Sonorans viewed collective land tenure as inferior to the "division of the great estates into small ranches and farms" through the process of *fraccionalización*. Even ejidal collectives formed as a result of dotación—which the Sonorans saw "as a way of creating small, technologically modern, capitalized, and productive estates . . . in which peons would evolve into proprietors"—were viewed as superior to the traditional peasant communities that restitución would help to reestablish.[15] Before the CNA considered a claim for restitución, then, peasants were asked to provide difficult-to-obtain documentary evidence of illegal usurpation of their lands.[16] As a result, most successful agrarian claims involved dotación,[17] which echoed colonial-era practices that rewarded service and loyalty to the Crown with grants of land and allowed the government to present itself as a generous, paternal institution.[18]

Many Mexican peasants viewed the dotación process with suspicion because ejidos were subject to new taxes (including a levy of 15 percent of each harvest)[19] and because those "who petitioned for land also wanted their own land. . . . Securing a restitution was justice, while securing a dotación was an insult, a matter of the state posturing as a patron."[20] This was especially true in communities such as those of the Gran Nayar, which demanded the recognition and/or restitución of territories that were synonymous with their political, cultural, and ethnic identities and integral to their practice of costumbre and understandings of space, time, and history. They justified their claims with reference to colonial-era títulos virreinales. The revolutionary state viewed these as relics of an obsolete tenancy system, but the Náayarite, Wixáritari, O'dam, and Mexicaneros regarded them as objects of supernatural power that were far more legitimate than anything produced by the new agrarian bureaucracy and demanded their territorial boundaries be recognized in line with them.

Given the slow, complicated, and conflicted nature of land reform in this period, the SEP, founded by revolutionary intellectual and politician José Vasconcelos in October 1921,[21] played a more salient role in early revolutionary state-building in much of Mexico, including the Gran Nayar. One of the SEP's most important divisions was the Departamento de Educación y Cultura Indígena (DECI), soon renamed the Departamento de Escuelas Rurales y Incorporación Cultural Indígena (DERICI), which was tasked with assimilating into the Mexican nation-state the approximately 30 percent of the population still living in a state of "physical and cultural isolation."[22] Throughout the 1920s, the SEP was dominated by "conservative urban social reformers and pedagogues influenced by U.S. social science," who perceived the problems of Mexico's rural population caused primarily by their "isolation . . . rather than structures of power that limited peasant access to land, capital and trade."[23] The DECI/DERICI therefore sought to introduce "new skills and behaviors" through the compulsory education of young Indigenous people, which would unite them and their communities around a nationalist ideal and liberate them from poverty by integrating them into the national economy. Such changes would in turn open up rural Mexico's previously untapped human and natural resources for the nation's benefit.[24]

The schools that would spearhead this program—first called *casas del pueblo* (houses of the pueblo) and later and less evocatively *escuelas rurales indígenas* (rural Indigenous schools)—were to be funded and supplied both by the SEP and, it was hoped, by local pupils and their families. Communities were expected to help construct their schools, while the agricultural labor of Indigenous pupils on the school's grounds would provide them (and their teachers) with food and demonstrate "improved" agricultural techniques to local people, which would help to "forge a physical connection between them and the patria." The implementation of this ambitious program was delegated to the SEP dependencies (*departamentos de educación federal*) set up in each of Mexico's states and territories, which would support the *maestros ambulantes* (itinerant teachers) sent to work in Indigenous regions. The itinerant teachers were soon renamed *maestros misioneros* (missionary teachers), reflecting Vasconcelos's hope that they would emulate the Catholic orders first tasked with "civilizing" Mexico's Indians. Clearly, the mindsets of many revolutionary educators still had much in common with those of their Porfirian predecessors, who had depended on similar "religious, even messianic, metaphors to describe the process of rural education."[25]

However, the maestros misioneros were handicapped by the fact that their actual roles still lacked definition: they were first instructed to explore their assigned regions with a view to founding casas del pueblo in remote communities,[26] then ordered to abandon exploration and focus on organizing literacy campaigns in their centers of residence,[27] and then to establish themselves in Indigenous communities where possible, until the DECI declared that as it was not possible to "determine the boundary between indigenous people and Indian peasants . . . the rural schools cannot distinguish between indigenous people and mestizos."[28] Federal education programs were also hindered by budgetary problems and the associated poor quality of the teachers willing to take up rural postings, many of whom were young men and women who had received only a limited education themselves.

FIGURE 1 Children in the Náayari Baja doing manual labor, carrying bricks for construction of a new classroom (AHSEP-84-85/C/38877/E/31, M. Durán Cárdenas, "Informe," July 10, 1932).

Above all, the success of the SEP's assimilative program was frustrated by the fact that much of Mexico's Indigenous population spurned the educational "missionaries," just as their ancestors had rebuffed the latter's religious predecessors. There were many reasons for this recalcitrance: some could not afford to pay contributions toward the building of schools; others believed that the schools would infect their children with Protestantism or disliked the SEP's often self-important teachers.[29] In many cases, Indigenous families simply couldn't afford to lose their children's contributions to the household economy,[30] especially as they did so much manual labor at school anyway: "'If the children are going to school to learn that,' they declared, 'it would be better if we taught them.'"[31]

Moreover, in the case of the Gran Nayar, local people were already wary of schools. The handful of teachers sent to the region during the Porfiriato had been untrustworthy and abusive, and many Náayarite, Wixáritari, O'dam, and Mexicaneros also believed that literacy and contact with outsiders would lead their children to "lose their native tongue and their ancient beliefs."[32] Such dramatic cultural change was exactly what Vasconcelos and other early SEP policy makers desired; for despite abandoning older doctrines of Indian racial inferiority, they still regarded Indigenous cultural and political and religious identities as barriers to their incorporation into a nation-state conceived of as inherently "mestizo."[33] Even Indigenista intellectuals such as Manuel Gamio, who "acclaimed the Indian as a model for the future of the nation," excluded from this vision all those peoples who had been "peripheral to the history of Central Mexico," including the Tarahumara, the Yaqui, and, as this chapter will show, the Indigenous inhabitants of the Gran Nayar.[34]

SEP policy goals therefore pitted teachers against the distinct beliefs, practices, and ways of life that many Náayarite, Wixáritari, O'dam, and Mexicaneros believed essential to the existence of the universe itself. SEP officials also offended their hosts by meddling in questions of local agrarian reform, by encouraging the mestizo colonization of Indigenous communities to help spread "civilized" values and by campaigning against "primitive" lifeways on which local people had long depended for survival. Worst of all, as teachers and other officials grew frustrated by local intransigence, some attempted to forcibly remove children from their families to send them to boarding schools where, free from the influence of their "primitive" material and cultural surroundings, they could be more easily "civilized."[35] Such radical tactics were also used against Indigenous students in the United States, Canada, and Australia[36] and against religious dissidents such as the Doukhobors in the Russian Empire.[37] In Mexico, the tactics became common from 1922, first to procure Indian children from peripheral regions for regional boarding schools and then, from 1925, for the national Indigenous boarding school—the Casa del Estudiante Indígena—in Mexico City.

Although in recent decades the toxic legacy of "residential schools" has been subject to high-profile debate and soul-searching in the United States, Canada, and Australia,[38] in Mexico neither the state nor civil society has addressed the historical abuses committed against Indigenous children by the SEP. Instead, the idea of Mexico's rural teachers as noble martyrs in the service of popular liberation from oppression, poverty, and "backwardness" remains pervasive.[39] Understandably, the families of the children kidnapped by SEP officials often regarded such actions in a less forgiving light. In the Gran Nayar, as in other regions that have suffered the effects of imperialist and racist education policies,[40] most local people resisted the SEP's program using "weapons of the weak" such as foot-dragging, noncompliance, evasiveness, and obfuscation[41] and, on occasion, resorting to less subtle methods, including murder.

As in rural communities across the country, however, other Náayarite, Wixáritari, O'dam, and Mexicaneros—above all, the commanders of communal defensas—had vested interests in the political and economic changes promoted by revolutionary policy makers.[42] The defensa commanders were less wary of outsiders than their fellows and often saw teachers and mestizo settlers as potential allies in their power struggles with local gobiernos tradicionales.[43] Many defensa commanders and their cosmopolitan followers therefore embraced the ideas of "progress," "productivity," and "civilization" that, as defined by mestizo government officials, were to be the foundation of the new Mexican nation-state. Some of them also saw compromise with these officials as the only way to preserve the integrity and autonomy of their communities.[44] However, this version of autonomy would be safely overseen by themselves and a few other members of the emerging elite of young, ambitious, and wealthy Indigenous men who had come into close contact with Mexican society thanks to the revolution.[45] During the early 1920s, then, Sonoran state-building exacerbated the factional power struggles that had already begun to emerge in many communities, with severe consequences both for the success of the state's programs in the Gran Nayar and for the lives and livelihoods of the region's inhabitants.

NAYARIT: THE NÁAYARITE

By the time that Obregón and his Sonoran allies overthrew Carranza, Nayarit had been largely "pacified" thanks to the efforts of the state's defensa forces, including those of the Sierra Náayari.[46] There, Mariano Mejía governed the Náayari Alta both politically and militarily (although the region remained part of the Subprefectura de la Sierra and was governed, in theory, from Tepic), while Domínguez controlled the communities of the Náayari Baja (in de jure terms still split amongst the municipalities of Rosamorada, Santiago Ixcuintla, and Acaponeta).[47] However, the fall of General de Santiago's state government in the wake of the Sonoran coup ushered in a period of renewed political instability comparable with that which Nayarit had suffered throughout much of the nineteenth century.[48] As deputies, federal military chiefs, and local political and commercial factions all fought for power, fifteen different administrations would govern the state over the next six years.[49]

Antonio Navarrete, the first maestro ambulante that the SEP posted to Nayarit, immediately gained firsthand experience of the chaotic situation, as on his arrival in Tepic in December 1921 he was caught up in fighting between rival claimants to the state governorship. As a result, Navarrete was convinced that the federal government should take total control of the provision of education in the state.[50] The federalization of education across Mexico as a whole was, in fact, already official policy: both Vasconcelos and President Obregón hoped that federal schools would strengthen popular support for the central government vis-à-vis the state administrations with which it competed for influence. However, "the impact of federalization . . . would depend on the political patterns of each state,"[51] and it was initially resisted in most of Nayarit. The one exception was the Sierra Náayari, where Navarrete's recommendations were adopted because neither the state nor municipal governments had any real control over local affairs. The running of schools in Náayari communities instead became the official preserve of Nayarit's federal education department, which would work closely to this end with both Mejía and Domínguez.

Navarrete took the issue of Indigenous education to heart, and only one month into his tenure in the state—and even before an SEP circular explicitly ordered all maestros misioneros to make their bases in "a rural settlement, preferably indigenous"[52]—he asked permission to leave his appointed scholastic zone on the coast to set up schools in the Náayari communities. He argued that this would be the best way of incorporating into the nation a region "that since 1914 has remained outside of government control," and by way of justification offered his superiors a detailed report on conditions in the Sierra Náayari—the first to be produced by an outsider since the late Porfiriato. Navarrete informed his superiors that the communities of San Juan Peyotán and Huaynamota were by now relatively compact settlements inhabited by "non-Indians" (whom he defined as anyone who could not speak an Indigenous language). Jesús María, San Francisco, La Mesa, Dolores, and Santa Teresa remained purely Náayari, however, and their inhabitants still lived for the most part in rancherías scattered across the "unlimited territory" that each community controlled—an exaggeration of their size, perhaps, but also an acknowledgement of the success of Náayari resistance to the division of their communal landholdings during the Porfiriato.

Navarrete believed that

> the unanimous instinct of the Náayarite and Wixáritari to leave their pueblos abandoned and flee from society and population centers, reveals a continued barbarous streak, as they prefer wild animals over their fellow men.[53]

At first glance, such a comment would seem to echo the disparaging views of Nayarit's nineteenth-century mestizo intellectuals who, like their peers throughout Porfirian Mexico,[54] stressed biological inferiority as the root cause of "the ignorance, the immorality and the lack of civilization of the indigenous race."[55] However, although revolutionary Indigenista intellectuals "still viewed living Indians as both inert and inferior,"[56] they tended to reject biological racism,[57] and Navarrete stressed that the Náayarite naturally possessed "robust and potent intellectual faculties" but had been denied access to "civilization" and its values by "nefarious governments that have dedicated themselves to increasing educational budgets by disparaging our natives."[58] Navarrete was also the first—and one of very few—government officials of the revolutionary period to recognize that the dispersed Náayari settlement pattern was also a product of economic necessity, as survival in the sierra depended on raising sheep for wool, making cheese, weaving palm fiber, beekeeping, and, most important, growing corn and beans—all of which required families to live in their rancherías "from June to December." Of course, the isolation of these rancherías, and their distance from the sites of prospective schools, would "severely impair the advance of schools." But only by teaching the Náayarite "cottage industries," and thus fundamentally changing the nature of their economy, could their settlement patterns be changed, which Navarrete acknowledged would be a long-term project.

In the meantime, Navarrete pointed to more immediate obstacles to the SEP's project in the Sierra Náayari. He claimed the SEP had failed to supply local teachers with enough food to last them the year, or to pay them enough to support themselves—especially given the inflated prices of transport and goods in the sierra. Since the Náayarite were either unwilling or unable to provision the teachers sent to the region, they risked starving to death—making such postings understandably unpopular amongst "teachers of recognized proficiency, whom are needed in the Sierra more than in any other scholastic zone." The problems that Náayari society itself presented the SEP were graver still. Navarrete claimed that their traditional authorities were dominated by "those so resistant to learning . . . that far from fomenting the schools' progress, they foment their decline."[59]

In many rural parts of Mexico, women were regarded as being more religious and conservative and more wedded to tradition than men,[60] and this was certainly true of the Náayari women whom Navarrete encountered. He noted that they were resolutely opposed to schools and refused even to allow their children to learn Spanish,

> although they all speak it, as the special tendency of those peoples is to conserve their language and customs, for all that the school focuses on children speaking and understanding Spanish, the household openly opposes it and formally counteracts these efforts, which will evidently retard greatly the education of the children.

Furthermore, Navarrete noted that Náayarite of all sexes thought that

> if their children are educated in schools, they will become malicious, lose their customs and quickly die, and they so strongly believe this that, when the authorities exhort parents to comply with the requirement of compulsory education, some move their ranches farther away so as to be less obliged in this respect.[61]

To overcome such resistance, Navarrete suggested that the region's authorities would have to depend on force to ensure that "parents and guardians obey the law of education, and send their children to school regardless of their ages." After thus strong-arming the region's families, every child would have to spend at least one year in intensive Spanish classes before they started the normal school curriculum, as teaching the national language and suppressing the use of "primitive dialects" was at this point seen not just by Navarrete but also by SEP officials throughout Mexico as a "critical means of racially improving and nationally assimilating indigenous children."[62] To implement his recommendations, Navarrete proposed that a school inspector be permanently posted to the sierra and, from his base in Jesús María (for inspectors, unlike teachers, were almost exclusively male),[63] charged with making regular visits to the rest of the region's schools, organizing and invigilating exams, giving talks during the holidays, and resolving "all the doubts and difficulties that teachers may have with regard to their work."[64]

Soon after submitting his report, Navarrete's superiors assigned him precisely this role. As the Sierra Náayari's supervisor, for the next two years the majority of his recommendations became SEP policy in the region. Jesús María was made the center of a new scholastic zone encompassing all of the Náayari communities; local authorities—in this case the regional caciques Mejía and Domínguez and their pro-government subordinates, the communal defensa commanders—were enjoined to guarantee both the safety of teachers and the attendance of pupils; and much of the curriculum consisted of teaching Náayari children to speak Spanish. However, despite his efforts, the progress of the new schools continued to be obstructed by the same basic problems that Navarrete had outlined: namely the poor quality of teachers, the state legislature's alternating neglect of and interference in the federal schools, and, most of all, resistance to the SEP's revolutionary state-building project on the part of both traditional authorities and the Náayari population as a whole.

Federal schools were first established in the communities of the Náayari Baja, which were more easily reached from Tepic than those of the Náayari Alta. In June 1922, after repeated requests to his superiors for permission and the payment of his travel expenses, Navarrete set out for the region on a "voyage of research and exploration,"[65] armed with thirty volumes of Tolstoy and seven of Romain Rolland (although exactly which titles remains unknown).[66] In line with instructions issued by the SEP, in each community he gave lectures on "the National Language, Arithmetic, Hygiene, Morality, and Civic Education" and decided that he would establish his base in Rosarito. Like many of the maestros misioneros of the time,[67] Navarrete saw himself as a man of action, describing his mission as "similar to that developed by the remarkable Booker T. Washington"[68] (whose work on African American education in the United States was an important influence on SEP policy in this period)[69] and declaring that while "in those distant pueblos the life of civilized people is always in imminent danger . . . when one bears a sacred mission, one fears nothing."[70] In spite of such "dangers" (which often necessitated the hiring of armed guards to accompany him on his tours of the sierra)[71] and the other cultural and economic obstacles outlined in his report, Navarrete was an active and enthusiastic educator, even offering to "renounce [his] right to any travel expenses" if it would secure his department's approval for his plans.[72]

In Rosarito, San Juan Corapan, and San Pedro Ixcatán, Navarrete reported that the locals were anxious to receive education[73] and asked that schools—which, in the quasi-religious discourse that characterized much revolutionary rhetoric,[74] he referred to as "Temples of Science"—be founded in each community in order to "emancipate them from the ignorance in which they have always lived."[75] Eutimio Domínguez agreed to guarantee local cooperation, and his support for government schools in this period is remembered in San Juan Corapan today, where the local primary school still carries his name.[76]

Domínguez's status as one of the few literate Náayarite of the period and his involvement in both the regional cattle trade and the revolution—which brought him into close contact with mestizos and with broader Mexican society—had no doubt made him aware of the advantages available to literate, Spanish-speaking Indians. As leaders in other rural parts of Mexico had done since the nineteenth century,[77] Domínguez had anticipated the arrival of the SEP in his community by "paying from his own pocket a man named Primitivo Mayorquín, to locally impart a basic understanding of the alphabet."[78] And like other, more contemporary, Indigenous caciques,[79] Domínguez saw supporting federal education policies as a convenient way of demonstrating his loyalty to the state and thus strengthening his own regional political position, as well as the position of his community in relation to its land-hungry mestizo neighbors. With his backing, the first school in the area was opened in San Pedro Ixcatán in August, its security guaranteed by Domínguez's subordinate Eusebio González, head of San Pedro's defensa. At the same time, Navarrete also worked to secure funds for a special "Agricultural and Industrial School" in San Juan Corapan, an ambitious project he hoped would prepare local children for a "practical life" and enable them to abandon their isolated rancherías and settle permanently in the community's cabecera.[80]

In July 1922, Heriberto Parra became the second maestro misionero to establish schools amongst the Náayarite,[81] in this case in the municipality of Acaponeta.[82] Parra seems to have been less clear than Navarrete as to the exact nature of his mission, blaming the region's poor communications, which prevented the (already rather confusing) circulars issued by his department from reaching him in good time. Was his primary role to found new schools or to supervise the few schools already in existence in Acaponeta? Should he actually be teaching literacy in these schools himself?[83] However, by September Parra had visited the Náayari communities of San Blasito and Saycota, the Mexicaneros of Saycota's anexo, Santa Cruz de Guajolota, and several of the mestizo-inhabited settlements that had recently sprung up within the traditional territories of both communities.[84] Parra reported that although their cabeceras were barely populated, each was surrounded by rancherías inhabited by numerous potential students, and he was initially enthusiastic about his successes, writing that the locals had promised him "after holding various meetings with them, not just to willingly accept schools, but to lend their moral and material support to them so that they can achieve the noble aims this Department has put forward."[85] In Saycota, he reported that he had been offered not one, but two different buildings for use as schools: one in the cabecera and the other in the settlement to which most inhabitants moved every summer, during the rains.[86]

However, Parra soon began to appreciate the difficulties of establishing schools in the region. Two seemingly contradictory statements he made regarding the Náayarite—that "their authorities are unable to do anything without the support of the majority of the Indians"[87] but also that "in all of the region's pueblos, and especially the indigenous ones, the inhabitants will do nothing without the approval of their Judges"[88]—indicate his growing awareness of the uneasy balance between caciquismo and consensus in Náayari communal politics. The support of the traditional government for Parra's projects did not necessarily guarantee that of the community as a whole, while at the same time a sudden change in the attitude of once-sympathetic leaders was enough to force the closure of previously flourishing schools.

For example, Parra complained that despite a promising start to his work in the region, local people "now aggressively refused to permit the establishment of schools." In part, Parra blamed Acaponeta's parish priest for this shift in popular attitudes but also hinted that there was more to the newfound opposition of many Náayarite to his activities. He noted that many Náayarite believed that once schools were established in their communities, the government would "introduce a levy on their real estate and the lands they cultivate."[89] The idea that federal teachers might also double as state or municipal tax collectors was clearly a misunderstanding of their role; but at the same time it does suggest that local people regarded the idea of materially supporting the schools established in their communities as an unwelcome imposition and, beyond this, perhaps recognized that the ultimate goal of the SEP's school-building program was to end the de facto autonomy—both political and fiscal—that the Náayarite currently enjoyed.[90] They were clearly not enthused by this prospect.

In November 1922, Parra did finally manage to open a school in Saycota,[91] where a relatively impressive total of twenty Náayari children were initially enrolled.[92] However, the friendly traditional cargo holders that Parra had first encountered were soon replaced by more hostile individuals, probably selected for precisely this reason by elders opposed to Parra's activities. Thus in August 1923, Parra complained that Saycota's new governor

> openly opposes pitching in for the progress of the Casa del Pueblo and intrigues so that the rest don't either. He refused the request of Municipal President [of Acaponeta] himself that he help secure land for the school's farm.[93]

The character of the teacher posted to Saycota, Pedro Flores, only made matters worse. Flores was apparently posted to Saycota because, although of "scarce enlightenment," he was familiar with the area, spoke some Náayari, and also had "the advantage of being acclimatized to the awful weather that prevails here."[94] However, in 1924, after two years in Saycota, Parra reported that

> the moral and social state of the Casa del Pueblo and the local people is one of complete desolation. In general, I believe that not only has [Flores] made no progress at the school during his time there; but that he has betrayed the hopes of this Department and butchered the pueblo's evolutionary process.[95]

Flores had been sending his superiors "fraudulent reports about the school's breakthroughs"[96] while apparently spending more time drinking and gambling than teaching. It is not difficult to see a connection between this loutish behavior and the growth of local opposition to Saycota's school. As one of his superiors noted, "Ultimately, it is strange that elements such as [Flores] have been chosen to better the customs of the natives and incorporate them into civilization."[97] However, no one could be found to replace him, and so he stayed in the community, which Nayarit's Department of Indigenous Education decided was preferable to shutting the school—although this ultimately caused more long-term damage to the SEP's project in the region than a temporary closure would have done.[98]

Flores was finally fired in late 1924, and Saycota's school was permanently closed, despite the ostensible protestations of "the community" and "the students"—whose letters claiming that Flores's accusers were "enemies of the indigenous race" and that his departure would leave them "submerged in ignorance"[99] were later discovered to be Flores's own forgeries.[100] The kinds of problems caused by teachers like Flores, which compounded popular suspicion of the SEP's objectives, only became more pronounced when SEP officials began to arrive in the Náayari Alta. Despite the support there of Mariano Mejía, these same issues—exacerbated by the interference of politicians seeking to use SEP programs to boost their own influence—would obstruct the attempts of the federal government to expand its power into the region.

In late 1923, Adolfo de la Huerta, backed by more than half the army, attempted to overthrow Obregón after the latter endorsed the candidacy of de la Huerta's rival, Plutarco Elías Calles, for the 1924 presidential election. The uprising caused turmoil across much of the country,[101] forcing many of Nayarit's schools to close.[102] However, both Domínguez and Mejía stayed loyal to the government, which quickly emerged victorious, and so the Sierra Náayari was largely untouched by the violence.[103] Even in the midst of the rebellion, Gonzalo Mota, head of the Nayarit's Department of Federal Education, continued to petition his superiors for support in establishing schools amongst the Náayarite.[104] Mota claimed that although the Náayarite "do not obey to any extent the civil authorities, but rather their own caciques . . . the natural distrust of these Indians, disappears with kind and generous treatment by outsiders." In line with Vasconcelos's goal of "harness[ing] rural society to the national project,"[105] SEP officials had also been ordered to investigate the natural resources found in their regions, and Mota reported that the sierra possessed "incalculable natural resources: wood of all kinds, pastures of excellent quality for cattle, fertile lands with abundant water . . .

and unexploited mines" and advocated the extension of state control over the region as a matter of urgent national economic interest.[106]

However, Bernardo J. Gastélum, the subsecretary of education, was displeased with the SEP's slow progress in the Sierra Náayari.[107] By early 1924, "the SEP oversaw 65,000 students in 1,089 schools, with 1,146 teachers and 102 missionaries" across Mexico as a whole.[108] The latest SEP budget provided an additional 200,000 pesos for the establishment of "indigenous cultural centers" for the Wixáritari, Tarahumaras, Chamulas, Yaquis, Mayos, Purépecha, Zapotecs, Mixtecs, the various peoples of the Sierra Norte de Puebla, and the O'dam of Durango.[109] But of an estimated 2,500 eligible Náayari youths, only 42 were then enrolled in the three or four federal schools still functioning in the sierra. Mota blamed this failure on dispersed Náayari settlement patterns, reporting that they came together "only from time to time in the pueblos to which they belong, to get drunk and dance around their patron saints." However, Gastélum blamed Antonio Navarrete, who was accused of supporting the Delahuertista rebels and dismissed from his post.[110] The national head of the DECI, Enrique Corona, was forced to step down soon afterward, on the grounds that so few Náayari, Wixárika, or Yaqui students had yet to be enrolled in federal schools.[111]

Aurelio Guerrero replaced Navarrete as chief maestro misionero in the Sierra Náayari. Attesting to the importance of the federal education program to the revolutionary state's plans, a grand banquet—attended by Gastélum himself and other notables, including Nayarit's military zone commander—was organized for Guerrero before he headed off to "exercise his influence over the tribes" in April 1924.[112] By the end of the year, he claimed to have cultivated friendly relations with the traditional authorities of various Náayari communities,[113] which won his superiors' approval for the establishment of an Indigenous boarding school (*internado*) in Jesús María (reflecting the growing popularity within the SEP of separating children from their "primitive" surroundings in order to "civilize" them more easily).[114] Guerrero also proposed setting up smaller schools in Dolores (where he was sure that reluctant parents could be forced to enroll their children by the "Governor of the Indians who is my good friend") and Santa Teresa (where again, he admitted that "the locals are not interested in schools, but I judge it necessary to establish one, assisted by the warm friendship I have cultivated with the community's Governor").[115]

Guerrero also launched an agrarian claim on behalf of Saycota, not for the certification of the community's traditional landholdings but rather for dotación de ejidos.[116] As explained earlier, independent-minded villagers across Mexico regarded state land grants not as justice but rather as an imposition,[117] and this was certainly the case in Saycota, where Guerrero's claim gave rise to conflicts between supporters and opponents of an exchange of political autonomy for territorial security. Guerrero's agitation in Saycota also alarmed Nayarit's agrarian authorities, who believed that "with the pretext of safeguarding their territory, the inhabitants may commit outrages against the other settlements that exist within these same lands and cause this Government problems that we wish at all cost to avoid."[118] We can assume that such worries were shared by the Náayarite of neighboring Rosarito and San Blasito and the Mexicaneros of San Buenaventura.

Ultimately, Guerrero would not be able to use his self-proclaimed influence over the Náayari communities' traditional authorities to establish successful schools in the sierra, as in January 1925 he suddenly lost his job. In a somewhat surprising turn of events, the SEP rehired the disgraced Antonio Navarrete and appointed him inspector in the Sierra Náayari in Guerrero's place.[119] This was probably linked to the accession of Calles to the Mexican presidency in December 1924, and his appointment of José Manuel Puig Casauranc as the new secretary of education. Puig Casauranc—or, more likely, his subsecretary, Moisés Sáenz—reorganized the DECI into the Departamento de Escuelas Rurales y Incorporación Cultural Indígena (DERICI), which prompted a reshuffling of SEP posts across the country. Nayarit's director of federal education, Gonzalo Mota—whom Navarrete had accused of being a well-known member of the Knights of Columbus,[120] a supporter of the "reactionary candidacy of Angel Flores,"[121] a partisan of the privileged, and neglecter of the Indians[122]—was transferred to Durango and replaced in Nayarit by Francisco Nicodemo. But it also seems that the machinations of an ambitious state deputy, Colonel Ismael Romero Gallardo—who saw the SEP's project as a way of boosting his own political influence in the state—played a part in Navarrete's return to the sierra.

Romero Gallardo first involved himself in the SEP's activities in Nayarit in June 1923. Presenting himself as an expert on Huajimic and the other mestizo pueblos to the south of the Sierra Náayari (where he had fought during the revolution), he warned Vasconcelos that local teachers were pretending to set up schools in settlements destroyed during the revolution and then appropriating the funds destined for their upkeep. Romero Gallardo pledged to investigate the situation personally and to bring supplies to any schools that really did exist, earning him Vasconcelos's personal praise.[123] In the following months, Romero Gallardo criticized many of Nayarit's other maestros misioneros, whom he claimed "dedicate themselves only to slandering the local Government and provoking conflicts around the question of education,"[124] and took it on himself to set up schools in rural communities across Nayarit (including in some that already had schools, prompting teachers to denounce his "interference" in their work).[125]

By appearing at the official openings of new schools, donating books to their libraries, and generally presenting himself as a bringer of education to the masses,[126] Romero Gallardo built himself a broad political base. By January 1925, he had become sufficiently influential in Nayarit to petition for Navarrete's reappointment and to propose teachers for a number of new schools recently approved for the Sierra Náayari, offering them a daily wage of three pesos (as opposed to the national standard of two).[127] However, although Navarrete and Mariano Mejía both tried hard to secure this sum from the SEP, whose budget for 1925 included an allowance for founding new schools in the Náayari Alta, Romero Gallardo's promises turned out to be empty. The new appointments were allotted two pesos as usual, and as a result, only two of them actually turned up at the start of the new term, allowing schools to be opened only in Huaynamota and Jesús María.[128]

Nayarit's director of federal education, Francisco Nicodemo, complained that Romero's meddling had undermined his authority and lamented that now his department did not know who or where the rest of Romero's new appointments were, adding that "if this state of affairs continues, the role left for the Director of Federal Education will be a tragic one."[129] Soon after, ex–maestro misionero Guerrero complained he had been removed from his post for political reasons (a claim backed up by several of his colleagues),[130] and he accused Romero Gallardo of "nominating as teachers his political supporters who have never before worked in such roles."[131] He was joined in his accusations by Nayarit's League of Agrarian Communities, who petitioned President Calles to "interpose his invaluable influence so that these wicked political reactionaries do not send us their teachers."[132]

Although the resultant departmental confusion and infighting combined with budgetary constraints to delay the establishment of the new schools proposed for the sierra, it seems that in those Náayari communities under the control of Mejía and Domínguez where schools were already operating, traditional governments amenable to their presence were—for the moment—in ascendance. Navarrete reported in March that in Jesús María, the traditional authorities had cooperated with Mejía in raising the average attendance at the school to thirty-two students and had managed to dispel the local belief that "the Government desires to educate the Indians in order to then kill them." Navarrete enthusiastically added—probably to impress his superiors and secure his position as inspector more than from any genuine conviction—that "the majority of the Indians will soon attend school," although he continued, rather disapprovingly, that "the majority of the children appear completely naked, as they wear only loin-cloths."[133]

However, as Mejía, Domínguez, and the SEP's local representatives began to encourage increasing numbers of mestizos to settle in the Sierra Náayari, tensions grew between Náayari conservatives on one side, and colonists, teachers, and defensas on the other. Before the revolution, around 100 mestizos lived amongst the 1,500 Náayarite of Jesús María, and a handful of others had settled in the cabeceras of San Francisco and Santa Teresa.[134] By the mid-1920s, however, many more had arrived in the region, displaced by revolutionary unrest in northern Jalisco, southern Zacatecas, and coastal Nayarit or drawn by the economic opportunities—especially those related to cattle ranching, seen as an ideal a way of developing the national economy[135]—that SEP officials like Gonzalo Mota had earlier enthused about to their superiors.[136]

As Mejía was himself a mestizo and Domínguez was a fluent Spanish-speaker who had fought alongside mestizos in the revolution,[137] neither man seems to have had much ideological opposition to the presence of mestizos—whether teachers or settlers—in the communities under their control. Mejía in particular had close personal ties with mestizos involved in the SEP's project in the sierra, including his comadre Petra Tovar de Aquino (a rural teacher initially charged with opening Jesús María's school)[138] and her husband Evaristo Aquino (who headed Jesús María's Indigenista organization, the Comité Cultural Pro-Raza: Estudio y Progreso).[139] And, both as relatively wealthy ranchers and as representatives of a government that encouraged ranching, Mejía and Domínguez had political and commercial interests in promoting the settlement of mestizo cattlemen so as to boost the local livestock trade.[140] Members of the region's communal defensas, who were often small-time ranchers themselves and were anyway under orders from Mejía and Domínguez, also generally supported mestizo settlement. In some cases, and usually without the general agreement of the community, they loaned, rented, or gifted land to the newcomers, generally near the cabeceras of their communities, which served as poles of attraction for scattered communal populations and were natural locations for shops and cattle markets as well as SEP schools.[141]

Local SEP officials also saw mestizo immigration as a positive cultural and economic development. Part of their official mission in the sierra was to open up the region's natural resources for exploitation, and given their tendency to infantilize the Náayarite, they saw mestizos as better equipped to pioneer such efforts, which would in turn provide the Náayarite with a positive example to follow, helping to educate them out of their dependence on subsistence agriculture. Furthermore, the SEP's teachers had much more in common, culturally speaking, with mestizo settlers living close by in the communal cabeceras than with Náayarite, who anyway lived in far-flung rancherías. Unlike in some of the less peripheral Indigenous regions of Mexico, where teachers formed close bonds with local people and as a result felt obliged to help and protect them,[142] in the Sierra Náayari most SEP officials preferred to establish social and commercial links with mestizo settlers,[143] who would soon constitute a local economic elite of shopkeepers and ranchers.[144]

However, Náayari elders remember today that "we were scared of the mestizos, because we couldn't understand them, not at all! They have their language, and we have our own separate one." Most Náayarite also believed that, given the political, economic, and cultural privileges that mestizos enjoyed as bearers of Mexico's "national" culture, it was necessary to "distance ourselves so as to conserve our traditions . . . we must never forget what our ancestors used to do."[145] Thus the conservative Náayari factions that had already begun to challenge the legitimacy of Mejía, Domínguez, and the local defensa commanders,[146] now ramped up their opposition to the activities of the SEP's teachers—the primary agents of cultural change within their communities[147]—in spite of Navarrete's optimistic reports about changing local attitudes toward schools. Náayari use of "weapons of the weak"—especially the withdrawal of their children from schools—was all the more effective in the context of Nayarit's chronic political instability. By the end of 1925, Náayari pressure had forced SEP officials to moderate their attempts to incorporate them into "civilization."

The political chaos elsewhere in Nayarit had little effect on the sierra until President Calles unseated Nayarit's governor, Pascual Villanueva, in February 1925. After this dramatic event, the factional infighting in Nayarit grew more intense,[148] and Mejía, Domínguez, and the SEP's local representatives were steadily drawn into questions of state-level politics. In April, Nayarit's state congress deposed Calles's new appointee as governor, General Miguel Díaz, and nominated Ismael Romero Gallardo in his place. Romero Gallardo was then besieged in Tepic by elements of the municipal police and the army, and the state capital was temporarily moved to Ixtlán del Río, before soldiers arrested the rebels. Coups, countercoups, and widespread political violence followed,[149] and the SEP was sucked into the conflict as Romero Gallardo attempted to persuade the federal teachers and inspectors—including Antonio Navarrete—to aid him "at all costs,"[150] which naturally interfered with their educational work. Just as in Chihuahua, where "national government and state government were [also] engaged in a ceaseless struggle to achieve political hegemony," the resultant "confusion and animosity between governing bodies" and the attempts of "state officials . . . to stop federal 'incursions' on state sovereignty" obstructed the SEP's program in the Sierra Náayari.[151]

In May, Leopoldo Rodríguez Calderón took over from Francisco Nicodemo as Nayarit's director of federal education. Describing himself as a "an old Teacher, who during 37 years of service in various of the Republic's States, has internalized the needs of teachers," Rodríguez promised to put an end to fraudulent or misleading reports and urged the inspectors to "correct by their own example the deficiencies they find"[152] and to stay out of politics.[153] This was evidently impossible, however, as Navarrete and other inspectors were accused of political campaigning on Romero Gallardo's behalf throughout 1925.[154]

In September, Rodríguez reported that Navarrete had not visited the sierra for three months.[155] Lucio Rosas was asked to take over his zone,[156] but it turned out he was on sabbatical while he ran for political office.[157] With both inspectors "supported by influential persons," Rodríguez complained that the schools of the sierra were left unsupervised while "this Directorate has constantly been circumvented."[158] Navarrete had in fact asked for authorization to leave the sierra in April 1925, citing the region's poor communications with the rest of the state,[159] and he finally departed for Tepic, without the permission of his superiors, in June, claiming that an illness brought on by the rains had forced him to do so.[160] He alleged that he only prolonged his stay in the state capital because his wife fell seriously ill and after her recovery had taken another ten days of preapproved leave.[161] Even if there was some truth to what Rodríguez dismissed as "a thousand pretexts,"[162] Navarrete's long and unauthorized stay in Tepic was likely also connected to his political campaigning on behalf of Romero Gallardo[163] and to the fact that both of the caciques of the sierra were partisans of his patron's rival, Francisco Ramírez Romano.[164]

Despite the repeated references by SEP officials to the remoteness of the Sierra Náayari and its lack of roads and communication channels,[165] life there did not exist in a vacuum, isolated from the rest of Mexico. And so, just as Mejía and Domínguez had made alliances with political and military forces based outside the region during the armed phase of the revolution (and would do so again during the Cristero Rebellion), it is not surprising to find that in this period they forged links with Ramírez Romano, who was backed both by President Calles and Nayarit's new zone commander, General Alejandro Mange. Mejía's support for Ramírez Romano against a third candidate for state governor, José de la Peña (a local client of Jalisco's powerful state governor and opponent of Calles, José Guadalupe Zuno), spurred rumors that Mejía and Ramírez Romano were literally related.

> [Ramírez Romano] has great standing among the natives of the sierra of Nayarit, because they are under the orders of an uncle of his, according to General Matías Ramos, who has communicated it to the President of the Republic. The Governor of Jalisco, a partisan of de la Peña, sent various individuals to the aforementioned sierra to win over the locals to de la Peña and so far I have heard nothing more of them, some say they were hanged by the Chief of that Tribe.[166]

Domínguez, too, was obviously in favor of Ramírez Romano in his struggle for the state governorship, as was Domínguez's subordinate, Eusebio González, who complained that the municipal government of Rosamorada foments in every way the imposition of the reactionary candidacy of José de la Peña, and has tried to force all of the Indians of this region to go to exercise their civic rights in the town of EL VENADO, 15 kilometres away, where they will set up the voting booths . . . they are denying us our rights as free citizens, and also depriving the entire tribe of voting for a man with a noble heart and the only one who has guaranteed the wellbeing of the humble classes that vegetate in these mountains: we refer to LICENCIADO FRANCISCO RAMIREZ ROMANO, who has always concerned himself with regional culture, and the intellectual betterment of those races . . . who currently have no support but for that of the waters of heaven, and the light of the Sun.[167]

That the sierra's caciques enthusiastically—and perhaps even violently—supported Ramírez Romano almost certainly unnerved Navarrete in light of his own association with Romero Gallardo and probably contributed to his decision to abscond from his post in Jesús María. The resultant lack of an inspector to supervise the sierra's schools, the resistance of the Náayari majority to the SEP's assimilatory efforts, and the ongoing state-level political conflicts (which prevented state and municipal authorities from assisting the maestros rurales)[168] outweighed the support of Domínguez, Mejía, and their local allies for the SEP's attempts to make "Mexicans" of the Náayarite, whom the increasingly embittered Navarrete now referred to as "indolent races who have never cared about the progress of that distant, abundant region."[169]

Although Mejía was at this point described as "a Cacique . . . who enjoys all the power of a king,"[170] his support for Jesús María's school (run by Petra Tovar, his mestiza comadre) was not enough to save it from closing its doors in August 1925, because of a lack of pupils. Although Mejía tried to explain away the low attendance as caused by an epidemic, which "in order to avoid contagion" prevented him from ordering parents to send their children to school,[171] Rodríguez reported that Náayari parents refused to send their children to the school because they "hate and fear the whites," which prompted him to recommend that any future teacher in the community "must be of indigenous features to avoid being attacked."[172] By this time schools in La Mesa and San Francisco had also been closed (if they had ever been open except on paper). Thus, the only schools still functioning in Mejía's cacicazgo by late 1925 were the two that had been established in the mestizo pueblos of San Juan Peyotán and Huaynamota (which resident priests accused of being "protestant schools")[173] and those in the Náayari communities of Dolores and Santa Teresa. The latter communities lacked priests, and so their schools were unaffected by the growing tensions between Calles and the church. However, they were nonetheless attended by few pupils, and the "mood" in Santa Teresa in particular was described as "completely adverse to our work" by one school inspector, who ultimately blamed this on Navarrete.

> From the humblest peasant, to the most eminent inhabitants of this region, all express nothing but unhappy memories of that Inspector, and such ideas become generalized (due to the ignorance that dominates) toward all of us, and even our Institution itself.[174]

The SEP had by this point little success in the Náayari Baja either. In San Juan Corapan, seat of Domínguez's cacicazgo, a school had been opened in early 1925 but was soon closed and its teacher transferred elsewhere.[175] It was reopened in October, but problems remained with its teacher, and its students were, in November, described as "still clumsy in speaking Spanish."[176] Meanwhile, in San Pedro Ixcatán, home to the oldest school in the entire Náayari region, attendance remained a major problem. Náayari parents told their children—quite rightly in the eyes of today's elders—that if they attend school, "you'll become a bum. You'll sell your land, you won't want to work, you won't continue to live here, you'll go off with the mestizos."[177] To improve attendance, Navarrete had the school's teacher replaced, and the traditional government sent its alguaciles to warn the community's dispersed inhabitants that "without excuses or pretexts, they present themselves within thirty days, to enroll those children and adults who remain in open rebellion against the alphabet."[178] But despite the support of Eutimio Domínguez, Eusebio González, and the rest of the community's authorities, the "Náayari children and adolescents who are accustomed to living in the mountains, far from all civilization" continued to shun the school, which presented a "bleak and miserable appearance."[179]

JALISCO: THE WIXÁRITARI

The assassination of Wixárika cacique Patricio Mezquite and the killing, exile, or absorption into the federal military of the rest of northern Jalisco's bandits and Villista guerrillas[180] left the region largely peaceful by 1920.[181] The mestizo-inhabited districts remained under the military, political, and economic control of caciques who had come to power during—or even, in some cases, before—the revolution.[182] In Huejuquilla and nearby parts of Zacatecas, defensa commander (and future cristero general) Pedro Quintanar remained a leading figure until 1923, when he was jailed for killing an agrarista rival at a rodeo.[183] Meanwhile, the municipal government of Mezquitic, whose de jure authority extended over most of the Wixárika population, was dominated by the large landowners of the municipal seat, led by the Robles clan.[184] The Robles were closely allied with the Guzmán, Valdés, and Sánchez families,[185] who ruled the municipalities of Chimaltitán, Bolaños, and El Salitre (renamed Villa Guerrero in 1921) to the southeast of the Sierra Wixárika.[186]

Thanks to their recent victories over their mestizo rivals, the Wixárika communities themselves remained autonomous, under the control of their own military leaders, traditional governments, and shamans. The death of Mezquite had deprived the Wixáritari as a whole of any politico-military unity—indicating a return to the prerevolutionary status quo—but in San Andrés, at least, Mezquite's lieutenant Clemente Villa remained influential into the 1920s. However, local "bandits" and the cacique of the nearby Náayari Alta region, Mariano Mejía, increasingly contested Villa's authority. In February 1921, Villa complained to the governor of Jalisco that

> Luis de la Torre, Felipe de la Cruz, Jose Chalate, and Paulo Chino, have destroyed the pueblo of San Andrés Cohamiata, carrying out infinite abuses and horrific cases, they murdered twenty-three Indians including women and children, robbed without compassion—these bandits are natives of this same pueblo and under the shadow of the revolution did whatever they wished and now it appears they have been pardoned by Mr. MARIANO MEXIA, MILITIA COMMANDER IN JESUS MARIA IN THE TERRITORY OF TEPIC NAYARITE [sic], the indigenous of this pueblo are timorous and are sure that whatever happens they will continue injuring the pueblo, annihilating Indians and their cattle. . . . The authorities must hate us.[187]

Of course, Villa was no stranger to violence himself, as Josefino missionaries and mestizo settlers living in San Andrés had discovered a few years before. He now played up the trope of Wixárika "timidity"—which had a long history as a flipside to Wixárika "savagery"—in the hope it would persuade Jalisco's government to intercede on his behalf and defend him against his local enemies and against Mejía, an interloper from a neighboring state. Villa's complaint also attests to the armed revolution's violent legacy in the Sierra Wixárika, which had prompted the exodus of not only mestizo colonists but as much as one-fifth of the Wixáritari themselves.[188]

These Wixárika exiles hailed not just from San Andrés but also from Tuxpan, where many residents had fled Villista raids and Mezquite's subsequent reign of terror for the municipal seat of Bolaños. Some families never returned home and instead assimilated into the regional mestizo population.[189] In San Sebastián, too, fighting had left "a portion of the pueblo . . . destroyed," while "many ranchos were heavily damaged, destroyed, and/or abandoned."[190] In 1920, some of these refugees still roamed the region around Camotlán, Nayarit,[191] while Cristobal Magallanes, the parish priest of Totatiche, reported that more than a hundred other Wixárika exiles—some of whom had been baptized at the Josefino mission in San Sebastián—had settled in a canyon just outside of Azqueltán.

> They live in caves and lean-tos, scattered throughout different parts of the same canyon, far from each other, and they only gather in one place during the many fiestas they celebrate throughout the year . . . all of which are idolatrous and superstitious, mixed with a little Christianity, given they do not lack in their shacks and at these same fiestas, the odd image of Our Lady of Guadalupe, or of Christ. . . . These colonists seek the baptism of their children, although some of the recent arrivals from Nayarit are often three or four years old and still unbaptized.[192]

Some of these armed exiles had apparently arrived in the Azqueltán Canyon in 1917 or 1918, and their continued presence there is clear evidence of the disruption that the revolution had caused to communal life. These and other contemporary mentions of the Wixárika presence in Nayarit meanwhile suggest that much of the modern Wixárika presence there is rooted in the flight of Wixáritari from Jalisco in this period.[193]

Most Wixáritari, however, continued to live within their traditional communal territories. Over the next few years, priests and missionaries paid little attention to them, focusing instead on reestablishing the nearby mestizo-inhabited parishes that had been dissolved, destroyed, or depopulated during the revolution, in some cases as a result of the depredations of the Wixáritari themselves.[194] But unlike the clergy, the mestizo ranchers of Mezquitic, Huejuquilla, Villa Guerrero, and Bolaños all coveted access to the forests, pastures, watering holes, and mineral riches of the Sierra Wixárika, and they began to plot their return to the lands from which they had been expelled during the revolution.[195] Such renewed threats to Wixárika control of their communal territories soon brought Wixárika leaders into more regular contact with representatives of the revolutionary state.

In December 1920, San Andrés's authorities bypassed the local CLA, based in the regional capital of Colotlán and dominated by antiagrarian elites, by sending an agrarian petition directly to the new governor of Jalisco, Basilio Vadillo, a "radical obregonista."[196] They claimed that their copy of the community's "primordial title" had been lost during the revolution and asked that a search be made for the original to prove their right to lands recently occupied by the hacienda of San Juan Capistrano in Zacatecas.[197] A few months later, Clemente Villa headed a commission to Guadalajara to reiterate his community's case against the hacienda and also to complain that

> our indigenous brothers from the neighboring pueblo of Santa Catarina, are wanting to invade a great part of our lands, so we thought it best put all this before you, that you

> might do us the favor of conceding us an authorized copy of our title with which to defend that which is legally our property.[198]

In May, Villa submitted a third petition (with an "uncertified copy" of the communal title attached), further accusing the inhabitants of Santa Catarina of being "extremely greedy people who survive by troubling their neighbors such as our Pueblo, and San Sebastián and Tenzompa, because of which we have only a small amount of land left to us, which is not sufficient to plant on."[199]

In the same month, Santa Catarina's authorities, who since before the revolution had also been seeking the restitution of lands seized by San Juan Capistrano, wrote to the governor of Jalisco, claiming in the name of 150 families that

> our community, exclusively dedicated to agriculture, possesses only a small extension of land that is insufficient to fulfil the needs of the inhabitants, who are forced to work as wage-laborers for a pittance. . . . Our communal territory is safeguarded by a title that we will present when we have the opportunity, so you can see that it covers a larger area, but that nearby landowners have laid claim to it under the shadow of previous Governments that have never cared about the improvement of the indigenous class.[200]

The leaders of both San Andrés and Santa Catarina demonstrated their awareness of the political shifts brought about by the revolution, and the changes in political discourse that accompanied it, by appealing directly to the new governor—a revolutionary intellectual—rather than to the regional elite, by concluding their petitions with the old Maderista slogan of "Effective Suffrage, No Reelection" while also playing up their sufferings under the Porfirian regime, and by linking their struggles for land with the transformation of the Indigenous population that the revolutionary government saw as essential to the nation's own transformation. Like many of their equivalents elsewhere in Mexico,[201] they sought to legitimize their demands by emphasizing their loyalty to, and their place within, both the revolution and Mexico itself.

This approach—a continuation of the "legalistic" defensive strategies used by many Indigenous groups since the colonial period—initially seemed to bear fruit. Governor Vadillo responded sympathetically to the Wixárika petitions, ordering a search of the state archives for San Andrés's title[202] and approving the beginning of the process of restitución de tierras for San Andrés[203] and of dotación de ejidos for Santa Catarina.[204] That San Andrés and Santa Catarina felt as threatened by each other as by a powerful local hacienda, and that Santa Catarina was also reported as harassing San Sebastián (which given their long-standing enmity does not seem unlikely), shows that—in contrast with the situation in the Sierra Náayari—territorial conflicts amongst the

Wixárika communities had again become as important a factor in Wixárika state relations as the threats posed to their communities by outside forces, despite Mezquite having momentarily brought much of the Sierra Wixárika together only a few years before.

Despite Vadillo's support, the inhabitants of Santa Catarina still felt sufficiently threatened by their neighbors to send a five-man commission—including a young leader named Agustín Carrillo, who soon emerged as the community's most important pro-government cacique—to Guadalajara in November 1922. They petitioned the governor for "civil protection" in the face of "the constant invasions of whites and mestizos"[205] and sought to emphasize the justness of their cause and their loyalty to the revolutionary regime by requesting that a school be established in their community. The arrival at the Palacio de Gobierno of these exotic, long-haired "primitives," armed with bows and arrows and wearing hats covered with "pictures of saints, feathers and knick-knacks," made the front page of Guadalajara's *El Informador*. The paper's correspondent presented the Wixáritari as "a race on the brink of extinction" but argued that a school might prove their salvation and beseeched the government to "take into consideration the aspirations of these natives, with the object of elevating them from the character of almost unconscious beings, to that of useful men."[206]

By this point, the SEP had sent a maestro misionero, Diego Hernández Topete, to incorporate into the Mexican nation northern Jalisco's estimated five thousand Wixárika inhabitants and their five hundred Tepecano neighbors.[207] Unlike the initially enthusiastic maestros misioneros then working in the Sierra Náayari, Hernández was reluctant to give up the comforts of urban life for the risks and privations of the Sierra Wixárika and settled instead in the mestizo town of Temastián, justifying this decision by blurring the lines between "Indians" and "mestizos."[208] Although in the 1920s it was not uncommon for SEP policy makers and teachers alike to struggle to define the difference between the two,[209] in this case Hernández deliberately misled his superiors by claiming that Temastián was still home to 250 O'dam, whom he characterized as fanatical Catholics and "averse to all progress."[210] In response to Santa Catarina's recent, well-publicized request for a school, Jalisco's Federal Education Department again ordered Hernández to visit the Sierra Wixárika,[211] but he managed to fudge the issue once more[212] and set himself up in another mestizo town that was closer to Guadalajara than to Santa Catarina—although, naturally, he again described it as an "indigenous community."[213]

Despite the SEP's early plans and the requests of the Wixáritari themselves, the first representative of the revolutionary state to visit the sierra was therefore not a teacher but an agronomist, S. Ramírez Martínez. In July 1923, the new state governor, José Guadalupe Zuno, sent him to investigate the agrarian claims then emanating from northern Jalisco. Colotlán's municipal president was a less-than-revolutionary figure, however, who used his control of the regional CLA to obstruct the agrarian claims of Wixáritari and mestizos alike, to forbid local people to rent Ramírez any horses and even to order the police to disarm him and his entourage.[214] Ramírez nonetheless managed to visit several local communities that had petitioned for agrarian reform. Although sympathetic to some of these claims, he dismissed those of San Andrés and Santa Catarina, using terms that echoed the Porfirian view of Indians as "primitive" and "lazy"—an idea that would dominate most government officials' perceptions of the Wixáritari into the 1950s.[215] In his report back to the CNA, Ramírez reported that the inhabitants of San Andrés and Santa Catarina possessed

> vast extensions of territory, which are of a superior class to the rest of the lands in those regions. . . . Their annual harvests are altogether small because they stop at sowing that on which they can just about survive, and do not bother about the exploitation of such rich lands.[216]

However, the leaders of San Andrés remained hopeful that the state would resolve their agrarian problems and continued to complain to Colotlán's municipal president that San Juan Capistrano had invaded their most productive lands, while those of the community's anexo, Guadalupe Ocotán, had been occupied by ranchers from Huajimic, including Petronilo Muñoz, son of Huajimic's most important cacique. They alleged that these thefts and invasions were a product of their own "ignorance and timidity," again using the trope of Wixárika "passivity" to encourage outside intervention on their behalf.[217]

Colotlán's president naturally received their petitions without sympathy, warning the regional CLA that "the complainants are individuals of the Wixárika race, lacking in any culture." He then informed San Andrés's authorities that despite their having made a claim for restitution already, they would need to make another request regarding "the lands that they say have been usurped" and that they themselves would need to notify any landowner who might be affected by it.[218] Thanks to the reductive and economistic views of Wixárika cultural ecology held by municipal and state officials alike, the prospect of Mexico's central CNA approving any Wixárika land claims remained a distant hope, even as the agrarian policies of Zuno's regional administration and Obregón's central government allowed for the successful settlement of numerous agrarian claims in other parts of Jalisco.[219]

Meanwhile, unlike San Andrés and Santa Catarina, neither San Sebastián nor Tuxpan made any agrarian claims in this period, despite their history of agrarian lobbying prior to the revolution[220] and the fact that mestizo ranchers from Villa Guerrero and Mezquitic had begun to graze their cattle on rich upland pastures close to San Sebastián. In 1922, the municipal government of Bolaños also started to rent to mestizo ranchers lands near Camotlán that Tuxpan claimed as its own.[221] Why then did they not attempt to secure the aid of the revolutionary state in defending and reclaiming their lands in the early 1920s? For a start, the inhabitants of San Sebastián had long been more recalcitrant than those of the other Wixárika communities. While the latter were willing to reach out to mestizo authorities for help, San Sebastián's long history of hostility toward outsiders (as Thord-Gray and the Josefino missionaries had experienced firsthand) and its status as "the largest, wealthiest and most conservative"[222] of the Wixárika communities might explain its reluctance to apply to the government for agrarian reform. The ambiguous contacts between the community's inhabitants and Carrancista forces—who had first empowered Mezquite and thus facilitated both his early victories and his later abuses and then turned against him in dramatic fashion when his capricious violence threatened regional stability—presumably buttressed traditional local distrust of outsiders. That former Carrancistas now dominated the state and federal governments probably further reduced the community's faith in the revolutionary state as a potential benefactor—especially as municipal governments also claiming to represent the new revolutionary order were now promoting the invasion of both San Sebastián's and Tuxpan's lands.

Despite Wixárika doubts about Sonoran commitment to agrarian reform, by early 1923 the atmosphere in Guadalajara was becoming increasingly radical, and Diego Hernández felt sufficiently pressured to demonstrate his commitment to Indigenous education that he finally began his work as a maestro misionero in earnest. The local antecedents for bringing "civilization" to the Wixáritari, whom Hernández described as "near savage, just like their customs,"[223] were far from positive, however. Both church and state had already tried, and failed, to "educate" the Wixáritari in the final years of the Porfiriato. Calixto Guerrero, head of the Josefino mission in San Sebastián, had earlier noted that any Wixárika attendance at government schools could only be achieved through "the threat of being thrown in jail" because

> some of those who received instruction in some government school, on their return, under the pretext of resolving local ownership of their lands, robbed them and abused them as much as they could. This explains the great horror they have of schools.

Even the few orphans and other exceptional cases who had been taken from their families to study at mission schools in the sierra itself, or at seminaries in Zacatecas, proved resistant to their custodians' efforts. Often, having learned to speak, read, and write in Spanish, dress like Mexicans, worship as Catholics, and even sing and play classical instruments, "they took off their clothes and threw them at the priests, saying 'you have it, Christian' and entirely naked headed back to join the others."[224] Wixárika elders today still recall their parents banning them from attending schools on the grounds that "you'll come back from school and never want to help, you'll sell out your community."[225]

Nonetheless, in May 1923, Hernández pressed for the establishment of schools for the Wixáritari to "make them reasonable men." He argued, as had Navarrete in the Sierra Náayari, that such a project would need to be fully funded by the federal government, as in the Sierra Wixárika "the action of the State Government is in many areas nonexistent, that of the municipalities completely nonexistent, and the assistance that individuals can provide is negligible given the economic conditions in which they live."[226] Enrique Corona, head of the DECI, rejected Hernández's suggestions because of the SEP's own budgetary restrictions[227] and also turned down the idea of funding a number of other projects that Hernández had tried to link to the cause of Wixárika education (such as bringing a choir of fifty Wixáritari to Mexico City to showcase traditional songs and dances).[228] Instead, Corona rebuked Hernández for reportedly dedicating "so much time to social celebrations such as dances, days out, etc., . . . we bring to your attention that, if true, you must turn your attentions to schools."[229]

Federal schools only arrived in the Sierra Wixárika in late 1923 after the new SEP budget allotted two hundred thousand pesos toward the founding of "indigenous cultural centers" across the country[230] and mandated the sending out of 690 rural "missionaries" into the Mexican countryside.[231] Hernández petitioned for teachers to be sent to San Sebastián and, especially, Santa Catarina, where he claimed that the inhabitants "usually so opposed to education, are interested in having schools."[232] However, the teachers Hernández nominated for these posts refused to leave their current posts in mestizo villages to work in either Wixárika community. Hernández therefore headed to the sierra himself to investigate potential locations for schools, visiting Santa Catarina, San Sebastián, Tuxpan, and Azqueltán.[233] He then organized the recruitment of two new teachers hired specifically for work in the sierra and in November oversaw the establishment of a school in Tuxpan and another amongst the Tepecanos of nearby Azqueltán.[234]

No informants in Tuxpan today remember a school opening in their community in this period and assert that most Wixárika parents were fiercely opposed to schools in general,[235] but the teacher whom Hernández left in charge of the institution described it as an extraordinary success. Apparently, forty-nine children and forty adults were initially enrolled,[236] and in December, attendance averaged at only one below the maximum possible, while in January, twenty-five new students enrolled, with average attendance now standing at ninety-five.[237] These figures were almost certainly grossly inflated, but the school's very existence, in the midst of test plantings of modern commercial crops such as coffee, oranges, avocados, and bananas,[238] at least shows that Hernández and his subordinates had become actively engaged, as they understood it, in transforming the Wixáritari into "true industrialists who would know how to exploit the natural resources they possess."[239]

As in the Sierra Náayari, the Sonoran state-building project in the Sierra Wixárika was interrupted by the outbreak of the Delahuertista rebellion in late 1923. Jalisco's zone commander, General Enrique Estrada, declared for the rebels, cut off the state's communications with the rest of the country, and overthrew Governor Zuno. Northern Jalisco was "overwhelmed by rebels," amongst whom were important regional figures like Pedro Quintanar (whom the rebels broke out of jail)[240] and Herminio Sánchez Sánchez, a Colotlán merchant and old associate of General de Santiago who raised a thousand-man force that came close to taking the city of Zacatecas.[241] Although the Delahuertistas were soon defeated and Zuno was reinstated, the Wixáritari of Santa Catarina reported that the rebellion "was very severe" in "the distant regions" in which they lived,[242] which had forced them to mobilize their defensa. Later that year, they asked Zuno to let them know if peace had yet returned to the rest of the state, as they wished to disband the defensa "so that we can live peacefully as we did before," hinting at the increasingly controversial status of such organizations throughout the Gran Nayar.[243]

Another commission from Santa Catarina, again headed by Agustín Carrillo, also informed Zuno in late 1924 that the rebellion had prevented them from meeting with an agronomist to discuss their agrarian claim.

> I earnestly beg you to do me the favor of pardoning me this failure, which was involuntary, as we feared the enemy would find us. Agustín is on his way to receive your orders, he goes as this pueblo's representative, he is very trustworthy and you can give him whichever orders you please.[244]

Although making use of a discourse of "absolute loyalty" instead of "timidity," the object of Carrillo's new commission was the same as that of the rest of Wixárika contacts with Zuno in this period: to legitimize long-standing communal agrarian goals in the eyes of Jalisco's state government. To this end the authorities in Santa Catarina wrote again to Zuno shortly after—presumably in response to information that Agustín Carrillo had brought back from the state capital—asking that he send someone to explain to them in more detail the process of agrarian reform. They also pledged their total allegiance to the state government once again and tied their protestations of loyalty to their agrarian claim by ending their petition with the explicit statement, designed to appeal to Zuno's sentiments, that "we are agraristas."[245] Their apparent loyalty was rewarded, a month later, with the publication of the community's agrarian claim (still for dotación rather than for restitución) in the *Periódico Oficial de Jalisco*.[246]

After the defeat of the Delahuertista rebels, a school was also finally approved for San Sebastián, headed by Federico Antuna, who was assigned a daily wage of three pesos—a third more than that earned by his colleagues in Nayarit and most other Mexican states. Forty-five students (twenty-one children and eighteen adults), all of them Wixárika and all of them male, were initially enrolled.[247] It is interesting that Tuxpan and San Sebastián—which had still not petitioned for agrarian reform—were chosen to receive the Sierra Wixárika's first schools, rather than San Andrés and Santa Catarina, whose leaders were in much closer contact with the revolutionary state. Perhaps precisely because they lacked such ties to the state, the federal government now prioritized bringing these communities into the national fold. However, it is more likely that members of the regional mestizo elite influenced the SEP's decision to establish schools in Tuxpan and San Sebastián to advance their own interests in these communities.

It is not clear to what extent Inspector Hernández was knowingly complicit in the attempts of local mestizo leaders to take control of communal landholdings in the eastern part of the Sierra Wixárika. Hernández certainly enjoyed a cordial relationship with the cacique of Villa Guerrero, Adolfo Valdés y Llanos, to whom he presented himself in October 1923 as a prelude to his first major expedition to the sierra and who, in place of the local military officer stipulated by the SEP, certified Hernández's loyalty to the government during investigations into his conduct during the Delahuertista rebellion (despite Hernández's commercial links with rebel leader Herminio Sánchez) and approved the validity of the unreliable reports emanating from Tuxpan's school (in place of the president of Bolaños, the municipality to which Tuxpan actually belonged).[248] Valdés y Llanos, whose family, together with the Sánchez clan, controlled the economic and political life of Villa Guerrero,[249] was linked by close commercial, familial, and political ties to the Guzmán family of Bolaños and the Muñoz family of Huajimic.[250] These families had, during the nineteenth century, seized most of the formerly communal lands on the eastern and southern edges of the Sierra Wixárika (particularly those of Azqueltán)[251] and were now attempting to penetrate deeper into Tuxpan's and San Sebastián's territories.[252]

Hernández, on his first visit to San Sebastián's new school, dedicated his time to what he called the "bringing together of mestizos and Indians." This involved inviting Luis Huerta, Petronilo Muñoz, and Leandro and J. Guadalupe Sánchez to visit the school and meet with the community's governor.[253] These men were representatives of the main cacical clans of the region. Leandro Sánchez, for example, was a rich landowner and rancher whose family led the takeover of the Azqueltán's lands during the Porfiriato,[254] while Petronilo Muñoz (son of Nieves Muñoz, cacique of Huajimic) had recently seized lands belonging to Guadalupe Ocotán[255] and in 1928, under cover of the cristiada, stole more than two thousand hectares of San Sebastián's communal territory.[256]

Seen in the light of Hernández's plans for the community's school and for the community itself and in the context of San Sebastián's past and future agrarian conflicts with these same men and their families, it is difficult to believe the meetings that Hernández organized and facilitated did not, at least in part, concern the potential settlement of the community's lands by mestizos. Typical of the Indigenista rhetoric espoused by SEP policy makers in this period,[257] Hernández saw the Wixáritari as "poor Indians, living monuments to our glorious people"[258] who failed to understand that "man needs to work, and he who works hardest will live most comfortably."[259] More controversially, Hernández also clung to Porfirian ideas of Indigenous people as requiring "a gradual process of regeneration and 'true redemption' through contact with their racial and cultural betters."[260] Thus he advocated that "the lands of the Sierra in which the 'Wixárika' lives, be populated by honest and hardworking [mestizo] families, whose resolve, honor and work will infect, forgive me the word, the semi-savage 'Wixárika.'" Only this, he believed, would bring about "the miracle of civilization in these lands abandoned to indifference and selfishness."[261]

Hernández's view of the commercial potential of Wixárika communal lands—which he claimed possessed "natural riches which have never been exploited to anyone's benefit; sites for bountiful timber, cattle, mineral and agricultural production"[262]—was similar to those of the region's mestizo caciques, who, using almost identical arguments, had long been trying to seize them.[263] Whether for reasons of ideology or economic self-interest, Hernández, Valdés y Llanos, and the scions of the cacical clans invited to San Sebastián's school all wanted the same thing: the colonization—or recolonization—of Indigenous lands by "hardworking" mestizos. Given that Hernández openly envisaged schools as springboards from which to launch such a project, it would not be surprising to find that he and the region's caciques had used their combined influence to persuade the SEP to establish the first federal schools in the Sierra Wixárika in precisely those communities whose lands they most coveted. Although there is no documentary smoking gun that proves beyond doubt that this was the case, Wixárika opposition to such plans on the part of Hernández and his mestizo allies would also help to explain both the subsequent complaints of San Sebastián's authorities that "the municipal authorities and private individuals have long abused our ignorance in order to rob us of our lands"[264] and the closure soon afterward of the schools in both San Sebastián and Tuxpan.[265]

Although DECI director Enrique Corona claimed that the Sierra Wixárika was one of "the most difficult regions in the country," his department's slow progress in establishing schools there and their lack of endurance contributed to his being forced to step down from his post in early 1924.[266] Throughout the year, Hernández petitioned Corona's successor, Ignacio Ramírez, to approve a replacement school for San Sebastián, as well as new schools for Santa Catarina and San Andrés.[267] However, Hernández's appeals fell on deaf ears until the reorganization of Indigenous education under newly elected President Calles in December 1924, who allotted more resources to "indigenous incorporation."

In April 1925, the SEP at last approved the establishment of a new school in the Sierra Wixárika—this time in San Andrés. However, the fate of the school and its teacher, Antonio Reza, soon brought into clearer relief the scale of Wixárika resistance to the SEP's activities and in particular to abuses committed in the name of "incorporation." San Andrés had once before hosted a government-run school, during the late Porfiriato, but its teacher had dedicated himself to local politicking and the sale of "alcohol and cloth" and was soon run out of town.[268] Unfortunately, Hernández now repeated the mistakes of his predecessors by appointing Antonio Reza—already an unpopular local figure—to take charge of the new school. Reza had been one of several "huicholitos" taken from San Andrés to Zacatecas before the revolution to receive the "great benefit" of a religious education. According to the head of San Sebastián's Josefino mission, these youths had been "corrupted by the vices" they were exposed to in the city and, on returning to their communities, became "real monsters of dishonesty and sin, forcing the Wixáritari, in view of the evils these learned men caused them, to join together in taking their lives or driving them into exile." The people of San Andrés killed some of them during the revolution, but Reza had managed to "miraculously" escape this fate by fleeing the community, in spite of the "continuous torment" he had inflicted on his fellows.[269] Despite this, however, Hernández assumed that as an educated, Spanish-speaking Wixárika, Reza would be well qualified to act as an intermediary between local people and the SEP and to help spread "civilized values" in the community.

Reza had returned to San Andrés by March 1925, when he reappears in the documentary record as having set up and headed a "special committee" to oversee the community's ongoing claim for "restitution."[270] Given that only a decade or so before, Reza's "educated" Wixárika peers had become notorious for attempting to steal communal land undercover of "helping" their communities lay legal claim to it,[271] it is likely that Reza's taking control of San Andrés's agrarian reform proceedings riled many of his peers. Any hostility this generated must have been compounded by the activities of several of Reza's colleagues, who in 1925 attempted to recruit Wixárika students for Mexico City's Casa del Estudiante Indígena through the use of "unconstitutional measures."[272] These included, in the words of one teacher, "seizing" Wixárika children from their "lairs."[273]

The SEP's use of "forced recruitment" in those regions of Mexico "where young Indians did not come forward voluntarily as prospective students"[274] was often counterproductive, prompting Indigenous parents who already "distrusted the intentions of the authorities" to refuse to allow their children to attend any kind of government school.[275] As a result, SEP officials faced severe problems recruiting Indigenous children for the Casa, not only in Jalisco and Nayarit but also in Chiapas, Sonora, Querétaro, Michoacán, and Quintana Roo.[276] Moreover, in the case of the Sierra Wixárika, the Josefinos had already "made the mistake of removing Wixárika children from the Sierra without the permission of their parents," which contributed to the eventual violent Wixárika expulsion of the missionaries during the revolution.[277] The inhabitants of San Andrés would therefore have been all the more sensitive to the recent renewal of such abusive practices by the SEP, with which Antonio Reza, as that institution's local representative, would have been popularly identified regardless of his actual direct involvement. It is perhaps not surprising, then, that Reza—a reputedly treacherous and exploitative representative of "outside forces" perceived as threatening both local landholdings and the integrity of local families—was "assassinated by the tribe" in September 1925. It was furthermore alleged that "they lynched [Reza] in the community's TUKI,"[278] suggesting that the community's kawiterusixi—guardians of the tuki—at least approved Reza's murder, even if they did not oversee it.

It seems that for Wixárika conservatives in San Andrés, opposing the work of the SEP and its cosmopolitan Wixárika representative had become a matter of life or death. To Hernández, however, Reza's murder was a humiliating rebuff to the efforts of the state government, the SEP, and himself to "benefit the poor natives" and a "clear demonstration of our own weakness in the face of the magnitude of this work." Like many SEP officials across Mexico in this period whose attitudes toward the country's Indigenous population "hardened when 'redemption' failed to occur on schedule,"[279] Hernández now stepped up his efforts to persuade the SEP that only the mestizo colonization of Wixárika lands could bring about "the transformation of these miserable, not just illiterate but semi-savage people" and implored his superiors to win President Calles's support for his colonization project in conjunction with Governor Zuno—an impossible dream, given the two men were now furiously struggling for control of Jalisco's state legislature.[280] Hernández declared that while he awaited the results of his petition, he would "go and prepare the families who, full of enthusiasm and faith, will abandon their provincial homes for the mountains to help us form the link through which the 'Wixárika' will save himself."[281]

There is no documentary evidence to suggest that Hernández's plan was taken seriously by the SEP, and no evidence on the ground that the colonization of the sierra, while it had long been encouraged by municipal authorities, became an official policy of either the state or federal governments in this period (although it would become just that in the 1940s). But the murder of Reza is a clear indication of the depth of Wixárika resistance to the practical application of the revolutionary state- and nation-building project. This resistance was increasingly matched by that of the region's mestizos, who were affronted by the increasing anticlericalism of both Calles and Zuno, who competed to demonstrate their revolutionary credentials by clamping down on Catholic lay organizations, raiding churches, and arresting those who demonstrated against such actions.[282] The rising regional tensions contributed to the outbreak of the Cristero Rebellion, which in turn forced the SEP to suspend its efforts to "incorporate" the Sierra Wixárika into the nation-state.

DURANGO: THE O'DAM AND MEXICANEROS

The O'dam and Mexicaneros are, of all the peoples of the Gran Nayar, the least represented in the documentary record for this period. Although there were genuine—if rather unsuccessful—efforts on the part of the revolutionary state to expand its influence into the sierras of Nayarit and Jalisco after 1920, the federal military, the SEP, and state authorities ignored the O'dam and Mexicanero communities in the far south of Durango, which continued to be stricken by intercommunal violence, cacical feuds, and anti-government rebellion. Not a single school had been established in this region by 1925, and so the SEP archives provide us with little information on events in the O'dam and Mexicanero homeland in this period.[283] The agrarian archives are similarly silent for these years, despite both Xoconoxtle and Santa María Ocotán having (separately) petitioned for agrarian reform on several different occasions between 1917 and 1919.[284]

What we do know is that while the overthrow and assassination of Carranza in April 1920 provided the last Villista bands in Nayarit, Jalisco, and Zacatecas with the opportunity to make peace with the victorious Sonorans, Carranza's downfall precipitated the outbreak of new violence in Durango. Pancho Villa himself—who only eight months before had been threatening the city of Durango—did accept the offer of Adolfo de la Huerta, the new interim president, to lay down his weapons and take up the life of a hacendado at Canutillo, in the far north of the state.[285] But Durango's governor, Domingo Arrieta, remained loyal to Carranza, fleeing the state capital in

May 1920 and leaving the governorship in the hands of Enrique R. Nájera.[286] Domingo's brother Mariano soon joined him in their clan's stronghold in the mountains of northwest Durango, and although their new rebellion had "no more justification or plan than that of opposition to the government of Adolfo de la Huerta and then that of Álvaro Obregón,"[287] the rebels, from being no more than a few "very small groups," grew in numbers as the Arrietas' former allies from across Durango—including the O'dam cacique of Temoaya, Dámaso Barraza—joined their movement.

While the Arrietas themselves led raids throughout northern Durango,[288] far to the south, Barraza and his followers in the Sierra O'dam attacked the regional municipal seat of Mezquital in February 1921.[289] A month later, Xoconoxtle's authorities reported that they were unable to send to the local CLA the documents needed to move their agrarian claim forward, "as due to being invaded by the rebels of Yonora . . . we are without contact with the municipal seat."[290] That Xoconoxtle's authorities described Barraza's men as "rebels" and were seemingly the victims of their attacks indicates that the community and its leaders (including Gregorio Aguilar) had pledged allegiance to the new regime, even as their former ally Barraza actively pursued the Arrietas' anti-Sonoran cause. However, government forces fought back against the rebels, and after they executed a large group of rebel captives in Mezquital in April,[291] Arrieta's support in southern Durango evaporated, and there are no archival references to further skirmishes there that year. On his own home turf, Arrieta himself, "without managing to rally popular support for his rebellion, lacking victuals and the opportunity to achieve anything militarily," laid down his arms (albeit temporarily) in December, having agreed to terms with General Juan Andreu Almazán, then zone commander in the Laguna region.[292]

Ironically, although the rebel Barraza survived the consequences of his uprising and by 1923 was back in command of Temoaya's defensa, neither of his one-time Carrancista counterparts in Santa María Ocotán or Huazamota lasted long into the Sonoran era. Primo Ortiz, the former cacique of Huazamota, was killed in May 1922. In separate articles published in the same regional newspaper, he was described first as the victim of a "cowardly assassination," carried out by local rebels who burst into his house and shot him seven times in an apparent case of mistaken identity,[293] then in the second article, published only ten days later, as a "rebel chieftain" who preyed on travelers heading to Huazamota from Nayarit. On this occasion, however, his would-be victims

> charged on their attackers . . . having first struck down their chieftain himself, which sowed panic amongst the rest, who took to their heels . . . henceforth the locals believe that they will now be free of the nuisances they have suffered since the outbreak of the revolution in those distant places.[294]

That such divergent accounts of the same event could appear in the same month in the same newspaper reflects the distance between the sierra and the urban centers in which newspapers were then being produced and consumed. It also reveals the extent to which caciquismo had divided Huazamota, where each rival faction now lived its own divergent reality. In fact, the people of Huazamota today continue to disagree as to whether Ortiz was a victim or a villain, showing the extent to which the factionalism of the revolutionary era is still alive in the minds of many in the region.[295]

What both parties agree on is that members of the Muñoz family led the attack, including a young man named Florencio Estrada, who through his marriage to Dolores Muñoz was the brother-in-law of clan leaders Tiburcio and Nabor Muñoz. However, rather than putting an end to factional conflicts in Huazamota, Ortiz's assassination marked the beginning of a new power struggle, as Estrada, his own brothers, and their allies now faced off against their cuñados "in a war that should be understood as a struggle for the throne of the vacant cacicazgo."[296] This conflict would come to a head several years later, when Florencio Estrada threw his lot in with the cristeros and became a regional rebel leader, while Tiburcio and Nabor Muñoz led Huazamota's pro-government defensa against cristero bands throughout the Gran Nayar.

A factional conflict involving another future cristero leader also led to the death of Ortiz's erstwhile enemy, Gregorio Aguilar, at around the same time. Aguilar was at his ranch near Agüita Zarca, an anexo of Xoconoxtle, when he heard that Santa María Ocotán's traditional authorities were plotting to kill him. Aguilar decided to launch a preemptive attack and, backed by loyalists within Santa María's defensa, "headed directly for Santa María, where on their arrival they killed the community's governor." The fatal rumor was apparently the work of a "jealous woman," who heard that Santa María's authorities had sent men to call Aguilar to attend a communal assembly and, motivated by a personal feud with the governor, "went to Agüita Zarca where Gregorio Aguilar had his home, and told him, 'some people are about to come here to kill you.'"[297]

Although a vague and typically "macho" interpretation of events, it is true that throughout the revolutionary period—and into the present day—communal gossip, perceptions of slighted honor, and fights between men over women—so-called *cuestiones de faldas* (questions of skirts)—frequently blended with and aggravated more explicitly "political" violence across Mexico.[298] So, too, in some cases did rivalry between the wives of caciques contribute to the development of feuds between different political factions, sometimes breaking apart formerly close alliances based on kinship or political allegiances.[299] At the same time, however, it is tempting to read more into this conflict between Aguilar (a native of Xoconoxtle who owed his influence in Santa María to arms supplied by outside forces) and Santa María's own traditional authorities (whose power was linked to their performance of communal costumbre and who likely resented Aguilar as an outsider who had usurped their legitimate authority).

Aguilar's interference in regional politics during the later stages of the revolution had already earned him the enmity of Mezquital's municipal authorities and Durango's federal military. In the wake of his murder of Santa María's governor, both institutions turned decisively against him, offering their full support to a young O'dam leader named Juan Andrés Soto, who assembled an armed force to avenge the governor's death. Gregorio, accompanied by his son Ascención "Chon" Aguilar, was hiding out in the mountains near his ranch, where, after a month of searching, Soto and his men "besieged him there, and at close range opened fire and killed him."[300]

Chon survived the shootout, obtained an amnesty from the state government, and returned to Agüita Zarca in peace.[301] Meanwhile, the victorious Juan Andrés Soto took Gregorio's place as commander of Santa María Ocotán's defensa, restoring it to the control of a native of the community.[302] The resultant feud between Juan Andrés Soto and Chon Aguilar would later help to determine the course of the cristiada in the Sierra O'dam, as the former became a cristero chieftain and the latter formed a powerful pro-government militia in his home community of Xoconoxtle.

In addition to factional violence in Santa María Ocotán and Huazamota, the region was also affected by the outbreak of a new anti-Sonoran rebellion in the second half of 1922, led by Francisco Murguía. Domingo Arrieta joined the movement in northern Durango, and General Juan Carrasco, who had been central to the Carrancista campaign in Sinaloa during the revolution, also declared for the rebels and marched through the southern part of the Sierra O'dam on his way to join forces with Murguía. As they crossed the mountains of Acaponeta and Huajicori, Carrasco and his men would have depended on the local O'dam and Mexicanero population for food supplies and guides. However, we do not know whether the region's Indigenous defensa forces participated in Carrasco's final battle on November 8, when federal troops commanded by Alfonso de la Huerta, brother of Adolfo, finally caught up with him near San Andrés Milpillas, on the Nayarit-Durango border. Carrasco was defeated and killed, and his body was taken back to Acaponeta to be put on public display before burial. Murguía was captured and executed soon after, and Arrieta fled to safety in the United States.[303]

Obregón's rule was more seriously threatened a year later by the Delahuertista rebellion. In Durango the revolt drew in ex-Villistas and some of the few Carranza loyalists who survived the 1922 revolt, including—of course—Domingo Arrieta, who returned from his American exile to join yet another rebellion against Obregón (even if, on this occasion, it was led by another of the Sonorans originally responsible for Carranza's overthrow). However, de la Huerta's uprising attracted less support in

Durango than it did in other parts of the country,[304] in part because the state's most important potential rebel commander, Pancho Villa, had been assassinated the previous July.[305] By February 1924, federal forces under Generals Jesús Agustín Castro and Eulogio Ortiz had crushed the rebels in Durango, and the mopping-up operations were left to armed members of the state's pro-government agrarista movement.[306]

Arrieta's participation was enough to persuade Dámaso Barraza to join the Delahuertista cause,[307] but Mezquital's municipal authorities stayed loyal to the government and in December 1923 rigorously enforced Jesús Agustín Castro's draconian orders for "the confiscation of horses, saddles and weapons found in the hands of private individuals, so as to supply with all haste the forces organized to combat the revolutionary movement."[308] That such orders needed to be issued suggests there was sufficient local support for Barraza's rebels that loyalist authorities feared any arms left in private hands would end up being used against them. But on May 7, 1924, Arrieta surrendered and was amnestied, stripped of his rank, and forced to retire to private life.[309] Barraza laid down his arms shortly after and was also amnestied, seemingly on more generous terms than Arrieta, since he continued to lead Temoaya's defensa until he joined the cristeros in a final act of rebellion in December 1926.

The existence of armed bands throughout Durango in the early 1920s obstructed the advance of the federal government's state-building project in much of the state. A plan to build a telegraph line between Durango and Yonora, passing through Mezquital and Temoaya, which would have been given over to the federal military once finished,[310] was abandoned because of regional instability. Meanwhile, the state government's coffers, already strained by the cumulative effects of a decade of intense conflict, were exhausted by the costs of combating the Arrietista and Delahuertista rebels. The violence that had wracked Durango since 1910 had already "paralyzed the majority of industries, mines, haciendas and cottage industries" and had a demographic cost, "taking into account inhabitants who were never born, emigrants, and deaths . . . of 48% of the population, compared to the 1910 figures, which is to say much more than in the other states of the Republic."[311] The state government therefore prioritized the restoration of industrial and agricultural production throughout the 1920s, and although Governor Castro "passed the principal laws essential for the crystallization of the revolution's ideals," he ignored educational programs entirely, to the extent that he "closed down the General Directorate of Primary Education."[312]

The Sierra O'dam, like Chihuahua's Sierra Tarahumara,[313] did not figure in SEP plans until the end of 1923, when its budget for the next year finally allotted two hundred thousand pesos for setting up "indigenous cultural centers" in various states, including Durango.[314] Everardo Gámiz Olivas, who served as a maestro misionero from late 1923 until mid-1924, was the first SEP official responsible for the municipalities of Mezquital and Huazamota. He reported that they possessed only a few "awful dirt roads" and were inhabited by Indigenous people who lived not in the cabeceras of their communities but in "homes disseminated at considerable distances from one another." He noted that the region would be hugely difficult to supervise, given "the difficulties of communication in the ex-Partido of Mezquital, and the fact that it is in this ex-Partido where there is the greatest aboriginal population." And reflecting the oft-stated views of the "missionaries" as to the perils inherent in their work (and probably the extent to which the identities of Durango's mestizo inhabitants had been influenced by collective memories of the colonial-era O'dam Rebellion),[315] Gámiz added that "due to the character of the natives," trying to educate them would be dangerous.[316] Such drastic views were a little extreme, however, given that according to O'dam elders today, their forebears would have feared Gámiz just as much as he feared them, to the extent that "in those days . . . when any mestizo arrived, the children ran away, and others too, because they were scared."[317]

Although by early 1924 Nayarit's Department of Federal Education had established a school for the O'dam and Mexicaneros of San Andrés Milpillas,[318] the rest of the year passed without a single school being set up for the O'dam and Mexicaneros of Durango. The state government's indifference to education, its budgetary problems, and rebel activity continued to obstruct SEP activity across Durango as a whole, which in the state's southern mountains was compounded by the inactivity of Gámiz, who was subsequently suspended for failing to submit regular reports. His superiors noted that although Gámiz appeared to be "a very cultured person . . . he demonstrated little activity in fulfilling his duties," and he finally left the SEP in June 1924 to pursue a career as an academic.[319]

The accession of Calles to the presidency in December 1924 brought fresh impetus at the national level to the revolutionary state's education and agrarian reform programs. The new governor of Durango, Enrique R. Nájera, set about locally accelerating "the distribution of land and the promotion of dotación de ejidos, with the aim of rewarding the hosts of agraristas who had combated the Delahuertista rebellion and contributed to his election." In this agrarian project Nájera was enthusiastically aided by the state's official peasant organizations, whose chiefs, "in full enjoyment of their governmental alliance, were put forward during the election as federal deputies."[320] Among these men was Alberto Terrones Benítez, who was appointed to the seat that Governor Nájera had previously occupied in the state senate.

Before the revolution, Terrones Benítez had worked as a lawyer for foreign mining companies with interests in Durango, and it was only in 1917, when he was elected deputy for Cuencamé, that he was "reincarnated as an agrarian reformer."[321] As a member of Durango's commission to the Constitutional Congress in Querétaro, he helped Pastor Rouaix to draft article 27 of the Mexican Constitution, which outlined the top-down basis for revolutionary land reform.[322] By 1925 he had become Durango's primary proponent of state-administered agrarian reform. In a report on the State Agrarian Congress of January 1925, which he had also presided over, Terrones Benítez advised Governor Nájera that

> the Federal Government must revise the titles, and demarcate all rural lands and properties, and the State Government must contribute to this task, thereby taking advantage of a magnificent opportunity to create a land registry . . . the lack of which allows the big landowners to annually defraud the tax authorities of many millions of pesos.

Terrones Benítez also reported on the particularities of land reform in the Sierra O'dam, where the "ignorance in which these natives are found" would, he predicted, complicate government efforts to defend them from the landowners then invading their lands. "The majority of these natives," he continued, "barely speak the Castilian language and are in such a state of misery and ruin, that they live on toasted maize, they lodge in rudimentary wooden shacks or in caves, and dress in rags even during the winter, which is exceedingly severe." Terrones Benítez concluded that the only solution to agrarian problems in these regions depended on "specific action on the part of the Government given we so need to incorporate them into civilization," which he saw as best accomplished through the establishment of schools for the O'dam of San Francisco de Lajas, Xoconoxtle, Taxicaringa, and Temoaya, the Mexicaneros of San Buenaventura, the Náayarite of San Lucas de Jalpa, and the mestizos of Huazamota.[323]

However, Terrones Benítez's advocacy was not enough to overcome the bureaucratic obstacles holding back the progress of the agrarian claims of Santa María Ocotán, Xoconoxtle, and Temoaya. The first two communities had already applied for restitución de tierras on several occasions even before Carranza's overthrow in 1920. Temoaya's claim was more recent and a response to the growing boldness with which members of Mezquital's politico-economic elite were now encroaching with their cattle onto pastures that belonged to the community. In so doing, they challenged local pride, communal territorial integrity, and the economic interests of Dámaso Barraza, who also possessed extensive herds of cattle.[324] However, all three communities' claims had stalled in the face of "the difficulties of communication with the inhabitants" and, more important, their failure to set up new agrarian authorities—the Comités Particulares Ejecutivos—to oversee the process of restitución.[325]

It is not surprising that the mainly illiterate O'dam of Durango, like their Wixárika neighbors and numerous other peasant groups throughout Mexico, did not well understand the bureaucratic requirements of the agrarian reform process (even if "practical knowledge" of the process often came down to "who to pay [and] how much").[326] Furthermore, the O'dam—like the Náayarite of Saycota or the mestizos of Namiquipa, Chihuahua[327]—were reluctant to compromise their autonomy and signal their acceptance of the Mexican state's guardianship of the nation's lands and other resources by establishing state-approved nontraditional power structures in their communities. But the fact that the claims of all three O'dam communities were severely delayed specifically because of Mezquital's CLA playing up their failure to establish Comités Particulares Ejecutivos also suggests that the elites who controlled the local agrarian bureaucracy took deliberate advantage of Indian intransigence to retard the progress of claims that would threaten their interests (just as their equivalents in northern Jalisco were doing with regard to Wixárika agrarian petitions). In Temoaya in particular, the community's resultant lack of faith in the revolutionary state's ability to resolve its conflicts with its mestizo neighbors would help to push Dámaso Barraza and his followers into forming an alliance with the cristeros.[328]

While agrarian reform remained a dead letter in the Sierra O'dam, plans were once again made to set up schools in the region in January 1925, after Puig Casauranc became the new education secretary and ordered Gonzalo Mota to take over Durango's Department of Federal Education. Mota had previously headed its counterpart in Nayarit and was well aware of the practical challenges of applying the SEP's education policies to the communities of the Gran Nayar.[329] Given Senator Terrones Benítez's recent petitions for schools to be established in Durango's "unexplored regions," and in line with the SEP's increasing emphasis on "cultural incorporation," Mota immediately began to pressure Ignacio Ramírez, head of the DERICI, for the resources needed to establish schools in the Sierra O'dam. He claimed the region was inhabited by a "multitude of indigenous pueblos that have remained excluded from civilization for want of schools and communication channels, and indolence, and the neglect of the political authorities" and asked Ramírez to assign two more school inspectors to Durango to spearhead the "redemption of our ignorant masses who in their majority make up the indigenous race."[330]

After Ramírez turned down Mota's requests on financial grounds,[331] Mota sent him a damning in-depth report on the state of Durango's Federal Education Department, whose functionaries had paid so little attention to rural schools in previous years that there was no information in their files as to how many had actually been established in the state nor how many still functioned. Furthermore, just as in the mountains of

Jalisco, Chihuahua, and (as Mota had previously complained) Nayarit, the low daily wage of two pesos paid to rural teachers only attracted individuals who "by their writings reveal their ineptitude for this work . . . and others who see the school as a secondary thing, given their primary focus revolves around their private businesses." In Durango, Mota continued, this was a particular problem because

> this State has been one of those that suffered most during the Revolution, its principal sources of wealth: mining, agriculture, and stockbreeding, were left paralyzed and as an immediate consequence of such disorganization, scarcity, lack of regional production and unemployment proliferated, circumstances that have made life extremely expensive throughout the State, which is only just entering a period of reconstruction.

Mota assured Ramírez that unless teachers' wages were raised, "the Rural Schools will continue in their decadent state," and he concluded that ultimately "it would be better to reduce the number of schools until we can appreciate their quality, if the National Budget cannot properly satisfy the needs of those that now exist in this Entity."[332]

On this last point, Ignacio Ramírez took Mota at his word and cut down the number of rural schools in Durango funded by the DERICI to only thirteen. Durango's new interim governor, Antonio Gutiérrez, was outraged and responded by writing directly to Ramírez's superior, Puig Casauranc, demanding for his state as many federal rural schools as were currently operating in Jalisco, Nayarit, and Guanajuato, "which have one hundred each." Like Mota, Gutiérrez also contrasted Durango's contribution to the revolution with the lack of federal attention it was now receiving, which he viewed as especially disgraceful given that Durango had "rendered to the Revolution its most contingents of blood and sacrifice and for having exhausted all of its sources of wealth in the holocaust of that same Revolution, not durangueña, but eminently nationalist."[333]

Despite the protestations of Gonzalo Mota, Governor Gutiérrez, and members of the state legislature,[334] Mezquital's single school (in the mestizo agrarista settlement of El Troncón) did not survive the federal government cuts. By July 1925, Mota was again desperately asking his superiors for increased funds for the SEP in Durango, as "the Municipalities . . . due to their scarce incomes cannot sustain schools even in their most important centers."[335] Little progress had been made by September, however, when Governor Nájera, after taking back control of the state from Gutiérrez, complained to Puig Casauranc that not a single rural teacher was working with Durango's Indigenous population.[336] The same day, Mota sent Ignacio Ramírez a proposed budget for the 1925/26 academic year in Durango totaling 105,740 pesos, of which the greatest cost by far was 43,800 pesos for sixty "directors of rural schools" earning 2 pesos a day, followed by 7,300 pesos for two "inspector-instructors" at 10 pesos a day to supervise them. He once again justified the size of these sums with the assertion that Durango "was the theater of the revolutionary movement during a long period of time and where there is most need for the Secretariat of Public Education to multiply its centers of culture."[337]

Only a week later, Governor Nájera again complained to the education secretary that of the thirty-four rural schools that had opened their doors across Durango earlier that year, fourteen had since been forced to close.[338] The secretary of education did at least promise Nájera that by the end of the year he would send to southern Durango "a group of teachers who will put themselves in contact with the educators and Indians of that region so to give them useful lessons."[339] By March 1926, however, these teachers had still not arrived, despite Mota's ambitious proposed education budget. In fact, by this point only two schools had been founded in all of the municipality of Mezquital: both of them in mestizo communities near the municipal seat, far from the region's O'dam and Mexicaneros.[340] Both groups were still regarded by outsiders as the isolated and recalcitrant guardians of immense untapped natural resources—including rich deposits of gold—who "oppose the entry of civilized people, whom they consider a danger to the interests of the tribes and for their customs and traditions; thus those who exploit metalliferous veins are expelled with arrows and bullets."[341]

CONCLUSIONS

By the end of 1925, the two federal agencies at the center of the Sonoran state-building project had done little to successfully "incorporate" into the revolutionary Mexican nation-state the peoples of the Gran Nayar. None of the local communities that applied for agrarian reform won a claim in this period, limiting the development of patron-client ties between their inhabitants and the state. The leaders of some communities—such as San Andrés and Santa Catarina in the Sierra Wixárika—did remain hopeful that either the federal or state government would eventually act to protect their lands from neighboring haciendas, mestizo ranchers, and rival communities. But the central CNA's lack of responsiveness to demands for the recognition of Indigenous communal territories and the ease with which the mestizo elites who controlled the regional CLAs blocked Indigenous petitions for agrarian reform at a lower level ended up turning other communities—such as Dámaso Barraza's stronghold of Temoaya—against a revolutionary regime that seemed to be working to obstruct long-standing communal goals.

Neither was the SEP much more successful in its aim of making "Mexicans" out of the Náayarite, Wixáritari, O'dam, and Mexicaneros. The geographical and cultural characteristics of the Gran Nayar presented numerous obstacles to the SEP's project, including difficult terrain, poor communications, dispersed local settlement patterns, strong traditions of communal autonomy, and generalized Indian distrust of mestizos. In Durango, additional problems related to the SEP's own lack of resources, the revolution's devastating effects on Durango's regional economy, Governor Castro's disparaging attitude toward education, and Barraza's close relations with rebellious strongman Domingo Arrieta meant that not a single school was founded in any of the state's O'dam or Mexicanero communities.

The SEP was more active in the Náayari and Wixárika homelands in Nayarit and Jalisco, where its local representatives enjoyed the qualified support of local leaders such as Mariano Mejía, Eutimio Domínguez, and Agustín Carrillo. However, teachers and inspectors continued to face intense hostility from conservative Indigenous elders and anxious parents. As opposed to the way in which some schools in other regions became sites of exchange between Indigenous people and the state and new public spaces where collective—and especially female—grievances and desires could be expressed for the first time,[342] in the Gran Nayar, schools became sites of conflict between two very different worlds. Even when teachers tried to avoid direct confrontation, the inherent clash between the SEP's scholarly calendar and local ritual cycles—between two rival conceptions of time itself—often led to conflict.[343] Indigenous parents refused to reorder their children's lives in line with school timetables, which they viewed as a threat both to communal- and family-level ritual life and the associated family-unit agricultural production on which they subsisted.[344]

Ultimately, then, the SEP's early activities in the Gran Nayar are examples not only of revolutionary efforts to *forjar patria* (forge the fatherland)[345] but also of the educational paradigm that Vaughan, drawing on the work of Becker and Street, describes as

> [that] undertaken for the purposes of promoting state control and market penetration . . . [and] conceptualised and carried out within cultural constructs oblivious to the logic of local practices of productive, reproductive, and ritual labor. [Such programmes] are disruptive of the delicate ecological and social balances that sustain life upon a precarious resource base. The discourse between community and teachers is likely to be antagonistic, characterised by resistance, or absent.[346]

The record of the forty or so Náayari pupils enrolled at the boarding school that finally opened in Jesús María in 1926 attests to the ineffectiveness of the SEP's four years of work in the region: only two of the pupils spoke Spanish, none could read or write, none had any knowledge of Mexican "heroes"—including Juárez and Madero—nor did any understand what either Nayarit or Mexico was or who the current president was. Not a single "civic festival" was celebrated in the community itself, which also lacked a Mexican flag, and the exasperated new scholastic zone inspector complained that there was an urgent need to "confer with the local authorities" to stop the Náayarite dumping their rubbish in the school grounds.[347]

Meanwhile, the SEP had been even more impotent in the Sierra Wixárika, thanks to maestro misionero Diego Hernández's poor choice of teachers, close relations with land-hungry regional caciques, support for the mestizo "colonization" of the sierra, and apparent complicity in the forcible recruitment of Wixárika students for the Casa del Estudiante Indígena.[348] In fact, Hernández's efforts did more to alienate those Wixárika communities that acquired federal schools—such as San Andrés, where local people eventually murdered the local teacher—than to bring them into the national fold.

Thus the Náayarite, Wixáritari, O'dam, and Mexicaneros all preserved throughout this period a higher level of cultural, political, and territorial autonomy than most of the country's other Indigenous peoples, including the highlanders of Chiapas, the Yucatec Maya, and Chihuahua's Tarahumara.[349] But the attempted expansion of the revolutionary state into the Gran Nayar and conflicts related to the political and economic dynamics of revolutionary caciquismo nonetheless shook the internal stability of many of the region's communities. In Santa María Ocotán, cosmopolitan cacique Gregorio Aguilar murdered the community's governor, only to be killed and replaced as defensa commander by Juan Andrés Soto. Meanwhile, the educational and economic programs promoted by Mejía and Domínguez in the mountains of Nayarit turned important factions in many Náayari communities against the local defensas and the mestizo settlers and teachers with whom the latter had allied.

Such conflicts would soon come to play an important role in defining the local dynamics of the Cristero Rebellion. When halfway through 1926 a local mestizo, Juan Sifuentes, was finally ordered to set up a school in Santa María Ocotán—in the process becoming the first teacher posted to the Sierra O'dam since the creation of the SEP—he "dedicated himself to political activities and failed to open the School"[350] and soon became one of the community's main cristero leaders. In Jalisco, the ties that up-and-coming politico-military leader Agustín Carrillo forged with the state and federal governments not only cemented his influence in Santa Catarina but also helped to determine the fates of his own community and of its long-standing rival, San Sebastián, during the cristiada. And in Nayarit, Náayari opposition to mestizo immigration, homegrown caciquismo, and state education policies had by 1927 grown strong enough to push some individuals or factions into taking up arms against the state itself, even as others stayed loyal to the cosmopolitan defensa leaders and fought as federal auxiliaries. Across the Gran Nayar, many Wixáritari, Náayarite, O'dam, and Mexicaneros would soon take up arms once again to fight as either cristero rebels or as allies of the revolutionary state, in spite of their continued independence from the influence of both orthodox Catholicism and revolutionary nationalism.

4

THE CRISTERO REBELLION IN THE GRAN NAYAR, 1926–1929

THE OUTBREAK OF the Cristero Rebellion in late 1926 brought to a head a decade of rising tensions between the Catholic Church and the revolutionary Mexican state. During the armed phase of the revolution, some insurgent forces had attacked churches, priests, and Catholic activists,[1] and the revolutionary constitution of 1917 challenged the cultural, political, and economic power of the church.[2] Presidents Carranza and Obregón were reluctant to enforce the constitution's anticlerical articles 3, 27, and 130, which restricted the activities of individual priests and of the institutional church, but various state governors experimented with applying them locally during the late 1910s and early 1920s.[3]

After Calles became president in December 1924, his outspoken anticlericalism emboldened more state governors, including those of Jalisco and Durango, to pass legislation limiting the numbers and activities of local priests. In response, violence broke out between gangs of Catholics and anticlericals in cities, towns, and villages across Mexico.[4] In March 1925, Catholic lay activists founded the Liga Nacional Defensora de la Libertad Religiosa (LNDLR, or National League for the Defense of Religious Liberty). The organization's goal was to "reconquer religious liberty and all the social and economic freedoms that derive from it," and reflecting the increasingly belligerent attitudes on both sides of the religious debate, to this end it claimed the right to use "the means that the circumstances may require."[5]

Church-state tensions reached a further nadir in June 1926 when the president promulgated the so-called Calles law—a legislative package designed to enforce, at the national level, the constitution's anticlerical provisions. Foreign priests were banned from working in Mexico, and the number of native priests was limited to one for every six thousand citizens. They were prohibited from participating in politics or associating with one another socially and wearing their vestments or holding masses outside their churches. The churches themselves became property of the nation, and municipal authorities were ordered to inventory their contents. Monasteries and convents were turned over to workers' and peasants' organizations, and monks and nuns were forced to rejoin secular society. Catholic political parties were banned, church schools were outlawed, and the qualifications they had issued were invalidated.[6] Transgressors faced fines, imprisonment, and, in the case of foreigners, expulsion from Mexico; and copies of the new laws were fixed to the doors of the nation's churches for all to see.

Mexico's episcopacy looked to the LNDLR and other Catholic lay organizations—amongst them the Mexican Catholic Youth Association (ACJM), the National Union of Catholic Ladies (UNDC), and the Knights of Columbus—to mobilize the nation's faithful against the new laws. Throughout the summer of 1926, tens of thousands of Mexicans took part in an economic boycott led by these organizations in an attempt to force Calles to back down. But Calles refused to compromise, and so in July 1926 Mexico's leading bishops withdrew the clergy from the nation's churches and suspended religious services. In some parts of Mexico, local officials made deals with priests that enabled village sacristans or neighborhood committees to take peaceful control of churches, dampening popular outrage. Elsewhere—including in Nayarit, Jalisco, Durango, and Zacatecas—rumors spread that Calles himself had ordered the churches closed, leading to riots in which a few soldiers and local politicians and significant numbers of Catholic protesters were killed.[7] In turn, Calles looked to the nation's landless peasants to shore up his rule, arming agrarista militias—many of them based in Indigenous communities—which soon began to invade disputed landholdings and launch attacks on their political rivals.[8]

By September 1926, the tensions between priests, devout civilians, and Catholic political organizations on the one side and government officials, the army, and agraristas on the other had sparked rebellions in a few key central and western states. By early 1927, rural populations in much of Jalisco, Zacatecas, Colima, Michoacán, Guanajuato, and Querétaro, and smaller parts of Nayarit, Durango, and Oaxaca—the great majority of them mestizos—had pledged themselves to "Christ the King" and declared holy war on the government. Like their revolutionary forebears, most of the cristero rebels remained loyal above all to local chiefs,[9] but tens of thousands also pledged broader allegiance to General Enrique Gorostieta,[10] who was first hired by the (by now outlawed) LNDLR as its military chief in Jalisco and who soon took command of the cristeros at the national level.[11] LNDLR agents and civilian supporters supplied the rebels with arms and ammunition, which were smuggled from the United States, stolen from local arms factories, or even bought directly from corrupt federal commanders (although the cristeros would be permanently handicapped by a shortage of materiel).[12]

As a result of the escalating conflict between government forces and these rural rebels, by spring 1927 the Gran Nayar—whose mountain paths connected the cristero strongholds of southern Zacatecas and Durango to those of northern Jalisco—once again became a strategically important theater of combat, as well as a refuge, recruiting ground, and source of food supplies for both cristero guerrillas and the army and its agrarista auxiliaries. The first half of this chapter presents a narrative of how the fighting between these groups played out in the Gran Nayar, based on contemporary documents, secondary accounts from publications like *David* (a monthly journal published by ex-cristeros between 1952 and 1968), oral histories, and ethnological studies of the Náayarite, Wixáritari, O'dam, and Mexicaneros from the 1930s onward. It shows that the Cristero Rebellion severely divided the region's inhabitants as the dynamics of the rebellion and the fluid nature of the Clausewitzian "facts on the ground"[13] pitted cacique against cacique, community against community, and faction against faction.[14]

The second part of this chapter analyzes the different factors that helped decide Náayari, Wixárika, O'dam, and Mexicanero loyalties (or, indeed, neutrality) during the cristiada. This brings into clearer relief the ways in which communal and individual sympathies were shaped by caciquismo and factionalism (often products of participation in the revolution of the previous decade), communal rivalries (often related to longer-running territorial conflicts), local cultural idiosyncrasies (which varied between "tribes," communities, and even families), and the nature of the relationships forged during the early 1920s between individual representatives of the state and the inhabitants of the Gran Nayar.

This analysis of Náayari, Wixáritari, O'dam, and Mexicanero participation in the cristiada challenges Jean Meyer's initial presentation of the cristiada as an inherently popular and religiously motivated rebellion[15] and his contention that, for the same reason, a majority of Wixáritari and O'dam supported the cristeros, while the Náayarite, although less enthusiastic backers of the rebellion, didn't oppose them either (he fails to mention the Mexicaneros).[16] Instead, it fits within a more recent historiographical tradition that stresses the importance of economic and political, as well as cultural and spiritual, factors in determining popular loyalties during the rebellion.[17] It also helps to complicate broad-brush regional analyses that, relying on "essentializing views of religion and regional cultures,"[18] characterize all of central-western Mexico as a monolithic "clerical heartland." For despite its proximity to the mestizo-dominated cristero strongholds of Jalisco, Zacatecas, and Durango, in 1926 the Gran Nayar was—and today remains—one of the least "clericalized" regions of the entire country.

In the former regions, cristero leaders were able to harness the support not only of devoutly Catholic peasants but also of local priests, lay organizations like the ACJM, and agrarian reform–fearing ranchero caciques who mobilized their supporters against the government.[19] Such actors were almost entirely absent from the Gran Nayar, lending weight to Knight's argument that geographical patterns of support for cristeros were also modified strongly by the effects of revolutionary agrarianism and federal education, which encouraged some communities to adopt anticlerical attitudes to gain lands and others "to look favourably on the Church and its strident defense of property rights."[20] Finally, in weighing the relative importance of all these factors in shaping the local progress and outcomes of the conflict, this chapter constitutes a case study of how, why, and with what results subaltern groups may decide to drop the "weapons of the weak" and take up rifles, rocks, or bows and arrows against those forces—whether local elites, regional rivals, or the self-declared representatives of God or the government—perceived as threatening their families, communities, and ways of life.[21]

REBELLION IN THE BORDERLANDS: THE CRISTERO UPRISINGS OF 1926 IN DURANGO, JALISCO, AND ZACATECAS

Of the rural uprisings that eventually merged together to become the cristiada, two of the earliest and most important broke out on the very edges of the Gran Nayar. The first was led by Huejuquilla's former defensa commander Pedro Quintanar, who in August 1926 took up arms against the government just to the east of the Sierra Wixárika. Quintanar's rebellion was directly precipitated by the murder of the parish priest of Chalchihuites, Father (and later Saint) Luis Bátiz, an outspoken defender of Catholic political rights.[22] On August 14, Bátiz and three local members of the ACJM were arrested by federal troops on the orders of Zacatecas zone commander General Eulogio Ortiz.[23] The next day, Quintanar and some friends tried to rescue them, leading to a gunfight in which all four prisoners were killed.[24] Quintanar "found himself in a de facto state of rebellion" and on August 29, 1926, at the head of "around a hundred men," attacked and took the devoutly Catholic town of Huejuquilla.[25] Many local people, including Huejuquilla's defensa, decided to join their holy war against the government.[26] Quintanar's rebellion soon spread south to Mezquitic, Jalisco, where an armed band led by a militant priest raided several villages before escaping "toward the mountains inhabited by the Wixáritari."[27] By January 1927, as Catholics across central and western Mexico answered the LNDLR's call for national rebellion, bands loyal to Quintanar were also operating in Villa Guerrero, Bolaños, and the Zacatecan canyons, on the fringes of the Sierra Wixárika.[28]

A similar rebellion broke out at around the same time in Durango, in the village of Santiago Bayacora, near the state capital. Although Meyer describes Bayacora's inhabitants as "acculturated O'dam" and contemporary sources often referred to them as "indios,"[29] it is clear that by the 1920s, Bayacora was linguistically, culturally, and sociopolitically a mestizo village,[30] albeit one with a reputation for rebelliousness.[31] Like Quintanar himself, however, the people of Santiago Bayacora took up arms against the state only in response to what they perceived as a direct attack on their faith.

On September 29, 1926, government officials arrived in the village to make an inventory of its church, as mandated by the ley Calles. Local people, many still drunk from a fiesta the day before, attacked the functionaries and ran them out of the village.[32] Federal troops soon arrived to restore order but were repulsed by the villagers, who elected the village sacristan, Trinidad Mora, as their leader. The federals returned with reinforcements under General Eliseo Páez, and although the defenders had seized weapons and ammunition after their initial victory, they would not have been able to hold out against their attackers had a nearby river not broken its banks, drowning various soldiers and again forcing their retreat. Mora's men, and the population as a whole, escaped the village before more troops could arrive.[33]

Some federals saw their defeat as the work of supernatural forces and claimed that in Santiago

> they are all sorcerers, led by a brave General mounted on a white horse, and a woman dressed in brown . . . and when we open fire on them, our arms fall down completely and we can't shoot.

Mora and his followers believed that the "general" and the "woman" were none other than the village's santitos, "Saint Santiago and the Most Saintly Virgin," in human form.[34] Encouraged by this evidence of divine support for their cause,[35] Mora and his eighty-eight armed men sent their families into hiding and then marched south into the mountains of Mezquital and Pueblo Nuevo.[36]

On October 26, near Mezquital's municipal seat, Mora's men ambushed a federal force, seizing horses, rifles, and ammunition[37] and killing fourteen men, including General Ismael Lares (who had asked Calles for permission to personally put down the rebellion).[38] News of this victory spread fast and, compounded by stories of Quintanar's successes in nearby parts of Zacatecas and Jalisco, won Mora's cristero rebels many new recruits. The most important of these was Porfirio Mayorquín, a butcher from Acaponeta, Nayarit, who had fled to Durango after killing a neighbor in a duel.[39] When a warrant for his arrest reached Durango, Mayorquín headed to Mora's camp, where he was taken for a spy and almost shot.[40] Luckily one of Mora's lieutenants

FIGURE 2 Cristero leader Porfirio Mayorquín with his lieutenants, somewhere between southern Durango and Northern Nayarit, ca. 1928 (ARA/Sección Gráfica/791).

was able to vouch for him and thanks to his natural military talent, ruthlessness, and charisma, Mayorquín soon became an important cristero commander.

Mora also sent out commissions to the commanders of southern Durango's defensas sociales, hoping that, like the pro-government militiamen who had rallied behind Quintanar, they could be persuaded to defect to the cristero cause.[41] Valente Acevedo, defensa commander in Llano Grande (a small mestizo settlement within the O'dam community of San Bernardino), agreed to join Mora's forces, bringing with him a group of armed and mounted followers estimated to have range from twenty-two to one hundred men (although the higher figure comes from Mora's lieutenant and cristero chronicler Francisco Campos, who often exaggerates such figures by a factor of ten).[42]

Campos's estimate should be viewed with even more caution because Campos was not present during Acevedo's arrival at Mora's camp. Instead, he and his friend Federico Vázquez—a mestizo from near Santiago who would become an important cristero leader himself—had gone in search of Dámaso Barraza, the O'dam revolutionary fighter, defensa commander, and cacique of Temoaya. According to Campos, Barraza was eager for news of Mora's uprising, and they quickly convinced the gruff O'dam cacique to bring his forces over to the cristero side.[43] Other accounts claim LNDLR envoys had in fact arrived in Yonora several weeks before, and Barraza had already agreed to join the rebellion as soon as he and his men had finished bringing in their harvests (and, we can assume, celebrating the rituals without which the sacred corn would remain inedible).[44] Either way, Barraza and the inhabitants of Temoaya and its anexo, Yonora, became the first O'dam recruits to the cristero cause.[45]

On January 1, 1927, Barraza and his O'dam fighters (who Campos claims numbered four hundred but are unlikely to have exceeded one hundred men)[46] joined Mora's forces near Mezquital. Although Mora remained the rebellion's supreme leader, he knew of Barraza's military prowess and put him in charge of his cristero forces. The same day, Barraza led them to victory over Mezquital's federal garrison and then ordered the town's inhabitants to assemble in the plaza. Reveling in the opportunity to settle accounts with his rivals in the municipal seat—and belying Meyer's assertions that the cristeros constituted an "army of volunteers"[47]—Barraza, pistol in hand and flanked by rifle-wielding O'dam,[48] conscripted all of the town's males above the age of twelve, declaring that

> we come defending Religion, all is well with he who desires to help us, and he who does not, let him step forward and you know what, he who refuses to help will be considered an enemy, and who knows what will happen to him.[49]

Alarmed by the fall of Mezquital, Calles ordered Generals Enrique León and Eliseo Páez to crush the burgeoning rebellion. However, on January 6, 1927, Barraza's enlarged cristero forces, freshly supplied in the wake of their recent victories, ambushed the federals at the Hacienda del Refugio (Barraza's headquarters in 1918). With knowledge of the terrain on their side, the cristeros routed the federals, managing to kill General Paéz himself and many of his men.[50]

This victory, however, went to Barraza's head, and on January 17, he abandoned his usual guerrilla tactics to fight a pitched battle against 250 federals under General Anacleto López.[51] Better disciplined and more accustomed to conventional styles of fighting, the federals trounced the cristeros. Barraza himself was crushed beneath his horse and killed soon after the battle began,[52] and his men fled into the surrounding countryside.[53] López retook Mezquital and hauled the bloodied body of the Sierra O'dam's most important cacique back to Durango for public display.[54] Most of Barraza's troops, either demoralized by the death of their chief or sensing an opportune moment to escape their conscript status,[55] surrendered to López soon afterward, "handing over all the materiel that they had originally seized from the [Federals]."[56]

Ultimately, only seventy-five of these men, under Barraza's *cuñados* (brothers-in-law), Macario and Ireneo Valdés, stayed loyal to the cristero cause,[57] regrouping with Mayorquín and Acevedo near the latter's village of Llano Grande.[58] Mora and the surviving rebels of Bayacora journeyed north toward their own home territory where they derailed and ambushed a trainload of soldiers whom they forced to join their ranks and also seized arms, ammunition, and cash. Their morale boosted, Mora's forces then set up a new camp in the Sierra O'dam with Mayorquín, Acevedo, Macario, and Ireneo Valdés and their remaining troops and many of their families.[59]

CRISTERO EXPANSION AND FEDERAL COUNTERINSURGENCY IN THE GRAN NAYAR

By the end of December 1926, cristero forces controlled much of northern Jalisco, southern Durango, and southern Zacatecas and were also well established in parts of Guanajuato and southern Jalisco. In the first weeks of 1927, thousands more men in Colima, Michoacán, and the "Los Altos" region of eastern Jalisco answered the LNDLR's call to mobilize against the government.[60] The cristeros continued to depend on hit-and-run tactics against their better-armed, better-supplied, and more numerous enemies, holding on to towns and larger villages for short periods before melting back into the countryside in the face of federal counterattacks. But a lack of support and supplies often forced the soldiers to return to their barracks soon after retaking a town,[61] and their lack of cavalry left them vulnerable to the lightning attacks of mounted cristeros, many of them revolutionary veterans who had spent their lives in the saddle.[62]

The momentum of the rebellion against Calles continued to grow, and by spring 1927 Quintanar's forces had obtained pledges of loyalty from formerly pro-government caciques across southern Zacatecas and northern Jalisco, including those of Mezquitic and its satellite pueblo of Nostic.[63] Quintanar's men remained unassailable in Huejuquilla, which served as the capital of the cristero "shadow state" that Quintanar's deputy and local LNDLR representative Aurelio Acevedo established in the region.[64] Like most twentieth-century Latin American insurgent movements, the cristeros saw the creation of alternate institutions as vital to formalizing and legitimizing their political program.[65] Acevedo oversaw the creation of a postal service, a system of archives (which preserved many of the documents cited in this chapter),[66] and offices responsible for regulating the cattle trade, overseeing the rationing of grain, and enforcing a "Catholic" moral code that banned civilians and soldiers alike from swearing, drinking, gambling, and engaging in sex outside of marriage and also mandated conservative dress for women.[67]

Meanwhile, in Durango, cristero bands led by Valente Acevedo, Porfirio Mayorquín, and Federico Vázquez left Mora's camp early in the new year and headed deep into the Sierra O'dam. Although suffering from a lack of arms and ammunition, they managed to recruit (or press-gang) many local men (and boys) into their ranks.

FIGURE 3 Children conscripted into Federico Vázquez's rebel forces in Durango (ARA/ Sección Gráfica/492).

Military intelligence described Acevedo as dominating by mid-1927 the western part of the Sierra O'dam,[68] while Vázquez, using a mixture of persuasion, coercion, and the promise of booty (mainly in the form of cattle), rallied much of the eastern sierra to the cristero cause.[69] In the latter region, Juan Andrés Soto, cacique of Santa María Ocotán and commander of the community's defensa, declared for Vázquez and in classic cacical style was backed by his brother Pedro, their close relatives Felipe, Gerardo, and José Soto Aguilar, and many of their familial-factional allies.[70]

Porfirio Mayorquín set up his base in Jacalitos, an anexo of Teneraca that lay in the center of the Sierra O'dam, along the camino real connecting Nayarit's coast to the city of Durango. From there he integrated into his forces around eighty O'dam from Teneraca under Dario Soto (unrelated to Juan Andrés)[71] and also persuaded José María Gutiérrez—one-time head of San Francisco Ocotán's defensa and the community's most important leader—to join him.[72] As one elderly O'dam informant from Teneraca explained, "As you should know, one who speaks well . . . can gather many followers."[73] Taking advantage of Jacalitos's proximity to his home turf in northern Nayarit, Mayorquín also recruited O'dam and Mexicaneros from San Andrés Milpillas[74] and a few conservative Náayarite from Dolores and Santa Teresa whose general hostility toward mestizos like Mayorquín was outweighed by their opposition to the cosmopolitan rule of Mariano Mejía and his Náayari allies.[75]

Farther to the southeast, Florencio Estrada launched a cristero uprising in Huazamota in January,[76] hoping to establish his own cacicazgo and unseat his cuñados, the pro-government Muñoz clan who had taken power in the region in the context of the factional, interethnic, and cross-state conflicts that accompanied the last years of the armed revolution in southern Durango.[77] Initially backed by few outside his immediate family (his twin brother, Frumencio, and younger brother, Jesús, were his first and most loyal followers), on February 20, 1927, he met up with Quintanar himself in Huejuquilla (a town historically linked to Huazamota by ties of marriage, trade, and the cult of Huejuquilla's miraculous image of the Divine Prisoner).[78] Estrada was officially incorporated into Quintanar's forces as "Squadron Commander" of the Huazamota region, with the rank of major.[79] Soon afterward, at the nearby hacienda of San Juan Capistrano, Zacatecas, Sebastián Arroyo raised a force of twenty-four men, "all of them well mounted, although lacking ammunition,"[80] who further facilitated communications amongst Quintanar to their east, Estrada to their west, and Mora's lieutenants in the O'dam communities to their north.[81]

In response to the cristeros' growing strength and organization, Generals Anacleto López and Eulogio Ortiz developed a "three-pronged counter-insurgency strategy" in the region, which centered on negotiating the surrender of cristero leaders, "reconcentrating" civilian populations, and arming civilian auxiliaries.[82] "Reconcentration" entailed forcing dispersed rural populations to leave their ranches, on pain of death, for towns garrisoned by federal troops, to choke off the rebels' supplies of food and new recruits. Meanwhile, Ortiz and López distributed weapons to loyalist regional caciques, who in turn offered protection from cristero raids and the possibility of state support for local agrarian struggles to anyone who pledged their loyalty to the Calles regime (and, naturally, to their own cacical authority).[83] Some civilians were thus persuaded to join pro-government agrarista defensas voluntarily, while others knew that if they refused, they would be persecuted as cristero sympathizers. These men quickly won for themselves a reputation for bravery and brutality matching that of the cristeros,[84] above all, according to their descendants, because of the hardship that such service entailed. "There weren't enough tortillas to go round, so they said, 'I'm hungry, I'm thirsty, and I'm angry, we've gotta shoot these bandits like we mean it!' Damn, how you suffer when you go off to fight."[85]

Agrarista militias were vital to the government's scorched-earth campaigns in southern Durango and northern Jalisco and Zacatecas, helping federal flying columns to destroy homes and crops and to corral dispersed rural populations into more easily defended towns (seen as the only way of isolating the cristeros from their civilian supporters).[86] Meyer is ultimately right in arguing that across rural Mexico this strategy "was overused, destroying without ever pacifying, waging the war ever further afield and making it ever more severe."[87] The violent repression of urban sympathizers and the military's murder of several priests (including Cristobal Magallanes in Colotlán) pushed many into joining the cristeros.[88] But López and Ortiz's counteroffensive also allowed them to take back the initiative from the cristeros in and around the Gran Nayar.

For example, in summer 1927, encouraged by the army's offers of support, many of the men of Nostic, led by Apolonio González, went back on their pledges of loyalty to Quintanar, ambushed and killed the village's main cristero commander, and drove his supporters from the village. They then marched on Mezquitic, where they were joined by the town's caciques and their followers and organized themselves into a new pro-government defensa force of around "sixty armed men and twenty without weapons."[89] Their maneuver prompted others in Tenzompa and La Soledad to abandon the cristero cause, allowing the influence of pro-government forces to creep ever closer to the Sierra Wixárika.[90]

In southern Durango, federal forces meanwhile established "garrisons from Durango to Mezquital, connected to one another by 110 km of telephone lines,"[91] before General Ortiz himself headed into the western Sierra O'dam in March 1927, in pursuit of "the forces commanded by the rebel chieftain Acevedo."[92] The return of federal troops to the region—and the arms, ammunition, and other supplies they brought with them—emboldened the remaining loyalist caciques of the Sierra O'dam, who organized their followers for battle against the cristeros. In Santa María Ocotán, for example, Cosme Solís, a local O'dam who also happened to speak Spanish, emerged as the leader of a small pro-government defensa, "as the government sent him weapons from Durango, for his followers . . . they gave him thirteen, with which to defend the family, and they named him 'Commander of the Militia' (Jefe de Armas)."[93]

At this stage, the Sierra Náayari remained relatively untouched by the upheaval in neighboring areas of Durango, Jalisco, and Zacatecas or by the smaller uprisings breaking out in other parts of Nayarit. Although by June it was rumored in Tepic that the Náayarite "have risen up in arms for religious reasons," in reality the situation in the sierra stayed calm enough for pro-government caciques Mariano Mejía and Eutimio Domínguez to continue supporting the SEP's "educational crusade . . . as they have enthusiasm and a great desire for the dissemination of education, in the places under their care and command."[94]

However, regional SEP inspector Florencio Orozco also warned that

> the Sierra is a complete nest of Indians and a nest that lacks light, where for this reason the gloom of obscurantism reigns . . . to combat this great evil, it is essential to put before every source of fanaticism, a light-bearing torch, or that which is the same thing, a School, with a true priesthood of science at its head, so that with their words, they dispel the shadows and create light, which is the precursor of civilization and progress, which once achieved, will bring the redemption of the Indian.[95]

Given the lack of Catholic influence on the Náayarite in this period, Orozco's emphasis on the need for churches to be replaced by schools is probably less evidence of Náayari "Catholicism" and more of an illustration of the reductionist nature of contemporary discourse on the "religious question" within the SEP, which led many officials to see all Indian ritual activity, however unorthodox, as Catholic "fanaticism."[96] However, his report, for all its messianic fervor, also indicates that the conflict was edging ever closer to the Náayari communities of Nayarit—hardly a surprise given that by now there were anywhere from seven thousand to twenty thousand cristero fighters active across the country.[97]

The cristiada finally arrived in the mountains of Nayarit in July 1927, when Porfirio Mayorquín launched a major cross-border offensive from his base in the Sierra O'dam, first raiding Huajicori and then descending on his hometown of Acaponeta.[98] The statements of eyewitnesses to Mayorquín's successful taking of both towns on July 27 hint at the success of his recruitment drive amongst the O'dam, describing his three-hundred-man force as formed entirely of "people from Durango, all Indians."[99] In the aftermath of these attacks, "all the prisoners they had liberated, and the police and their commander" were forced to join Mayorquín's forces;[100] which further supports the assertions of informants in the Gran Nayar today that cristero recruitment strategies depended more on the time-honored Mexican tradition of *la leva* (press-gang) than on inspiring local Indigenous people to "defend" a faith that, in their own communities, Calles's anticlericalism had never really threatened.

Farther south, a significant number of Náayarite from San Pedro Ixcatán, San Juan Corapan, and Rosarito now declared for the cristeros, setting up camp with their families in a nearby canyon and raiding the surrounding rancherías.[101] Some were motivated by their opposition to Eutimio Domínguez's cosmopolitan cacicazgo in the Náayari Baja, but according to local informants, others wanted no more than to "rob and eat meat."[102] These Náayari rebels likely cooperated with another band of cristeros, active nearby, whose attacks "forced the female teachers of Teponahuastla, Paramita and San Juan Bautista to flee for the town of Rosa Morada."[103] The increasing violence hit the economy of the entire Sierra Náayari, disrupting the harvest and local trade routes and causing "an absolute shortage of everything that could be called an item of basic necessity."[104]

At this stage of the conflict, however, the majority of those Náayarite who were actively involved in the fighting—themselves a minority compared with the neutral civilians, known as *pacíficos*—were members of defensas loyal to either Eutimio Domínguez or Mariano Mejía. Domínguez and his followers soon tracked down the local cristeros. Spotting the smoke from their fires at dawn, they attacked their camp from two sides but found most of their enemies had already fled: "The only one they killed was someone still bathing himself." In a shocking demonstration of the cruelty with which both sides treated civilians accused of sympathizing with the enemy, Domínguez's infuriated militiamen—many of whom had lost cattle to cristero raids—then murdered the women and children left behind in the rebel encampment: "Over there was a baby, which they lifted up with a knife. . . . And an old woman, old, who was eating meat, and my grandfather grabbed the hot meat and smacked her in the face with it, 'Look, you're eating the meat from my cow!' No, so his companion, so she didn't suffer, shot her there and then."[105] Thanks in part to such brutality, by October 1927 the two caciques of the Sierra Naáyari had crushed the initial outbreaks of cristero activity in the region. One newspaper article, which declared that "In Nayarit the Natives Fight for the Return of Peace," described them as commanding a total force of "more than 600 natives fully armed and munitioned," which had "efficiently contributed to the extermination of the bands of rebels that were threatening the tranquility of the Northern regions of this Entity."[106]

Elsewhere in Nayarit, however, it was soon reported that as "the battalions and regiments are of very recent formation, the recruits pass with arms and munitions to the side of the rebels." Cristero forces regained the initiative in many areas, "assaulting pueblos and shooting any agraristas and obregonistas they find."[107] These failures were blamed on Nayarit's military zone commander, General Teodoro Escalona, a veteran Carrancista from Veracruz who "knew absolutely nothing of the local terrain and could do little to pursue these rebel groups." Calles therefore replaced Escalona with Juventino Espinosa, "a Nayarit-born General who knows the state perfectly and can go after and perhaps completely destroy the rebels who refuse to leave the inhabitants of smaller settlements in peace." But top-level personnel changes could not solve the problem of lower-level defections to the cristeros, especially in the Sierra Náayari, where a local SEP official warned that Mejía and Domínguez were increasingly struggling to maintain control of

> the Indians, as commissions from various states such as Durango, Zacatecas and Jalisco arrive amongst them, desiring that they raise up all of the Náayarite and Wixáritari against the Federal Government . . . [which] would pose a full-blown military challenge given the Indians populating those regions number more than 10,000.[108]

Increasing cristero incursions into Nayarit point to both the increasing strength of the cristero movement across Mexico as a whole and the growing coordination of insurgent groups in Durango, Jalisco, and Zacatecas. In autumn 1927, a cristero commission left San Juan Capistrano, Zacatecas, to "conquer for our Cause the cacique Mejía of the pueblo of Jesús María, Nayarit."[109] Around the same time, Felipe Sánchez, cristero leader in the southern Zacatecan canyons, gained the allegiance of "the people of the Bolaños River and Azqueltán and the Wixáritari pueblo of San Sebastián,

FIGURE 4 Wixárika cristero leader Juan Bautista and his lieutenants (ARA/Sección Gráfica/792).

forming a contingent of around 500 men" (although Sánchez admitted that, like most of the cristero troops, they were "much lacking in ammunition").[110]

In the Sierra Wixárika, as in the Sierra O'dam, costumbre defined the limits of the regional campaigning season. Under their leader Juan Bautista, alias "El Tzakaka" (for the shape of his sombrero, which resembled the cones of unrefined cane sugar called *piloncillo* in Spanish, or *tzakaka* in Wixárika),[111] the Wixáritari of San Sebastián joined the cristeros only after they had taken in that autumn's harvest and ritually transformed the sacred corn into the stuff of human sustenance. It was also, unsurprisingly, around this time that many of their Wixárika rivals in Santa Catarina, angered by cristero depredations, declared for the government. The communal assembly "arrived at an agreement to request weapons and all that"[112] and asked Agustín Carrillo—the community's preferred intermediary in its dealings with the state—to organize a communal defensa.[113] Carrillo traveled to Zacatecas to meet with General Anacleto López and "bring back guns and ammunition."[114] López rewarded Carrillo's loyalty by assigning him the rank of colonel[115] and sent for five members of the community to come to his headquarters at the hacienda de Las Víboras "for training. In those days the men wore their hair in plaits, [but] as they'd been called up for training they shaved their heads. . . . My father spoke little Spanish, but there they taught him to speak, too."[116] However, the weapons that López sent back with these men to Santa Catarina were less than the community had hoped for, and many of Carrillo's fighters were forced to face their cristero enemies with no more than "bows and arrows, and slingshots, and rocks. It wasn't much progress at all, was it?"[117]

HUNGER, VIOLENCE, AND THE INTENSIFICATION OF THE CONFLICT IN THE GRAN NAYAR, SPRING/SUMMER 1928

The intensity and geographical spread of the Cristero Rebellion increased throughout 1928.[118] By January of that year an estimated 23,400 cristeros had taken up arms, and huge swathes of the northern, western, and central Mexican countryside were in flames.[119] In the Sierra O'dam, the fighting had prevented many families from planting their crops and still more from bringing in the harvest, leaving local cristeros, pro-government defensas, and federal troops alike dependent for sustenance on the age-old local practice of cattle rustling.[120] Food shortages and cattle rustling encouraged more local people to take up arms on either side to protect scarce supplies or to gain more through raiding. By the beginning of 1928, most O'dam and Mexicaneros had abandoned their homes and were either hiding out in caves and canyons and surviving on wild greens, tubers, and other traditional famine food, or they were taking part in guerrilla warfare throughout the sierra.

Farther south, federal confiscations of comestibles also hit Quintanar's forces hard,[121] but they were cheered by cristero commander-in-chief General Gorostieta's recognition of Quintanar as leader of all the cristeros of northern Jalisco—a zone whose importance as a center of cristero activity was exceeded only by Gorostieta's own stronghold in the Altos de Jalisco.[122] Quintanar's fighters, who now numbered several thousand men,[123] were further emboldened by their chief's successful efforts to secure new allies amongst the O'dam, Náayarite, and Wixáritari, boosting the regional momentum of the rebellion.

In January 1928, Federico Vázquez's forces left the Sierra O'dam to help Quintanar rout a federal force based near Huejuquilla,[124] and the Wixáritari of San Sebastián joined mestizo cristeros under Quintanar and his lieutenants Justo Ávila, Felipe Sánchez, and José "Pepe" Sánchez in the conquest of Mezquitic.[125] Their victory neutralized the threat that Mezquitic's pro-government forces had posed to the cristero "capital" of Huejuquilla[126] and dramatically inverted the power relations between the Wixáritari and the local municipal seat, whose inhabitants had frequently encroached on San Sebastián's lands.[127] Unsurprisingly, Bautista's men and their allies celebrated their victory by burning much of the town and systematically "confiscating" all the cattle they could find.[128] Local caciques Luz and Natividad Robles were killed, pro-government defensa commanders Apolonio González and Griseldo Salazar were forced into hiding, and a cristero civil administration was established in the ruins of the pueblo.[129]

Government loyalists in the Sierra Náayari suffered an even more dramatic reversal in the first days of 1928, as Mariano Mejía, under pressure from cristero commissions and rebel raids, decided to switch his allegiance to the cristeros. The Náayari forces under his command—the same men once lauded by government officials as "the only ones who have been bothered to defend their communities"—now chose, or were forced, to follow Mejía in his defection, prompting the few teachers left amongst the Náayarite to flee from "the fanatical hordes."[130] Náayari conservatives who already sympathized with the cristeros were thus temporarily reunited with Mejía's cosmopolitan allies under the banner of their joint rebellion against the revolutionary state. Many more of the Náayari pacíficos who had so far avoided involvement in the fighting on either side were incorporated into the ranks of Mejía's rebel army on the strength of promises of arms and booty and the threat of violence against those who refused to join what, at this point, must have appeared to be the winning side.[131] "He grabbed them all by the balls. Some without weapons, just like that, others with bows, or slingshots, others with hoes, with which to stab when the fighting was face-to-face; that was what that war was like."[132]

From being a pro-government bulwark against the incursions of cristeros from neighboring states, the Náayari Alta was transformed into a center of rebel activity only a few days' march from Tepic. Mejía quickly began an audacious advance on the state capital. Where the sierra gives way to Nayarit's central altiplano at Pochotitán, Mejía's army was finally stopped by loyalist local defensas and a detachment of federal troops under Major Reyes Orozco in a battle still remembered throughout the region.[133] Mejía's forces took up positions on the hills surrounding the town, and using mortars that the government had given them before their defection, destroyed houses, shops, and a school that federal troops had been using as their barracks.[134] Pochotitán's defenders repulsed Mejía's repeated attempts to capture the town; "Mariano's Náayari soldiers couldn't go any further, the military met them with bullets and forced them back."[135] Running out of ammunition and increasingly demoralized, the rebels retreated into the sierra. "When [the defenders] made it up the hill, there were no cristeros left there, they were already crossing the river, leaving their blankets and sombreros and the rest of their shit there in their dugouts."[136] The pro-government forces gave chase,[137] but the Náayarite, experts at guerrilla fighting, "positioned themselves on the crests, and when the soldiers came up the slopes, they used levers to roll boulders down on top of them . . . the Náayarite eventually fled, but only after killing plenty of soldiers."[138]

Despite Mejía's defeat, Calles feared that "the subversive movement developing in Nayarit was fairly significant" and ordered General Antonio Ríos Zertuche, Sonora's zone commander, to march south "with sufficient forces . . . to combat the sedition threatening to unfold there."[139] Eutimio Domínguez remained loyal to the government in the face of Mejía's defection and played a key role in federal efforts to "take on the rebels of Jesús María."[140] Although not as devastating as the internecine conflicts between their Wixárika neighbors,[141] the differing loyalties of the Sierra Náayari's caciques provoked a rare burst of intercommunal Náayari conflict, as Domínguez, according to informants in Jesús María, "came to fight against the Náayarite from here; yes, I remember well . . . the multitude there rose up, they are Náayarite too, brothers of ours. They burned a load of nearby houses, Náayari houses . . . and they stole cattle, took all the bulls back down [to the Náayari Baja], all rustled cattle, it was 'let's go!' with any that they found."[142]

Oral testimony from the Náayari Baja presents Domínguez, a local hero, as fiercely opposed to such looting.

> He said, "Take care, boys! I don't want you to go robbing things. . . . If you find money, leave it! Because we are not going there to steal. If you see a horse with a new saddle, leave it! 'Cos whoever I find untying it, 'BANG!' I'll leave you right there, because you're a bandit too. Equally, if you see a girl approaching, leave her! Don't grab her, don't embrace her, because it is bad!"[143]

But in addition to the defensas of the Náayari Baja, Domínguez was accompanied by Náayarite from La Mesa, under former bandit chief Mariano Solís,[144] who had no such qualms. "It suited him to go over there with [Domínguez] because there was cattle, probably someone else's, and money, maize, whatever one might find, and also women to make tortillas. . . . Everything that was there, they took."[145] Informants in Jesús María agree, adding that "they chased our fathers away with bullets, many of the Náayarite here were rich in cattle, but most of it they took away back down there."[146]

Despite his continuing losses, Mejía rejected a federal attempt to win his surrender—allegedly on the advice of Nayarit's governor, Francisco Ramírez Romano, who was an anticlerical in public but "privately maintained close relationships with Catholic leaders, including the head of Nayarit's Knights of Columbus."[147] Instead, Mejía and his remaining followers fled to his birthplace, Huaynamota, where they "constructed walls of stone, lots of fortifications."[148] From here they could more easily obtain supplies in Tepic and launch raids on the towns of Nayarit's altiplano[149] and were also protected from federal counterattacks by the Río Santiago on one side and "the beautiful mountains" on the other.[150]

Worried by the stalling of Mejía's rebellion, the cristero leadership sent José Gutiérrez to Huaynamota in late January to put an end to "the anarchy and impose discipline on certain elements who appear to confuse the defence of 'the cause' with their personal interests."[151] In his memoirs, Gutiérrez leaves an interesting description of the cristero bands of the Sierra Náayari, whose numerous chiefs by this point commanded only

> small groups which together would scarcely have amounted to a regiment, picturesque and genial to be sure, as it would have been made up of soldiers of very varied types; from

> the well-formed white, well-dressed and with some learning, to the humble and ignorant Wixárika Indian, dressed miserably and armed with a bow and a handful of arrows.

As well as lacking weapons and ammunition, Mejía's failed attack on Pochotitán demonstrated a shortage of strategic know-how. Mejía and his lieutenants therefore claimed that

> we have no ambitions to lead; we want an able cristero chief to come and organise us; we want ammunition and only ammunition; we want to work together so that the campaign is truly effective, that our enemies would really feel it.[152]

Gutiérrez assured Mejía that such help would arrive soon and hurried back to Guadalajara. A friend of General Gorostieta, José Posada Ortiz, was offered command of Nayarit's cristero forces, but he rejected the post. Soon, "seeing the promises the Western Cristero Command had authorised us to make them going unfulfilled,"[153] Mejía returned to Pochotitán in early March 1928, this time to sign a peace deal with Nayarit's zone commander Juventino Espinosa.[154]

In Pochotitán's central plaza, Mejía's dispirited cristeros, "passing in two files with their blankets on their shoulders and their barrels of their weapons pointing to the ground," heaped their weapons together before "dousing them with petrol and setting them on fire in a symbolic act marking the end of the social struggle."[155] Granted amnesty, many of them returned to their roles as federal auxiliaries, serving in the Náayari Alta's reconstituted defensa forces under Mejía's Náayari compadre and former lieutenant León Contreras. Mejía himself was meanwhile imprisoned in Tepic, where, the story goes, he miraculously survived three separate assassination attempts[156] before he was finally sent to the notorious Islas Marías prison colony off the coast of Nayarit.[157] Mejía's rebellion thus came to a desultory end, and Nayarit's pro-government press triumphantly announced that in the Sierra Náayari "pacification is now complete, thanks to the energetic incursion that the Federal troops have carried out in that region."[158]

SCORCHED-EARTH TACTICS AND "SHADOW STATE-BUILDING" IN THE GRAN NAYAR

While the government made momentary gains in Nayarit, the O'dam and Mexicaneros of Durango remained under heavy pressure from both sides. In March 1928, the army defeated Valente Acevedo near his home at Llano Grande.[159] Trinidad Mora and Porfirio Mayorquín arrived with reinforcements too late to help Acevedo defend his village, which the soldiers razed before heading on toward San Bernardino. The second aspect of federal counterinsurgency strategy came into play soon after, as the federals returned from San Bernardino backed by a large number of what the cristeros called "agraristas"—presumably local O'dam, given the cristeros at first mistook them for "people who had stayed in order to join our forces." Acevedo, Mora, and Mayorquín were again defeated and forced to retreat deeper into the sierra, whose inhabitants vanished at the first sign of their approach. Francisco Campos writes that

> we arrived at an Indian ranch, but there was no one there, we saw steam coming from one place and went to see what it was and it was an oven in which they had been cooking agave, but obviously the *inditos* felt something bad and fled their ranch; we took the roast agave out to eat it, but it was completely raw. We couldn't eat anything.[160]

As the violence caused food shortages and general hardship for the region's inhabitants, increasing numbers of local men and boys began to join the region's pro-government defensas,[161] including those headed by Cosme Solís in Santa María Ocotán and Chon Aguilar and José Flores in Xoconoxtle. By this point, Solís had pledged himself to the miraculous patron saint of the Mexicanero community of San Pedro Jícoras, receiving in return both physical and spiritual power.[162] Building on this connection, in April 1928, a group of O'dam "enemies of the cause" from Santa María Ocotán, led by Solís's cousins Gregorio, Sixto, and Hilario Mendía and their friends Manuel, Saturnino, and Hilario Flores, established a base in San Pedro and set about incorporating the local Mexicaneros into their pro-government force.[163]

Santa María's cristero leader Juan Andrés Soto reacted quickly to the emergence of this new threat, attacking San Pedro, defeating the Mendía clan and their local allies, and seizing their horses, cattle, and weapons. His cristero forces also murdered the elder in charge of San Pedro's communal mitote patio as he tried to stop them kidnapping his wife. This sacrilegious act caused a storm to flood the community, followed by a plague of locusts, which together wiped out the year's harvest[164] and forced San Pedro's remaining civilian inhabitants to flee their homes.[165] But despite this victory, a month later Soto reported that in Santa María "other new government loyalists . . . joined the pro-Calles Mendía and Flores families, creating a larger number of enemies."[166] Around the same time, many of the Mexicaneros of San Buenaventura, which bordered the Náayari community of Santa Teresa, and those of Santa Cruz de Guajolota, an anexo of the Náayari community of Saycota, were conscripted into pro-government Náayari defensas.[167]

The newly reconstituted Náayari defensas of Nayarit, aided by federal troops, put new pressure on the Wixáritari of northern Jalisco, pressing toward San Andrés Cohamiata from the south and west. The inhabitants of San Andrés found themselves

FIGURE 5 Wixárika cristeros, somewhere in Jalisco—note the child soldiers on the far right (ARA/Sección Gráfica/798).

caught between pro-government forces and the cristeros of Huejuquilla, Tenzompa, Mezquitic, and San Sebastián to their north and east. This likely explains the strenuous efforts of San Andrés's leaders to remain neutral.[168] However, Juan Bautista and his Wixárika cristeros demanded they join their cause[169] and launched punitive raids against San Andrés's government sympathizers and neutral civilians alike.

Bautista's forces were more determined still to punish the inhabitants of San Sebastián's main political and territorial rival, pro-government Santa Catarina, and those of Tuxpan, whose leaders Cenobio Sánchez de la Cruz and Zenón Romero had resisted Bautista's influence and remained loyal to the government.[170] The Wixárika cristeros and their mestizo allies "took away the cattle, killed people, and robbed maize, leaving the people without food."[171] They also killed and kidnapped civilians with impunity: murdering elderly women by impaling them on stakes[172] and abducting younger women to work for them as cooks and porters: "If they liked a woman, they'd take them away and no one could say anything."[173]

The inhabitants of Tuxpan and Santa Catarina also feared that Bautista would destroy or steal their santitos and other sacred images. Iconoclastic soldiers and government officials often committed such acts in this period.[174] However, as an active participant in the Wixárika cult of the saints, Bautista—like his predecessor Mezquite—was no Jacobin; rather, he wanted to debilitate his enemies by taking control of their most prized, powerful possessions. In both Tuxpan and Santa Catarina "they took all of the saints out, and went around hiding them, in this cave, over here or over there, like that, it was terrible!"[175]

For the same reasons, Bautista and his men also destroyed the tukite, as well as shrines known as *xirikite,* that were affiliated with their pro-government rivals. Informants in Las Latas, one of Santa Catarina's most important anexos, bitterly remember Bautista's raids.

> That was when they razed the ceremonial center, you can still see the burn marks. . . . They burned all of the roof, and the little houses [of the peyote pilgrims] and their fields, everything was lost. All of the place's blessings were looted and destroyed, that which is tradition, the trajectory of the past, the survivals from before, the culture, which enables life, for all humanity, and for all of nature.[176]

Bautista's cristero forces also sacrilegiously attacked the inhabitants of Pochotita—another of Santa Catarina's main anexos—as they celebrated the Fiesta of the Peyote, one of the most important dates in the Wixárika ritual calendar.

> People from San Sebastián came, armed with machetes and bows and arrows, and cerrojos, and some also had rifles. In those times my father Pablo was commander of the defensa. He thought [the cristeros] were his comrades, with another two or three of his men they went on foot to greet them, but they were forced back by gunfire. . . . The rebels chased Pablo's men and arrived in Pochotita, where many people were gathered. Pablo and his men shouted at their fellows, "they're coming! They're attacking us!" and everybody went running, to the caves, to hide themselves. They burned our tuki temples, the maize, food, houses, they burned everything.[177]

Naturally the cristeros stole what they could from the many "rich people" then living in Las Latas and Pochotita, but Bautista's main aim, according to local informants, was to seize Santa Catarina's título virreinal.[178] However, "an old lady, eighty years old, hid it in her skirts . . . who knows, she was probably crossing herself or something, so they didn't kill her."[179] The community's claim to territory long disputed with San Sebastián was thus preserved. However, Bautista's depredations forced Santa Catarina's population to abandon their homes for "the roughest places possible, which most people can't enter."[180] Unable to make fires for fear of revealing their positions to the enemy or to plant corn or carry out their pilgrimages, they were effectively forced to abandon their costumbre. As a result, "there was lots and lots of sickness, and floods . . . because the offerings were lacking in those days."[181] Because of Bautista's raids, Tuxpan also effectively ceased to exist: "after the war started, there were no topiles, or governors. . . . Up there above they celebrated fiestas, but here in Tuxpan they couldn't. There were no people here."[182] Some left the Sierra Wixárika altogether, taking refuge "in the neighboring pueblos, such as Bolaños and Villa Guerrero, with the object of saving the lives of themselves and their families."[183]

Inevitably, in San Sebastián itself, those who "disagreed with the preaching of the Holy War . . . were [also] forced to flee."[184] They were replaced by mestizo cristeros and refugees from across the region (including Wixáritari, mestizos, and even a few rebel priests)[185] who helped to defend the community against the advances of the defensas that once again dominated the sierras of Nayarit.[186] However, these forces were increasingly unable to withstand the attacks of their rivals in Huajimic, "fiefdom of los Muñoz, caciques hostile to the cristeros and allies of the Guzmán clan of Bolaños."[187] As well as attacking Bautista and his allies, stealing cattle, and terrorizing Wixárika civilians, Huajimic's caciques used their support for the government's cause as a pretext to continue their invasions of San Sebastián's communal territory, two thousand hectares of which Petronilo Muñoz laid claim to in 1928 alone.[188]

Regional cristero commanders warned Quintanar that "those Pharisees are getting stronger with every day,"[189] prompting him to try to put a definitive end to the threat that Huajimic posed to his Wixárika allies and simultaneously strike a blow against the resurgent pro-government forces of the Náayari Alta. In early May, Quintanar ordered mestizo, Wixárika, and O'dam cristeros to advance on Huajimic, Jesús María, San Juan Peyotán, and Huazamota. If they were victorious, they stood to gain control of the strategically important Jesús María Canyon.[190] On May 6, Florencio Estrada led one hundred men in an attack on Huazamota,[191] which had become a pro-government enclave surrounded by "throngs of revolutionaries." After several hours of "hard fighting," the village's defensa, commanded by Estrada's brother-in-law Tiburcio Muñoz, retreated to the tower of the church, where they surrendered soon after. Four were promptly shot,[192] but the violence did not stop there; while Florencio celebrated his victory, his men

> began to put under the knife those who had resisted them. Only the women begging Florencio to save the lives of los Muñoz prevented the massacre of Huazamota's pacíficos and government loyalists, and prolonged the vengeful wrath of los Muñoz.[193]

Farther to the south, federal forces arrived in time to help León Contreras and his Náayari fighters repel an attack on Jesús María, and Bautista's Wixárika rebels, backed by mestizo cristeros from Zacatecas, were forced to draw back from Huajimic after the arrival there of pro-government reinforcements from Huaynamota.[194] On May 20, the cristeros who remained in the area briefly occupied San Juan Peyotán but were forced to make a final, definitive retreat at the approach of federal reinforcements from Jesús María.[195] However, the operation marked the start of a new phase of increased cooperation amongst all the Gran Nayar's cristero forces, regardless of which side of the local state borders they happened to be on. And soon after, during a near-identical second joint offensive,[196] Juan Bautista and his allies managed to raze much of Huajimic to the ground.[197]

Around the same time, Juan Andrés Soto proved that he and his men were more than just cattle rustlers during the infamous battle at Cerro de las Papas. For more than a year, southern Durango's cristero bands had been struggling with federal forces under Colonel José Ruiz for control of "the gorges of Taxicaringa, Teneraca and other indigenous pueblos."[198] In June 1928, Ruiz heard that Trinidad Mora was camped near Santa María Ocotán and decided to surprise him there.[199] Mora and various followers were heading to Huejuquilla for a meeting with Quintanar and had stopped en route at a ranch where pro-cristero O'dam were "celebrating a mitote according to their custom"[200] (implying that, unlike the Wixáritari, many O'dam and Mexicaneros were still able to perform their descent group rituals).[201] Mora continued on toward Huejuquilla the next morning with a small escort, and the rest of his men remained at the ranch, where they held their own impromptu fiesta. However, that afternoon

> two worried-looking O'dam arrived and talked to us in O'dam, they made signs in one direction and the other, but we didn't understand them, nor they us. . . . Eventually they left, and we thought that there must be some kind of danger. . . . We halted our fiesta and sat there thinking about this indigenous embassy, and then at five in the afternoon there came another two O'dam who spoke more Spanish and told us that two Federal columns were approaching, trying to surround us.[202]

The cristeros decided to ambush the soldiers within a high-walled canyon at Cerro de las Papas.[203] Knowing the federals would contract local men as guides, Juan Andrés Soto sent his lieutenant, Luciano Carrillo, and a few other trusted men to volunteer their services and lead Ruiz's column into a trap, agreeing they should wear red bandanas to distinguish themselves.

Colonel Ruiz accepted Carrillo's offer and put the O'dam at the head of his column.[204] "Once they had nearly arrived at the hill, [Carrillo] took out his red handkerchief. . . . As if sensing that something was happening, the soldiers asked him why, but he said 'No, it's just to wipe away the sweat.' 'Ah okay,' they said, 'let's keep going.'"[205] But once the unfortunate soldiers entered the canyon, the cristeros hidden above began shooting and rolling boulders down on top of them.[206] "They could only hear the gunfire, they couldn't see who was shooting because they were lying flat up there, hidden. The mestizos couldn't do anything but drop."[207] Ruiz was wounded in the hand, "but with his left hand took out his pistol"[208] and "continued firing even after he fell. He began to crawl and crawl until he took shelter in a cave. . . . They came closer to him and Juan Andrés asked, 'So what, you came for my head?' 'Yes, but I couldn't, you're a real devil, more than I am,' said the mestizo. 'I've fought in many places and I was always far above everyone, but I couldn't defeat you, despite the fact you're just any old O'dam.'" Juan Andrés then removed the mestizo's hat (today believed to have contained a protective charm) and dealt him the coup de grace.[209]

It is unclear how many soldiers died in the ambush, but although it likely resulted in fewer casualties than the three hundred local sources often claim,[210] it is clear that, in the words of an informant from Yonora, "there they caused a lot of death. . . . Yes, they were nasty those scuffles!"[211] The story highlights the vulnerability of federal troops—many of them conscripts unfamiliar with guerrilla warfare in unforgiving mountain terrain—when faced with enemy forces who had spent their whole lives in the sierra. It also underscores the dangers inherent in the federals' reliance on civilian auxiliaries and is further evidence of the difficulties that outsiders—both mestizo soldiers and cristeros alike—faced in trying to communicate with the inhabitants of the Gran Nayar in this period, increasing their dependence on bilingual Indigenous leaders.

Rebel O'dam caciques took advantage of their positions as mediators between mestizo cristero commanders and the local population to consolidate their regional political influence, just as their predecessors had done during the decade of armed revolution. Juan Andrés Soto, after his victory at Cerro de las Papas, attempted to cement his control over the eastern Sierra O'dam, sending seventy men to Santa María Ocotán to track down "the authority . . . named by the Government, who was already dead when they got him, as he had tried to run as soon as he saw our comrades." Luciano Carrillo meanwhile led an attack on a pro-government O'dam defensa being formed in San Francisco Ocotán, "where the Callista chieftain who had tried to lead that movement was successfully caught and immediately exterminated."[212]

However, just as Quintanar himself struggled to maintain discipline and enforce "Catholic morality" amongst the diverse coalition of cristero bands he commanded,[213] so too Juan Andrés Soto faced a serious challenge in trying to curb the excesses of his followers—an essential step in legitimizing their politico-military control of the sierra. In June, he asked for Quintanar's advice regarding the complaints of civilians in Santa María, who accused some of the local rebels of being far from austere soldiers of Christ.

> They are always trying to enjoy entertainments like dances and drunken sprees, all of them scandalous; for which reason I have seen to write to you, so that you might remedy these difficulties and order these abuses to be stopped, because it does not benefit in any way those who are defending our cause that they have gatherings in those ranches as attested by said complainants.[214]

Quintanar's second-in-command in Huejuquilla, Luis Montellano, responded by warning Soto to act with "prudence, much prudence, so that it is not because of bad feelings or a trivial act that you come to the wrong conclusions and commit some injustice."[215] But he also sent Soto a copy of the General Regulations recently drafted by the cristero civil authorities and, seeing an opportunity to expand the reach of the cristero "shadow state" into the Sierra O'dam, stressed the need for Soto to organize an effective civil-military administration in the areas under his control, which meant establishing a postal service, sending weekly reports to Huejuquilla, forming his men into squadrons "organized according to the guidelines set out for this by the League," and fighting "without respite . . . [against] all those who refuse to subject themselves to order."[216]

In response, Soto and his men elected the mestizo Juan Sifuentes as civil-military chief of the entire Sierra O'dam, "as he is more capable in the performance of such a role."[217] Sifuentes, a close friend and compadre of Juan Andrés Soto, had married an O'dam woman and settled in Santa María Ocotán before the outbreak of the rebellion[218] but was also a Spanish speaker who had completed four years of primary school and was literate enough to have briefly served as a rural teacher.[219] He was therefore an ideal figure to bridge the cultural and ideological distance between Quintanar's mestizo cristeros and the O'dam rebels. His appointment was quickly approved by Montellano,[220] who hoped he would be able to "unify where possible the command of the contingents disseminated throughout the sierra of Santa María Ocotán and the neighboring pueblos."[221]

However, Sifuentes still depended on Soto and other O'dam chiefs for the support of the local population. Despite the efforts of Quintanar's cristero administration to increase its authority over the Sierra O'dam, Soto therefore remained preeminent in Santa María Ocotán and tried to legitimize his power by taking control of communal costumbre from the local elders,[222] bypassing their traditional authority by imposing his ally Fernando Cumplido as the community's governor, a move that Quintanar backed by officially recognizing Cumplido in his position "in light of your sympathy for our Holy Cause."[223] Although followers of the rival Solís and Mendía families undermined such efforts by hiding the community's varas and santitos,[224] these pro-government O'dam were forced to request a new official seal—an important traditional symbol of authority—for "our Governor . . . because the rebels have seized it from us."[225]

Disputes over control of objects and rituals associated with legitimate authority are often central to Indigenous power struggles,[226] so it is not surprising to find that many O'dam communities were wracked by such conflicts. Teneraca's pro-government faction took the community's varas de mando with them into exile in San Andrés Milpillas after their cristero rivals forced them to flee.[227] And O'dam and Mexicanero descent groups broken apart by conflicting allegiances during the cristiada established new spaces in which to practice their costumbre free from the ritual pollution of relatives who were now factional enemies.[228] Such actions utterly undermined everything that O'dam and Mexicanero costumbre was meant to maintain—the internal unity of communities and descent groups, the integrity of their territories, and peace and tranquility not only in the Sierra O'dam but throughout the universe—and demonstrated the extent to which local leaders on both sides of the national-level conflict subverted local gerontocratic power structures, which had traditionally overseen both communal and descent group ceremonialism.

At this point the cristero shadow state was also expanding into the Sierra Wixárika, where San Sebastián's cristero chief Juan Bautista and his followers, who enjoyed complete politico-military autonomy when not taking part in "official" campaigns, continued to mercilessly target all those who refused to join them. By now, much of the Wixárika population knew cristero forces dominated northern Jalisco, southern Zacatecas, and southern Durango and continued to ravage the Sierra Náayari. Many were also aware of president-elect Álvaro Obregón's assassination by a lone Catholic militant in July 1928[229] and of the publication of the cristeros' official political manifesto, the Plan de Los Altos, in October.[230] In this context, growing numbers of Wixáritari believed the cristeros, despite their chronic lack of ammunition, would emerge victorious. So despite the continued presence of pro-government forces in San Andrés and Santa Catarina,[231] rival factions in both communities tried to use Quintanar's increasing politico-military reach to win concessions, just as they had previously sought to take advantage of the Sonoran regime's state-building efforts.

One group in San Andrés, although still not sufficiently convinced of cristero victory to fully throw themselves into the fighting, wrote to Quintanar "manifesting our desire to not be considered supporters of the tyrant Calles and his associates." They asked that he send "some members of the Catholic forces" to the region to help them arrest a local pro-government leader who had fled for the protection of Agustín Carrillo in Santa Catarina. They alleged he had offered to guide federal troops to San Andrés, threatening both the neutrality and the safety of their community. Their actions appear to have been based on personal grudges as much as political considerations, however, as he "took away the wife" of one of them as punishment for not joining his pro-government force and "for that reason we are wanting you to give us guarantees so we can sort out our issues."[232]

Huejuquilla's cristero commanders recognized that maintaining control of the Sierra Wixárika was important to the success of their wider regional campaigns and therefore granted to the pro-cristeros of San Andrés "full protection so you may live in peace and dedicate to your habitual labors."[233] In response to a similar petition launched on behalf of Santa Catarina's neutral inhabitants by Juan García, a local leader formerly considered an agrarista,[234] they also agreed to curb cristero raids on that community's pacíficos. García alleged that

> because of . . . Agustín Carrillo, Antonio Ávila and others who have taken up arms against the [cristero] party that you defend, we are suffering and have suffered cruel discomforts, and, as all of these armed men have withdrawn from these ranches, there remain only those peaceful people who have never mixed themselves up in anything, working only to maintain our families, worrying daily that we will be troubled by these [pro-government] forces and also by the Wixáritari of the Pueblo of San Sebastián.[235]

García and his copetitioners pledged to remain neutral, but this was not enough for Huejuquilla's cristero commanders, who in return for halting their attacks demanded that

> you give us immediate warning of whatever movements our enemies make in those regions, and that if any Wixárika or mestizo of those who took up arms against our religion presents himself, you take him prisoner and deliver him to the military command of Tenzompa or to this headquarters.[236]

Shortly after this exchange, and at the explicit request of Juan Bautista, the cristeros of Tenzompa delivered arms to García's pro-cristero faction in Santa Catarina's anexos of Taimarita and Pedernales.[237] Their combined forces then went on the offensive and secured "the surrender of thirty-four indigenous government loyalists distributed throughout the Sierra of Mezquitic." In the same month a separate cristero expedition surprised and defeated Santa Catarina's defensa (which had retained control of the community's cabecera), "almost managing to take prisoner the Wixárika Agustín Carrillo."[238] Despite these cristero victories, however, the majority of the Wixárika population continued to try to avoid involvement on either side, either by hiding out in the Sierra Wixárika or by seeking refuge in nearby mestizo pueblos or in the Náayari communities of Nayarit.[239]

THE APOGEE OF THE CRISTIADA IN THE GRAN NAYAR, WINTER 1928

Fighting throughout the Gran Nayar reached a peak during the harvest months toward the end of 1928.[240] Quintanar's cristero command became concerned that pro-government O'dam forces, "which we believed almost completely extinguished,"[241] were once again "entering into activity and which before long might constitute a real threat to the security of the sierra."[242] After Santa María Ocotán's pro-government defensa, led by the Mendías, ambushed and killed Luciano Carrillo,[243] Huazamota's cristero chief Florencio Estrada was ordered to march on Santa María and

> give encouragement with your example to the O'dam, obliging them to not delay any further an offensive against these enemies who have not stopped being, if not a danger to the Movement as a whole, then a serious obstacle to our communications and a constant threat to our comrades in the sierra.[244]

However, cristero ammunition shortages impeded their planned counteroffensive,[245] allowing the defensas of Santa María and Xoconoxtle—who possessed such a surfeit of ammunition that in just two skirmishes with Estrada and Juan Andrés Soto's forces, they used up well over one thousand cartridges—to retain the local initiative.[246] Estrada was forced to beg Quintanar to send "some two hundred bullets to the followers of Pedro Soto who have nothing in their rifles, and from whom los Mendía recently carried away some cattle, and have not been able to take them back because effectively many of them have not a single cartridge."[247]

Federal forces meanwhile readied themselves for an ambitious new campaign across much of the Gran Nayar, targeting "the remains of the vandals still roaming over there, and who one hopes will very soon receive the severest chastisement." General Eulogio Ortiz marched south from Durango into the Sierra O'dam, General Juventino Espinosa set off from Tepic into the Sierra Náayari at the head of more than six hundred cavalry,[248] and General Desiderio García led a third federal flying column to San Juan Peyotán. There, the federals were reinforced by the defensas of the Náayari Baja under Eutimio Domínguez,[249] the defensas of the Náayari Alta under León Contreras and Mariano Solís, the pro-government exiles of Huazamota under Tiburcio Muñoz, and the O'dam defensas, whose knowledge of southern Durango's mountains would be of vital importance to the success of the offensive, billed as "a gathering together of all the Sierra's pueblos in a concerted attack on the enemy."[250]

In the ensuing campaign, federal forces and their local auxiliaries took decisive control of the Jesús María Canyon.[251] At the same time, on the other side of the mountains, defensas from the Bolaños and Zacatecan canyons and southern Nayarit[252] and one thousand well-armed and supplied federal troops (including cavalry) routed local cristero forces,[253] allowing the Guzmán family, under military commander José Guzmán "el Chico," to take back control of the area.[254] The onslaught continued into 1929, as Durango's zone commander Francisco Urbalejo, working closely with the well-supplied O'dam defensas and Huazamota's pro-government exiles,[255] pursued the local cristeros almost as far as Huejuquilla itself.[256] Federal troops also embarked on a new round of "reconcentration" to "deprive the rebels of provisions and bring the campaign to a quick finish."[257] Throughout the Gran Nayar, "hunger began to overwhelm those families who had decided to stay in the mountains to protect their property," forcing many O'dam, for example, to subsist on "no more than cowhide because they were dying of hunger."[258]

Despite the government's advances, cristero forces still dominated the Sierra Wixárika and much of the Sierra O'dam. Meanwhile, the Sierra Náayari remained a war zone. Although Jesús María was garrisoned by federal troops and León Contreras's defensa, other Náayari communities continued to suffer from cristero raids and the "absolute absence of guarantees caused by the ongoing religious revolution."[259] The ongoing violence blocked the return of Náayari refugees to their homes and of teachers and other SEP officials to the region's ruined government schools.[260] Local informants remember cristero raids making the practice of costumbre nearly impossible, as "the bandits burned everything... they burst into the middle of the fiestas, 'bang!' Son of a bitch, no one could celebrate their fiestas properly, because of those bandits arriving."[261]

Given their suffering at the hands of government forces during Mejía's rebellion, however, few Náayarite trusted the federal military either: "When the government came, we hid ourselves. Because we didn't know what they were after. We'd run off to the river, to the canyons, to hide there perhaps two or three days." In the face of terror and worsening famine, which forced them to depend on famine foods such as breadnuts, ever more Náayari civilians either fled their communities or took up arms themselves.[262]

SNATCHING DEFEAT FROM THE JAWS OF VICTORY: FROM THE ESCOBARISTA REBELLION TO "LOS ARREGLOS"

By early 1929, the Cristero Rebellion had reached a critical stage across all of central-western Mexico. Federal "reconcentration" efforts inflicted misery on hundreds of thousands of civilians without seriously threatening the cristeros, whose numbers were constantly increasing. January alone saw 135 combats between cristeros and government forces, while in February, functionaries' wages were cut by 30 percent to finance federal campaigns in Jalisco, Michoacán, and Guanajuato.[263] Throughout the spring, cristero General Gorostieta toured the Jalisco-Zacatecas borderlands in an attempt to "give a more militarized form to the cristero forces."[264] Federico Vázquez and Florencio Estrada left their mountain strongholds to meet with Gorostieta in Huejuquilla before joining the rest of southern Durango's cristeros in an attack on Mezquital a few weeks later. They routed the troops General Urbalejo sent to defend the town, killing around two hundred of them.[265] If we believe the naturally rather partisan cristero sources, the humiliation of this defeat helped push both Urbalejo and Durango's governor Juan Gualberto Amaya into joining Coahuila zone commander José Gonzalo Escobar in revolting against Calles on March 3, 1929.[266]

The so-called Escobarista rebels were mainly followers of the slain president-elect Álvaro Obregón. They aimed to depose Obregón's replacement, Emilio Portes Gil, and the man they accused of being behind his assassination, Plutarco Elías Calles, who as the so-called Jefe Máximo de la Revolución remained Mexico's de facto supreme leader. In addition to General Urbalejo and Governor Amaya, Escobar won the support of the zone commanders of Sonora, Veracruz, and Chihuahua, along with a third of federal officers and some thirty thousand troops.[267] The uprising naturally undermined the government's anti-cristero campaign, but more worrying still for Calles and his allies was Escobar's announcement that he would work with the cristeros to overthrow the government, an offer the LNDLR readily accepted.[268]

Although a unified cristero-Escobarista rebel command was never established, complicating their effective coordination, the new uprising reinvigorated cristero forces, who stormed towns and even cities across the country and suddenly seemed on the brink of victory. In Durango, the forces of Trinidad Mora and Valente Acevedo managed to work with Escobarista battalions under Juan Gualberto Amaya to take control of the state capital, while their allies completely dominated the Sierra O'dam.[269] In Nayarit, federal troops from the north of the state were sent to fight rebel troops in Sinaloa,[270] allowing Porfirio Mayorquín to raid across the region, challenging Major Reyes Orozco for control of Acaponeta and again taking Huajicori, killing the commander of its defensa in the process.[271] Loyalist troops were also withdrawn from Jalisco and Zacatecas and sent to fight the Escobaristas in Coahuila, Sonora, and Chihuahua. In both of the former states,

> all of the areas left ungarrisoned were occupied by the rebel fanatics who gave themselves over to every kind of excess and depredation, thus sowing panic and obliging a general reconcentration of all parts of society.[272]

Quintanar's cristeros occupied Colotlán, and then in combination with rebel forces from neighboring areas looked likely to take Zacatecas itself.[273]

But then the Escobarista uprising imploded. The United States cut supplies to the rebels and sent new weapons to Calles, who distributed them to agraristas across Mexico, above all in the north.[274] Agrarista militias and federal forces together defeated General Urbalejo in central Zacatecas on March 9, as Calles loyalists in Veracruz defeated rebellious naval units and a planned revolt in Oaxaca stalled. Durango's rebel governor Juan Gualberto Amaya panicked and fled the state capital,[275] allowing loyalist soldiers and agrarista militias from northern Durango to retake the city and force Trinidad Mora and Valente Acevedo to retreat back into the sierra.[276] Federal units from central Mexico defeated Escobar himself at Torreón on March 17, while General Lázaro Cárdenas, backed by airplanes and gunboats, crushed the rebels of Sinaloa and Sonora.[277]

Gorostieta was disillusioned by the disintegration of the Escobaristas, whose leaders seemed more concerned with robbing banks than overthrowing the government.[278] In late March he complained to Aurelio Acevedo that

> our situation, instead of having improved, has worsened with the military uprising. . . . If that movement ends in failure, "The Turk" [Calles] will turn back to us. And he will come with many men, enthusiastic and proud of their victories against the military rebellion, and they will face off against our forces, lacking in ammunition as usual, but now compounded by the lack of civilian support, and I do not doubt that then, they might indeed manage to put a stop to our movement.[279]

On May 3, just as Gorostieta had feared, Calles declared the Escobarista revolt officially defeated and turned his fully mobilized forces on the cristeros. General Saturnino Cedillo and his well-trained twelve-thousand-man militia arrived in Jalisco from San Luis Potosí, severing lines of communication and supply between the cristeros of Huejuquilla and their allies in Los Altos.[280] Presidential decrees mandated the deportation to the Islas Marías of any woman caught supporting the LNDLR—constricting flows of ammunition to the cristeros—and the confiscation of property belonging to civilian sympathizers, encouraging the army and its auxiliaries to systematically pillage rural communities across central-western Mexico.[281] In southern Durango, this looting caused "a fifty percent reduction in agricultural production" and "the destruction of [the state's] cattle wealth."[282] On June 2, 1929, in a further blow to cristero morale, General Gorostieta himself was killed in an ambush.[283]

On June 29, after months of secret negotiations, the Mexican episcopacy, backed by the Vatican, signed a peace treaty—referred to euphemistically as *los arreglos* (the arrangements)—with President Portes Gil, supervised, of course, by "el jefe máximo" Calles. The cristero political leaders within the LNDLR were forced by their clerical superiors to accept the treaty and in turn ordered the cristero army to follow suit. Although they had appeared close to victory only a few months before, in July 1929 the cristeros' rebellion officially came to an abrupt end. In the Gran Nayar, as in many of the peripheral regions of western Mexico where support for the rebels had been strongest,[284] the fighting between pro-government forces and cristeros did not come to an immediate halt.[285] But deprived of the material and moral support of the LNDLR, lacking the church's blessing to legitimize their struggle, and subjected to continued federal military pressure on the one hand and constant offers of amnesty on the other, most of the Gran Nayar's cristeros had demobilized by the end of the year and a fragile peace returned to the region.

EXPLAINING NÁAYARI, WIXÁRIKA, O'DAM, AND MEXICANERO PARTICIPATION IN THE CRISTERO REBELLION

Few in the Gran Nayar today use the terms *Cristero Rebellion* or *cristiada* to refer to the conflict that devastated the region between 1927 and 1929. But tales of leaders like Mariano Mejía, Juan Bautista, and Juan Andrés Soto and of battles between pro-government and rebel forces during the late 1920s dominate local oral traditions of "the revolution." In fact, this bloody and traumatic period still serves as a common point of reference for Náayarite, Wixáritari, O'dam, and Mexicaneros of all ages when they try to explain more recent local violence, such as that associated with Mexico's ongoing "drug war."

To many in the Gran Nayar today, the Cristero Rebellion was above all defined by banditry and especially by cattle rustling carried out by the cristeros, who are often accused of rising against the government only in order to "go and steal things."[286] Taken at face value, such statements suggest that the conflict was in part a class struggle: a rebellion of poor subsistence agriculturalists against wealthy cattle-ranching elites. The rise of many of the revolutionary era's pro-government caciques had been tied up with their ownership of cattle, which inherently challenged both the political and economic dominance of local elders who had previously controlled both communal governments and the provision of shamanic services paid for in livestock. Thus economic rivalries, mainly centered around cattle ownership, inflected the political conflicts that were the primary motive for the participation of the Gran Nayar's population in the cristiada.

However, material factors rarely "generate revolt in isolation . . . even when mediated by the attitudes and traditional value systems of the population."[287] Moreover, in the Gran Nayar, both pro-government and pro-cristero factions were made up, for the most part, of poor subsistence farmers. Their leaders, meanwhile, whether conservative or cosmopolitan, Indian or mestizo, tended to be amongst the wealthiest members of their communities. As neither side in the cristiada locally represented either "the rich" or "the poor," the conflict cannot have been a class struggle per se.[288] Instead, the stress that oral accounts of the cristiada put on material factors in explaining local mobilization has more to do with local informants' "peasant's eye view" of the world. Friedrich observed that in rural Michoacán, peasants explained social conflict "in terms of such ultimate life symbols as corn, a shortage of tortillas, and the expropriation of the land."[289] In relation to the cristiada in the Gran Nayar, the "confiscation" of cattle seems to be precisely such a life symbol, rather than a material cause of local mobilization.[290]

But if we cannot take at face value the retroactive analysis of local informants alone,[291] then how can we explain why so many in the Gran Nayar fought for or against the rebels during the cristiada? The answer lies in respecting informants' explanations of particular behaviors and actions while also, in line with the exhortations of James C. Scott, supplementing—rather than trying to replace—these with information taken from sources unavailable to local people.[292] The following section therefore combines oral accounts with historical documents, anthropological literature, and a critical analysis of the (limited) extant historiography in an attempt to, in the words of both Friedrich and Thucydides, "expose and make fully intelligible" the factors—not only material but also political, social, and religious—that shaped Náayari, Wixárika, O'dam, and Mexicanero participation in the first Cristero Rebellion.[293]

NAYARIT: THE NÁAYARITE

Academics have tended to overlook the Cristero Rebellion in Nayarit in part because of the grander and more dramatic nature of the conflict in other parts of the country and in part because of the popular myth, widely propagated by successive state governments, that "no cristeros existed" in Nayarit.[294] If scholars have paid little attention to the role that the state's mestizo majority played in the cristiada, most have completely ignored the participation of Nayarit's Náayari minority. Even Avitia Hernández, whose work on the rebellion in southern Durango frequently touches on events in the north of Nayarit, writes that "as far as we know, the Náayarite stayed on the margins of the conflict."[295]

The most important exception to this rule is Jean Meyer, who has long taken a special interest in the history of Nayarit. In *La cristiada*, Meyer briefly mentions the Náayarite as having taken part in the rebellion "as individuals and not collectively."[296] Meyer is right in that there was no "mass" Náayari cristero movement. Some Náayarite fought as pro-cristero rebels, others as auxiliaries of federal forces. Many of them actually fought on both sides, first as members of pro-government defensas, and then, after Mariano Mejía defected to the cristeros, as rebels, before switching their allegiance back to the government following Mejía's surrender. Many more abandoned their homes so as to escape the conflict, leaving their rancherías and communal cabeceras uninhabited and the agricultural cycle and the costumbre that went with it neglected.

Meyer argues that the Náayarite did not join the cristeros en masse because they were "less Catholic" than the Wixáritari and O'dam, whom he claims overwhelmingly supported the rebellion.[297] Meyer is right to see the Náayarite as disconnected from orthodox Catholic beliefs. Despite the church's efforts to extend its influence over regions of Indian religious heterodoxy (or outright "heathenism") during the Porfiriato,[298] Preuss reported of the Náayarite just before the outbreak of the revolution that the "ceremonies they celebrate on the feast days of the Catholic calendar . . . contain almost no Christian elements."[299] In fact, he argued that in general, they had "in no way understood the doctrines of the Christian religion,"[300] given that

> their desires are all of a worldly character, and do not refer to the beyond. They do not know the concept of sin, except in the sense of violating the rule of fasting and maintaining sexual abstinence in the run-up to a ceremony. The consequences of these kinds of transgressions are that the rituals will not have the desired positive effect, and that the participants will end up harmed.[301]

This situation had changed little by the 1920s, during which period most Náayarite, even those with ties to cosmopolitan communal political factions, continued to practice their traditional costumbre both inside and outside of churches.[302] They had little contact with priests, who tended to side "with regional Vecino cattle merchants and politicians" against traditional Náayari authorities[303] and encouraged mestizo settlement in the sierra. Most Náayarite in fact remained hostile to "official" clerical Catholicism into the 1940s, when they were still described as reluctant to "attend the rites of the church" and distrustful of priests in general, "above all those wearing habits, because they say that these ask for too much money and carry diseases under their robes."[304]

It is worth noting that despite their distance from orthodox Catholicism, the cults of Catholic santitos did play an important part in Náayari costumbre. This meant that during the cristiada, Náayari fighters—like the Yaqui rebels of the nineteenth century[305] or the Zapatista fighters during the revolution[306]—often rallied around images of saints when going into battle. This was not a phenomenon limited to pro-cristero factions, however, and thus cannot be interpreted as evidence of "Catholic" beliefs as motives for Náayari sympathies for the rebels. In fact, the anti-cristero fighters of Eutimio Domínguez were perhaps more devoted to their local saints than were their local cristero rivals; they boasted that "no one was ever wounded . . . because we carried our 'images,' which help you so that no bullets or anything else can touch you."[307] Domínguez himself was reputed to have enjoyed a special relationship with his community's patron, San Juan: "That santito still belongs to him, really . . . he had special prayers to make sure nothing happened to anyone, and those five bodyguards of his, and the rest of the soldiers too, no one ever killed any of them."[308]

Meyer is therefore right to rule out "Catholicism" as a factor that directly influenced Náayari participation in the cristiada. However, popular religious feeling, the influence of priests, and the suspension of Catholic services did generate sympathy for the cristeros amongst many of the sierra's mestizos and probably had an indirect effect on the loyalties of some Náayarite. By early 1927, members of the clergy were preaching against the government in mestizo Rosamorada and El Venado, on the borders of the Náayari Baja, and in San Juan Peyotán, within the Náayari Alta itself, where "by means of leaflets, flyers, and their own voices they exhort mothers not to send their children to the Federal Rural School because it is atheist, protestant and heretical, and the female teacher suffers insults and harassment from the most fanatical locals."[309] In San Juan, the priest even "excommunicated all those parents who sent their children to the school."[310] Local mestizos who were thus persuaded to turn against the government probably helped to win over some of their Náayari neighbors to the cristero cause. Other Náayarite reacted against the cristero sympathies of their rivals by seeking an alliance of convenience with the state.

The most important example of Catholic pressure indirectly influencing Náayari participation in the cristiada can be found in Mejía's defection to the cristeros in late 1927, precipitated as it was by the arrival in Jesús María of a cristero commission headed by Father José Cabral. Almost all of the members of the communal defensas under Mejía's control were forced to follow him over to the cristero side.[311] "Mejía used to call the people together, inviting them to take part in some work, or to attend some meeting or other business, and they always answered the call, so they trusted him when he asked them to go [against the government]."[312] It seems likely that Mejía's decision to join the cristeros was influenced by some ideological sympathy toward the church and its representatives and perhaps even by the "Catholic" political ideologies they promoted. After all, Mejía was a mestizo who had been partly raised and educated by a priest, had married in a church,[313] and was described by the cristero José Gutiérrez as a "Christian man."[314] His defection was certainly legitimized in his own eyes by the sermons of Father Cabral, which helped to convince many of Jesús María's other mestizo residents to join the cristero cause. Cabral's preaching may even have inspired a few local Náayarite to join the rebels, likely prompting the complaint of Nayarit's director of federal education that "the Indians are extremely ignorant and fanatic and as the priests who used to officiate [elsewhere] in the state live amongst them, they incite them and as Federal forces have never managed to get to those distant places, the instigators enjoy almost complete impunity."[315]

Despite such complaints, it seems clear that relatively few Náayarite—especially outside Jesús María—threw in their lot with the cristeros on the basis of anti-government preaching or their outrage at the suspension of church services that they rarely attended in the first place. The historian Enrique Bautista González, in a short monograph on the cristiada in Nayarit, instead suggests that local agrarian tensions generated Náayari sympathy for the rebels, arguing that "groups of Náayarite pushed forward their agrarian demands" by joining the cristeros.[316] But although agrarian problems influenced the decisions of many Mexican peasants—including O'dam and Wixáritari—to join the cristeros or, conversely, to fight as federal auxiliaries, this cannot have been the case in the Náayari Alta. There, thanks to Lozada's rebellion, the difficult local geography, the power of intercommunal Náayari costumbre, and Mejía's unifying military leadership during the armed revolution of the previous decade, intercommunal agrarian tensions simply did not exist in this period, to the extent that not a single petition for dotación or restitución was launched from any Náayari Alta community before the early 1940s.

Although Bautista González's assertion that agrarian conflicts encouraged Náayarite to become cristeros is untenable, it does seem that, in the Náayari Baja at least, such conflicts had the opposite effect, helping to shore up Domínguez's pro-government stance and by extension the loyalties of the men and women of the communities under his control. Unlike the communities of the Náayari Alta, Eutimio Domínguez's strongholds in the Náayari Baja had faced threats to their landholdings during the Porfiriato.[317] These became more acute in the immediate postrevolutionary era, thanks to the region's geographical proximity to the land-hungry villages and haciendas of the coast and because elites in Acaponeta, Rosamorada, and Santiago Ixcuintla sought to use their jurisdiction over the communities of the Náayari Baja to seize their communal lands. In response, San Pedro Ixcatán unsuccessfully petitioned the federal government for a copy of its título virreinal in 1922;[318] in 1924 a maestro misionero was able to apply for a dotación on behalf of Saycota, and Eutimio Domínguez's community of San Juan Corapan began to petition for official recognition of its traditional landholdings in 1927.[319]

This early agrarista activity in the Náayari Baja directly involved only a few individuals but constituted a reaction to pressures that affected many more local people besides. As the authorities of Corapan and Ixcatán would not have been able to launch their agrarian petitions in this period without at least the tacit support of Eutimio Domínguez, it would seem that the Náayari Baja's most important leader sympathized with the form of agrarismo they professed (especially given his own need for secure access to communal landholdings on which to graze his cattle). Like many contemporary Mexican caciques, whether Indian or mestizo,[320] Domínguez's participation in—and even patronage of—local agrarian claims no doubt reinforced his own ties to the revolutionary state, influencing his decision to remain loyal to Calles throughout the Cristero Rebellion, even in the face of Mejía's defection to the rebels.

Both Catholic fervor (or lack of it) and agrarian commitments (or lack of them) had important, direct, and immediate effects on Mejía's and Domínguez's ultimately divergent loyalties. In turn, the power of these two caciques was the most important single factor in determining the allegiances of the Náayari majority.[321] Meyer hints this was the case, asserting that after Mejía's detention and exile, the Náayarite were left without leaders to "incorporate them into one or other cause."[322] But his assumption that Mejía was the only cacique of any importance in the Sierra Náayari during the Cristero Rebellion and that his role had been an exclusively unifying one oversimplifies the complex effects of caciquismo on the Náayari population.

As discussed in the previous chapter, the armed power of the region's two caciques and of their subordinate defensa commanders posed a serious challenge to the authority of traditional Náayari cargo holders and elders, around whom opposition factions soon coalesced. The growing influence of these "conservatives" prompted many defensa commanders to fortify their own positions by more closely associating themselves with Mejía, Domínguez, mestizo colonists, and local SEP officials, further inflaming factional tensions. When cristero rebels began to arrive in the sierra in early 1927, many Náayari conservatives saw them as potential allies in their conflicts with pro-government caciques, especially as both groups found common ground in their opposition to government education programs.[323] Thus although the cristeros were mainly Catholic mestizos who regarded Náayari religious practices as heretical, small groups of Náayarite in both the Náayari Alta and Baja regions joined cristero bands. Meanwhile, Mejía and Domínguez called on the communal defensa commanders (who were less autonomous than their equivalents amongst the Wixáritari or O'dam), together with their cosmopolitan Náayari allies, to help defend the Callista order.

The influence of caciquismo and factionalism on popular Náayari loyalties was compounded by the local population's need for security amidst widespread violence. Many factionally neutral Náayarite were swayed toward the pro-government side by the coercive power of Mejía and Domínguez. These caciques commanded forces that were better armed and organized than the small bands of conservative Náayarite who initially sided with the cristeros. Choosing the stronger side by joining either Mejía or Domínguez was almost a form of self-defense. "Náayarite, Wixáritari and mestizos . . . he had them all by the balls. Without blankets, without anything, with no more than what they could grab, and 'Let's go! If you have weapons, bring them, and if you don't, here are some weapons!' And like that, who could stay behind?"[324] Such press-ganging was all the easier given that many of those conscripted were mere children at the time: "Whoever could carry a weapon went along, or was taken along. Like don Chano, they say he could barely hold a rifle, you know, he was only about twelve, or less, maybe eight or ten years old."[325] The importance of caciquismo and the need for physical security—a constant concern for peasants across Mexico in times of conflict[326]—in deciding Náayari allegiances is further substantiated by the fact that the members of many Náayari defensas became cristeros almost overnight, following the defection of their leader, Mariano Mejía, before again changing sides after his surrender to the government.

The coercive pressures that caciques on both sides of the Cristero Rebellion applied to the bulk of the Náayari population were compounded by the economic attractions of joining the fighting. Although the cristiada in the Sierra Náayari was not an economic conflict per se, it was certainly a conflict inflected by economic considerations, as both sides took advantage of the tumult to attack political opponents and rival descent groups and, above all, to steal (or "confiscate") cattle and other goods for economic gain.[327] As the fighting caused ever more disruption to local agricultural production, many more politically neutral and religiously disinterested Náayarite took up arms to defend their families and livestock from raiders or to obtain food by becoming raiders themselves. It is hardly surprising, then, that the cristiada is locally remembered today as less of a political or religious conflict than as a war between rival bands of cattle rustlers.

The last major factor determining Náayari participation was geography. Simple geographic circumstance played a key role in deciding Mejía's defection to the cristeros, Domínguez's loyalty to the federals, and the attitudes of the rest of the Náayari population to either side. Mejía's base in the Náayari Alta was far closer to areas of cristero influence—southern Zacatecas, southern Durango, and northern Jalisco—than were Domínguez's strongholds in the Náayari Baja. The cristero commission that visited Mejía in late 1927 would have no doubt reminded him that he was surrounded by cristero forces on three sides, at the same time proclaiming the "justness" of the cristero cause. The commission also arrived at a time when the cristeros appeared increasingly ascendant across central-western Mexico, Mayorquín's forces were actively raiding throughout the north of Nayarit, including within his own cacicazgo, and the position of Mejía's most important ally, State Governor Francisco Ramírez Romano, had become unsteady because of accusations that he tacitly supported the rebels. Mejía hedged his bets and defected to the cristeros.

Domínguez faced less cristero pressure than Mejía, as the Náayari Baja was far from any major rebel power centers. And he was also subject to more serious sanctions from the government if suspected of disloyalty, as his cacicazgo lay much closer than Mejía's to the government-dominated central and coastal regions of Nayarit (and to the Guadalajara-Tepic-Mazatlán railway, an important federal military thoroughfare).[328] Domínguez therefore stayed loyal to the government. The allegiances of Náayari civilians were influenced by these same military-geographical pressures twice over: both indirectly, in that such pressures helped to determine the loyalties of the Náayari caciques, and directly, in that their relative distance from either cristero or pro-government strongholds made declaring for one side or the other a better bet in their search for security.

JALISCO: THE WIXÁRITARI

The participation of the Wixáritari in the Cristero Rebellion has been subject to more academic analysis than that of their Náayari, O'dam, or Mexicanero neighbors. However, the shortage of documents relating to the Wixáritari in this period, and the difficulties of conducting historical research in the Gran Nayar, have left many scholarly assertions about the dynamics of Wixárika participation dependent on sources that actually concern the second Cristero Rebellion (1934–40).[329] Local oral accounts also frequently conflate the first rebellion with the second because "history" for many Wixáritari remains "a reflective history embodied in ritual and myth, rather than a recitation of events or a chronicle in the strict sense of the word." Furthermore, although some local narratives of the cristiada are actually good examples of history as "described in a chronicle rather than a ceremonial format,"[330] most of the stories of the period that circulate in the sierra today have been passed on to informants by their parents and grandparents, "when during the night, we watch the fire, sitting there and talking."[331] As a result of this mode of transmission, these tales often anachronistically compress together the first cristiada with the second, as well as with the revolution and even the rebellion of Manuel Lozada.

Historians, anthropologists, and many Wixáritari themselves therefore contest even such basic facts as the relative sympathies of each Wixárika community during the first cristiada.[332] The documentary and oral evidence presented earlier in this chapter indicates that Santa Catarina was mainly pro-government, San Sebastián pro-cristero, and San Andrés vaguely neutral. But it also substantiates the idea that Wixáritari who dissented from their community's majority opinion were forced to flee to outlying ranches within their communal territories, or farther afield to new settlements in Nayarit and Durango.

A second debate surrounds the issue of why the dominant factions within each of these communities (or in the case of Guadalupe Ocotán and Tuxpan, semiautonomous anexos) chose to take such differing paths and, in the words of Beatriz Rojas, "join the struggles of people apparently so different from themselves."[333] Meyer maintains that Wixárika religious feeling and friendships between many Wixáritari and Cristóbal Magallanes—the mestizo parish priest of Totatiche, murdered in 1927 by the army and later canonized as a saint and Catholic martyr—generated solid Wixárika support for the cristeros.[334] These two assertions are closely connected, as Meyer claims that Magallanes was responsible for what he qualifies as the church's successful "resumption of the Jesuit missions of the Gran Nayar" between 1860 and 1925[335] and thus of the conversion of many Wixáritari to a form of Catholicism that engendered sympathy for the cristeros.[336]

Before the revolution, however, Lumholtz and other foreign visitors observed that many Wixáritari were "clever enough to put on an external show of Christianity toward people from whom they expect some favour" but that in reality "the ancient beliefs, customs, and ceremonies still have a firm hold on the minds of the people," who snubbed priests and mainly celebrated non-Catholic rituals in their churches.[337] The violent expulsion of the Josefinos from their communities during the revolution is further testament to Wixárika hostility toward the church and its representatives. Meanwhile, there is no archival evidence that Magallanes ever visited San Sebastián, calling into question his relevance to cristero sympathies in that community. Magallanes did work toward the "evangelization of the Colony of Wixáritari" near Azqueltán—outside the Sierra Wixárika proper—between 1920 and 1921.[338] But he described the Wixáritari settled there as "entirely savage and idolatrous" (which he blamed on the Josefinos' earlier failures in the region)[339] and soon abandoned this mission in favor of catechistic work in the mestizo parishes of northern Jalisco that had been dissolved during the revolution.[340] It is difficult, then, to accept that Magallanes's death or the existence of a "Christian" component within Wixárika costumbre inspired many Wixáritari to mobilize against the government.

However, religious (rather than strictly Catholic) beliefs and practices did influence individual Wixárika sympathies during the cristiada, as well as the local dynamics of the conflict itself. Saints and holy images were important figures within Wixárika costumbre, and it is natural that both cristero and pro-government Wixáritari often rallied around them or, indeed, tried to steal them from their rivals. Attempted thefts of santitos were thus as common an occurrence in the Sierra Wixárika as in the rest of the Gran Nayar, to the extent that these sometimes motivated attacks on rival communities.[341]

Weigand also argues that the preaching of an individual clergyman—not Magallanes but an unnamed "cristero priest"—helped to persuade the Wixáritari of San Sebastián to join the rebels. This figure, who arrived in the community in late 1926, is probably the same "fanatical priest" who a regional SEP inspector claimed went into hiding in the Sierra Wixárika around the same time,[342] likely the militant padre Herculano Cabral, who was definitely living in San Sebastián by 1928.[343] Whoever he was, he told Juan Bautista and his allies that "the Federal Government was an instrument of Satan and, therefore, should be destroyed in the name of Christ the King."[344] The fact that such a message found a particularly receptive audience in San Sebastián's cabecera might be connected to the greater influence of Catholicism there relative to other Wixárika settlements. But it is unlikely that local people would have been won over to the cristero side by the priest's words alone, particularly as only a few spoke any Spanish and far fewer would have understood the apocalyptic references running through his anti-government discourse. Instead, the backing of a priest above all helped to legitimize Juan Bautista's own anti-government message.

Caciquismo, in the form of Bautista's leadership, was more critical than religious sentiment in generating Wixárika support for the cristeros in San Sebastián. Likewise, Agustín Carrillo's leadership played an essential role in shoring up the loyalty of most of Santa Catarina's inhabitants for the government. Meyer, who emphasizes the importance of both Bautista and Carrillo in this period, agrees that caciquismo was key to deciding Wixárika allegiances during the cristiada.[345] Carrillo and Bautista were able to exercise such power over their fellows because of their command of Spanish[346] and their ability as orators in their native tongue,[347] which had transformed them into influential mediators between their communities and the outside world in the immediate postrevolutionary period. This was not unusual, for as Benítez found in the Gran Nayar in the 1970s, "a people accustomed to the recitation of myths is sensitive to 'fine speech.'"[348] Patricio Mezquite had risen to power in a similar way a decade before,[349] and even today, Johannes Neurath notes that within Wixárika communal assemblies "that which [often] triumphs is not common sense, but rhetoric."[350]

It is hardly surprising then that Bautista in particular—described in the early 1930s as "friendly, gay, objective, and critical"[351] and "the Indian who is most influential, intelligent, and with the ambitions that most stand out" in all of San Sebastián—was able to rise to a position of great power within his community.[352] The charisma he radiated is reflected in the stories still told about his supernatural invulnerability, often attributed to a magical amulet he carried with him, made up of pieces of "a hawk, and the claws of a coyote . . . and also the tail of a horse . . . apparently he wore them around his sombrero, and because of it they couldn't kill him."[353] Thanks to the charismatic pull and political influence of both Bautista and his rival, Carrillo—along with their relative youth (a typical attribute of successful caciques across Mexico and beyond)[354]—they were able to persuade a significant number of their fellows to follow them into battle.

Although caciquismo was vital in shaping Wixárika participation in the cristiada (as it was throughout Mexico),[355] it was not completely decisive. After all, many Wixáritari ignored local leaders and attempted to stay neutral or even went against the sentiments of communal majorities and were forced to leave their homes. Bautista, Carrillo, and other Wixárika leaders must themselves also have had reasons for their radically different allegiances during the cristiada. To explain their divergent sympathies, as well as their success in mobilizing majority factions to their causes, we must look beyond the realm of religious belief and cacical charisma, which would have had less impact on popular sympathies if they had not somehow tied into the preexisting sentiments of many of their compatriots.

Archival and oral evidence points to Wixárika participation in the cristiada as ultimately determined by *serrano* impulses, encapsulated by Weigand as "a single basic idea: the preservation and defence of their communities, of their communal structures, and the cultural autonomy of the area."[356] Mestizo land grabs had long threatened the stability and cohesion of all the different Wixárika territories, while in the years immediately preceding the outbreak of the cristiada, their autonomy was threatened by the expansion of the revolutionary Mexican state into the Sierra Wixárika. Just as Purnell found for many villages in Michoacán,[357] amongst the Wixáritari it was therefore communal rivalries and land disputes, together with the effects of the Mexican state's agrarian reform and school-building programs, that played the pivotal role in shaping both popular and cacical sympathies at the outset of the cristiada.

Maintaining or reclaiming control of their communal territories had driven Wixárika participation in the armed phase of the revolution. Subsequently, Santa Catarina and San Andrés put their faith in the authorities in Guadalajara for a solution to their agrarian problems. The existence of such patron-client relationships defined their attitudes toward the Mexican state for much of the 1920s (at least until the people of San Andrés violently rejected a government school in 1925). In the case of Santa Catarina, they can clearly be seen coming into play during the cristiada itself, as in October 1927, Jalisco's interim government backed Santa Catarina's claim before the federal authorities in the same month as Agustín Carrillo became a colonel in the federal army and began to take part in the regional anti-cristero campaign.[358] A few months later, the federal government officially recognized his community's agrarian petitions.[359]

The de facto alliance between agrarista factions in San Andrés and Santa Catarina and the state and federal authorities was compounded by the fact that both communities' longstanding mestizo rivals—namely Huejuquilla, Tenzompa, and San Juan Capistrano—sided with the cristeros. Thus it is hardly surprising that most of San Andrés's and Santa Catarina's inhabitants declared against the rebels, even if we discount the rather reductive assertion of former cristero leader Aurelio Acevedo that Agustín Carrillo's anti-cristero position had been "dictated by the rich merchants (los Robles) of Mezquitic, a town which practically controlled life in Santa Catarina."[360] Conversely, because of their reluctance to engage in agrarian petitioning in the 1920s, San Sebastián's authorities lacked allies in the government at the outbreak of the cristiada, while the community's mestizo enemies in Mezquitic, Villa Guerrero, Bolaños, and Huajimic and their Wixárika rivals in Santa Catarina all remained loyal to the state. San Sebastián's leaders therefore decided that an alliance with the cristeros was the best way to "protect the community from outsiders, whether mestizos or Indians."[361]

The long-running dyadic conflict between Santa Catarina and San Sebastián helped to condition the radically divergent positions of the leaders of each community, positions which the majority in each community was naturally inclined to support.[362] But because of the tensions that had long existed between San Sebastián and its semi-autonomous anexo of Tuxpan, the inhabitants of the latter refused to rally to Bautista's leadership and declare allegiance to the cristeros, despite sharing San Sebastián's territorial problems. Tuxpan's loyalty to the government, which seems a little perplexing if viewed in purely agrarian terms, in fact lends weight to the idea that communal rivalry and territorial disputes played the most important role in deciding Wixárika allegiances during the cristiada.

The recent activities of the SEP also shaped Wixárika participation in the cristiada, mainly by tempering local support for the government that had been inspired by its promises of agrarian reform. The unsavory characters frequently employed as teachers, the meddling of these teachers in the agrarian reform process, and the threat the SEP's curriculum posed to Wixárika costumbre turned many Wixáritari against the revolutionary state that these teachers officially represented (as had also occurred in the Sierra Náayari and other comparable regions).[363] As no school had been established in Santa Catarina between 1920 and 1296, there had been no chance for drunken, abusive, or exploitative teachers to cast the Mexican state in a bad light in that community and undermine local support for the government. But San Andrés enjoyed a far more ambiguous relationship with the state. Although the community's leaders had faith that the federal authorities would help them resolve their agrarian conflicts, many local families received the rural teachers sent to their community with undisguised hostility, expressed violently in the case of Antonio Reza's lynching. The tension between these two opposing attitudes toward the state and its representatives accounts for San Andrés's generally noncommittal stance during the cristiada and the contacts that different members of the community established with either cristero or federal commanders.

Meanwhile, both the leaders and much of the general population of San Sebastián had come to the conclusion that the revolutionary Mexican state was impotent to help them with their agrarian problems, while the SEP—in view of the controversial initiatives of Inspector Hernández and his close association with the community's traditional enemies—actively threatened their political and territorial autonomy and the cohesion of their society. Such perceptions, combined with the added moral authority that a cristero preacher lent to the anti-government stance of a persuasive communal cacique, paved the way for San Sebastián to become a cristero stronghold.

As in the Sierra Náayari, such generalized anti-government sentiments took hold in San Sebastián all the more easily thanks to memories of their forebears' participation in previous rebellions. As Neil Harvey has shown in relation to highland Chiapas, any "process of mobilization will draw upon historical memory, cultural practices, and political symbols as much as on legal norms."[364] A connection between Bautista's rebels and their

Lozadista forebears is explicit in the statement of a mestizo informant from Tenzompa, who in the 1960s told Jean Meyer that "the Wixárika cristeros spoke of Lozada and said that he would have been their leader and would have led them to victory."[365] The more recent mobilization of many of the community's inhabitants under Patricio Mezquite must also have played a part in encouraging them to take up arms again under Bautista. Although informants agree that Bautista was still too "young and tender" to have served under Mezquite, he, like many young men in San Sebastián, "started to hear and know of" the many stories told about the Wixárika general's adventures, "and I think that Juan liked all of that. And that's why he must have risen up."[366] While the opposition of many in San Sebastián to the government and its regional allies led them to take up arms as cristeros, their decisions were compounded by memories of their recent "victories over the vecinos during the revolution proper."[367]

The motivations for Wixárika allegiances relative to the Mexican state or rebel forces during the first cristiada naturally helped to determine the way each community, or different groups within each community, participated in the rebellion itself. So too did the general desire for booty shared by Wixáritari on both sides of the conflict. The enthusiastic participation of Juan Bautista's men in the taking of Mezquitic, for example, was in part due to the town's status as a regional commercial center[368] whose leading citizens possessed large herds of cattle,[369] which were "highly revered" by the Wixáritari in religious terms and a key signifier of wealth and prestige.[370] Cattle rustling and generalized raiding became still more prevalent as people faced starvation as a consequence of the conflict's disruption of local agriculture. Thus, just as in the Sierra Náayari, many Wixáritari today remember the cristiada primarily in terms of the raiding that defined their forebears' participation in the conflict rather than the ideological or practical considerations that had prompted their joining either cristero or pro-government forces in the first place.

DURANGO: THE O'DAM AND MEXICANEROS

There has been less scholarly discussion of O'dam participation in the cristiada than that of the Wixáritari, and from fewer writers: namely Meyer, Avitia, and Antonio Estrada (son of cristero chief Florencio Estrada and author of *Rescoldo*, a novel based on his experiences during the second cristiada). All three present the vast majority of the O'dam as supporting the rebels; according to Meyer, "seventy-five percent of them were cristeros."[371] Meanwhile, only one scholar, the ethnologist Neyra Alvarado Solís, has ever mentioned the role of the Mexicaneros in the rebellion and asserts they were mainly the victims of cristero "thefts and violations."[372] However, many O'dam elders today are fiercely critical of cristeros, dismissing their actions as "nothing more than robbery,"[373] while the evidence presented in the first half of this chapter indicates that some Mexicaneros also took part in the conflict as fighters: "Those who liked to shoot their guns got involved. Some of them with Juan Andrés Soto, others with the government of Durango,"[374] and yet others as allies of the defensas of Náayari communities like Santa Teresa.[375]

It is clear, then, that the cristiada in the south of Durango was in reality a highly divisive conflict. But why was this the case, given that the region's O'dam and Mexicanero communities had had almost no contact with either church or state in the years leading up to the rebellion? Unsurprisingly, Meyer believes that religion was a key factor, arguing that the O'dam were "the most acculturated and the most Catholic of the Sierra's Indians" and so were naturally inclined to support the cristeros.[376] However, there is no evidence to support the idea that most O'dam (and by implication Mexicaneros) were essentially mestizo Catholics who happened to speak an Indigenous language (expressed in Meyer's description of mestizo cristero leaders Valente Acevedo, Trinidad Mora, and Federico Vázquez as "acculturated O'dam" and their forces being made up of "those who had once been or only just stopped being Indians").[377] It is clear that Mora, Acevedo, and Vázquez were actually Spanish-speaking, conventionally Catholic mestizos,[378] while anthropologists have shown that shaman-led mitote ceremonialism has always been as vital to O'dam and Mexicanero belief systems, sociopolitical organization, and agricultural practices as it is to their Wixárika or Náayari neighbors and that O'dam and Mexicanero "Catholicism" is very distinct from that practiced by their mestizo neighbors.[379]

This does not mean, of course, that holy images played no role in defining O'dam and Mexicanero participation in the cristiada. Like their Náayari and Wixárika neighbors, the Indigenous people of southern Durango rallied around particular santitos during the rebellion and also went to great pains to hide their most precious images in caves or canyons for fear they would be seized or destroyed by their enemies.[380] But as in the rest of the Gran Nayar, such behavior applied equally to members of both pro-cristero and pro-government factions. The pro-government leader Cosme Solís was regarded as having obtained such charismatic power through an alliance with the patron of San Pedro Jícoras.[381] And the cristero Juan Andrés Soto is said to have consecrated himself to either the patron of San Andrés Milpillas (through typically O'dam offerings of flowers and ritual fasting) or, according to the descendants of his enemies, to the devil himself, whom he fought and defeated one night in a canyon (synonymous with "dark forces" in O'dam culture), winning for himself a huge black horse and invulnerability from federal bullets: "Even when they shot at him point blank they couldn't get him."[382] The existence of such beliefs does little to substantiate the idea that the O'dam and Mexicaneros shared the same kind of Catholic faith that pushed so many of western Mexico's mestizos to back the cristeros.

Avitia acknowledges the implausibility of Meyer's argument and instead builds on the work of Fernando Benítez to argue that O'dam participation in the cristiada was the culmination of a history of fierce "messianic" resistance to the power of the Spanish Crown and the Mexican state.[383] Just as Van Young argued that "messianism" has historically motivated many of the rebellions of both Indians and mestizos across northern Mexico,[384] Avitia asserts that southern Durango's O'dam shared the (pagan) faith of their colonial-era ancestors in the existence of a warrior's paradise, which "partly explains the constant participation of the O'dam in rebellions and wars of resistance against whites and mestizos."[385] However, this is based on yet more poor ethnology, in this case that of local maestro misionero-turned-scholar Everardo Gámiz, who was the first to mention the O'dam creator god Sahuatoba and his Valhalla-like paradise at Masada[386]—much to the surprise of the O'dam themselves, who had yet to hear of either.[387] Thus it seems doubtful that some kind of O'dam "warrior religion" generated support for the cristeros in southern Durango.

Meyer and Avitia also argue that more worldly conflicts, related to the exploitation of the Sierra O'dam's forests, helped to push many O'dam into rebelling against the government. They portray the pro-government O'dam cacique of Xoconoxtle, Chon Aguilar, as "the first to open the forests to the logging companies"[388] and posit that he and his supporters were therefore allied to politicians and businessmen in Durango and Mexico City with interests in the region's virgin pine forests.[389] Avitia even goes so far as to describe the cristiada in the sierra as "the struggle for the sacred forest."[390] This stress on logging as a key point of conflict is predicated on a passage in Estrada's *Rescoldo* in which an O'dam character, Chano Gurrola—portrayed as an important cristero chief—complains that (in mock O'dam-accented Spanish) "Mezquital mestizo go always further into sierra. All sierra becoming bare of branches. O'dam cannot live without pines."[391]

However, Chano Gurrola seems to be less a real historical personage than a literary invention, created by Antonio Estrada as a way of representing O'dam culture, beliefs, and actions in the form of a single character in his novel. This does not mean we should simply disregard this character's statements, which Estrada likely based on the words of the O'dam individuals with whom he lived in the sierra between 1934 and 1936, during the second cristiada. But the fact that *Rescoldo* is set in those years also means that using Estrada's novel to explain the dynamics of the first cristiada risks engaging in anachronism. In fact, it is clear from both oral and documentary evidence that in 1926, Chon Aguilar was not yet a particularly influential cacique; the pine forests of Santa María Ocotán and Xoconoxtle had been little exploited; and those of the other O'dam communities were still completely untouched.[392] According to Saturnino Solís, an elder from Santa María Ocotán,

> in those days, we didn't fell the pines. People just cut a few slender little pines to make boards, and a few beams, but only using axes. There were no chainsaws. [The cristeros] were no longer alive when the logging industry arrived here, they'd all been killed before that.[393]

Neither logging nor Chon Aguilar's then-limited regional influence could therefore have done much to shape O'dam participation in the first cristiada. However, the power of other local caciques did play key roles in deciding O'dam and Mexicanero allegiances in this period. Meyer regards caciquismo as vital to securing the loyalty of what he claims was only a small O'dam "minority" for the revolutionary government (as he also argues for a few other regions, such as Puebla, that do not fit with his thesis of a causal link between popular Catholic religiosity and support for the cristeros).[394] Meyer's vision of severely limited O'dam support for the government is linked to his exaggerated view of O'dam acculturation, which leads him to misidentify Sixto Mendía and Cosme Solís—two of the most important pro-government O'dam leaders—as mestizos. Thus Chon Aguilar becomes "the only Indian leader" to back the state during the first Cristero Rebellion,[395] allowing Meyer to assign more "noble" religious motives to the O'dam "majority" he presents as supporting the cristeros.

The evidence instead suggests that it was not cacical ideologies but internal factional conflicts related to the dynamics of caciquismo itself that played the biggest role in determining the loyalties of different O'dam and Mexicanero caciques and thus of the local population as a whole. Geographical circumstance, forced recruitment, and the logic of violence subsequently cemented factional divides and swelled the numbers of each cacique's followers, although these remained a minority in relation to those forced to abandon their communities "to safeguard their lives and protect the women from rape and avoid being press-ganged into the ranks of the rebels and Federals alike."[396]

It is tempting to try to associate the O'dam and Mexicanero factions that declared for Calles with cosmopolitans and to characterize those who allied with the cristeros as members of conservative factions aligned with traditional authorities threatened by the expansion of the revolutionary state (as was the case in Nayarit's Náayari communities). But many pro-cristero O'dam leaders, such as Juan Andrés Soto in Santa María Ocotán, José María Gutiérrez in San Francisco Ocotán, and Dámaso Barraza in Temoaya and Yonora, had, like Pedro Quintanar in Huejuquilla, until recently been defensa commanders officially aligned with the government. If anything, these defectors to the cristero cause were more powerful at the outbreak of the cristiada than government loyalists like Sixto Mendía, Cosme Solís, or Chon Aguilar. Having served as commander of a defensa was therefore rarely evidence of ideological support for the Mexican state. This is probably because in the early 1920s the influence of both federal and state authorities in the Sierra O'dam was so weak that they had no choice but to lend official recognition, ex post facto and irrespective of their political leanings, to any local leader able to exercise politico-military control over a community, just as they had done before the revolution.

The idea that rival ideological positions vis-à-vis "tradition" or "modernity," or church or state, genuinely determined local allegiances during the first Cristero Rebellion also invites anachronism, as most O'dam and Mexicaneros only came into contact with agrarista or cristero ideologues after they had been incorporated into either side's armed forces.[397] Such ideological differences would eventually come to dominate communal politics throughout the Sierra O'dam: by 1959, anthropologists Carroll L. Riley and John Hobgood noted everywhere strong divisions between conservatives, "those individuals who are determined to retain the old ways of life, and especially to resist any further intrusion on the part of Mexican nationals," and liberals, consisting of those "interested in the benefits of outside contacts, and . . . more receptive to outside ideas."[398] But divisions between these "political parties" cannot have influenced local mobilization during the first cristiada because they did not yet exist—as a brief revision of the careers of local caciques clearly demonstrates.

Juan Andrés Soto, for example, did defend his community's traditional authorities by killing Gregorio Aguilar and, in the mid-1930s, destroying a government boarding school in Santa María Ocotán to "protect costumbre."[399] But would a dedicated conservative have pursued Aguilar with the full backing of the region's mestizo authorities, put himself under the authority of the mestizo former teacher Juan Sifuentes during the first Cristero Rebellion, collaborated with the SEP in the early 1930s, and again worked closely with mestizo rebels throughout the second cristiada?

Likewise, eventual cristero leader José María Gutiérrez had been both a traditional authority and a defensa commander in San Francisco before the rebellion, had been in extensive contact with Durango's state government during the later stages of the revolution, and had pledged loyalty to the new revolutionary order in 1919. Did Gutiérrez sympathize more closely with the revolutionary regime, with his community's traditional power structures, or with the cristeros? The archival evidence provides no easy answer, but oral accounts agree that his early contacts with the state and later declaration for the cristeros were motivated less by ideology than by a desire to preserve his local influence in the face of wider macroregional power shifts.

Even for Chon Aguilar—a self-proclaimed agrarista held up by Meyer and Avitia as a quintessential Callista cacique—ideology was a secondary concern when it came to choosing sides. His father, Gregorio, had been in close contact with agrarista revolutionaries during the revolution and had advocated for agrarian reform in Santa María and Xoconoxtle. He might therefore have passed down pro-agrarista sentiments to his son (if, indeed, he supported agrarian reform in search of more than just personal and communal gain). But given that Chon accompanied Gregorio when the latter went on the run and was only reconciled with the state and municipal governments—by this time purged of their Arrietista elements—after Gregorio's death, his later allegiance to Calles was likely determined more by the nature of his reconciliation with the regional authorities (who gave him arms after his surrender)[400] and, above all, by the urge to revenge himself on the man who killed his father—cristero chief Juan Andrés Soto.

More than ideology, then, the old dictum that "the enemy of my enemy is my friend" and the local dynamics of caciquismo were at the heart of most O'dam (and, we can assume, Mexicanero) caciques' loyalties during the cristiada. Internal power struggles had developed within many of the region's communities not, as in the rest of the Gran Nayar, as a result of state expansion but rather as a consequence of the revolution and the Arrietista and Delahuertista uprisings. These conflicts had allowed relatively wealthy, Spanish-speaking, and often semiliterate young men to gain access to weapons and outside political support and to begin challenging their communities' traditional governments. When another round of generalized violence arrived on their doorsteps in late 1926 and groups of armed outsiders, led by charismatic figures like Porfirio Mayorquín and Federico Vázquez on the one hand and Eulogio Ortiz and Anacleto López on the other, once again attempted to win over local allies to their respective causes, rival leaders within each community rallied their followers together and, to safeguard or to bolster their own personal political and economic positions, threw themselves into the fighting.

The decisions of these caciques to declare for either the government or the cristeros was in turn influenced by territorial conflicts both within and between their communities, which had been exacerbated by population movements during the convulsions of the previous decade. For example, within Santa María Ocotán, tensions had long existed between descent groups living close to the communal cabecera and those who lived far to the north, around the anexo of Candelaria.[401] During the second cristiada, the conflict between these groups pushed many in Candelaria to side with rebel forces against the pro-government majority in and around Santa María itself. It would be surprising if similar considerations had not also influenced the support of Candelaria's caciques for the cristeros during their first rebellion.[402]

Territorial disputes between communities were still more important in determining local loyalties. The anthropologist José Sánchez Olmedo goes too far in asserting, on the basis of evidence presented in Meyer's la cristiada, that "land was the primary motive for O'dam involvement in this struggle."[403] But it is nonetheless true that conflicts over land were at the root of Dámaso Barraza's rivalry with Mezquital's rancher caciques, who were allies of the revolutionary state. "It was for that reason that [the latter] went after don Dámaso, because he kicked the landlords out [of Temoaya and Yonora], to whom a few local people had sold land."[404] The arrival of a rebel army committed to overthrowing these local elites and their protectors in Durango—which had already won a series of God-given victories against federal forces—must have seemed providential to Barraza, who needed little persuasion to join them.

Juan Andrés Soto, a native of Platanitos—an anexo of Santa María Ocotán that bordered Barraza's stronghold of Yonora—soon heard about Barraza's decision, and to avoid conflict with his powerful neighbor, he abandoned his own allegiance to the government. He likely also believed that Barraza's support for the cristeros augured their victory. Soon afterward, armed and mounted cristeros arrived in Taxicaringa (also located close to Yonora), Teneraca (in whose anexo of Jacalitos, Porfirio Mayorquín established his headquarters), and San Bernardino (a stone's throw from Valente Acevedo's headquarters at Llano Grande), promising wealth in terms of "confiscated" cattle to those who joined them and death to those who refused to pledge loyalty to their cause.[405] Naturally, many local people declared for the cristeros.

At the same time, Chon Aguilar—still a relatively minor figure in his home community of Xoconoxtle—saw in declaring for the government an opportunity to obtain vengeance for his father's death, boost his own regional influence,[406] and win federal support for his community in its territorial conflict with the cristeros of neighboring Huejuquilla.[407] Aguilar and his followers were probably also antagonistic toward Barraza because in 1921 the latter had broken with his former ally, Gregorio Aguilar, and raided Xoconoxtle.[408]

Sixto Mendía, who hailed from Santa María's southern anexo of La Laguna del Burro, also declared against the cristeros. If we can take Media's grandson Asiano De la Rosa Calleros at his word, Mendía and his relatives received arms from General Eliseo Páez himself (which, as Páez died in battle in January 1927, would make Mendía the first O'dam leader to declare against the cristeros).[409] If Páez visited Mendía before cristero forces were active in the area, Mendía would have had little choice but to form an alliance with the federals. His decision was also likely influenced by his power base's location far from pro-cristero Yonora and close to pro-government Huazamota, which was itself close to the headquarters of Mariano Mejía, at this point the most powerful representative of the Mexican state in the entire Gran Nayar.

Each O'dam or Mexicanero leader could depend on a core of loyal supporters bound to them through ties of blood, ceremonial kinship, and clientelist self-interest. Temoaya's influential Valdés clan, led by Macario and Ireneo, backed Barraza, their relative through marriage; Juan Andrés Soto's most loyal lieutenants were his brothers, Pedro and Casimiro Soto, his cousin, Juan Soto,[410] and other members of his descent group, such as Jacinto Soto and Gerardo Aguilar Soto, all of whom danced the same mitote at a patio near Candelaria;[411] while Sixto Mendía's brothers, Gregorio and Hilario, and their cousins Cosme, Agustín, Fernando, and Benito Solís, whose family mitote patio was located near La Laguna del Burro, formed the core of Santa María Ocotán's pro-government faction.

Once these groups gained weapons and outside support, they set about extending their political, territorial, and military influence out from their local strongholds toward neighboring rancherías and, ultimately, the cabeceras of their communities. They promised booty to those who would join them and declared those who resisted to be their enemies. "That's how they got us, they'd kill you if you didn't go with them. . . . They said, 'If you're not going to come with us, then you can stay here permanently, fucker!' That's what the people here suffered."[412] Not even the elders in charge of communal mitote patios and other traditional authorities—who before the revolution had been the ultimate decision-makers in their communities and whose persons were regarded as sacrosanct—were exempt from such pressures.

Most O'dam and Mexicaneros attempted to escape conscription by trying to physically remove themselves from the theater of conflict. "Those who weren't caught went off running, because if you stayed in one place, they wouldn't let you be."[413] Just as in the sierras of Nayarit and Jalisco, this exodus interrupted the agricultural cycle, and local people "were forced to live on tortillas made from the *aviet* fruit, which must be cooked for hours to take away its bitterness. . . . All had to endure this penury for years, and so the equilibrium of communal costumbre, rooted in the complementary actions of men and women, was violently torn apart."[414] Both pro-cristero and pro-government forces therefore became ever more dependent on robbery and cattle rustling for survival, leaving many of those who had initially escaped conscription with no choice but to take up arms to defend their cattle from such "banditry" or, starving and desperate, to obtain food for themselves and their families. Ultimately, then, it is not hard to see why so many of those who lived through the conflict claim that "what happened was nothing more than robbery . . . that's the only reason they fought, and that way they were able to get more and more people to join them."[415]

CONCLUSIONS

Ultimately, despite their limited numbers, the actions of Náayari, Wixárika, O'dam, and Mexicanero fighters on either side of the Cristero Rebellion had important effects on the progress and outcomes of the conflict. Initially, the Gran Nayar—and in particular the Sierra O'dam—served as an incubator for regional cristero movements under Trinidad Mora and, to a lesser extent, Pedro Quintanar. The region's loyalist forces gave a similar boost to Eulogio Ortiz and Anacleto López's regional counteroffensives. Later, Náayari, Wixárika, O'dam, and Mexicanero cristeros, alongside their mestizo allies, participated in the conquests of Mezquital, Mezquitic, and Acaponeta and even, for a short period, occupied the city of Durango. Their activities also contributed to the fall of Governor Francisco Ramírez Romano of Nayarit in early 1928 and a year later helped to push Governor Juan Gualberto Amaya, General Francisco Urbalejo, and other high-ranking members of Durango's political elite to throw in their lot with the Escobaristas. Conversely, Náayari, Wixárika, O'dam, and Mexicanero defensas also prevented cristero forces from consolidating their hold on the Gran Nayar and going on to seriously threaten government control of nearby cities such as Tepic and Zacatecas. They later played a decisive role in defeating the Escobarista rebellion, which marked the end of Amaya's and Urbajelo's careers and the beginning of a new period of Callista consolidation across the country. Together with loyalist army units, agrarista militias, and the rest of central and western Mexico's rural defensas, the pro-government forces of the Gran Nayar subsequently helped to reverse the momentum of the Cristero Rebellion as a whole, which came to an official end soon after.

Six basic, interlinked factors helped to determine the allegiances and actions of the Gran Nayar's rival pro- and anti-government forces: (1) the influence of religious (although not necessarily Catholic) belief, (2) the local dynamics of caciquismo, (3) intracommunal factional tensions, (4) intercommunal agrarian conflicts, (5) the search for security in the context of generalized violence, and (6) simple, unabashed coercion. All of these were, whether at individual, factional, communal, or "tribal" level, inflected by geographical circumstance, state-level political developments, local cultural idiosyncrasies and emerging economic divisions, and, of course, the changing "facts on the ground," for as Clausewitz points out, in any conflict "the original political objects can greatly alter during the course of the war and may finally change entirely since they are influenced by events and their probable consequences."[416]

Given their lack of contact with both priests and Catholic doctrine since the late eighteenth century, Náayari, Wixárika, O'dam, and Mexicanero mobilizations during the cristiada were less influenced by religious belief than those of central and western Mexico's mestizo population. However, the actions of mestizo cristeros inspired by Catholic religious doctrine, political ideology, and the sociocultural authority of priests—which ranged from peaceful proselytism to violent coercion, raiding, and cattle rustling—helped to persuade some Náayarite, Wixáritari, O'dam, and Mexicaneros to align themselves with the rebels while pushing others to declare for the government. Similarly, "popular piety"—mainly in the form of the heterodox practices, beliefs, and worldviews bound up with local costumbre—also helped to condition the activities and behavior of Indigenous fighters and civilians once the conflict was underway. Faith in the power of local santitos and other deities and in the supernatural abilities of shamans drove fighters on both sides to raid the sacred spaces of their rivals. The ceremonies that rendered the local corn crop edible defined the limits of the regional "campaigning season" and the timings of military offensives rather than the actual harvest itself, and rituals also shaped preparations for raids or measures to defend communities from raiders. Even the directions in which civilians fled were informed by older routes of pilgrimage, which linked the communities of the Gran Nayar to the sacred caves and forest groves that now became the hideouts of desperate pacíficos.

Caciquismo and factionalism played even more important roles in shaping Náayari, Wixárika, O'dam, and Mexicanero participation in the cristiada. These phenomena were in themselves still influenced by costumbre, which defined the conceptions of kinship through which caciques harnessed support, as well as the charismatic power that helped them to hold their factional groupings together under enemy pressure. Amongst the Náayarite and Wixáritari, the perceived threats that revolutionary state-building posed to ways of life defined by ritual and subsistence agriculture also gave rise to the factional conflicts that pushed conservatives into backing the cristeros and their cosmopolitan rivals into allying with government forces. More conventional ideological, political, and economic concerns were similarly central to some caciques' support for government schools, mestizo immigration, and agrarian reform through which they sought to demonstrate their loyalty to the government, boost the local economy, bring the region's children the advantages that came with literacy, and secure their lands against rival communities. Such concerns similarly influenced the arguments of their conservative rivals, who saw these developments as threatening the integrity of their families, the functionality of the household labor unit, the continued communal control of traditional landholdings, and their own shamanically derived cattle wealth.

Political conflicts between Indigenous communities and land-hungry regional mestizo elites, long-standing territorial rivalries amongst the communities of the Gran Nayar, and regional political developments also helped to generate the conditions for local mobilizations on both sides. In Nayarit, Náayari loyalties were conditioned not only by the decisions of caciques but also by state-level political and military concerns, the effects of cristero raids and proselytizing, and, in the Náayari Baja, by the existence of agrarian conflicts with neighboring mestizo pueblos. In Jalisco, Wixárika participation was likewise influenced by the nature of recent contacts between the revolutionary state and communal leaders, by political and territorial disputes amongst their own communities, and by their conflicts with nearby mestizo pueblos, some of which became pro-government strongholds and others bastions of pro-cristero sentiment. Meanwhile, Durango's Sierra O'dam had been, in the years immediately following the revolution, the section of the Gran Nayar most affected by rebellion and least touched by state-building. As a result, internal power struggles developed throughout the region's communities, pitting younger leaders against traditional political systems and also, in many cases, against one another. These conflicts played the greatest role in determining the loyalties of O'dam and Mexicanero caciques and their followers at the outbreak of the cristiada, sometimes in combination with inter- and intracommunal territorial disputes.

Naturally, as the conflict progressed, state-level developments also influenced the progress of the conflict in the Gran Nayar's constituent regions. In Durango, the success of Trinidad Mora's initial rebellion in Santiago Bayacora, the subsequent emergence of a powerful armed agrarian movement in the north of the state, and, later, the defection of Durango's military and political leaders to the Escobaristas helped to shape the scope of the rebellion in the Sierra O'dam, the goals of its participants, and the way in which the conflict there was eventually brought to an end. Mariano Mejía's rebellion in the Náayari Alta and Eutimio Domínguez's decision not to rebel were similarly tied to the increasingly shaky position of state governor Ramírez Romano (a close ally of Mariano Mejía) or, conversely, to the growing strength of the federal forces stationed on the edges of Eutimio Domínguez's cacicazgo.

As the region became an important theater of conflict in itself, the location of state borders within the Gran Nayar grew ever more irrelevant. Both cristero and pro-government forces took advantage of its mountain paths and canyon systems to raid and recruit throughout the region. By late 1927, initially distinct conflicts in the Sierra O'dam, the Sierra Wixárika, and the Sierra Náayari had become closely interconnected and by early 1928 had more in common with one another than with the fighting going on elsewhere in their respective states. By this point, too, all of the inhabitants of the Gran Nayar were, regardless of their original factional loyalties or attempts to remain neutral, increasingly concerned with a single common goal: survival. As a result, the popular search for security became a defining local feature of the cristiada (as it was in much of the rest of the country and had been during other previous conflicts).[417] Civilians who failed to flee contested areas were swayed toward one side or another by the coercive power of local cristero or pro-government forces or by the need to feed themselves and their families given the widespread theft or destruction of crops and livestock.

Ultimately, violence and hunger combined to further atomize dispersed populations, force traditional communal governments to disband, and bring the sacred practice of subsistence agriculture to a standstill. This disruption to local social, religious, and economic life, compounded by the tendency of armed bands to attack their targets in the midst of fiestas, led to the temporary disintegration of Náayari, Wixárika, O'dam, and Mexicanero costumbre at anything beyond the individual or immediate family level. "They were scared that the rebels would arrive. No, it was not until things calmed down that they could once again practice costumbre."[418] In turn, this undermined traditional mechanisms for resolving conflicts and maintaining solidarity within each of the region's communities and between the different communities themselves, exacerbating the ongoing violence.

As the Cristero Rebellion went on, feuds amongst communities, factions, families, and individuals became ever more entrenched in local life, as did the importance of revenge as a factor driving local people to take up arms. Over the course of the subsequent decade, it would become increasingly clear that national-level agreements between the church and state could do little to moderate the vicious cycle that the violence of the armed revolution and the Cristero Rebellion, together with the divisive activities of an expansionist state, had unleashed on the Gran Nayar and its inhabitants.

5

BOARDING SCHOOLS, FACTIONAL FEUDS, AND UNLIKELY ALLIANCES DURING THE MAXIMATO, 1929–1934

THREE PRESIDENTS OFFICIALLY ruled Mexico between 1929 and 1934: Emilio Portes Gil, Pascual Ortiz Rubio, and Abelardo L. Rodríguez. Yet Plutarco Elías Calles continued to hold real power as jefe máximo throughout this period, known as the *Maximato*. Following on from the devastation of the Cristero Rebellion, which had killed an estimated ninety thousand soldiers and cristero rebels and thousands more civilians besides,[1] the Maximato was in some ways a replay of the period of revolutionary consolidation that followed the end of the armed phase of the revolution in 1920. In the Gran Nayar, the Maximato regime's local representatives—namely military officers, SEP inspectors and teachers, state government officials, regional mestizo caciques, and a handful of agronomists—carried out a census, forced local children to attend boarding schools, installed the symbols of state in sacred Indigenous spaces, and cut political deals with former rebels in a renewed attempt to incorporate the Náayarite, Wixáritari, O'dam, and Mexicaneros into the fabric of the Mexican nation.

Thanks to its efforts to crush the Cristero Rebellion, the military's presence in the Gran Nayar had expanded significantly. However, its role in local state-building efforts remained limited. Although military officers assigned to Jesús María and Santa María Ocotán were tasked with maintaining order in the surrounding areas, there was no military occupation of the region as a whole. Instead, although in much of Mexico the army now disbanded communal defensas and agrarista militias,[2] such semiautonomous forces still dominated the Gran Nayar militarily and politically. Because of their role in defeating local cristeros, the commanders of the Gran Nayar's defensas had become more influential than ever and continued to mediate between their communities and the SEP officials who again spearheaded "Indian incorporation" programs across the region.

Despite the previous efforts of the SEP, in 1930 a quarter of Mexico's Indigenous-language speakers—around three hundred thousand individuals—spoke no Spanish.[3] The proportion of monolingual Indians was higher still in the Gran Nayar and included most women, children, and older men.[4] But the high cost of recent counterinsurgency campaigns had forced cuts to the SEP's budget, leaving it financially ill placed to embark on major Indigenous education drives.[5] At this point, the SEP employed only 6,504 rural teachers to minister to a rural population of more than eleven million people, including 1,185,073 speakers of Indigenous languages.[6] The SEP's renewed efforts to incorporate the country's Indigenous peoples—including the Náayarite, Wixáritari, O'dam, and Mexicaneros—therefore centered, initially, on their (often coercive) recruitment as pupils for the Casa del Estudiante Indígena in Mexico City. However, although 5 Náayarite and 6 Wixáritari—and not a single O'dam or Mexicanero—were listed amongst the Casa's 212 students in 1931,[7] like many of Mexico's Indians, most Náayarite and Wixáritari opposed sending their children to a faraway institution run by strange mestizos.[8]

In 1931, Calles appointed a close ally, Narciso Bassols, to replace José Manuel Puig Casauranc as education secretary. In the context of budgetary problems and controversies relating to the Casa's disastrous attrition rate (averaging 30 percent),[9] poor living conditions for the students, and the small percentage of alumni who returned to their communities as rural teachers (supposedly the Casa's raison d'être), the reorganized SEP administration closed the school in mid-1932[10] and instead concentrated on establishing new Indigenous boarding schools in communities across the country. These schools—called *internados indígenas*—sought to "replicate the successes of the [Casa] without simultaneously disconnecting students from their place of origin" and would function as the nuclei of networks of smaller rural schools, reflecting a shift in the SEP toward "incorporating communities, rather than simply individuals."[11] Critics such as Manuel Gamio argued that the internados would cause problems similar to the Casa, as their alumni would either refuse to return to their "primitive" villages or would become a divisive presence there because of their having adopted contentious new "mestizo" customs.[12] But many within the SEP saw internados as the best way to transform rural Indians into "productive" members of Mexican society,[13] and their construction soon began in Indigenous communities throughout Mexico, including those of the Sierra Náayari, the Sierra Wixárika, and, for the first time, the Sierra O'dam.

Bassols also transformed the content of the SEP's curriculum. A Marxist anticlerical and leading agrarista lawyer,[14] Bassols was still more radical as head of the SEP, introducing the doctrine of "socialist education" to the federal education system, which "supplemented existing policy emphasising peasant behaviour reform with an intensified attack on superstition [and] religious practice."[15] These were to be replaced with civic fiestas or repackaged as "folklore."[16] Stressing the material origins of Indian poverty and marginalization, Bassols's socialist curriculum also focused on teaching Indigenous youths Spanish, basic literacy and numeracy, improved agricultural techniques, and small-scale industries such as logging and tanning.[17] Teachers were ordered to promote anti-alcohol and sanitation programs,[18] to establish local postal services and village cooperatives, and to organize regular sporting events, which Bassols saw as "a panacea for masculine degeneration."[19] And just as in U.S. and Australian Indigenous residential schools, child labor would be central to keeping Mexico's "socialist" internados and rural schools running.[20]

Alexander Dawson argues that Bassols's promotion of internados "embodied a realization that the homogenizing project earlier articulated through the Casa was neither possible nor desirable."[21] However, this underplays the extent to which socialist education, despite paying lip service to an idealized model of the "noble Indian," actively sought to destroy the bases of Indigenous political and cultural autonomy. In the Gran Nayar, as in comparable regions of Oaxaca and Campeche,[22] teachers aided defensa commanders and mestizo settlers in their often-violent efforts to overthrow traditional civil-religious hierarchies and suppress "superstition," Indigenous languages, the use of alcohol, and traditional agricultural techniques. All of this threatened to destroy the costumbre that had long regulated local social, political, economic, and religious life. Naturally, as in previous years, conservative elders, traditional office holders, and anxious parents contested the SEP's antagonistic project as well as the influence of the local defensas and mestizo settlers who supported it. Maximato-era state-building efforts in the Gran Nayar thus exacerbated preexisting conflicts between cosmopolitan and conservative Indian factions, rooted both in long-running territorial disputes and clan rivalries and in newer feuds generated by more recent violence and political upheaval.

The story of Náayari, Wixárika, O'dam, and Mexicanero responses to the pressures and opportunities of the Maximato also complicates traditional narratives of church-state conflict during the period. Ben Fallaw has shown that in Campeche, the anticlericalism of SEP officials who arrived there from elsewhere in Mexico pushed local Catholics to ally with homegrown, "socialist" caciques. In exchange for their help in preventing SEP "outsiders" from meddling in local politics, the caciques rewarded the Catholics by rolling back their own anticlerical campaigns. Similarly counterintuitive coalitions emerged in parts of the Gran Nayar, as the dynamics of communal factionalism forced amnestied cristeros to work with their former enemies—including anticlerical educators, military officials, and even Callista politicians—to advance their local political goals.

The developments described in this chapter also attest to the revolutionary state's continued reluctance to implement agrarian reform.[23] Indeed, some of the state's local representatives—either in the name of increasing rural "productivity" or with a view to personal gain—assisted local mestizo ranchers in their efforts to appropriate Indigenous lands. This fact further undermines the hagiographic portrayals of rural teachers that characterize traditional Mexican historiography, as well as more recent sympathetic accounts of education policy and indigenismo in this period. Ultimately, then, this chapter shows how state policies and the divisive actions of government officials aggravated preexisting cultural, political, and territorial conflicts both within and between the communities of the Gran Nayar. By the end of the Maximato, many Náayarite, Wixáritari, O'dam, and Mexicaneros believed that the revolutionary regime posed an existential threat to their communities and cultures. As these local tensions peaked, the resurgence of national-level conflict between church and state prompted the Gran Nayar's military authorities and pro-government defensas to attack amnestied local cristeros.[24] Such heavy-handed actions shattered the uneasy peace that had settled over the region, driving many of the Gran Nayar's inhabitants to once again take up arms against the government just as Lázaro Cárdenas acceded to the presidency in December 1934.

NAYARIT: THE NÁAYARITE

In the wake of los arreglos, Mariano Mejía, once the Sierra Náayari's most powerful cacique, was released from the Islas Marías prison colony. "He returned home a changed man; he was no longer the courageous leader of before, he came back completely subdued."[25] The military prestige Mejía had earned during the revolution had evaporated following his defeats during the cristiada, while the army had "confiscated" his vast herds of cattle—the foundation of his former wealth and political influence.[26] In penury and with few allies left, he never recovered from "the blows that the government had dealt him" and retreated back into private life as a small-time rancher,[27] dying in obscurity fifteen or so years later.[28] However, memories of Mejía live on not just in the Gran Nayar but across Mexico, thanks to the famous ballad "Valentín de la Sierra," which mentions the "ochocientos soldados / Que trae por la sierra / Mariano Mejía" (eight hundred soldiers / that through the sierra brought / Mariano Mejía) at the height of the Cristero Rebellion.[29]

In Mejía's place, two mestizo government officials—a "municipal commissioner" appointed by the state governor and a military officer, Major J. Jesús Meza, appointed by Nayarit's zone commander—were sent to Jesús María to take civil and military control of the Náayari Alta (still a subprefecture of the municipality of Tepic rather than a free municipality in itself).[30] Meanwhile, although the municipal governments of Acaponeta, Rosamorada, and Santiago Ixcuintla continued to claim jurisdiction

FIGURE 6 Pro-government defensa commanders of the Sierra Náayari gathered for a meeting in Jesús María, Nayarit, in the mid-1930s (AHSEP-84-85/C/38886/E/14, Joaquín Rivera, "Informe," Apr. 25, 1936).

over the Náayari Baja, Eutimio Domínguez remained that region's most important politico-military authority. The local defensas commanded by Domínguez and Major Meza were integrated into Nayarit's "peasant corps," which, as a federal reserve corps, now constituted an "integral part of the army."[31] Together with SEP inspectors and teachers, the commanders of these paramilitary forces continued to be the Mexican state's primary local representatives throughout the Maximato.

Traditional authorities meanwhile continued to govern the civil and religious affairs of each of the Náayari communities. But the feuds, population displacements, and disruption to annual ritual cycles generated by the cristiada had weakened the legitimacy and power of these cargo holders, over whom the defensas and their allies wielded increasing influence. Factions led by conservative elders continued to contest the power of the defensas, however, and by extension the local authority of the Mexican state. In the five years between the end of the first Cristero Rebellion and the outbreak of the second, the renewed activities of the SEP and the acceleration of agrarian reform in Nayarit—which, as across much of Mexico, encouraged mestizo immigration and the expansion of mestizo ejidos into peripheral, Indigenous-majority areas[32]—further fractured the internal cohesion of the Náayari communities.

The Mexican census of 1930 officially registered a total Náayari population of 900 individuals.[33] However, an examination of original census documents reveals that some 2,459 Náayari-speaking individuals above the age of five then lived in Nayarit, and three years later SEP officials estimated the Náayari population at around 4,000.[34] The discrepancies between these numbers attest to the continued dispersion of the Náayari population and to the weakness of the state's regional presence, preventing it from collating reliable population figures. The tenuousness of the state's grip over the Sierra Náayari is further evident from the fact that in 1930, the SEP managed to establish only two new schools there: one in San Juan Peyotán, inhabited by mestizos and a few Wixárika refugees, and another in Eutimio Dominguez's home community of San Juan Corapan. Even here the local SEP inspector stressed that intensive "social work" would be necessary to attract "the few Náayari families living in the Pueblo [and] familiarize them with the School." In the hope of guaranteeing the school's success, he gave Domínguez—who, despite the SEP's efforts in the 1920s, remained "the only inhabitant who can read"—control of the community's "Educational Committee."[35] SEP officials also established a postal service linking La Mesa, Jesús María, San Francisco, and San Juan Peyotán with Tepic[36] and set up "Anti-Alcohol Leagues" in each of these communities.[37]

DERICI director Rafael Ramírez asked that Náayari children be recruited for the Casa del Estudiante Indígena, where it was hoped that their becoming "fully modernized (and for that matter, mexicanized)"[38] would demonstrate that despite widespread local resistance to earlier SEP programs, the Náayarite were capable of being "incorporated" into Mexican society. Five Náayari students were eventually recruited in Jesús María, La Mesa, and San Juan Corapan,[39] the respective strongholds of pro-government caciques León Contreras, Mariano Solís, and Eutimio Domínguez. These men saw in acceding to the SEP's demands a chance to display their loyalty and to endow local children with literacy and other skills needed "for them to be able to defend their community" (indeed, several of those educated at the Casa were later elected as agrarian representatives of their communities).[40] Yet the Náayari population as a whole remained distrustful of the SEP's intentions. As no Náayari parents would entrust their children to the care of mestizo strangers,[41] the students were all orphans, and even then their enrollment was made possible only "due to the mediation of Eutimio Domínguez and León Contreras," who traveled to Mexico City "to see where the Indian students would stay and . . . report back to and reassure their relatives."[42]

In early 1931, Manuel Durán Cárdenas became the Sierra Náayari's new SEP inspector. With the Casa falling from official favor, Durán tried to set up schools in Jesús María, Santa Teresa, La Mesa, San Francisco, Dolores, and Ixcatán. He described life in these communities as "completely miserable," adding that the inhabitants possessed

> a marked and hereditary aversion to being part of society, and even more to forming relationships with mestizos; they lead a primitive life, as many wander around naked

> except for a truss. . . . While the indolent husband lies back and suns himself, the women do all of the work, from fetching water and firewood and grinding corn for tortillas, even tending to the animals.

Durán's disparaging outlook was compounded by the apparent desolation of these communities' cabeceras. He reported that only "ten or twelve Náayari families and those of a few mestizos" lived in Jesús María, except on the few occasions each year when "the Náayarite leave their incipient homes to live temporarily, two or three days, in the center of their cacicazgos, and celebrate their race's profane religious festivals." In La Mesa, too, only three houses were inhabited, while only the community's governor, mayordomo, and a teacher lived permanently in Santa Teresa's cabecera, which he described as

> two dozen sagging and destroyed houses, disseminated across a plateau and uninhabited . . . the place is grim and miserable because of its desolation and the lack of cultivation of its lands, which could produce great benefits and secure the well-being of the inhabitants.

Of course, Náayari settlement patterns had always been dispersed, especially at the time of year that Durán was writing—a few weeks after Easter—when most Náayari families headed to their rancherías to take part in descent group mitotes and sow their crops. However, taken together with his reports of an "absolute shortage of maize" in the region, Durán's descriptions also indicate the destruction that the cristiada had wrought on the region, forcing many Náayarite to abandon their homes.

Naturally, Durán saw education as the key to the "transformation" of the Náayarite and tried to persuade each community's traditional authorities to promote attendance at the new schools, which focused on teaching children Spanish and "cleanliness and a few orderly habits." In Santa Teresa, however, the traditional governor insisted that the five students who occasionally attended were the only children in the region, and Durán was reluctant to press the point further given "the uselessness of insisting on anything with these Indians, especially when first entering into relations with them." Instead, he encouraged the local teacher to win favor with Santa Teresa's authorities by working as their scribe and advised his superiors that "one needs patience to deal with the indigenous race, overcoming difficulties little by little, you have to proceed slowly if you want to obtain a satisfactory result."[43]

In Jesús María, too, although more than one hundred children were officially enrolled at the school, only twenty-five actually attended.[44] As in much of rural Mexico, local families needed their children's help in the fields,[45] and the community's governor "asked insistently" that the children attending the local school be given

FIGURE 7 Young Náayari pupils of Santa Teresa's new school, 1932. According to the community's traditional governor, the only children to be found in the entire region (AHSEP-84-85/C/38877/E/31, M. Durán Cárdenas, "Informe," July 10, 1932).

leave to go "to the ranches and plots where they had their crops." Anxious not to lose the fragile support of the communal authorities, Durán accepted this request and arranged a festival "in honor of the Náayari children as a farewell," an opportunity he used to "speak on behalf of the Secretariat of Education and ask [the community's] decisive cooperation in the new year . . . soon I managed to defeat the typical apathy of their race, leaving the field clear for future projects."[46]

Despite Inspector Durán's assertions that a gentle approach would be necessary to overcome Náayari resistance to government schooling, over the next year he and the teachers under his authority increasingly challenged long-established Náayari customs, in line with official SEP policy in many Indigenous regions.[47] In La Mesa, Durán went so far as to destroy the community's *cepo*, a kind of wooden stocks that played an important role in the complex traditional Náayari judicial system but which Durán described as an "an instrument of punishment and torture."[48] Even though he claimed that, after much deliberation, the community's elders gave him permission to hack apart and burn part of the stocks and use the rest to build stools for his classroom, his actions must surely have offended local conservatives. So would Durán's other attempts to crack down on what SEP doctrine now condemned as Indian "vices," particularly the drinking of locally produced alcohol,[49] which had a "special religious significance" in most of Mexico's Indigenous cultures[50] and played a key part in Náayari rituals and fiestas.[51]

Mary Vaughan notes that most SEP officials "seemed oblivious to liquor's intimate role in sacralizing every event in the life cycle from birth to death,"[52] and anti-alcohol campaigns therefore caused controversy throughout Indigenous Mexico.[53] The people of the Sierra Náayari were certainly less than pleased with Durán's demands—translated into Náayari for the benefit of monolingual elders—that they not only support new schools but also moderate "the drunkenness which is for them frequent and ritualistic, as in their festivities it is usual to get extremely drunk."[54] But as local discontent at Durán's officiousness grew, his attitude to Náayari culture seems to have only hardened further. From Jesús María, for example, he reported that

> with intimate satisfaction we have seen that ancestral customs have been disappearing amongst the children and youths who attend [the school]; in the orgies, which constitute the obligatory final act in their idolatrous religious fiestas, those natives who have frequent contact with the educational center, no longer participate, which is a positive triumph for the school and for the educational work carried out there.[55]

As well as challenging Náayari costumbre, SEP officials continued to encourage mestizo immigration to the sierra. Somewhat surprisingly, given his usual willingness to cooperate with the government, Eutimio Domínguez prevented mestizos from settling permanently in Corapan,[56] but by 1932 a number of mestizo families lived in nearby Ixcatán.[57] The first of these settlers had formally requested permission from defensa commander Eusebio González to make his home there. González told the communal assembly that this mestizo "will help us, will sell us everything we lack here, like salt and soap." Others argued that the mestizo "will be like a strangler-fig,[58] will bring his little ones with him, and they will grow up and make their homes here. And once they start their own families, when will we ever be able to get rid of them? Never!" But González's arguments prevailed, and soon, as predicted, "his friends began to arrive, and these others didn't ask for permission."[59]

Various mestizos also lived in Santa Teresa, under the protection of defensa commander Evaristo Castañeda,[60] and five mestizo families had settled in Dolores, whose defensa was itself commanded by a mestizo.[61] Meanwhile, the more long-standing mestizo presence in Jesús María and San Francisco, which had increased significantly under Mejía's rule,[62] continued to grow during the Maximato. These settlers tended to be natives of nearby mestizo-inhabited towns and were a mixture of refugees fleeing the revolution or the cristiada, and merchants and ranchers in search of land and commercial opportunities.[63]

FIGURE 8 Meeting of the traditional Náayari authorities of Jesús María (AHSEP-84-85/C/38877/E/31, M. Durán Cárdenas, "Informe," July 10, 1932).

Mestizo immigrants, mestizo teachers, and the mestizo authorities in Jesús María had long been closely associated with one another; one teacher, Petra Tovar de Aquino, was Mariano Mejía's comadre, and it was reported that she and many others "have married, although not civilly, and their husbands and the material interests they have there, influence their work and the life of the school."[64] Like Eusebio González, the commanders of the Náayari Alta's defensas argued that mestizo settlers would help to improve the material quality of local life[65] and also saw these outsiders as a useful counterweight to the power of the conservative elders. However, the growing power of mestizo submunicipal authorities in Jesús María, increasing mestizo immigration, and SEP officials' attacks on local costumbre angered even moderate conservatives to the extent that by July 1932, Inspector Durán was complaining that "the Governors of the tribe are disrupting our work."[66]

In Jesús María, for example, Durán caused a scandal by making Náayari students stitch together a Mexican flag, which he then hung from "the pueblo's principle edifice, which is the ruined church of the Franciscans." Durán, in line with usual SEP discourse, framed the ensuing dispute in nationalist terms,[67] reporting that "the Náayari Indians view all acts or manifestations of patriotism with much wariness."[68] But it is obvious that hanging an essentially "foreign" banner in a sacred ritual space constituted a symbolic challenge on the part of the Mexican state to the authority of the community's elders.[69] In response, the traditional authorities withdrew their cautious support for the school, which Durán reported soon afterward

> is sometimes without pupils because the Governor of the Náayarite orders it thus, advised by the Council of Elders, who are markedly adverse to the school, and even more that [local children] begin to pronounce words in a language that is not their own.[70]

Meanwhile, in Santa Teresa, tensions between conservative and cosmopolitan factions resulted in violent incidents being played out in the realm of ritual and belief. The most dramatic of these was the beating to death and then burning of a man accused of sorcery, an act allegedly carried out by one of the traditional authorities charged with leading the community's often unruly Easter festival. In response, and in line with policies then being promoted by the SEP, Evaristo Castañeda warned that neither drunkenness nor the participation of children would be allowed during that year's festival and ordered the latter to attend school instead.[71]

The mestizo defensa commander in nearby Dolores also attempted to force Náayari attendance at the community's new school, whose teacher, much to the disgust of local parents, "employed blows in dealing with the children."[72] He also organized the repair of the one road leading to the town, which Náayari elders, like conservatives in many Indigenous communities even today,[73] "considered a future threat." In response, the "old Indians, custodians of tradition and racial hatreds," embarked on "a true campaign of caste conflict" and in April 1932 "forced the mestizo families to leave the pueblo."[74] The teacher naturally took the side of the exiled mestizos and "constantly threatened the Indians with the intervention of higher authorities and severe punishments which had them in constant unease" until "they retreated to the hills and hid themselves in the canyons and today the pueblo is without families, and it doesn't appear they will return."[75]

In the face of such resistance, Nayarit's director of federal education accused Durán of laziness and ordered him to redouble his efforts in the sierra.[76] Durán therefore turned to the region's mestizo authorities to help force Náayari attendance, writing to the municipal commissioner in Jesús María that

> our teachers have really struggled with the deceptions of the old Indians, and with profound surprise I have seen that in isolated places one finds the children, completely naked, looking after an incipient herd of sheep, and that the Náayari Authorities have ignored my appeals that our school should accommodate these unfortunate children.

Durán then asked both the commissioner and Major Meza to ensure that "the Náayari Governors and Authorities do not use subterfuges and tricks, stowing away the majority of the children in the canyons, especially the females" and that "the children are not removed from the school for any reason whatsoever."[77] In response, Meza and the commissioner ordered the dispersed Náayari population to settle permanently in the cabeceras of their communities so that their children could attend school.[78] Some Náayari families initially obeyed,[79] and Durán optimistically assured his superiors that soon "the admission of these people into civilization will be a reality."[80] Bolstered by this momentary success, he intensified his campaign against Náayari costumbre, ordering teachers to crack down on drunkenness at festivals[81] and to "stamp out the use of noxious herbs, the practice of superstition and the meddling of so-called 'tatoanes' [Indian lords], 'cantadores' [singing-shamans] or 'hechiceros' [sorcerers] . . . so that these absurd practices would disappear."[82]

In the communities of the Náayari Baja, the authority of Eutimio Domínguez checked the resentment that this campaign would otherwise have generated. Durán reported in April 1933 that in Rosarito, San Juan Corapan, and San Pedro Ixcatán "the Authorities have carefully brought together the individuals of their race and accustomed them to living in society," and that the local teachers had experienced few problems and were quickly teaching their Náayari charges to speak Spanish.[83] The government's official newspaper, *El Nacional*, applauded these "triumphs," which it announced had required "many sacrifices" on the part of Durán and his subordinates in the Náayari Baja.[84]

However, the communities of the Náayari Alta, described in the same article as "absent of any of civilization's influence," became ever more hostile both to schools and mestizo settlers. By mid-1933, Durán was complaining that even though Jesús María's inhabitants were well used to contact with outsiders, they still resented sending their children to school and that as he "lacked the influence of those entrusted with authority, the Indians do not feel this pressure and little by little, as they know how, they withdraw their children." Likewise, he described the inhabitants of San Francisco and La Mesa as "very recalcitrant" and constantly looking for "ways to dodge the rules and live freely without any subordination at all." Worse still, he was forced to withdraw Santa Teresa's teacher, who local people accused of "not dedicat[ing] himself to work, or to teaching the classes that he is supposed to give . . . [instead] dedicat[ing] himself to his commercial enterprise."[85] Thus by August 1933, in all Nayarit, official figures for Náayari enrollment in government schools totaled a pitiful 126 male and 104 female Náayari students—just over 3 percent of the total Náayari population—while actual attendance was likely far lower still.[86]

● ● ● ●

Just as the SEP's attempts to "incorporate" the Náayarite seemed to be bearing fruit in the Náayari Baja, a second strand of the revolutionary regime's state-building and social reformist project—corporatist agrarian reform—began to alienate many of its formerly cooperative inhabitants. Although the communities of the Náayari Alta were still little affected by agrarian issues, "conserv[ing] their lands according to tradition, each pueblo having its property titles which date to the era of the viceroyalty,"[87] communal landholdings in the Náayari Baja had been threatened by nearby haciendas and neighboring mestizo pueblos since the Porfiriato. The attempts of local and national politicians to expand the state's reach into rural Nayarit in the early 1930s, by dividing local haciendas into ejidos administered by their supporters, left the communities of the Náayari Baja still more vulnerable to mestizo land grabs.

Nayarit's agrarian movement had been gathering force since 1931, when state senator Guillermo Flores Muñoz, kick-starting his career as one of Nayarit's most important and enduring political figures, "mobilised the Agrarian League and launched agitatory commissions across the state."[88] In May 1934, the passing of the "law of division of the state's large landholdings" cemented regional agrarista influence. Over the next six years they made some 300 agrarian claims, of which 280 were approved (compared with just 135 put forward and 39 approved between 1917 and 1934).[89] However, newly created ejidos on the edge of the Náayari Baja and groups of mestizos already settled in the region itself now began to claim ownership of Náayari landholdings. For example, in 1934, mestizo ranchers living on lands jointly owned by Saycota and San Blasito applied for a dotación de ejido for themselves,[90] while the ejido of El Venado, backed by the state government, invaded the territory of San Pedro Ixcatán.[91] A year later, San Juan Corapan suffered a similar government-sponsored land grab, with a local newspaper reporting that "600 indigenous families . . . by decree of the Government of the same state, have been robbed of the lands that they have possessed since time immemorial."[92]

Ritual practices such as mitotes and pilgrimages and the existence of colonial-era titles left most Náayarite convinced of their legal, moral, and spiritual ownership of their traditional territories. Like many rural Mexicans with *serrano* tendencies,[93] they wanted no more than the government's certification of these rights, along with the restitución of territory lost to mestizo land grabs, rather than the dotación of state lands that would oblige them to pay fees and new annual taxes of 15 percent of each harvest.[94] In fact, even restitución was viewed with suspicion by many Náayarite, as making such a claim required registering the names of all those entitled to work communal lands, which facilitated the enclosure of individual plots where previously "everyone planted wherever they wanted to plant, and the next year planted somewhere else. They didn't claim ownership of the land, it was all free."[95] Communities were also reluctant to set up the new state-sanctioned agrarian authorities—the Consejo de Vigilancia (Supervisory Board) and Comisario de Bienes Comunales (Communal Property Commission)—whose formation constituted an essential part of the restitución process and would have added a confusing third tier to communal governments, even as elders and traditional cargo holders were still struggling for power with recently created defensas.[96]

The establishment of these communal agrarian authorities—which, as products of national legislation, existed apart from Náayari costumbre and were open to mestizo membership—presented settlers, teachers, and cosmopolitan Náayarite with a way of wresting power from traditional governments with the full backing of the state. According to an elderly informant in Ixcatán,

> the Náayarite, as always, knew that this community is a community, not an ejido. . . . But the mestizos already said, "We're going to get approval for a commission. Because a commissioner is strong, he's an important authority." The government quickly gave them that, because the government helped the mestizos more than the Náayarite in those days. Soon they received a commissioner's seal, and named a certain man as commissioner.[97]

As in much of *serrano* Mexico, state-backed agrarian reform in the Náayari Baja therefore empowered cosmopolitan caciques and their mestizo allies[98] and distanced members of defensas from traditional communal authorities, where previously they had been united by a shared belief system and subordination to Eutimio Domínguez. In the second half of the 1930s, this would serve to undermine the regional Náayari population's political and cultural autonomy and also deal a death blow to San Pedro Ixcatán's very existence as an Indigenous community.

Meanwhile, in the Náayari Alta, Inspector Durán remained blind to the growing resistance engendered by the threat that the SEP's program of cultural "transformation" posed to Náayari beliefs, practices, and ways of life. He instead placed the blame for Náayari intransigence on the failings of local teachers, accusing them of unduly adapting to the local environment so that they now lived "in a state of intellectual and economic misery greater than that of the inhabitants themselves."[99] Since the SEP could not afford better-trained teachers[100] and the use of force had failed to improve Náayari attendance at the region's schools, Durán turned to technology to try to convey the wonders of modern Mexican "civilization" to those whom he now defined as "the most neglected Indians in all our Republic." Together with Nayarit's new director of federal education, Celso Flores Zamora, and a team that included teachers, a film operator, and two full-time porters, in early 1934, Durán traveled through the sierra armed with reels of film and a portable cinema projector.[101] He reported that

> the cinematographic exhibitions caused a profound impression amongst the people who turned out in large numbers, one naturally noted the effect the different stages of the

> projections, the electric lighting, etc., all new to them, produced on their spirits; it was a true spiritual revolution that will go down in history in that forgotten region.[102]

During this trip, Durán also persuaded Flores Zamora to authorize the establishment of an internado in Jesús María.[103] Although the traditional governors of Jesús María, Santa Teresa, and La Mesa had already refused to contribute "any material assistance whatsoever" to the project on the grounds that they lacked "life's essentials" even for their own families, Durán secured land in Jesús María on which to build the boarding school and a plot by the river on which to grow food for the students and showcase modern agricultural techniques.[104] The school opened its doors toward the end of the year, which inevitably worsened factional and interethnic tensions.

Many Náayarite opposed the school on the grounds it threatened the integrity of their families, communities, and cultures as well as their agricultural activities, in which children played an important role.[105] One of the internado's first students, recruited in Santa Teresa, remembered that

> like all of the rest of the Náayari students there, he was locked into the school at night for fear that he or the other students might flee. . . . After a few years in the school, however, [he] proved his faithfulness and was given permission to return to Santa Teresa to visit his parents, whereupon they refused to let him return to Jesus Maria. Instead, they fled the town with their 12-year-old son in order to avoid the teacher who came after him.[106]

Many other parents "didn't want their children to learn to write, or speak Spanish," to the extent that the father of one student "left offerings on his behalf on the sacred mountain . . . and fasted for five days, so he would forget how to read, and, well, the child forgot."[107] The internado became a focal point in the long-running struggles between Náayari conservatives and cosmopolitans, which might have led to all-out civil war between them, had it not been for the outbreak of the second Cristero Rebellion in late 1934.

As rebels from neighboring parts of Jalisco, Durango, and Zacatecas began raiding the Náayari communities once more, the connection between political disunity and military weakness became painfully clear to local people. At the same time, the unpopular defensas were given a renewed raison d'être in defending their communities against armed outsiders. Just as case studies have shown for rural communities throughout revolutionary Mexico,[108] the eruption of a new round of brutal, generalized violence across the Gran Nayar pushed most Náayarite to set aside—at least temporarily—their factional struggles and restored to their divided communities a level of political and military cohesion that had not existed since the revolution.

JALISCO: THE WIXÁRITARI

In northern Jalisco, where the cristero movement had been stronger than in Nayarit, the signing of los arreglos did not bring instant peace. Although most cristero fighters returned to their homes, key rebel leaders remained distrustful of their local enemies' willingness to observe government promises of amnesty. Pedro Quintanar remained active around Mezquitic and Huejuquilla, and federal troops and Mezquitic's defensa, now commanded by local notable Griseldo Salazar, continually raided his ranch, "confiscated" his cattle and grain, and eventually took his family hostage.[109]

In early 1930, Quintanar reluctantly accepted an amnesty offered to him by General Eulogio Ortiz. Fearing for his life if he returned home, Quintanar accompanied Ortiz's entourage when the general was transferred to Chihuahua soon afterward. His enemies caught up with him in June, however, and Quintanar, now sixty-nine years old, "was trapped naked in a public bath and stabbed to death."[110] Quintanar's assassination was a good example of the dangers now faced by amnestied cristero leaders across Mexico and was followed a few months later by the murder of Porfirio Mayorquín in Durango. Such threats led Nostic's cristero leader Pepe Sánchez—by now the compadre of Wixárika rebel Juan Bautista—to refuse amnesty until early 1932.[111]

Federal forces and their local auxiliaries did not just target cristero leaders. Generals Anacleto López and Maximino Ávila Camacho became rich by systematically robbing cattle across northern Jalisco and southern Zacatecas,[112] much of it taken from "the fields of peaceful civilians."[113] In May 1930, the Wixáritari of San Sebastián complained that Griseldo Salazar "is taking all the little cattle we have left,"[114] while the defensas of Mezquitic and other mestizo pueblos used continued local unrest as a pretext to seize the community's lands, compounding invasions already carried out during the cristiada by the caciques of Huajimic.[115]

The other Wixárika communities had also suffered famine, depopulation, and the destruction of homes and ceremonial centers between 1926 and 1930, weakening their grip on communal landholdings. Tuxpan had been abandoned in the face of cristero attacks, enabling members of the defensas of Bolaños, Villa Guerrero, and Huajimic to lay claim to much of the community's land.[116] San Andrés's hold on its traditional territories was also increasingly precarious, especially after its claim for restitución was declared null and void by Mezquitic's CLA, "due to it expiring . . . before the corresponding judgement and governmental resolution could be produced."[117] Even pro-government Santa Catarina found itself in a desperate position. In 1930, one of the community's representatives, Emiterio Mijares Cosío, traveled all the way to Mexico City "to discuss boundaries because [their mestizo neighbors] have tried to seize their lands."[118] His son Agustín accompanied him on the journey, an experience that paved the way for his becoming Santa Catarina's teacher and an important local pro-government figure.[119]

The attacks of the army and its mestizo allies on the Wixárika communities were complemented by the more peaceful expansion of the state into the region. Census takers arrived in 1930, officially recording only 1,888 of the estimated 5,000 Wixáritari reported as living in the sierra in the mid-1920s. However, analysis of the original census documents reveals that 3,328 speakers of the Wixárika language were actually registered, of whom around 42 percent were living in Nayarit, scattered throughout the Sierra Náayari and the mestizo lands of the Nayarit coast.[120] In the same year, the SEP renewed its attempts to bring about "a new era of peace and progress" in the Wixárika homeland.[121] Just as in the Sierra Náayari, the SEP's efforts would have been impossible without the mediation of pro-government Wixárika leaders. But conservative traditional office holders, and anxious Wixárika parents, continued to contest the influence of mestizo schoolteachers and their Wixárika allies, especially as SEP campaigns against "superstition" increasingly targeted their costumbre,[122] while certain SEP officials encouraged the mestizo "colonization" of Wixárika lands to increase rural "productivity" (or with a view to personal gain).[123]

In early 1930, Inspector Ramón Durand was sent to the Sierra Wixárika to recruit students for the Casa del Estudiante Indígena.[124] Victorio Poirett, a teacher working near Colotlán, warned Durand that "we will never be able to recruit them by way of persuasion" and, just as SEP officials had attempted to do in 1925, recommended using "some armed men to surprise them in their huts and grab their kids." He added that "various inhabitants of Mezquitic, Bolaños or Chimaltitán, who are those closest to the places in which the Indians live," could be counted on to help, attesting to the violence that defined relations between the Wixáritari and their mestizo neighbors. Alternatively, Poirett suggested that "a very pro-government Wixárika friend of mine" could assist them, as long as they did not try to recruit children in San Sebastián, as "this Wixárika cannot meet those Indians because they are cristeros"—demonstrating the extent to which tensions between pro- and anti-government groups continued to dominate relations between the different Wixárika communities themselves.[125]

DERICI director Rafael Ramírez recognized that forcibly recruiting Wixárika students would only create new tensions between the Wixáritari and the state and told Durand that "if it is not possible to get the Indians to come of their own free will, it would be better to not bring them at all."[126] Shortly afterward, however, a local teacher delivered five Wixárika children to the Casa.[127] He did not explain how he had recruited them, but Wixárika elders remember that teachers "carried away various little children, about six years old . . . grabbing them and taking them away."[128] The trauma of such forced recruitment is referenced in a short story by contemporary Indigenista author Ramón Rubin, which describes an encounter between a Wixárika child and an armed group

> composed of various mestizos and mestizoised Indians, who frequented the places of the Wixárika region on behalf of the white man, hunting the school-age aboriginal children to take them away, tied up, to the school where they were reputed to fatten them up and eat them. . . . On sighting the [former], a paralysing and animalistic panic shook [the Wixárika child] and made his tender, not even ten-year-old body tremble.[129]

It is likely that the Wixáritari recruited for the Casa in this period were the victims of such practices. Rafael Ramírez's criticisms were quickly justified, however, as the five students, unenthusiastic about being ripped away from their families for an education in Mexico City, escaped the Casa within a month and returned to their homes.[130]

In late 1930, with national education policy moving back toward a strategy of educating Indigenous children within their own communities,[131] Inocencio Ramos replaced Durand as inspector in the Sierra Wixárika. Ramos took more seriously than many of his contemporaries the increasingly radical Indigenista discourses emanating from the SEP's national offices.[132] In sharp contrast to SEP officials previously sent to the region, he was determined to defend "the interests of the Indian . . . with a prudent attitude and within constitutional norms"[133] and won the cooperation of Wixárika leaders by bringing their problems to the attention of the federal government.

In San Sebastián, Ramos complained on behalf of the communal authorities that the local defensas "seize their cattle and instead of providing guarantees do the opposite" and asked that the federal government intervene to defend them "because otherwise such dangers will continue, and you have said we must open the eyes of the Indian."[134] Ramos also began to help the Wixárika communities with their agrarian claims, whose "case files . . . have been unable to be collated . . . as an inescapable consequence of the state of rebellion in which this Entity has found itself since 1926"[135] and which the municipal authorities leading the invasion of Wixárika lands were trying their best to block.

Ramos's advocacy in San Sebastián secured him the friendship of Juan Bautista, who had by now returned peacefully to his community, where Ramos described him as "the Indian President."[136] Bautista saw supporting the government school as a way of reconciling with the state and protecting himself and his followers. He agreed to become head of the local "education committee,"[137] facilitating a meeting at

San Sebastián's courthouse (casa real) between Ramos, the community's traditional authorities, and a representative of the federal military. With Bautista serving as his interpreter, Ramos explained to the community

> the mission that these teachers bring to the region on behalf of the State Directorate of Federal Education, which in its deep desire for education, intends to nurture the Wixárika Tribe with the aim of reconciling it with the Civilized Pueblos. Informed of this, the Authorities of the Tribe, and the principles of the aforementioned settlement, understand they must present their children at the College that, the 1st of the present month, will be open for their instruction, declaring they are in agreement with the benefits that the Government gives them.

In return, the communal authorities demanded "greater security for their personal interests and their lives" and "the frank and effective protection of the Government, given that said tribe has been harassed for many years by various elements at the service of the Authorities of the neighboring Municipalities."[138] Ramos's support for these claims was at odds with the attitudes of many of his peers, such as the SEP officials then active in the Sierra Tarahumara, who saw "the theft of [Indian] land and resources by mestizos" as "secondary to . . . building additional schools in the region."[139] Indeed, Ramos's enthusiasm seems to have surprised and perhaps even worried Jalisco's director of federal education, who warned Rafael Ramírez that "I am about to take the Indians' complaints to the relevant authorities, which I consider one of my professional obligations, but I inform you in advance in case in doing so I provoke any difficulties"[140]—probably a reference to potential conflicts between government agencies sympathetic to the plight of the Wixáritari and the municipal authorities accused of persecuting them.

Neither Ramírez nor the openly pro-agrarista education secretary Narciso Bassols[141] obstructed Ramos's backing for Wixárika land claims, which encouraged Ramos to travel to Guadalajara in late 1931 to secure a land registry certificate for San Sebastián.[142] By the end of the year, he had also launched a joint claim for restitución de tierras on behalf of San Sebastián and Tuxpan, which the traditional governors of both communities, along with local caciques Cenobio Sánchez, Zenón Romero, Santos de la Cruz, Pascual González, and Juan Bautista, all signed. These men had fought one another during the cristiada and would soon be divided again by the second cristiada. But for the moment, their anxiety over the security of San Sebastián and Tuxpan's joint landholdings trumped long-standing personal and intercommunal tensions.

The authorities in Mezquitic naturally opposed restitución for San Sebastián and Tuxpan, informing the state agrarian commission that

> no titles or documents exist that deal with the seizure of lands that the natives of the Pueblo of San Sebastián complain. . . . Furthermore I bring to your attention that this Authority is not the cause of the imaginary dispossession of which these natives complain, because currently that which the natives of this pueblo possess, is the same they have enjoyed for hundreds of years.[143]

However, in July 1932, Ramos and a Wixárika commission including Zenón Romero, Pascual Chino, and Cenobio Sánchez again traveled to Guadalajara,[144] where they received a provisional communal land title. Three agronomists subsequently began surveying San Sebastián territory, which they tried to surreptitiously reduce by around thirty thousand hectares.[145] However, their activities aroused Wixárika suspicions, and Ramos accompanied the community's authorities to Mexico City "to prove their case with titles in hand at the National Land Registry." There they managed to have the agronomists' decision overturned and filed a new claim for the restitution of all their traditional territory.[146]

In return for Ramos's assistance in such matters, all of the Wixárika communities approved the establishment of schools in their cabeceras.[147] However, few Wixárika families agreed to enroll their children. In San Sebastián, where Ramos organized farming and logging cooperatives, built two separate classrooms for boys and girls, and sowed five hectares of communal land to supply grain for the school and its pupils,[148] attendance at the school remained pitiful. Like most of Mexico's Indigenous communities, San Sebastián was a patriarchal place, and local people were additionally sensitive to centuries of mestizo sexual predation on Wixárika women.[149] They therefore refused to allow girls to attend the school until a female teacher could be found for them. Even the school's few male students were for the most part "orphans missing both mother and father and others who have only mothers," sent to the school by relatives to receive free clothes and food. Ramos obtained five hectoliters of corn for these pupils from the authorities in Mezquitic but reported that much more would be needed if all of the community's children were to attend.[150] Then, as in the Sierra Náayari, at the approach of the rainy season the few parents who had enrolled their children demanded that Ramos "let them take back their children, because, to a greater extent than in mestizo pueblos, they go to far distant places to plant their crops."[151]

Worse still, the schools established in San Andrés, Tuxpan, and Santa Catarina soon ceased to function, as "the teachers designated to run these schools, failed lamentably . . . because these are places inhabited by natives and are an enormous distance away, and thus very difficult for this Inspectorate to control."[152] Ramos suggested that Luis Carrillo—one of the few Wixárika alumni of the Casa del Estudiante Indígena not to have returned to "the customs of his race, with tendencies to continue the nomadic life of their ancestors"[153]—could take over the school in Santa Catarina.[154]

However, as Ramos's superiors refused to dismiss the sierra's indifferent and inefficient teachers, preferring instead to transfer them to mestizo settlements in less remote areas,[155] there were no openings available for Carrillo, nor for any other teachers who might have been willing to serve amongst the Wixáritari.[156]

Conflicts within Jalisco's SEP administration,[157] together with the brief rebellion of a group of ex-cristeros in the Jalisco-Zacatecas borderlands, forced San Sebastián's school—the only one left in the sierra—to close[158] and delayed any further regional SEP initiatives. Tensions between municipal authorities and amnestied local rebels had been rising because of the systematic assassination of former cristero leaders[159] and the Jalisco state government's introduction of new anticlerical legislation.[160] Among those who rose up in December 1932 was Pepe Sánchez, whom Griseldo Salazar, leader of Mezquitic's defensa, had threatened with summary execution if he showed his face in the town. This had stopped him from collecting the safe conduct that local authorities owed him, which Salazar and his men used as a pretext to further "harass and accuse him of not having turned in his arms."[161]

Federal forces entered into "great activity to suffocate the uprisings at their outbreak, and Zacatecas's zone commander himself had to personally travel to this area."[162] By mid-January, the rebels, suffering from organizational problems and a lack of arms and ammunition, had demobilized and gone into hiding in the sierra.[163] The rebels' defeat and the appointment of Erasto Valle as Jalisco's director of federal education, which put an end to conflicts within Jalisco's SEP administration,[164] allowed the SEP to renew its work in the Sierra Wixárika. In February 1933, Ramos reopened San Sebastián's school,[165] and in March a one-room school was established in Santa Catarina, where Valle followed Ramos's earlier recommendations and appointed Luis Carrillo as its teacher.[166] Valle also began to push for the establishment of boarding schools for the Wixáritari. Referencing the colonial policy of "congregation" and Vasconcelos's more recent ideas of teachers as "missionaries,"[167] Valle envisaged government land grants to families who agreed to make their homes close to these schools as a way of concentrating the scattered Wixárika population "as in the remote past they congregated around churches," solving the problems that dispersed local settlement patterns had long presented the SEP.[168]

In March, Valle set off on a tour of the sierra to find potential sites for the planned internados. On his return, he reported that the Wixáritari numbered around five thousand, were "greatly attached to their customs and reluctant to assimilate themselves to the customs of the whites and mestizos," and lived "miserable" lives because of their "ancestral laziness . . . preferring to hunt rather than raise animals and [being] resistant to farming, except in a small scale and rudimentary manner."[169] He also noted that "their arms are reduced to small bows and arrows." His report suggests the grim reality of the regional post-cristiada settlement. Federal troops and defensas had stolen most Wixárika livestock, confiscated many of their rifles, and forced them to conceal the rest. Valle concluded that despite active Wixárika participation in the revolution and the cristiada, they were not a "warrior race" and in the face of threats "confine themselves to fleeing."[170]

As for the SEP's current efforts in the region, Valle reported that the school in San Sebastián consisted of only a few huts made of straw and lacked enough pupils to justify its continued existence. He declined to close it as he viewed Inocencio Ramos's continued presence in the community essential to preventing the exploitation of local people by mestizos. Instead, he ordered Ramos to boost attendance but recognized this was difficult given that local families, who had to help feed the pupils, saw the school as a burden. Furthermore, he observed that when supplies of "tortillas and ground or toasted maize"—the only food available—were exhausted, the pupils were forced to return to their homes until Ramos could secure enough grain to feed them again.[171]

Valle therefore continued to view internados as the best way to assimilate the Wixáritari, despite having suffered "the worst disillusion on realizing that from this tribe one can expect neither material nor moral aid," meaning such schools would have to depend entirely on government funding.[172] Valle suggested establishing internados in San Sebastián, San Andrés, and Las Latas (one of Santa Catarina's most important anexos). Foreshadowing the emphasis the SEP would put on improving material conditions in Mexico's Indigenous communities during the presidency of Lázaro Cárdenas,[173] each of Valle's planned Wixárika internados would be staffed by a male director and a female assistant. Together they would teach fifty pupils to speak, read, and write Spanish, raise crops and animals more efficiently, build "better" houses, eat "better" food, and wear "better" clothes, attesting to the overwhelming ethnocentrism of SEP policy and its representatives' faith in the superiority of mestizo Mexican culture over long-standing Indian lifeways.[174] Once they had been trained, Wixárika graduates would be given agricultural equipment and plots of land near the school, while local teachers would ensure that the graduates "do not disconnect themselves morally or intellectually from [either] their relatives or from the internado."[175]

However, the project's huge projected cost—at 42,300 pesos a year, or around 0.14 percent of the SEP's total budget for 1934[176]—led Rafael Ramírez to reject Valle's plans.[177] The Wixáritari themselves also undermined Valle's attempts to impose a "foreign" culture on their children, using mestizo ignorance of the Wixárika language to their advantage.[178] In San Andrés, for example, one of Valle's subordinates managed to win the communal governor's approval for an internado. However, just as the latter was about to officially confirm the community's support,

> an old Wixárika man squatted down, lifting his arms up and turning toward the governor, and asked in his language that he pause, and then bowing his head three times spoke a few words [in Wixárika] to the others, which they discussed animatedly. Then the Governor asked me: "You will yourself to direct the school and will be responsible for the other teachers who come?" "No," I said, "I have no academic titles or diplomas and furthermore, the government will decide whom to send." He replied: "The community doesn't want the school if you will not direct it, and so we will not [approve it]."[179]

Given their past experiences with mestizo teachers, it is not surprising that the elders of San Andrés would trust only those whom they had already met and who would take personal responsibility for any conflicts that their presence might cause. Thus the errors of Valle's predecessors now scuppered his own efforts to establish internados in the Wixárika communities.

Meanwhile the ex-cristeros of northern Jalisco were again on the warpath, transforming the mestizo-inhabited areas bordering the Sierra Wixárika into notorious hotbeds of anti-SEP sentiment and forcing many of the region's schools to close.[180] In January 1934, local rebels and Catholic civilians alike were further enraged by the addition of sexual education classes to Bassols's controversial "socialist" curriculum,[181] which led many of them to imagine that teachers "were going to undress the boys and girls in the classroom, in order to commit immoralities."[182] In February, the leaders of the nation's resuscitated cristero movement—who now called themselves the Guardia Nacional (GN)—declared war on the revolutionary state, announcing that anyone caught selling or drinking alcohol, playing pool, dancing, or going to the cinema or theater would be fined by the Guardia's local representatives, "as it is not just that while some groan under the upheavals and calamities of war, the rest give themselves over to pleasure."[183] Calles responded by declaring his own war on the church in the famous "Cry of Guadalajara" in July 1934, which was followed by constitutional reforms that officially positioned the SEP as the vanguard of the state's campaign against Catholicism, fanning the flames of the diverse local uprisings that collectively constituted the second Cristero Rebellion.[184]

In the face of this new rebellion, Santa Catarina's authorities remained loyal to the government. Although the community's school had suffered poor attendance because of local distrust and the demands of the agricultural cycle,[185] its Wixárika teacher managed to avoid seriously offending local sensibilities. The community's leaders therefore continued to tolerate the school's existence, especially because it served as a direct link with the government officials to whom they looked for the protection of the community's patrimony. Tuxpan's leaders were similarly hopeful that the federal government would protect them from their mestizo neighbors,[186] and with Ramos's recent support and their feud with San Sebastián's ex-cristeros still fresh in their minds, they also declared against the rebels. Under the leadership of José Sánchez, son of communal cacique Cenobio, Tuxpan's defensa obtained weapons from the state and played a key role in regional anti-cristero campaigns.[187]

However, cristeros and pro-government militiamen posed equal threats to the traditional landholdings of San Andrés. "Unscrupulous individuals" from pro-cristero Huejuquilla had, "with illicit intentions," recently launched a claim for lands belonging to San Andrés,[188] as at the same time pro-cristero San Juan Capistrano continued to invade the community's territory. But the authorities of San Andrés's anexo, Guadalupe Ocotán, alleged that government loyalists in Nayarit threatened their lands, and the community therefore attempted to remain neutral once again.[189]

Meanwhile, just as in the years preceding the cristiada, the provocations of a teacher pushed many in San Sebastián to side with the rebels. In August 1933, Inocencio Ramos was dismissed from his post on charges of "exploiting the Wixáritari." These accusations were never substantiated and seem unlikely given his well-documented support for Tuxpan's and San Sebastián's agrarian claims,[190] with which he persisted for many years afterward.[191] In fact, the ire such advocacy aroused amongst the region's mestizo caciques likely led one of them to level these accusations against him in the first place. After all, Valle himself had noted that those who exploited Mexico's Indigenous population often used the support of "very influential persons" to evade charges brought against them by conscientious Indigenista teachers, allowing them to

> tear everything apart, and sometimes secure the punishment of the teacher himself, which makes the Indian lose his faith on seeing that [the teacher] is powerless to do anything in his favor.[192]

Reinforcing the hypothesis that powerful local interests orchestrated Ramos's dismissal is the fact that he was replaced by Apolonio González, a member of the region's mestizo elite and cofounder of Mezquitic's pro-government defensa,[193] which his close friend Griseldo Salazar had transformed into a vehicle for harassing San Sebastián. Soon after González arrived in the community, he and Salazar, "with wicked intentions and [taking] advantage of the ignorance of the Wixárika Indians," together applied for a dotación de ejidos on behalf of San Sebastián in an attempt to void the community's existing agrarian claims and "take control of these lands for themselves."[194] González's flagrant abuse of his position, in partnership with no less than the hated Salazar, was compounded by other unprofessional actions. Juan Bautista himself complained to Inocencio Ramos, who continued to work as an advocate for the community, that González

> has days when he gives lessons and days when he doesn't and when he does it's only for a bit. The patios of the houses of the Wixáritari are clearer than the school. In the school he sells liquor, that's what [Bautista] told me, and asked me what he should do, I advised him to chuck the [barrel of mezcal] out of the classroom.[195]

González's actions led many of San Sebastián's inhabitants to connect the invasion of their communal lands by mestizo municipal authorities, such as Salazar, with the presence of the school in their community as well as with state-promoted agrarismo. Such an association ruptured Juan Bautista's momentary reconciliation with the revolutionary government and pushed him and his allies back into the arms of Pepe Sánchez and the rest of the region's resurgent ex-cristeros. However, given their suffering during the first cristiada and the positive relationship they had enjoyed with Inocencio Ramos, San Sebastián's traditional authorities refused to back Bautista's new rebellion.[196] The community was left divided,[197] and many of San Sebastián's families fled to pro-government Tuxpan to escape involvement in the new conflict.[198]

DURANGO: THE O'DAM AND MEXICANEROS

Of all the Gran Nayar's constituent regions, the Sierra O'dam had been home to the strongest cristero mobilization. Many of Durango's cristeros therefore viewed the signing of los arreglos as "treachery" on the part of the Mexican episcopate and the LNDLR, and Trinidad Mora, Federico Vázquez, Valente Acevedo, Porfirio Mayorquín, Florencio Estrada, and Juan Andrés Soto initially refused to sacrifice their hard-won regional gains for an uncertain peace with a regime they had vowed to destroy. Although they lacked ammunition and lost much of their cattle to agrarista militias and General Jaime Carrillo's Yaqui battalions, they continued to attack southern Durango's railways and even the train station itself at Acaponeta.[199] Eventually, Alberto Terrones Benítez, whom Calles had appointed Durango's interim state governor after Amaya's defection to the Escobaristas,[200] enlisted a priest to intercede with the rebels. At a meeting in Mezquital on July 16, Father Abundio Nájera duly warned Trinidad Mora that

> the Church will no longer support he who continues with the struggle, because now there is no longer reason for it, if he goes somewhere to take food, it is a robbery, and if

the victim appeals for help and the army arrives and gives chase, and they fight and he is killed, this will be classed as a suicide.[201]

The church's attitude to Durango's recalcitrant cristeros complemented that of Calles's, who promised that those who continued to refuse amnesty "will be pursued and crushed, and considered as bandits, as this is the only way to view those who continue in arms without a banner or other motive."[202] But Terrones Benítez also sweetened the deal by offering the cristero leaders government posts or the chance to incorporate themselves into new defensa forces, which, amid growing banditry across Durango, would be entrusted with "the persecution of robbers, and the punishment of the same."[203]

In a deal that echoed the terms of Pancho Villa's settlement with the Sonoran regime in 1920,[204] the cristeros of Santiago Bayacora demobilized after the expropriation of "the hacienda of Santa Rosa . . . which would serve as an ejidal grant to the combatants."[205] Their leader, Trinidad Mora, was given a potentially profitable position as a forestry chief in Bayacora, responsible for issuing permissions and collecting payments for "the exploitation of the land" around his pueblo.[206] Ex-cristeros, led by Dámaso Barraza's compadres Macario and Ireneo Valdés, also dominated Temoaya and Yonora, and San Bernardino remained enough of a pro-cristero stronghold for Valente Acevedo to return to his ranch in nearby Llano Grande.[207] Acevedo subsequently took up a post as defensa commander in Taxicaringa, which became a refuge for former rebels from across the Sierra O'dam and beyond as far as Jalisco and Zacatecas.[208]

Meanwhile the revolutionary strongman of Acaponeta, General Juventino Espinosa, sent his brother to the sierra to persuade Porfirio Mayorquín to lay down his arms. The latter eventually accepted Espinosa's offer and returned to his former base near Teneraca with ten of his followers,[209] leaving control of Teneraca's cabecera in the hands of ex-cristeros led by José Gallardo Aguilar,[210] which encouraged demobilized rebels from across the sierra to settle there.[211] San Francisco de Lajas remained largely deserted, inhabited by only four families whom the municipal authorities of Pueblo Nuevo accused of being "amnestied rebels . . . who dedicate themselves to dodgy dealings in Cattle." The rest of the community's population was divided between pro-cristeros who had taken refuge in San Bernardino and a rival pro-government faction of some "seventy families made up of more than two hundred individuals . . . who were forced to flee the territory of Durango having been robbed of all their property by the cristero rebels."[212]

Huazamota remained in the hands of its pro-government caciques, and although Florencio Estrada and his followers accepted amnesty in September 1929,[213] they were unable to return to their homes "because Misters Muñoz and Gutiérrez, who constitute the civil and rural [militia] authorities . . . have not provided us with guarantees."

In line with a Mexican tradition of co-opting rebels through military service that goes back to at least the mid-nineteenth century, they were therefore incorporated, along with Juan Andrés Soto and his O'dam rebel forces, into Santa María Ocotán's reformed defensa.[214] However, they were forced to settle at ranches far from the cabecera, where Sixto Mendía, Cosme Solís, and the rest of the community's pro-government Callista faction constituted a rival paramilitary force and continued to control the traditional government, having recently secured the reelection of Cosme's brother Francisco Solís as governor on the grounds that "if we nominated one of the surrendered [rebels] it would cause us difficulties."[215] Xoconoxtle also remained a pro-government stronghold dominated by Chon Aguilar and José Flores.[216]

Although the rancor between Durango's former rebels and the state government began to subside by 1930, the rival pro-government and pro-cristero factions of the Sierra O'dam itself remained bitterly opposed to each other, which compounded older feuds between descent groups and communities and led to frequent threats of violence and occasional tit-for-tat killings. Lajas's ex-cristeros begged Governor Terrones Benítez to prevent their pro-government rivals from returning to the community, claiming that "they have always harassed us, for that reason we do not like them, it is better that they be absent so they do not trouble us."[217] Similarly, Francisco Solís, governor of Santa María Ocotán, complained to Mezquital's municipal authorities that the community's amnestied cristeros "had fooled the Government, turning in only the weapons that they do not need" and that because of their previous cattle rustling, an innocent female member of the Solís clan had recently died of hunger, while

> many of the people who were battered by the cristero revolution find themselves in the same condition . . . they are infuriated and demand with all their energy that they be returned at least half of the animals that still remain in the hands of the surrendered cristeros, whom they also complain still have weapons and have not ceased to threaten them.[218]

Durango's Confederation of Peasant and Worker Unions heard of these complaints and urged Terrones Benítez to "disarm these unfaithful leaders who do not warrant any trust."[219] However, the latter's position as governor was increasingly precarious: Durango's military authorities were plotting to overthrow him,[220] and his former allies in the state's agrarista organizations had turned against him after he disarmed their militias and clamped down on agrarian reform in line with Calles's recent antiagrarian policy shift.[221] Given that the Sierra O'dam's ex-cristeros had spent the last three years fighting both of these groups, Terrones Benítez saw them as potentially useful allies and refused to disarm them. Instead, he ordered Pueblo Nuevo's municipal authorities to reconcile the rival factions in Lajas and arrange for the peaceful return of the pro-government exiles,[222] and those of Mezquital to use "conciliatory measures to make the [former cristeros of Santa María Ocotán] drop the threatening attitude that they have assumed,"[223] saving Juan Andrés Soto and his followers from the slaughter that their former compatriots across the rest of the country were now suffering.[224]

The uneasy peace that finally settled over the Sierra O'dam enabled the Mexican state, for the first time since the early 1920s, to attempt to assimilate the region's inhabitants into the nation. The first step in this process was carrying out the 1930 census in the region's communities, which, as in the rest of the Gran Nayar, only officially registered a fraction of the local population: the O'dam were reported to consist of only 1,048 individuals, and the Mexicaneros were not counted at all. However, the participation in the census-taking process of the region's ex-cristero caciques resulted in a much more accurate count made at the communal level. The data they collated reveal that southern Durango was home to at least 3,650 O'dam-language speakers (2,835 in Mezquital and another 815 in Pueblo Nuevo), while another 531 O'dam were reported to be living in Nayarit, around half of whom were exiles from Durango (figures that surely fail to take into account refugees still hiding in more inaccessible areas). Another 479 speakers of Mexicanero were also counted, many of whom now lived alongside Durango's O'dam and mestizos and around 50 of whom were natives of Nayarit.

The SEP also announced plans to establish schools in the Sierra O'dam to foment the region's "economic, social, and cultural improvement, given that indolence, vice, fanaticism, and lack of knowledge of our language, and obscurantism, that predominate amongst the inhabitants of these regions."[225] In December 1930, Durango's director of federal education, Rafael Villeda, set out on his first visit to the Sierra O'dam, accompanied by Terrones Benítez, who had finally been ousted from the governorship and was replaced by José Ramón Valdez (head of Durango's Syndicate of Agrarista Peasants but also the state's branch of Calles's newly organized National Revolutionary Party [PNR]).[226]

Having worked in mining before entering politics, Terrones Benítez was "very knowledgeable about mining" and spent much of the trip collecting data on the sierra's "metallic riches," which Villeda noted were currently "unexploited because the Indians do not allow the residence of whites in their dominions." On his return, Villeda announced the formation of a new scholastic zone in southern Durango, which would be supervised by an inspector, based in Mezquital, responsible for establishing schools in "all of the indigenous nuclei which exist in a semi-savage state completely outside of Government influence." Influenced by Terrones Benítez's ideas for the sierra's economic development, Villeda also asked that roads be built to link the region with Nayarit, Jalisco, and Zacatecas, facilitating the exploitation of the region's "great natural resources" by both the state and private companies (often one and the same in this period, given how many generals and politicians used their positions "to foster their own private enterprises").[227] The interest of both Villeda and Terrones Benítez in the region's natural resources anticipated the controversial intervention of soon-to-be state governor Carlos Real in Santa María's and Xoconoxtle's agrarian claims, on behalf of companies seeking to exploit local pine forests.

Villeda also requested funding to establish seventeen schools in the sierra.[228] In May, a school was approved for the Mexicaneros of San Buenaventura if they agreed to provide it with "a sufficient extension of land for cultivation,"[229] but the project seems to have fallen through. In August 1931, a school opened in Huazamota in response to the petitions of the community's Callista caciques.[230] The similarly pro-government Aguilar and Flores families also set aside communal land for a school in Xoconoxtle.[231] It closed after a matter of months, however, "because the Indians began to harass the teacher whom they threatened with death, because they grew to believe that what the Government desired to do was to seize their lands because they are so fertile."[232] This proved an early example of the way in which the growing politico-economic ties between the SEP, Durango's political elite, and pro-government O'dam caciques would exacerbate the factional conflicts within communities already divided by the cristiada.

For the moment, however, the state government did its best to keep the peace in the sierra. Governor Valdez ignored the warnings of Sixto Mendía that Teneraca and other "indigenous pueblos have once again rebelled"[233] and instead sent ten rolls of manta to Teneraca as a gift.[234] He also backed the inhabitants of San Bernardino Milpillas against the defensa of Pueblo Nuevo, who had raided several of the community's rancherías and stolen

> maize, wax, a shawl, a pair of trousers, clothes made by the white man, needles, any centavos they found, nets, some cheeses, the strings of a guitar, some metal plates, maize seed, a calf which they killed, age two years, a black horse which they took away, a mule belonging to Mr. Pablo Ríos; two weapons, a .44 and a 30 calibre, and a saddled and bridled mule, and some spurs.[235]

Although the defensa's commander claimed he only targeted local rebels,[236] Valdez ordered him to halt his attacks on San Bernardino and return the stolen items[237] and ordered Durango's zone commander to "proceed militarily against this defensa if cases such as this should be repeated."[238]

From mid-1931, local factional tensions mounted in the context of renewed state-level political instability and in some cases proved too powerful for Valdez to keep in check. He could do little to prevent the assassination of Porfirio Mayorquín at his ranch, at the hands of Acaponeta's defensa. The attack was led by Captain Andrés Rodríguez, who sought vengeance for the death of a relative whom Mayorquín had killed during the cristiada. Although oral narratives attest that Mayorquín had retired to private life and was killed by Rodríguez's men early one morning before he even had time to put on his shirt,[239] the regional press celebrated his assassination as the just and inevitable end of a "well-known miscreant,"[240] who had feigned acceptance of a government amnesty but "soon returned to his forays, putting together a gang that distinguished itself for its vicious exploits."[241] The newspapers triumphantly concluded that "with the death of Mayorquín, the Southwest Region of the State [of Durango] is now entirely free of robbers, allowing the hardworking inhabitants to dedicate themselves to their labors."[242]

The overthrow in August 1931 of Governor Valdez, who had done his best to protect Durango's amnestied cristeros, rather ironically triggered a series of events that ultimately saved them from Mayorquín's fate. Valdez was deposed on account of his continued agrarista sympathies, in defiance of Calles's recent declaration that he would "set a relatively short period within which to request lands and . . . then not one more word about the issue."[243] Calles was unable to install his preferred candidate in Valdez's place and so Pastor Rouaix became a caretaker governor until June 1932, when elections for a new constitutional governor would be held. Valdez, who remained head of Durango's PNR, was put forward as the party's official candidate with the backing of the state's agrarista organizations. This was an obvious challenge to Calles's authority, and his response was to create a new political party, the PID (Partido Institucional Durangueño),[244] from loyalist elements of the PNR and the CROM (Confederación Regional Obrera Mexicana, the nation's most important trade union). General Carlos Real was named the PID's candidate.[245]

The caciques of southern Durango who had fought for Calles during the cristiada were caught out by this high-level political maneuvering. By now they identified as agraristas and PNR loyalists and were confused by Calles's clampdown on agrarian reform and his promotion of an "independent" candidate for governor. Mezquital's interim municipal president, Antonio Heredía (a dedicated anticlerical who had commanded the town's pro-government defensa during the cristiada),[246] and agrarista O'dam defensa leaders, including Chon Aguilar, therefore remained loyal to Valdez, even if it meant going against Calles's preferred candidate for governor.

In response, the sierra's amnestied cristero leaders turned against Valdez—who until now had been their chief protector—and instead entered into an unlikely alliance with Carlos Real, despite his being a close associate of Calles, their former archnemesis. Florencio Estrada, for example, actively campaigned for Real's victory "wherever we were able to: helping to control the pueblos of Temoaya, Santa María, Teneraca and even Huazamota: managing to win round of the greater part of the inhabitants, to deposit their votes in favor of [Real] . . . with the sincere goal of there being Peace in our neglected pueblo."[247]

The Sierra O'dam's ex-cristeros thus allied with national forces to head off the threats posed to them by their own local enemies—a situation that contrasted markedly with the contemporary state of affairs in many other regions, where "recalcitrant Catholics [made] common cause with regional revolutionaries who wanted to keep Mexico City at arm's length."[248] The former strategy worked, albeit temporarily. The inevitable victory of Calles's candidate as Durango's governor ushered in, rather counterintuitively, the beginning of a short-lived "golden age" for the Sierra O'dam's amnestied rebels, whom Governor Real rewarded with positions of political and military power. The former rebels Zacarías Rodríguez and Apolinar Flores became Mezquital's municipal president and commander of its defensa;[249] and in Santa María Ocotán, Jesús Soto, a close relative of Juan Andrés, became communal governor with the help of local ex-cristeros.[250]

This unlikely shift in regional political dynamics naturally inflamed tensions between ex-cristero and pro-government factions. In Santa María, Sixto Mendía, Cosme Solis, and other confused former Callistas complained that "the most important fanatics better said robbers of this sierra . . . despite having submitted, are working constantly to get us in trouble with the Government, prejudicing us where they can and then heaping the blame on us" and asked that "the bad elements, instigators of uprisings, Judases and robbers be removed from our region . . . [because] we don't want to be mixed up in any more revolts."[251] In Huazamota, pro-government cacique Nabor Muñoz also "warned" Governor Real that the amnestied cristeros "caused many evils" in the sierras of Durango and Nayarit,

> leaving mothers without their children, in all this region more than forty men were assassinated by them and their companions, it would be too long to enumerate the all the barbarous acts committed even against defenceless people, killing even women of advanced age.[252]

Muñoz asked that a commission be sent to investigate his claims and to prevent atrocities being carried out against himself and other "honorable men."[253] Real ordered Mezquital's new municipal president to investigate the allegations, but as an ex-cristero himself, Rodríguez inevitably reported that the conduct of his former allies "has been impeccable according to the investigations I was able to make regarding the matter" and added that Muñoz was a notorious partisan of Valdez, who "overreached himself far more during his time as a revolutionary."[254]

Backed by Florencio Estrada,[255] Rodríguez also accused Xoconoxtle's defensa, under Chon Aguilar, of trying to assassinate him, since shortly after the confirmation of Real's victory

> with the cry of "Viva Valdez," the members of said Defensa sallied out into the streets of the town, firing their weapons and in his own home killed one Realista comrade, who died shouting "que Viva Real," and they beat others and one of their mothers and came to my house looking for me around three times.[256]

Governor Real endorsed the ex-cristeros' complaints and ordered a federal detachment to keep the peace in Santa María, accused Sixto Mendía of "undertaking imprudent actions . . . which cause unease in the inhabitants of the region,"[257] and ordered Rodríguez to "reconcile the interests of the different groups that may exist in the Municipality," despite Rodríguez himself being a member of one of these rival factions.[258]

The tactical alliance between Durango's state government and amnestied cristeros meant the Sierra O'dam remained calm even as relations between church and state deteriorated at the national level.[259] Durango's zone commander Pablo Macías was sure that a second Catholic uprising was imminent and urged Calles to send him extra troops "as a preventative measure, because the State of Durango is very fanatical." Macías predicted that the inhabitants of the Sierra O'dam would be the first to revolt,[260] and a month later a brief cristero rebellion erupted in neighboring parts of Zacatecas and Jalisco. But none of southern Durango's former rebels mobilized against the government.

Pedro Quintanar's former lieutenant Aurelio Acevedo did travel to the Sierra O'dam in late 1932, to establish communications between the region's ex-cristeros and the rebel forces now active in nearby parts of Zacatecas. He optimistically reported that the sierra's former cristeros "are now tired of their exile in the sierra where they live in the cruelest misery. They are likely to do something, and soon, given that all are armed and live more or less separate from any outside elements, [although] they have no cartridges."[261] However, Acevedo found Trinidad Mora to "enjoy little prestige because of his inactivity, and it is well-known that few people follow him," while Florencio Estrada failed to show up to their scheduled meetings. Acevedo instead named Federico Vázquez, who still had many followers and a flair for combat, as commander-in-chief of a prospective new regional uprising and appointed Valente Acevedo, who was better organized, as Vázquez's second-in-command.

This decision offended Florencio Estrada and Macario Valdés, who requested any potential uprising be delayed a few days while they waited for delivery of "the weapons that the Government offered them to arm some Defensas" and then went back on their promises to Acevedo and fell into inactivity. Juan Andrés Soto also failed to join the new rebellion, despite Acevedo's assessment that "despite his Indian manner regarding unknown or little-known persons, declared his eagerness to work and even suggested a meeting of Chiefs to arrange this." Juan Sifuentes, whom Acevedo described as "a mestizo of average education, whom the O'dam have as an advisor and secretary to their Chief," meanwhile refused to "go forward with anything without orders from his compadre Juan Andrés." In the end, even Vázquez and Valente Acevedo failed to organize a rebel campaign in the sierra,[262] forcing Aurelio Acevedo to conclude that "unfortunately there exists no unity between them, for lack of a Chief who can control them all."[263]

The former cristeros of the Sierra O'dam instead remained loyal to Governor Real. Incredibly, at a time when peasants throughout the neighboring regions were revolting against the Calles regime's renewed anticlericalism, the O'dam of Teneraca felt so assured in their alliance with Real that they asked this close associate of Calles to help them repair their church. They earnestly asked him to send them the "little bell and the devotion that belong to Lord Saint Santiago which were lost during the past revolution, and also they say you could send me some colored ink to paint the church."[264] Soon afterward, and in further contrast to most of Mexico's other ex-cristeros, some of Durango's amnestied rebels became promoters of the SEP's anticlerical socialist education program in their communities.

● ● ● ●

From the moment of his accession to the state governorship, Carlos Real had worked closely with Durango's new director of federal education, Ramón Méndez, to try to "incorporate into our civilization those aboriginals whose current situation still completely separates them from the rudimentary characteristics of humanity relative to the general environment in our Nation."[265] Elsewhere in Mexico, most former cristeros—with the exception of Juan Bautista in the Sierra Wixárika—repudiated the SEP's radical new "socialist" curriculum.[266] But Real saw the SEP's program in the Sierra O'dam as an opportunity to reinforce the local influence of his ex-cristero allies, whom he believed would return the favor by helping to persuade their followers to welcome mestizo teachers into their communities. He therefore won Ramón Méndez's approval for an internado in Santa María Ocotán, where former rural teacher-turned-cristero leader Juan Sifuentes would serve as a teacher, and Florencio Estrada would provide it with supplies.[267]

The internado opened its doors in April 1933.[268] But as well as facing the perennial problems posed by the Gran Nayar's poor communications, bad roads, and dispersed population patterns, the internado's staff, despite the backing of Sifuentes and Estrada, found themselves "in a hostile environment, to the extent they have been called foreigners or Government spies, who have come with the deliberate purpose of taking away their customs, their religion and their properties."[269] The teachers complained that even the few families who had agreed to send their children to the school "withdraw their sons whenever they like, saying they need them; they haven't sent a single female because they distrust coeducation and . . . for the apparently sacred dances celebrated by each family, they are incessantly asking that they be granted freedom to dispose of their children [as they wish]."[270] After several visits to Santa María, Ramón Méndez managed to extract promises from a number of families that, after the harvest, they would send their children to the internado, but he remained far from convinced that the school would fare any better the next year, noting that "the Indian is fickle in his decisions whenever it suits him, and it is impossible to know if on this occasion he will fulfil his promise to send a larger contingent of boys, and perhaps even girls, and build up the school."[271]

The success of the internado was further hindered by Durango's military authorities, headed by General Anacleto López since early 1933. Doubting the loyalty of the sierra's amnestied cristeros, López decided to "neutralize" former cristero leaders, despite their recent reconciliation with the state government. Already notorious for abusing civilians and enriching himself at their expense, López also doubtless wanted to seize the former rebels' cattle in the process.[272] In February, López brought the state's defensas, dominated by the agrarista archrivals of the amnestied cristeros, under his own direct control[273] on the grounds they officially constituted "Reserves of the National Army."[274] In so doing, he deprived Mezquital's municipal authorities, made up of ex-cristeros, of any power over the defensas of Xoconoxtle, Santa María Ocotán, and Huazamota, which were headed by their old enemies. López then ordered these defensas, together with troops under Lieutenant Colonel Guadalupe Contreras, to confiscate the weapons of anyone not officially registered as a defensa member.[275] This became the pretext for raids on ex-cristeros across the region.[276]

Tensions between former rebels and the federal troops and defensas charged with their persecution intensified throughout the year.[277] In September, López and his allies went a step further and tried to take control of Mezquital's municipal government. Chon Aguilar demanded the dismissal of new municipal president Ángel Guzmán—an ex-cristero and close ally of Carlos Real—on the grounds that Guzmán had insulted him and threatened him at gunpoint and was a member of a Catholic prayer group, arguing that "we don't think it prudent that an authority be a member of a grouping that is opposed to the policies laid down by THE SUPREME GOVERNMENT."[278] In turn, Guzmán accused Aguilar and his allies amongst the defensas of Mezquital and Xoconoxtle of being "the same Agraristas and the same who were also opposed to the Realista Party, and for that reason it has not been possible for them and myself to come together in agreement."[279]

A few weeks later, Teneraca's governor protested (not for the first time) that Lieutenant Colonel Contreras was confiscating cattle that members of the community had purchased legitimately or had been given by the federal government in return for accepting amnesty.[280] Teneraca's complaints were taken up by the rest of the region's ex-cristero leaders, who called on Governor Real to replace both General López and his subordinate, Contreras, "for being those who agitate and support the Valdecista Defensa commanders . . . unjustifiably ordering them to arrest and disarm us wherever they find us; which, knowing how they act, causes great intranquility in this peaceful region." Furthermore, they demanded Chon Aguilar be tried for sheltering local bandits and rustling cows, horses, and mules and accused defensa commanders Cosme Solís and Sixto Mendía of stealing their cattle. Finally, reflecting the strange political situation that had transformed ex-cristeros into allies of the SEP, they also alleged that their agrarista enemies in Santa María Ocotán "are opposed to the Establishment of the Internado and in many ways hassle its co-operators."[281] Ramón Méndez backed this last allegation, reporting that Santa María's ex-cristero faction "responded from the beginning to the call I made to them" and blaming the internado's poor attendance figures on the refusal of local agrarista leaders to "willingly contribute their part."[282] The presence of ex-cristeros amongst the school's staff probably inspired this opposition to the school on the part of the latter faction, which otherwise claimed to support the Callista order in their community.

Ironically, however, Méndez's own superiors within the SEP further hampered the progress of the internado. In November 1933, DERICI director Rafael Ramírez fired Juan Sifuentes, whom Méndez defended as an "element indispensable to the internado's function"[283] but whom Ramírez argued was insufficiently qualified to be a rural teacher.[284] Méndez then began "a full-blown campaign by way of appeals to the Commander of [Military] Operations in this Entity" in an attempt to win the support of the local defensas for the internado.[285] But the commanders of these defensas, with the help of the regional military authorities, instead persuaded Méndez's bosses to dismiss Florencio Estrada from his post at the school, accusing him of "improper handling of funds and food supplies."[286] With time, Sifuentes and Estrada might have helped to bridge the cultural differences between O'dam civilians and the mestizos who ran the internado, just as they had mediated between O'dam rebels and Quintanar's mestizo cristero forces a few years before. But this chance was lost because of the bitterness of local factional feuds and the belligerence of Durango's military authorities and the national-level SEP administration, whose actions put ever greater strain on the fragile alliance between Governor Real, state-level SEP officials, and the Sierra O'dam's amnestied cristeros.

Real, Méndez, and other regional officials remained blind to the threat that the increasing tensions in the sierra and the departure of Sifuentes and Estrada from the internado posed to their efforts to "civilize" the O'dam and Mexicaneros. Instead, Méndez reported that local confidence in the internado was increasing and asked for resources to expand the SEP's program in the sierra by establishing schools in Xoconoxtle, Temoaya, Teneraca, San Francisco de Ocotán, and San Lucas de Jalpa.[287] In line with Narcisco Bassols's vision of teachers as champions of revolutionary ideals, Méndez also promoted agrarian reform in the sierra. The amount of lands distributed to Durango's peasants had increased during Real's term as governor, but this had depended on the *fraccionamiento* of hacienda lands to benefit the peons already working them rather than on the dotación of privately owned landholdings to benefit landless peasants. Real also exempted the state's biggest landowners from the effects of reform, while taking advantage of state agrarian policy to increase his own landholdings.[288]

It was not until September 1933, when Méndez informed Bassols that Santa María Ocotán had been waiting fifteen years for a response to its claim against the hacienda of San Juan Capistrano, that the state government turned its attention to the agrarian problems in the Sierra O'dam. Méndez noted that Santa María's authorities had already sent maps, plans, and a copy of their colonial title to the CNA and asked that their claim be given preferential attention.[289] The SEP informed both the CNA and Governor Real about this situation, but the CNA denied all knowledge of Santa María's claim,[290] prompting Real to send agronomists to carry out "topographical studies related to the restitution of lands to the pueblos of Xoconoxtle and Santa María Ocotán."[291]

The arrival of these agronomists in the sierra renewed a controversy over the ownership of more than 120,000 hectares of communal territory—the Predio de la Montaña—that a lawyer had taken from Santa María and Xoconoxtle during the Porfiriato and that had since passed into the hands of the state government. Although the land had remained in the de facto possession of the local O'dam,[292] in 1933 Governor Real sold the Predio—now apparently measuring 177,105 hectares—to a "well-known businessman" with extensive logging interests throughout Durango.[293] Santa María's inhabitants denounced this sale as "a despoilment that the authorities of that State and various capitalists have attempted to carry out,"[294] which they saw as also having been facilitated by the SEP, given Méndez's close relationship with Carlos Real, his role in bringing government engineers to the community, his attempts to secure a larger plot of communal land on which to build a larger coeducational school, and his plan to "establish a saw-mill, in which work the students will participate."[295]

These initiatives were likely motivated by Mendez's genuine belief that despite "the immense natural riches which they have at their fingertips, [the O'dam] live miserable lives, hemmed in by the impossibility of exploitation imposed by the awful roads." But they stoked local fears that the establishment of the internado was part of a government plot to strip Santa María Ocotán of its communal lands and resources. By June 1933, local tempers had risen to the extent that the lives of the internado's teachers were rumored to be in danger, and Méndez ordered them to stay alert and to avoid inflaming local tensions by avoiding arguments with local people and using only "scientific persuasion in general meetings, or in personal conversations with the locals."[296]

If the internado was in an increasingly precarious position, so too were the region's ex-cristeros. The controversy over Santa María's lands weakened the political position of their protector, Carlos Real, as former governor Terrones Benítez seized on his "counter-revolutionary" behavior to tarnish his rival's reputation.[297] Real was increasingly impotent to protect his local allies from the federal military and the Valdecista defensas, which had gained additional power as a consequence of the outbreak, in February 1934, of the second cristiada in neighboring parts of Jalisco and Zacatecas. In August 1934, Governor Real informed Florencio Estrada that his life was now in danger and offered to help him flee Durango with his family.[298] Similar messages reached Trinidad Mora,[299] who was outraged, declaring, "Who has any right to stop me from rising in arms to escape being murdered in my own home? At the very least we must be allowed to defend ourselves."[300] Together with around fifty followers from Bayacora he took up arms again in late October[301] and headed into the sierra to meet with Federico Vázquez, Valence Acevedo, Florencio Estrada, and Juan Andres Soto, who agreed to "form a single group" and appointed Mora the leader of a new rebellion that would devastate the Gran Nayar until the early 1940s.[302]

CONCLUSIONS

Between 1930 and 1934, the efforts of SEP officials, federal commanders, and local caciques to promote the revolutionary regime's state-building policies in the Gran Nayar had a divisive impact on the Náayari, Wixárika, O'dam, and Mexicanero communities of the Gran Nayar. Indigenous communities in less peripheral regions of Mexico had already suffered a similar fate during the Porfiriato, when state-promoted mestizo immigration, division of lands, and the decline of cargo hierarchies led to the emergence of rival communal factions with "distinctive attitudes toward mestizo immigrants, the national state, and the Revolution."[303] Given the extent to which earlier Liberal projects to create "Mexican individuals" from Indigenous corporate bodies influenced Maximato-era Indigenous policy, it is perhaps not surprising that state-building efforts in the Gran Nayar in this period further fractured communities already riven by political conflicts and clan rivalries.

Throughout the region, then, cosmopolitan factions tried to use revolutionary state-building efforts to their own advantage, actively promoting corporatist agrarian reform and the radical cultural and political programs of the SEP. At the same time, rival groups of Náayari, Wixárika, O'dam, and Mexicanero conservatives steadfastly opposed government policies and their promotion by representatives of the Mexican state, including teachers and other SEP officials, federal military officers, municipal authorities, and, above all, the commanders of local defensas. Such overtly political and cultural conflicts were compounded by the meddling of teachers, politicians, and regional mestizo caciques in communal agrarian conflicts and by the federal government's failure to address resultant local concerns. Across the Gran Nayar, conservatives increasingly saw the SEP's activities as threatening not only costumbre but also communal landholdings. Such suspicions were often hard to refute, especially in the cases of San Sebastián, where a local teacher colluded with the region's mestizo elite in an attempt to dismember the community's territory, and of Santa María Ocotán, whose school was caught up in a controversy over sales of communal land and dragged into a violent conflict between armed factions linked to rival pro- or anti-cristero caciques.

While the tensions within and between communities mounted, Catholic opposition to anticlerical legislation and the SEP's increasingly radical curriculum grew across the country. The federal military therefore increased its repression of the Gran Nayar's amnestied cristero commanders in an attempt to prevent a new uprising in the region. The ensuing violence—employed primarily by the coercive forces of the state and their local allies—ultimately sabotaged the attempts of other state bodies, including regional governments and SEP administrations, to reconcile the Gran Nayar's former cristeros with the national post-cristiada settlement. The chance to establish a stable peace in the Gran Nayar was lost, and national tensions instead combined with worsening local factional and intercommunal conflicts to drive many former cristeros, along with a few sympathetic conservatives, to take up arms against the state once more. Across the region, the resultant violence would define the six years of incoming president Lazar Cárdenas's rule: a period regarded in much of Mexico as one of radical, pro-Indian reform and political consolidation[304] but which, in contrast, is remembered by most Náayarite, Wixáritari, O'dam, and Mexicaneros as the final, ferocious climax of a long-running war that had started with the overthrow of Porfirio Díaz in 1911.

6

CARDENISMO AND THE SECOND CRISTERO REBELLION IN THE GRAN NAYAR, 1935–1940

UNLIKE HIS PREDECESSORS, who had served as frontmen for Calles's continued rule as jefe máximo, General Lázaro Cárdenas demonstrated "a wayward heterodoxy" even before he acceded to the presidency.[1] A former governor of Michoacán on the left wing of the PNR, once Cárdenas became president in December 1934, he distanced himself from Calles and pushed for the application of the 1917 Constitution's more radical ideas. He organized the working classes into unions that would form a key pillar of PNR (and later PRI) rule into the 1990s and nationalized the railways and the oil industry, causing international controversy but gaining him the support of sectors of society otherwise wary of his "socialist" leanings. He also backed wholesale agrarian reform in the countryside,[2] replacing the conservative and inefficient CNA with a new federal body, the Departamento Agrario (DA), which between 1935 and 1940 distributed 18,786,000 hectares of land—60 percent more than the combined total given out by his predecessors since 1915.[3]

Cárdenas also set out to further institutionalize the army and encouraged it to exercise "solidarity with the peasantry and proletarian classes." He gave the nation's defensas "a more explicit social rationale," arguing that "the militia should include only peasants who had received government grants of land."[4] Finally, he stepped up the intensity and extended the reach of the SEP's educational programs, more than doubling the SEP's budget over the course of his presidency. By 1936, the number of teachers in the Mexican countryside had reached 16,079—more than two and a half times their number in 1930.[5] However, this expansion came at the cost of a decline in the quality of teachers and the effectiveness of their supervision by inspectors, which in many cases increased local opposition to the SEP's project.[6] Neither did Cárdenas initially do much to reorient the SEP from its controversial position as the vanguard of state campaigns against Catholicism.[7] Although Bassols stepped down as education secretary shortly before Cárdenas became president, his successor, Ignacio García Téllez, continued to promote anticlerical "socialist education," while SEP officials, backed by state governors, military officers, and other officials who remained loyal to Calles's Jacobinic project, trashed churches and burned sacred images from Chiapas to Sonora.[8]

Such policies earned Cárdenas numerous enemies, and his presidency was characterized by social and political ferment. Landlords, businessmen, foreign companies, and Callista political rivals all tried to destabilize his regime,[9] which also faced down widespread Catholic-led demonstrations and boycotts[10] and a coup attempt by General Saturnino Cedillo.[11] Meanwhile, the second cristiada, inspired by state government policies enacted during the Maximato, raged across more rural areas, including the Gran Nayar, throughout Cárdenas's rule. The secretariat of war dismissed the rebellion as no more than a few isolated flare-ups of violent "fanaticism" and "banditry," involving fewer than a thousand rebels active only in peripheral regions of Jalisco, Durango, Zacatecas, Guanajuato, and Colima.[12] However, the politico-military leaders of the rebel Guardia Nacional claimed their uprising was far more significant and had the support of many thousands of Catholics opposed to "atheist communism," radical agrarian reform, and socialist education.[13] Historians have lent some credence to the Guardia's claims,[14] with Jean Meyer estimating a total of 7,500 rebel guerrillas active across thirteen different states, not just in the central-western heartland of the first cristiada but also in Sonora, Oaxaca, the highlands around Mexico City, and on the Gulf Coast.[15]

Cárdenas was a pragmatist, and to hold on to power, he "cut deals right and left" throughout his presidency.[16] From early 1935, he rolled back official anticlericalism, to dampen the Catholic resistance that was complicating his efforts to wrest power from the jefe máximo.[17] After further shoring up his political position through alliances with conservative provincial caudillos,[18] in May 1935, he purged Calles loyalists from state governorships and the cabinet and appointed a new education secretary, Gonzalo Vázquez Vela, who "soft-pedalled the religious question."[19] Less than a year later, Cárdenas ordered the SEP to abandon all "anti-fanatic" activity and eased restrictions on the clergy.[20] In return, the church "demonized hardline elements" such as the Guardia Nacional, disbanded militant lay organizations, and corralled "Catholic energies" into new groups under its direct control.[21] In April 1936, Cárdenas forced Calles, Mexico's most important anticlerical politician, into exile in the United States, and by 1937 a combination of federal and popular pressure had forced state and municipal governments to completely abandon even the most localized anticlerical campaigns.

Even so, Catholic doctrine still permitted the use of "proportional" and "defensive" violence and priests continued to rail against the dangers of "socialist education." The church could do little to prevent individual Catholics resorting to armed resistance against those they perceived as their oppressors, and rebel violence continued unabated in parts of Jalisco, Guanajuato, and, as this chapter shows, Durango and Nayarit.[22] In fact, in the Sierra O'dam, Federico Vázquez and his primarily Indigenous guerrilla fighters mounted the longest running of all these local rebellions, raiding rural schools and skirmishing with agrarista defensa units and only finally laying down their weapons in 1941. Violence against schools and agraristas typified the second cristiada in most regions,[23] often encouraged by landlords and hacendados seeking to sabotage Cárdenas's agrarian project.[24] However, the second cristiada in the Gran Nayar was different. Landlords barely existed in the region, or else supported the state rather than the rebels. And although many of the Gran Nayar's rebel rank and file, like their mestizo compatriots elsewhere in Mexico, mobilized in opposition to socialist education and agrarian reform, this opposition was predicated less on their allegiance to political Catholicism and more on the dynamics of local factional conflict, combined with popular hostility to state policies that, even after Cárdenas put a stop to official anticlericalism, continued to target the "symbolic base of . . . [Indigenous] social, political and ceremonial organization."[25]

Such policies were intertwined with Cárdenas's efforts to organize the nation's "popular sectors"—workers, peasants, Indigenous groups, soldiers, and militiamen—in support of his regime. To this end, he encouraged the integration of peasants into the state's corporatist political system through their enrollment into peasant leagues associated with the PNR and promoted the formation of ejidos, which "depended upon government credit banks for finance and sold [their] product through government marketing organisations," depriving their members of "their independence as individual producers."[26] Many ejidatarios were also incorporated into the institutional army through enrollment in local defensas. By 1939, these militias had around sixty thousand members, which Cárdenas presented as a dual victory for both the DA and the secretariat of war.[27]

Cárdenas had a similar vision for the nation's Indians, establishing the Departamento de Asuntos Indígenas (Indigenous Affairs Department, DAI) in 1936 to conduct research into, consult with, and officially represent Indigenous communities within an increasingly corporatist national political system.[28] In many regions, Cardenista policies—including agrarian reform, the outlawing of peonage, and the organization of hacienda laborers into unions—benefited Indigenous people in numerous ways. At the same time, representatives of the DI, along with teachers, agronomists, and military officers, became less concerned with racially assimilating "degenerate" Indians into the Mexican body politic and instead focused on mobilizing them in support of the government. But these policies were also designed to co-opt potentially troublesome Indigenous leaders and harness to the state "the very community structures previously identified with resistance to outside intervention and exploitation."[29]

The Gran Nayar's cosmopolitan factions, headed by defensa commanders by now closely associated with local teachers, mestizo settlers, and regional military officials, enthusiastically backed corporatist agrarian and political reform. They saw these policies as offering them opportunities to enrich themselves, bolster their influence vis-à-vis both the state and their Indigenous compatriots, and also, they hoped, protect their communities' landholdings while preserving for them a measure of self-rule—which would be overseen, of course, by themselves and their allies. However, many other Náayarite, Wixáritari, O'dam, and Mexicaneros remained fiercely defensive of their political and cultural autonomy and hostile to the idea of ejidal land regimes and therefore vigorously opposed reformist state programs. Local Indigenista officials regarded such resistance as evidence that the Gran Nayar's inhabitants were wretched primitives, which prevented the kind of wholesale rapprochement between local communities and state representatives that in many other similarly peripheral regions led to "the triumph of the government programme."[30]

Of course, given the climate of political radicalism that prevailed during much of Cárdenas's sexenio, officials working in the Gran Nayar often paid lip service to the problems caused there by "every kind of parasite" who "sucked on the peasant blood of indigenous groups." However, most teachers and school inspectors remained determined to destroy local languages, political systems, and religious, economic, and ecological practices, which they saw as "the main reason for the backwardness of these ancient races."[31] Worse still, government officials and regional politicians often applied state policies with a view to their own personal gain. They helped mestizo settlers carry out land grabs under cover of agrarian reform in return for cash, land, or favors and shored up their local influence by backing abusive military officers and defensa commanders in their conflicts with conservative Indigenous factions. The fact that Indigenous people who opposed such threats were dismissed as "barbarians, fanatics, and . . . primitives who needed to be dragged into the twentieth century"[32] only hardened the resolve of the Gran Nayar's recalcitrant conservatives, who believed their costumbre alone was capable of holding together an increasingly chaotic and violent universe.

The evidence from the Gran Nayar therefore undermines the idea put forward by scholars such as Vaughan that in this period most teachers moved away from viewing rural resistance to SEP programs as simple "backwardness" and instead tried to make state directives more palatable to peasants while defending them against "new abusers of power within the emerging state."[33] Some postrevisionist historians have also argued that during this period the power of the Mexican military declined sharply, with the Cárdenas regime instead managing to end endemic violence across the country through its genuine willingness to compromise with local communities.[34] But in the Gran Nayar it was rather the strength of the military response to the second cristiada—on the part of both local defensa forces and a modernizing federal army equipped with airplanes and radio equipment—that enabled the government to defeat the uprising, just as it had overcome Yaqui rebels in Sonora a decade previously.[35] Further parallels can be drawn between the Gran Nayar and Sonora in this period in the sense that the Náayarite, Wixáritari, O'dam, and Mexicaneros, like their Yaqui and Mayo contemporaries,[36] used a mixture of collaboration and rebellion to compel the government to halt its attacks on their costumbre. By the end of Cárdenas's presidency, this dual strategy had enabled most of the Gran Nayar's communities to hold on—in the short term at least—to both their political autonomy and control of their lands.

NAYARIT: THE NÁAYARITE

Rebel violence in neighboring regions spread quickly to the Sierra Náayari, where SEP Inspector Durán reported in December 1934 that because of the activities of the Sierra O'dam's rebels, "Nayarit's border communities find themselves unprotected . . . and the schools located in the heart of the sierra have suffered from a lack of students and the cooperation of locals and authorities due to the alarm, not unjustified, that reigns in those places."[37] However, despite the government's persecution of Catholics throughout Nayarit,[38] and the optimistic assertion of Acaponeta's cristero chief Pablo Rangel that the Náayarite "say there is no God more beautiful than ours and that they are with us,"[39] of all the peoples of the Gran Nayar the Náayarite would provide the least support for the second cristiada.

Opposition to compulsory schooling, mestizo immigration, and the support of the defensas for both did push a few Náayarite into rebellion. So did personal feuds and the desire to win cattle and other booty. Other Náayarite were press-ganged into the rebel ranks. But few Náayarite sympathized with them for religious reasons, and most who had fought in the first Cristero Rebellion had ended up on the winning government side by the end of that conflict and doubted that the outcome of the second would be any different. Thus there was little popular enthusiasm for the new uprising. Meanwhile, despite the death of Eutimio Domínguez (from natural causes) in 1934,[40] the defensas of the Sierra Náayari remained well armed and organized and were backed by "a shitload of Federal soldiers" under the command of Major Jesús Meza,[41] which served to further deter recalcitrant Náayarite from joining the rebels.

In the eyes of many Náayarite, the rebels "were not defending a cause, they just went around robbing [and] killing cows and eating them, and everywhere causing disturbances."[42] For them, the resultant conflict was defined more by ethnicity than ideology, as the loyalist Náayari majority faced off against "Wixáritari, O'dam and mestizos . . . who wanted to steal whatever riches and cattle were found here."[43] The raids of these outsiders on their communities boosted Náayari support for the defensas charged with defending them. Although Major Meza "looked after the mestizos in Jesús María, those who owned the shops,"[44] cristero attacks also prompted the flight of mestizo teachers and settlers and the closure of schools in many communities, which temporarily placated discontented Náayarite. Much of the civilian population would also go into hiding, surviving on maize saved from previous harvests and whatever they could hunt or gather, dispersing feuding factional groups and freezing the conflicts between them.

Despite Meza's efforts, the response of Nayarit's federal forces to the new rebellion was widely criticized for its slackness,[45] and local informants assert that "many of the Federal soldiers died, because they couldn't run fast [enough]."[46] By contrast, the Náayarite "were really swift" and had intimate knowledge of local terrain and were thus better suited than the federals to guerrilla warfare in the sierra. Náayari defensas spearheaded regional counterinsurgency campaigns, often pursuing rebel bands across the state border into Durango, Zacatecas, and Jalisco, where they frequently collaborated with pro-government Wixárika and O'dam forces.[47] In December 1935, near San Juan Capistrano, Zacatecas, "four hundred government loyalists including Náayarite, O'dam and Federals" forced seventy cristeros to make a disorderly retreat towards Huazamota, Durango, in the process losing several men and their flag.[48] Rebels under Juan Bautista's compadre Pepe Sánchez, whose forces included "many Wixáritari from the sierra of Jalisco,"[49] counterattacked the Náayarite near San Juan a few days later but were obliged to retreat back into the Sierra Wixárika, as Náayari forces hidden "in the heights of the Sierra . . . hit us on our left flank when we least expected it, we had to kill some of them point blank to escape."[50]

The regional conflict continued to grow in intensity, and in January 1936, rebels based in Acaponeta penetrated almost as far south into Nayarit as Tepic.[51] Across the Náayari Alta, cristero forces burned rancherías, stole food supplies, and murdered or conscripted any civilians they could find.[52] Náayari families fled their homes at the first sign of dust raised by the rebel cavalry on the horizon:[53] "We fled, taking the santitos with us to the crevices up in the mountains, because those who stayed, the elderly, were killed. . . . That's how it went, everyone who could left, even the heavily pregnant women, I think two of them even gave birth on the road up into the mountains."[54] In one particularly brutal attack on La Mesa, O'dam raiders "killed fifteen Náayarite, all of them elders; as it was the festival of the new year, no one thought they'd come and many people got drunk there, and all of them were murdered."[55] On another occasion, a large group of refugees from San Juan Peyotán, including "many children, women and elderly people," were burned to death when rebels set fire to a cane field in which they were hiding.[56] Wixárika and O'dam informants meanwhile still remember the huge herds of cattle that local rebels brought back from raids on Náayari communities.[57]

The local defensas did their best to fight back. The members of these groups were mostly Náayarite, plus a few mestizos, all "good in a ruckus, many of them from [Arroyo de Santiago], San Francisco, Jesús María, Huaynamota, Santa Rosa, San Juan Peyotán, Santa Teresa and La Mesa."[58] Not all were men: some were eleven- or twelve-year-old conscripts, chosen because they were tall for their age.[59] As the rebellion wore on, even these child soldiers "no longer felt fear, only rage! Why? Because they were hungry! Why? Because of the bandits!"[60] In May 1936, two hundred of these Náayari *gobiernistas* again attacked rebel forces near San Juan Capistrano, forcing Zacatecan rebel chief Guadalupe Pedroza to retreat from the area, and then pillaged nearby rancherías.[61] Keen to retain the initiative, the Náayari defensas then marched into the Sierra O'dam. According to elders in the Náayari Baja,

> those of San Pedro Ixcatán, Corapan, la Mesa, Jesús María, and San Francisco, all joined together, lots of them, pure Náayarite, indigenous people. They were all united, that's what I remember from when I was a kid. They headed up past Jesús María until they arrived among the O'dam. Because the O'dam came here, fighting and killing, so the Náayarite followed them. And they no longer respected them, they went after them to kill them.[62]

The extent of Náayari fury became clear when they reached San Francisco, at this point a rebel stronghold. After securing the area,

> they went into the church, and the soldiers from here took out the O'dam saints, put them outside and began to bash them with sticks. "So you know what it feels like, when the people that believe in you kill those who owe them nothing." They smashed all of them there just like that, like they were punishing them too.[63]

The Náayarite then headed toward San Pedro Jícoras, where they used the same brutal tactics as the rebels and "set the fields on fire. They burned up many horses and many O'dam."[64] Then they joined pro-government O'dam forces in an attack on a rebel encampment by the Mezquital River,

> where there is a big cave. There [the rebels] had their animals, and that which they ate. They had a lot of cattle there. The [pro-government fighters] attacked them there, had them besieged three days in the cave until forcing them out. They let most of them live,

let them run off with their wounded. But they killed around three of them, the fiercest of them. . . . Then what was left of the animals, the Náayarite took half back there to Santa Teresa. The O'dam took the rest to Santa María Ocotán.[65]

The siege mentality that prevailed in the Sierra Náayari at the height of the second cristiada mitigated—for the time being—internecine conflict. Groups of cosmopolitans and conservatives worked together to protect their communities, with ritual specialists using their supernatural abilities to augment the military strength of local defensas. In Santa Teresa, for example, "an elderly man worked spiritually," hiding "small clay figures of soldiers" around the communal cabecera. Whenever the rebels tried to enter, "soldiers appeared, well they weren't really soldiers, not actually, but they did talk, and, well, they were enough to make the rebels turn back."[66] Other elders prayed to santitos and left offerings of ground maize to gods and ancestors to ensure that "there weren't too many deaths, that there wasn't a massacre . . . that's how the men from here always won."[67]

But as the threat posed by the rebels slowly began to fade, dormant local tensions were rekindled by the reopening of Jesús María's unpopular internado in 1936. Federal forces under Major Meza, along with the men of León Contreras's defensa, guaranteed its safety. Local SEP inspector Joaquín Rivera regarded Contreras as a positive, "progressive" presence in Jesús María, reporting that he and his family were "perfectly clean in their persons and their clothes, which shows us that victory is not impossible."[68] He added that many other Náayari families had also by now been convinced of "the advantages they will receive on enrolling in the Internado." Given that rebel violence had compounded the normal hardships of the lean months prior to harvest, the most obvious of these "advantages" was probably the daily rations allotted to each pupil, which in addition to tortillas apparently included "62 g oats, 120 g meat, 280 g bread . . . 30 g pasta, 30 g rice . . . 60 g sugar, 75 g lard, 62 g raw sugar and 225 g of beans."[69]

Even so, Nayarit's director of federal education noted, contrary to Rivera's reports, most of the Náayari students "were recruited almost by force and of the maximum of twenty-five we've had here, today there are barely eight left and the teachers have to watch them carefully so they are not furtively withdrawn from the school."[70] The continued attempts of government officials to force attendance at the school—which often entailed imprisoning defiant Náayari parents and ambushing and carrying away Náayari children as though they were "wild horses"[71]—together with the exploitation of the Náayari population by local mestizos "in an iniquitous manner . . . and by every means possible," compounded Náayari opposition to the internado and to the mestizo authorities and settlers associated with it.[72]

In March 1936, Rivera and the staff of the internado decided to take the few students they had managed to enroll—a mixture of Náayarite, Wixáritari, and mestizos from across the Náayari Alta—on a trip to the state capital. The children were accompanied by some of their parents and, given that the rebels continued to raid across the sierra, "some natives from the Defensas of la Mesa del Nayar and Huaynamota, making up a total of forty-five including students and adults."[73] The trip took place during Semana Santa, in which Náayari children were normally important participants.[74] Thus the excursion, during which the students competed in basketball and athletics competitions[75] and took part in marches and other "revolutionary" celebrations with the mestizo children of Tepic, was also designed to "decouple [the Náayarite] from their ancient traditions, practiced assiduously despite the absence of members of the clergy."[76] The trip was also envisaged as "the first link in the future understanding between the Wixárika and Náayari races and the mestizos," and Rivera reported enthusiastically that on their return to the sierra, the children from San Juan Peyotán,

> almost white due to their little admixture . . . without anyone telling them, guided only by their sentiments of comradeship, bid farewell to those [of la Mesa], stretching out their hands and calling them by their names, and the latter, all of them Náayarite, answered them with unabashed joy. . . . Considering this friendship has begun under such good auspices, we must continue cultivating it so as to erase the barrier that until today has existed between the two races.

These glowing reports were overoptimistic, however, as SEP pressure on local people to "carry out their dances and rituals in a non-religious way" caused the resurgence of violent factional conflicts between Náayari conservatives on the one side and teachers, defensa members, and their mestizo settler allies on the other.[77] Tensions came to a head after the region's mestizo authorities tried to concentrate Náayari populations around each community's cabecera. In La Mesa, for example, Rivera reported that murders connected to accusations of sorcery had become a common occurrence. In one particularly brutal incident—a semi-fictionalized account of which constitutes the final, climactic chapter of Miguel Ángel Menéndez's classic Indigenista novel, *Nayar*[78]—the local teacher intervened in an attack on an individual "accused of practicing witchcraft to cause incurable evils" and managed to prevent a group of men from burning their victim alive. But in a clear challenge to the teacher's authority, "as soon as they were out of the female teacher's sight they stabbed him to death and then hanged him."[79]

Santa Teresa had also been seriously split by "estrangements between the Náayarite themselves, because some of them allowed a mestizo to settle here against the wishes of the majority."[80] Open interfactional warfare was subsequently triggered by the acquiescence of the local defensa commander Evaristo Castañeda to the SEP's request to cut wood in forests near the community's boundary with Jesús María with which to repair the internado's roof. Many in Santa Teresa saw this as a threat to the integrity of the community's territory, and in response, the traditional governor and other conservative communal authorities attempted to assassinate Castañeda. As scholars have observed throughout the world, public celebrations—especially those that involve the reversal of everyday rules and norms—are "a time-honoured and near-universal site" for class struggles, political protests, and other forms of conflict.[81] It is not surprising, then, that Santa Teresa's conservatives used the community's raucous Easter festival, which featured the temporary inversion of traditional power relations, as the setting for their plot.

Castañeda, along with other defensa members, was seized by a group of "devils"—young men representing the chaotic and sometimes destructive forces of fertility—and taken to the communal jail, where conservative cargo system officers planned to execute him. However,

> as he was being jailed [Castañeda] managed to get hold of a knife. In the struggle he was stabbed deeply in the stomach, leaving his intestines exposed. Government officials soon heard of this rebellion, and sent soldiers from Jesús María, Mesa del Nayar, and San Francisco. These soldiers freed [Castañeda] and his men, and took the two cargo-system Governors who had seemingly been involved in planning the attack into custody. These Governors were initially jailed in Jesus Maria while [Castañeda] was taken overland to Tepic to undergo surgery for his wound. This surgery was successful, and [Castañeda] returned to supervise the execution of the former Governors who had been returned to his custody.[82]

In the wake of this dramatic confrontation between Santa Teresa's two conflicting forms of authority, the defeated conservatives fled to Dolores and Saycota. They took with them the staffs of traditional office and other objects essential to local costumbre—including the flag used during the Lenten Pachitas festival—which left the new cosmopolitan traditional authorities installed by Castañeda without the customary symbols of their legitimacy. These "thefts" paved the way for the people of Dolores to "declare their traditional fiestas independent" and so set themselves up as a separate community to Santa Teresa.[83] The episode is an early indication of the way in which the political and economic integration of the Sierra Náayari into the Mexican nation exacerbated internal conflicts over cultural and political autonomy and created new intercommunal disputes over the control of natural resources.

In the Náayari Baja, territorial conflicts of the kind only just emerging between Santa Teresa and Jesús María were more severe. The violence of the second cristiada spurred increasing mestizo immigration into the region from Jalisco, Durango, and Zacatecas, compounding existing conflicts and creating new ones in communities that had been, until now, less affected by factional conflict than those of the Náayari Alta. By 1937, San Pedro Ixcatán, San Juan Corapan, Rosarito, San Pedro de Honor, and Saycota and San Blasito (whose inhabitants owned joint title to some of their lands) were all threatened by mestizo settlers and neighboring mestizo ejidos and had therefore filed requests for the confirmation of their colonial land titles and the demarcation of their communal territories. A sympathetic agrarian official recommended that these requests be granted free of charge to facilitate the "incorporation of these Tribes into civilization."[84] However, most were transmuted at the communal, state, or federal level into petitions for dotación. Three factors were at work: the ambiguity surrounding the legal status of communal, rather than ejidal, lands;[85] the state's preference for the creation of new ejidos controlled by its agrarista clients over the simple titling of existing landholdings;[86] and, as in Indigenous communities across Mexico in this period,[87] the opportunities to gain power and money that control of agrarian authorities offered to mestizo settlers and their local allies, in this case the cosmopolitan Náayarite who dominated the local defensas.[88]

Both mestizos and cosmopolitans therefore pushed for dotación of lands, against the wishes of local majorities who wanted only the validation of communal land titles. In San Diego de Alcalá, for example, a petition for dotación was launched on the community's behalf by a single mestizo, who,

> for political reasons and availing himself of trickery, made them sign blank papers which he then used to put together a request for ejidos, and thus put himself in the good books of the then-state governor as a propagator of agrarista doctrines.[89]

The Náayari authorities of Saycota similarly rejected a request for dotación that a teacher had made in their name more than a decade earlier, dismissing it as the product of "political agitation by political actors trying to disorganize us." They informed a government agronomist that they were still in control of their "communal lands that they cultivate while . . . the lands that surround their community . . . also belong to them."[90]

Although most Náayarite "conceive as something severe and illegal, that a pueblo would try to transform itself into an Agrarian Community,"[91] the Agrarian Department refused to nullify false agrarian claims made on their behalf by mestizo agraristas, as most government agronomists, like their contemporaries in the SEP, saw Indigenous lands as underexploited and mestizo colonists as more industrious than their Indian counterparts.[92] As a result, in Saycota some Náayarite eventually abandoned their principles and joined with mestizo colonists in trying to take control of lands traditionally shared with San Blasito, rupturing the formerly close political and ritual bonds between the two communities.[93] In turn, growing internal conflict set the stage for further mestizo invasions of San Diego and Santa Cruz.[94] The local Náayarite (and a few Mexicaneros) complained bitterly they had

> permitted those now petitioning for an ejido to live in their territory, on condition that they respect the Indigenous Authorities of Saycota . . . the native complainants consider what the mestizos are trying to do as unjust and inappropriate . . . given that they have always seen them as members of the community and have never harassed them in any way.[95]

Meanwhile, as the number of mestizos settled in San Pedro Ixcatán grew, so too did disputes between Náayarite who desired only the validation of the community's title and mestizos who petitioned for restitución so as to force the establishment of an agrarian committee (through which they sought to take political control of the community). A severe interethnic conflict ensued. A mestizo settler, Fidencio Salas, became the community's first official agrarian representative and soon "asked for credit for barbed wire from the government. [The mestizos] began to seize the lands, fencing them off, while the Náayarite still said, 'It's communal land, why would we fence it?' But the mestizos didn't respect that."[96] Local tensions were further inflamed by the success of mestizo settlers in winning the dotación of lands they had seized from Ixcatán a few years before, resulting in the establishment of an ejido at El Zopilote.[97]

As agrarian conflicts in the Náayari Baja—and from late 1938, the Sierra Wixárika—mounted, the communities of the Náayari Alta, sandwiched between these two regions, began to face unprecedented pressure on their own landholdings. Surveys of Náayari Baja and Wixárika communal boundaries were often understood by the inhabitants of neighboring Náayari Alta communities, already on edge because of rebel raids and outbreaks of factional violence, as preludes to the "invasion" of their lands. The Náayari Alta's pro-government leaders therefore became increasingly receptive to the agrarista propaganda of state officials,[98] and of mestizo settlers who hoped to use agrarian reform to their own advantage.

Territorial tensions were compounded by the SEP's acceleration of its attempts to integrate the Náayarite, like the rest of the country's Indigenous peoples, into the regional and national economies.[99] Rafael Villeda, formerly head of federal schooling in Durango and now director of Indigenous education in Nayarit, noted that the "prolonged and almost utopic hope of redeeming these races through education" had been largely unsuccessful and that "a practical program of exclusively economic action" was the only real way to "bring them under control."[100] He promoted a range of new projects across the region, including the provision of loans from the state Agricultural Bank "for dairy production and raising cattle," which aimed to reduce Náayari reliance on subsistence agriculture, and a scheme to halt the "felling of forests" associated with slash-and-burn farming so that the sierra's forests could instead be logged "efficiently" (and thus more profitably for whoever would manage the new industry).[101]

These SEP-administered economic programs mainly worked to the advantage of the local mestizos and in fact encouraged more mestizo settlers to arrive in the region. As usual, the newly arrived mestizo loggers and ranchers quickly established links with the local mestizo military and civil authorities, who helped them secure communal land for planting, raising cattle, and logging. SEP policies that set out to transform not only the sierra's economy but also traditional settlement patterns and even the very landscape itself, disrupted subsistence strategies that local people had developed over thousands of years to survive in the mountains. The government's promotion of logging and "modern" cattle rearing and campaigns against slash-and-burn cultivation also increased the awareness of Náayari leaders of the monetary value of their lands and resources, which had previously formed part of a landscape defined by ritual rather than by its potential for profit.[102]

By 1937, agrarian petitions began to emanate from communities throughout the Náayari Alta. León Contreras and the traditional authorities of Jesús María petitioned President Cárdenas to meet with them to discuss, amongst other problems, the issue of local land titles.[103] Soon afterward, regional SEP inspectors Amado González Davila and Manuel Durán Cárdenas founded the Nayarit Indigenista Front, which aimed, in typical Cardenista style, to establish "a Bridge between the natives of our state and the federal and local authorities." The organization's members included long-serving local teachers Petra Romero and Heriberto Parra as well as "representatives" of the local Náayari and Wixárika traditional authorities. In 1939, the Front wrote to the president seeking federal intervention in the region on the grounds that "the Tribes of Nayarit . . . are victims of mestizo exploiters backed by the local authorities, who seize the lands and properties of the natives of the Sierra." They singled out for particular blame "the nefarious preponderance of the military sector who with various merchants despoil [the Náayarite]." The

Front reported that the theft of Náayari lands was aggravated by other forms of economic exploitation, such as the tendency of mestizo merchants to charge the local Náayarite "a cow or a bull for a few grams of maize or beans" during the hunger gap before the harvest.[104]

In response, the regime's official newspaper, *El Nacional*, published an editorial praising the Front for working to "re-create with the remains of those tribes the greatness that they undoubtedly once had, during their respective ancient eras," so that "with their Yaqui and Mayo brothers," they might "cease to be . . . simple biological reserves and transform themselves into social organizations, with all of the rights and problems that modern life imposes upon men." In line with the Cárdenas regime's emphasis on class struggle and the Front's own complaints, the editorial in *El Nacional* denounced mestizo traders' exploitative practices, which had begun to provoke amongst the Náayarite an "exodus toward lands even further away from civilized areas." For the first time, the federal government thus signaled its recognition that the problems of the Sierra Náayari went beyond the age-old "total absence of technical assistance, of schools, and of roads."

Yet the editorial made no mention of abusive military officers, the pitfalls of corporatist agrarian reform, or the fact that the conflicts wracking the region were ethnic and political as much as economic. Cardenista intellectuals still failed to understand that insensitive state-building programs, and the manipulation of these by local political, military, and commercial elites, were at the heart of the issues the Náayarite were now facing. Confusing the symptoms of the problem with its causes, the government sought to resolve conflicts engendered by state-building with more of the same, announcing that it would accelerate the building of "roads across the sierra of Nayarit; boarding schools . . . [and] that necessary for commerce and the scientific exploitation of land and cattle."[105] In so doing, Cardenista policy entrenched the conflicts that were tearing the Náayari communities apart.

Burgeoning political, economic, and territorial conflicts steadily undermined the legitimacy of cosmopolitan members of Náayari traditional governments, who were seen as having failed to challenge the abuses of teachers, military officers, mestizo settlers, and defensa commanders. In many communities, conservative factions regained strength. In La Mesa and Santa Teresa, the local SEP inspector complained that although "the representatives of the indigenous Náayari tribe, whom they are accustomed to calling 'governors,'" had pledged to support the schools in their communities, their efforts to increase attendance had been strongly resisted by many parents "because they fear that their children will be taken away by force to the rural school or Internado Indígena, as has happened in some cases, and which they categorically oppose."[106] The response of other SEP officials was to double down on such practices, kidnapping children with the help of

> the armed soldiers of the Defensa Rural, tying them up like dangerous prisoners; children who live far distant from the school, and who for reasons previously noted and without understanding a single word of the teacher's classes, flee their homes to hide themselves in the forest, seeking the company of wild beasts and preferring the feral life to the lessons of the teacher.[107]

The legitimation crisis suffered by Náayari cargo holders was compounded by the disruptive effects of rebel raids on the communal ceremonialism that traditionally invested them with their authority, prompting the governors of several communities to complain that now "their authority is not respected." They attempted to reassert themselves by appealing for official recognition by Nayarit's newly elected state governor, General Juventino Espinosa (at whose own inauguration they had, in typical Cardenista fashion, been guests of honor, along with regional trades union officials and agrarian leaders).[108] The crisis in Santa Teresa was particularly serious, given that compliant traditional authorities had been imposed there by Evaristo Castañeda on the back of the execution of the office holders who had tried to murder him. The community's conservative exiles formed an armed group in 1938 and threatened to attack their rivals, causing anxiety amongst both Santa Teresa's cosmopolitans and the mestizo authorities in Jesús María.[109] However, while SEP officials recognized that tensions in the Sierra Náayari obstructed their civilizing mission, most of them continued to identify the Náayarite, rather than their own activities, as the problem, complaining that "the minor caciques . . . have exploited the ignorant folk, undermining the most noble campaign there is, making it seem threatening in the sense that the Government wants to instruct the adults to turn them into soldiers, or agraristas, communists, etc."[110]

Ultimately, such ongoing conflicts meant that by the end of Cárdenas's presidency, despite the state's increased investment in education, there remained only eighteen schools throughout the entire Sierra Náayari, which could naturally provide an education to only a fraction of the six thousand Indigenous children now estimated to live in the region. Similarly, popular Náayari resistance continued to obstruct the state's efforts to take control of their homeland's "immense natural resources; its mines, its vast extensions of land ideal for cultivation, its wide meadows where ranching could be easily carried out, its mountains covered with tall pines that enclose great fortunes waiting to be exploited."[111]

JALISCO: THE WIXÁRITARI

By late 1934, rebel forces were active throughout the mestizo-inhabited regions surrounding the Sierra Wixárika, despite the church's refusal to support their uprising.[112]

The new conflict reached the sierra itself in December, when two bodies were found near San Sebastián's contested boundary with Santa Catarina. They likely belonged to the pair of mestizo merchants who Wixárika informants agree were the first local victims of the second cristiada. "They were selling things, like cloth, in San Sebastián, and [Juan Bautista] spied them on the road, and killed them there."[113] Another Wixárika elder added dryly that "he didn't like them, because they were from Mezquitic... and also they must have been rich, so to get their money he fucked them over."[114] Mezquitic's defensa, led by Griseldo Salazar, used their murder as a pretext for attacking San Sebastián,[115] "and from there the new war began."[116]

A few weeks later, Salazar's close associate Apolonio González, fearing for his life, abandoned his post as teacher in San Sebastián for his native Nostic.[117] But he remained at risk, and a few weeks later he and his brother, Pablo, were killed there by local ex-cristeros led by Pepe Sánchez.[118] It is possible that Sánchez's Wixárika allies took part in this attack as retribution for González's machinations as head of San Sebastián's school. After the murder of the Mezquitic merchants and the pernicious González, Bautista drove out the colonists who had recently settled San Sebastián's territory. Many of them were signatories of Salazar and González's fraudulent claim for dotación on the community's behalf,[119] clearly indicating that mestizo designs on the community's lands influenced Bautista's decision to once again take up arms.

Long-standing disputes amongst the Wixáritari themselves also shaped Bautista's actions. As well as raiding pro-government mestizo pueblos and the communities of the Náayari Alta,[120] Bautista—backed by mestizo rebels from Tenzompa, Huejuquilla, and Nostic[121]—attacked the Wixáritari of Santa Catarina, Tuxpan, and San Andrés, stealing cattle, burning rancherías and ceremonial centers, and attempting to take their santitos. According to informants in Santa Catarina, "They burned anything they could! There were rich people living here, but they rounded up all their cattle and took them [to San Sebastián]."[122] Elders in Tuxpan similarly remember that Bautista "went around eating lots of meat, pure meat and soup, wherever he wanted"[123] and "killed many people, women and men alike."[124] Even children were targets, including Rosalio Salvador, then living with his family close to San Andrés: "When I was just a little kid, they nearly hanged me. But I was crying so much, and my brother too, that one of them said, 'Leave him, he's too little, he hasn't done anything,' and so finally they left us alone."[125]

• • • •

The majority in San Sebastián remained reluctant to support Bautista's rebellion, however, and appealed to President Cárdenas for protection against Mezquitic's defensa.[126] The community, and even individual descent groups, were therefore seriously divided by the second cristiada. Even members of Bautista's family turned against him: one of his uncles, on being asked to lend him a rifle, "rather than giving him the weapon, wanted to fuck [Bautista] up" and ended up joining Tuxpan's pro-government defensa.[127]

The loyalist stance of Tuxpan's caciques, meanwhile, entailed, somewhat counterintuitively, their fighting alongside regional mestizo caciques, such as José Guzmán, who had obstructed their agrarian claims,[128] or even—as in the case of Huajimic's defensa commander Petronilo Muñoz—actively usurping their lands.[129] Long-running tensions between San Sebastián and Tuxpan and the faith of the latter's leaders in the agrarian reform process initiated by Inocencio Ramos, and now facilitated by a recently arrived American anthropologist, Robert Zingg,[130] evidently trumped the threats that the Guzmán or Muñoz clans posed to them; especially as in March 1935, Guzmán's loyalist forces provided the guarantees necessary for agronomists to begin surveying Tuxpan's lands.[131]

The caciques of Santa Catarina also remained loyal to the government. They enjoyed personal links, forged during the first cristiada, with military commanders like General Anacleto López[132] and were confident that the revolutionary state would favorably resolve their territorial disputes, which, at the outbreak of the second Cristero Rebellion, involved rebel strongholds like San Sebastián and Tenzompa. Declaring war on the rebels gave leaders like Agustín Carrillo a chance to forcibly reclaim territory from rival communities and settle scores with old enemies, such as Juan Bautista, as well as win cattle and other booty for themselves.

However, the general populations of Santa Catarina and Tuxpan lacked personal connections with mestizo military commanders, teachers, or other representatives of the state. They had also long been suspicious of—or even actively hostile to—the SEP's local activities, to the extent that Santa Catarina's school was closed in April 1935 "due to the tenacious resistance of the Wixáritari to the cultural project of the National Government."[133] In fact, a few of Santa Catarina's inhabitants—perhaps those who had sided with the rebels during the first cristiada—so opposed schools that they again joined the rebels. Some of them were killed by their compatriots, who "were not willing to pardon them for their misdeeds because they were from our own community. For that reason our people decided to hang them."[134] But the risks associated with actively supporting the government were just as high, as federal arms were few and scattered rancherías were easy targets for cristero raiders. Most of the inhabitants of both Tuxpan and Santa Catarina tried to avoid taking any side in the new conflict, as did both the leaders and general population of San Andrés. Few in the latter community had strong personal or ideological links to either the state or the rebels, and the community's territorial conflicts involved both rebel and pro-government strongholds.[135] San Andrés's leaders no doubt feared that a tacit alliance with one side would justify raiding by the other and further weaken the community's threatened landholdings.

The professed neutrality of the Wixárika pacíficos did nothing to guarantee their safety, as they now faced attack from cristero rebels, federal troops, and Wixárika, Náayari, and mestizo defensa forces alike. As a result, the violence of the second Cristero Rebellion, like that of the first, sparked an exodus of Wixárika civilians from their rancherías. Parts of San Andrés, such as the "densely populated valley of [H]uastita"—in Preuss's time "perhaps the most prosperous part of all the Wixárika territory"[136]—were left almost completely deserted.[137] So, too, was Tuxpan, where for fear of rebel raids, "there was no one there, they went to live far away."[138] According to an agronomist's report, even San Sebastián was abandoned because "fanatic elements have, with guns in hand, managed to divide the [inhabitants], who are currently divided from one another."[139]

The suffering of the Wixárika refugees remains keenly remembered today. "We lived outside, in caves, wherever, up in the hills, without fire."[140] With their animals stolen and their harvests burned, they subsisted on "wild yams [and] various herbs,"[141] but hunger remained a constant and "some starved to death because they couldn't withstand it."[142] The disruption of the agricultural cycle, the impossibility of making pilgrimages, and the destruction of ceremonial centers, santitos, and ritual objects (such as the varas de mando of Tuxpan's traditional authorities)[143] also paralyzed costumbre: "Everything stopped! It could only be recovered once the conflict ended."[144] Another elder remembered that "we hid our seeds in the caves. Once things calmed down, we took them out again and planted them."[145]

Many Wixáritari sought refuge in Nayarit. They joined their compatriots who had fled there during the revolution or the first cristiada, many of whom still lived "without fixed abode or defined settlement . . . they are disliked by the Náayarite and this animadversion means the races do not mix."[146] The bulk of the exiles did settle there permanently, however, either in the Sierra Náayari or in the state's coastal lowlands and in such numbers that they fundamentally altered Nayarit's ethnic composition. Other refugees headed west, where, rejected by the mestizos of towns such as Villa Guerrero, they were given sanctuary by the Tepecanos of Azqueltán (where other Wixáritari had settled during the revolution). This paved the way for Azqueltán's evolution into its modern form as a mixed Tepecano and Wixárika community.[147]

The Sierra Wixárika was rapidly devastated by the violence of the second cristiada. By the time President Cárdenas ordered Jalisco's state government to put a stop to the attacks of Mezquitic's defensa on San Sebastián,[148] rebel forces under Bautista and

FIGURE 9 Wixárika man in Jesús María, Nayarit, who was "persuaded to pose for the camera together with SEP inspector Joaquín Rivera (right) and a local mestizo (left)" (AHSEP-84-85/C/38886/E/14, Joaquín Rivera, "Informe," Apr. 25, 1936).

Sánchez had succeeded in killing its commander, Griseldo Salazar. His successor complained he could not combat the rebels effectively because of a shortage of men and asked that federal reinforcements be sent to the region to allow his forces to take care of the harvest.[149]

Despite his victories, however, Bautista remained unable to rally San Sebastián as a whole. In July 1935, he requested Zacatecan cristero chief Guadalupe Pedroza and his men help him "persuade" his community to join the rebellion. Pedroza visited San Sebastián but failed to inspire a mass cristero uprising there and remained unable even to "estimate the number of men [Bautista] has, because he was unable to assemble them all, as they live isolated from one another and their work does not allow them to go as soon as they are called, with three days not sufficient for them to muster."[150] Local informants estimate that Bautista had at his command "at most, I think around fifty or sixty men, no more," most of them armed with "bows and machetes and ropes" rather than rifles, although those who did have guns "were really good shots."[151] Far fewer Wixáritari therefore joined the second cristiada than had joined the first rebellion. This is hardly surprising given the new rebellion was generally smaller in scale than the first cristiada had been, with the number of regional mestizo rebels under Pepe Sánchez and a few other chiefs estimated by the secretariat of war to number only ninety-seven men.[152]

That said, pro-government forces were still hard-pressed to inflict serious losses on the rebels, who knew the Sierra Wixárika intimately and were highly mobile, living off the cattle they raided from beleaguered civilians and sheltering "wherever they liked, in 'houses' made of the hides of stolen cattle."[153] In September 1935, federal troops under Zacatecas zone commander Pánfilo Natera, accompanied by Mezquitic's defensa and the town's municipal president, occupied San Sebastián, spending ten days "in search of the bandits and carrying out other related investigations, in the knowledge that the chieftain José [Pepe] Sánchez and his men pass most of their time in this pueblo." Mezquitic's municipal president added that San Sebastián

> has always distinguished itself for its disobedience to every Government order, none of which it respects, and are always the first to support any revolutionary movement against the Constitutional Government; so that to attract them to civilization one needs to establish at least two internados in the indigenous pueblos, backed by permanent federal forces to impose respect.[154]

The occupation did little to curb rebel raids, which in early October prompted Santa Catarina's defensa commander Agustín Carrillo to petition President Cárdenas for "assistance" and "protection."[155] Support arrived a few weeks later in the form of a federal regiment under General Salinas, who occupied Tenzompa and, according to rebel reports, "looted the chapel, taking the chalice and the best ornaments and the carpet. They used the clothes of the venerated image of 'the Lord of Tensompa' for disgusting things." Although Salinas then campaigned across the Sierra Wixárika, his troops did little more than raid the region's rancherías, "accusing them of being rebels and taking whatever they could get their hands on."[156]

Despite the violence wracking the region, the SEP was anxious to use its increasing resources and political influence to continue to "civilize" peripheral regions such as the Sierra Wixárika.[157] Since it was currently impossible to establish schools in the sierra itself, an internado for Wixárika children was established in Bolaños under José Guzmán's protection. Once again, the SEP hoped to congregate the dispersed Wixárika population around the school to better "attract them to culture" while its staff would "dedicate special attention to the exploitation of the region's raw materials . . . taking into account that the Wixárika Indians are above all hunters, and therefore have the elements necessary for the manufacture of footwear."[158] Among the teachers hired to run the internado was Agustín Mijares Cosío, son of one of Santa Catarina's agrarian representatives and, according to *El Nacional*, a "Wixárika co-opted into civilization."[159] He had studied in a private college in San Luis Potosí and later worked in Mexico City "as a perfume salesman, then as a mechanic and, lastly, manufacturing chocolate." Eventually, Mijares Cosío returned home to take up the position of teacher in Santa Catarina, a decision his superiors in the SEP, in line with Cardenista discourse, viewed as the result of a desire to "contribute his grain of sand to rescuing from illiteracy those of his race."[160] Like many city-educated Indigenous youths who returned to their communities,[161] he soon became an influential local leader, acting as an interpreter for Jalisco's director of federal education, Luis Tijerina Almaguer, who visited the sierra to help set up the internado. He also led commissions into the sierra "to gather the boys who must come to the boarding school."[162]

Juan Bautista and Pepe Sánchez responded to the SEP's efforts by attacking these commissions and their defensa escorts.[163] Despite such threats, the internado opened its doors in late 1936, although it was soon moved from Bolaños to Mezquitic after the intervention of Mezquitic's municipal president, who sought to reinforce his claim to political authority (and by extension the influence of Mezquitic's mestizo elite) over the Wixárika communities "so that natives do not obstruct the commendable project that we hope to establish for their own benefit and for that of outsiders."[164] Unsurprisingly, few Wixáritari were enthusiastic about sending their children to the internado, prompting the school's director to request that federal troops "visit the indigenous pueblos to convince them to provide their quota of students for this school."[165] Less than a year later, Tijerina Almaguer was forced to admit that the internado

> has not yielded the fruits we expected, because the Roman clergy has made every kind of [obstructionist] effort, by way of constant propaganda on the one hand, and on the other via a band of armed fanatics who stalk the region, who have threatened with death the natives who send their children to that school, which added to their ancestral reluctance, completes their absolute resistance.[166]

Rebel attacks similarly obstructed the DA's activities in the Sierra Wixárika. An agronomist was sent to Tuxpan in early 1936, but "given the insecurity found in that region, devastated in those days by groups of cristeros . . . he was unable to undertake his fieldwork with the accuracy required."[167] Land surveying near San Andrés and San Sebastián was similarly postponed because of widespread violence and the hostility of local people.[168]

In mid-1936, additional federal troops were sent to protect the internado and hunt down "the cristero José Sánchez who for a trifling seven years has roamed the Wixárika region as a rebel, together with his friend, the Wixárika Juan Bautista."[169] But attacks on teachers and Wixárika students continued: In February 1937, near Santa Catarina,

> the rebel, Vidal, who was only just amnestied by General Manuel Ballesteros, assassinated the indigenous [teachers] Domingo Carrillo and Pablo Cosío, as they were taking their children to the Internado. . . . They were hanged by the heartless murderer, while Luis Carrillo and Pascual Pineda escaped, and are currently in hiding for fear of meeting the same fate as their comrades.

The author of this report, a Wixárika teacher and member of Santa Catarina's defensa,[170] dramatically proclaimed, "Those of my race, Mr. President, are also Mexicans or better said the true Mexicans, and their blood calls out for vengeance. Do something for them, and if my life had help in any way, I will give it up gladly for the well-being of my people."[171]

Yet the apparent failure of Santa Catarina's defensa to protect the community caused more disillusionment than thirst for vengeance. In December 1937, the inhabitants of several outlying rancherías asked the president to send to Santa Catarina "a detachment to provide us with security, that would not exploit us as do those who are up in arms, who are finishing us off, killing civilians and stealing our cows." They added that by accepting federal arms themselves, the members of Santa Catarina's defensa

> have done no more than compromise us . . . as when they arrive, they waste their extravagant force and their bullets in scandalizing, and on hearing the shots the rebels come to batter the peaceful inhabitants. We are all willing to serve the Government, but to take up arms we need the presence of a detachment in our pueblos, and then the majority of the locals, in this form, will take arms.[172]

Ongoing regional violence also prompted the governor of Zacatecas, Félix Bañuelos, to echo the previous proposals of local SEP officials by asking the president to establish military colonies throughout the sierra, to "foment cattle-ranching for the benefit of the colonists . . . and achieve the complete pacification of the borderlands of the States of Jalisco and Zacatecas."[173] In his reply, Cárdenas noted that "the expansion of ranching and agriculture always redound to the benefit of the corresponding region and the country in general" and agreed that military veterans would be a "civilizing" presence amongst the Wixáritari. But he turned down the plan on the grounds it was insufficiently developed.[174]

The internado in Mezquital finally closed in early 1938 because of rebel raids and the opposition of Wixárika parents to enrolling their children, particularly since the building was in terrible condition and a child had recently died there.[175] In the eyes of pro-government Wixárika leaders, the internado's failure compounded the lasting problems caused by "teachers who are inept and without appreciation for those poor people whom the great majority of [the teachers] do not understand."[176] They regarded the other representatives of the state sent to the region, such as the agronomists charged with bringing Wixárika land claims to fruition, as having similarly failed in their duties. Perhaps worried by talk of military colonies being established in the sierra, Agustín Mijares Cosío began aggressively petitioning the DA to recognize and confirm Wixárika land titles, complaining that all of their communities

> have had many difficulties with the Municipalities of Bolaños, Mezquitic and Huejuquilla . . . as various landowners in said Municipalities have invaded their properties in an improper and undocumented way . . . [the Wixárika] are also compromised by the haciendas of San Antonio and San Juan Capistrano, of the Municipality of Valparaíso, Zacatecas . . . said INVASIONS have been committed for more than fifty years, while in addition, for many years now the indigenous Wixáritari of the different communities have themselves been appealing these cases.

Mijares defined his letter as a "demand for justice in the interest of his brothers by blood and language, who remain thirsty for justice but because of their cultural retardation are found to be timid before the most legitimate GOVERNMENT."[177] His petition resembled many of those launched by Indigenous leaders during the Cárdenas era, which were less "compliant supplications . . . designed simply to curry favour or represent the Indian in a favourable light" and more "statements of the modern political identities of these communities." However, the SEP, the DA, and the DAI continued to differentiate between Indigenous groups "that deserved the rights of citizenship, and those that did not."[178] Despite the increasing political astuteness of Wixárika leaders such as Mijares Cosío, the peoples of the Gran Nayar remained firmly in the latter category. Thus Mijares and his compatriots grew increasingly disenchanted with the government's response to their long-standing demands for agrarian reform, demanding that a DAI official be appointed to the region to represent their petitions directly to the government and counteract the tendency of other "persons of official character," such as the agronomists of the DA, to resist traveling to the Wixárika communities themselves, instead "on many occasions making do with only somewhat credible information obtained in the adjacent mestizo pueblos as to the current state of 'the Indians.'"[179]

• • • •

Bautista and Sánchez's forces now numbered only "forty to fifty men," but Mijares complained that "for my poor Indian bothers," rebel attacks still constituted a "pretty severe problem, given that more than fifty indigenous men succumbed to them; some for being supporters of the government and others for being considered their enemies." To that end, he begged the president to launch a "war without quarter to achieve the quickest possible extermination of these rebels."[180] Although the government also ignored this element of Mijares's petition and no new federal campaign was launched in the Sierra Wixárika in this period, local violence did at last begin to subside toward the end of 1938. Many of Jalisco's most important rebel commanders had been killed by this point,[181] and the government had cracked down on the corrupt officers who supplied the rebels from the army's own stocks.[182] Federal victories in other parts of Jalisco, as well as in Durango and Zacatecas, put additional pressure on the Wixárika rebels.

The growing strength of the pro-government Wixárika forces of Santa Catarina and Tuxpan and the increasing strategic collaboration between these groups and the defensas of the Sierra Náayari further restricted the operational abilities of the local rebels. By the late 1930s, government weapons consignments had allowed Tuxpan's defensa to expand to "more or less, eighty or ninety men."[183] The ranks of Santa Catarina's defensa, originally made up of around twenty men armed with rifles, also swelled as "many others joined, armed with bows and arrows, stakes, machetes, anything"[184] "because it made no sense for so many to be dying, so they had to rise up [to defeat the rebels]. Yes, they had to leave their families and everything, it was ugly."[185]

These groups worked closely with Náayarite defensas and federal troops, led by Major Jesús Meza, who penetrated deep into the Sierra Wixárika in search of Bautista and his dwindling forces.[186] According to Fernando Muñíz—a Náayari elder who, aged twelve, was conscripted into Meza's forces—they found the region largely desolate: "We went two days without eating, up there in the Sierra. There were small Wixárika ranches, but the inhabitants had fled, because of the rebels that roamed around there, killing them or snatching them and forcing them to accompany them. . . . Thus it was as solitary there as it is at sea, they had nothing to eat and neither did we."[187] Meza incorporated into his forces some of the Wixárika refugees, who helped him track Bautista to Santa Catarina, where they ambushed the rebel chief but managed only to knock his hat off, thanks to the speed of his "pale horse, quick as a hummingbird."[188]

Rebel military defeats were compounded by the state's increasing rapprochement with the church.[189] In return for the government's relaxation of previous restrictions on the numbers and activities of priests,[190] the clergy stepped up its condemnation of the rebels, which reduced civilian support for the rebels and their access to weapons, ammunition, foodstuffs, and new recruits.[191] In late 1938, Pepe Sánchez retired to Guadalajara, where he died peacefully many years later.[192] Bautista remained in arms for a few years more, raiding the sierra's more remote rancherías and occasionally attacking teachers and other government officials. In December 1938, his band even managed to ambush and kill Agustín Mijares Cosío, the "progressive" Wixárika leader who had so vociferously demanded their extermination.[193] But the second cristiada as a major revolutionary conflagration affecting all of the Gran Nayar was drawing definitively to an end.

As the threat posed by the rebels subsided, in late 1938, Cardenista agrarian reform finally reached the Sierra Wixárika. A year before, Cárdenas had announced the massive redistribution of lands in Sonora's Yaqui Valley, which, in a "noteworthy departure from previous governmental policies at both the state and national levels," ceded to the Yaqui "a territory reserved for their exclusive occupation . . . encompass[ing] approximately one-third of the area that the Yaquis claimed as theirs by colonial tradition." This ended more than a century of conflict between recalcitrant Yaquis and the Mexican state, binding them together in a firm patron-client relationship that, in combination with regional infrastructure projects, significantly reduced Yaqui autonomy.[194] It would seem that Cárdenas envisaged a similar settlement for the Sierra Wixárika when he ordered the DA to fix the boundaries of the region's communities, which, he hoped, would put a definitive end to the conflicts wracking the region.[195]

This news was optimistically received in Tuxpan, Santa Catarina, and San Andrés. A representative of the latter community explained to the DA that

> previously we didn't even try to complain, because we understood that no one would do us justice, but now that the Government of Mr. General Cárdenas has taken it upon himself to liberate the indigenous tribes of the Republic, we have written to you to make public our plea, hoping that you would be good enough to attend to it, so that those lands which we mention be returned to us.[196]

However, rather than mark out the Wixárika communal territories in line with their colonial land titles, as Wixárika leaders had been demanding since the Porfiriato, the agronomists who now arrived in the region concluded that "demarcation will not resolve the Indians' problems, as these are not to do with land, but are economic, racial and environmental." They instead reiterated the earlier proposals of SEP officials and Governor Bañuelos by suggesting that to "improve the fatal issues previously signaled . . . migratory currents must be triggered in both directions, that is, foment the colonization of Wixárika lands, and draw large groups of the latter to the larger population centers." With Agustín Mijares's death depriving the Wixáritari of a politically sophisticated bicultural leader who might have contested the DA's condescending policies, the Sierra Wixárika was divided into three zones. In the first, mestizo colonists "will teach the Indians to plant, making them realize the advantages that agriculture will bring them"; in the second, the settlers would teach the Wixáritari modern logging techniques; and in the third, they would teach them to raise cattle.[197]

The loyalty of Santa Catarina's leaders to the state—which had cost the lives of so many of the community's inhabitants—was further insulted by a presidential resolution awarding the community a paltry 15,837 hectares of land[198] (only a fifth of what it would receive in a second presidential resolution in 1960 and a fraction of the total territory still claimed by the community today).[199] Meanwhile, the redistribution of ex-hacienda lands near Camotlán, over which the government of Nayarit now asserted its control, threatened Tuxpan, whose authorities feared "that the repartition [would] extend to their territory . . . given the inhabitants of the hacienda have always been interested in their community's lands."[200] The redistribution threatened to fragment their communal territory and put it at the mercy of Huajimic's caciques, who were backed by the authorities in Nayarit.

The Cárdenas regime's betrayal of its Wixárika allies was but one example of the ways in which, from 1938 onward, it curbed or even reversed its reformist program in the face of "serious economic difficulties and political challenges." Although such moves "alienated many of [the regime's] erstwhile supporters" throughout the country,[201] Tuxpan's caciques nonetheless remained loyal to the state. They continued to pursue the last of the region's rebel bands, and their forces finally killed Juan Bautista in September 1940, as he celebrated a harvest ritual.[202] Oral accounts of Bautista's death conclude the cycle of "the revolution" as remembered today in Tuxpan and San Sebastián. They coincide with newspaper reports in describing federal troops based in Villa Guerrero as cooperating with Tuxpan's defensa in an attack on Bautista's headquarters at a fortified cave near San Sebastián.[203] But Wixárika informants are clear that José Sánchez—son of Tuxpan's defensa commander Cenobio Sánchez—dealt the deathblow to the notorious Wixárika rebel. According to José's son, Salvador,

> leader to leader they fought. . . . My father got to a place below the caves where Juan [Bautista] stored his weapons. When [Bautista] arrived there, my father was already in position, and when [Bautista] entered, he gave him one to the head, but he didn't fall down, they say he ran off below, but my father followed, shooting at him. They got to a plateau, where there was an stream with water in it, [Bautista] didn't manage to jump it and fell in the water, he turned to face my father and jumped up and grabbed him, as my father couldn't load his weapon because he was too close. [Bautista] had a pistol, but he couldn't load it either, it was really "Will he go down or won't he?" but in the end my father managed to overpower him.

Wixárika narratives of this event, like so many of the stories told about the Gran Nayar's caciques, emphasize Bautista's supernatural powers, attesting to his extraordinary charisma. According to Salvador Sánchez, Bautista "didn't die quickly, not at all, the first blow was my father's bullet in his head. Listen, how his head must have ended up! But he continued to shoot back, and they yelled at each other, he was yelling! But while he was already all fucked up, can you believe it?"[204] Some informants put this down to the fetishes that Bautista wore around his neck: "Even seven bullets didn't kill him, because he had these amulets or something, which were helping him. So they took them off, and it was only then that, you know, 'have a nice trip to wherever you're going!'"[205]

Bautista's death marked the end of nearly thirty years of revolutionary conflict in the Sierra Wixárika. However, it did little to alleviate Wixárika territorial conflicts with nearby mestizo pueblos. San Sebastían suffered worst of all. Surviving members of Bautista's band reached their community in time to "warn the people to hide the santitos," preventing them from falling into the hands of pro-government Wixárika militiamen.[206] But the human inhabitants of the community were not so lucky: their enemies "avenged themselves there, apparently they carried away young women, and cattle, maize, because the people [of Santa Catarina] were dying of hunger."[207] Worse was to come, as mestizo cattlemen from Huajimic and Mezquitic invaded the community's lands in such numbers that they "nearly ended Wixárika control over San Sebastián."[208]

The fighting had also left the cabeceras of San Andrés and its anexo Guadalupe Ocotán "much destroyed" and "their courthouses falling down," and forced much of the community's population to flee into exile in Nayarit and Durango. The community's authorities complained these refugees

> no longer want to return to the pueblos, although we call them they refuse. We see the other tribes like the Náayarite and the O'dam, because they always remain on their lands they are better off than us. Why? Because they have not left the lands that, as we know, the Supreme Government has given them.[209]

Much of the community's territory, like that of Tuxpan and San Sebastián, was dismembered by the caciques of Huajimic, who took control of Guadalupe Ocotán with the backing of Nayarit's state government.[210] Even informants from Wixárika communities that had long disputed their borders with San Andrés felt sympathy for their old rivals: "apparently in the community of San Andrés they lost lots of land, I think there were three or four changes to the location of Jalisco's borders, which shrank [their territory]."[211] These annexations constituted an existential threat to San Andrés, whose leaders begged President Cárdenas to order the demarcation of our communal lands, in accordance with the communal property title that we have in our power, because mestizo elements, among them the current Municipal President of La Yesca [en Nayarit], have seized parts of our territory.

However, lacking the funds to pursue such a complex legal case without the federal government's support,[212] Guadalupe Ocotán remained, de facto, within Nayarit, its inhabitants adding to the numbers of Wixáritari now living permanently in that state. Many of these Wixárika exiles remained in hiding in the mountains near Huaynamota.[213] In the late 1930s, Nayarit state governor Juventino Espinosa and local SEP officials attempted to permanently settle the refugees,[214] whom they regarded as "underage wards in need of guardianship in order to enter the life of society and be able to be taken into account as adults."[215] Modern Wixárika colonies at Huaynamota and Zoquipan, and other Wixárika ejidos (rather than traditional "communities") farther to the south and west, have their roots in the SEP-administered resettlement plans in this period.

DURANGO: THE O'DAM AND MEXICANEROS

Of the three constituent regions of the Gran Nayar, the Sierra O'dam was the most fertile ground for renewed rebel mobilization. Support for the rebels was generated by the same factors that led so many O'dam and Mexicaneros to join the cristeros in 1926. Personal connections forged between local people and rebel leaders during the earlier conflict, together with opposition to more recent federal school-building efforts, helped to shore up this support.

In Temoaya and Yonora, late cacique Dámaso Barraza's compadres Macario and Ireneo Valdés persuaded much of the population to pledge allegiance to Trinidad Mora in early November.[216] In Santa María Ocotán, too, Juan Andrés Soto persuaded most of his relatives and factional allies to support the rebellion and won the backing of others angered by the state government's involvement in the recent "despoilment" of communal lands. Local support for the rebels rose further after their first major action—a raid on Santa María's unpopular boarding school. After leveling the building,[217] the rebels kidnapped Héctor Méndez, the agriculture teacher at the school and the son of Ramón Méndez, head of Durango's Department of Federal Education. Much to the fury of the teachers across the country who took up Méndez's cause with the government, the rebels used their hostage as a bargaining chip, "threatening him with death as 'chastisement for the teachers because of Socialist Education' and imposing a large ransom in exchange for his life."[218]

Although the rebels lacked the support of the church, Trinidad Mora justified the raid as a "Catholic" attack on "an internado established by the government to throw children and youths into perdition."[219] Conversely, Juan Andrés Soto announced that his men had acted in defense of O'dam costumbre. They were applauded by "conservative" factions throughout the sierra, thanks to widespread fears that children who attended government schools "would abandon their customs, and the traditions that we have. For that reason the elders hated the school."[220] Thus both in Santa María itself and in other communities, such as Taxicaringa, "Juan Andrés gained strength, there were lots of cristeros, he had many followers."[221]

However, as in neighboring parts of the Gran Nayar and much of the rest of Mexico, the people of the Sierra O'dam were less supportive of the second than they had been of the first Cristero Rebellion. Like the Náayarite and Wixáritari, the O'dam and Mexicaneros had lived through thirty years of conflict. Many were tired of fighting and wanted to return to their old lives as agriculturalists and devout practitioners of costumbre. In Temoaya and Yonora, many former rebels "didn't believe Federico [Vázquez], that he was fighting for the faith," and sent "warnings" to other communities "so they would not believe Federico's men, because they went around robbing, they were abusing people over there."[222] As before, rebel leaders were often forced to depend on conscription, backed by terror, to fill their ranks. In Teneraca, for example, "they killed those who refused to go with Federico [Vázquez]. They say there was a huge *chalate* tree,[223] from which the people were hanged when Federico arrived."[224]

By now, many O'dam communities also harbored powerful pro-government factions. In Taxicaringa, amnestied Zacatecan cristero leader Francisco Sánchez was killed in April 1934, along with "his wife, his sister and his parents," by "the same locals who had previously served the cristero Movement and were later at the orders of Callismo."[225] In Teneraca, too, pro-government defensa commander Simón Enríquez replaced former cristero José Gallardo Aguilar as governor in 1935, suggesting that a pro-government faction now dominated the community's Consejo de Ancianos.[226] Both the traditional authorities and the defensa of Xoconoxtle were under the control of the pro-government Flores and Aguilar families,[227] and in Santa María, a close relative of pro-government cacique Sixto Mendía was elected traditional governor in 1935.[228] Even Santa María's ex-cristeros did not join the rebels en masse. Scholars have observed that the bonds of political allegiance and friendship that hold together factional groupings often weaken in the wake of defeat,[229] and this had evidently occurred in Santa María after the first cristiada. In April 1935, for example, Durango's governor commended Juan José María Gurrola, a former lieutenant of Andrés Soto, for his cooperation "with this Administration in the fight against the cristeros which has been conducted in the State."[230]

Yet the rebels still posed a threat to the incipient revolutionary project in southern Durango. Despite the availability of airplanes, which the government used against the Yaqui in 1927[231] and Escobarista rebels in 1929,[232] federal forces initially failed to penetrate the Sierra O'dam because of "the topography of the terrain . . . with huge mountains separated by deep canyons . . . [and] covered in thick forests which hide some areas from the sight of airplanes."[233] Untroubled by federal attacks, the rebels' main encampment at Cerro Gordo, in the heart of the sierra, grew to accommodate more than two hundred men as well as their families.[234] They stocked up on supplies through raids: "They seized animals and plundered maize and whatever else people had. They burned the houses, and caused a lot of damage."[235]

In December, the first federal column to venture into the sierra was ambushed by Federico Vázquez, near Cerro Gordo, and forced to retreat with heavy losses. Durango's chastened federal forces, under General Anacleto López, postponed further attacks on the rebels and instead dedicated themselves to "confiscating" "all of the cattle and maize" they could find near Trinidad Mora's native Bayacora.[236] In January 1935, Saturnino Cedillo—whose humane treatment of captured rebels had been key to his success in smothering the first Cristero Rebellion[237]—warned that such looting would only inflame the rebellion, writing to President Cárdenas that López

> used poor tactics in the cristero campaign of 1929, as far from keeping the pueblos contented, he turned even most of their cattle into cristeros. It pains me to say, but it is necessary, and I believe that in these moments of discontent, if General López is left to himself any longer, one runs the risk that rebel outbreaks in said State will continue [to occur].[238]

As in the Sierra Náayari, federal failures left O'dam defensas to spearhead the campaign against their old rivals. The guerrilla war that followed was brutal, soon costing the life of Mezquital's municipal president and forcing many O'dam and Mexicaneros to flee their homes.[239] These pacíficos often followed traditional routes of trade and pilgrimage into Nayarit: many of Teneraca's inhabitants settled in towns like Quiviquinta, which had been inhabited by O'dam and Mexicaneros until the late Porfiriato,[240] while refugees from Santa María and San Francisco Ocotán found refuge amongst the Náayarite of Santa Teresa and San Pedro Ixcatán.[241] Others stayed in Durango, settling in the Mexicanero communities of San Pedro Jícoras and San Buenaventura or heading in the opposite direction to towns along the border with Zacatecas, to "maintain themselves through begging."[242]

Federal commanders regarded the flight of these refugees as evidence of collaboration with the rebels. Despite Cardenista rhetoric about the army as a force for proletarian liberation, it used harsh scorched-earth tactics across the Sierra O'dam (just as it had done in southern Sonora a year before, in response to a short-lived Mayo uprising).[243] Forces under Brigadier General José Cortés Ortiz destroyed Teneraca, Lajas, Taxicaringa, San Bernardino, and Valente Acevedo's stronghold of Llano Grande. They left "not a single house" standing on the grounds that "the families that existed here are found with the rebels living in the canyons." O'dam elders today remember that the soldiers "burned pretty much all of the pueblos. . . . Because the bad guys were roaming around there, and because of them everyone was hit [by the violence]."[244]

General Cortés was unapologetic about such brutality. He accused the exiled inhabitants of San Bernardino of "making common cause with banditry,"[245] despite communal leaders claiming they had been forced to "wander strange lands so that our families might escape the rebels' clutches," leaving them "in an awful condition to the extent we are dying of hunger."[246] He similarly reported, rather triumphantly, that because the inhabitants of Teneraca had fled their homes for "the caves and canyons," his troops burned what had once been "[the] only pueblo consisting of well-constructed houses in all the vast expanses stalked by the enemy."[247]

Teneraca also lost its santito, Saint Santiago, in this attack. The army remained a bastion of anticlericalism in this period,[248] and on finding the saint in a nearby cave, iconoclastic soldiers "shot it with their rifles."[249] Miraculously, the santito survived the attack: "The shots never hit it, the bullets disintegrated."[250] Chon Aguilar witnessed this marvel and, "as this man was from here, was of our people, knew how to speak O'dam, he realized it was a miracle, he said, 'This santito is powerful. It's coming with me.'" He took the saint back to his native Xoconoxtle, where it remains hidden today, much to the frustration of Teneraca's inhabitants.[251]

Memories of hunger and other privations still dominate O'dam and Mexicanero narratives of the second Cristero Rebellion, as they do the accounts of this conflict told throughout the rest of the Gran Nayar. As federal troops and cristero rebels alike "killed cows and goats in order to eat meat and they had plenty of water," civilians faced extreme hardship,

> suffering much hunger, thirst, cold and heat, they could only eat raw animal skins, the roots of certain plants, wild limes, honeycomb, and the raw flower-stalks of agave. Sometimes they made fires at twelve or one in the afternoon, because at that time it doesn't smoke as much, because if the bad guys saw the smoke, they would immediately head for that place to kill the people there.[252]

In the face of Cedillo's recent complaints and mounting federal losses (to say nothing of defensa and civilian casualties), the military shifted its strategy, attempting to negotiate the surrender of rebel leaders. Cárdenas authorized General Mariano Arrieta, one of Durango's most important revolutionary veterans and an implacable enemy of Calles, to travel to Durango, where he offered amnesty to the local rebels. Mora angrily rejected Arrieta's offer, replying that

> it is painful that persons such as yourself would be willing in any way to obey the orders of a tyrant. Surely you must understand . . . that my attitude is not due, in any way, to lust for power or personal prosperity, but rather, as a citizen conscious of my rights, and seeing those violated in the filthiest manner, by a group constituting a government at the point of a bayonet, simple human dignity has forced me to defend, with the same force, that which the tyrants would try to snatch.

Mora instead invited Arrieta to join "our cause together with all those men who have even a hint of patriotism."[253] However, Valente Acevedo (earlier described by Mora as "amongst the least willing to join up")[254] did accept amnesty along with many of his men, and in August, General López induced Cárdenas to pay Acevedo three hundred pesos, with fifty more for "each one of his companions."[255] Further amnesties were granted to members of Macario Valdés's group and then to several of Vázquez's fighters,[256] before Vázquez himself finally accepted amnesty.[257]

The sierra's pro-government leaders were incensed by the negotiations. Mezquital's authorities denounced the inhabitants of Yonora—their enemies since before the revolution—as murderers and demanded that even if they gave up their weapons, they be forced to settle outside the state. They suggested the community's lands could be given to their own O'dam allies in Santa María and Xoconoxtle, who "have always given proof of being loyal to the Government, as they are currently demonstrating with their acts in combating those disturbers of order, and have known how to suffer with resignation the terrible consequences."[258] The suspicions of pro-government caciques were substantiated when Vázquez's surrender was revealed to be a feint. He bought arms and ammunition with the three thousand pesos that General Jesús Agustín Castro, Durango's newly appointed zone commander, had raised in donations from the state's Chamber of Commerce for himself and his men.[259] Then, having tended to their harvests during the pause in the fighting, they launched a new campaign across the Sierra O'dam and into Nayarit.[260]

As in the Sierra Wixárika, the government recognized that it would be able to crush the second cristiada in southern Durango only with the help of local communities. It therefore did its best to consolidate its alliances with local caciques and, to win further popular support, pushed forward with the surveying of Santa María Ocotán and Xoconoxtle's communal territories. This process had been set to begin in June 1935, but given the threat posed by rebel groups and the cost of sending five engineers, twenty assistants, and a fifty-man military escort to the region for five months,[261] the project was postponed until December, when national and local politics meshed together to transform the issue of O'dam land titles into a matter of political significance for President Cárdenas.

Since May 1935, Calles had been loudly criticizing Cárdenas's reformist agenda. Fearing that Calles would try to unseat him, in late 1935, Cárdenas purged Calles's most important political allies, including the state governors of Durango, Sonora, Sinaloa, and Guanajuato, paving the way for the arrest and exile of Calles himself in April 1936. In some states, Cárdenas was forced to compromise with local conservatives to oust his Callista enemies.[262] But in Durango, where conservative politicians and military commanders remained loyal to the jefe máximo, Cárdenas undermined Callista influence by empowering local radicals and political independents, such as military strongman General Jesús Agustín Castro (who had retired into private life after breaking with Obregón in 1928) and former state governor Alberto Terrones Benítez (deposed by Calles in 1930).

Terrones Benítez used his knowledge of agrarian problems in the Sierra O'dam to his and Cárdenas's advantage, accusing his old rival, Governor Carlos Real, of orchestrating "the despoilment of its lands and forests that the settlement of Xoconoxtle has suffered in favor of capitalist enemies of the revolution."[263] Cosme Solís, who spoke with Cárdenas in Mexico City in November, backed up Terrones Benítez's accusations and complained that

> the seizure of which we have been the object, has left us in misery . . . as we lack the right to use any wood in the construction of our shacks, far less to make planks for our own benefit. For many years we have been supporting the constitutional Government, combating the reactionaries and cristeros as we are able to prove, with many of the Zone Commanders who have been in Durango.[264]

The issue became a national scandal, which enabled Cárdenas to maneuver Governor Real from power in December 1935. General Castro, whom Cárdenas had appointed as Durango's zone commander, took over temporary control of the state government before a local Cardenista, Enrique Calderón, was installed as governor.[265]

In return for O'dam assistance in deposing his enemies in Durango, Cárdenas ordered the immediate joint confirmation of Santa María Ocotán's and Xoconoxtle's territorial claims. Though each community still maintained its own traditional government, the resolution assigned them joint title to the lands that each claimed, effectively fusing the communities. While this was accepted by the pro-government caciques of each—who together took control of the agrarian council established to exercise jurisdiction over what was now the community of Santa María Ocotán y Xoconoxtle—they launched a legal challenge against the resolution because it failed to assign them the Predio de la Montaña.[266] In response, Cárdenas ordered the full return of all 421,139 hectares outlined in these communities' original agrarian petitions,[267] creating what is today Mexico's largest communally owned territory. Along with a title, the community also acquired a "telephonic radio,"[268] "an emergency landing-strip,"[269] and a federal garrison.[270]

The transformation of Santa María's cabecera into an important federal base spelled disaster for the region's cristeros. Frumencio Estrada soon died during a raid on the nearby anexo of Llano Grande, where the Solís clan had their mitote patio.[271] A large group of "pro-government O'dam had taken refuge there . . . they had their cattle, and their houses, and they were celebrating their mitote because, well, they thought that there, far away, the cristeros wouldn't come looking for them. But [Frumencio] Estrada, Federico Vázquez and Juan Andrés got together and went to attack them there."[272] As the rebels "went into the houses, burning some of them," Cosme Solís, Sixto Mendía, and the rest of those "who had weapons, ran off to one side. . . . [They asked themselves], 'Where is their leader?' Then they saw where Frumencio was, and shot at him, hitting him with their bullets and killing him." The rebels panicked and fled, taking with Frumencio's body with them, which they buried in a nearby forest.[273]

Frumecio's twin brother, Florencio Estrada, who still claimed to lead "many O'dam" and around 170 mestizos on the Durango-Zacatecas border,[274] was killed soon afterward. In *Rescoldo*, Antonio Estrada writes that his father had just begun to prepare breakfast at his camp near San Juan Capistrano when federal troops and their Náayari and O'dam auxiliaries attacked.[275] Although the federal commander, Estrada's former compadre, urged him to surrender, the defiant cristero chief tried to escape and was shot in the leg. "Now he shouted, 'Long live Christ the King' and 'Death to the government,' while continuing to shoot at whoever stuck his head out." But Estrada's pistol jammed, and while trying to reload it, he was mortally wounded. This didn't stop a group of soldiers from torturing him to death, much to the disgust of their commander, who immediately ordered the execution of the man who fired the fatal shot. The corpses of Estrada and several of his men were taken to Huejuquilla, where they were paraded around the town accompanied by a brass band and a military escort.[276]

Estrada's death prompted Macario and Ireneo Valdés, together with the remaining forty-three rebels of Temoaya and Yonora, to accept amnesty. General Agustín Castro planned to use them as guides and boasted to the president that

> with this surrender I can assure you that the State has been pacified, as Federico Vázquez has lost his best men and according to the reports of the amnestied, he will leave the region or they will take charge of capturing him. Permit me to congratulate you, because with this I declare the end of the campaign in all of the State of Durango.[277]

After General Castro, bolstered by this victory, overstepped the mark by trying to overthrow Durango's governor and install a puppet administration,[278] Cárdenas transferred command of the state's federal forces to General Miguel Henríquez. He pressed home the army's advantage by organizing an advance on rebel strongholds near San Francisco de Lajas, in conjunction with the region's defensas.[279] Although the rebels had lost several of their most important leaders, Vázquez's forces, estimated to number one hundred and ninety men,[280] together with reinforcements from the Zacatecas and Jalisco under Pepe Sánchez and Florencio Estrada's younger brother, Jesús, still managed to inflict a humiliating defeat on their enemies near Lajas.

> The rebels employed a decent amount of dynamite . . . which they caused to explode once the vanguard of this large column were within the canyon, subsequently letting loose a hail of gunfire on our troops from their advantageous positions, also using rudimentary hand grenades made from cowhides . . . and a landslide of huge boulders.[281]

Despite using over five thousand cartridges in their desperate defense, the federals lost twenty-five men, a "regrettable result" that Henríquez blamed on

> the Lieutenant Colonel's confidence in the inferiority of the bandits . . . despite my personally recommending him, on repeated occasions, to take every sort of precaution, considering that the topography of the terrain is extremely advantageous to the rebels.

However, the men of Santa María's defensa, better suited to guerrilla fighting than the federals but much better equipped than their enemies, swiftly counterattacked and managed to kill several of the rebels.[282] Xoconoxtle's defensa struck a further blow against them soon afterward, killing the most important O'dam rebel leader, Juan Andrés Soto, in an ambush near Santa María Ocotán.[283]

> [Chon] Aguilar had come from where he lived, from Agüita Zarca, to see if [Juan Andrés] was in the area. From afar [Chon and his men] saw two people walking. They had a telescope, and they were observing them with it. "It's Juan Andrés, he's coming this way!" they said. "He's very close!" They ran to meet him further down the hill, where they could [more easily] take him out, and dug themselves in. And so, when Juan Andrés went past, they shot at him and felled him, but he was still alive, he could still talk. "Who

are you?" they asked him, as he lay there dying. "I am Juan Andrés Soto," he said. "Ah yes, the man who killed my father," said Chon.[284]

Chon Aguilar then gave Juan Andrés Soto a final bullet to the head, avenging the death of his father, Gregorio, and putting an end to a feud that had riven the northern Sierra O'dam since the early 1920s.

General Henríquez capitalized on the deaths of Florencio and Frumencio Estrada and Juan Andrés Soto by launching an all-out campaign against the region's remaining rebel forces in December 1936. He sent four federal columns to San Andrés Milpillas, which "had not yet been touched by our forces and has always been a refuge for fugitives from justice whom this time I assure you will be liquidated." The five hundred soldiers carried Mendoza automatic rifles and portable radios and were accompanied by surveillance airplanes, which, since the construction of an airstrip in Santa María Ocotán, had begun to undermine the natural advantage that the rebel guerrillas had enjoyed in the mountains. The federals also had eighty cargo mules and could count on "posts where they will find provisions for their support."[285] In the face of overwhelming pressure, numerous local rebels surrendered.[286] Juan Sifuentes, who had taken refuge in San Andrés, was killed by pro-government O'dam shortly after, having been betrayed by his brothers-in-law who "were after his animals.... Thus the Mendía [were able to] kill him, and took all of the cattle he possessed."[287]

In the same month, federal forces finally killed Trinidad Mora, who had been secretly living in Durango while recovering from an injury.[288] In a Guardia Nacional manifesto released shortly afterward, Federico Vázquez was declared the new commander-in-chief of Durango's rebels. This document, authored by the Guardia's new delegate in Durango, Jesús Sanz Cerrada (who used the alias Héctor Martínez de los Ríos), also announced that

> in all ways and whatever form, will struggle against the nefarious socialist education that, on the orders of Jewish Russia, is being implemented in our country.... We are not rebels, nor bandits, nor murderers but, as the liberators of our Motherland, we will try to save it from communism.[289]

Such rhetoric was by now typical of the second cristiada's main ideologues, many of whom would later join right-wing political movements such as the Sinarquistas or the PAN.[290] But references to Russia, communism, and "the Jews" had little meaning for Gran Nayar's Wixárika, O'dam, and mestizo rebels, suggesting the growing disconnect between the rebel rank and file and the Guardia Nacional's political arm in Mexico City, even as federal campaigns continued to take their toll on the numbers and morale of both.

As relations between the church and state steadily improved, even the most militant members of Durango's clergy had withdrawn their tacit support for the rebel cause by early 1937. Sanz Cerrada described this as "yet another blow that they give us, as they nullify the few sympathetic priests and demoralize completely the civilians who in various forms once helped us."[291] Short of ammunition and unsettled by the killings of most of the Sierra O'dam's other rebel leaders, Federico Vázquez lay low. Rather than carry out new attacks, he concentrated on organizing his reserve forces and planning the assassination of Valente Acevedo, who since accepting amnesty had accompanied General Henríquez "in his frequent air-raids in order to indicate the hideouts and encampments of the rebels." In time-honored Mexican tradition,[292] Vázquez lured Acevedo to a meeting in the sierra to discuss his possible surrender and then shot his unfortunate former compadre, "thus paying with his life a long and interminable list of treacheries."[293]

With the local rebels on the back foot, the federal government stepped up its state-building project in the Sierra O'dam. In January 1937, officials from the newly founded DAI traveled through the region. After two decades of revolutionary efforts to develop the Mexican countryside and impose peace and order on its inhabitants, it is significant that these officials used almost exactly the same words their early 1920s predecessors used to describe local conditions, reporting that because of "the frequent raids of armed groups," its inhabitants were living in "a condition of misery that is truly lamentable." In response, the federal government distributed "50 hoes, 50 axes, 15 pickaxes, 10 crowbars y 10 shovels," plus 5,325 pesos worth of clothes and 800 pesos worth of "maize, beans, salt and chillies," to "the O'dam of Santa María Ocotán and nearby pueblos."[294] A few months later, as the federal government's Office of Rural Hygiene began "sanitary expeditions throughout the majority of the States of the Republic," a brigade of health workers also headed to the sierra, "where never before have the benefits of modern healthcare arrived." They visited Santa María Ocotán, San Pedro Jícoras, and San Buenaventura, vaccinating 1,247 O'dam and Mexicaneros against smallpox and carrying out "other prophylactic projects in this zone, giving advice to its inhabitants about questions of hygiene via the interpreters they bought with them, given that the majority of the region's inhabitants are ignorant of Spanish." Using data from this trip, the Office of Rural Hygiene would formulate "a program of action . . . aiming to protect the health of the thousands of natives who live apart from civilization."[295]

Plans were also made to rebuild Santa María's internado. Former maestro misionero Everardo Gámiz, now an important member of Durango's intellectual elite, applauded this project in an article for a regional newspaper and called for schools for the rest of the region's communities. However, in line with the more radical Indigenista currents then gaining ground in Mexico and no doubt influenced by his own experiences of O'dam and Mexicanero resistance to schools, he warned that only teachers who "know the language, customs, defects, virtues, etc., of those distant pueblos" be chosen to serve in the sierra. To this end, he saw as "indispensable" the prior foundation of "a special school to which a good number of natives be brought so they can be trained as teachers," a project he was sure that President Cárdenas, "who has preoccupied himself with the true redemption of the aboriginals," would support.[296]

Encouraged by the lull in the fighting and the government's renewed interest in the region, many O'dam refugees now requested the state to help them improve their living conditions, or even to return home. The inhabitants of San Bernardino, housed by federal forces in temporary camps near Llano Grande, complained they lacked food and petitioned for permission to at least "go to the ravines to collect plantains, the only crop which can provide for their daily needs."[297] General Henríquez, however, insisted that their rations were generous,[298] and they were forced to wait another year before they were allowed to return to their community.[299]

Teneraca's pro-government leader Simón Enríquez, who had fled to Tamazole (an anexo of San Andrés Milpillas in Nayarit) with much of the community's population, similarly complained to Governor Enrique Calderón that they lived in "lamentable conditions, due to being in places in which it is impossible to dedicate oneself to work and whose climate is unhealthy for our families." They requested that a federal detachment accompany them back to Teneraca, where they were desperate to begin preparing their lands for planting.[300] This would allow them to renew their practice of costumbre, which—given that Enríquez had now been traditional governor for three years running—had obviously been seriously disrupted by the conflict.[301] General Henríquez offered them land near Santa María Ocotán, "selected as fulfilling the conditions for their easy subsistence, and where the forces dependent on this Military Zone who are found in that region can furthermore provide for their security."[302] But the exiles insisted on returning home, as they had heard that "the bandit Vázquez . . . has now retreated from Teneraca and taken up in the higher parts of the Sierra Madre."[303] As they "came here without arms, bringing only their animals,"[304] the army gave them "a few old weapons and a few cartridges with which to defend themselves," and local government officials reassured them "the rebels are only ten or fifteen strong and are poorly armed."[305]

However, the rebels were still far from defeated, and according to their own internal reports, Vázquez's fifty-man force was made up "of the best"[306] and was well armed with pistols and semiautomatic rifles.[307] Local informants today agree that "they were excellent shots":[308] "With those guys, every single bullet was a killer bullet!"[309] The rebels had also seized plentiful food supplies from O'dam civilians, which they

FIGURE 10 Federico Vázquez (center), last of the Gran Nayar's cristero chieftains, with his O'dam and mestizo lieutenants, including Florencio Estrada (center left) (ARA/Sección Gráfica/499-1).

euphemistically described as "aid . . . received in the region in which they operate." Although few of Vázquez's men were willing to leave their home territory, they were eager to attack local targets and soon descended on Teneraca, killing thirty members of the community's reconstituted defensa and seizing clothes and cattle.[310] Then the self-declared "defenders of the faith" burned the village, including its church. Once again, Teneraca's hard-pressed inhabitants were forced to flee, this time toward Chon Aguilar's base at Xoconoxtle.[311]

A few weeks later, Vázquez's men attacked their demobilized former allies in Temoaya (whom they now referred to as *agraristas*), killing three and taking rifles and still more cattle. In response, two hundred federal troops set out from Santa María Ocotán to hunt them down, and printed offers of amnesty were dropped across the sierra from airplanes. However, Sanz Cerrada reported that "the most eloquent responses to this invitation have been the two blows that the forces of General Vázquez has given the Federals, acts that naturally have silenced the local newspapers as well as the radio stations."[312] In August, Mezquital's municipal president complained that "those bandits, rather than being exterminated, are prospering day by day and as I have said: with grave harm to the poor peasants who are frequently suffering assaults, robberies and murders."[313] In October, he requested federal reinforcements, claiming that the number of rebels under Vázquez had risen to three hundred.[314]

Throughout 1938, although rebel violence was subsiding in Jalisco and Nayarit, a low-intensity war continued to rage across southern Durango. But Vázquez was handicapped by a shortage of ammunition, "to the extent that of the one hundred and fifty men who are currently operating, close to a third have absolutely no ammunition."[315] Sanz Cerrada later wrote that the situation was still more difficult

> because of having to attend to two encampments, one constituted of the fighters and the other of their relatives, wives and children, who are unable to stay in their places of origin due to the fierce persecution of which they were victims. We were constantly running, our messengers were murdered, [and] important battles could not take place for lack of ammunition.[316]

Demoralized and desperate, some of the rebels deserted, giving away information that allowed federal forces to capture and kill four of Vázquez's couriers. Vázquez's second-in-command, Magdaleno Noriega, subsequently died in battle in November; Durango's zone commander, General Matías Ramos, sent President Cárdenas photographs of the dead rebel and added he was sure that "the few groups that remain in the State will dissolve or amnesty themselves, because Noriega was Vázquez's mentor. Furthermore I have ordered the intensification of their persecution until we achieve their extermination."[317] Further setbacks followed, including a "betrayal" in Durango that forced Sanz Cerrada himself to go underground.[318] He advised Vázquez that "there is no longer any point in continuing with a sterile struggle in the midst of so many enemies, especially those who were [previously] with us," and retired to Ciudad Juárez, depriving Vázquez of the supplies that Sanz Cerrada had previously secured him as well as his most reliable connection to the GN's political command.[319]

By 1939, the danger posed by the rebels had diminished enough for the government to accelerate local agrarian reform. The region's most consistently pro-government communities and their leaders were the primary beneficiaries. Chon Aguilar was elected to Mezquital's municipal government[320] and played a key role in local land distributions. After the state government announced that the inhabitants of Temoaya, abandoned in the face of both federal and rebel attacks, were free to return to their homes, along with anyone else interested in colonizing the community's lands, Aguilar "took official possession of the Pueblo of Temoaya."[321] Although twenty-nine families from Chon's native Xoconoxtle joined him there, many mestizo settlers also took advantage of the government's offer of lands. Their arrival in the community constituted a final blow to its Indigenous identity, already weakened by war, exile, and mestizo colonization.[322] In the words of one local elder, "Because of that everything changed. The O'dam here were finished, because while the father of my mother still danced the mitote, he had a patio here and everything . . . the rest of the family, they no longer [celebrated costumbre]."[323]

Meanwhile, Durango's state government helped Cosme Solís's faction retain control of Santa María Ocotán,[324] in the face of DAI-backed challenges to their authority, which destabilized Indigenous communities across Mexico in this period.[325] The community's governor accused the DAI's representative in Santa María of plotting to assassinate Solís, of fomenting "disorder amongst the natives of this place," and of inflicting "privations and miseries" on the community.[326] The state government backed its long-standing local allies and forced the meddlesome federal official to "suspend the hostilities against Mr. Cosme Solís . . . promising that from now on he will do everything in his power to economically benefit all of the inhabitants of this region."[327]

Local pro-government caciques had no such conflicts with the SEP, however. Buoyed by Everardo Gámiz's public support for the intensification of SEP activities in the sierra, Durango's director of federal education planned to establish numerous new schools in the region, noting that previous efforts had been "notoriously insufficient for its 7000 inhabitants." He wrote to his superiors that

> as one is dealing with an indigenous group almost left to their own fate, and we have a commitment to rehabilitating them through education, in the most considerate way we beg you to be good enough to concede us ten teaching posts, with the aim of founding many other schools that might be transmitters of culture in those places most densely populated by natives.[328]

Meanwhile, although Vázquez remained a disruptive regional presence, he was increasingly short of supplies, ammunition, and men. In February 1939, he launched his last major attack, leading forty rebels in a raid on Mezquital, "which they would have taken if help had not reached the Callistas, who numbering six hundred forced our men to retreat."[329] A few months later, President Cárdenas authorized a regional Villista veterans' organization to negotiate Vázquez's surrender.[330] General Lorenzo Ávalos, secretary general of the Legión de Veteranos de la Revolución (Division del Norte), reached out to the rebels, who offered to accept a government amnesty in exchange for the return of their lands.[331] Vázquez passed over his own destruction of rancherías across the Sierra O'dam and declared that

> the motive for our taking up arms against the Government was the seizure of our properties to deliver them to the Ejido, knowing that it is the smallholding that we depend on to obtain bread for our children, tearing down our pueblos such as Santiago Bayacora,

> Temoaya, Taxicaringa, and Teneraca[.] [W]hat reason did the Government have to carry out such destruction[?] Only because we claimed that which is ours, [they] moreover persecuted our families murdering our children, without their being responsible for our attitude.[332]

Although the language now used by Vázquez contrasted dramatically with the messianic anticommunism of former cristero ideologues like Sanz Cerrada, his emphasis on the right to private property gelled with the rhetoric of the nascent Sinarquista movement and was also likely intended to prevent his being labeled an agent of the reactionary clergy.[333] Instead, by railing against injustice in the countryside, he presented his movement—accurately, to an extent—as one made up of campesinos, which in the context of the radicalism of the Cárdenas period meant he could hope for a measure of political sympathy. At the same time, Vázquez's new emphasis on agrarian issues was also a late admission of the fact that many O'dam, Mexicaneros, and Wixáritari had taken up arms to defend the physical integrity of their communities against threats posed by local authorities and state governments alike.

In May, the rebels began to turn over their weapons to local federal forces, and General Ávalos congratulated President Cárdenas on the final defeat of Durango's rebel forces.[334] But Vázquez and a core of followers remained suspicious of the government's promises and refused to surrender. They remained a force to be reckoned with late into the next year,[335] at one point feigning acceptance of an amnesty in order to lure their old enemy, Lieutenant Coronel Guadalupe Contreras, into a fatal ambush near El Salto.[336] Vázquez and his men, by now the last active cristero rebels in all of Mexico, finally agreed to demobilize only after Lázaro Cárdenas's term came to an end and he was succeeded by Manuel Ávila Camacho, the first postrevolutionary president to publicly proclaim himself "a believer."

The handover of power at the national level coincided with a change of governors in Durango, with Enrique Calderón succeeded by Elpidio Velázquez. In late 1940, Velázquez commissioned an employee of the Cooper Lumber Company to meet with the Sierra O'dam's remaining rebels.

> Already very late at night, the cristeros and Federico Vázquez arrived, all of them distrustful and with their weapons ready. They were in bad shape; dirty, ill and tired. They had their meeting and I noted everything down. They asked for economic assistance, food and grains, medicines, education for their children, schools, logs to use for planting with animals, and that they be given the lands of Taxicaringa (an O'dam ceremonial center) but what they wanted above all was for their lives to be respected.[337]

Governor Velazquez assured Vázquez he would respect these conditions, writing to him that with Ávila Camacho now in power and the conflict between church and state definitively over,

> the entire Nation has given itself over in these moments to its reconstruction, all of the citizens desire to work for the aggrandizement of the Motherland, you and yours are almost the only elements that remain beyond the borders of this administration. . . . In the name of the administration I represent, I formally invite you to embrace the guarantees that the government offers you, sure that you will receive the stimulus necessary to immerse yourselves in work with total tranquility and honor, closely united forever with our administration.[338]

Soon afterward, Governor Velázquez and General Ávalos met with Vázquez in the sierra, where he agreed to terms almost identical to those that had secured the surrender of his former commander, Trinidad Mora, more than a decade before. The government guaranteed the safety of Vázquez and his men, the restitution of Bayacora's lands to the community's former cristeros and their families,[339] and named Vázquez southern Durango's "forestry chief."[340] An article in the *Siglo de Torreón* celebrated the return of peace, declaring that now the Sierra O'dam, "the richest in almost all kinds of tropical products . . . it could be a tourist attraction for its magnificent climate and beautiful landscapes . . . at once the most abrupt and the most scenic."[341]

CONCLUSIONS

Throughout Cárdenas's presidency, rebel violence and radical reform constituted a reciprocal phenomenon in the Gran Nayar, the dynamics of which varied in accordance with the cultural and historical idiosyncrasies of the region's four peoples, the vagaries of ammunition and food supplies, evolving factional alliances and conflicts, and the interventions of santitos and shamans. But by 1941, federal troops and local defensas had defeated the Gran Nayar's last remaining rebels. Most of their leaders—including Juan Bautista, Juan Andrés Soto, and Florencio Estrada—were dead, the rest amnestied. Their followers demobilized, accepting that the army—by now well supplied in terms of food, weapons, ammunition, horses, and cargo mules, equipped with modern communications equipment, and backed by surveillance aircraft—was unbeatable by poorly armed guerrillas, even within the mountainous terrain of their homeland.

However, the government and its local allies had not been able to overcome the hostility of recalcitrant Náayari, Wixárika, O'dam, and Mexicanero factions to being "incorporated" into the Mexican nation. The violence of the second Cristero Rebellion—in large part an expression of local resistance to state-building—had disrupted SEP programs and blocked the application of "antifanatic" policies that threatened local costumbre. At the same time, to secure the allegiance of the Gran Nayar's pro-government factions, the state had finally been forced to institute the agrarian reform that many communities had been demanding since before the revolution. Thus most Náayari, Wixárika, O'dam, and Mexicanero communities managed to safeguard their cultural autonomy and win for their landholdings a modicum of security, in defiance of the predictions of Lumholtz and other prerevolutionary anthropologists that they would "soon disappear by fusion with the great nation to whom they belong."[342]

But rebel raids, federal and defensa counterattacks, and violent intra- and inter-community conflicts had left the Gran Nayar's communities in ruins, its inhabitants exhausted, and their costumbre in crisis. Post-1940, then, those who had survived the violence of the revolution and the two cristero rebellions faced the challenge of rebuilding the ritual-political foundations of descent group and communal life torn apart by conflict and exile. In the Náayari communities of Nayarit, traditional governments under the renewed influence of conservative factions continued to campaign for state recognition and struggled to restore the ritual-political unity of what they described as the "League of Indigenous Pueblos of Náayari origin that . . . recognizes as its principal center the Pueblo of Jesús María."[343] Náayari individuals, descent groups, and whole communities brought their santitos out of hiding, recommenced the pilgrimages that rebel violence had forced them to postpone, and returned to their mitote patios to celebrate the rites that linked together the cycles of agriculture and human life, bringing balance to an unstable universe.[344]

The Wixáritari began similar attempts to return to their ancestral practices, desperate to win back the favor of gods whose cults had been neglected during the second cristiada. "It was five, six, seven, maybe eight years that no one could plant, thus [the gods] did not make it rain."[345] However, without corn they lacked an element vital for the proper performance of costumbre, while few had been able to make pilgrimages to collect peyote in San Luis Potosí, and many of the shamans who had best known the intricacies of Wixárika costumbre had died or remained in exile. According to local informants, "it wasn't an easy thing for everything to return to normal."[346] But with the help of spirits and animal gods, each community began to reconstruct its ceremonial centers and gather essential materials for rituals. "It was difficult, but when they brought [the gods] their offerings, it began to rain, and the illness went away. From then until now, everything has remained normal, and there hasn't been any new turmoil."[347]

Meanwhile, throughout southern Durango, O'dam and Mexicaneros "carried on the struggle there in the communal mitote patio, because so many had suffered, many poor people were left without cattle, without anything to eat, they survived only on things from the bush. When peace returned, they began to ask God, that he would never again make war here between the Indians."[348] In fact, as much of the rest of the world was now consumed by the Second World War, "there in the patio they asked that Our Lord leave in peace all of the countries there are," in line with local conceptions of their costumbre as essential to the health and stability of the world as a whole.[349] The people of Teneraca, still reeling from the loss of their patron saint, also "arranged for a copy to be made of their original saint . . . they brought the one that is here [now]." In order to imbue it with the spiritual powers of its predecessor, the community's chief shamans "had to perform their costumbre, staying awake, fasting, they had to do that for one month [a year] for five years. They had to make offerings, too, so that it would become powerful."[350]

Concerted efforts to reestablish communities on the basis of costumbre went hand-in-hand with more explicitly political struggles. Political reforms, state-backed economic programs, and corporatist agrarian policies had caused an upsurge in intercommunal conflict and in many communities enabled mestizo settlers to claim communal lands for themselves, regardless of whether the community in question had chosen to resist or accommodate the growing power of the revolutionary regime. Furthermore, the partnerships formed between pro-government caciques, mestizo settlers, and local teachers and military officials and the continued efforts of a widening cast of municipal, state, and federal actors to integrate the Gran Nayar socially, politically, and economically into the Mexican nation continued to create, or exacerbate, internal communal conflicts. By 1940, growing numbers of Náayarite, Wixáritari, O'dam, and Mexicaneros therefore regarded state governments and federal agencies alike as determined to destroy their communities and accused many local leaders of active involvement in such efforts.

In Nayarit, Governor Espinosa had promoted the Subprefectura de la Sierra to the status of a municipality (renamed El Nayar) in 1939,[351] while in the Náayari Baja, San Pedro Ixcatán became part of another new municipality, Ruiz, carved out of Santiago Ixcuintla.[352] These changes increased the reach of primarily mestizo municipal authorities over the Sierra Náayari as a whole but, given increasing local animosity toward mestizos, further undermined the stability of a region already divided by factional conflicts, mestizo immigration, the diminishing legitimacy of traditional communal governments, and the emergence of intercommunal agrarian conflicts. Testament to this was a spate of killings of Náayari caciques during communal fiestas, which illustrates the way in which Náayari costumbre became a "battleground within a long-term factional struggle between intruding non-indigenous people (and their [Náayari] supporters) and the other [Náayarite] who opposed the policies of these outsiders."[353]

El Nayar's first municipal president, the pro-government Náayari cacique Mariano Solís, was shot down in 1941 while dancing at a festival in San Francisco. Solís "was one of those real fierce types" and made many enemies during his earlier career as a "bandit."[354] Apparently his murderers were men from Jesús María whom he had previously "threatened with his pistol . . . for that reason they ended him."[355] His killing was welcomed by many Náayarite, whom he had tried to control through violence and who regarded him as a "tyrant,"[356] to the extent that "the entire Sierra was against his municipal government."[357] A year later, Santa Teresa's defensa commander Evaristo Castañeda was assassinated as the community celebrated the festival of Santo Santiago.

> Mr. [Castañeda] was patrolling the area and had apprehended a subject who is a native of Dolores, and struggling arm-to-arm with said individual a soldier of the Rural Defense Brigade fired a shot to defend the commandant, instead hitting him five or six centimetres from the right ear, causing him to fall dead.

The new mestizo president of El Nayar—a nephew of Mariano Mejía—dismissed the killing as the result of a "vulgar dispute amongst drunks."[358] However, that Castañeda's adversary was from Dolores, the refuge of Santa Teresa's conservative exiles, and that he was killed only "five metres from the door of the courthouse," the seat of traditional authority in the community, suggest that factional tensions played a part in the death of this stalwart supporter of compulsory schooling, mestizo immigration, and the sierra's integration into the national economy.[359]

Similar conflicts wracked the Sierra Wixárika. In some communities, disaffected Wixáritari attacked pro-government caciques, as in Santa Catarina, where angry locals accused Emeterio Mijares Cosío, father of the late Agustín, of seizing the community's título virreinal and one of its traditional stamps of office. Mijares was forced to appeal to the president for "guarantees . . . because without this support I will be forced to wander, suffering, far from my home and my lands."[360] Their declining popularity prompted some formerly pro-government leaders to change their tactics and adopt a more combative position in their dealings with the SEP, the DA, and other state institutions.[361] In Tuxpan, for example, Cenobio Sánchez and other leaders complained that the agronomist sent to demarcate the community's landholdings "decided to draw up the maps from his house, without having gone to check any of his work in the field and using data supplied by the adjacent landowners themselves."[362] They also demanded that both the federal government and the municipality of Bolaños put a stop to mestizo invasions backed by state authorities in Nayarit.[363] Meanwhile, in San Sebastián the government's brutal treatment of local people after the death of Juan Bautista became "a central theme in their oral and cultural history, and is referred to on almost every occasion when government agencies present themselves as working on their behalf."[364]

The arrival of extractive industry in the Sierra O'dam—which government officials had long promoted as essential to the region's economic development and the incorporation of its inhabitants into "civilization"—also provoked renewed violence, just as it had done a few years before in the Sierra Náayari. Rival O'dam caciques struggled "for control of the economic resources derived from said industry, and also because of the resulting conflicts over communal borders."[365] For example, Chon Aguilar, now Mezquital's municipal president, supported the efforts of the Cooper Lumber Company to dominate the incipient regional logging industry, but his former ally, José Flores, at this point an unspecified "communal authority" in the recently amalgamated communities of Santa María Ocotán and Xoconoxtle,[366] favored the rival Thomas Brooke Company. A violent conflict ensued, which exacerbated latent tensions within the Aguilar family in a way that reshaped local factional allegiances and ultimately cost Chon his life.[367] "They killed him in Santa María. Because of the forests, and also the lands themselves. . . . They say that Chon's own brother, Eleuterio, ordered José Flores to kill Chon, over some lands and some cattle that Chon got from their father, from Gregorio [Aguilar]."[368] Flores himself was killed soon afterward, however, leaving control of Santa María and Xoconoxtle in the hands of Sixto Mendía and Cosme Solís.

Federico Vázquez was assassinated in a separate dispute over logging rights a few years later.[369] Now a regional forestry official, he had signed agreements with both Temoaya and Taxicaringa granting him permission to oversee the logging of their forests. However, many in the former community "wouldn't give him the opportunity. They said they didn't want to see him. Because he had fucked them over, robbed so much money, so many animals." Vázquez therefore "went to once again organize the people of Taxicaringa, because it's pure forests over there where they live,"[370] but Vázquez's enemies in Temoaya suspected him of encroaching into their territory. On May 20, 1945, as he rode through the sierra with two nephews, the veteran former cristero was ambushed by gunmen,[371] "various of those who had something against him, or were paid to kill him, and also wanted to get ahead."[372] Although Durango's military authorities ordered the persecution of attackers, they were never captured.

The nature of the postrevolutionary settlement in the Gran Nayar, which had failed to meet the hopes of most Náayarite, Wixáritari, O'dam, and Mexicaneros—and had even managed to disillusion many of the region's most reliably pro-government caciques—rekindled local opposition to the government's state-building project and led to the murders of many of the era's surviving politico-military leaders. Popular discontent with these caciques, and with the state itself, also led to the emergence of a new generation of local leaders, most of whom, like their predecessors, were young men able to serve as bridges between their communities and the emergent PRIísta regime.[373]

Some of these leaders, particularly in historically pro-government communities like Tuxpan or those of the Náayari Baja, continued to look to the state for support in their agrarian struggles, legitimizing their demands, like their peers in other regions of Mexico, with reference to their previous contributions to the revolutionary project.[374] Thus one emerging leader in San Pedro Ixcatán argued the DA should protect the community because its inhabitants "have provided their forces to the Federal Government in the different rebellions that have been organized with bastard aims . . . in which the blood of the Nayarit Indians has contributed to the consolidation of peace not just in the region, but in lands far distant from their homes."[375] Others, however, combined the militant tactics of the previous generation of revolutionary leaders with the calculated use of official discourses of "patriotism" to which they had been recently exposed (whether in schools, government agrarian offices, or through service in the region's defensas), in order to protect what they saw as their own Indigenous patrimony in the form of cultural, political, and territorial autonomy. Such political maneuvering went hand in hand with the restoration and revindication of Náayari, Wixárika, O'dam, and Mexicanero costumbre in the years following the Cárdenas era and did much to obstruct government efforts to "incorporate" them through the second half of the twentieth century and to the present day.

had narrowly escaped the slaughter of her father and most of his men at the hands of Tuxpan's defensa. I showed him the photo and he instantly burst into tears, overwhelmed with emotion as he recalled his ancestor's fate.

The revolution has similarly shaped the political identities of many communities as a whole. Teneraca, for example, is today seen as the most conservative of all the O'dam communities, despite its caciques' formerly close alliance with the revolutionary state. It is in part because of this alliance—and the violence and suffering it brought on the community during the second cristiada—that Teneraca turned so definitively against the government in the 1940s.[3] From then on, the community's inhabitants rejected government schools, logging contracts, and mestizo settlement and even held a special mitote to ask that a new road planned by the state government not reach them.[4] The Wixáritari of Santa Catarina, also one-time allies of the revolutionary state, underwent a similar conversion to conservatism after the community's best lands were invaded by mestizo ranchers.

> Yes, many [mestizos] became rich here! Many! But after a while, from 1970 it seems to me, those people were kicked out, now no more tenants were permitted, they refused to give permission for them to come here, better that they left, no? They expelled all of them in one go. And until today, here [in Santa Catarina], there's no mixing with [mestizos], there are only Wixárika people within the community.[5]

The revolution's legacy is also appreciable in terms of relationships between communities. Some intercommunal conflicts—like that between Santa Catarina and San Sebastián—stretch back to the Porfiriato but were exacerbated by atrocities committed during the cristero rebellions. Contentious SEP programs, agrarista agitation, federal military crackdowns, and cacical rivalry also caused the emergence of new intercommunal tensions in regions like the Sierra Náayari, which had previously been free of such strife. These factors pushed the Náayarite of Dolores, for example, to declare themselves independent of their former sister community of Santa Teresa. Today they define themselves in opposition to the inhabitants of the latter, who in turn resent them for having "ruptured" the community.[6] Similarly, Jesús María, after becoming the seat of the newly formed municipality of El Nayar, lost its position as the politico-religious center of a Náayari world defined by costumbre and quickly became enmeshed in political conflicts with its neighbors, who were envious of the "privileged position in terms of political posts" that its inhabitants enjoyed.[7]

Given the local inseparability of politics and costumbre, the cultural identities of many of the Gran Nayar's inhabitants have been strongly influenced by the revolution. Decades of violence, exile, mestizo settlement, political maneuvering by agrarista factions, and state-promoted shifts from subsistence agriculture to extractive industry transformed a few Indian communities into mestizo settlements. One illustrative case is that of San Pedro Ixcatán, which by the 1950s was taken over by mestizo colonists who forced the community's original Náayari inhabitants into exile. The Náayarite of San Lucas de Jalpa and the O'dam of Temoaya and Yonora managed to keep hold of their lands, but in the face of similar pressures abandoned their costumbre and now identify as mestizos.[8] Meanwhile many Mexicaneros intermarried with the O'dam and Náayari refugees who settled in their communities during the cristero rebellions. The children of such unions were often raised within the more dominant O'dam and Náayari cultures and have in turn passed these, rather than a Mexicanero identity, down to their own children.[9]

The costumbre of those who maintained their original ethnocultural identities was also changed by the revolution. In some cases, communal costumbre was all but abandoned in the face of factional splits, which resulted in descent group rituals becoming preeminent. Violence and exile forced many groups to abandon particular pilgrimages, likely dealing the deathblow to Náayari peyote-gathering expeditions to San Luis Potosí. At the same time, the revolution gave rise to ritual innovations. New territories occupied by Wixárika exiles in Nayarit and Durango were integrated into older mythical-historical cycles, and their "traditional" worldview expanded to dominate the greater space they now occupied as a people.[10] Caricatures of bandits, agronomists, and military officers were integrated into costumbre throughout the Gran Nayar, thus "traditionalizing" collective memories of the revolution, in the same way earlier contacts with missionaries had spawned fiestas parodying Catholic ceremonialism. Perhaps most dramatic of all, conservative O'dam, like their equivalents in many of the country's other Indigenous communities, legitimized their opposition to government programs and mestizo settlement through participation in religious revivals prompted by visions of the Virgin Mary.[11]

> A Virgin appeared in 1952 . . . [because] the people began to wear jeans, some no longer used manta, they say the Virgin told a twelve-year-old girl, that they must put aside their jeans, throw them away, "because these are not meant for you indigenous people."[12]

In addition to purging their communities of mestizo-produced goods, the Virgin told local people that the world would soon end unless they renewed the practice of a "pure" form of costumbre and sold their corn only at cost, "because it is life."[13] Such messianic religious revivals still periodically erupt in the Sierra O'dam today.

For most of the Gran Nayar's inhabitants, however, deciding what place they would occupy in postrevolutionary Mexico was less a black-and-white choice between staying completely "Indian" or becoming totally "mestizo" and more about the extent to which they took on dual identities that were at once "Indian *and* mestizo."[14] Across the region, then, the postrevolutionary years saw the emergence of new "bicultural" leaders, who continued to employ the age-old strategies of subversion, accommodation, evasion, and active, sometimes violent, resistance to keep hold of their lands, their political autonomy, and their communal identities. Hence the Náayarite, Wixáritari, O'dam, and Mexicaneros are still very much alive in the present day, even if some of the meanings bound up with these labels have changed.

Such transformations have given rise to unique local understandings of the revolution itself—which brought to their communities literacy, time as defined in the classroom rather than in the field, and new chronicle formats for recording and recounting "history" itself—as a watershed between a time when people practiced costumbre "properly" but were also "savage" and a modern era of "civilization" that has been accompanied by deep cultural loss. Before the revolution, for instance, "there were people who transformed themselves into wolves. . . . But from 1945 up till now, there haven't been such people."[15] Today, many local people read and write, drive pickup trucks, get elected to positions in municipal governments, and contact their relatives using phones and walkie-talkies—but at the same time lament that they no longer dress like "Indians," respect their elders, or practice costumbre as "purely" as before. This collective judgment on the revolution's legacy, phrased first and foremost in cultural terms, bridges the gap between the views of the two primarily political factions whose enmity defined the local dynamics of the revolution: that of the conservatives, dismissed by their enemies as "savages" who rejected the revolution as a threat to their beliefs and practices, and that of the cosmopolitans, who saw in the revolution a chance to become rich, literate, and win outside support for their struggles, no matter if this undermined costumbre.

Ultimately, after thirty years of resistance and accommodation, rebellion and state-building, and conflicts between caciquismo and costumbre, the nature of the regional postrevolutionary settlement constituted an unsatisfactory compromise between the fundamentally incompatible aims of conservatives and cosmopolitans. Local understandings of the revolution are therefore also a kind of compromise, which combines the rival visions of each faction into a synthetic vision of the revolution as a cultural moment, traversing ongoing political divides over its rights and wrongs. The story of the revolution in the Gran Nayar, then, contributes to our understanding, as outsiders, of the complex intersections between culture, ethnicity, politics, religion, geography, history, and memory. But it remains, above all, its own story: one defined by courage, resilience, tragedy, and, ultimately, adaptability. As the inhabitants of the Gran Nayar fought to leave their mark on an immense national event, they were at the same time marked by it in ways that attest to the immense flexibility of Indigenous cultures and the fact that even in societies stereotyped as "ancient," change is a constant. There is no doubt that many things have been lost since the beginning of the "civilized" era ushered in by the revolution. But it is worth noting that the ever-growing number of Náayarite, Wixáritari, O'dam, and Mexicaneros who own camera phones today also use them to record their participation in the costumbre that is still so central to life in the Gran Nayar.

NOTES

INTRODUCTION

1. Butler, *Popular Piety*, 2. These Catholic rebels were first called *cristeros* by their enemies, in mockery of their battle cry of "Viva Cristo Rey!" (Long live Christ the King!), but many soon adopted the term themselves.
2. In the Gran Nayar, mestizos are defined as those local people who do not participate in Indigenous rituals or speak an Indigenous language. For studies of the ways *mestizaje* is conceived in other regions, see Lomnitz-Adler, *Exits*; Bonfil Batalla, *México profundo*; Friedlander, *Being Indian in Hueyapan*.
3. Particularly well studied are the Tepehuan Revolt of 1616–20 (Deeds, *Defiance and Deference*), the Spanish-Náayari wars of the seventeenth and early eighteenth centuries (Magriñá, *Los coras*), and the mid-nineteenth-century rebellion of Manuel Lozada (Meyer, *Esperando a Lozada*; Jáuregui and Meyer, *El Tigre de Alica*; Aldana, *La rebelión agraria*).
4. Peyote (*Lophophora williamsii*) is a small spineless cactus. Its main active ingredient is mescaline, which produces visual and auditory hallucinations.
5. Vaughan, *Cultural Politics*, 25–26; Bonfil Batalla, *México profundo*, 229; Lomnitz-Adler, *Exits*, 276.
6. Purnell, *Popular Movements*, 124–33; Butler, *Popular Piety*, 3.
7. Especially within the English-speaking world, the use of the word *shaman* and its derivatives has in recent years become contentious. It is certainly true that it is vague and unhelpful as a generic term for Indigenous ritual specialists. However, many scholars

continue to classify as shamans those men and women who mediate between human and nonhuman worlds. In the Gran Nayar, local people similarly tend to refer to such figures, when talking to outsiders, using the Spanish-language cognate *chamán* (although in the Wixárika language, they are called *mara'kate*, in O'dam, *ma'g+m*, and so on). To avoid overcomplicating this book and to facilitate comparisons between the four peoples of the Gran Nayar, I will therefore use the term *shaman* as a synonym for the ritual specialists, who, in mediating between humans, deities, spirits, and ancestors, are central to Indigenous religious and, indeed, political life throughout the region.

8. Nahmad, "Coras, huicholes y tepehuanes," 160.
9. Knight, "Interpreting the Mexican Revolution," 21–22.
10. Knight, "Peasant and Caudillo," 35.
11. Knight, *Mexican Revolution*, i, 78–127.
12. Knight, "Peasant and Caudillo," 27.
13. Hobsbawm, "Introduction," 1–12.
14. Joseph and Nugent, *Everyday Forms*, 14.
15. Vaughan, *Cultural Politics*, 46, and *The State, Education*, 238–66; Marak, "Failed Assimilation," 415.
16. Cf. Rockwell, "Schools," 188, 203; Rus, "The 'Comunidad Revolucionaria Institucional,'" 272–78.
17. The factions that grew up around these caciques often referred to themselves, and were referred to by their mestizo allies, as *progressives*, while their opponents were often termed, and indeed termed themselves, as *traditionalists*. Using less loaded language, Knight defines such factions respectively as *cosmopolitans* and *conservatives* ("Caciquismo," 37). I use the latter terms to avoid echoing the value judgments inherent in the former.
18. Vaughan, *Cultural Politics*, 8–20, 15–59.
19. Vaughan, *Cultural Politics*, 19–20, 35–36.
20. Vaughan, 6.
21. Bantjes, *As if Jesus*, 46–50; Meyer, *La cristiada*, iii, 366–83; Vaughan, *Cultural Politics*, 34–35, 90.
22. Starn, *Nightwatch*; Gitlitz, *Administrando justiciar*. The communal paramilitary groups of the revolutionary-era Gran Nayar closely resemble indigenous militias that emerged elsewhere in Latin America during the later twentieth century, such as Peru's Indigenous *rondas campesinas* (peasant patrols).
23. In particular, they complement works on Indigenous-Sandinista relations in Nicaragua, such as Gould, *To Die In This Way*; Hale, *Resistance and Contradiction*; Morris, "Between Two Fires"; and also studies of the relations between Indigenous peoples and revolutionary movements in India and Vietnam, e.g., Goscha, *Modern Vietnam*; Miklian, "The Purification Hunt."
24. Chakrabarty, "Minority Histories," 15–29.

25. The use of oral accounts as sources for Indigenous history is often fraught with such difficulties; cf. Coyle, *From Flowers*, 183; Friedrich, *Agrarian Revolt*, 140; Rus, "The 'Caste War,'" 1033–47.
26. Friedrich, *The Princes*, 216.
27. Unfortunately, no functioning state archive yet exists in Nayarit.
28. In particular, I was able to better understand "traditionalization," that is, "the active creation of a connection linking current discourse to past discourse" (Liffman, *Huichol Territory*, 84–87). Thus politicians and drug lords are today referenced in ritual contexts that reveal the community's conception of its position in the national context and reaffirm the power of local identity and practices (see Fikes, Weigand, and García de Weigand, "Introduction," xxviii).
29. The 1998 murder of American journalist Philip True in the Sierra Wixárika remains well known throughout the Gran Nayar. Local people often hint True's death was the result of his sticking his nose where he shouldn't have (i.e., into illicit poppy or marihuana plantations). I therefore tried to err on the side of caution during my fieldwork. For more on True's death, see Rivard, *Trail of Feathers*, and Liffman, *Huichol Territoriality*, 166–204.
30. Hrdlička, "The Region of the Ancient 'Chichimecs,'" 411; Lumholtz, *Unknown Mexico*, i, 741–42.
31. Preuss, *Fiesta, literatura y magia*, 207–8.
32. E.g., Myerhoff, *Peyote Hunt*; Schaefer and Furst, *People of the Peyote*. Critiques of this peyote-centric approach can be found in Neurath, *Las fiestas* (e.g., 14), and especially in Fikes, *Carlos Castañeda*.
33. Alvarado Solís, *Atar la vida*; Coyle, *From Flowers*; Jáuregui, "Del reino de Lozada"; Jáuregui and Neurath, *Flechadores*; Neurath, *Las fiestas*; Magriñá, *Los Coras*; Reyes, *Los que están benditos*; Valdovinos, "Los mitotes"; Lira Larios, "De buenos mexicanos."
34. Levi-Strauss, *Tristes Tropiques*, quoted in Gow, *An Amazonion Myth*, 9.
35. Neurath and Bahr, "Cosmogonic Myths," 601; Coyle, *From Flowers*, 146; Reyes, *Los que están*, 205–14.
36. The PRI was founded by President Calles as the National Revolutionary Party (PNR) in 1929 to represent his victorious revolutionary faction in a single bloc. The party was renamed and reorganized in 1938 (as the Partido de la Revolución Mexicana, PRM) and again in 1946 (as the PRI). It held uninterrupted power until 2000, when it was defeated by the Catholic, right-wing National Action Party (Partido de Acción Nacional, PAN).

CHAPTER 1

1. San Lucas de Jalpa, in Durango, was the exception to this rule, remaining a primarily Náayari community until the revolution (de la Rosa, *Historia de la política*; Felipe Salas García).

2. CONAPO, *Indices de marginacion*. In fact, in 2017 the rate of food deficit in the Sierra O'dam was higher than in war-torn Syria or Afghanistan ("Mezquital Supera Pobreza de Africa," *Siglo de Durango*, Oct. 16, 2017).
3. Wolf, *Europe and the People Without History*, 3–9, 113, 234. The publication of Wolf's book proved particularly stimulating in this regard.
4. Neurath, *Las fiestas*, 23; Liffman, *Huichol Territory*, 166–204; Coyle, *From Flowers*, xii, 3.
5. Otis, "Clasificacion y aprovechamiento," 135–40; Reyes, "La familia del maíz," 6–7.
6. Lumholtz, *Unknown Mexico*, ii, 10.
7. Otis, "Clasificacion y aprovechamiento," 142.
8. Weigand, "Co-operative Labor Groups"; Neurath, *Las fiestas*, 141–42; Liffman, *Huichol Territory*, 41; Coyle, *From Flowers*, 32–33.
9. Neurath, *Las fiestas*, 139–40; Preuss, *Fiesta, literatura y magia*, 144.
10. Gómez, "Mujeres y propiedad," 546; see also Stauffer, "Community, Identity."
11. Neurath, *Las fiestas*, 130; Craumausell, "Personajes," 190.
12. Shelton, "Huichol Natural Philosophy," 339–54.
13. Preuss, *Fiesta, literatura y magia*, 145.
14. Preuss, 174.
15. Neurath, "Ambivalencias del poder," 124; Alvarado, *Atar la vida*, 299–300.
16. Liffman, *Huichol Territory*, 41–42; Neurath and Bahr, "Cosmogonic Myths," 3; Alvarado, *Atar la vida*, 38.
17. Lumholtz, *Unknown Mexico*, i, 492; Neurath, *Las fiestas*, 21–22, 121–32; Coyle, *From Flowers*, 211.
18. Liffman, *Huichol Territory*, 128.
19. Neurath, *Las fiestas*, 63; Reyes, "The Perpetual Return," 198–99; Magriñá, *Los Coras*, 228, 242.
20. Neurath, *Las fiestas*, 197–240.
21. Chatwin, *The Songlines*.
22. Shelton, "The Recollection," 365.
23. Preuss, *Fiesta, literatura y magia*, 218–19.
24. Liffman, *Huichol Territory*, 65.
25. Coyle, *From Flowers*, 58, 69–72; Neurath, *Las fiestas*, 159–240.
26. Coyle, *From Flowers*, 36–73; Neurath, *Las fiestas*, 159–96; Reyes, *Los que están*, 159–88.
27. The ritualized maintenance of communal or descent group territorial boundaries was common to many different Indigenous peoples, including the Yucatec Maya; see Eiss, "Beyond the Land," 513–15.
28. Coyle, *From Flowers*, 87–95; Liffman, *Huichol Territory*, 45.
29. Liffman, *Huichol Territory*, 21–30, 64–68.
30. Shelton, "Huichol Natural Philosophy," 339–54.
31. Neurath and Bahr, "Cosmogonic Myths," 601.

32. Gerhard, *La frontera Norte*, 55–58.
33. See Scott, *The Art of Not Being Governed*, 8.
34. Weigand and García de Weigand, "Huichol Society," 23.
35. Deeds, *Defiance and Deference*, 29–33.
36. Gerhard, *La frontera Norte*, 252, 264.
37. Francisco del Barrio, quoted in Weigand and García de Weigand, "Huichol Society," 28.
38. Deeds, "Los tepehuanes en misiones jesuitas," 220–21.
39. Riley, "Los tepehuanes del sur," 129.
40. Cramaussel, "Historia del poblamiento," 12.
41. Gerhard, *La frontera Norte*, 266.
42. Reyes, "The Perpetual Return," 16.
43. Reyes, 92.
44. Weigand, and García de Weigand, "'Huichol Society,'" 28.
45. Gerhard, *La frontera Norte*, 142–45.
46. The skull of Nayarit, the eponymous founder of the Náayari kingdom, is kept in La Mesa's church and remains an object of veneration for the Náayarite.
47. Coyle, *From Flowers*, 75.
48. Neurath, *Las fiestas*, 21.
49. Neurath, *Las fiestas*, 21–28; Hinton, "Pre-conquest Acculturation," 166.
50. Coyle, *From Flowers*, 82.
51. Jáuregui, *Los Coras*, 12.
52. Ortega, in Coyle, "The Customs," 516.
53. Güereca, "Las milicias," 92.
54. Liffman, *Huichol Territory*, 42.
55. Gerhard, *La frontera Norte*, 102.
56. Gerhard, 101.
57. Gerhard, 100.
58. AGA-BC/276.1/411/leg.1/Comunal/Restitución/Santa María Ocotán y Xoconoxtle, INI Report, n.d.
59. Güereca, "Las milicias," 99.
60. Weigand and García de Weigand, "Huichol Society," 24–25.
61. Liffman, *Huichol Territory*, 42. However, conflicts between kawiterusixi and cargo hierarchies also help to prevent the centralization of power in Wixárika communities (Neurath, "Ambivalencias del poder," 122–23).
62. Gerhard, *La frontera Norte*, 147.
63. Gómez, "Huicot," 138; Jáuregui and Magriñá, "Estudio ethnohistorico," 43.
64. Alvarado, *Mexicaneros*, 11.
65. Hinton, "Indian Acculturation," 22.
66. Coyle, *From Flowers*, 85.

67. Hinton, "Indian Acculturation," 22.
68. Rojas, *Los huicholes*, 117–18; Gerhard, *La frontera Norte*, 265; García, *Mezquital*, 52.
69. Jáuregui and Magriñá, "Estudio etnohistórico," 64–66. This hypothesis remains rather controversial, however. For a strong critique, see Alvarado, *Atar la vida*, 58–69.
70. Wright-Rios, "A Revolution in Local Catholicism?" 244–45; Knight, "Superstition," 259.
71. Coyle, *From Flowers*, 88.
72. Rojas, *Los huicholes*, 126.
73. Osnaya Velázquez, *Los misioneros josefinos*, 10–11; Rojas, *Los huicholes*, 26–30.
74. Rojas, *Los huicholes*, 126–43.
75. Cerda Silva, "Los coras," 112.
76. For a detailed account of Náayari and Wixarika participation in the movements headed by Manuel Lozada, see Lira Larios, "De buenos mexicanos."
77. Hernández, "Lozada no muere," 209–20.
78. Struggles over local religious autonomy were also key to Lozada's mobilization of the mestizos of Nayarit's lowlands; see Van Oosterhout, "Popular Conservatism."
79. Jáuregui, "El reino de Lozada," 149–50; Coyle, *From Flowers*, 89.
80. Jáuregui, "El reino de Lozada," 159.
81. Liffman, *Huichol Territory*, 45; Rojas, *Los huicholes*, 129–33, 138–39, 147–48; Meyer, *Manuel Lozada*, 229.
82. Meyer, "El reino de Lozada," 250–51.
83. Quevedo, *México*, 140. See also Van Oosterhout, "Popular Conservatism," 221–22.
84. See Harvey, *The Chiapas Rebellion*, 41; Knight, "Superstition," 257.
85. Neurath, *Las fiestas*, 214–15; Liffman, *Huichol Territory*, 70–72.
86. Rugeley, *Of Wonders*, 113–14. The Maya communities of Yucatán enjoyed similar levels of popular religious autonomy during the nineteenth century.
87. Liffman, *Huichol Territory*, 45; Neurath, *Las fiestas*, 81–91; Reyes, *Los que están*, 177–87; Coyle, *From Flowers*, 115–76.
88. Preuss, *Fiesta, literatura y magia*, 218.
89. Liffman, *Huichol Territory*, 65; Reyes, *Los que están*, 86–93.
90. Preuss, *Fiesta, literatura y magia*, 86.
91. Lumholtz, *Unknown Mexico*, ii, 187–88.
92. Interviews with José Flores; Felipe Salas Ramírez.
93. Reichel-Dolmatoff, *The People of Aritama*, 14; Radding, "Peasant Resistance," 337; Walsham, "Introduction," 18.
94. Harvey, *The Chiapas Rebellion*, 54–55; Hu-Dehart, *Yaqui Resistance*, 217.
95. Alvarado, *Atar la vida*, 165–67.
96. Durin and Rojas, "El conflicto," 162.
97. Gillingham, "The Strange Business," 212–13.
98. Radding, "Peasant Resistance," 336.

99. Since the 1930s, cabeceras have also functioned as the headquarters of agrarian authorities established in accordance with national agrarian reform legislation, and today host schools, clinics, government offices, and state-run shops. As families keen to access these services settled permanently nearby, many have grown into mid-sized villages.
100. Salazar, "Migración y jornaleros," 100–108; Craumausell, "Personajes," 190.
101. Dennis, "The Oaxacan Village President," 421.
102. Shelton, "The Recollection," 373.
103. Medina, "'Aún no hablan.'" The link between objects and political legitimacy is common in many cultures; cf. Walsham, "Introduction," 27.
104. Güereca, "Las milicias."
105. Mallón, "Reflections," 90–92; Friedlander, "The Secularization of the Cargo System," 138.
106. Throughout the Gran Nayar, women prepared the feasts that were central to ritual events (Lumholtz, *Unknown Mexico*, 519–20; Alvarado Solís, *Atar la vida*, 86). Wixárika women also took charge of the cults of female deities in various tuki temples and with their husbands served as *jicareras*, responsible for carrying out pilgrimages to San Luis Potosí (Neurath, *Las fiestas*, 225). Amongst the O'dam, responsibility for female-specific elements of communal costumbre was also traditionally assigned to two women, who enjoyed their cargos for life (Willett, "The Dual Festival System," 197–213).
107. Harvey, *The Chiapas Rebellion*, 78.
108. Neurath, "Ambivalencias del poder," 122.
109. Benítez, *Los indios*, iii, 321; cf. Radding, "Peasant Resistance," 354; Dawson, "From Models," 299.
110. Alvarado, *Atar la vida*, 87.
111. Neurath, *Las fiestas*, 138–45; Coyle, *From Flowers*, 26–35. In theory one could also be affiliated with the descent groups of one's great-grandparents and so on ad infinitum, but this would entail taking part in more rituals than is physically possible.
112. Reyes, *Los que están*, 40–42; Alvarado, *Atar la vida*, 85–93.
113. In the 1990s, the active members of different descent groups amongst the Náayarite of Santa Teresa varied from twenty (considered small) to more than one hundred (Coyle, pers. comm., Nov. 22, 2016), while today the participants in familial Wixárika rituals can reach two hundred (Neurath, pers. comm., Nov. 21, 2016). In the late nineteenth century, descent groups, like the overall population itself, were likely much smaller.
114. Lumholtz, *Unknown Mexico*, i, 510.
115. Lumholtz, i, 465–69; ii, 92–97; Sánchez, *Etnografía de la Sierra Madre Occidental*, 142.
116. Coyle, *From Flowers*, 78. For analyses of this institution's role in other Indigenous regions, see Friedrich, *The Princes*, 124; Torres, "Nahuat Factionalism," 466.
117. Cf. Friedrich, *Agrarian Revolt*, 22–27, and *The Princes*, 100–14.
118. Several of the Indigenous caciques of the revolutionary-era Gran Nayar became the compadres of their mestizo allies. This was not a new phenomenon; after the conquest of the

Náayari priest-kingdom, the defeated Tonatí became compadre to one of the victorious Spanish commanders (Coyle, *From Flowers*, 82), while today, many mestizo activists working for NGOs in the Sierra Wixárika seek to establish such ritual kinship with local Wixáritari (Liffman, *Huichol Territory*, 144; Myerhoff, *Peyote Hunt*, 67). Such ties were also common amongst the Yaqui of Sonora, see Radding, "Peasant Resistance," 35–56.

119. Jáuregui, *Los coras*, 12.
120. For a detailed account of the development and nature of these ritual bonds, see Morris, "¿'Forjando Patria'?"
121. Lozada, "Plan Libertador." In *Las rebeliones campesinas en México, 1819-1906*, edited by Leticia Reina.
122. Hernández, "Lozada no muere," 211.
123. Meyer, *De cantón*, 158.
124. Hu-Dehart, *Yaqui Resistance*, 140–41, 152–53; Radding, "Peasant Resistance," 336–40.
125. Friedrich, *Agrarian Revolt*, 100; Purnell, *Popular Movements*, 139.
126. Mallón, "Reflections"; Rus, "Las revoluciones contenidas," 79–80.
127. Coyle, *From Flowers*, 181. See also Falcón, "Force," 113.
128. AHSEP-84-85/C/38877, E/36, Navarro to DEFN, 26 Oct. 1927; cf. Coyle, *From Flowers*, 135–38.
129. Cerda Silva, "Los coras," 111.
130. Lumholtz, *Unknown Mexico*, 457–59, 491; Osnaya Velázquez, *Los misioneros josefinos*, 34–36.
131. Rojas, *Los huicholes*, 154, 161–62.
132. E.g., Rus, "The 'Comunidad Revolucionaria Institucional,'" 269.
133. Rojas, *Los huicholes*, 154. Similar laws were enacted in much of Mexico "to promote culture by improving the appearance of the natives" (Lumholtz, *Unknown Mexico*, ii, 289) and to assert the government's power and raise money from fines (Wright-Rios, "A Revolution in Local Catholicism?" 243).
134. Preuss, *Fiesta, literatura y magia*, 166.
135. Friedlander, "The Secularization of the Cargo System," 135–36.
136. Radding, "Peasant Resistance," 337–38; Eiss, "Beyond the Land," 515; Rus and Wasserstrom, "Civil-Religious Hierarchies," 3–11.
137. Diguet, "La sierra nayar," 92; Preuss, *Fiesta, literatura y magia*, 223.
138. Lumholtz, *Unknown Mexico*, ii, 24; Reyes, "La familia del maize," 8–9; Neurath, *Las fiestas*, 172.
139. Interview with Saturnino Solís.
140. Lumholtz, *Unknown Mexico*, ii, 250–53.
141. Lumholtz, 23.
142. Lumholtz, 250–54, see also 188.
143. Lumholtz, i, 485.

144. Lumholtz, ii, 253–54.

145. Coyle, *From Flowers*, 181; see also Knight, *Mexican Revolution*, ii, 239; Hu-DeHart, *Yaqui Resistance*, 118; Stauffer, "Community, Identity," 154–58.

146. Lumholtz, *Unknown Mexico*, ii, 253–54.

147. Diguet, *Por tierras occidentales*, 109; Lumholtz, *Unknown Mexico*, i, 494.

148. Preuss, *Fiesta, literatura y magia*, 98, 207.

149. Neurath, *Las fiestas*, 14.

150. Preuss, *Fiesta, literatura y magia*, 170.

151. In 1895, the Zapotec population was estimated at 48,885; the Tzotzils, 44,781; the Tarahumara, 18,320 (INEGI, *Estadísticas Históricas*, i, 109), compared with a possible combined total of 13,200 Náayarite, Wixáritari, O'dam, and Mexicaneros.

152. Coyle, *From Flowers*, 94.

153. Most of these had been inhabited until the early nineteenth century by people still identifying as Tepecanos, Wixáritari, or (Nahuatl-speaking) Tlaxcaltecans (Rojas, *Los huicholes*, 132–46; Hrdlička, "The Region of the Ancient 'Chichimecs,'" 388–89, 409, 425–30).

154. Lumholtz, *Unknown Mexico*, i, 491–92; Diguet, 91–92.

155. Radding, "Peasant Resistance," 343–47.

156. Coyle, *From Flowers*, 94.

157. Preuss, *Fiesta, literatura y magia*, 177.

158. Rojas, *Los huicholes*, 144.

159. Rojas, 146–47, 150–51, 160.

160. Shadow, *Tierra, trabajo*, 81–97; Shadow, "Production, Social Identity," 39–45; Alden Mason, "The Ceremonialism," 62–77.

161. AHAG-Amatlan de Jora/C/1, del Real to Arz., Dec. 13, 1904.

162. Preuss, *Fiesta, literatura y magia*, 172; Lumholtz, *Unknown Mexico*, ii, 22–23.

163. Osnaya Velázquez, *Los misioneros josefinos*, 34–36.

164. Rojas, *Los huicholes*, 157.

165. Weigand, "Aculturación diferencial," 156.

166. Preuss, *Fiesta, literatura y magia*, 145.

167. For example, Lumholtz noted the Wixáritari "do not care very much for their [Náayari] relatives," while the Náayarite were angered at the Wixáritari leaving charms "in the trails leading out of their country, to prevent the rain from coming to us" (*Unknown Mexico*, i, 492, 520).

168. Dennis, "The Oaxacan Village President," 421–22.

169. Rojas, *Los huicholes*, 145–58.

170. Preuss, *Fiesta, literatura y magia*, 168.

171. Interviews with Gregorio Villa; Magdaleno Arrellano; Felipe Salas Ramírez.

172. Lumholtz, *Unknown Mexico*, i, 469.

173. AGA-BC/276.1/411/leg.1/Comunal/Restitución/Santa María Ocotán y Xoconoxtle, INI Report, n.d.
174. AHED-L/C/1/E/16, Gob. de Dgo. to Gob. Zac., Apr. 30, 1909; AHED-M/C/16/E/114, Cosme Solís to Gob. Dgo, Aug. 20, 1937.
175. Geographical space similarly defined Indigenous political factions in both Michoacán and the Sierra Norte de Puebla (Friedrich, *The Princes*, 101–3; Torres, "Nahuatl Factionalism").
176. AHED-C/3/E/25, residents of Candelaria to Gob. Dgo., May 30, 1908.
177. AGA-D/276.1/12/leg.1/Comunal/Restitución/Taxicaringa, Roberto Barrios to Asuntos Agrarios Dgo., Dec. 17, 1960; AHED-D/C/1/E/66, residents of Taxicaringa to Gob. Dgo., May 22, 1907; AGA-D/276.1/31/leg.1/Comunal/RTBC/San Francisco de Lajas, Salvador Molinar Flores to Supreme Court, Mar. 11, 1966.
178. AHED-PN/C/3E/45, Gob. Dgo. to Prefecto Político Acaponeta, Nay., Aug. 17, 1901.
179. Meyer, *De cantón*, 139–49.
180. Mestizos, however, were "never allowed to settle within the confines of the village" (Lumholtz, *Unknown Mexico*, i, 473).
181. Pennington, *Tepehuan of Chihuahua*, 26.
182. Preuss, *Fiesta, literatura y magia*, 84.
183. Preuss, 168; Huaynamota was home to speakers of Nahuatl until at least the end of Manuel Lozada's rule, when many were deported to the Yucatán. But even in 1927, a school inspector described the community's three hundred inhabitants as "una mescla de vecinos, astecas y coras, dominando los segundos" (AHSEP-84-85/C/38876/E/17, Insp. Instructor Florencio Orozco, to Dir. Ed. Fed. de Nay., June 15, 1927). By this point, however, only a few elders could still speak Nahuatl and reserved it use for ritual contexts (Juáregui and Magriñá, "Estudio etnohistórico," 55–56).
184. Meyer, *De cantón*, 162–63; Jáuregui, "Del reino de Lozada," 182–83.
185. AHED-A/C/3/E/19, residents of San Lucas to Gob. Jal., Feb. 14, 1910; AHED-A/C/3/E/19, Martínez to Jefe Pol. Huazamota, Mar. 4, 1910.
186. Coyle, *From Flowers*, 181–82.
187. Lumholtz, *Unknown Mexico*, i, 509.
188. Meyer, *De cantón*, 139–49.
189. Lumholtz, *Unknown Mexico*, i, 505; Preuss, *Fiesta, literatura y magia*, 173.
190. Lumholtz, *Unknown Mexico*, 491.
191. Preuss, *Fiesta, Literatura y Magia*, 172.
192. Lumholtz, *Unknown Mexico*, i, 492.
193. Lumholtz, *Unknown Mexico*, 474, 496, ii, 23. Weigand reported that in the 1960s, the Wixáritari still regarded mestizos "as the lowest form of human life" ("Co-operative Labor Groups," 85).
194. Lumholtz, *Unknown Mexico*, i, 486. Indian communities in many other regions reacted similarly to such threats (Stauffer, "Community, Identity," 172).

195. Lumholtz, *Unknown Mexico*, 496.
196. Lumholtz, 469.
197. Fernando Benítez, *Los indios*, v, 420.
198. Rojas, *Los huicholes*, 234, 246.
199. Preuss, *Fiesta, literatura y magia*, 170.
200. Alvarado, *Atar la vida*, 34; interview with Saturnino Solís.
201. Preuss, *Fiesta, literatura y magia*, 145.
202. Preuss, 220.
203. E.g., Radding, "Peasant Resistance"; Smith, "Defending 'Our Beautiful Freedom,'" 131–39; Eiss, "Beyond the Land," 515–19; Friedrich, *Agrarian Revolt*, 46; Rus and Wasserstrom, "Civil-Religious Hierarchies," 466–73.
204. Hrdlička, *Observations*, 35.
205. Pérez, *Ensayo estadístico*, 10.
206. Dawson, "From Models," 291.
207. Lumholtz, *Unknown Mexico*, i, xvi; cf. Preuss, *Fiesta, literatura y magia*, 91; Diguet, *Por tierras occidentales*, 41.
208. Hrdlička, *Observations*, 35.

CHAPTER 2

1. Rus, "Revoluciones contenidas," 57–85.
2. Clausewitz, *On War*, 92.
3. Nugent, *Spent Cartridges*, 98–99; Wasserman, *Persistent Oligarchs*, 48–53.
4. These Maderista leaders all became important revolutionary leaders and statesmen, above all Pánfilo Natera (Knight, *Mexican Revolution*, ii, 43, 187; 'Félix Bañuelos,' *Mi Pueblo*, Jan. 1995; Meyer, *La cristiada*, iii, 186).
5. AHJ-G-12-911/C/331/E/18852, Manuel Camargo to Gob. Jal., Jan. 23, 1911; Jefe Pol. de Colotlán to Gob. Jal., Mar. 30, 1911.
6. Avitia, *Los Alacranes*, 23.
7. AHSDN-C/C/105/E/XI/481.5/187, Mariano Ruiz to Sec. de Guerra, Mar. 27, 1911.
8. Meyer, *De cantón*, 191.
9. AHJ-G-12-911/C/332/E/18865, Manuel Muro to Gob. Jal., May 18, 1911.
10. AHJ-G-5-912/C/34/E/7786, Jalisco state government decree, Apr. 2, 1912.
11. AHJ-G-5-912-913/C/34/E/7787, Jalisco state government decree, Sept. 11, 1913.
12. AHJ-G-5-912-913/C/34/E/7787, Mariano de la Torre to Gob. Jal., Dec. 11, 1912.
13. AHJ-G-5-912-913/C/34/E/7787, Mariano de la Torre to Gob. Jal., Aug. 10, 1912.
14. Rojas, *Los huicholes*, 161–62.
15. AGMJ/FUN-01-MJ, Calixto Guerrero, "Informe," Oct. 22, 1917.
16. Lumholtz, *Unknown Mexico*, ii, 153.

17. Rojas, *Huicholes: Documentos*, 243–44. As Rentería had seconded Pascual Orozco's recent rebellion against Madero, he was by extension a loose ally of Zapata (Flores Flores and Flores Sánchez, *Memorias políticas*, 29).
18. Campos was an Orozquista from the Laguna region, who "espoused a form of *de facto* agrarian reform" (Knight, *Mexican Revolution*, ii, 287).
19. Rojas, *Los huicholes*, 162; see also "Exposición," *Mi Pueblo*, Mar. 1995, 10.
20. Rojas, *Los huicholes*, 162.
21. Guerrero had been lauded as a hero in 1911 for his role in the defense of Tijuana against Magonista revolutionaries, regarded by many Mexicans as a front for a U.S. invasion (Samaniego, "La revolución mexicana," 172–74).
22. AHSDN-C/C/105/XI/481.5/188, Unsigned military report, Mar. 28, 1912.
23. Flores Flores and Flores Sánchez, *Memorias políticas*, 29.
24. AHSDN-C/C/105/XI/481.5/188, Unsigned military report, Apr. 29, 1912.
25. AHSDN-C/C/105/XI/481.5/188, Reps of Cámara Nacional de Comercio, Tepic, to Madero, May11, 1912.
26. Pérez, *Ensayo estadístico*, 560; López, *Fuego*, 150. Indeed, elite groups across Mexico used the specter of "caste wars" to undermine the political programs of their opponents; see Rugeley, *Yucatán's Maya Peasantry*, 33–60; Nugent, *Spent Cartridges*, 95–96.
27. Rojas, *Los huicholes*, 162.
28. Such memories remained strong well into the twentieth century; see Meyer, *Manuel Lozada: El Tigre*, 229, and the numerous oral histories collected in Jáuregui and Meyer, *El Tigre de Alica*.
29. AHSDN-C/C/105/XI/481.5/188, Juan Castillo to Sec. Guerra, May 22, 1912.
30. AHSDN-C/C/105/XI/481.5/188, Unsigned military report, July 8, 1912.
31. Joseph, "Caciquismo and the Revolution," 200–201; see also Hobsbawm, *Bandit*.
32. AHSDN-C/C/124/XI/481.5/250, J. Arzamendi to Sec. Gob., July 23, 1912.
33. AHAG-Amatlan de Jora/C/1, Francisco del Real to Arz., Oct. 19, 1912.
34. Gámiz Olivas, *La revolución*, 39–40.
35. AHED-R/C/3/E/122, Jefe Pol. Mezquital to Gob. Dgo., Dec 1, 1912.
36. Sánchez Olmedo, *Etnografía*, 42.
37. Rouaix, *Diccionario geográfico*, 261–62.
38. Knight, *Mexican Revolution*, i, 323–24.
39. Joseph, "Caciquismo and the Revolution," 200–201; Eiss, "Beyond the Land," 525.
40. Knight, "Peasant and Caudillo," 34.
41. AHJ-G-5-912-913/C/34/E/7787, L. Sanibañez, "Cuestionario," Feb. 2, 1913; Dir. Pol. Mezquitic to Gob. Jal., Feb. 1, 1913.
42. AHJ-G-15-913/C/436/E/32389, Maximiliano Rangel to Gob. Jal., Mar. 11, 1913.
43. AHJ-G-15-913/C/436/E/32389, Bernabé Salazar to Gob. Jal., Apr. 11, 1913.
44. AHJ-G-15-913/C/436/E/32389, Luis Gutiérrez Pérez to Gob. Jal., May 22, 1913.

45. AHAG-Totatiche/C/5/E/83, Magallanes Jara to Arz., Feb. 25, 1914.
46. Gámiz Olivas, *La revolución*, 44.
47. Valadés, *Rafael Buelna*, 50.
48. Thord-Gray, *Gringo Rebel*, 237–44.
49. Thord-Gray, 277–84.
50. Thord-Gray, 296–314.
51. Thord-Gray, 234; see also Hu-DeHart, *Yaqui Resistance*, 9.
52. Thord-Gray, *Gringo Rebel*, 234.
53. Thord-Gray, 282.
54. Thord-Gray, 302.
55. AHAG-Totatiche/C/3/E/13, Magallanes to Arz., July 6, 1920.
56. Knight characterizes "regional caciques"—those controlling several municipalities—as "notable for their longevity, for their ubiquitous archival presence, and for the key role they have played in the construction and maintenance of the postrevolutionary political system." "Municipal" caciques are those who control a single municipality or town and often become regional caciques through "preferment from above, or mobilization from below." Local "mini-caciques," meanwhile, rule "pueblos, villages, even street blocks" and constitute caciquismo's "hidden capillary roots, digging deep into the earth, drawing sustenance for the proliferating branches above" (Knight, "Caciquismo," 27–29).
57. Knight, *Mexican Revolution*, ii, 81.
58. Knight, 437; see also Almada, *La revolución*, 326–31.
59. The coa is "an indispensable tool for the peasant of Nayar; it replaces the crowbar, the pick-axe, the shovel, the machete, the knife and, if need be, teeth and nails" (Menéndez, *Nayar*, 102).
60. See Smith, *Politics and Pistoleros*, 67; I. Landa and P. Landa, in Caldera and de la Torre, *Pueblos*, 49, 55–56.
61. Mariano Mejía, commander of eleven men in Jesús María, could also assemble a combined force of around one hundred fighters from communities across the Náayari Alta (Enendino Escobedo Mejía; Juventino Mejía Rivera; Cándido Contreras Rosales).
62. Neurath, "Fricciones ontológicas," 15 (emphasis mine).
63. Nugent, *Spent Cartridges*, 83.
64. Knight, "Peasant and Caudillo," 52.
65. Knight, 25–30; see also Nugent, *Spent Cartridges*, 83–85.
66. AHED-FR/C/5/E/274, Circular 15 to Jefes de Defensa, Aug. 28, 1919.
67. Knight, "Caciquismo," 44.
68. Knight, *Mexican Revolution*, ii, 438.
69. Brewster, *Militarism, Ethnicity, and Politics*, 43–45; Nugent, *Spent Cartridges*, 83–85.
70. Smith, "Defending 'Our Beautiful Freedom,'" 139.
71. Liffman, *Huichol Territory*, 86.

72. Weigand, "Differential Acculturation," quoted in Liffman, *Huichol Territory*, 46. So too amongst northern groups such as the Yaqui; see Radding, "Peasant Resistance," 339.
73. Rus, "Revoluciones contenidas," 14–16; Hu-Dehart, *Yaqui Resistance*, 59–86; Friedrich, *The Princes*, 142–43; Knight, "Peasant and Caudillo," 25.
74. Goldkind, "Class Conflict," 325–45, cited in Joseph, "Caciquismo and the Revolution," 200.
75. Joseph, "Caciquismo and the Revolution," 200–201.
76. Neurath, "Ambivalencias del poder," 117–43.
77. Testament to the Gran Nayar's high level of autonomy is that in many other Indigenous regions, similar "generational and patriarchal" struggles broke out much earlier, during the nineteenth century (Radding, "Peasant Resistance," 339; Mallón, "Reflections," 96–101).
78. Knight, "Cardenismo," 97.
79. I. Landa Rentería, in Caldera and de la Torre, *Pueblos*, 49.
80. Zingg, *Los huicholes*, i, 132–33.
81. Rojas, *Los huicholes*, 163.
82. Weigand, "Co-operative Labor Groups," 19.
83. AGMJ/FUN-01-MJ, Calixto Guerrero, "Informe," Oct. 22, 1917.
84. Joseph, "Caciquismo and the Revolution," 198; Smith, *Politics and Pistoleros*, 65.
85. This Félix Díaz should not be confused with Porfirio Díaz's better-known nephew, then a rebel commander in Veracruz.
86. AGMJ/FUN-01-MJ, Calixto Guerrero, "Informe," Oct. 22, 1917.
87. See Knight, *Mexican Revolution*, ii, 220–21.
88. AGMJ/FUN-01-MJ, Calixto Guerrero, "Informe," Oct. 22, 1917.
89. Guerrero, as above.
90. R. Cosío Alvarez, in Caldera and de la Torre, *Pueblos*, 60.
91. "Huaynamota fue quitado a los bandidos a sangre a fuego," *Informador*, Nov. 1, 1918.
92. I. Landa Rentería, in Caldera and de la Torre, *Pueblos*, 50.
93. E.g., José Ramírez, in Caldera and de la Torre, 65–70.
94. AHAG-Amatlán, Francisco del Real to Arz., Sept. 3, 1920.
95. AHAG-Amatlán, Francisco del Real to Arz., Apr. 11, 1919.
96. Villista attacks had already forced the people of both these pueblos to evacuate to San Martín de Bolaños (AHAG-Bolaños/C/3/E/14, Pbro. San Martín de Bolaños to Arz., July 2, 1918).
97. AHAG-Amatlán, Francisco del Real to Arz., Apr. 11, 1919.
98. Knight, *Mexican Revolution*, ii, 235–36; Knight, "The Mentality," 21–56.
99. Geary, *Furta Sacra*, xi, 154–59.
100. Walsham, "Introduction," 31.
101. Hrdlička, "The Region of the Ancient 'Chichimecs,'" 410.

102. Van Oosterhout, "Popular Conservatism in Mexico," 208–9.
103. This was all the more likely because San José was especially venerated by the Wixáritari (Neurath, *Las fiestas*, 302–3).
104. Weigand, "El papel," 125. The Tzotzils of Chenalhó, Chiapas, also allied with the Carrancistas to drive mestizos from their lands and saw the revolution in a similarly positive light (Rus, "La revolución contenida," 75–76).
105. Interview with Salvador Sánchez.
106. Interview with Xuturima Hernández.
107. Weigand, "El papel," 125.
108. Salvador Sánchez; Zingg, *Los huicholes*, i, 88.
109. Weigand, "El papel," 125.
110. Interview with Salvador Sánchez.
111. Zingg, *Los huicholes*, i, 133.
112. As "patriotic liberals," the Carrancistas would "no more tolerate the creation or survival of *republiquetas de indios* within the state than had their Porfirian predecessors" and assassinated overly independent Indigenous leaders across Mexico (Knight, "Peasant and Caudillo," 29; see also Rus, "La revolución en los Altos de Chiapas," 18).
113. Weigand, "Differential Acculturation," 14.
114. The last primary source that directly mentions Mezquite's recent activities was written in April 1919, so he was likely arrested soon after.
115. Weigand, "El papel," 126.
116. Interview with Salvador Sanchez.
117. Avitia, *El caudillo*, 117.
118. Knight, "Peasant and Caudillo," 52.
119. AGN-G-195/C/48/E/46, J. Torres Sur to Carranza, Oct. 20, 1916.
120. Meyer, *Del canton*, 192.
121. AGN-G-195/C/42/E/7, Ferreira to Carranza, May 15, 1917.
122. AHSDN-C/C/105/XI/481.5/193, M. Diéguez to Carranza, Jan. 19, 1918.
123. Rojas, *Los huicholes*, 163–64.
124. Meyer, *De cantón*, 193.
125. AHSEP-84-85/C/X/E/60, Martimiano Serrano to DEFN, May 21, 1961.
126. AGN-Censo/1930/Nayarit/San Juan Corapan.
127. Interview with Filiberto Sánchez, "Aurelio Chavez,"
128. AHSEP-84-85/C/38876/E/17, Orozco to DEFN, Feb. 9, 1928.
129. Interviews with Sandalio Sánchez; Filiberto Sánchez; Agustín Lamas.
130. Interviews with Erasmo González and Filiberto Sánchez.
131. Interviews with Filiberto Sánchez, Sandalio Sánchez, and Celestino Lamas.
132. AHSEP-45/C/36301/E/29, Navarrete to DECI, May 4, 1925.
133. Cf. Friedrich, *Agrarian Revolt*, 71–72; Smith, *Pistoleros and Popular Movements*, 141–42.

134. AGN-Censo/1930/Nayarit/Arroyo de Santiago.
135. Rulfo, "Valentín de la Sierra," 162.
136. Oral sources are unclear as to her actual ethnicity, which given Huaynamota's history as a mixed Náayari-Mexicanero community very close to the Sierra Wixárika could reasonably have been Náayari, Wixárika, or Mexicanero.
137. Interviews with Enendino Escobedo; Juventino Mejía; Cándido Contreras.
138. See Rugeley, *Yucatán's Maya Peasantry*, 117–47; Fallaw and Rugeley, "Redrafting History," 16–17.
139. AHSEP-45/C/36301/E/29, San Lucas de Jalpa, to Pres., Mar. 12, 1925; AHJ-G-9-920-921/C/52/E/11171, Clemente Villa to Gob. Jal., Feb. 17, 1921.
140. Interviews with Enendino Escobedo; Juventino Mejía; Cándido Contreras.
141. Interview with Juventino Mejía.
142. Interview with Enendino Escobedo.
143. Interview with Juventino Mejía; cf. Coyle, *From Flowers*, 185–86.
144. Interview with Enendino Escobedo Mejía.
145. Scott, "Patron-Client Politics," 92.
146. Rojas, *Los huicholes*, 164.
147. Knight, *Mexican Revolution*, i, 115–27; see also Rugeley, *Yucatan's Maya Peasantry*, 101, and, more generally, Brewster, *Militarism, Ethnicity, and Politics*.
148. Rojas, *Los huicholes*, 164.
149. Perhaps in late 1916, when the defensas sociales of Chihuahua were also first established by Carrancista General Enríquez (Almada, *La revolución*, ii, 326); Nugent, *Spent Cartridges*, 83.
150. Torres notes that these same relationships defined factional politics amongst the Nahuas of highland Puebla ("Nahuat Factionalism," 467–68).
151. Interviews with Enendino Escobedo; Cándido Contreras.
152. Mejía's career trajectory was therefore similar to that of many regional caciques in this period, who "enjoyed prestige in their communities, and were therefore natural leaders of any armed movement that arose there," which then allowed them to further extend their influence "by usurping the powers of the former ruling class" (which usually consisted of "landlords and politicians" but in the case of the Gran Nayar was made up of elders, shamans, and cargo holders) (Ankerson, "Cedillo," 140).
153. Interviews with Juventino Mejía; Enendino Escobedo; Cándido Contreras.
154. Manuel Lozada is also said to have used a magical machete rather than a firearm (Meyer, *Manuel Lozada*, 220).
155. Interview with Juventino Mejía.
156. In nineteenth-century Colombia, for example, the rumor that a particular Conservative general was "imbued with great magical powers which made him invulnerable to the enemies' bullets" was enough to prompt the Indigenous inhabitants of Aritama to defect

en masse from the Liberal side and join their former enemies. However, "as soon as the general was killed by the counter-magic of the enemy, the villagers deserted and returned to their mountains" (Reichel-Dolmatoff, *The People of Aritama*, 15–16).

157. Weber, *On Charisma*, 19; see also Lomnitz-Adler, *Exits from the Labyrinth*, 350.
158. Brunk, *Emiliano Zapata*, 238–39. In the Sierra Norte de Puebla, Gabriel Barrios Cabrera was similarly viewed by local Nahuas (Brewster, *Militarism, Ethnicity, and Politics*, 57–61).
159. Jáuregui and Meyer, *El Tigre de Alica*.
160. The Yaquis have traditionally had a similar tendency to greatly distrust mestizos while following those identified as "benevolent patrones" (Radding, "Peasant Resistance," 352).
161. AHED-FR/C/5/E/54, Mariano Mejía to D. Arrieta, July 24, 1919; AHSEP-45/C/36301/E/29, Residents of San Lucas de Jalpa to Gob. Dgo., Mar. 12, 1925.
162. AHJ-G-9-920-921/C/52/E/11171, Clemente Villa to Gob. Jal., Feb. 17, 1921.
163. Aldana, *La rebelión agraria*, 181–209.
164. Nugent and Alonso, "Multiple Selective Traditions," 244.
165. Joseph, "Rethinking Mexican Revolutionary Mobilization," 157–65; Mallón, "Reflections," 98–100.
166. Interviews with Bruno Gómez and Nemesio Rodríguez.
167. Interview with Juventino Mejía.
168. AHED-FR/C/5/E/54, D. Arrieta to Mejía, Aug. 9, 1919.
169. Marriage certificate of Damazo [sic] Barraza and Nieves Valdés, June 20, 1907.
170. Meyer, *La cristiada*, i, 143.
171. Meyer, iii, 29.
172. Interviews with Manuel Arrellano and Felipe Salas Ramirez.
173. Meyer, *La cristiada*, i, 143.
174. Marriage certificate of Damazo [sic] Barraza and Nieves Valdés, June 20, 1907.
175. AHED-M/C/3/E/151, "Cuerpo Rural de Barraza," Oct. 6, 1918.
176. F. Campos, "Santiago," *David*, Dec. 22, 1955.
177. Meyer, *La cristiada*, iii, 94. Meyer evidently makes this assertion based on Naranjo, *Diccionario biográfico*, 43.
178. The Arrietas themselves worked closely with Durango's Villistas before 1914 (Knight, *Mexican Revolution*, ii, 220).
179. In addition to all owning relatively large herds of cattle, these men were of the same generation, and in fact Mejía and Barraza were both born in 1879.
180. Barraza's revolutionary career may well have started as early as 1912, when the inhabitants of Yonora first came into contact with rebel groups.
181. Domingo Arrieta, the most important of the nine Arrieta brothers, was a "'rugged, earthy, uneducated leader,'" "'illiterate but endowed with a phenomenal memory,'" who enjoyed "'a sort of tribal leadership of the inhabitants of the Sierra Madre'" (Knight, *Mexican Revolution*, ii, 482–85).

182. AHED-D/C/13/E/161, Apolinar Venegas to Gob. Dgo., Aug. 25, 1935.
183. Interview with Felipe Salas Ramírez.
184. AHED-FR/C/1/E/6, Gob. Dgo. to Barraza, Aug. 2, 1917.
185. AHED-FR/C/1/E/6, Gob. Dgo. to Carranza, Aug. 5, 1917.
186. AHED-A/C/3/E/55, PM Mezquital to Gob. Dgo., Aug. 15, 1917.
187. The situation was so bad that by the end of the year, the municipal president urgently requested state government funds for the construction of a new graveyard, "por haberse llenado de cadaveres el [panteón] de esta Cabecera, con motivo de la epidemia" (AHED-M/C/3/E/206, PM Mezquital to Gob. Dgo., Dec. 7, 1918).
188. Avitia, *Los Alacranes*, 110. In Morelos, too, "many villages were empty shells" by 1918 (Knight, *Mexican Revolution*, ii, 371). Conversely, Spanish influenza, drought, and banditry had devastated Michoacán a year earlier, and thus 1917 was remembered there as "el año del hambre" (González y González, *Pueblo en vilo*, 127).
189. AHED-M/C/3/E/175, PM Mezquital to Gob. Dgo., Oct. 30, 1918.
190. AHED-M/C/3/E/57, Visitador de Munic. to Gob. Dgo., Mar. 7, 1918.
191. AHED-M/C/3/E/175, PM Mezquital to Gob. Dgo., Oct. 30, 1918.
192. Avitia, *El caudillo*, 84–85.
193. AHED-M/C/3/E/127, M. Rojas et al. to Gob. Dgo., Aug. 10, 1918.
194. Knight, *Mexican Revolution*, i, 78–114, 150–70.
195. AHED-M/C/3/E/175, PM Mezquital to Gob. Dgo., Oct. 30, 1918.
196. Local banditry reached such levels that the state government banned "la salida de mulada, caballada y de ganado en general de [la región], sin el previo permiso de ese Supremo Gobierno, a efecto de que, en lo sucesivo, se siga comerciando con animales robados" (AHED-M/C/3/E/151, "Circular 19," Oct. 23, 1918).
197. AHED-M/C/4/E/136, [illegible] Zepeda, Gobernador de Milpillas Chico, to Domingo Arrieta, Gob.Dgo, Dec. 27, 1919; also P. Munic PN, Manuel Valles, to Gob. Dgo., June 2, 1918; AHED-M/C/3/E/45, Gob. Dgo. to P. Munic PN, March 1, 1918.
198. AHED-M/C/4/E/136, P. Munic PN, Manuel Valles, to Gob. Dgo., June 2, 1918.
199. AHED-M/C/3/E/45, P. Munic PN, to Gob Dgo., Feb. 20, 1918; AHED-M/C/3/E/45, Gob. Dgo. to P. Munic PN, March 1, 1918.
200. AHED-M/C/3/E/200, José Gutiérrez to Gob. Dgo., Dec. 31, 1918.
201. AHED-M/C/3/E/200, Gob. Dgo. to Gutiérrez, Jan. 21, 1919.
202. See Orozco y Berra, *Geografía de las lenguas*, 281.
203. AHED-M/C/3/E/200, José Gutiérrez to Gob. Dgo., Dec. 31, 1918.
204. AHED-M/C/3/E/200, Gob. Dgo. to Jefes de Cuarteles de San Andrés and Picachos, Jan. 21, 1919.
205. AHED-M/C/3/E/200, Gob. Dgo. to Auts. Trads. San Buenaventura, Jan. 21, 1919.
206. AHED-M/C/3/E/200, José Gutiérrez to Gob. Dgo., Dec. 31, 1919.
207. In many parts of Mexico, other similarly "self-declared," "disciplined," and "obedient" Indigenous military forces, including the Juchitecos of the Isthmus and many Yaquis,

also took advantage of "ingrained fears of Indian revolt, [to] carve out distinct spaces of local control" (Smith, "Heliodoro Charis," 128).

208. AHED-M/C/4/E/24, Vicente Muñoz to Gob. Dgo., Oct. 4, 1919.
209. AHED-FR/C/5/E/38, P. Ortiz to Gob. Dgo., July 2, 1919.
210. Ángeles was captured and executed by the Carrancista government in November 1919 (Almada, *La revolución*, ii, 347).
211. AHED-FR/C/5/E/38, P. Ortiz to Gob. Dgo., July 2, 1919.
212. AHED-FR/C/5/E/38, Gob. Dgo. to P. Ortiz., July 26, 1919.
213. AHED-HZ/C/4/E/106, Mejía to "autoridades militares de Dgo.," July 24, 1919.
214. AHED-FR/C/5/E/54, Mejía to Gob. Dgo., July 24, 1919.
215. AHED-FR/C/5/E/38, P. Ortiz to Gob. Dgo., July 2, 1919.
216. AHED-FR/C/5/E/54, Gob. Dgo. to Mejía, Aug. 9, 1919.
217. AHED-FR/C/5/E/54, V. Muñoz to Gob. Dgo., Aug. 29, 1919.
218. AHED-M/C/4/E/24, J. Tello Herrera to Gob. Dgo., Sept. 2, 1919; Avelino Rimoldi to Gob. Dgo., Sept. 2, 1919; Regino López to Gob. Dgo., Oct. 3, 1919.
219. AHED-M/C/4/E/24, Residents of San Juan Capistrano to Gob. Dgo., Sept. 3, 1919.
220. AHED-FR/C/5/E/38, P. Ortiz to Gob. Dgo., July 2, 1919.
221. AHED-FR/C/5/E/54, Gob. Dgo. to V. Muñoz, Sept. 4, 1919.
222. AHED-R/C/6/E/85, PM Mezquital to Gob. Dgo., Feb. 1, 1915.
223. AHED-M/C/3/E/175, PM Mezquital to Gob. Dgo., Oct. 30, 1918; PM Mezquital to Gob. Dgo., Nov. 17, 1918.
224. AHED-FR/C/5/E/38, Gob. Dgo. to P. Ortiz, May 31, 1919. Ortiz himself vigorously rejected such claims and counteraccused Aguilar of committing "muchas arbitrariedades, en terrenos de esta jurisdicción; pero tiene la palabra favorita que todo lo hace con acuerdo de esa Supremo Gobierno" (AHED-FR/C/5/E/41, P. Ortiz to Gob.Dgo., May 11, 1919).
225. Cf. Dennis, *Intervillage Conflict*, 49–94.
226. AHED-M/C/4/E/24, V. Estrada to Gob. Dgo., Sept. 30, 1919.
227. AHED-M/C/4/E/24, R. López to Gob. Dgo., Oct. 3, 1919.
228. AHED-M/C/4/E/24, G. Aguilar to Gob. Dgo., Oct. 7, 1919.
229. AHED-C/C/10/E/3, G. Aguilar to Gob. Dgo., Oct. 6, 1919.
230. Interview with Saturnino Solís.
231. AHED-M/C/4/E/24, Gob. Dgo. to Gutiérrez., Oct. 11, 1919.
232. AHED-FR/C/5/E/21, Gob. Dgo. to Bermúdez, Oct. 19, 1919.
233. AHED-FR/C/5/E/21, Bermúdez to Gob. Dgo., Nov. 12, 1919.
234. AHED-M/C/4/E/24, Gob. Dgo. to Sec. Gob., Nov. 26, 1919.
235. AHED-FR/C/5/E/21, Bermúdez to Gob. Dgo., Nov. 12, 1919.
236. Cf. Knight, "Caciquismo," 27.
237. Scott, *Weapons*, 136–37.
238. Knight, "Cardenismo," 97; cf. Friedrich, *The Princes*, 100.

CHAPTER 3

1. Rath, "Revolutionary Citizenship," 175.
2. Rath, *Myths*, 23–30; Fallaw and Rugeley, "Redrafting History," 7.
3. Fallaw and Rugeley, "Redrafting History," 8–9.
4. Many generals became rich through investment in land and industry, racketeering, the provision of "protection," and simple theft (Gillingham, "Military Caciquismo," 219; Tobler, "Las Paradojas," 62).
5. Marak, "Failed Assimilation," 412.
6. Mallón, "Reflections," 97–100.
7. Rus, "The 'Comunidad Revolucionaria Institucional,'" 278; Torres Trueba, "Nahuat Factionalism," 468–69; for a more extensive analysis of such dynamics, see Friedrich, *The Princes*.
8. Falcón, "Force," 115, citing Corrigan and Sayer, *The Great Arch*, 22.
9. AGN/Censo/1921/Nayarit, Durango, Jalisco.
10. Eiss, "Beyond the Land," 527.
11. Friedrich, *The Princes*, 41.
12. Gómez Santana, "Mujeres y propiedad," 555.
13. Nugent and Alonso, "Multiple Selective Traditions," 226.
14. In particular, in Veracruz, Aguascalientes, Michoacán, Puebla, and Guerrero; cf. Tobler, "Las Paradojas," 53–60.
15. Escobar and Butler, "Transitions and Closures," 57–58.
16. Birrichaga, "¿Ejidatarios o comuneros?" 321–53.
17. From 1916 to 1980, "only 17 percent of requests for restitution were granted, in contrast to 79 percent of the requests for *dotación*. During the same period only 214 restitutions were made, compared to 21,289 *dotaciones*" (Nugent and Alsonso, "Multiple Selective Traditions," note 38 to page 229).
18. Nugent and Alonso, 226–27, 236–37.
19. Nugent, *Spent Cartridges*, 98–99.
20. Nugent, 91 (italics mine); cf. 87–90, 98–99.
21. Vaughan, *Cultural Politics*, 44.
22. Loyo, "La empresa redentora," 101.
23. Vaughan, *Cultural Politics*, 29; cf. Eiss, "Deconstructing Indians," 135.
24. Aguirre Beltrán, *Teoría y práctica*, 97, 114–16, 125; Dawson, *Indian and Nation*, 8–20; Vaughan, *Cultural Politics*, 27–29, 46; see also the essays in Esobar and Butler, *Mexico in Transition*.
25. Eiss, "Deconstructing Indians," 130; see also Fallaw, "'Anti-Priests,'" 206–7.
26. AHSEP-42/C/36051/E/76.38, Circular No. 5, May 15, 1922.
27. AHSEP-42/C/35981/E/8.54, Parra to DECI, July 27, 1922.

28. AHSEP-45/C/36339/E/13, "Primer Congreso de Misioneros: dictamenes y proposiciones aprobadas," Sept. 18, 1922; cf. Eiss, "Deconstructing Indians," 137; Dawson, "'Wild Indians,'" 336; Lewis, "Collective Psychological Experiment," 14; Loyo, "La empresa redentora," 118.
29. Rockwell, "Schools," 198; Vaughan, *Cultural Politics*, 15–16; Dawson, *Indian and Nation*, 29; Rus, "The 'Comunidad Revolucionaria Institucional,'" 271; Lewis, *The Ambivalent Revolution*, 37–38.
30. Loyo, "La empresa redentora," 121; Eiss, "Deconstructing Indians," 135.
31. Eiss, "Deconstructing Indians," 142.
32. Lumholtz, *Unknown Mexico*, i, 458; see also AGMJ/FUN-01-MJ, Calixto Guerrero, "Informe," Oct. 22, 1917; Dawson, "'Wild Indians,'" 337.
33. Vaughan, *Cultural Politics*, 46, and *The State, Education*, 238–66; Eiss, "Deconstructing Indians," 129–31, 141; Marak, "Failed Assimilation," 418–19; De Giuseppe, "'El Indio Gabriel,'" 229.
34. Dawson, "From Models," 282–83, see also 292.
35. Loyo, "La empresa redentora," 103–4.
36. Carroll, "The Smell," 35.
37. Kropotkin, *Memoirs*, ii, 103–4.
38. Woolford, *This Benevolent Experiment*, 259–88.
39. Thus Andrae Marak, for example, writes that "the oppression that the Tarahumara suffered . . . at the hands of the SEP, for whatever it was worth, was meant to improve their lives. Given the weakness of the federal government and its inability to prevent local authorities from taking advantage of the Tarahumara, it is hard to conceive what other path the SEP might have taken" ("Failed Assimilation," 428–29).
40. See Segalla, *Moroccan Soul*; Woolford, *This Benevolent Experiment*.
41. Scott, *Weapons*, xvi, 29–35; Elsie Rockwell has also noted Tlaxcalan inhabitants' use of their native languages to confuse teachers and other outsiders; "Schools," 195–96.
42. E.g., Rockwell, "Schools," 188; Nugent, *Spent Cartridges*, 106–8.
43. For case studies of the same phenomenon in Puebla, Tlaxcala, Chiapas, and Oaxaca, see Torres, "Nahuat Facionalism," 463; Rockwell, "Schools," 200–202; Rus, "The 'Comunidad Revolucionaria Institucional,'" 278; Smith, "Defending 'Our Beautiful Freedom,'" 140–41.
44. Vaughan, *Cultural Politics*, 13–14; Rockwell, "Schools of the Revolution," 181.
45. Cf. Smith, "Defending 'Our Beautiful Freedom,'" 141.
46. Meyer, *De Cantón*, 193; AHSDN-C/C/105/E/XI/481.5/193, Col. Esquivel to JOM Nay., Feb. 3, 1920; Col. Esquivel to JOM Nay., Feb. 10, 1920.
47. Interview with Filiberto Sánchez.
48. Meyer, *Manuel Lozada*, 259.
49. Meyer, *De Cantón*, 193.

50. AHSEP-42/C/35987/E/12.2, Navarrete to DECI, Jan. 10, 1922.
51. Rockwell, "Schools," 186.
52. AHSEP-42/C/36051/E/76.38, "Circular No. 5," May 15, 1922.
53. AHSEP-42/C/35987/E/12.2, Navarrete to DECI, Jan. 25, 1922.
54. Eiss, "Deconstructing Indians," 119–50.
55. Pérez, *Ensayo estadístico*, 560.
56. Dawson, "'Wild Indians,'" 334.
57. Vaughan, *Cultural Politics*, 28–29; Dawson, "From Models," 279–308. However, Dawson also notes that Porfirian views of "the Aztecs as savages" and modern Indigenous peoples as "irredeemable" remained "present in school textbooks well into the 1920s."
58. AHSEP-42/C/35987/E/12.2, Navarrete to DECI, Jan. 25, 1922.
59. AHSEP-42/C/35987/E/12.2, Navarrete to DECI, Jan. 25, 1922.
60. Vaughan, *Cultural Politics*, 153; Mallón, "Reflections," 84; De Giuseppe, "'El Indio Gabriel,'" 235.
61. AHSEP-42/C/35987/E/12.2, Navarrete to DECI, Jan. 25, 1922.
62. Eiss, "Deconstructing Indians," 130–31.
63. Both the SEP's education programs and the institution itself were highly gendered; see Vaughan, *Cultural Politics*, 42–44, 49, 108; Rockwell, "Schools," 194; Lewis, *The Ambivalent Revolution*, 60, 90–95; Butler, *Popular Piety*, 80–104.
64. AHSEP-42/C/35987/E/12.2, Navarrete to DECI, Jan. 25, 1922.
65. AHSEP-42/C/35987/E/12.2, Navarrete to DECI, June 2, 1922.
66. AHSEP-42/C/35987/E/12.2, Jefe del Dept. Escolar to Dept. Bibliotecas, Mar. 7, 1922. This was in line with Vasconcelos's basic eurocentrism, for more on which, see Butler, *Popular Piety*, 83.
67. Maestros charged with "incorporating" Indigenous communities in Chiapas also wrote constantly of the "martyrdom" and "deprivation" they faced in the "wilderness" (Lewis, *The Ambivalent Revolution*, 25).
68. AHSEP-42/C/35987/E/12.2, Navarrete to DECI, Nov. 20, 1922.
69. Eiss, "Deconstructing Indians," 135.
70. AHSEP-42/C/35987/E/12.2, Navarrete to DECI, Nov. 20, 1922.
71. AHSEP-42/C/35987/E/12.2, Navarrete to DECI, Sept. 25, 1925.
72. AHSEP-42/C/35987/E/12.2, Navarrete to DECI, June 2, 1922.
73. AHSEP-42/C/35987/E/12.2, Navarrete to DECI, Aug. 20, 1922.
74. Cf. Butler, "A Revolution in Spirit?" 5; Eiss, "Beyond the Land," 521–22.
75. AHSEP-42/C/35987/E/12.2, Navarrete to DECI, Oct. 26, 1922.
76. Interviews with Filiberto Sánchez; Sandalio Sánchez Sánchez.
77. Rockwell, "Schools," 172.
78. AHSEP-45/C/36301/E/29, Navarrete, "Informe," May 4, 1925; cf. Filiberto Sánchez, "Aurelio Chavez."

79. Smith, "Heliodoro Charis," 121.
80. AHSEP-42/C/35987/E/12.2, Navarrete to DECI, Aug. 20, 1922.
81. AHSEP-42/C/35981/E/8.54, Parra to DECI, July 10, 1922.
82. The Náayarite of Acaponeta were few in number compared with the municipality's mestizos. They shared close linguistic, cultural, and politico-religious links with inhabitants of both the Náayari Baja and Alta, although they were not under the direct control of either Mariano Mejía or Eutimio Domínguez (cf. González, *Los coras*, 82–86).
83. AHSEP-42/C/35981/E/8.54, Parra to DECI, July 27, 1922.
84. The hamlets explicitly mentioned by Parra as inhabited by mestizos in this period were El Oro and Pedro Pablo, today anexos of Saycota, and El Motaje, an anexo of San Blasito.
85. AHSEP-42/C/35981/E/8.54, Parra to DECI, Sept. 29, 1922.
86. AHSEP-42/C/35981/E/8.54, Parra to DECI, Aug. 8, 1922.
87. AHSEP-42/C/35981/E/8.54, Parra to DECI, Nov. 19, 1922.
88. AHSEP-42/C/36023/E/48.13, Parra to DECI, Aug. 31, 1923.
89. AHSEP-42/C/35981/E/8.54, Parra to DECI, Nov. 19, 1922.
90. In this, SEP aims were in line with those of modernizing states the world over, where schools promote "state simplification" of national economy, ecology, and population, in order to facilitate state control (Scott, *Seeing Like a State*, 53–83, 309–57).
91. AHSEP-42/C/35981/E/8.54, Parra to DECI, Nov. 24, 1922.
92. AHSEP-42/C/35981/E/8.54, Saycota: school statistics, Dec. 21, 1922.
93. AHSEP-42/C/36023/E/48.13, Parra to DECI, Aug. 31, 1923.
94. AHSEP-42/C/36051/E/76.20, DEFN to DECI, June 16, 1923.
95. AHSEP-45/C/36330/E/32, Loyola to DEFN, Aug. 13, 1924.
96. AHSEP-45/C/36330/E/32, DEFN to "residents of Saycota," Feb. 17, 1925.
97. AHSEP-45/C/36304/E.27, Loyola to DEFN, June 9, 1924.
98. AHSEP-42/C/36023/E/48.13, DEFN to DECI, n.d., 1923.
99. AHSEP-45/C/36330/E/32, Flores (in name of "residents of Saycota") to DEFN, Dec. 10, 1924.
100. AHSEP-45/C/36330/E/32, DEFN to "residents of Saycota," Feb. 17, 1925.
101. Purnell, *Popular Movements*, 67–68.
102. AHSEP-45/C/36335/E/10, Navarrete to DECI, May 1 1924.
103. Davila, "General Francisco de Santiago Villegas." *Colotlán en llamas*. Accessed July 29, 2011. http://colotlanenllamas.blogspot.mx/.
104. AHSEP-45/C/36301/E/16, DEFN to DECI, Jan. 24, 1924.
105. Vaughan, *Cultural Politics*, 28.
106. AHSEP-45/C/36301/E/16, DEFN to DECI, Jan. 24, 1924.
107. "Cuales fueron las causas," *Demócrata*, May 13, 1924.
108. Dawson, "'Wild Indians,'" 333.
109. AHSEP-45/C/36322/E?24, "SEP Presupuesto 1923–24," July 10, 1923.

110. AHSEP-45/C/36335/E/10, DEFN to DECI, Feb. 19, 1924.
111. "Cuales fueron las causas," *Demócrata*, May 13, 1924.
112. AHSEP-45/C/36337/E/29, clipping from "Eco de Nayarit," Apr. 14, 1924.
113. AHSEP-45/C/36301/E/29, Guerrero to DEFN, Dec. 27, 1924.
114. Loyo, "La empresa redentora," 103–4.
115. AHSEP-45/C/36301/E/29, Guerrero to DEFN, Dec. 29, 1924; Guerrero to DEFN, Dec. 31, 1924.
116. AGA-D/23/147/leg.1/CCA/Dotación/Saycota, Guerrero to CNA, n.d., 1924.
117. Nugent, *Spent Cartridges*, 87.
118. AGA-D/23/147/leg.1/CCA/Dotación/Saycota, CLA to Aurelio Guerrero, Dec. 24, 1924.
119. AHSEP-45/C/36301/E/29, DECI to DEFN, Jan. 16, 1925.
120. The Knights of Columbus (Caballeros de Colón) was an influential international Catholic lay organization, founded in the United States but with branches across Mexico. Linked as it was to the Vatican, the "gringos," and Catholic political resistance to the 1917 Constitution, the organization was a frequent target of revolutionary ire in this period.
121. Flores had been Calles's opponent during the recent presidential elections.
122. AHSEP-45/C/36335/E/10, Navarrete to DECI, Dec. 10, 1924.
123. AHSEP-42/C/36023/E/48.60, Romero Gallardo to Vasconcelos, June 9, 1923; Vasconcelos to Romero Gallardo, June 13, 1923.
124. AHSEP-42/C/36023/E/48.60, Romero Gallardo to Vasconcelos, n.d., 1923.
125. AHSEP-42/C/36023/E/48.60, DEFN to DECI, Sept. 12, 1923.
126. AHSEP-42/C/36056/E/81.24, Enrique Maldonado to Vasconcelos, Oct. 14, 1924.
127. AHSEP-45/C/36326/E/6, Romero Gallardo to DEFN, Feb. 10, 1925; Marak, "Failed Assimilation," 420.
128. AHSEP-45/C/36326/E/6, Navarrete to DERICI, Feb. 17, 1925.
129. AHSEP-45/C/36326/E/6, DEFN to DERICI, Mar. 5, 1925.
130. AHSEP-45/C/36348/E/7, Juana Rocha et al. to DEFN, Mar. 27, 1925.
131. AHSEP-42/C/36059/E/84.29, Guerrero to DECI, Mar. 11, 1925.
132. AHSEP-45/C/36301/E/29, Liga de Coms. Agrarias Nay. to Pres., Mar. 9, 1925.
133. AHSEP-45/C/36301/E/29, Navarrete to DERICI, Mar. 25, 1925.
134. Lumholtz, *Unknown Mexico*, 491, 509; Preuss, *Fiesta, literatura y magia*, 127.
135. The Mexican state's support for—and the ties of its officials to—cattle ranching was a constant throughout the twentieth century; see Harvey, *The Chiapas Rebellion*, 73.
136. AHSEP-45/C/36301/E/16, DEFN to DECI, Jan. 24, 1924.
137. AHSEP-84-85/C/859/E/60, Meza to DEI, May 21, 1961.
138. AHSEP-45/C/36326/E/6, DEFN to DERICI, Aug. 31, 1925.
139. AGN/O-C/728-J-5, Evaristo Aquino to Pres., Apr. 15, 1925.
140. In this period the regional cattle trade does indeed seem to have recovered, at least partially, from the disruption of the revolution; see Coyle, *From Flowers*, 185–86.

141. In Jesús María, for example, the family of Mejía's Náayari second-in-command León Contreras grew so rich that "cuando se puso en paz, el papá de Don León Contreras, tenía ganados desde el cerro, todo el arroyo, mucho ganado!" (Candido Contreras).
142. Rockwell, "Schools," 202–3.
143. AHSEP-84-85/C/38874/E/8, Durán Cárdenas to DEFN, Jan. 25, 1933.
144. Interview with Fernando Muñíz.
145. Interview with Aurelio Cánare.
146. See Coyle, *From Flowers*, 186.
147. Interview with Erasmo González.
148. Villanueva was an ally of the governor of Jalisco, José Guadalupe Zuno, with whom Calles was then engaged in conflict, and he had also previously supported the candidature of Ángel Flores, Calles's rival in the presidential elections of 1924.
149. Meyer, *De Cantón*, 194–95.
150. AHSEP-45/C/36330/E/11, DEFN to DERICI, May 11, 1926.
151. Marak, "Failed Assimilation," 421.
152. AHSEP-45/C/36301/E/29, DEFN, "Circular 8," May 6, 1925.
153. AHSEP-45/C/36301/E/29, DEFN to Inspectores, Aug. 4, 1925.
154. AHSEP-42/C/36056/E/81.24, clipping from *El Socialista*, Sept. 14, 1925; AHSEP-45/C/36301, E/29, DEFN to DERICI, Sept. 14, 1925; AHSEP-45/C/36330/E/11, DEFN to DERICI, May 11, 1926.
155. AHSEP-45/C/36301/E/29, DEFN to DERICI, Sept. 22, 1925.
156. AHSEP-45/C/36301/E/29, Inspector Gral. del Pacífico to DERICI, June 17, 1925.
157. AHSEP-45/C/36301/E/29, Lucio Rosas, political propaganda, n.d., 1925.
158. AHSEP-45/C/36301/E/29, DEFN to DERICI, Sept. 22, 1925.
159. AHSEP-45/C/36301/E/29, Navarrete to DEFN, Apr. 10, 1925.
160. AHSEP-45/C/36301/E/29, Inspector Gral. del Pacífico to DERICI, June 17, 1925.
161. AHSEP-45/C/36335/E/10, Navarrete to DEFN, Sept. 25, 1925.
162. AHSEP-45/C/36335/E/10, DEFN to DERICI, Sept. 30, 1925.
163. AHSEP-45/C/36301/E/29, DEFN to DERICI, Sept. 14, 1925.
164. Meyer, *De Cantón*, 195.
165. AHSEP-45/C/36335/E/10, Navarrete to DEFN, Sept. 25, 1925.
166. AGN-DGIPS/C/169/E/2, Confidential report on Nayarit elections, Nov. 6, 1925. These claims were reaffirmed by a DGIPS agent a few years later in the context of both Mejía's and Ramírez Romano's alleged support for the Cristero Rebellion (AGN-DGIPS/C/232/E/22, G. Ortega to Francisco Delgado, Jan. 2, 1928).
167. AGN-DGIPS/C/169/E/2, E. González to Sec. Gob., Oct. 25, 1925.
168. AHSEP-45/C/36301/E/29, DEFN to DERICI, Nov. 23, 1925.
169. AHSEP-45/C/36301/E/29, Navarrete to DEFN, Sept. 25, 1925.
170. AHSEP-45/C/36301/E/29, DEFN to DERICI, Sept. 22, 1925.

171. AHSEP-45/C/36326/E/6, Mejía to DEFN, Aug. 25, 1925.
172. AHSEP-45/C/36326/E/6, DEFN to DERICI, Aug. 31, 1925.
173. AHSEP-45/C/36301/E/29, Navarrete to DEFN, Mar. 25, 1925.
174. AHSEP-45/C/36340/E/22, Loyola to Francisco Castorena, Sept. 4, 1925.
175. AHSEP-45/C/36301/E/29, Calderón to all Nayarit's teachers, Oct. 10, 1925.
176. AHSEP-45/C/36326/E/6, Navarrete to DEFN, Nov. 9, 1925.
177. Interview with Erasmo González.
178. AHSEP-45/C/36303/E/27, Navarrete to DEFN, Nov. 3, 1925.
179. AHSEP-45/C/36301/E/29, Navarrete to DEFN, Nov. 9, 1925.
180. I. Landa Rentería, in Caldera and de la Torre, *Pueblos*, 41.
181. Félix Bañuelos, for example, had been a loyal companion of Villa from the early stages of the revolution. However, after joining Obregón's rebellion against Carranza, he became zone commander in Querétaro and later enjoyed a successful political career ("Felix Bañuelos," *Mi Pueblo*, Jan. 1995, 6).
182. The Sánchez family of El Salitre and the Robles of Mezquitic, for instance, had been wealthy landowners, ranchers, and merchants since the Porfiriato.
183. Meyer, *La cristiada*, i, 107–8.
184. De la Torre, *1926*, 30.
185. P. N. Valdés, in Meyer, *La cristiada*, iii, 42.
186. The town of El Salitre originally belonged to the municipality of Totatiche, but during the late nineteenth century became an important commercial center in itself. In April 1921, it was transformed into the seat of a new municipality and changed its name soon after.
187. AHJ-G-9-920-921/C/52/E/11171, Villa to Gob. Jal., Feb 17, 1921.
188. Grimes and Hinton, "The Huichol and the Cora," 799.
189. Zingg, *Los huicholes*, i, 88.
190. Weigand, "Co-operative Labor Groups," 18.
191. AHAG-Amatlán, Lauro Márquez to Arz., Mar. 1, 1920.
192. AHAG-Totatiche/C/3/E/13, Magallanes to Arz., July 6, 1920.
193. AHSEP-42/C/35987/E/12.2, Navarrete to DEFN, Nov. 20, 1922; AHSEP-42/C/35984/E/9.15, J. G. González to Vasconcelos, Apr. 12, 1922.
194. Thus in 1920, the churches of Huajimic, Camotlán, and Amatlán were all in ruins (AHAG-Amatlan/C/1, Sánchez Gómez, to Arz., Abril 20, 1920, Dec. 21, 1921).
195. Shadow and Rodríguez, "Religión, economía," 681–89; Meyer, *La cristiada* iii, 19–20, 33–34.
196. Fernández, "José Guadalupe Zuno," 98.
197. AHJ-G-9-920-921/C/52/E/11171, de la Cruz to Gob. Jal., Dec. 31, 1920.
198. AHJ-G-9-920-921/C/52/E/11171, Villa to Gob. Jal., Feb. 27, 1921.
199. AGA-D/276.1/103/leg.1/SRA/RTBC/San Andrés, Villa to Gob. Jal., May 20, 1921.

200. AGA-D/23/8465/leg.1/SRA/Dotación/Sta. Catarina, Juan García et al. to Gob. Jal., May 7, 1921.
201. See Stauffer, "Community, Identity," 158–59; Preciado, "Conciencia histórica," 489; Smith, "Heliodoro Charis," 128.
202. AGA-D/276.1/103/leg.1/SRA/RTBC/San Andrés, Gob. Jal. to Archivo de Instrumentos, Mar. 5, 1921.
203. AGA-D/276.1/103/leg.1/SRA/RTBC/San Andrés, "Solicitud de restitución," May 20, 1921.
204. POEJ, May 28, 1921.
205. AHSEP-42/C/35980/E/27, Juan de la Cruz, Agustín Carrillo, et al. to Gob. Jal., Nov. 2, 1922.
206. "Una comisión de huicholes que piden escuelas," *Informador*, Nov. 7, 1922.
207. Boletín de la SEP, Jan. 1, 1924, 490.
208. The people of Temastián had by this point lost any distinctive Indigenous identity (Shadow and Rodríguez, "Religión, economía," 681; Hrdlička, "The Region of the Ancient 'Chichimecs,'" 425–26).
209. AHSEP-45/C/36339/E/13, "Primer Congreso de Misioneros: dictamenes y proposiciones aprobadas," Sept. 18, 1922. Only a month later, a teacher in Colotlán described the town's mestizo inhabitants as "huicholes de habla Española" (AHSEP-42/C/35980/E/5.64, Maria Macías to DECI, Oct. 19, 1922).
210. AHSEP-42/C/35980/E/27, Hernández to DECI, July 20, 1922.
211. AHSEP-42/C/35980/E/27, Gob. Jal. to DEFJ, Nov. 16, 1922; AHSEP-42/C/35980/E/27, DEFJ to Hernández, Nov. 21, 1922.
212. AHSEP-42/C/35980/E/27, PM Colotlán to DEFJ, Dec. 4, 1922; Hernández to DEFJ, Dec. 14, 1922.
213. AHSEP-42/C/35980/E/27, Hernández to DECI, July 20, 1922.
214. AGA-D/23/1425/leg.2/CCA/Dotación/Sta Catarina, Ramírez to CNA, July 25, 1923.
215. Dawson, "From Models," 282–83.
216. AGA-D/23/1425/leg.2/CCA/Dotación/Sta Catarina, Ramírez to CNA, July 25, 1923.
217. AGA-D/23/242/leg.1/CCA/Dotación/San Andrés, Auts. Trads. to J. Martínez, Oct. 22, 1923.
218. AGA-D/23/242/leg.1/CCA/Dotación/San Andrés, J. Martínez to CLA, Nov. 16, 1923, (emphasis mine).
219. However, most of Jalisco's forty-six successful agrarian claims in this period emanated from the central region, and none were in the far north of the state (Gómez Santana, "Mujeres y propiedad," 548).
220. Rojas, *Huicholes: Documentos*, 236, 237–38.
221. J. García, "Ramón Muro," *Mi Pueblo*, June 1996, 19; AGN-LC/C/611/E/524/60, Agronomist's report on Tuxpan, Apr. 25, 1935. In fact Weigand asserts that of all the Wixárika

communities, it was San Sebastián and Tuxpan that in this period "suffered the most pressure" from mestizo land grabbers ("El papel," 126).

222. Weigand, "El papel," 126.
223. AHSEP-42/C/35980/E/27, Hernández to DECI, June 26, 1922.
224. AGMJ/FUN-01-MJ, Calixto Guerrero, "Informe," Oct. 22, 1917.
225. Interview with Julio Robles and Antonio Candelario.
226. AHSEP-42/C/36013/E/38.71, Hernández to DECI, May 7, 1923.
227. AHSEP-42/C/36013/E/38.71, DECI to Hernández, June 9, 1923.
228. AHSEP-42/C/36013/E/38.71, Hernández to DECI, May 30, 1923.
229. AHSEP-42/C/36013/E/38.71, DECI to Hernández, June 6, 1923.
230. AHSEP-45/C/36322/E.24, "SEP Presupuesto 1923–24," July 10, 1923.
231. Vaughan, *Cultural Politics*, 12.
232. AHSEP-42/C/36013/E/38.71, Hernández to DECI, Oct. 25, 1923.
233. AHSEP-42/C/36013/E/38.71, Hernández to DECI, Oct. 30, 1923.
234. AHSEP-42/C/36013/E/38.71, Hernández to DECI, Sept. 25, 1923.
235. Interview with Salvador Sánchez.
236. AHSEP-42/C/36013/E/38.71, Rodríguez, "Informe," Nov. 1923.
237. AHSEP-45/C/36292/E/75, Rodríguez, "Informes" from Dec. 1923 and Jan. 1924.
238. AHSEP-45/C/36292/E/75, Rodríguez, "Informe," May 1924.
239. AHSEP-45/C/36292/E/37, Hernández to DECI, June 4, 1924.
240. Meyer, *La cristiada*, iii, 96.
241. Davila, "General Francisco de Santiago Villegas." *Colotlán en llamas*. Accessed July 29, 2011. http://colotlanenllamas.blogspot.mx/.
242. AGA-D/23/1425/leg.2/CCA/Dotación/Sta. Catarina, de la Cruz to Gob. Jal., Sept. 8, 1924.
243. AGA-D/23/1425, leg. 2, CCA/Dotación/Sta. Catarina, de la Cruz to Gob. Jal., Nov. 11, 1924.
244. AGA-D/23/1425/leg.2/CCA/Dotación/Sta. Catarina, de la Cruz to Gob. Jal., Sept. 8, 1924.
245. AGA-D/23/1425/leg.2/CCA/Dotación/Sta. Catarina, de la Cruz to Gob. Jal., Dec. 29, 1924.
246. POEJ, Jan. 17, 1925.
247. AHSEP-45/C/36292/E/37, Antuna, "Informe," Mar. 1924.
248. AHSEP-45/C/36342/E/1, Valdés y Llanos to DECI, Apr. 9, 1924; AHSEP-42/C/36013/E/38.71, Hernández to DECI, Oct. 30, 1923; AHSEP-45/C/36342/E/1, Valdés y Llanos to DECI, Apr. 9, 1924; AHSEP-42/C/36013/E/38.71, PM Sta María to DECI, Oct. 11, 1923; AHSEP-45/C/36292/E/37, Hernández to DECI, June 15, 1924.
249. Shadow and Rodríguez, "Religión, economía," 673.
250. Meyer, *La cristiada*, i, 215.

251. Shadow, "Production, Social Identity," 40–42.
252. These mestizo towns are still engaged in violent territorial conflicts with Tuxpan and San Sebastián (Juan Partida, "Recuperan huicholes de Jalisco tierras en Nayarit," *La Jornada*, Sept. 24, 2016).
253. AHSEP-45/C/36292/E/37, Antuna, "Informe," Apr. 1924.
254. Shadow and Rodríguez, "Religión, economía," 689.
255. AGA-D/23/242/leg.1/CCA/Dotación/San Andrés, Auts. Trads. to J. Martínez, Oct. 22, 1923.
256. AGA-D/276.1/79/leg.4/CCA/RTBC/San Sebastián, Unnamed Agronomist's Report, June 5, 1939.
257. Dawson, "From Models," 280, 284–88; Lewis, *The Ambivalent Revolution*, 25.
258. AHSEP-42/C/36013/E/38.71, Hernández to DECI, May 17, 1923.
259. AHSEP-45/C/36293/E/12, Hernández to DECI, Apr. 14, 1924.
260. See Eiss, "Deconstructing Indians," 140, who notes that such attitudes were prevalent amongst many SEP officials in the 1920s, above all in Yucatán.
261. AHSEP-45/C/36291/E/2, Hernández to DERICI, Sept. 8, 1925.
262. Hernández.
263. Rojas, *Los huicholes*, 129–48.
264. AGA-D/24/1680/leg.1/CCA/Restitución/San Sebastián, Inocencio Ramos to Gob.Jal, Dec. 27, 1931.
265. AHSEP-45/C/36291/E/2, Hernández to DECI, Jan. 13, 1925.
266. AHSEP-45/C/36335/E/10, DEFN to DECI, Feb. 19, 1924; "Cuales Fueron las Causas de la Renuncia del Profesor Enrique Corona," *El Democrata*, May 13, 1924, 7.
267. AHSEP-45/C/36291/E/2, Hernández to DECI, Jan. 13, 1925.
268. Rojas, *Huicholes: Documentos*, 246–47.
269. AGMJ/FUN-01-MJ, Calixto Guerrero, "Informe," Oct. 22, 1917.
270. AGA-D/276.1/103/leg.1/SRA/RTBC/San Andrés, Reza to CNA, Mar. 4, 1925.
271. AGMJ/FUN-01-MJ, Calixto Guerrero, "Informe," Oct. 22, 1917.
272. AHSEP-78-79/C/38283/E/28, V. Poirett to R. Durand, Jan. 16, 1930.
273. AHSEP-78-79/C/38283/E/28, G. Rodríguez to R. Durand, n.d., quoted in R. Durand to DERICI, Jan. 22, 1930.
274. Dawson, "'Wild Indians,'" 337.
275. Loyo, "La empresa redentora," 106.
276. Lewis, "Collective Psychological Experiment," 14–16; Eiss, "Deconstructing Indians," 138.
277. Guerrero, "Informe," Oct. 22, 1917.
278. AHSEP-45/C/36321/E.1, DERICI, informe sobre Jalisco, Nov. 1925 (capitals in original).
279. Eiss, "Deconstructing Indians," 141.
280. Fernández, "José Guadalupe Zuno," 101.
281. AHSEP-45/C/36291/E/2, Hernández to DERICI, Sept. 8, 1925.

282. Curley, "Anticlericalism," 527–32; Bantjes, "Regional Dynamics," 114.
283. Between 1923 and 1926, schools *did* apparently function in the small part of northern Nayarit inhabited by these groups, namely in San Andrés Milpillas and Santa Maria de Picachos (AHSEP-42/C/36023/E/48.6, Statistics for School in Milpillas, 1923 [no exact date given]; AHSEP-42/C/36023/E/48.10, Statistics for School in Picachos, 1923 [no exact date given]; AHSEP-84-85/C/38873/E/31, Calderón to DERICI, Jan. 6, 1927).
284. AGA-D/leg.1/Comunal/Restitución/Santa María Ocotán y Xoconoxtle, Reps. of Santa María to CNA, Mar. 1918; AGN-LC/C/207/E/404.1/177, G. Vázquez to Cárdenas, Oct. 26, 1936.
285. Katz, *The Life and Times*, 719–23.
286. Gámiz, *La revolución*, 62.
287. Avitia, *Los Alacranes*, 117.
288. Avitia, 118.
289. Avitia, *El caudillo*, 85.
290. AGA-D/leg.1/Comunal/Restitución/Sta. María Ocotán y Xoconoxtle, Gob. Dgo. to CLA, Mar. 30, 1921.
291. Avitia, *El caudillo*, 85.
292. Avitia, *Los Alacranes*, 121.
293. "Mezquital," *Siglo de Torreón*, May 10, 1922.
294. "Fue muerto el rebelde Primo Ortiz," *Siglo de Torreón*, May 20, 1922.
295. Interviews with Santiago Ortega; Félix Muñoz Estrada.
296. Avitia, *Los Alacranes*, 121–22.
297. Interview with Saturnino Solís.
298. Greenberg, *Blood Ties*, 216–17; Knight, "War, Violence and Homicide," 44–45; Friedrich, *The Princes*, 15–17, 39–40, 59–62, 274–75.
299. Friedrich, *The Princes*, 164.
300. Interview with Saturnino Solís.
301. Interview with Saturnino Solís.
302. AHED-FR/C/5/E/3, Gómez to Gob. Dgo., May 31, 1922.
303. Dulles, *Yesterday in Mexico*, 115–17.
304. Navarro, *El cardenismo*, 35.
305. The conspiracy that led to Villa's death probably had Obregón's approval and certainly involved War Secretary Joaquín Amaro, Interior Minister Plutarco Elías Calles, and Durango's governor, Jesús Agustín Castro (Katz, *The Life and Times*, 775–78).
306. Navarro, *El cardenismo*, 36.
307. AHSEP-68-69/C/37416/E/15, A. García, "Informe," Apr. 30, 1926.
308. AHED-FR/C/4/E/7, Miguel Gavila to Gob. Dgo., May 18, 1925.
309. Avitia, *Los alacranes alzados*, 129.

310. AGN/O-C/243-D-1, Obregón to Sec. de Hacienda, Aug. 10, 1921.

311. Avitia, *El caudillo*, 87–88. This includes even Morelos, which in comparison lost two-fifths of its population (Knight, *Mexican Revolution*, ii, 371, 420–22).

312. Gámiz, *La revolución*, 62.

313. Marak, "Failed Assimilation," 415.

314. AHSEP-45/C/36322/E.24, "SEP Budget 1923–24," July 10, 1923.

315. Christophe Giudicelli, "El mestizaje en movimiento," 106–7.

316. AHSEP-45/C/36281/E/39, E. Gámiz to DEFD, Dec. 27, 1923.

317. Interview with Evaristo Mendoza.

318. AHSEP-42/C/36023/E/48.10, San Andrés Milpillas School Statistics, 1923 (no exact date given).

319. AHSEP-45/C/36277/E/14, DEFD to DERICI, Mar. 20, 1925.

320. Navarro, *El cardenismo*, 37.

321. Walker, "The Villista Legacy." Paper presented at the Rocky Mountain Council for Latin American Studies, 1995.

322. Rouaix was a revolutionary intellectual and agrarian reformer from Puebla who also twice served as governor of Durango (Knight, *Mexican Revolution*, ii, 475).

323. AGN/O-C/818-D-14, Terrones Benítez, "Informe del 5/o Congreso Agrarista del Estado," Jan. 1, 1925.

324. Gámiz, in Avitia, *El caudillo*, 155. According to Gámiz's (almost certainly inflated) figures, Barraza amassed "un capital de más de 100,000 pesos, pues en Yonora poseía más de 1,000 cabezas de ganado."

325. AGN/O-C/818-D-14, Terrones Benítez, "Informe del 5/o Congreso Agrarista del Estado," Jan. 1, 1925.

326. Friedrich, *The Princes*, 127.

327. Nugent, *Spent Cartridges*, 87.

328. Interview with Felipe Salas Ramírez.

329. AHSEP-45/C/36348 E/6, DEFD to DERICI, July 15, 1925.

330. AHSEP-45/C/36277/E/14, DEFD to DERICI, Feb. 17, 1925.

331. AHSEP-45/C/36277/E/14, DERICI to DEFD, Feb. 23, 1925.

332. AHSEP-45/C/36277/E/14, DEFD to DERICI, Mar. 20, 1925; emphasis per the original.

333. AHSEP-45/C/36277/E/14, Gob. Dgo. to Puig Casauranc, May 27, 1925.

334. AHSEP-45/C/36277/E/14, Diputado Díaz Prendis to DERICI, May 21, 1925.

335. AHSEP-45/C/36277/E/14, DEFD to DERICI, July 9, 1925.

336. AHSEP-45/C/36277/E/14, Gob. Dgo. to Puig Casauranc, Sept. 1, 1925.

337. AHSEP-45/C/36277/E/14, DEFD to DERICI, Sept. 1, 1925.

338. AHSEP-45/C/36277/E/14, Nájera to Puig Casauranc, Sept. 7, 1925.

339. AHSEP-45/C/36277/E/14, Puig Casauranc to Nájera, Sept. 23, 1925.

340. AHSEP-68-69/C/37428/E/12, DEFD to DERICI, Mar. 3, 1926.
341. Luis Zubiría y Campa, "La Región del Mezquital," *Siglo de Torreón*, Feb. 16, 1927; "Las Minas del Mezquital," *Siglo de Torreón*, Feb. 18, 1927.
342. Rockwell, "Schools," 200.
343. Similar clashes accompanied the imposition of a modern industrial work regimen on the British laboring classes during the Industrial Revolution, as described by Thompson in his seminal article, "Time, Work-Discipline, and Industrial Capitalism."
344. Durin, Rojas, "El conflicto," 152–53; Schools raised similar heckles across rural Mexico (Mallón, "Reflections," 84), and even in Tlaxcala, where relationships were less conflictive, villagers still challenged the official conceptions of time introduced by teachers—designed as they were to transform children into potential urban workers—with their own temporal definitions and priorities (Rockwell, "Schools," 200).
345. The original manifesto for this state-building program, and the origin of the famous phrase used to describe it, is Manuel Gamio's *Forjando patria*, first published in 1916.
346. Vaughan, *Cultural Politics*, 15–16; cf. Becker, "Black and White," 163–79; Street, *Literacy*, 95–128, 183–212.
347. AHSEP-84-85/C/38861/E/18, León Sánchez to DEFN, Jan. 19, 1926.
348. Loyo, "La empresa redentora," 103–4.
349. Rus, "The 'Comunidad Revolucionaria Institucional,'" 269–70; Eiss, "Deconstructing Indians," 142; Marak, "Failed Assimilation," 415–18.
350. AHSEP-68-69/C/37436/E/35, DEFD to DERICI, July 2, 1926.

CHAPTER 4

1. Knight, "The Mentality," 25–26.
2. Butler, "A Revolution in Spirit?" 1–20; Knight, "The Mentality," 111–12.
3. Thanks to Graham Greene's *The Power and the Glory* and *The Lawless Roads*, Garrido Canabal's anticlerical clampdowns in Tabasco are well known. But Adalberto Tejeda in Veracruz and Carrillo Puerto in Yucatán carried out similar campaigns (Bantjes, "Regional Dynamics," 113–14; Eiss, "Beyond the Land," 520–21).
4. Bantjes, "Regional Dynamics," 113.
5. Lira and Villanueva, "La Constitución," 18.
6. Bantjes, "Regional Dynamics," 112.
7. In Nayarit, for example, in May 1926 the president of the State Congress attacked "one of [Xalisco's] main churches with pistol in hand . . . and with a rope to lasso the images and drag them through the streets." He was promptly mobbed and beaten to death by a crowd of furious women (AHSEP-84-85/C/38873/E/21, DEFN to Sec. Gob., May 18, 1926); see also Purnell, *Popular Movements*, 77–78.

8. Preciado, "Conciencia histórica," 485–508; Stauffer, "Community, Identity," 149–80; for an in-depth case study, see Friedrich, *The Princes*. "Community, Identity, and the Limits of Liberal State Formation in Michoacán's Coastal Sierra: Coalcomán, 1869–1940." In *Mexico in Transition: New Perspectives on Mexican Agrarian History, 19th and 20th Centuries*, edited by Antonio Escobar Ohmstede and Matthew Butler, 149–80. México: CIESAS, 2013.
9. Purnell, *Popular Movements*, 83, Knight, "Peasant and Caudillo," 44.
10. Meyer, *La cristiada*, iii, 104.
11. Purnell, *Popular Movements*, 85; Meyer, *La cristiada*, i, 199–204.
12. Meyer, *La cristiada*, i, 59–60, 167.
13. Clausewitz, *On War*, 92.
14. Rangel, *Imágenes e imaginarios*, 456; Rangel and Marín, "Desplazamientos territoriales," 12; Cramaussel, "Historia del poblamiento," 20–21; Alvarado, *Atar la vida*, 140; Coyle, *From Flowers*, 183–86; Weigand, "Role of the Huichols," 169.
15. Meyer, *La cristiada*, i, 386–91.
16. Meyer, 28–31. Despite taking up so little of Meyer's thousand-page epic, this analysis has informed most other references to the dynamics of the cristiada in the Gran Nayar, including Avitia, *El caudillo*; Sánchez Olmedo, *Etnografía*; and Bautista, *La guerra olvidada*.
17. E.g., Purnell, *Popular Movements*, 149–58, 124–33; Butler, *Popular Piety*, 3, and "The 'Liberal' Cristero," 670–71; Fallaw, "'Anti-Priests,'" 217–18; Stauffer, "Community, Identity," 173. Today, Meyer himself ("Review of Matthew Butler," 1248) also backs this more nuanced view.
18. Bantjes, "Regional Dynamics," 122; see also Smith, *The Roots*.
19. Shadow, *Tierra, trabajo*, 98; Bantjes, *As if Jesus*, 46–53; Vaughan, *Cultural Politics*, 62–63, 122–24; Shadow and Rodríguez, "Religión, economía," 679, 692–93.
20. Knight, "The Mentality," 33–34.
21. Scott, *Weapons*, 220–48.
22. Bátiz was beatified by Pope John Paul II on November 22, 1992, and canonized around eight years later.
23. Meyer, *La cristiada*, i, 220–21. For details of Ortiz's military and political careers, see Fallaw, "Eulogio Ortiz."
24. Arroyo, "Memorias," *David*, Feb. 4, 1954.
25. Caldera and de la Torre, *Pueblos*, 84.
26. ARA/C/13/E/54/Doc/6237, E. Madera to Quintanar, n.d.
27. AHSEP-78-79/C/38281/E/17, González to DEFJ, Oct. 27, 1926.
28. Meyer, *La cristiada*, iii, 126.
29. E.g., "Campesinos sublevados en Durango," *El Porvenir*, Oct. 1, 1926.

30. Cramaussel, "El fracaso," 154–99.
31. Rouaix, *Diccionario geográfico*, 252. Communal control over local forests seem to have been a key factor in tensions between Bayacora and the state ("Campesinos sublevados en Durango," *El Porvenir*, Oct. 1, 1926; "Permiso para extraer carbón y leña en los montes de Bayacora," *Siglo de Torreón*, Jan. 18, 1932).
32. Alcohol has long played a key role in rural rebellion in Mexico, explored in detail in Taylor, *Drinking, Homicide, and Rebellion*.
33. F. Campos, "Santiago," *David*, Apr. 22, 1955.
34. F. Campos, "Santiago Bayacora (Cont.)," *David*, Nov. 22, 1955.
35. "Se combatió durante tres horas en las cercanías de Durango," *El Porvenir*, Oct. 4, 1926.
36. F. Campos, "Santiago," *David*, June 22, 1955.
37. ARA/C/12/E/48/Doc/5774, Trinidad Mora, "Informe," Aug. 11, 1927.
38. As chief of Durango's *rurales* in 1919, Lares had been Dámaso Barraza's commanding officer during several regional campaigns (AHED-FR/C/5/E/206, Unsigned Military Report, Oct. 1919). As a result, he overestimated his familiarity with the local terrain and fell into Mora's trap.
39. Mayorquín's rival was a fellow butcher who goaded him about his height. Even after he became a feared rebel leader, he could not escape comments about his size; a government warrant for Mayorquín's arrest for "rebellion, robbery and firestarting" notably describes him as "of short stature" (AHJ-G-15-928/ C/454/E/32877, Agente del Ministerio Publico Fed. to Gob. Jal., Nov. 27, 1928).
40. F. Campos, "Santiago," *David*, Jan. 22, 1956; Chávez Gradilla, in Rangel, *Imágenes e imaginarios*, 452.
41. Many other defensa commanders also defected to the rebel side during the cristiada, including Andrés Salazar in Colima and Ezequiel Mendoza, Serapio Sifuentes, and Antonio Larios in Michoacán (Meyer, *La cristiada*, iii, 96).
42. "El regimento de Valparaíso y la Segunda Cristiada," *Mi Pueblo*, March–May 1996, vs. F. Campos, "Santiago," *David*, Jan. 22, 1956; see also Avitia, *El caudillo*, 186.
43. F. Campos, "Santiago," *David*, Jan. 22, 1956.
44. "Felipe de Jesús," "A proposito de las bajas callistas," *David*, Feb. 22, 1956.
45. Interview with Felipe Salas Ramírez.
46. F. Campos, "Santiago Bayacora (Cont.)," *David*, Jan. 22, 1956.
47. Meyer, *La cristiada*, iii, 100, 215–17.
48. AHED-M/C/10/E/29, Vecinos de Mezquital to Gob.Dgo., Sept. 7, 1932.
49. F. Campos, "Santiago," *David*, Mar. 22, 1956.
50. ARA/C/12/E/48/Doc/5774, Trinidad Mora, "Informe," Aug. 11, 1927.
51. Mora, "Informe."
52. Interview with Felipe Salas Ramírez.
53. Avitia, *El caudillo*, 185.

54. Avitia, *El caudillo*, 187; interview with Felipe Salas Ramírez.
55. "Numerosos rebeldes," *El Porvenir*, Jan. 27, 1927, page 9.
56. ARA/C/12/E/48/Doc/5774, Trinidad Mora, "Informe," Aug. 11, 1927.
57. Mora, "Informe."
58. F. Campos, "Santiago," *David*, Mar. 22, 1956.
59. Avitia, *El caudillo*, 192.
60. Meyer, *La cristiada*, i, 120–31; iii, 103.
61. Meyer, i, 95.
62. Meyer, 196.
63. ARA/C/13/E/56/Doc/6771, Cruz de la Torre, Apolonio González, to Pablo Robles, Aug. 23, 1927.
64. Meyer, *La cristiada*, i, 187. A similar "shadow state" was also established in the Altos region of Jalisco (Jim Tuck, *The Holy War in Los Altos*).
65. Wickham-Crowley, *Exploring Revolution*, 30–61.
66. The cristeros also systematically destroyed official government offices, including municipal archives (AHEJ-G-15-927/C/452/E/32805, W. Robles to Sec. Gob. Jal., Sept. 5, 1927). Without Acevedo's efforts to preserve rebel paperwork, few sources would exist for local events in this period. But this fact has also allowed cristero archivists like Acevedo and Nicolás Valdés much influence over the narrative of the cristiada presented by historians.
67. ARA/C/13/E/54/Doc/6323, "GN" to Gil Sánchez (Torreon), n.d.; Meyer, *La cristiada*, iii, 134.
68. AGN-DGIPS/C/212/E/3, Unsigned military report, n.d., mid-1927.
69. Interviews with Magdaleno Arrellano; Genaro Santillán.
70. Rangel, *Imágenes e imaginarios*, 461; Friedrich, for example, argues that "the nucleus of a cacicazgo always includes the brothers and sons of a cacique" (*The Princes*, 101).
71. Interview with Magdaleno Arrellano.
72. Interviews with Basilio de la Cruz; Pedro de la Cruz.
73. Interview with Magdaleno Arrellano.
74. Rangel, *Imágenes e imaginarios*, 461; interview with Magdaleno Arrellano.
75. Interviews with Basilio de la Cruz; Pedro de la Cruz; Nabor Castañeda.
76. "El Mayor Florencio," *David*, June 22, 1955.
77. Avitia, *El caudillo*, 86.
78. Interview with Santiago Ortega.
79. "El Mayor Florencio," *David*, June 22, 1955.
80. Arroyo, "Memorias," *David*, Oct. 22, 1960.
81. "El regimento de Valparaíso," *Mi Pueblo*, March–May 1996.
82. Fallaw, "Eulogio Ortiz," 140.
83. The government sponsored the formation of similar militias in many other hotbeds of cristero activity ("Rebels beaten says Mexico," *Binghampton Press*, Jan. 17, 1927).

84. Meyer, *La cristiada*, iii, 73–74.
85. Interview with Agustín Lamas.
86. Meyer, *La cristiada*, i, 220.
87. Meyer, 196.
88. Meyer, 220.
89. S. Martínez, in Caldera and de la Torre, *Pueblos*, 122–23.
90. Arroyo, "Memorias," *David*, Jan. 22, 1961.
91. Meyer, *La cristiada*, i, 185.
92. AGN-DGIPS/C/212/E/3, Unsigned military report, n.d., mid-1927.
93. Interview with Saturnino Solís.
94. AHSEP-84-85/C/38876/E/17, Florencio Orozco to DEFN, June 15, 1927.
95. Orozco to DEFN.
96. See Vaughan, *Cultural Politics*, 61–62.
97. Meyer, *La cristiada*, i, 197, citing LNDLR reports, puts this figure at twenty thousand; Purnell, *Popular Movements*, 87, citing the U.S. ambassador's estimates, posits some seven to eight thousand active rebels.
98. Rangel, *Imágenes e imaginarios*, 449–84.
99. P. Guzmán Juárez, in Rangel, 456.
100. Guzmán Juárez, 458.
101. Interviews with Agustín Lamas; Erasmo González; Filiberto Sánchez.
102. Interview with Agustín Lamas.
103. AHSEP-84-85/C/38873/E/76, DEFN to DERICI, Dec. 31, 1927.
104. AHSEP-84-85/C/38877/E/36, Navarro to DEFN, Oct. 26, 1927.
105. Interview with Agustín Lamas.
106. *El Fronterizo*, Oct. 14, 1927.
107. AHSEP-84-85/C/38896/E/29, DEFN to Dir. Misiones Culturales, Nov. 11, 1927.
108. AHSEP-84-85/C/38873/E/31, DEFN, "Informe," Nov. 30, 1927.
109. Arroyo, "Memorias," *David*, March 22, 1961.
110. F. Sánchez, "La Brigada," *David*, Apr. 22, 1958.
111. Interview with Vázquez Campos.
112. Interview with Xuturima Hernández.
113. Interview with Antonio Candelario.
114. Interview with Xuturima Hernández.
115. Arroyo, "Memorias," *David*, Aug. 1965; Meyer, *La cristiada*, iii, 30.
116. Interviews with Julio Robles and Antonio Candelario.
117. Interview with Antonio Candelario.
118. Meyer, *La cristiada*, i, 211–55; Purnell, *Popular Movements*, 85–87, 176.
119. Meyer, i, 247.

120. ARA/C13/E56/Doc/6782, Sebastián Arroyo to Aurelio Acevedo, Dec. 23, 1927. During the War of Independence, royalists' tactics in the Gran Nayar had also centered around confiscating the Indigenous inhabitants' grain and cattle (Santoscoy, *Colección de documentos*, 62).
121. "Combate en San Antonio," *David*, July 22, 1961.
122. Meyer, *La cristiada*, iii, 105–7; cf. Tuck, *Holy War*, 110.
123. Meyer, iii, 106.
124. "Combate en San Antonio," *David*, July 22, 1961; Meyer, *La cristiada*, i, 219.
125. Arroyo, "Memorias," *David*, Apr. 22, 1963. Ávila was a former Villista commander; Pepe Sánchez a native of Nostic who, motivated by a personal feud, defected from his village's defensa to the cristeros (S. Martínez and Pablo Bañuelos Martínez, in Caldera and de la Torre, *Pueblos*, 122–23, 166).
126. ARA/C/13/E/54/Doc/6381, Quintanar to A. Acevedo, Jan. 1928.
127. García Landa, "Ramón," *Mi Pueblo*, June 1996.
128. Carlos de la Torre, in Caldera and de la Torre, *Pueblos*, 126–28; Mercado, "Me Casé," *Mi Pueblo*, Jan. 1996.
129. Bañuelos, in Caldera and de la Torre, *Pueblos*, 166.
130. AHSEP-84-85/C/38897/E/9, Calderón, "Informe," Jan. 31, 1928.
131. Interviews with Fernando Muñíz Rafael; Aurelio Cánare; Enendino Escobeda Mejía.
132. Interview with Fernando Muñíz.
133. Meza, *Nayarit Memoria Oral*, 52–53.
134. Interview with Francisco Gómez and Alberto Casas.
135. Interview with Aurelio Cánare.
136. Interview with Francisco Gómez and Alberto Casas.
137. Interview with Bruno Gómez and Nemesio Rodríguez.
138. Interviews with Fernando Muñíz; Aurelio Cánare. Náayari insurgents had used similar tactics during the War of Independence (Santoscoy, *Colección de documentos*, 63) and the rebellion of Manuel Lozada (Meyer, *Manuel Lozada*, 239, 220).
139. AGN-DGIPS/C/220/E/1, clipping from "Excelsior de México," Mar. 2, 1928.
140. AHSEP-84-85/C/38876/E/17, Orozco to Jefe del Dept., Feb. 9, 1928.
141. Weigand, "Role of the Huichols," 169.
142. Interview with Aurelio Cánare.
143. Interview with Agustín Lamas.
144. Interview with Aurelio Cánare.
145. Interviews with Filiberto Sánchez, Sandalio Sánchez Chávez, and Celestino Lamas.
146. Interview with Aurelio Cánare.
147. AGN-DGIPS/C/232/E/22, Galicia Ortega to Francisco Delgado, Jan. 2, 1928. Ramírez himself was soon deposed, after "his tailor found a scapular in his suit and denounced him" (Fallaw, *Religion*, 3).

148. Interview with Aurelio Cánare.
149. Gutiérrez, "El Que Escarba, Encuentra," *David*, Nov. 22, 1953.
150. Gutiérrez, *Mis recuerdos*, ii, 25.
151. Gutiérrez, i, 227.
152. Gutiérrez, ii, 30–33.
153. Gutiérrez, 39–40.
154. Interview with Juventino Mejía.
155. Meza Aguirre, *Nayarit Memoria Oral*, 52–53.
156. Interview with Juventino Mejía.
157. Meyer, *La cristiada*, iii, 104.
158. AGN-DGIPS/C/220/E/1, clipping from *Eco de Nayarit*, n.d., early 1928.
159. F. Campos, "Santiago," *David*, Mar. 22, 1956.
160. F. Campos, "Santiago," *David*, Apr. 22, 1956.
161. Interviews with Arturo Soto; Saturnino Solís.
162. Interview with Saturnino Solís.
163. ARA/C/14/E/58/Doc/7029, Juan Andrés Soto et al. to Quintanar, June 23, 1928.
164. Alvarado, *Atar la vida*, 70.
165. Alvarado, 53–54.
166. ARA/C/14/E/58/Doc/7029, Juan Andrés Soto et al. to Quintanar, June 23, 1928.
167. Interviews with Sandalio Sánchez; Saturnino Solís; Bruno Gómez and Nemesio Rodríguez.
168. J. Antonio de la Cruz to Quintanar, n.d., in Meyer, *La cristiada*, iii, 30.
169. Juan Bautista to Quintanar, Mar. 17, 1928, in Meyer.
170. Interviews with Jesús Mercado; Julio Robles; Antonio Candelario; Xuturima Hernández; Salvador Sánchez.
171. Interview with Miguel Carrillo.
172. Interview with Xuturima Hernández.
173. Interview with Salvador Sánchez.
174. Butler, *Popular Piety*, 34, 211–15; Bantjes, *As if Jesus*, 11–5, 34–35; De Giuseppe, "'El Indio Gabriel,'" 230.
175. Interview with Salvador Sánchez.
176. Interview with Antonio Candelario.
177. Interview with Xuturima Hernández.
178. Interview with Julio Robles and Antonio Candelario.
179. Interview with Xuturima Hernández.
180. Interview with Antonio Candelario.
181. Interview with Mauricio Montellano.
182. Interview with Salvador Sánchez.
183. AGA-D/276.1/79/leg.1/CCA/RTBC/Tuxpan, Eleuterio Torres to DA, May 8, 1949.

184. Weigand, "Co-operative Labour Groups," 20.
185. ARA/C/14/E/58/Doc/6951, H. Cabral to A. Acevedo, June 1, 1928.
186. AHSEP-84-85/C/38873/E/76, Calderón, "Informe," Apr. 30, 1928.
187. Meyer, *La cristiada*, i, 215.
188. AGA-D/276.1/79/leg.4/CCA/RTBC/San Sebastián, DA Report, June 5, 1939.
189. ARA/C/14/E/57/Doc/6864, Rafael Acevedo to Quintanar, Apr. 26, 1928.
190. ARA/C/14/E/57/Doc/6877, A. Acevedo to LNDLR Valparaíso, May 9, 1928.
191. Arroyo, "Memorias," *David*, Mar. 1965.
192. AHED-M/C/5/E/137, Antonio Gutiérrez to Gob. Dgo., Apr. 1, 1928.
193. A. Estrada, quoted in Avitia, *El caudillo*, 159.
194. ARA/C/14/E/57/Doc/6904, A. Ramírez to Col. R. R. Cárdenas, May 23, 1928; ARA/C/14/E/57/Doc/6877, A. Acevedo to LNDLR Valparaíso, May 9, 1928; ARA/C/14/E/57/Doc/6925, F. Romero to Quintanar, May 29, 1928; Acevedo, "Los Renovadores (Escobaristas)," *David*, Feb. 1965; interviews with Ramón Gamboa, Primo Taizán.
195. ARA/C/14/E/57/Doc/6904, A. Ramírez to Col. R. R. Cárdenas, May 23, 1928.
196. ARA/C/14/E/58/Doc/7025, Montellano to A. Ramírez, June 20, 1928.
197. AHSEP-84-85/C/38858/E/16, Durán Cárdenas to DEFN, Oct. 13, 1930.
198. A. Campos, "Santiago," *David*, 22 June 1961.
199. Interview with Saturnino Solís.
200. A. Campos, "El Combate del Cerro de las Papas," July 22, 1964, 391.
201. In this they were helped by the greater ease with which they could consecrate new mitote patios, which required only ashes taken from the sacred bonfire of a "parent" patio and the observance of ritual abstinences (Manuel Arrellano; see also Alvarado, *Atar la vida*, 140).
202. A. Campos, "El Combate del Cerro de las Papas," July 22, 1964, 391.
203. Interview with Felipe Salas Ramírez.
204. Elpidio Reyes Flores, *Dhi u'uan*, 51–57.
205. Interview with Arturo Soto.
206. Interview with Felipe Salas Ramírez.
207. Elpidio Reyes Flores, *Dhi u'uan*, 51–57.
208. Interview with Arturo Soto.
209. Elpidio Reyes Flores, *Dhi u'uan*, 51–57.
210. Estrada, *Rescoldo*, 128; Manuel Arrellano; "Corrido de Cerro de las Papas."
211. Interview with Felipe Salas Ramírez.
212. ARA/C/14/E/58/Doc/7029, Juan Andrés Soto et al. to Quintanar, June 23, 1928.
213. ARA/C/13/E/54/Doc/6323, "GN" to Gil Sánchez (Torreon), n.d.
214. ARA/C/14/E/58/Doc/7059, Juan Andrés Soto, Gerardo Aguilar, to Quintanar, June 22, 1928.
215. ARA/C/14/E/59/Doc/7189, Montellano to Juan Andrés Soto, June 28, 1928.

216. ARA/C/14/E/58/Doc/7056, Montellano to Juan Andrés Soto, July 3, 1928.
217. ARA/C/14/E/58/Doc/7036, Juan Andrés Soto et al. to Quintanar, June 30, 1928.
218. Interview with Saturnino Solís.
219. AHSEP-68-69/C/37441/E/10, DEFD to DERICI, Nov. 13, 1933.
220. ARA/C/12/E/47/Doc/5747, Montellano to J. Sifuentes, July 28, 1928.
221. ARA/C/14/E/59/Doc/7191, Montellano to Estrada, Aug. 4, 1928.
222. Interviews with Eulogio Ciriano; Trinidad Morales.
223. ARA/C/12/E/47/Doc/5754, Quintanar to F. Cumplido, Oct. 15, 1928; ARA/C/12/E/48/Doc/5764, Quintanar to J. Jesús García, Nov. 26, 1928.
224. Interview with Saturnino Solís.
225. ARA/C/14/E/60/Doc/7395, Saturnino Flores to Residents of Sta. María Ocotán, Sept. 19, 1928.
226. Friedrich, *The Princes*, 120.
227. Meyer, *La cristiada*, i, 345–46.
228. Evaristo Mendoza; see also Alvarado, *Atar la vida*, 140.
229. ARA/C/14/E/59/Doc/7227, A. Acevedo to Estrada, Aug. 10, 1928.
230. The *Plan*, drafted by Miguel Palomar y Vizcarra, announced that after the cristeros' inevitable victory, the Liberal Constitution of 1857, stripped of the anticlerical reform laws, would replace the revolutionary Constitution of 1917 (Meyer, *La cristiada*, i, 68–69).
231. Interview with Xuturima Hernández.
232. ARA/C/13/E/55/Doc/6599, "Residents" of San Andrés to Quintanar, n.d., 1928.
233. ARA/C/14/E/60/Doc/7429, Luis Montellano to "Residents" of San Andrés, Sept. 30, 1928.
234. AGA-D/23/8465/leg.1/SRA/Dotación, Juan García et al. to Gob. Jal., May 7, 1921.
235. ARA/C/14/E/59/Doc/7215, Juan García to Montellano, Aug. 4, 1928.
236. ARA/C/14/E/59/Doc/7243, Montellano to Juan Garcia, Aug. 13, 1928.
237. ARA/C/14/E/60/Doc/7381, Pilar Herrera to Quintanar, Sept. 17, 1928.
238. Arroyo, "Memorias," *David*, Aug. 1965.
239. Téllez, "Lozadistas, revolucionarios y cristeros," 238.
240. ARA/C/12/E/50/Doc/5931, Juan Andrés Soto to Quintanar, July 22, 1928.
241. ARA/C/14/E/59/Doc/7191, Montellano to Estrada, Aug. 4, 1928.
242. ARA/C/14/E/59/Doc/7189, Montellano to Juan Andrés Soto, Aug. 4, 1928.
243. ARA/C/12/E/50/Doc/5931, Juan Andrés Soto to Pedro Quintanar, July 22, 1928.
244. ARA/C/14/E/59/Doc/7191, Montellano to Estrada, Aug. 4, 1928.
245. ARA/C/14/E/59/Doc/7208, Florencio Estrada to A. Acevedo, Aug. 7, 1928.
246. ARA/C/14/E/59/Doc/7258, Saturnino Flores to Urbajelo, Aug. 18, 1928.
247. ARA/C/14/E/59/Doc/7210, Florencio Estrada to Quintanar, Aug. 7, 1928.
248. AHSEP-45/C/36351/E/2, clipping from *Eco de Nayarit*, Sept. 13, 1928.
249. ARA/C/14/E/60/Doc/7359, Tiburcio Muñoz to Saturnino Flores, Sept. 12, 1928.

250. ARA/C/14/E/60/Doc/7387, Tiburcio Muñoz to Saturnino Flores, Sept. 18, 1928.
251. Arroyo, "Memorias," *David*, Aug. 1965.
252. Flores Flores and Flores Sánchez, "Memorias Políticas," 108–9.
253. P. Delgadillo Galindo, in de la Torre, *1926*, 158.
254. Meyer, *La cristiada*, i, 264.
255. AHED-FR/C/4/E/2, Vicente Lemus to Urbalejo, Jan. 11, 1929; AHED-FR/C/4E/ "Armas y parque," PM Suchil to Gob. Dgo, Feb. 12, 1929; AHED-FR/C/4/E/ "Armas y parque," Urbalejo to Gob. Dgo., Feb. 12, 1929.
256. AHED-FR/C/4/E/Armas y parque, PM Suchil to Gob. Dgo., Feb. 12, 1929.
257. AHSEP-84-85/C/38873/E/21, I. Rivera to DEFN, Feb. 16, 1929. One of the largest population transfers apparently involved "todos los habitantes de la ex-Municipalidad de Huazamota" being moved to Jesús María (AHED-FR/C/4/E/2, Antonio Gutiérrez to Gral. Amaya, Jan. 11, 1929).
258. Rangel, Marín, "Desplazamientos territoriales," 165.
259. AHSEP-45/C/36353/E/2, DEFN to DERICI, Sept. 25, 1928; AHSEP-84-85/ C/38861/E/15, DEFN, "Informe: San Francisco," Jan. 1, 1929; AHSEP-84-85/ C/38857/E/25, DEFN, "Informe: La Mesa," Jan. 1, 1929.
260. AHSEP-45/C/36353/E/2, DEFN to DERICI, Sept. 25, 1928.
261. Interview with Agustín Lamas.
262. Interview with Candido Contreras.
263. Meyer, *La cristiada*, i, 282–84.
264. Avitia, *El caudillo*, 213.
265. Meyer, *La cristiada*, i, 260.
266. "El Mayor Florencio," *David*, June 22, 1955.
267. Dulles, *Yesterday in Mexico*, 441–43; Rath, *Myths*, 24.
268. ARA/C/12/E/46/Doc/5640, Santiago Guerra to all cristero forces, Mar. 5, 1929.
269. "En El Mezquital," *Siglo de Torreón*, Apr. 30, 1929.
270. AHSEP-84-85/C/38873/E/21, DEFN to DERICI, Apr. 12, 1929.
271. Rangel, *Imagenes y imaginarios*, 469.
272. AHSEP-78-79/C/38284/E/8, Durand, "Informe," Apr. 1, 1929.
273. Meyer, *La cristiada*, i, 295.
274. Meyer, Meyer, *La cristiada*, i, 291–92.
275. Tuck, *Holy War*, 148.
276. Avitia, *El caudillo*, 220–21.
277. Dulles, *Yesterday in Mexico*, 441–55.
278. Tuck, *Holy War*, 151.
279. ARA/C/14/E/57/Doc/6902, Gorostieta to A. Acevedo, Mar. 31, 1929.
280. Tuck, *Holy War*, 162.
281. "Deportación de las mujeres," *Siglo de Torreón*, Abril 26, 1929.

282. Meyer, *La cristiada*, i, 147; "Agraristas Desarmados," *Siglo de Torreón*, April 13, 1929.
283. Tuck, *Holy War*, 174.
284. Meyer, *La cristiada*, i, 326–28.
285. Avitia, *El caudillo*, 224, 245, 151; Dulles, *Yesterday in Mexico*, 447.
286. Interview with Aurelio Cánare.
287. Friedrich, *Agrarian Revolt*, 127.
288. Scott has observed similar dynamics at play in factional conflicts in Malaysia (*Weapons*, 147–48).
289. Friedrich, *Agrarian Revolt*, 136.
290. Interview with Agustín Lamas.
291. Indeed, Joseph points out that "in the tumultuous context of riots and rebellions, the insurgents themselves may not even be conscious, at the moment they join a band, of what motivates them" ("Rethinking Mexican Revolutionary Upheaval," 148, and also 150–51).
292. Scott, *Weapons*, 46–47, see also 139–40.
293. Friedrich, *Agrarian Revolt*, 135; Thucydides, *The History*, I.22.
294. Durán, C. "Presentarán investigación."
295. Avitia, *El caudillo*, 160.
296. Meyer, *La cristiada*, iii, 30.
297. Meyer, iii, 30.
298. See Rugeley, *Of Wonders*, 113–15, 247; Starr, *Notes*, i, 17–23, 55–63.
299. Preuss, *Fiesta, literatura y magia*, 188.
300. Preuss, 223–24.
301. Preuss, 184.
302. Interviews with Nabor Castañeda; Nemesio Rodríguez; Filiberto Sánchez.
303. Coyle, *From Flowers*, 181–82.
304. De la Cerda, "Los coras," 112.
305. Radding, "Peasant Resistance," 339.
306. Brunk, *Emiliano Zapata*, 68.
307. Interview with Erasmo González.
308. Interview with Filiberto Sánchez.
309. AHSEP-84-85/C/38873/E/31, DEFN, "Informe Annual, 1926," Jan. 6, 1927.
310. AHSEP-84-85/C/38861/E/10, DEFN to DERICI, Jan. 14, 1927.
311. Interview with Fernando Muñíz.
312. Interview with Candido Contreras.
313. AGN-Censo/1930/Nayarit/Arroyo de Santiago.
314. J. Gutiérrez, *Mis recuerdos*, 39-40.
315. AHSEP-84-85/C/38873/E/31, DEFN. "Informe Mensual," Nov. 30, 1927.
316. Bautista, *La guerra olvidada*, 130.

317. Jáuregui, "Del reino de Lozada," 182–83.
318. AGA-D/276.1/14/leg.1/Comunal/RTBC/San Pedro Ixcatán, Reps. to CNA, July 9, 1922.
319. AGA-D/276.1/485/leg.1/CCA/RTBC/San Juan Corapan, Reps. to DAI, May 16, 1936.
320. Nugent, *Spent Cartridges*, 113.
321. Interview with Fernando Muñíz.
322. Meyer, *La cristiada*, iii, 30.
323. AHSEP-84-85/C/38873/E/31, DEFN to DERICI, Jan. 6, 1927.
324. Interview with Fernando Muñíz.
325. Interview with Filiberto Sánchez.
326. Brewster, *Militarism, Ethnicity, and Politics*, 65.
327. Interviews with Erasmo González; Agustín Lamas; Nabor Castañeda; Aurelio Cánare.
328. Meyer, *De cantón*, 217.
329. Both Meyer, *La cristiada*, and Avitia, *El caudillo*, are cases in point.
330. Fikes, Weigand, and García de Weigand, "Introduction," xxviii.
331. Interview with Xuturima Hernández.
332. Juan Negrín writes that "Most Wixárika were anti-cristeros," except for those of San Sebastián ("Recent History," 1). Weigand argues that San Sebastián was split between "neutrals" and cristeros, San Andrés was largely "pro-government," and Santa Catarina for the most part "neutral" ("Role of the Huichols," 171). Meyer asserts that "two-thirds of the Wixáritari opted for the cristeros," including those of San Andrés, while Santa Catarina at first supported the government but later opted for "absolute neutrality" (*La cristiada*, iii, 28–31).
333. Rojas, *Los huicholes*, 170.
334. Meyer, *La cristiada*, iii, 28.
335. Meyer, 306. Here he confuses the Wixáritari, evangelized by the Franciscans, with the Náyarite, organized into missions by the Jesuits.
336. This idea seems to be founded on a visit to Santa Catarina in 1968, where Meyer found "Christian Wixáritari" living "without problems with the others" (*La cristiada*, iii, 29–30). Many of these so-called Christians, however, were not actually Catholic at all but recently converted evangelical Protestants who were soon expelled from Santa Catarina precisely because they were "practicing a different religion . . . and have diverged from the rites and ceremonies of el costumbre" (Torres, *Relaciones de frontera*, 90; Julio Robles and Antonio Candelario).
337. Lumholtz, *Unknown Mexico*, ii, 22–23, 158–59, 258; see also Preuss, 145.
338. AHAG-Totatiche/C/3/E/13, Magallanes to Arz., July 4, 1920.
339. AHAG-Totatiche/C/3/E/13, Magallanes to Arz., Nov. 15, 1920.
340. AHAG-Bolaños/C/3/E/14, Magallanes to Arz., July 6, 1920; Zepeda to Arz., Nov. 30, 1921; José Zepeda to Arz., Feb. 2, 1922.

341. Interviews with Pedro de la Cruz; Salvador Sánchez.
342. AHSEP-78-79/C/38281/E/17, González to DFEJ, Oct. 27, 1926.
343. ARA/C/14/E/57/Doc/6907, J. Ávila to Quintanar, May 24, 1928.
344. Weigand, "Co-operative Labor Groups," 20.
345. Meyer, *La cristiada*, iii, 29–31.
346. In 1922, Carrillo was described as speaking a "mix of bad Spanish and indigenous dialect" ("Una comisión," *Informador*, Nov. 7, 1922). His command of the national language likely improved as his contact with government officials increased.
347. Weigand, "Co-operative Labor Groups," 19.
348. Benítez, *Los indios*, iii, 321.
349. Similar factors were central to the rise of many other Indigenous leaders in this period (De Giuseppe, "'El Indio Gabriel,'" 234).
350. Neurath, "Ambivalencias del poder," 122.
351. Klineberg, "Notes on the Huichol," 457.
352. AHSEP-78-79/C/38267/E/35, I. Ramos, "Informe," Nov. 21, 1931.
353. Interviews with Raul Vázquez; Gilberto Bautista.
354. Friedrich, *Agrarian Revolt*, 78–90, 19–20; Brunk, *Emiliano Zapata*, 72–73.
355. Meyer, *La cristiada*, iii, 33–34.
356. Weigand, "El papel," 10.
357. Purnell, *Popular Movements*, 149–58, 124–33.
358. AGA-D/23/1425/leg.3/CCA/Restitución/Santa Catarina, Gob.Jal. to Dir. de POEJ, Oct. 7, 1927.
359. POEJ, Jan. 17, 1928.
360. Aurelio Acevedo, in Meyer, *La cristiada*, iii, 30.
361. Weigand, "El papel," 5–6.
362. See Dennis, *Intervillage Conflict*, 49–94, for similar examples in Oaxaca.
363. Smith, *The Roots*, 232; Bantjes, *As if Jesus*, 33–35.
364. Harvey, *The Chiapas Rebellion*, 41.
365. Meyer, *Manuel Lozada*, 229.
366. Interview with Salvador Sánchez.
367. Weigand, "Co-operative Labor Groups," 20.
368. Meyer, "La revolución en occidente," 262.
369. ARA/C/14/E/58/Doc/6980, PM Mezquitic to Montellano, June 8, 1928.
370. Fikes, "Huichol Indian Ceremonial Cycle," 80–82.
371. Meyer, *La cristiada*, iii, 29.
372. Alvarado, *Oralidad y ritual*, 44, 53–54.
373. Interview with José Flores.
374. Interview with Saturnino Solís.
375. Interview with Bruno Gómez and Nemesio Rodríguez.

376. Meyer, *La cristiada*, iii, 29. His argument is based on a paper from the 1940s, which describes the O'dam as Catholics who followed "the same customs as the mestizos" and amongst whom "the priest has great influence" (Cerda Silva, "Los Tepehuanes," 564).
377. Meyer, *La cristiada*, iii, 29.
378. Estrada, *Rescoldo*, 74–75, 154, 163; interviews with Felipe Salas Ramírez; Eulogio Ciriano; Magdaleno Arrellano.
379. Reyes, *Los que están*, 189–226, see also "Their Gods," 2–10, and "The Perpetual Return"; Benítez, *Los indios*, v, 192; Cramaussel, "El sistema de cargos," 75, 94; Preuss, *Fiesta, literatura y magia*, 173, 155; Alvarado, *Mexicaneros*, 43–44, and *Atar la vida*, 166–67.
380. Interviews with Felipe Salas Ramírez; Saturnino Solís.
381. Interview with Saturnino Solís.
382. Interview with José Flores.
383. Avitia, *El caudillo*, 6, 406; Benítez, *Los indios*, v, 57–58.
384. Young, "Millenium on the Northern Marches," 385–413.
385. Avitia, *El caudillo*, 162.
386. Everardo Gámiz, *Monografía de la nación tepehuana*, 69–77.
387. Antonio Reyes, pers. comm., April 2, 2014.
388. Meyer, *La cristiada*, iii, 29; also Avitia, *El caudillo*, 164–66.
389. Meyer, *La cristiada*, 18.
390. Avitia, *El caudillo*, 164–66.
391. Estrada, *Rescoldo*, 150.
392. AGA-BC/276.1/411/leg.1/Comunal/Restitución/Santa María Ocotán y Xoconoxtle, INI Report, n.d.
393. Interview with Saturnino Solís; also Evaristo Mendoza. By the mid-1920s, logging *had* become an important industry in other areas of Durango (Cramaussel, "Historia del poblamiento," 22–23), and in the mid-1930s, politicians and businessmen with interests in logging tried to seize forested lands within the territory of Santa María Ocotán, which influenced O'dam participation in the second cristiada (see chapter 5 of this volume).
394. Meyer, *La cristiada*, iii, 104, 310.
395. Meyer, 29.
396. Rangel, Marín, "Desplazamientos," 16.
397. Knight discusses such ideological "contagion" in *Mexican Revolution*, ii, 494–516.
398. Riley, Hobgood, "A Recent Nativistic Movement," 356.
399. Interview with Trinidad Morales Rodríguez.
400. Interview with Saturnino Solís.
401. Riley, Hobgood, "A Recent Nativistic Movement," 356; de la Rosa, *Historia de la política*, 64; Reyes, *Los que están*, 41.
402. Estrada, *Rescoldo*, 150; A. Campos, "El Combate," *David*, July 22, 1964.
403. Sánchez Olmedo, *Etnografía*, 38, citing Meyer, *La cristiada*, iii, 20.

404. Interview with Felipe Salas Ramírez.
405. Interviews with Gregorio Villa; Manuel Arrellano.
406. Interview with Saturnino Solís.
407. POED, Aug. 31, 1924.
408. AGA-D/leg.1/Comunal/Restitución/Sta. María Ocotán y Xoconoxtle, Gob. Dgo. to CLA. Mezquital, Mar. 30, 1921.
409. De la Rosa, *Historia de la política*, 128.
410. Interview with Saturnino Solís.
411. Interview with Eulogio Ciriano.
412. Interview with José Flores.
413. Interview with José Flores.
414. Alvarado, *Atar la vida*, 70.
415. Interview with José Flores.
416. Clausewitz, *On War*, 92.
417. Meyer, *La cristiada*, i, 93–125; Butler, *Popular Piety*, 179–212; Rus, "The 'Comunidad Revolucionaria Institucional.'"
418. Interviews with Saturnino Solís; José Flores.

CHAPTER 5

1. Bantjes, "Regional Dynamics," 114.
2. Tobler, "Las Paradojas," 50, note 17.
3. Loyo, "Los centros," 141.
4. AGN-Censo/1930/Nayarit, Durango, Jalisco.
5. Marak, "Failed Assimilation," 422.
6. Vaughan, *Cultural Politics*, 25; INEGI, *Estadísticas históricas*, i, 110.
7. Loyo, "La empresa redentora," 126–29. The majority of the students were from larger Indigenous groups, including the Tarahumaras, Mixtecs, Mayos, Tzotzils, and Nahuas (SEP 45, C/36339 E/2, "Report on la Casa," October 31, 1931).
8. Loyo, "La empresa redentora," 106–7.
9. Vaughan, *Cultural Politics*, 111.
10. Loyo, "La empresa redentora," 112–14.
11. Dawson, "'Wild Indians,'" 353.
12. Engracia Loyo, "La empresa redentora," 99–124.
13. Vaughan, *Cultural Politics*, 155–57.
14. Simpson, *The Ejido*, 27–29, 81–97.
15. Vaughan, *Cultural Politics*, 5.
16. Vaughan, 46, 93–95, 125.
17. DEFJ to DERICI, Mar. 1, 1931, AHSEP-78-79/C/38260/E/5.

18. Vaughan, *Cultural Politics*, 5; Marak, "Failed Assimilation," 421–23.
19. Vaughan, 42, 31–35; see also Joseph, "Rethinking Mexican Revolutionary Upheaval," 147.
20. Carroll, "The Smell," 35.
21. Dawson, "'Wild Indians,'" 361; see also Dawson, "From Models," 282–83.
22. Smith, "Defending 'Our Beautiful Freedom,'" 140–41; Fallaw, "'Anti-Priests,'" 206.
23. Simpson, *The Ejido*, 112–27.
24. Knight, "The Mentality," 26.
25. Interview with Fernando Muñíz.
26. Interview with Juventino Mejía.
27. Interview with Fernando Muñíz.
28. Interview with Enendino Escobeda.
29. "Corrido de Valentín de la Sierra."
30. AHSEP-84-85/C/38877/E/31, Durán Cárdenas to DEFN, Nov. 2, 1932.
31. "Reorganización de las fuerzas campesinas," *Nacional*, Nov. 22, 1931, page 10.
32. Stauffer, "Community, Identity," 173.
33. AGN-Censo/1930/Nayarit.
34. AHSEP-84-85/C/38877/E/31, Durán Cárdenas to DEFN, Aug. 5, 1933.
35. AHSEP-84-85/C/38859/E/2, Magdaleno Vázquez to Jacinto E. Téllez (DEFN), Aug. 7, 1930.
36. AHSEP-84-85/C/38861/E/10, Vázquez to DEFN, Aug. 23, 1930.
37. AHSEP-84-85/C/38877/E/26, DEFN circular, Oct. 27, 1930.
38. Dawson, "'Wild Indians,'" 336.
39. AHSEP-84-85/C/38874/E/8, DEFN to DERICI, Feb. 14, 1930.
40. Interview with Filiberto Sánchez.
41. Interviews with Filiberto Sánchez, Sandalio Sánchez, Celestino Lamas.
42. AHSEP-84-85/C/38874/E/8, DEFN to DERICI, Feb. 14, 1930.
43. AHSEP-84-85/C/38861/E/16, Durán Cárdenas to DEFN, Apr. 18, 1931.
44. AHSEP-84-85/C/38861/E/18, Durán Cárdenas to DEFN, Mar. 28, 1931.
45. Vaughan, *Cultural Politics*, 80, 154, 96–97.
46. AHSEP-84-85/C/38861/E/18, Durán Cárdenas to DEFN, June 20, 1931.
47. E.g., Smith, "Defending 'Our Beautiful Freedom,'" 141.
48. AHSEP-84-85/C/38877/E/31, Durán Cárdenas to DEFN, Dec. 5, 1932.
49. Lewis, *Ambivalent Revolution*, 100–109.
50. Marak, "'Failed Assimilation,'" 421–43; Knight, "'Superstition,'" 261.
51. Preuss, *Fiesta, literatura y magia*, 171.
52. Vaughan, *Cultural Politics*, 122.
53. Bantjes, *As if Jesus*, 33; Lewis, *Ambivalent Revolution*, 100–109.
54. AHSEP 84-85, C/38857, E/25, Durán Cárdenas to DEFN, Nov. 4, 1932.
55. AHSEP-84-85/C/38877/E/31, Durán Cárdenas to DEFN, July 10, 1932.

56. AHSEP-84-85/C/38859/E/2, Eulogio Ulloa, "Informe," Nov. 23, 1932.
57. AHSEP-84-85/C/38877/E/31, Durán Cárdenas to DEFN, Dec. 5, 1932.
58. Such trees grow to envelop and kill the host trees to which they attach themselves.
59. Interview with Agustín Lamas.
60. AHSEP-84-85/C/38861/E/16, "Censo Escolar: Santa Teresa," Oct. 14, 1931; interviews with Nabor Castañeda; Gonzalo Ramírez; Bruno Gómez.
61. AHSEP-84-85/C/38860/E/16, "Censo Escolar: Dolores," May 21, 1931.
62. AGN-Censo/1930/Nayarit/Arroyo de Santiago.
63. AHSEP-84-85/C/38874/E/8, Durán Cárdenas to DEFN, Jan. 25, 1933; interviews with Gonzalo Ramírez; Bruno Gómez.
64. AHSEP-84-85/C/38874/E/8, Durán Cárdenas to DEFN, Jan. 25, 1933.
65. Interviews with Aurelio Cánare; Bruno Gómez and Nemesio Rodríguez.
66. AHSEP-84-85/C/38877/E/31, Durán Cárdenas, "Informe anual," July 31, 1932.
67. Joseph, "Caciquismo and the Revolution," 216.
68. AHSEP-84-85/C/38877/E/31, Durán Cárdenas to DEFN, May 10, 1932.
69. See Bantjes, *As if Jesus*, 12–13: "Since symbols are at the heart of man's attempts to understand the world, it is obvious that a struggle between Weltanschauungen involves an effort to eliminate the symbols of one legitimating system and replace these with new ones or imbue them with new meaning."
70. AHSEP-84-85/C/38877/E/31, Durán Cárdenas, "Informe annual," July 31, 1932.
71. Coyle, *From Flowers*, 186–87.
72. AHSEP-84-85/C/38860/E/16, Durán Cárdenas to DEFN, Apr. 24, 1932.
73. Contemporary road-building projects often involved coercive labor practices, while roads themselves were rightly seen by many Indigenous people as accelerators of sociocultural change and, by extension, loss (Friedrich, *The Princes*, 165; Vaughan, *Cultural Politics*, 85; Brewster, *Militarism, Ethnicity, and Politics*, 137–51). Their construction still remains controversial in the Gran Nayar (Liffman, *Huichol Territory*, 179; Neurath, "Fricciones ontológicos").
74. AHSEP-84-85/C/38860/E/16, Durán Cárdenas to DEFN, Apr. 24, 1932.
75. AHSEP-84-85/C/38877/E/31, Durán Cárdenas to DEFN, Mar. 19, 1933.
76. AHSEP-84-85/C/38873/E/3, DEFN to DERICI, Mar. 7, 1932.
77. AHSEP-84-85/C/38877/E/31, Durán Cárdenas to Comisario Municipal, Oct. 22, 1932.
78. AHSEP-84-85/C/38877/E/31, Durán Cárdenas to DEFN, Oct. 30, 1932.
79. AHSEP-84-85/C/38877/E/31, Durán Cárdenas to DEFN, Nov. 6, 1932.
80. AHSEP-84-85/C/38877/E/31, Durán Cárdenas to DEFN, Nov. 1, 1932.
81. AHSEP-84-85/C/38857/E/25, Durán Cárdenas to DEFN, Mar. 8, 1933.
82. AHSEP-84-85/C/38877/E/31, Durán Cárdenas to DEFN, Aug. 5, 1933.
83. AHSEP-84-85/C/38877/E/31, Durán Cárdenas, "Informe," Apr. 4, 1933.
84. "Ha penetrado ya en la conciencia del indio la nueva escuela rural," *Nacional*, June 3, 1933.

85. Mercurio Flores to Unknown, in Coyle, *From Flowers*, 188; see also AHSEP-84-85/C/38877/E/31, Durán Cárdenas, "Informe," Apr. 4, 1933.
86. AHSEP-84-85/C/38877/E/31, Durán Cárdenas to DEFN, Aug. 5, 1933.
87. Interview with Durán Cárdenas.
88. Meyer, "Historia del reparto," 243.
89. Meyer, 244–45.
90. AGA-D/23/225/leg.1/CAM/Dotación/Saycota, "Informe: El Motaje," July 23, 1934.
91. AGA-D/276.1/14/leg.1/Comunal/RTBC/San Pedro Ixcatán, Proc. de Pueblos to DA, Oct. 6, 1937.
92. AGN-LC/C/198/E/403/726/San Juan Corapan, clipping from "El Universal," Nov. 27, 1935.
93. Nugent, *Spent Cartridges*, 87–99; Shadow, "Production, Social Identity," 43–45; Purnell, *Popular Movements*, 192.
94. AGA-D/276.1/14/leg.1/Comunal/RTBC/San Pedro Ixcatán, Cruz Salas to Proc. de Pueblos, Nov. 23, 1935.
95. Interview with Erasmo González.
96. AGA-D/23/120/leg.1/CAM/Dotación/Saycota, Residents to Ing. Flores Vega, June 27, 1945; AGA-D/24/1163/leg.1/SRA/Restitución/Saycota, Ing. Zazueta G. to CLA Nay., Dec. 19, 1932.
97. Interview with Erasmo González.
98. See Nugent, *Spent Cartridges*, 129–30; Friedrich, *The Princes*, 142–43, 158; Harvey, *The Chiapas Rebellion*, 72–73.
99. AHSEP-84-85/C/38877/E/31, Durán Cárdenas to DEFN, Sept. 13, 1933.
100. AHSEP-84-85/C/38877/E/31, Durán Cárdenas to DERICI, Oct. 23, 1933.
101. AHSEP-84-85/C/38877/E/31, Durán Cárdenas to DEFN, Mar. 25, 1934.
102. AHSEP-84-85/C/38877/E/31, Durán Cárdenas to DEFN, Mar. 26, 1934.
103. AHSEP-84-85/C/38874/E/18, Durán Cárdenas to DEFN, Jan 7, 1934.
104. AHSEP-84-85/C/38877/E/31, Durán Cárdenas to DEFN, Jan. 28, 1934.
105. Interview with Durán Cárdenas.
106. Coyle, *From Flowers*, 188.
107. Interviews with Bruno Gómez and Nemesio Rodríguez.
108. Joseph, "Rethinking Mexican Revolutionary Upheaval," 198; Friedrich, *The Princes*, 239–40; Torres, "Nahuat Factionalism," 465.
109. J. Guadalupe Ceniceros, in Caldera and de la Torre, *Pueblos*, 206.
110. Fallaw, "Eulogio Ortiz," 141–42; see also Tuck, *Holy War*, 182.
111. J. García, "Juan Landa," *Mi Pueblo*, March 1996.
112. Rath, *Myths*, 107.
113. J. G. Ceniceros, in Caldera and de la Torre, *Pueblos*, 206.
114. AHSEP-78-79/C/38267/E/35, I. Ramos to DEFJ, Rafael Jiménez, n.d. (late 1930).

115. AGA-D/276.1/79/leg.4/CCA/RTBC/San Sebastián, lands sold by "indígenas de Nostic" to vecinos of Mezquitic, n.d.; José Sánchez buys land from Adelaido Quintanilla, April 28, 1930; Petronilo Muñoz sells Nieves Muñoz 2,000 hectares for 300 pesos, December 15, 1928; agronomist's report, Sept. 24, 1954.
116. Zingg, *Los huicholes*, i, 157.
117. AGA-D/276.1/103/leg.1/SRA/RTBC/San Andrés, CNA to PM Mezquitic, Sept. 18, 1929.
118. AHSEP-78-79/C/38288/E/25, Ezequiel Haro to Puig Casauranc, Aug. 25, 1933.
119. AHSEP-78-79/C/38285/E/9, Tijerina Almaguer, "Informe," Nov. 16, 1935.
120. AGN-Censo/1930/Jalisco, Nayarit.
121. AHSEP-78-79/C/38283/E/25, Ramón Durand, "Informe," Jan. 14, 1930.
122. Vaughan, *Cultural Politics*, 31–35.
123. Simpson, *The Ejido*, 112–27.
124. AHSEP-78-79/C/38283/E/28, Durand to DERICI, Jan. 9, 1930.
125. AHSEP-78-79/C/38283/E/28, Poirett to Durand, Jan. 22, 1930.
126. AHSEP-78-79/C/38283/E/28, DERICI to Durand, Feb. 4, 1930.
127. AHSEP-78-79/C/38283/E/28, DERICI to Rodríguez, Feb. 20, 1930.
128. Interview with Julio Robles and Antonio Candelario.
129. Rubin, "Caza Menor," *Informador*, Dec. 23, 1956; see also Rubin, *La Bruma*.
130. AHSEP-78-79/C/38283/E/28, DERICI to Rodríguez, Mar. 26, 1930.
131. Dawson, "'Wild Indians,'" 352–53.
132. Dawson, "From Models," 299–300.
133. AHSEP-78-79/C/38267/E/35, DEFJ, to DERICI, July 11, 1931.
134. AHSEP-78-79/C/38267/E/35, Ramos to DEFJ, n.d. (late 1930).
135. AGA-D/276.1/103/leg.1/SRA/RTBC/San Sebastián, CLA Mezquitic to Gob. Jal., June 12, 1929.
136. AHSEP-78-79/C/38267/E/35, Ramos to DEFJ, n.d. (late 1930). Belying Weigand's assertion that "Bautista retreated to the mountains to fight a defensive battle" in this period ("Los huicholes en las revoluciones," 6).
137. AHSEP-78-79/C/38267/E/35, Ramos, "Informe," Nov. 21, 1931.
138. AHSEP-78-79/C/38267/E/35, Ramos, "Informe," July 12, 1931.
139. Marak, "Failed Assimilation," 430.
140. AHSEP-78-79/C/38267/E/35, DEFJ to DERICI, July 11, 1931.
141. Simpson, *The Ejido*, 27–29, 81–97; Aguirre Beltrán, *Teoría y práctica*, 120–26.
142. AGA-D/24/1680/leg.2/CCA/Restitución/San Sebastián, Ing. Balderas, "Informe," Nov. 7, 1936.
143. AGA-D/24/1680/leg.1/CCA/Restitución/San Sebastián, José Egurvido to CLA, Feb. 1, 1932.
144. Interview with Raul Vázquez Campos.

145. AGA-D/24/1680/leg.2/CCA/Restitución/San Sebastián, Ing. Balderas, "Informe," Nov. 7, 1936.
146. AHSEP-78-79/C/38284/E/17, Ramos to DEFJ, Aug. 18, 1932.
147. AHSEP-78-79/C/38283/E/22, Ramos, "Informe," Nov. 17, 1930; AHSEP-78-79/C/38260/E/5, DEFJ to DERICI, Mar. 1, 1931.
148. AHSEP-78-79/C/38267/E/35, Ramos, "Informe," Nov. 21, 1931.
149. Cf. Liffman, *Huichol Territory*, 179–81; see also Vaughan, *Cultural Politics*, 80–81, 126.
150. AHSEP-78-79/C/38267/E/35, Ramos to DEFJ, May 8, 1932.
151. AHSEP-78-79/C/38286/E/21, Sevilla to DEFJ, May 14, 1932.
152. AHSEP78-79: C/38280/E/10, DEFJ to DERICI, July 15, 1932; AHSEP-78-79/C/38280/E/10, Sevilla to DEFJ, May 25, 1932.
153. AHSEP-78-79/C/38282/E/5, clipping from "Las Noticias," Mar. 25, 1933.
154. AHSEP-78-79/C/38267/E/35, Ramos to DEFJ, May 8, 1932.
155. AHSEP-78-79/C/38280/E/10, Sevilla, "Informe," July 15, 1932.
156. AHSEP-78-79/C/38280/E/10, DEFJ to Sevilla, July 28, 1932.
157. Michel, *Episodios históricos*, 96.
158. AHSEP-78-79/C/38280/E/10, Ramos, "Informe," Apr. 17, 1933.
159. Bantjes, "Regional Dynamics," 115.
160. M. Rivera, "Yo era Sacristán," *Mi Pueblo*, Oct. 1995, 7; AHAG-Bolaños/C/3/E/30, PM San Martín to Arz, Aug. 11, 1934.
161. E. Bañuelos Villagrán, in Caldera and de la Torre, *Pueblos*, 242–43.
162. AHSEP-78-79/C/38280/E/10, Sevilla, "Informe," June 12, 1933.
163. AHAG-MC/1928-1975/C/2/E/22, Acevedo, "Escrito sobre la cristiada," Jan. 1933.
164. Michel, *Episodios históricos*, 96; see also Vaughan, *Cultural Politics*, 33.
165. AHSEP-78-79/C/38280/E/10, Sevilla to DEFJ, Apr. 18, 1933.
166. AHSEP-78-79/C/38280/E/10, Sevilla, "Informe," Apr. 19, 1933.
167. Gómez, "'Huicot,'" 94–145.
168. AHSEP-78-79/C/38282/E/15, DEFJ to DERICI, Feb. 6, 1933.
169. AHSEP-78-79/C/38282/E/5, clipping from "Las Noticias," Mar. 25, 1933.
170. AHSEP-78-79/C/38282/E/12, DEFJ to DERICI, Mar. 30, 1933. The Wixárika have long been stereotyped as a "timid" people (e.g., Hrdlička, *Medical Observations*, 35), as opposed to "warlike" groups such as their Náayari neighbors (Thord-Gray, *Gringo Rebel*, 278), the Purépecha (Lumholtz, *Unknown Mexico*, ii, 413), or, most famously, the Yaqui (Hu-Dehart, *Yaqui Resistance*, xvii).
171. AHSEP-78-79/C/38282/E/12, DEFJ to DERICI, Mar. 30, 1933.
172. AHSEP-78-79/C/38282/E/5, clipping from "Las Noticias," Mar. 25, 1933.
173. Dawson, "From Models," 300–305.
174. See Vaughan, *Cultural Politics*, 26–29, 151–54.
175. AHSEP-78-79/C/38282/E/4, Valle, "Plan educativo," May 25, 1933.

176. INEGI, *Estadísticas Históricas*, i, 98.
177. AHSEP-78-79/C/38282/E/4, Ramírez to Valle, June 13, 1933.
178. For other cases of such linguistic resistance, see Scott, *Weapons*, 19-21; Rosebery, "Hegemony," 364.
179. AHSEP-78-79/C/38265/E/31, Macías to DEI, Feb. 12, 1942.
180. AHSEP-78-79/C/38282/E/6, Valle, "Informe anual," Aug. 18, 1933; AHSEP-78-79/C/38281/E/8, Rubalcaba to DERICI, Dec. 31, 1933; Raby, "Los maestros rurales," 194–97.
181. AHSEP-78-79/C/38280/E/5, Braulio Rodríguez, "Circular," Jan. 30, 1934.
182. AHSEP-78-79/C/38280/E/7, DEFJ to DERICI, June 29, 1935.
183. ARA/C/12/E/46/Doc/5663, GN "Circular # 4," Feb. 4, 1934.
184. Vaughan, *Cultural Politics*, 34.
185. AHSEP-78-79/C/38280/E/10, Sevilla, "Informe," June 12, 1933.
186. AHSEP-78-79/C/38260/E/2, María García M. to DEFJ, Jan. 15, 1934; AGA-D/276.1/137/leg.1/SRA/RTBC/Tuxpan, de la Cruz et al. to CNA, Mar. 26, 1935.
187. Interview with Salvador Sánchez.
188. AGA-D/24/1680/leg.2/CCA/Restitución/San Sebastián, Balderas, "Informe," Nov. 7, 1936.
189. AGA-D/276.1/103/leg.1/SRA/RTBC/San Andrés, Communal leaders to CNA, May 19, 1933; AGA-D/24/1680/leg.2/CCA/Restitución/San Sebastián, Balderas, "Informe," Nov. 7, 1936.
190. AHSEP-78-79/C/38267/E/35, Valle to DERICI, Mar. 13, 1934.
191. AGA-D/276.1/36/leg.1/CCA/RTBC/Tuxpan, Alonso Guerrero to Jefe del Dept., April 13, 1940.
192. AHSEP-78-79/C/38282/E/15, Valle to DERICI, Feb. 6, 1933.
193. Martínez, in Caldera and de la Torre, *Pueblos*, 122–23.
194. AGA-D/276.1/103/Leg.1/SRA/Restitución/San Andrés, Enrique Cárdenas, "Informe," Nov. 7, 1936.
195. AHSEP-78-79/C/38267/E/35, Ramos to DEFJ, Feb. 7, 1934.
196. AGN-LC/559.1/67, de la Rosa to Pres. Cárdenas, Dec. 30, 1934.
197. AGA-D/24/1680/leg.2/CCA/Restitución/San Sebastián, Julio Vindiola to DA, Sept. 30, 1937.
198. AHSEP-78-79/C/38260/E/2, Ramos (now working for the DAI) to DEI, Oct. 24, 1940.
199. Meyer, *La cristiada*, i, 151; Avitia, *El caudillo*, 224.
200. Dulles, *Yesterday in Mexico*, 447.
201. A. Campos, "Santiago," *David*, Dec. 22, 1960.
202. "Un llamado a los Rebeldes," *Siglo de Torreón*, June 28, 1929.
203. AHED-FR/C/4/E/1423, Terrones Benítez, "Circular 35," Nov. 1, 1929.
204. Katz, *The Life and Times*, 719–23.
205. Avitia, *El caudillo*, 246.

206. AHED-AG/C/2/E/102, José Ramón Valdez, to Bayacora Reps., Apr. 30, 1931.
207. AHED-M/C8/E/45, Gobernador de Lajas to Gob. Dgo., July 16, 1930.
208. AHED-FR/C/1/E/226, PM Mezquital to Gob. Dgo., May 4, 1934; "Coronel Francisco Sánchez Hernández," *David*, Aug. 22, 1956.
209. Chávez, *Porfirio Mallorquin*, 11–12.
210. "División territorial de la municipalidad del Mezquital," *Periodico oficial del estado de Durango*, Oct. 16, 1930, 9; ARA/C/14/E/59/Doc/7258, Saturnino Flores to Gob. Dgo., Aug 18, 1928.
211. Interviews with Magdaleno Arrellano; José Flores.
212. AHED-M/C/8/E/45, Pres. de Junta Prov. PN to Gob. Dgo., July 30, 1930.
213. "Amnestía," *Nacional*, Sept. 11, 1929.
214. AHED-AR/C/4/E/83, Florencio Estrada to Gob. Dgo., Oct. 24, 1932.
215. AHED-M/C/7/E/89, Cosme Solís et al. to Gob. Dgo., Dec. 25, 1929.
216. AHED-M/C/11/E/35, Chon Aguilar et al. to Gob. Dgo., Sept. 11, 1933.
217. AHED-M/C/8/E/45, Merced Ríos to Gob. Dgo, Julio 16, 1930.
218. AHED-AR/C/2/E/14, PM Mezquital to Gob. Dgo., Feb. 10, 1930.
219. AHED-AG/C/1/E/77, PM Mezquital to Gob. Dgo., Feb. 8, 1930.
220. AGN-POR/1930/E/111/F/1546-8290, Jaime Carrillo to Pres., Mar. 5, 1930; Fallaw, "Eulogio Ortiz," 154; Rath, *Myths*, 158.
221. AGN-POR/1930/E/111/F/1546-8290, CSOC to Pres., Mar. 30, 1930; Wasserman, *Persistent Oligarchs*, 157.
222. AHED-M/C/8/E/45, Pres. Junta Prov. PN to Rafael Torrijos, Aug. 19, 1930.
223. AHED-AR/C/2/E/14, Gob. Dgo. to PM Mezquital, Feb. 21, 1930.
224. Meyer, *La cristiada*, i, 345–46.
225. AHSEP-68-69/C/37438/E/2, Maurilio Náñez, "Informe," June 20, 1929.
226. Navarro, *El cardenismo*, 54–56.
227. AHSEP-68-69/C/37434/E/4, DEFD to DERICI, Dec. 27, 1930. For more on the links between generals and businessmen, see Gillingham, "Military Caciquismo," 219; Rath, *Myths*, 104, 131; Wasserman, *Pesos and Politics*, 20–21, 87.
228. AHSEP-68-69/C/37432/E/18, DEFD to DERICI, Feb. 10, 1931.
229. AHSEP-68-69/C/37416/E/2622, DERICI to DEFD, May 15, 1931.
230. AHSEP-68-69/C/37416/E/25, T. Muñoz et al. to Gob. Dgo., Apr. 10, 1931.
231. AHSEP-68-69/C/37416/E/24, DEFD to DERICI, Apr. 10, 1931.
232. AHSEP-68-69/C/37431/E/3, DEFD to DERICI, Nov. 1, 1931.
233. AHED-M/C/8/E/121, Alejandro Santana, Hilario Soto, to Gob. Dgo., May 13, 1931.
234. AHED-M/C/8/E/121, Gob. Dgo. to Santana, May 22, 1931.
235. AHED-FR/C/4/E/1426, Andrés Aguilar, to Gob. Dgo., Apr. 19, 1931.
236. AHED-FR/C/4/E/1426, Facundo García to Gob. Dgo., Apr. 29, 1931.
237. AHED-FR/C/4/E/1426, Gob. Dgo. to García, Apr. 24, 1931.

238. AHED-FR/C/4/E/1426, JOM Dgo. to García, Apr. 24, 1931.
239. Genaro Santillán; Chávez, *Porfirio Mayorquín*, 117–18.
240. "Murió Conocido Fascineroso," *Siglo de Torreón*, July 16, 1931.
241. "Fue muerto ya el conocido bandido 'El Pillaco,'" *Informador*, July 23, 1931.
242. "Murió Conocido Fascineroso," *Siglo de Torreón*, July 16, 1931.
243. Falcón, "El surgimiento," 355–56.
244. This was perhaps the first of Mexico's "Institucional" parties.
245. Navarro, *El cardenismo*, 54–56.
246. AHED-AR/C/4/E/3, Gob.Dgo., Circular to PMs, June 25, 1931; AHED-AR/C/3/E/41, Heredía to Flores, June 19, 1931; AHED-AR/C/3/E/41, Heredía to Gob. Dgo., July 9, 1931.
247. AHED-AR/C/4/E/83, Florencio Estrada to Gob. Dgo., Oct. 24, 1932.
248. Fallaw, "'Anti-Priests,'" 217.
249. AHED-FR/C/4/E/353, Reps of El Troncón to Gob. Dgo., Sept. 8, 1932.
250. AHED-M/C/10/E/34, Gob. Dgo. to PM Mezquital, Oct. 13, 1932.
251. AHED-FR/C/4/E/452, Francisco Solís et al. to Gob. Dgo., Oct. 28, 1932.
252. AHED-FR/C/4/E/453, Nabor Muñoz to Gob. Dgo., 22 Oct. 22, 1932.
253. AHED-FR/C/4/E/453, Nabor Muñoz to Gob. Dgo., Oct. 22, 1932.
254. AHED-FR/C/4/E/453, PM Mezquital to Gob. Dgo., Nov. 19, 1932.
255. AHED-AR/C/4/E/83, Estrada to Gob. Dgo. Oct. 24, 1932.
256. AHED-M/C/10/E/34, PM Mezquital to Gob. Dgo., Sept. 20, 1932.
257. AHED-M/C/10/E/34, Gob. Dgo. to Jefe de Destacamiento Fed., Oct. 13, 1932.
258. AHED-FR/C/4/E/452, Gob. Dgo to PM Mezquital, Nov. 7, 1932.
259. Vaughan, *Cultural Politics*, 31.
260. AGN-ALR/C/159/E/541/9, Gral. Macías to Pres., Oct. 14, 1932.
261. AHAG-MC/1928-1975/C/2/E/22, Acevedo, "Escrito sobre la cristiada," Jan. 1933.
262. ARA/C/12/E/46/Doc/5669, GN to Vázquez, Sept. 15, 1932; GN to Acevedo, Sept. 15, 1932; GN to Vázquez, Oct. 26, 1932.
263. AHAG-MC/1928-1975/C/2/E/22, Acevedo, "Escrito sobre la cristiada," Jan. 1933.
264. AHED-AS/C/4/E/88, Gob. Teneraca, Francisco Nolasco, to Gob. Dgo., Dec. 4, 1932.
265. AHSEP-68-69/C/37431/E/6, Gob. Dgo. to Bassols, Nov. 25, 1932.
266. Vaughan, *Cultural Politics*, 34–35; Purnell, *Popular Movements*, 132, 193.
267. AHSEP-68-69/C/37432/E/6, DEFD to DERICI, May 19, 1933; AHSEP-68-69/C/37441 E/10, DEFD to DERICI, Oct. 31, 1933.
268. AHSEP-68-69/C/37432/E/6, DEFD to DERICI, Apr. 25, 1933.
269. AHSEP-68-69/C/37432/E/6, DEFD to DERICI, Mar. 31, 1933.
270. AHSEP-68-69/C/37432/E/6, DEFD to DERICI, May 19, 1933.
271. AHSEP-68-69/C/37432/E/6, DEFD to DERICI, June 14, 1933.
272. Tobler, "Las Paradojas," 74.
273. AHED-FR/C/4/E/400, Gral. López, Circular 114 to PMs, Feb. 24, 1933.

274. AHED-FR/C/4/E/2150, SDN Circular 16, June 6, 1930.
275. AHED-FR/C/4/E/400, López to Contraras, Mar. 30, 1933.
276. AHED-M/C/11/E/96, Gob. Teneraca to Julián Rivera, May 13, 1933.
277. AHED-FR/C/4/E/400, Florencio and Eleuterio Estrada to Gob.Dgo., Apr. 8, 1933; AHED-FR/C/4/E/400, PM Mezquital to Gob. Dgo., Apr. 27, 1933.
278. AHED-M/C/11/E/35, Chon Aguilar, José Flores et al. to Gob. Dgo., Sept. 11, 1933.
279. AHED-M/C/10/E/34, PM Mezquital to Gob. Dgo., Sept. 23, 1933.
280. AGN-ALR/C/161/E/542.7/45, Residents of Teneraca to Gob. Dgo., Oct. 15, 1933.
281. AHED-FR/C/1/E/404, Cumplido to Gob. Dgo., Oct. 15, 1933.
282. AHSEP-68-69/C/37432/E/6, DEFD to DERICI, Nov. 21, 1933.
283. AHSEP-68-69/C/37441/E/10, DEFD to DERICI, Oct. 31, 1933.
284. AHSEP-68-69/C/37441/E/10, DEFD to DERICI, Nov. 13, 1933.
285. AHSEP-68-69/C/37432/E/6, DEFD to DERICI, Nov. 21, 1933.
286. Avitia, *El caudillo*, 295.
287. AHSEP-68-69/C/37435/E/18, DEFD to DERICI, Jan. 17, 1934.
288. Navarro, *El cardenismo*, 54–56; Fallaw, "Eulogio Ortiz," 159.
289. AHSEP-68-69/C/37431/E/28, DEFD to DERICI, Sept. 6, 1933.
290. AHSEP-68-69/C/37431/E/28, Antonio Hidalgo to CNA, Oct. 6, 1933.
291. AHED-M/C/10/E/34, Gob. Dgo. to PM Mezquital, Jan. 1, 1934.
292. AGA-BC/276.1/411/leg.1/Comunal/Restitución/Santa María Ocotán y Xoconoxtle, INI Report, n.d.
293. "Noticias de Durango," *Siglo de Torreón*, Jan. 18, 1932.
294. AGN-ALR/C/184/E/552.5/459, León García to Pres., May 9, 1934.
295. AHSEP-68-69/C/37432/E/6, DEFD to DERICI, Oct. 26, 1933.
296. AHSEP-68-69/C/37429/E/12, DEFD to DERICI, June 20, 1934.
297. AGN-LC/C/207/E/404.1/177, Terrones Benítez to Pres., Nov. 3, 1934.
298. Estrada, *Rescoldo*, 57.
299. AGN-LC/C/58/E/120/558, Unknown to Pres., n.d.
300. "El Mayor Florencio," *David*, June 22, 1955.
301. AGN-LC/C/58/E/120/558, Unknown to Pres., n.d.
302. ARA/C/12/E/44/Doc/5562, "Acta levantada en Cerrito Gordo," Nov. 22, 1934.
303. Stauffer, "Community, Identity," 173, 153; see also Kourí, *A Pueblo Divided*.
304. Knight, "Cardenismo," 77; Rus, "The 'Comunidad Revolucionaria Institucional,'" 267.

CHAPTER 6

1. Knight, "The Rise and Fall," 249.
2. Hamilton, *The Limits*, 108, 140, 105.
3. Escobar and Butler, "Introduction," 59.

4. Rath, "Revolutionary Citizenship," 180–83.
5. Vaughan, *Cultural Politics*, 34–36, 12.
6. Gillingham, "Ambiguous Missionaries," 338.
7. Vaughan, *Cultural Politics*, 34–35.
8. Bantjes, "Regional Dynamics," 119; Bantjes, *As if Jesus*, 34–35.
9. Knight, "Cardenismo," 83–102.
10. Vaughan, *Cultural Politics*, 35; Meyer, "Religious Conflict," 185.
11. See Ankerson, "Cedillo."
12. "Rebeldes," *Siglo de Torreón*, June 6, 1936, quoting Secretariat of War official estimates of 288 rebels in Jalisco, 190 in Durango, 97 in Zacatecas, 130 in Guanajuato, and 286 in Colima.
13. Meyer, *La cristiada*, i, 367; "Martínez," "Manifiesto al pueblo de Durango," in Avitia, *El caudillo*, 349–50.
14. Raby, "Los maestros rurales," 194–97; Bantjes, "Regional Dynamics," 119; Bantjes, *As if Jesus*, 24–60.
15. Meyer, *La cristiada*, i, 374–75.
16. Knight, "Cardenismo," 104.
17. Bantjes, *As if Jesus*, 76; Vaughan, *Cultural Politics*, 35.
18. Knight, "Cardenismo," 104.
19. Vaughan, *Cultural Politics*, 35.
20. Bantjes, "Regional Dynamics," 121–25.
21. Meyer, "Religious Conflict," 185.
22. Meyer, "Religious Conflict," 198; Bantjes, "Regional Dynamics," 125.
23. Vaughan, *Cultural Politics*, 91–162; Purnell, *Popular Movements*, 132; Raby, "Los maestros rurales."
24. Fallaw, *Religion*, 121–56.
25. Bantjes, *As if Jesus*, 34; see also Rus, "The 'Comunidad Revolucionaria Institucional.'"
26. Ankerson, "Cedillo," 158–59.
27. Rath, "Revolutionary Citizenship," 183.
28. Loyo, *Para Entender*, 180.
29. Dawson, "From Models," 284–94.
30. Smith, "Defending 'Our Beautiful Freedom,'" 140–43.
31. "Opinión Editorial: Acción en Bien de los Indios," *Nacional*, July 25, 1939.
32. Dawson, "From Models," 306–8.
33. Vaughan, *Cultural Politics*, 19–20.
34. Vaughan, 35–36; Ai Camp, *Generals*, 24; cf. Smith, "Defending 'Our Beautiful Freedom,'" 144.
35. Radding, "Peasant Resistance," 349; Hu-Dehart, *Yaqui Resistance*, 210–11.
36. See Bantjes, *As if Jesus*, 10, 75–78.

37. AHSEP-84-85/C/38877/E/31, Durán Cárdenas, "Informe," Jan. 12, 1935.
38. Bantjes, "Regional Dynamics," 117–18.
39. ARA/C/13/E/55/Doc/6707, Pablo Rangel to GN., June 18, 1935.
40. Interview with Filiberto Sánchez, Sandalio Sánchez, Celestino Lamas; see also Filiberto Sánchez, "Aurelio Chavez."
41. Interviews with Fernando Muñíz; Candido Contreras.
42. Interview with Enendino Escobeda.
43. Interviews with Fernando Muñíz; Erasmo González; Bruno Gómez and Nemesio Rodríguez.
44. Interview with Fernando Muñíz.
45. AHSEP-84-85/C/38873/E/2, Lucas Ortiz to JOM Nay., May 21, 1935.
46. Interview with Fernando Muñíz.
47. Avitia, *El caudillo*, 305; Interview with Saturnino Solís.
48. ARA/C/13/E/54/Doc/6309, Cristero Military Report, Dec. 14, 1935; see also Juventino Mejía.
49. Interview with Enendino Escobeda.
50. ARA/C/12/E/51/Doc/6006, Guadalupe Pedroza to GN, Dec. 27, 1935.
51. ARA/C/12/E/48/Doc/5853, Cristero Report, "Parte NE de Nayarit," Jan. 8, 1936.
52. Interviews with Nabor Castañeda; Juventino Mejía; Nemesio Rodríguez.
53. Interviews with Candido Contreras; Nabor Castañeda.
54. Interview with Fernando Muñíz.
55. Interview with Erasmo González.
56. Interview with Magdaleno Arrellano.
57. Interviews with Rosalio Salvador; Pedro de la Cruz.
58. Interview with Enendino Escobeda.
59. Interview with Fernando Muñíz.
60. Interview with Agustín Lamas.
61. ARA/C/12/E/51/Doc/6021, Pedroza to GN, May 31, 1936.
62. Interview with Erasmo González.
63. Interview with Erasmo González.
64. Interview with Bruno Gómez and Nemesio Rodríguez.
65. Interview with Saturnino Solís.
66. Interview with Bruno Gómez and Nemesio Rodríguez.
67. Interview with Nabor Castañeda.
68. AHSEP-84-85/C/38886/E/14, Joaquín Rivera, "Informe annual," July 16, 1936.
69. AHSEP-84-85/C/38886/E/14, Rivera to DEFN, July 14, 1936.
70. AHSEP-84-85/C/38891/E/7, DEFN, "Informe General," Aug. 19, 1936.
71. Interview with Enendino Mejía.
72. AHSEP-84-85/C/38891/E/7, DEFN, "Informe General," Aug. 19, 1936.

73. AHSEP-84-85/C/38886/E/12, Gonález Sánchez to DEFN, Apr. 1936.
74. The Náayari Easter Week festival was key to legitimizing traditional communal power structures and also helped to initiate children into communal life (Coyle, *From Flowers*, 143–50). Amongst the Yaqui, SEP officials also deliberately disrupted the Lent festival, which played a similar role in Yaqui society (Vaughan, *Cultural Politics*, 148–49).
75. Such activities were commonly organized throughout Mexico; see Vaughan, *Cultural Politics*, 42; cf. 75, 94–95.
76. AHSEP-84-85/C/38886/E/14, Rivera to DEFN, Mar. 31, 1936.
77. AHSEP-84-85/C/38886/E/14, Rivera to DEFN, Apr. 25, 1936.
78. Menéndez, *Nayar*, 256–77.
79. AHSEP-84-85/C/38886/E/14, Rivera to DEFN, May 12, 1936.
80. AHSEP-84-85/C/38886/E/14, Rivera to DEFN, Mar. 31, 1936.
81. Gillingham, "Maximino's Bulls," 203, citing Ladurie, *Carnival*, 318–22.
82. Coyle, *From Flowers*, 190.
83. Interview with Bruno Gómez and Nemesio Rodríguez.
84. AGA-D/276.1/14/leg.1/Comunal/RTBC/San Pedro Ixcatán, Proc. de Pueblos to DA, July 20, 1937.
85. Simpson, *The Ejido*, 81–97, 482–88.
86. Dulles, *Yesterday in Mexico*, 599; Nugent, *Spent Cartridges*, 91; Purnell, *Popular Movements*, 156–57.
87. Friedrich, *The Princes*, 142–43; Harvey, *The Chiapas Rebellion*, 72–73.
88. The same dynamic was also at play in mestizo Namiquipa; see Nugent, *Spent Cartridges*, 129–30.
89. AGA-D/24/1163/leg.1/SRA/Restitución/Saycota, Ing. Zazueta to CLA, Dec. 19, 1932; for the rather similar story of Primo Tapia's request for dotación in Naranja, see Friedrich, *Agrarian Revolt*, 91.
90. AGA-D/24/1163/leg.1/SRA/Restitución/Saycota, "Residents of Saycota" to Ing. Flores Vega, June 27, 1945.
91. AGA/D/23/92/leg.1/SRA/Dotación/Saycota, Proc. de Comunidades, Ruiz, to DA., Dec. 9, 1939.
92. Preciado, "Conciencia histórica," 495.
93. AGA-D/23/225/leg.1/CAM/Dotación/Sayocta, "Informe: El Motaje," May 31, 1946.
94. AGA-D23/92/leg.1/SRA/Dotación/Saycota, San Diego and Santa Cruz to Gob Nay., Nov. 18, 1939.
95. AGA/D/23/92/leg.1/SRA/Dotación/Saycota, Proc. de Comunidades, Ruiz, to DA., Dec. 9, 1939.
96. Interview with Erasmo González.
97. AGA-D/276.1/14/leg.1/Comunal/RTBC/San Pedro Ixcatán, "Informe: El Zopilote," ND, 1939.

98. See Vaughan, *Cultural Politics*, 30–31.
99. Vaughan, 190–91.
100. AHSEP-84-85/C/38887/E/11, DEFN to Felipe Madera, Mar. 28, 1938.
101. AHSEP-84-85/C/38877/E/25, Madera, "Informe," Dec. 26, 1936.
102. Jáuregui, *Los coras*, 23–24; see also Boyer, *Political Landscapes*, 3.
103. AGN-LC/C/77/E/121/52, León Contreras et al. to Pres., Sept. 20, 1937.
104. AGN-LC/C/156/E/151.3/1251, "Frente" to Pres., July 20, 1939.
105. "Opinión Editorial: Acción en Bien de los Indios," *Nacional*, July 25, 1939.
106. AHSEP-84-85/C/38861/E/19, Madera to Gob Nay., Feb. 25, 1938.
107. AHSEP-84-85/C/38887/E/3, Felipe Madera, "Informe," Jan. 24, 1940.
108. "Gráficas de la toma de posesión," *Nacional*, Jan. 15, 1938.
109. Coyle, *From Flowers*, 12.
110. AHSEP-84-85/CC/38887/E/3, Madera, "Informe," Jan 24, 1940.
111. AGN-LC/C/156/E/151.3/1251, "Frente" to Pres., July 20, 1939.
112. ARA/C/12/E/51/Doc/6013, J. Martínez to GN, Feb. 29, 1936.
113. Interview with Jesús Mercado.
114. Interview with Salvador Sánchez; cf. Fikes, "Serratos."
115. AGN-LC/559.1/67, Tomas de la Rosa Estrada to Pres., Dec. 30, 1934.
116. Interview with Jesús Mercado.
117. AHSEP-78-79/C/38280/E/7, Samuel Pérez to DEFJ, Apr. 20, 1935.
118. AHSEP-78-79/C/38285/E/18, Federación de Maestros Feds. de Jal. to Gob.Jal., Apr. 15, 1935; Sánchez Martínez, *A contra corriente*, 38.
119. AGA-D/24/1680/leg.2/CCA/Restitución/San Sebastián, Ing. Balderas, "Informe," Nov. 7, 1936.
120. Interview with Jesús Mercado.
121. Interview with Miguel Carrillo.
122. Interview with Julio Robles and Antonio Candelario.
123. Interview with Jesús Mercado.
124. Interview with Raul Vázquez.
125. Interview with Rosalio Salvador.
126. AGN-LC/559.1/67, Tomas de la Rosa Estrada to Pres., Dec. 30, 1934; AGN-LC/559.1/67, Sec. Gob. to Gob. Jal., June 3, 1935.
127. Interview with Salvador Sanchez.
128. AGA-D/276.1/137/Leg.1/SRA/Restitución, Sánchez, Romero, and Chino to DA, March 26, 1935; AGN-LC/C/611/E/524/60, PM Bolanos to Pres., Feb. 12, 1936.
129. Interview with Salvador Sánchez.
130. According to Fikes, Weigand, and García de Weigand, Zingg's political advocacy on behalf of the Wixáritari won him their trust and cooperation in his anthropological studies ("Introduction," xxxi).

131. AHSEP-78-79/C/38280/E/7, DEFJ to Samuel Pérez, Apr. 20, 1935.
132. Interview with Jesús Mercado.
133. AHSEP-78-79/C/38268/E/18, DEFJ to Samuel Pérez, Apr. 4, 1935.
134. Fikes, "Serratos."
135. AGN-LC/C/567/E/503.11/259/San Andrés, Reps. to DA, Nov. 24, 1937; Nov. 25, 1938.
136. Preuss, *Fiesta, literatura y magia*, 140.
137. Interviews with Rosalio Salvador; Jesús Mercado.
138. Interview with Salvador Sánchez.
139. AGA-D/24/1680/leg.2/CCA/Restitución/San Sebastián, Julio Vindiola to DA, Sept. 30, 1937.
140. Interview with Jesús Mercado.
141. Interview with Antonio Candelario.
142. Interview with Xuturima Hernández.
143. Interview with Jesús Mercado.
144. Interview with Salvador Sánchez.
145. Interview with Rosalio Salvador.
146. AHSEP-84-85/C/38877/E/31, Durán Cárdenas to DEFN, Aug. 5, 1933.
147. Interview with Davíd Chino.
148. AGN-LC/E559.1/67, Sec. Gob. to Gob. Jal., June 3, 1935.
149. AGN-LC/E/555/21, Aurelio Muñiz Vargas to Pres., June 16, 1935.
150. ARA/C/12/E/51/Doc/5994, Pedroza to GN, July 18, 1935.
151. Interview with Salvador Sánchez.
152. "Los Rebeldes," *Siglo de Torreón*, June 6, 1936.
153. Interview with Jesús Mercado.
154. AHSEP-78-79/C/38281/E/5, PM Mezquitic to Gob. Jal., Sept. 12, 1935.
155. AGN-LC/C/611/E/524/60, Agustín Carrillo Ávila, Pascual Ávila, to Pres., Oct. 1, 1935.
156. ARA/C/12/E/45/Doc/5627, "Boletín de Zacatecas," ca. Oct. 14, 1935.
157. Vaughan, *Cultural Politics*, 12.
158. AHSEP-78-79/C/38286/E/5, clipping from "Las Noticias," Sept. 18, 1935.
159. "Internado Indígena," *Nacional*, Aug. 28, 1935, 5.
160. AHSEP-78-79/C/38288/E/25, Ezequiel Haro al SEP, Aug. 25, 1933.
161. Loyo, "La empresa redentora," 121.
162. AHSEP-78-79/C/38285/E/9, Tijerina Almaguer, "Informe," Nov. 16, 1935.
163. AHSEP-78-79/C/38281/E/5, G. Ceja Torres to DEFJ, Nov. 15, 1935.
164. AHJ-G-9-935/C/11183/E/53, Eliseo Robles to Gob. Jal, Aug. 28, 1935.
165. AGN-LC/C/967/E/559.1/23, Ávila Vázquez to Pres., Oct. 29, 1935.
166. "Mejoramiento de los internados indígenas," *Nacional*, June 6, 1936, 7.
167. AGA-D/276.1/137/leg.1/SRA/RTBC/Tuxpan, Llamas Quezada, "Informe," Nov. 15, 1944.

168. AGA-D/24/1680/leg.2/CCA/Restitución/San Sebastián, Balderas, "Informe," Nov. 7, 1936.
169. "El Internado de Mexquitic," *Nacional*, Aug. 20, 1936, 15.
170. AGN-LC/C/760, JOM Zac. to Gob. Jal., Feb. 19, 1936.
171. AGN-LC/C/760, Antonio López Mendoza, Feb. 19, 1937.
172. AGN-LC/C/967/E/559.1/23, Montoya to Pres., Dec. 13, 1937.
173. AGN-LC/C/567/E/503.11/259, Bañuelos to Pres., n.d. (mid-1937).
174. AGN-LC/C/567/E/503.11/259, Pres. to Bañuelos, July 5, 1937.
175. Dawson, *Indian and Nation*, 48.
176. AGN-LC/C/567/E/503.11/259, Mijares Cosío to Pres., July 26, 1938.
177. AGA-D/24/1680/leg.2/CCA/Restitución/Santa Catarina, Mijares Cosío to Gabino Vázquez, Feb. 16, 1938.
178. Dawson, "From Models," 303–6.
179. AGN-LC/C/567/E/503.11/259, Mijares Cosío to Pres., July 26, 1938.
180. Interview with Mijares Cosío.
181. Bantjes, "Regional Dynamics," 117.
182. "Contrabando de armamento," *Siglo de Torreón*, Nov. 18, 1936.
183. Interview with Salvador Sánchez.
184. Interview with Xuturima Hernández.
185. Interview with Salvador Sánchez.
186. Interviews with Salvador Sánchez; Rosalio Salvador; Ramón Gamboa; Fernando Muñíz.
187. Interview with Fernando Muñíz.
188. Téllez Lozano, "Lozadistas, revolucionarios y cristeros," 239.
189. Fallaw, "'Anti-Priests,'" 214; Smith, *The Roots*, 247–9; AHAG-Bolaños/C/3/E/29, Arz. to Cura Valdés, March 20, 1937; Pbro Jose Quezada to Arz., March 25, 1937.
190. Smith, *The Roots*, 247–49.
191. ARA/C/12/E/49/Doc/5891, Hector Martínez to GN, Sept. 19, 1938.
192. Vela del Real, "Nuestra Tierra," *Mi Pueblo*, Mar. 1996; Enendino Escobeda.
193. AGN-LC/C/1103/E/201.5/ Emeterio Mijares Cosío to Pres., Jan. 17, 1939.
194. Radding, "Peasant Resistance," 349; Bantjes, *As if Jesus*, 134–37.
195. AGN-LC/C/567/E/503.11/259, Pres. to DA, Sept. 14, 1938.
196. AGA-D/23/242/leg.1/CCA/Dotación/San Andrés, Juan Carrillo to DA, Nov. 25, 1938.
197. AGA-D/276.1/36/leg.1/CCA/RTBC/Tuxpan, Alonso Guerrero to Jefe del Dept., Apr. 13, 1940.
198. AGA-D/276.1/98/leg.11/SRA/Trabajos Tecnicos Informativos/Sta. Catarina, Res. Pres., July 17, 1940.
199. AGA-D/276.1/98/leg.11/SRA/Trabajos Tecnicos Informativos/Sta. Catarina, Res. Pres., Aug 9, 1960.

200. AGN-LC/C/611/E/524/60, PM Bolaños to Pres., Nov. 24, 1938; AGN-DGIPS/C/109/E/18, "Informe: Puente de Camotlán," Nov. 3, 1938.
201. Knight, "Cardenismo," 105.
202. Although both Weigand and Meyer date Bautista's death to 1935 ("Role of the Huichol," 171; "La revolución en occidente," 263), Wixárika petitions show that Bautista remained active throughout 1938 (AGN-LC/C/567/E/503.11/259, Cristóbal Rodríguez et al. to Pres., Apr. 7, 1939), while an article in Monterrey's *El Porvenir* proves that he was finally killed in 1940 ("Murió en un tiroteo el rebelde Bautista," Sept. 9, 1940).
203. Interviews with Raúl Vázquez; Salvador Sánchez.
204. Interview with Salvador Sánchez.
205. Interview with Julio Robles and Antonio Candelario.
206. Interview with Raul Vázquez.
207. Interview with Xuturima Hernández.
208. Weigand, "Differential Acculturation," 14.
209. AGN-LC/C/567/E/503.11/259, José María de la Cruz to Pres., Mar. 18, 1939.
210. Téllez Lozano, "Lozadistas, revolucionarios y cristeros," 239.
211. Interview with Antonio Candelario.
212. AGA-D/23/242/leg.1/CCA/Dotación/San Andrés, Juan Carrillo to DA, Oct. 14, 1939.
213. AHSEP-84-85/C/38861/E/19, Felipe Madera to DEFN, Mar. 12, 1938.
214. AHSEP-84-85/C/38861/E/19, Espinosa to DEFN, Mar. 18, 1938.
215. AHSEP-84-85/CC/38887/E/3, Madera, "Informe," Jan. 24, 1940.
216. ARA/C/12/E/48/Doc/5775, Mora to GN, n.d. (ca. Dec. 1934).
217. Interview with Trinidad Morales.
218. AHSEP-68-69/C/37438 E/14, Prof. Filemon Alvarado to DERICI, Jan 9, 1935.
219. ARA/C/12/E/48/Doc/5775, Mora to GN, n.d. (ca. Dec. 1934).
220. Interview with Magdaleno Arrellano; see also Trinidad Morales; Arturo Soto.
221. Interview with Eulogio Ciriano; see also Evaristo Mendoza; Magdaleno Arrellano.
222. Interview with Manuel Arrellano.
223. *Ficus Crocata*, a large species of tropical fig with a stout trunk and long spreading branches.
224. Magdaleno Arrellano; see also José Flores Díaz.
225. "Francisco Sánchez," *David*, Aug. 22, 1956.
226. AHED-M/C/13/E/6, PM Mezquital to Gob. Dgo., Jan. 19, 1935.
227. AHED-M/C/13/E/6, PM Mezquital to Gob. Dgo., Jan. 1, 1935.
228. AHED-M/C/13/E/6, PM Mezquital to Gob. Dgo., Jan. 25, 1935.
229. Friedrich, *The Princes*, 89–97.
230. AHED-M/C/13/E/119, Gob. Dgo. to José María Gurrola, Apr. 29, 1935.
231. Hu-Dehart, *Yaqui Resistance*, 210–11; Rath, *Myths*, 25; Dulles, *Yesterday in Mexico*, 311–12.
232. Meyer, *La cristiada*, i, 157; Dulles, *Yesterday in Mexico*, 454.
233. AGN-LC/C/58/E/120/558, Gral. Cortés Ortiz to Pres., Mar. 20, 1935.
234. AGN-LC/C/58/E/120/558, Unknown to Pres., n.d., 1935.

235. Interview with Saturnino Solís.
236. Avitia, *El caudillo*, 305–6.
237. Ankerson, "Cedillo," 152.
238. AGN-LC/C/958/E/556.4/219, Cedillo to Pres., Jan. 13, 1935.
239. AGN-LC/C/58/E/120/558, Cortés Ortiz to Pres., Mar. 4, 1935; AGN-LC/C/58/E/120/558, Gral. Diaz González to Pres., Mar. 3, 1935; AGN-LC/C/58/E/120/558, Gral. Matías Ramos to Pres., Mar. 26, 1935.
240. Interview with Magdaleno Arrellano.
241. Interviews with Bruno Gómez and Nemesio Rodríguez; Erasmo González.
242. Interview with Felipe Salas Ramírez.
243. Bantjes, *As if Jesus*, 11.
244. Interview with Manuel Arrellano.
245. AGN-LC/C/58/E/120/558, Cortés Ortiz to Pres., Mar. 20, 1935.
246. AHED-M/C/13/E/163, Geronimo Santillán et al. to Gob. Dgo., Sept. 4, 1935.
247. AGN-LC/C/58/E/120/558, Cortés Ortiz to Pres., Mar. 20, 1935.
248. Bantjes, *As if Jesus*, 13–15.
249. Interview with Manuel Arrellano.
250. Interview with Genaro Santillán.
251. Interview with Manuel Arrellano; see also interviews with Magdaleno Arrellano; José Flores Díaz.
252. Cervantes, "Una escalofriante matanza," 20–21.
253. ARA/C/16/E/72/Doc/9328, Mora to Arrieta, Apr. 22, 1935.
254. ARA/C/12/E/48/Doc/5775, Mora to GN, n.d. (ca. Dec. 1935).
255. AGN-LC/E/120/1458, Lopez to Gral. Castro, Aug. 5, 1935; Pres. to Castro, Nov. 19, 1935.
256. "La tranquilidad en Durango se considera un hecho," *Siglo de Torreón*, Jul. 6, 1935; Avitia, *El caudillo*, 318.
257. Avitia, *El caudillo*, 318.
258. AGN-LC/C/972/E/559.4.1, PM Mezquital to Pres., Mar. 30, 1935.
259. Avitia, *El caudillo*, 318.
260. ARA/C/12/E/51/Doc/6007, Pedroza to GN, Oct. 9, 1935; ARA/C/12/E/48/Doc/5852, R. de León to GN, Nov. 13, 1935; ARA/C/12/E/49/Doc/5885, R. de León to GN, Feb. 9, 1936.
261. AGN-LC/C/207/E/404.1/177, Gabino Vázquez, "Informe," July 20, 1935.
262. Cf. Bantjes, *As if Jesus*, 78; Fallaw, *Cárdenas Compromised*.
263. Navarro, *El cardenismo*, 104.
264. AGN-LC/C/207/E/404.1/177, Pres. to Gob. Dgo., Jan. 3, 1936.
265. Navarro, *El cardenismo*, 104.
266. AGN-LC/C/207/E/404.1/177, Gabino Vázquez to Pres., Jan. 23, 1936; "Debida aclaración," *Nacional*, Jan. 21, 1936.
267. AGN-LC/C/207/E/404.1/177, Pres. to Hilario Mendía et al., July 31, 1936.

268. AGN-LC/C/606.3/E/62, Military report, May 20, 1936.
269. Avitia, *El caudillo*, 332.
270. AGN-LC/C/207/E/404.1/177, Pres. to Hilario Mendía et al., July 31, 1936.
271. Interview with Eulogio Ciriano; see also "Nueva Derrota a Una Gavilla," *Siglo de Torreón*, April 19, 1936.
272. Interview with Eulogio Ciriano.
273. Interview with Evaristo Mendoza.
274. ARA/C/13/E/54/Doc/6262, Estrada to GN, n.d. (mid-1936).
275. ARA/C/12/E/51/Doc/6026, Pedroza to GN, June 30, 1936; see also Coyle, *From Flowers*, 184; interviews with Nabor Castañeda; Eulogio Ciriano.
276. Estrada, *Rescoldo*, 257–61.
277. AGN-LC/C/606.3/62, Gral. Castro to Pres., Aug. 12, 1936.
278. Rath, "Revolutionary Citizenship," 189; Navarro, *El cardenismo*, 91–104, 242–52.
279. AGN-LC/C/606.3/62, Álvarez to Pres., Nov. 21, 1936.
280. "Rebeldes de Durango," *Siglo de Torreón*, June 6, 1936.
281. AGN-LC/C/58/E/120/558, Henríquez Guzmán to Pres., Nov. 27, 1936.
282. AGN-LC/C/58/E/120/558, Henríquez Guzmán to Pres., Nov. 27, 1936.
283. Interviews with Eulogio Ciriano; Arturo Soto; Saturnino Solís.
284. Interview with Eulogio Ciriano.
285. AGN-LC/C/58/E/120/558, Henríquez Guzmán to Pres., Nov. 27, 1936.
286. AGN-LC/C/606.3/62, Alvarez to Pres., Nov. 30, 1936.
287. Interview with Saturnino Solís.
288. Avitia, *El caudillo*, 345–47.
289. "Martínez," "Manifiesto al pueblo de Durango," in Avitia, 349–50.
290. F. Brondo to Meyer, in Meyer, *Pro domo mea*, 30; Avitia, *El caudillo*, 359–61.
291. ARA/C/12/E/49/Doc/5886, "Martínez" to GN, Apr. 1937.
292. E.g., Brunk, *Emiliano Zapata*, 224–25.
293. ARA/C/12/E/49/Doc/5886, "Martínez" to GN, Apr. 1937.
294. "Ayuda a los indígenas de Durango," *Nacional*, Jan. 26, 1937.
295. "Exploración Sanitaria en los Estados," *Nacional*, March 5, 1937.
296. "La incorporación," *Siglo de Torreón*, April 18, 1937.
297. AHED-FR/C/2/E/271, Luis Ramírez de Arellano to Henríquez Guzmán, Mar. 18, 1937.
298. AHED-FR/C/2/E/271, Henríquez Guzmán to Ramírez de Arellano, Mar. 19, 1937.
299. AGN-LC/C/555/E/21, PM Mezquital to Pres., Dec. 13, 1937.
300. AHED-FR/C/2/Sin Expediente, Enríquez, to Gob. Dgo., Feb. 28, 1937.
301. AHED-M/C/16/E/114, Gob. Dgo. to PM Mezquital, Nov. 26, 1937; see also Genaro Santillán.
302. AHED-FR/C/2/Sin Expediente, Henriquez Guzmán to Ramírez Arellano, Mar. 20, 1937.

303. AHED-FR/C/2/Sin Expediente, A. Heredia to Gob. Dgo., June 22, 1937.
304. Magdaleno Arrellano Soto.
305. AGN/-LC/C/207/E/404.1/177, Antonio Heredia to Gob. Dgo., Aug. 15, 1937.
306. ARA/C/12/E/51/Doc/6040, Froylan Diéguez to GN, June 2, 1937.
307. ARA/C/12/E/49/Doc/5887, "Martínez," "Informe," July 2, 1937.
308. Interview with Saturnino Solís.
309. Interview with Felipe Salas Ramírez.
310. ARA/C/12/E/49/Doc/5888, "Martínez," "Informe," June 1937.
311. Interview with Manuel Arrellano.
312. ARA/C/12/E/49/Doc/5888, "Martínez," "Informe," June 1937.
313. AGN-LC/C/207/E/404.1/177, PM Mezquital to Gob. Dgo., Aug. 15, 1937.
314. AHED-FR/C/2/Sin Expediente, Ramírez de Arellano to JOM Dgo., Oct. 8, 1937.
315. ARA/C/12/E/49/Doc/5890, "Martínez," "Informe," Apr. 11, 1938.
316. F. Brondo to Meyer, in Meyer, *Pro domo mea*, 30.
317. AGN-LC/C/959/E/556.7/11, Gral. Matías Ramos to Pres., Nov. 12, 1938.
318. ARA/C/12/E/49/Doc/5891, Martinez to GN, Sept. 19, 1938.
319. F. Brondo to Meyer, in Meyer, *Pro domo mea*, 30.
320. AHED-M/C/17/E/4, PM Mezquital to Gob. Dgo., Jan. 1, 1939.
321. AHED-M/C/18/E/54, PM Mezquital to Gob. Dgo., Aug. 23, 1939.
322. Interview with Manuel Arrellano.
323. Interview with Felipe Salas Ramírez.
324. AHED-M/C/18/E/54, Angél Hernández to Gob. Dgo., Apr. 20, 1939; AHED-M/C/18/E/7, Cosme Solís to Gob. Dgo., Mar. 22, 1939; AHED-M/C/18/E/54, Gob. Dgo. to Angél Hernández, Apr. 28, 1939.
325. See Smith, "Defending 'Our Beautiful Freedom,'" 146.
326. AHED-M/C/18/E/54, Ángel Hernández to Gob. Dgo., April 20, 1939.
327. AHED-M/C/18/E/54, Sec. Gral de Gob. Dgo. to Ángel Hernández, April 28, 1939.
328. AHSEP-68-69/C/37487 E/25, DEFD to DEI, Aug. 24, 1939.
329. ARA/C/12/E/51/Doc/6075, Unknown to GN, Feb. 22, 1939.
330. In an effort to counter the opposition to his rule by the right-wing UNVR veterans' organization (Schreyer, *The Rancheros*, 95), Cárdenas had cultivated ties with left-wing veterans' groups and also began "a first tentative reconciliation with organized groups of Villista veterans." In Durango, Cardenista governor Enrique Calderón also emphasized his government's ties with Villismo to win over both agraristas and conservative Villistas for whom Villa remained a hero. The leader of the latter faction, ex-Villista general (and Terrones Benítez's former rival to the state governorship) Máximo García, obtained one of two posts for state senator in 1940 (Rath, *Myths*, 158).
331. AGN-LC/C/58/E/120/558, Ávalos to Pres., Apr. 8, 1939.
332. AGN-LC/C/606.3/62, Ávalos to Pres., May 1, 1939.

333. Purnell, *Popular Movements*, 193–94; Sanz Cerrada had by now become a propagandist for the Sinarquistas (Avitia, *El Caudillo*, 359), and would later become a PAN deputy in Chihuahua (F. Brondo to Meyer, in Meyer, *Pro domo mea*, 30).
334. AGN-LC/C/58/E/120/558, Ávalos, Gral. Nicolás Fernandez, to Pres., May 27, 1939.
335. "Combate en Durango," *Siglo de Torreón*, Oct. 21, 1940.
336. "Rebeldes muertos en el E. de Durango," *Informador*, Sept. 5, 1940.
337. Walter Bishop, in Avitia, *El caudillo*, 362.
338. "Amnistía," *Siglo de Torreón*, Feb. 27, 1941, quoting letter from Velázquez to Vázquez, Feb. 8, 1941.
339. "Restitución de Tierras a los Indios de Bayacora," *Siglo de Torreón*, Feb. 26, 1939.
340. F. Campos, in Avitia, *El caudillo*, 368.
341. "Amnistía," *Siglo de Torreón*, Feb. 27, 1941.
342. C. S. Lumholtz, *Unknown Mexico*, i, xvi.
343. AGA-D/276.1/14/leg.3/Comunal/RTBC/San Pedro Ixcatán, Fausto Iriarte Luna to DA, July 25, 1943.
344. Interviews with Aurelio Cánare; Agustín Lamas.
345. Interview with Antonio Candelario.
346. Interview with Antonio Candelario.
347. Interview with Julio Robles and Antonio Candelario.
348. Interviews with Saturnino Solís; see also Manuel Arrellano.
349. Interviews with Saturnino Solís.
350. Interviews with Manuel Arrellano.
351. POEN, Gral. Juventino Espinosa, Decreto, Sept. 6, 1939.
352. POEN, Gral. Juventino Espinosa, Decreto, Mar. 15, 1940.
353. Coyle, *From Flowers*, 237.
354. Interview with Aurelio Cánare.
355. Interview with Fernando Muñíz.
356. Interview with Bruno Gómez and Nemesio Rodríguez.
357. Interview with Fernando Muñíz.
358. Coyle, *From Flowers*, 191–92.
359. Interview with Bruno Gómez and Nemesio Rodríguez.
360. AGN-AC/542.1/847, Emeterio Mijares Cosío to Pres., Feb. 4, 1943.
361. AGA-D/276.1/36/leg.1/CCA/RTBC/San Sebastián, Reps. to DA, Feb. 21, 1944.
362. AGN-AC/404.1/3381, Cenobio Sánchez, Juan González, Prof. Nabor Hurtado, to Pres., March 18, 1943.
363. AGN-AC/404.1/3381, Juan Chiu Rodríguez, Vice-PM. de Bolaños, to Pres., Feb. 26, 1943.
364. Fikes, Weigand, and García de Weigand, "Introduction," xxvii.
365. Reyes, "Pueblos Indígenas de Dgo.," 400–401.

366. AGA-BC/276.1/411/leg.1/Comunal/Restitución/Santa María Ocotán y Xoconoxtle, INI report, n.d.
367. Friedrich observed similar processes at work in Naranja after the conclusion of local agrarian reform; see *The Princes*, 136, 168.
368. Interview with Saturnino Solís.
369. F. Campos, in Avitia, *El caudillo*, 368.
370. Interview with Magdaleno Arrellano.
371. "El cristero F. Vázquez," *Siglo de Torreón*, May 21, 1945.
372. Interview with Saturnino Solís.
373. Weigand, "El papel"; Torres, *Relaciones de frontera*; Benítez, *Los indios*, ii.
374. E.g., Preciado, "Conciencia histórica," 489; Rus, "La revolución en los Altos de Chiapas," 26–27.
375. AGA-D/276.1/14/leg.3/Comunal/RTBC/San Pedro Ixcatán, Fausto Iriarte Luna to DA, July 25, 1943.

EPILOGUE

1. Wasserman, *Persistent Oligarchs*, 53; Purnell, *Popular Movements*, 150.
2. Turkey under Erdoğan and Brazil under Bolsonaro provide good examples of the centrality of schooling to recent efforts to transform societies.
3. Riley and Hobgood, "A Recent Nativistic Movement," 356.
4. Reyes, pers. comm., Apr. 2, 2014; interview with Magdaleno Arrellano.
5. Interview with Antonio Candelario.
6. Interview with Bruno Gómez and Nemesio Rodríguez.
7. Valdovinos, "Acciones e interacciones," 85.
8. Cramaussel, "Historia del poblamiento," 25–26.
9. Interviews with Saturnino Solís; Bruno Gómez and Nemesio Rodríguez.
10. Medina Miranda, "Aún no hablan," 88.
11. Riley and Hobgood, "A Recent Nativistic Movement," 357. Similar apparitions had already occurred elsewhere during the revolutionary period as expressions of religious resistance to anticlericalism and "expression[s] of ethnic defiance against mestizo interlopers" (Butler, "A Revolution in Spirit?" 13).
12. Interview with Saturnino Solís.
13. Coyle, "The Customs," 511; Reyes, "The Perpetual Return," 193.
14. Neurath, "Fricciones ontológicas," 15.
15. Interview with Antonio Candelario and Julio Robles.

BIBLIOGRAPHY

PRIMARY ARCHIVAL SOURCES

AGA (Archivo General Agraria)
AGA-BC (Ramo Bienes Comunales)
AGA-D (Ramo Delegación)
AGMJ (Archivo General de los Misioneros Josefinos)
AGN (Archivo General de la Nación)
AGN-ALR (Ramo Presidentes, Abelardo L. Rodríguez)
AGN-Censo (Censos de Población)
AGN-DGIPS (Dirección General de Investigaciones Políticas y Sociales)
AGN-G-195 (Secretaría de Gobernación, Período Revolucionario)
AGN-LC (Ramo Presidentes, Ramo Presidentes, Lázaro Cárdenas)
AGN-O-C (Ramo Presidentes, Álvaro Obregón-Plutarco Elías Calles)
AGN-POR (Ramo Presidentes, Emilio Cándido Portes-Gil)
AHAG (Archivo Histórico del Arquidiócesis de Guadalajara)
AHAG-Amatlán (Gobierno Eclesiástico: Municipios: Amatlán de Jora)
AHAG-MC (Movimiento Cristero)
AHAG-Totatiche (Gobierno Eclesiástico: Municipios: Totatiche)
AHED (Archivo Histórico del Estado de Durango)
AHED-A (Siglo XX, Administración)
AHED-AG (Siglo XX, Secretaría de Gobierno, Agricultura y Ganadería)
AHED-AR (Siglo XX, Secretaría de Gobierno, Asuntos Religiosos)

AHED-AY (Beneficencia: Ayudas)
AHED-C (Siglo XX, Secretaría de Gobierno, Correspondencia)
AHED-D (Siglo XX, Secretaría de Gobierno, Municipios: Durango)
AHED-FR (Siglo XX, Secretaría de Gobierno, Fuerzas Rurales)
AHED-HZ (Siglo XX, Secretaría de Gobierno, Municipios: Huazamota)
AHED-L (Límites)
AHED-M (Siglo XX, Secretaría de Gobierno, Municipios: Mezquital)
AHED-PN (Siglo XX, Secretaría de Gobierno, Municipios: Pueblo Nuevo)
AHED-R (Revolución)
AHJ (Archivo Histórico de Jalisco)
AHJ-G-2 (Secretaría de Gobernación-Guerra)
AHJ-G-5 (Secretaría de Gobernación-Divisiones Políticas y Territoriales)
AHJ-G-9 (Secretaría de Gobernación-Indios)
AHJ-G-12 (Secretaría de Gobernación-Correspondencia)
AHJ-G-15 (Secretaría de Gobernación-Seguridad Pública)
AHSDN (Archivo Histórico de la Secretaria de la Defensa Nacional)
AHSDN-C (Correspondecia)
AHSEP (Archivo Histórico de la Secretaria de Educación Pública)
AHSEP-42 (Departamento de Educación y Cultura Indígena)
AHSEP-45 (Departamento de Escuelas Rurales y Incorporacion Cultural Indigena)
AHSEP-68-69 (Dirección de Educación Federal Durango)
AHSEP-78-79 (Dirección de Educación Federal Jalisco)
AHSEP-84-85 (Dirección de Educación Federal Nayarit)
ARA (Archivo Aurelio Robles Acevedo)

PRIMARY PRINTED AND PUBLISHED SOURCES

GOVERNMENT BULLETINS

DOF (*Diario Oficial de la Federación*)
POED (*Periódico Oficial del Estado de Durango*)
POEJ (*Periódico Oficial del Estado de Jalisco*)
POEN (*Periódico Oficial del Estado de Nayarit*)

NEWSPAPERS

David
El Demócrata
El Eco de Nayarit

El Informador
El Nacional
El Siglo de Torreón
La Jornada
Mi Pueblo

SECONDARY SOURCES

Aguirre Beltrán, Gonzalo. *Teoría y práctica de la educación indígena*. Mexico City: SEP, 1973 [1953].

Ai Camp, Roderic. *Generals in the Palacio: The Military in Modern Mexico*. Oxford: Oxford University Press, 1992.

Aldana Rendón, Mario. *La rebelión agraria de Manuel Lozada, 1873*. Mexico City: SEP, 1983.

Alden Mason, John. "The Ceremonialism of the Tepecan Indians of Azqueltan." In *Themes of Indigenous Acculturation in Northwest Mexico*, edited by Thomas Hinton and Phil Weigand, 6–76. Tucson: University of Arizona Press, 1981.

Almada, Francisco R. *La revolución en Chihuahua*. 2 vols. Chihuahua: Talleres Gráficos de la Nación, 1964.

Alvarado Solís, Neyra P. *Atar la vida, trozar la muerte: El sistema ritual de los mexicaneros de Durango*. Morelia: Universidad Michoacana-San Nicolás de Hidalgo, 2004.

Alvarado Solís, Neyra P. *Oralidad y ritual: "El dar parte" en el xuravet de San Pedro Jícoras, Durango*. Morelia: Universidad Michoacana-San Nicolás de Hidalgo, 1996.

Alvarado Solís, Neyra P. *Los mexicaneros*. Mexico City: CDI, 2008.

Ankerson, Dudley. "Saturnino Cedillo, a Traditional Caudillo in San Luis Potosí, 1890–1938." In *Caudillo and Peasant in the Mexican Revolution*, edited by D. A. Brading, 140–68. Cambridge: Cambridge University Press, 2008.

Avitia Hernández, Antonio. *El caudillo sagrado: Historia de las rebeliones cristeras en el estado de Durango*. Mexico City: Impresos Castellanos, 2000.

Avitia Hernández, Antonio. *Los alacranes alzados*. Durango: Instituto Municipal del Arte y Cultura, 1998.

Bantjes, Adrian A. *As if Jesus Walked the Earth: Cardenismo, Sonora, and the Mexican Revolution*. Wilmington, DE: SR Books, 1998.

Bantjes, Adrian A. "The Regional Dynamics of Anticlericalism and Defanatizaction in Revolutionary Mexico." In *Faith and Impiety in Revolutionary Mexico*, edited by Matthew Butler, 111–30. New York: Palgrave Macmillan, 2007.

Bautista González, Enrique. *La guerra olvidada: La cristera en Nayarit, 1926–1929*. Guadalajara: Taller Editorial La Casa del Mago, 2008.

Becker, Marjorie. "Black and White and Color: Cardenismo and the Search for a Campesino Ideology." *Comparative Studies in Society and History* 29, no. 3 (1987): 453–65.

Benítez, Fernando. *Los indios de México*. 5 vols. Mexico City: Ediciones Era, 1968.

Bonfil Batalla, Guillermo. *México profundo*. Mexico City: SEP/CIESAS, 1987.

Boyer, Christopher R. *Political Landscapes: Forests, Conservation, and Community in Mexico*. Durham: Duke University Press, 2015.

Brading, David A. *Caudillo and Peasant in the Mexican Revolution*. Cambridge: Cambridge University Press, 1980.

Brewster, Keith. *Militarism, Ethnicity, and Politics in the Sierra Norte de Puebla, 1917–1930*. Tucson: University of Arizona Press, 2003.

Brunk, Samuel. *Emiliano Zapata: Revolution and Betrayal in Mexico*. Albuquerque: University of New Mexico Press, 1995.

Butler, Matthew. "A Revolution in Spirit? Mexico, 1910–40," In *Faith and Impiety in Revolutionary Mexico*, edited by Matthew Butler, 1–20. New York: Palgrave Macmillan, 2007.

Butler, Matthew. "The 'Liberal' Cristero: Ladislao Molina and the Cristero Rebellion in Michoacan." *Journal of Latin American Studies* 31, no. 3 (1999): 645–71.

Butler, Matthew. *Popular Piety and Political Identity in Mexico's Cristero Rebellion*. Oxford: Oxford University Press, 2004.

Butler, Matthew, ed. *Faith and Impiety in Revolutionary Mexico*. London: Institute for the Study of the Americas, 2007.

Caldera, Manuel, and Luis de la Torre, eds. *Pueblos del Viento Norte*. Guadalajara: Secretaría de Cultura de Jalisco, 1994.

Cambré, Manuel. *La guerra de tres años en Tepic*. Guadalajara: Imprenta José Cabrera, 1904.

Carroll, James. "The Smell of the White Man Is Killing Us: Education and Assimilation Among Indigenous Peoples." *U.S. Catholic Historian* 27, no. 1 (2009): 21–48.

Cerda Silva, Roberto de la. "Los coras." *Revista Mexicana de Sociología* 5, no. 1 (1943): 89–117.

Cerda Silva, Roberto de la. "Los Tepehuanes." *Revista Mexicana de Sociología* 5, no. 4 (1943): 541–67.

Cervantes, Eder U. "Una escalofriante matanza en toda la región indígena." In *Lo que hemos pasado: historias sobre la participación de los pueblos originarios en la Independencia Nacional y la Revolución Mexicana*, 20–21. Mexico City: SEP, 2012.

Chakrabarty, Dipesh. "Minority Histories, Subaltern Pasts." *Postcolonial Studies* 1, no. 1 (1998): 473–79.

Chatwin, Bruce. *The Songlines*. London: Penguin, 1988.

Clausewitz, Carl von. *On War*. Edited and translated by Michael Howard and Peter Paret. Princeton: Princeton University Press, 1984.

Coyle, Philip E. *From Flowers to Ash: Náyari History, Politics, and Violence*. Tucson: University of Arizona Press, 2001.

Coyle, Philip E. "The Customs of Our Ancestors: Cora Religious Conversion and Millennialism, 2000-1722." *Ethnohistory* 45, no. 3 (1998): 509–42.

Cramaussel, Chantal. "El fracaso de la evangelización en la Sierra Tepehuana y Pueblo Nuevo." In *Historia general del estado de Durango*, edited by Miguel Vallebueno, ii, 154–99. Durango: Universidad Juárez del Estado de Durango, 2013.

Cramaussel, Chantal. "El sistema de cargos en San Bernardino de Milpillas Chico, Durango." *Culturales* 1, no. 1 (2013): 69–106.

Cramaussel, Chantal. "Historia del poblamiento del municipio de Pueblo Nuevo, Durango." *Revista de Historia de la UJED*, no. 37 (2009): 10–36.

Cramaussel, Chantal. "Personajes de la Sierra Tepehuana: Don Calixto Contreras, el jefe de la danza en San Francisco de Lajas." *Revista de la Historia de la UJED*, no. 7 (2015): 187–92.

Cramaussel, Chantal, and Sara Ortelli, eds. *La sierra tepehuana: asentamientos y movimientos de población*. Zamora: El Colegio de Michoacán, 2006.

Curley, Robert. "Anticlericalism and Public Space in Revolutionary Jalisco." *The Americas* 65, no. 4 (2009): 511–33.

Dawson, Alexander S. *Indian and State in Revolutionary Mexico*. Tucson: University of Arizona Press, 2004.

Dawson, Alexander S. "From Models for the Nation to Model Citizens: Indigenismo and the 'Revindication' of the Mexican Indian, 1920–40." *Journal of Latin American Studies* 30, no. 2 (1998): 279–308.

Dawson, Alexander S. "'Wild Indians,' 'Mexican Gentlemen,' and the Lessons Learned in the Casa del Estudiante Indígena, 1926–1932." *The Americas* 57 no. 3, 2001: 329–61.

Deeds, Susan M. *Defiance and Deference in Mexico's Colonial North: Indians Under Spanish Rule in Nueva Vizcaya*. Austin: University of Texas Press, 2003.

Deeds, Susan M. "Los tepehuanes en misiones jesuitas. Cambios étnicos y culturales en los siglos xvii y xviii." In *La sierra tepehuana: asentamientos y movimientos de población*, edited by Chantal Cramaussel and S. Ortelli, 219–29. Zamora: El Colegio de Michoacán, 2006.

De Giuseppe, Massimo. "'El Indio Gabriel': New Religious Perspectives Among the Indigenous in Garrido Canabal's Tabasco (1927–30)." In *Faith and Impiety in Revolutionary Mexico*, edited by Matthew Butler, 225–43. New York: Palgrave Macmillan, 2007.

Dennis, Philip A. *Intervillage Conflict in Oaxaca*. New Brunswick: Rutgers University Press, 1987.

Dennis, Philip A. "The Oaxacan Village President as Political Middleman." *Ethnology* 12, no. 4 (1973): 419–27.

Diguet, Léon. *Por tierras occidentales: Entre sierras y barrancas*. Mexico City: Centro de Estudios Mexicanos y Centroamericanos, 2005.

Dulles, John W. F. *Yesterday in Mexico: A Chronicle of the Revolution, 1919–1936*. Austin: University of Texas Press, 1967.

Durin, Séverine, and Angélica Rojas Cortés. "El conflicto entre la escuela y la cultura huichola: Traslape y negociación de tiempos." *Relaciones* 101, no. 26 (2005): 149–90.

Eiss, Paul K. "Beyond the Land: Memory, Community, and the Meanings of El Pueblo in Yucatán." In *Mexico in Transition: New Perspectives on Mexican Agrarian History, 19th and 20th Centuries*, edited by Antonio Escobar Ohmstede and Matthew Butler, 511–40. Mexico City: CIESAS, 2013.

Eiss, Paul K. "Deconstructing Indians, Reconstructing Patria: Indigenous Education in Yucatan from the Porfiriato to the Mexican Revolution." *Journal of Latin American Anthropology* 9, no. 1 (2004): 119–50.

Escobar Ohmstede, Antonio, and Matthew Butler, eds. *Mexico in Transition: New Perspectives on Mexican Agrarian History, 19th and 20th Centuries*. Mexico City: CIESAS, 2013.

Estrada, Antonio, *Rescoldo: Los últimos cristeros*. Mexico City: Editorial Jus, 1961.

Fallaw, Ben. "'Anti-Priests' versus Catholic-Socialists in 1930s Campeche: Federal Teachers, Revolutionary Communes, and Anticlericalism." In *Faith and Impiety in Revolutionary Mexico*, edited by Matthew Butler, 203–23. New York: Palgrave Macmillan, 2007.

Fallaw, Ben. "Eulogio Ortiz: The Army and the Antipolitics of Postrevolutionary State Formation, 1920–1935." In *Forced Marches: Soldiers and Military Caciques in Modern Mexico*, edited by Ben Fallaw and Terry Rugeley, 172–209. Tucson: University of Arizona Press, 2012.

Fallaw, Ben. *Cárdenas Compromised: The Failure of Reform in Postrevolutionary Yucatán*. Durham: Duke University Press, 2001.

Fallaw, Ben. *Religion and State Formation in Postrevolutionary Mexico*. Durham: Duke University Press, 2013.

Fallaw, Ben, and Terry Rugeley, eds. *Forced Marches: Soldiers and Military Caciques in Modern Mexico*. Tucson: University of Arizona Press, 2012.

Fallaw, Ben, and Terry Rugeley. "Redrafting History: The Challenges of Scholarship on the Mexican Military Experience." In *Forced Marches: Soldiers and Military Caciques in Modern Mexico*, edited by Ben Fallaw and Terry Rugeley, 1–22. Tucson: University of Arizona Press, 2012.

Fernández Aceves, María. "José Guadalupe Zuno Hernández and the Revolutionary Process in Jalisco." In *State Governors in the Mexican Revolution, 1910–1952: Portraits in Conflict, Courage, and Corruption*, edited by Jürgen Buchenau and William Beezley, 95–108. Lanham: Rowman and Littlefield, 2009.

Fikes, Jay C., *Carlos Castañeda: Academic Opportunism and the Psychedelic Sixties*. Victoria: Millenia Press, 1993.

Fikes, Jay C., Philip C. Weigand, and Acelia García de Weigand. "Introduction." In Robert M. Zingg, *Huichol Mythology*, edited by Jay C. Fikes, Phil C. Weigand, and Acelia García de Weigland, xiii–xxxvi. Tucson: University of Arizona Press, 2004.

Flores Flores, Manuel, and Eliseo Flores Sánchez. *Memorias políticas de Manuel Flores Flores: La Revolución Mexicana y la Guerra Cristera en el municipio de La Yesca*. Mexico City: Arlequín Editorial, 2000.

Friedlander, Judith. *Being Indian in Hueyapan: A Study of Forced Identity in Contemporary Mexico*. New York: St. Martin's Press, 1975.

Friedlander, Judith. "The Secularization of the Cargo System: An Example from Postrevolutionary Central Mexico," *Latin American Research Review* 16, no. 2 (1981): 132–43.

Friedrich, Paul. *Agrarian Revolt in a Mexican Village*. Chicago: University of Chicago Press, 1977.

Friedrich, Paul. *The Princes of Naranja: An Essay in Anthrohistorical Method*. Austin: University of Texas Press, 1986.

Gamio, Manuel. *Forjando Patria: Pro-Nacionalismo*. Translated by Fernando Armstrong-Fumero. Boulder: University Press of Colorado, (1916) 2010.

Gamíz Olivas, Everardo. *La revolución en el estado de Durango*. Mexico City: Instituto Nacional de Estudios Historicos de la Revolución Mexicana, 1963.

Gamíz Olivas, Everardo. *Monografía de la nación tepehuana que habita en la región del sur del estado de Durango*. Mexico City: Ediciones Gámiz, 1948.

Geary, Patrick J. *Furta Sacra*. Princeton: Princeton University Press, 1978.

Gerhard, Peter. *La frontera Norte de la Nueva España*. Mexico City: UNAM, 1996.

Gillingham, Paul. "Ambiguous Missionaries: Rural Teachers and State Facades in Guerrero, 1930–1950." *Mexican Studies/Estudios Mexicanos* 22, no. 2 (2006): 331–60.

Gillingham, Paul. "Maximino's Bulls: Popular Protest after the Mexican Revolution 1940–1952." *Past and Present* 206, no. (2010): 175–211.

Gillingham, Paul. "Military Caciquismo in the PRIísta State: General Mange's Command in Veracruz." In *Forced Marches: Soldiers and Military Caciques in Modern Mexico*, edited by Ben Fallaw and Terry Rugeley, 210–37. Tucson: University of Arizona Press, 2012.

Gillingham, Paul. "The Strange Business of Memory: Relic Forgery in Latin America." *Past & Present* 206, no. 5 (2010): 199–226.

Gitlitz, John S. *Administrando justicia al margen del Estado: Las rondas campesinas de Cajamarca*. Lima: Instituto De Estudios Peruanos, 2013.

Giudicelli, Christophe. "El mestizaje en movimiento: Guerra y creación identitaria en la guerra de los tepehuanes." In *Colonización, resistencia y mestizaje en las Américas*, (siglos XVI-XX), edited by Guillaume Boccara, 105–38. Quito: Editorial Abya Yala, 2002.

Goldkind, Victor. "Class Conflict and Cacique in Chan Kom." *Southwestern Journal of Anthropology* 22, no. 4 (1966): 325–45.

Gómez Canedo, Lino. "Huicot: Antecendentes Misionales." *Estudios de Historia Novohispana* 9, no. 9 (1987): 95–145.

Gómez Santana, Laura G. "Mujeres y propiedad social en Jalisco, 1876–1924." In *Mexico in Transition: New Perspectives on Mexican Agrarian History, 19th and 20th Centuries*, edited by Antonio Escobar Ohmstede and Matthew Butler, 545–63. Mexico City: CIESAS, 2013.

González Ramos, Gildardo. *Los coras*. Mexico City: INI, 1972.

González y González, Luis. *Pueblo en vilo: Microhistoria de San José de Gracia*. Mexico City: El Colegio de México, 1968.

Goscha, Christopher. *The Penguin History of Modern Vietnam*. London: Penguin, 2016.

Gould, Jeffrey L., *To Die in This Way: Nicaraguan Indians and the Myth of Mestizaje, 1880–1965*. Durham: Duke University Press, 1998.

Gow, Peter. *An Amazonian Myth and Its History*. Oxford: Oxford University Press, 2001.

Greenberg, James B. *Blood Ties: Life and Violence in Rural Mexico*. Tucson: University of Arizona Press, 1989.

Greene, Graham. *The Lawless Roads*. London: Penguin, (1939) 2006.

Greene, Graham. *The Power and the Glory*. London: Penguin, (1940) 1991.

Grimes, Joseph E., and Thomas B. Hinton. "The Huichol and the Cora." In *Handbook of Middle American Indians: Ethnology*, edited by Evan Z. Vogt, 792–813. Austin: University of Texas Press, 1969.

Gutiérrez y Gutiérrez, José. *Mis recuerdos de la gesta cristera*. 2 vols. Guadalajara: Editorial Deli, 1975.

Hale, Charles R. *Resistance and Contradiction: Miskitu Indians and the Nicaraguan State, 1894–1987*. Stanford: Stanford University Press, 1994.

Harvey, Neil. *The Chiapas Rebellion: The Struggle for Land and Liberty*. Durham: Duke University Press, 1998.

Hamilton, Nora. *The Limits of State Autonomy*. Princeton: Princeton University Press, 1982.

Hernández Chávez, Alicia. "Lozada no muere." In *De Cantón de Tepic a Estado de Nayarit, 1810–1940*, edited by Jean Meyer, 209–19. Guadalajara: Universidad de Guadalajara, 1990.

Hinton, Thomas B. *Coras, Huichols y Tepehuanos*. Mexico City: Dirección General de Publicaciones del Consejo Nacional para la Cultura y las Artes, 1990.

Hinton, Thomas B. "Indian Acculturation in Nayarit: The Cora Response to Mestizoization." In *The Social Anthropology of Latin America: Essays in Honor of Ralph Leon Beals*, edited by Walter Goldschmidt and Harry Hoijer, 16–35. Los Angeles: University of California Press, 1970.

Hinton, Thomas B. "Pre-conquest Acculturation of the Cora." *Journal of the Arizona Archaeological and Historical Society* 37, no. 4 (1972): 161–68.

Hinton, Thomas B., and Philip C. Weigand, eds. *Themes of Indigenous Acculturation in Northwest Mexico*. Tucson: University of Arizona Press, 1981.

Hobsbawm, Eric. *Bandits*. New York: Delacorte, 1969.

Hobsbawm, Eric. "Introduction: Inventing Traditions." In *The Invention of Tradition*, edited by Eric Hobsbawm and Terence Ranger, 1–14. Cambridge: Cambridge University Press, 1983.

Hrdlička, Aleš. *Physiological and Medical Observations Among the Indians of Southwestern United States and Northern Mexico*. Washington, DC: Government Printing Office, 1908.

Hrdlička, Aleš. "The Region of the Ancient 'Chichimecs,' with Notes on the Tepecanos and the Ruin of La Quemada, Mexico." *American Anthropologist* 5, no. 3 (1903): 385–440.

Hu-Dehart, Evelyn. *Yaqui Resistance and Survival: The Struggle for Land and Autonomy, 1821–1910*. Madison: University of Wisconsin Press, 1984.

INEGI. *Estadísticas Historicas de Mexico*. 2 vols. Mexico City: INEGI, 1998.

Jáuregui, Jesús. "Del reino de Lozada y la segunda conquista de el nayarit a la revolución mexicana: La resistencia cora en el movimiento lozadeño (1853–1912)." In *Participación indígena en los procesos de Independencia y Revolución Mexicana*, edited by Rojo Leyva, Victor, José Luis Reyes Utrera, and Adrián Rangel Aguilar, 149–94. Mexico City: CDI, 2011.

Jáuregui, Jesús. *Los Coras*. Mexico City: CDI, 2004.

Jáuregui, Jesús, and Laura Magriñá. "Estudio etnohistórico acerca del origen de los mexicaneros (hablantes del náhuatl) de la Sierra Madre Occidental," *Dimensión Antropológica* 26 (September–December, 2002): 27–81.

Jáuregui, Jesús, and Jean Meyer, eds. *El Tigre de Alica: Mitos e historia de Manuel Lozada*. Mexico City: SEP-CONAFE, 1997.

Jáuregui, Jesús, and Johannes Neurath, eds. *Flechadores de estrellas: Nuevas aportaciones a la etnología de coras y huicholes*. Mexico City: INAH-Universidad de Guadalajara, 2003.

Jáuregui, Jesús, and Johannes Neurath. "La expedición de Konrad Theodor Preuss al Nayarit (1905–1907) y su contribución a la mexicanística." In *Fiesta, literatura y magia en el Nayarit: Ensayos sobre coras, huicholes y mexicaneros de Konrad Theodor Preuss*, edited by Jesús Jáuregui and Johannes Neurath, 15–60. Mexico City: Centro de Estudios Mexicanos y Centroamericanos, 1998.

Joseph, Gilbert. "Caciquismo and the Revolution: Carrillo Puerto in Yucatán." In *Caudillo and Peasant in the Mexican Revolution*, edited by D. A. Brading, 193–221. Cambridge: Cambridge University Press, 1980.

Joseph, Gilbert. "Rethinking Mexican Revolutionary Mobilization: Yucatán's Seasons of Upheaval, 1909–1915." In *Everyday Forms of State Formation: Revolution and the Negotiation of Rule in Modern Mexico*, edited by Gilbert Joseph and Daniel Nugent, 135–69. Durham: Duke University Press, 1994.

Joseph, Gilbert, and Daniel Nugent, eds. *Everyday Forms of State Formation: Revolution and the Negotiation of Rule in Modern Mexico*. Durham: Duke University Press, 1994.

Jrade, Ramon. "Inquiries into the Cristero Insurrection Against the Mexican Revolution." *Latin American Research Review* 20 no. 2 (1985): 53–69.

Katz, Friedrich. *The Life and Times of Pancho Villa*. Stanford: Stanford University Press, 1998.

Klineberg, Otto. "Notes on the Huichol." *American Anthropologist* 36, no. 3 (1934): 446–60.

Knight, Alan. "Caciquismo in Twentieth-Century Mexico." In *Caciquismo in Twentieth-Century Mexico*, edited by Alan Knight and W. G. Pansters, 3–48. London: Institute for the Study of the Americas, 2005.

Knight, Alan. "Cardenismo: Juggernaut or Jalopy?" *Journal of Latin American Studies* 26, no. 1 (1994): 43–107.

Knight, Alan. "Peasant and Caudillo." In *Caudillo and Peasant in the Mexican Revolution*, edited by D. A. Brading, 17–58. Cambridge: Cambridge University Press, 1980.

Knight, Alan. "The Mentality and Modus Operandi of Revolutionary Anticlericalism." In *Faith and Impiety in Revolutionary Mexico*, edited by Matthew Butler, 21–56. New York: Palgrave Macmillan, 2007.

Knight, Alan. *The Mexican Revolution, 1910–1920*. 2 vols. Cambridge: Cambridge University Press, 1986.

Knight, Alan. "Superstition in Mexico: From Colonial Church to Secular State." In *Religion of Fools? Superstition Past and Present*, edited by Alan Knight and Stephen Anthony Smith. Past and Present supplements, 229–70, vol.199, issue 3. Oxford: Oxford University Press, 2008.

Knight, Alan. "The Rise and Fall of Cardenismo, c.1930–c.1946." In *Mexico Since Independence*, edited by Leslie Bethell, 241–320. Cambridge: Cambridge University Press, 1991.

Knight, Alan. "War, Violence and Homicide in Modern Mexico." In *Murder and Violence in Modern Latin America*, edited by Eric A. Johnson, Ricardo Salvatore, and Pieter Spierenburg, 12–48. London: SLAS-Wiley-Blackwell, 2013.

Knight, Alan, and Wil Pansters, eds. *Caciquismo in Twentieth-Century Mexico*. London: Institute for the Study of the Americas, 2005.

Kourí, Emilio. *A Pueblo Divided: Business, Property, and Community in Papantla, Mexico*. Stanford: Stanford University Press, 2004.

Kropotkin, Peter. *Memoirs of a Revolutionist*. 2 vols. London: Smith, Elder, 1899.

LeRoy Ladurie, Emmanuel. *Carnival: A People's Uprising at Romans, 1579–1580*. Translated by Mary Feeney. London: Scolar Press, 1980.

Levi-Strauss, Claude. *Tristes Tropiques*. London: Penguin, (1942) 1976.

Lewis, Stephen E. *The Ambivalent Revolution: Forging State and Nation in Chiapas, 1910–1945*. Albuquerque: University of New Mexico, 2005.

Liffman, Paul M. *Huichol Territory and the Mexican Nation: Indigenous Ritual, Land Conflict, and Sovereignty Claims*. Tucson: University of Arizona Press, 2011.

Lira, Enrique, and Gustavo Villanueva Bazán, eds. *La constitución del os cristeros y otros documentos*. Mexico: UNAM/CESU, 2005.

Lira Larios, Regina, "De buenos mexicanos, cristianos, soldados y valientes: Pueblos coras y huicholes en la configuración de una región, 1840 a 1880." *Historia mexicana* 69, no. 3 (Ene-Marzo 2020): 1091–1142.

Lomnitz-Adler, Claudio. *Exits from the Labyrinth: Culture and Ideology in the Mexican National Space*. Berkeley: University of California Press, 1992.

López Díaz, Pedro. *Fuego en Nayarit*. Guadalajara: Editorial Gráfica, 1957.

Loyo, Engracia. "La empresa redentora: La Casa del Estudiante Indígena." *Historia Mexicana* 46, no. 1 (1996): 99–131.

Loyo, Engracia. "Los centros de educación indígena y su papel en el medio rural." In *Educación rural e indígena en Iberoamérica*, edited by Pilar Gonzalbo, 139–59. Mexico City: El Colegio de Mexico City, 1996.

Loyo, Engracia. *Para entender el Sistema Educativo*. Mexico City: Nostra Ediciones, 2010.

Lozada, Manuel. "Plan Libertador proclamado en la sierra de Álica por los pueblos de Nayarit" (originally published Jan. 17, 1873). In *Las rebeliones campesinas en México, 1819-1906*, edited by Leticia Reina, 223–28. Mexico City: Siglo Veintiuno, 1988.

Lumholtz, Carl S. *Unknown Mexico*. 2 vols. New York: Scriber and Sons, 1902.

Magriñá, Laura. *Los Coras entre 1531 y 1722: ¿Indios de Guerra o de Paz?* Mexico City: INAH, 2002.

Mallón, Florencia E. "Reflections on the Ruins: Everyday Forms of State Formation in Nineteenth-Century Mexico." In *Everyday Forms of State Formation: Revolution and the Negotiation of Rule in Modern Mexico*, edited by Gilbert Joseph and Daniel Nugent, 69–106. Durham: Duke University Press, 1994.

Marak, Andrae M. "The Failed Assimilation of the Tarahumara in Postrevolutionary Mexico." *Journal of the Southwest* 45, no. 3 (2003): 411–35.

Medina Miranda, Héctor. "'Aún no hablan': Varas de mando y fundación de comunidades huicholas en Durango." *Dimensión Antropológica* 12, no. 34 (2005): 87–105.

Menéndez Reyes, Miguel Ángel. *Nayar*. Mexico City: Editorial Zamná, 1940.

Meyer, Jean. *De Cantón de Tepic a Estado de Nayarit, 1810–1940*. Guadalajara: Universidad de Guadalajara, 1990.

Meyer, Jean. "El reino de Lozada en Tepic." In *Esperando a Lozada*, edited by Jean Meyer. 235–56. Zamora: El Colegio de Michoacán, 1984.

Meyer, Jean, ed. *Esperando a Lozada*. Zamora: El Colegio de Michoacán, 1984.

Meyer, Jean. "Historia del reparto agrario en Nayarit, 1915–1934." *Revista Mexicana de Sociología* 51, no. 2 (1989): 237–46.

Meyer, Jean. *La cristiada*. 3 vols. Mexico City: Siglo Veintiuno, 1974.

Meyer, Jean. *Manuel Lozada: El Tigre de Álica, general, revolucionario, rebelde*. Mexico City: Editorial Tusquets, 2015.

Meyer, Jean. *Pro domo mea: 'La Cristiada' a la distancia*. Mexico City: Siglo Veintiuno, 2004.

Meyer, Jean. "La revolución en occidente: el caso especial de los huicholes." In *Los Huicholes: Documentos históricos*, edited by Beatriz Rojas, 259–63. Mexico City: CIESAS, 1992.

Meyer, Jean. "Religious Conflict and Catholic Resistance in 1930s Oaxaca." In *Faith and Impiety in Revolutionary Mexico*, edited by Matthew Butler, 185–202. New York: Palgrave Macmillan, 2007.

Meyer, Jean. "Review of Matthew Butler, 'Popular Piety and Political Identity in Mexico's Cristero Rebellion. Michoacan, 1927–1929." *Historia Mexicana* 54, no. 4 (2005): 1242–49.

Meza Aguirre, Ramón. *Nayarit Memoria Oral: Cachirul, cabalgando con Lozada*. Tepic: Universidad Autónoma de Nayarit, 1996.

Michel Pimienta, Zenaido. *Episodios históricos de la educación en Jalisco*. Guadalajara: Talleres Vera, 1960.

Miklian, Jason. "The Purification Hunt: The Salwa Judum Counterinsurgency in Chhattisgarh, India." *Dialectical Anthropology* 33, no. 3/4 (2009): 441–59.

Morris, Nathaniel. "'Between Two Fires: Mayangna Indians in Post-Revolutionary Nicaragua, 1979–1990." *Bulletin of Latin American Research* 33, no. 2 (2014): 203–18.

Morris, Nathaniel. "¿'Forjando Patria'? Indigenismo, agrarismo, y el ocaso de los vínculos intercomunales coras en la Sierra del Nayar." *Relaciones* 39, no. 156 (2018): 13–48.

Myerhoff, Barbara G. *Peyote Hunt: The Sacred Journey of the Huichol Indians*. Ithaca: Cornell University Press, 1976.

Naranjo, Francisco. *Diccionario biográfico revolucionario*. Mexico City: Imprenta Editorial Cosmos, 1935.

Navarro Valdez, Pavel L. *El cardenismo en Durango: Historia y política regional, 1934–40*. Durango: ICED, 2005.

Neurath, Johannes. "Ambivalencias del don y de poder en el sistema político ritual wixarika." In *Los Pueblos Amerindios más allá del estado*, edited by Berenice Alcántara Rojas and Federico Navarrete Linares, 117–43. Mexico City: UNAM, 2011.

Neurath, Johannes. *Las fiestas de la casa grande: Procesos rituales, cosmovisión y estructura social en una comunidad huichola*. Mexico City: CONACULTA-INAH, 2002.

Neurath, Johannes. "Fricciones ontológicas en las colaboraciones entre huicholes y ambientalistas." *Relaciones* 39, no. 156 (2018): 167–94.

Neurath, Johannes, and Donald Bahr. "Cosmogonic Myths, Ritual Groups, and Initiation: Toward a New Comparative Ethnology of the Gran Nayar and the Southwest of the U.S." *Journal of the Southwest* 47, no. 4 (2005): 571–614.

Nugent, Daniel. *Spent Cartridges of Revolution: An Anthropological History of Namiquipa, Chihuahua*. Chicago: University of Chicago Press, 1993.

Nugent, Daniel, and Ana María Alonso. "Multiple Selective Traditions in Agrarian Reform and Agrarian Struggle: Popular Culture and State Formation in the Ejido of Namiquipa. Chihuahua." In *Everyday Forms of State Formation: Revolution and the Negotiation of Rule in Modern Mexico*, edited by Gilbert Joseph and Daniel Nugent, 207–46. Durham: Duke University Press, 1994.

Orozco y Berra, Manuel. *Geografía de las lenguas y carta etnográfica de México: precedidas de un ensayo de clasificación de las mismas lenguas y de apuntes para las inmigraciones de las tribus*. Mexico City: J.M. Andrade y F. Escalante, 1864.

Osnaya Velázquez, Salvador. *Los misioneros josefinos e la Diócesis de Zacatecas: Sierra del Nayar y Santuario de Plateros (1901–1922)*. Mexico City: Ediciones Familia Josefina, 2007.

Otis, George. "Clasificación y aprovechamiento del paisaje entre los coras." In *Flechadores de estrellas: Nuevas aportaciones a la etnología de coras y huicholes*, edited by Jesús Jáuregui and Johannes Neurath, 133–42. Mexico City: INAH-Universidad de Guadalajara, 2003.

Pennington, Campbell W. *Tepehuan of Chihuahua: Their Material Culture*. Salt Lake City: University of Utah Press, 1969.

Pérez González, Julio. *Ensayo estadístico y geográfico de Territorio de Tepic*. Tepic: Imprimador de Retes, 1894.

Plan Lerma. *Operacion huicot: asistencia técnica*. Guadalajara: Poder Ejecutivo Federal, 1966.

Preciado Zamora, Julia. "Conciencia histórica y reforma agraria: el Estado mexicano y los indígenas de Suchitlán, Colima." In *Mexico in Transition: New Perspectives on Mexican Agrarian History, 19th and 20th Centuries*, edited by Antonio Escobar Ohmstede and Matthew Butler, 485–510. Mexico City: CIESAS, 2013.

Preuss, Konrad T. *Fiesta, literatura y magia en el Nayarit*. Edited by Jesús Jáuregui and Johannes Neurath. Mexico City: Centro de Estudios Mexicanos y Centroamericanos, 1998.

Puente Lutteroth, María. *Movimiento Cristera: una pluralidad desconocida*. Mexico City: Editorial Progreso, 2002.

Purnell, Jennie. *Popular Movements and State Formation in Revolutionary Mexico: The Agraristas and Cristeros of Michoacán*. Durham: Duke University Press, 1999.

Quevedo y Zuvieta, Salvador. *México: Recuerdos de un emigrado*. Madrid: Estudio Tipográfico de los Sucesores de Rivadeneyra, 1883.

Raby, D. L. "Los maestros rurales y los conflictos sociales en México, 1931–1940." *Historia Mexicana* 18, no. 2 (1968): 190–226.

Radding, Cynthia. "Peasant Resistance on the Yaqui Delta: An Historical Inquiry into the Meaning of Ethnicity." *Journal of the Southwest* 31, no. 3 (1989): 330–61.

Rangel Guzmán, Efraín. *Imágenes e imaginarios: Construcción de la región cultural de Nuestra Señora de Huajicori*. Zamora: El Colegio de Michoacán, 2012.

Rangel Guzmán, Efraín, and Jorge L. Marín García. "Desplazamientos territoriales y nuevos asentamientos tepehuanes." *Relaciones*, no. 137 (2014): 149–78.

Rath, Thomas G. *Myths of Demilitarization in Postrevolutionary Mexico, 1920–1960*. Chapel Hill: University of North Carolina Press, 2013.

Rath, Thomas G. "Revolutionary Citizenship Against Institutional Inertia: Cardenismo and the Mexican Army, 1934–1940." In *Forced Marches: Soldiers and Military Caciques in Modern Mexico*, edited by Ben Fallaw and Terry Rugeley, 507–32. Tucson: University of Arizona Press, 2012.

Reichel-Dolmatoff, Alicia, and Gerardo Reichel-Dolmatoff. *The People of Aritama. The Cultural Personality of a Colombian Mestizo Village*. Chicago: University of Chicago Press, 1961.

Reyes Flores, Elpidio, ed. *Dhi u'uan na bix aixim mi tu ua'ñix o'dam ki'n* (Libro de literature en lengua tepehuana Durango). Mexico City: SEP, 2003. (Relevant sections kindly translated into Spanish for me by the wonderful Selene Galindo Cumplido.)

Reyes Valdez, J. Antonio. "La familia del maíz: Prácticas agrícolas y reproducción social entre los tepehuanes de Durango." *Memoria bio-cultural en las regiones indígenas de México*. Mexico City: INAH, 2015.

Reyes Valdez, J. Antonio. *Los que están benditos: el mitote comunal de los tepehuanes de Santa María de Ocotán, Durango*. Mexico City: INAH, 2006.

Riley, Carroll L. "Los tepehuanes del sur y los tepecanos." In *Coras, Huichols y Tepehuanos*, edited by Thomas B. Hinton, 127–36. Mexico City: Dirección General de Publicaciones del Consejo Nacional para la Cultura y las Artes, 1990.

Riley, Carroll L., and John Hobgood. "A Recent Nativistic Movement among the Southern Tepehuan Indians." *Southwestern Journal of Anthropology* 15, no. 4 (1959): 355–60.

Rivard, Robert. *Trail of Feathers: Searching for Philip True*. New York: Public Affairs, 2005.

Rockwell, Elsie. "Schools of the Revolution: Enacting and Contesting State Forms in Tlaxcala, 1910–1930." In *Everyday Forms of State Formation: Revolution and the Negotiation of Rule in Modern Mexico*, edited by Gilbert Joseph and Daniel Nugent, 170–246. Durham: Duke University Press, 1994.

Rojas, Beatriz. *Huicholes: Documentos históricos*. Mexico City: INI, 1992.

Rojas, Beatriz. *Los huicholes en la historia*. Mexico City: Centro de Estudios Mexicanos y Centroamericanos, 1993.

Rojo Leyva, Víctor, José Reyes Utrera, and Adrián Rangel Aguilar, eds. *Participación indígena en los procesos de Independencia y Revolución Mexicana*. Mexico City: CDI, 2011.

Rosa Calleros, Asiano de la. *Historia de la política y de la justicia del tepehuano del Mezquital, Durango*. Mexico City: CDI, 2003.

Rosebery, William. "Hegemony and the Language of Contention." In *Everyday Forms of State Formation: Revolution and the Negotiation of Rule in Modern Mexico*, edited by Gilbert Joseph and Daniel Nugent, 355–66. Durham: Duke University Press, 1994.

Rouaix, Pastor. *Diccionario geográfico, histórico y biográfico del estado de Durango*. Mexico City: Instituto Panamerico de Geografía e Historia, 1946.

Rubín, Ramón. *La bruma lo vuelve azul*. Mexico City: Fondo de Cultura Economica, 1954.

Rugeley, Terry. *Of Wonders and Wise Men: Religion and Popular Culture in Southeast Mexico, 1800–1876*. Austin: University of Texas Press, 2001.

Rugeley, Terry. *Yucatán's Maya Peasantry and the Origins of the Caste War*. Austin: University of Texas Press, 1996.

Rulfo, Juan. "Valentín de la Sierra: Historia de un mito." *Relaciones*, no. 25 (1986): 157–64.

Rus, Jan. "Revoluciones contenidas: El pueblo indígena y la lucha por los Altos de Chiapas, 1910–1925." *Mesoamérica*, no. 46 (2004): 57–85.

Rus, Jan. "The 'Caste War of 1869' from the Indians' Perspective: A Challenge for Ethnohistory." *Memorias del Segundo Coloquio Internacional de Mayistas*, 2 Mexico City: Centro de Estudios Mayas, UNAM, 1989.

Rus, Jan. "The 'Comunidad Revolucionaria Institucional': The Subversion of Native Government in Highland Chiapas, 1936–1968." In *Everyday Forms of State Formation: Revolution and the Negotiation of Rule in Modern Mexico*, edited by Gilbert Joseph and Daniel Nugent, 265–300. Durham: Duke University Press, 1994.

Rus, Jan, and Robert Wasserstrom. "Civil Religious Hierarchies in Central Chiapas: A Critical Perspective," *American Ethnologist* 7, no. 3 (1980): 466–78.

Samaniego, Marco A. "La revolución mexicana en Baja California: maderismo, magonismo, filibusterismo y la pequeña revuelta local." *Historia Mexicana* 56, no. 4 (2007): 1201–62.

Sánchez Martínez, Jesús M. *A contra corriente: Compendio*. Guadalajara: Palibrio, 2011.

Sánchez Olmedo, José G. *Etnografía de la Sierra Madre: tepehuanes y mexicaneros*. Mexico City: SEP-INAH, 1980.

Santoscoy, Alberto. *Nayarit: Colección de documentos, inéditos, historicos y etnograficos, acerca de la Sierra de ese Nombre*. Guadalajara: Tipo-Lit. y Enc. de J. Maria Yguíniz, 1899.

Schaefer, Stacey B., and Peter T. Furst, eds. *People of the Peyote: Huichol Indian History, Religion, and Survival*. Albuquerque: University of New Mexico Press, 1997.

Schryer, Frans J. *The Rancheros of Pisaflores: The History of a Peasant Bourgeoisie in Twentieth-Century Mexico*. Toronto: University of Toronto Press, 1980.

Scott, James C. "Patron-Client Politics and Political Change in Southeast Asia." *The American Political Science Review* 66, no. 1 (1972): 91–113.

Scott, James C. *Seeing Like a State: How Certain Schemes to Improve the Human Condition Have Failed*. New Haven: Yale University Press, 1998.

Scott, James C. *The Art of Not Being Governed: An Anarchist History of Upland Southeast Asia*. New Haven: Yale University Press, 2009.

Scott, James C. *Weapons of the Weak: Everyday Forms of Peasant Resistance*. New Haven: Yale University Press, 1986.

Segalla, Spencer. *The Moroccan Soul: French Education, Colonial Ethnology, and Muslim Resistance, 1912–1956*. Lincoln: University of Nebraska Press, 2009.

Shadow, Robert D. "Production, Social Identity, and Agrarian Struggle Among the Tepecano Indians of Northern Jalisco." In *Ejidos and Regions of Refuge in Northwest Mexico*, edited by Ross Crumrine and Philip C. Weigand, 39–46. Tucson: University of Arizona Press, 1987.

Shadow, Robert D. *Tierra, trabajo y ganado en la región norte de Jalisco: una historia agraria*. Zamora: El Colegio de Michoacán, 2002.

Shadow, Robert D., and María Rodríguez Shadow. "Religión, economía y política en la rebelión cristera: el caso de los gobernistas de Villa Guerrero." *Historia Mexicana* 43, no. 4 (1994): 657–99.

Shelton, Anthony. "Huichol Natural Philosophy." *Cosmos: Yearbook of the Traditional Cosmology Society*, iv, 339–54. Edinburgh: Edinburgh University Press, 1988.

Shelton, Anthony. "The Recollection of Times Past: Memory and Event in Huichol Narrative." *History and Anthropology* 2, no. 2 (1986): 355–78.

Simpson, Eyler N. *The Ejido: Mexico's Way Out*. Chapel Hill: University of North Carolina Press, 1937.

Smith, Benjamin T. "Defending 'Our Beautiful Freedom': State Formation and Local Autonomy in Oaxaca, 1930–1940." *Mexican Studies/Estudios Mexicanos* 23, no. 1 (2007): 125–53.

Smith, Benjamin T. "Heliodoro Charis Castro and the Soldiers of Juchitán: Indigenous Militarism, Local Rule, and the Mexican State." In *Forced Marches: Soldiers and Military Caciques in Modern Mexico*, edited by Ben Fallaw and Terry Rugeley, 110–35. Tucson: University of Arizona Press, 2012.

Smith, Benjamin T. *Pistoleros and Popular Movements: The Politics of State Formation in Postrevolutionary Oaxaca*. Lincoln: University of Nebraska Press, 2009.

Smith, Benjamin T. *The Roots of Conservatism: Catholicism, Society, and Politics in the Mixteca Baja, 1750–1962*. Albuquerque: University of New Mexico Press, 2012.

Starn, Orin. *Nightwatch: The Politics of Protest in the Andes*. Durham: Duke University Press, 1999.

Starr, Frederick. *Notes Upon the Ethnography of Southern Mexico*. 2 vols. Proceedings of the Davenport Academy of Sciences, 1902.

Stauffer, Brian A. "Community, Identity, and the Limits of Liberal State Formation in Michoacán's Coastal Sierra: Coalcomán, 1869–1940." In *Mexico in Transition: New Perspectives on Mexican Agrarian History, 19th and 20th Centuries*, edited by Antonio Escobar Ohmstede and Matthew Butler, 149–80. Mexico City: CIESAS, 2013.

Taylor, William B. *Drinking, Homicide, and Rebellion in Colonial Mexican Villages*. Stanford: Stanford University Press, 1979.

Téllez Lozano, Víctor M. "Lozadistas, revolucionarios y cristeros: movimientos armados y reorganización territorial entre los huicholes." In *Participación indígena en los procesos de Independencia y Revolución Mexicana*, edited by Leyva, Victor, José Luis Reyes Utrera, and Adrián Rangel Aguilar, 225–48. Mexico City: CDI, 2011.

Thompson, Edward P. "Time, Work-Discipline, and Industrial Capitalism." *Past and Present*, no. 38 (1967): 56–97.

Thord-Gray, Ivor. *Gringo Rebel: Mexico 1913–1914*. Coral Gables: University of Miami Press, 1960.

Thucydides. *The History of the Peloponnesian War*. Loeb Classical Library. Cambridge: Harvard University Press, 1919.

Tobler, Hans-Werner. "Las Paradojas Del Ejército Revolucionario: Su Papel Social En La Reforma Agraria Mexicana, 1920–1935." *Historia Mexicana* 21, no. 1 (1971): 38–79.

Torre, Luis de la. *1926: Ecos de la cristiada*. Zapopan: Amat Editorial, 2008.

Torres Contreras, J. Jesús. *Relaciones de frontera entre los huicholes y sus vecinos mestizos: Santa Catarina y Huejuquilla el Alto*. Zapopan: Colegio de Jalisco, 2009.

Tuck, Jim. *The Holy War in Los Altos: A Regional Analysis of Mexico's Cristero Rebellion*. Tucson: University of Arizona Press, 1982.

Torres Trueba, Henry. "Nahuat Factionalism." *Ethnology* 12, no. 4 (1973): 463–74.

Valadés, José C. *Rafael Buelna: las caballerías de la revolución*. Culiacán: Universidad Autónoma de Sinaloa, 1932.

Valdovinos Alba, Margarita. "Acciones e interacciones en el sistema normativo cora." In *Sistemas normativos indígenas huichol, cora, tepehuano y mexicanero*, edited by Alvarado Solís, 77–134. Mexico City: CDI, 2009.

Valdovinos Alba, Margarita. "Los mitotes y sus cantos: las transformaciones de las prácticas culturales y de la lengua en dos comunidades coras." *Dimensión Antropológica*, no. 34 (2005): 67–86.

Van Young, Eric. "Millennium on the Northern Marches: The Mad Messiah of Durango and Popular Rebellion in Mexico, 1800–1815." *Comparative Studies in Society and History* 28, no. 3 (1986): 385–413.

Vaughan, Mary K. *The State, Education, and Social Class in Mexico, 1880–1928*. DeKalb: Northern Illinois University Press, 1982.

Vaughan, Mary K. *Cultural Politics in Revolution: Teachers, Peasants, and Schools in Mexico, 1910–1940*. Tucson: University of Arizona Press, 1997.

Walsham, Alexandra. "Introduction: Relics and Remains." *Past and Present* 1, no. 206 (2010): 9–36.

Wasserman, Mark. *Persistent Oligarchs: Elites and Politics in Chihuahua, Mexico 1910–1940*. Durham: Duke University Press, 1993.

Wasserman, Mark. *Pesos and Politics. Business, Elites, Foreigners, and Government in Mexico, 1854–1940*. Redwood, CA: Stanford University Press, 2015.

Weber, Max. *On Charisma and Institution Building*. Edited by Shmuel N. Eisenstadt. Chicago: University of Chicago Press, 1968.

Weigand, Philip C. "Differential Acculturation Among the Huichol Indians." In *Themes of Indigenous Acculturation in Northwest Mexico*, edited by Thomas B. Hinton and Philip C. Weigand, 9–21. Tucson: University of Arizona Press, 1981.

Weigand, Philip C. "El papel de los indios huicholes en las revoluciones del Occidente de México." In *Ensayos sobre el Gran Nayar. Entre coras, huicholes y tepehuanos*, edited by Philip C. Weigand, 121–30. Mexico City: CEMC-INI, 1992.

Weigand, Philip C. "Review of Meyer, 'La cristiada.'" *American Anthropologist* 80, no. 2 (1978): 432–33.

Weigand, Philip C. "Role of the Huichol Indians in the Revolutions of Western Mexico." In *Revolution in the Americas*, edited by Lewis Tambs, 167–76. Proceedings of the Pacific Coast Council on Latin American Studies, 1977.

Weigand, Philip C., and Alicia García de Weigand. "Huichol Society Before the Arrival of the Spanish." *Journal of the Southwest* 42, no. 1 (2000): 12–36.

Wickham-Crowley, Timothy P. *Exploring Revolution: Essays on Latin American Insurgency and Revolutionary Theory*. New York: M. E. Sharpe, 1991.

Willett, Elizabeth R. "The Dual Festival System of the Southern Tepehuan of Mexico." *Journal of the Southwest* 38, no. 2 (1996): 197–213.

Wolf, Eric R. *Europe and the People Without History*. Berkeley: University of California Press, 1982.

Woolford, Andrew. *This Benevolent Experiment: Indigenous Boarding Schools, Genocide, and Redress in Canada and the United States*. Lincoln: University of Nebraska Press, 2015.

Wright-Rios, Edgar. "A Revolution in Local Catholicism? Oaxaca, 1928–34." In *Faith and Impiety in Revolutionary Mexico*, edited by Matthew Butler, 243–60. New York: Palgrave Macmillan, 2007.

Zingg, Robert M. *Huichol Mythology*. Edited by Jay C. Fikes, Philip C. Weigand, and Alicia García de Weigand. Tucson: University of Arizona Press, 2004.

Zingg, Robert M. *Los huicholes: una tribu de artistas*. 2 vols. Mexico City: INI, 1982.

UNPUBLISHED THESES AND PAPERS

Chávez Gradilla, Néstor. "Porfirio Mallorquin: El Pillaco." Unpublished manuscript, author's own copy, 2015. PDF.

Fikes, Jay C. "Transcription of Interview with 'Serratos': An Anonymous Huichol Shaman." Pers. comm., Dec. 3, 2013.

Güereca Durán, Raquel E. "Las milicias de indios flecheros en la nueva españa, siglos xvi-xviii." Master's thesis, Universidad Nacional Autónoma de México, 2013.

Lewis, Stephen E. "A 'Collective Psychological Experiment' for the Mexican Nation: The Success and Failure of the Casa del Estudiante Indígena, 1926–1932." Paper presented at the Rocky Mountain Council for Latin American Studies, 1999.

Reyes Valdez, J. Antonio. "Their Gods Our Customs: Native Catholic Practices Among the Tepehuan People of Northern Mexico." Presentation at University of St. Andrews, 2014.

Reyes Valdez, J. Antonio. "The Perpetual Return of the Ancestors: An Ethnographic Account of the Southern Tepehuan of Mexico and their Deities." PhD thesis, University of St. Andrews, 2015.

Salazar Martínez, María de Lourdes. "Migración y jornaleros agrícolas en San Pedro Jícoras, Durango." Bachelor's thesis, Escuela Nacional de Antropología y Historia, Mexico, 2007.

Van Oosterhout, Aaron. "Popular Conservatism in Mexico: Religion, Land, and Popular Politics in Nayarit and Querétaro, 1750–1873." PhD diss., Michigan State University, 2014.

Walker, David W. "The Villista Legacy and Agrarian Radicalism in Eastern Durango, Mexico, 1913–1930." Paper presented at the Rocky Mountain Council for Latin American Studies, 1995.

Weigand, Philip C. "Co-operative Labor Groups in Subsistence Activities Among the Huichol Indians of San Sebastián Teponahuastlán." PhD thesis, Southern Illinois University, 1970.

ONLINE RESOURCES

CONAPO, *Indices de marginacion por entidad federativa y municipio (2010)*. Accessed August 14, 2014. http://www.conapo.gob.mx/es/CONAPO/Indices_de_Marginacion_2010_por_entidad_federativa_y_municipio.

Davila, René. "General Francisco de Santiago Villegas." *Colotlán en llamas*. Accessed July 29, 2011. http://colotlanenllamas.blogspot.mx/.

Durán, C. 'Presentarán investigación sobre el movimiento cristero en Nayarit.' *La jornada de Guerrero*. Accessed March 23, 2013. http://www1.lajornadaguerrero.com.mx/2009/01/26/index.php?section=cultura&article=011n1cul.

"Indios Coras Baten a los Rebeldes: En Nayarit Los Nativos Luchan Por Que Vuelva La Paz." *El Fronterizo*. Accessed Jan. 7, 2013. http://content.library.arizona.edu/cdm/ref/collection/p15399coll11/id/95.

"México matrimonios 1570–1950: Damazo Barraza y Nieves Valdes, 20 June 1907." Accessed Oct. 10, 2014. https://familysearch.org/pal:/MM9.1.1/ND5K-JYH.

Negrin, Juan. "Recent History." Accessed Feb. 15, 2012. wixarika.mediapark.net/en/assets/pdf/RecentHistory.pdf.

INTERVIEWS

Arrellano, Manuel, Santiago Teneraca, Durango, 23 Apr. 2015

Arrellano Soto, Magdaleno, Santiago Teneraca, Durango, 22 Apr. 2015

Bautista, Gilberto, San Sebastián, Jalisco, 9 Sept. 2014

Cánare, Aurelio, Jesús María, Nayarit, 26 Oct. 2013

Candelario, Antonio, Las Latas (anexo of Santa Catarina Cuexcomatitlán), Jalisco, 14 Apr. 2015

Castañeda Lemús, Nabor, Santa Teresa, Nayarit, 26 Oct. 2012 (trans. Andrés Castañeda)

Chino Carrillo, David, Tuxpan de Bolaños, Jalisco, 21 Mar. 2015

Ciriano Flores, Eulogio, Santa María Ocotán, Durango, 9 Nov. 2012

Contreras, Candido, Piedra de la Iglesia, (anexo of Jesús María), Nayarit, 28 Oct. 2013

de la Cruz Gutiérrez, Basilio, San Francisco de Ocotán, Durango, 29 Apr. 2015

de la Cruz Ramírez, Pedro, San Francisco de Ocotán, Durango, 29 Apr. 2015

Escobeda Mejía, Enendino, Arroyo de Santiago, Nayarit, 27 Oct. 2013

Flores Díaz, José, Santiago Teneraca, Durango, 21 Apr. 2015

Gamboa, Ramón, Huajimic, Nayarit, 18 Mar. 2015

Gómez Estrada, Bruno, Santa Teresa, Nayarit 3 Nov. 2013

Gómez Rosales, Francisco, and Alberto Casas Barrada, Pochotitán, Nayarit, 4 Feb. 2015

González, Erasmo, Presidio de los Reyes (anexo of San Pedro Ixcatán), Nayarit, 7 Apr. 2014

González, Leocadio, Puente de Camotlán, Nayarit, 20 Mar. 2015

Hernández García, Emelia (Xuturima), Nueva Colonia (anexo of Santa Catarina Cuexcomatitlán), Jalisco, 13 Apr. 2015

Lamas, Agustín, Presidio de los Reyes (anexo of San Pedro Ixcatán), Nayarit, 7 Apr. 2014

Mejía Rivera, Juventino, Arroyo de Santiago (anexo of Jesús María), Nayarit, 27 Oct. 2013

Mendoza Calleros, Evaristo, La Cebolleta (anexo of Santa María Ocotán), Durango, 12 Nov. 2012

Mercado González, Jesús, Tuxpan de Bolaños, Jalisco, 20 Feb. 2014

Montellano, Mauricio, San Andrés Cohamiata, Jalisco, 25 Mar. 2015

Morales Rodríguez, Trinidad, Santa María Ocotán, Durango, 8 Nov. 2012

Muñíz Rafael, Fernando, San Francisco de Paula, Nayarit, 22 Oct. 2013

Muñoz Estrada, Félix, Huazamota, Durango, 3 May 2015

Ortega, Santiago, Huazamota, Durango, 1 May 2015

Ramírez, Gonzalo, Santa Teresa, Nayarit, 26 Oct. 2012

Robles Robles, Julio, Las Latas (anexo of Santa Catarina Cuexcomatitlán), Jalisco, 14 Apr. 2015

Rodríguez Rodríguez, Nemesio, Santa Teresa, Nayarit, 3 Nov. 2013

Salas García, Felipe, San Lucas de Jalpa, Durango, 2 May 2015

Salas Ramírez, Felipe, Yonora, Durango, 25 Apr. 2015

Salvador Carrillo, Rosalio, San Miguel Huastita (anexo of San Andrés Cohamiata), Jalisco, 14 Feb. 2014

Sánchez, Salvador, Tuxpan de Bolaños, Jalisco, 21 Mar. 2015

Sánchez Lovato, Filiberto, San Juan Corapan, Nayarit, 5 Apr. 2014

Sánchez Lovato, Filiberto, Sandalio Sánchez Chávez, Celestino Lamas Chávez, San Juan Corapan, Nayarit, 4 Apr. 2014

Santillán Carrillo, Genaro, Santiago Teneraca, Durango, 21 Apr. 2015

Serio de la Cruz, José Guadalupe, San Sebastián, Jalisco, 4 Mar. 2014

Solís Mendoza, Saturnino, Cerro de las Papas (anexo of Santa María Ocotán), Durango, 17 May 2014, and again on 24 Apr. 2015

Soto Reyes, Arturo, Santa María Ocotán, Durango, 11 Nov. 2012

Taizán Martínez, Primo, Huaynamota, Nayarit, 1 October 2017

Vázquez Campos, Raul, Tuxpan de Bolaños, Jalisco, 23 Feb. 2014

Villa Rangel, Gregorio, El Carrizal (anexo of Santa María Magdalena Taxicaringa), Durango, 26 Apr. 2015

CORRIDOS

"Corrido de Cerro de las Papas" (trad.). Performed by unknown musicians, Santa María Ocotán, 18 May 2014.

"Corrido de Mariano Solís" (trad.). Performed by unknown musicians, Jesús María, 25 October 2013.

"Corrido de Valentín de la Sierra" (trad.). Recording by Antonio Aguilar, 1968.

INDEX

ABOUT THE AUTHOR

Nathaniel Morris is the Leverhulme Early Career Research Fellow at University College London. He received his PhD in history from Oxford University in 2015. His research interests include Indigenous vigilante organizations in Mexico, the Mexican Revolution, the history of the Mexican drug trade, and Indigenous responses to the Nicaraguan Civil War. His work has been published in such journals as *Journal of Latin American Studies*, *Bulletin of Latin American Research*, and *Relaciones*. Morris is also the co-founder of Vlax Records, a project to recover the Golden Age of Yugoslav Roma music.